ACADÉMIE DE DROIT INTERNATIONAL
DE LA HAYE

HAGUE ACADEMY
OF INTERNATIONAL LAW

D1806942

COLLOQUE 2007

WORKSHOP 2007

L'Académie remercie tous ceux qui par leur appui ont contribué à la tenue du présent colloque, et notamment :

The Academy wishes to thank all those who, by their support, have contributed to the holding of the present Workshop, especially:

Ministère néerlandais des Affaires étrangères/Dutch Ministry of Foreign Affairs

Ambassade de France aux Pays-Bas/Embassy of France in the Netherlands

Cour permanente d'arbitrage/Permanent Court of Arbitration

ISBN (volume relié/Hard-back Volume)   978-90-04-17421-4
ISBN (volume broché/Soft-cover Volume)   978-90-04-17422-1

Printed by/Imprimé par Triangle Bleu, 59600 Maubeuge, France

ACADÉMIE DE DROIT INTERNATIONAL DE LA HAYE
HAGUE ACADEMY OF INTERNATIONAL LAW

ACTUALITÉ
DE LA CONFÉRENCE DE LA HAYE DE 1907, DEUXIÈME CONFÉRENCE DE LA PAIX

TOPICALITY
OF THE 1907 HAGUE CONFERENCE, THE SECOND PEACE CONFERENCE

COLLOQUE
LA HAYE, 6-7 SEPTEMBRE 2007

WORKSHOP
THE HAGUE, 6-7 SEPTEMBER 2007

Préparé par/Edited by: YVES DAUDET

2008
MARTINUS NIJHOFF PUBLISHERS
Leiden/London

LISTE DES PARTICIPANTS

LIST OF PARTICIPANTS

Abi-Saab, G.,	professeur honoraire, Institut universitaire de hautes études internationales, Genève ; membre de l'Organe d'appel de l'Organisation mondiale du commerce.
Argent, P. d',	professeur à l'Université catholique de Louvain.
Baldewsingh, S.,	Alderman, The Hague.
Bennouna, M.,	juge à la Cour internationale de Justice.
Boisson de Chazournes, L.,	professeur à l'Université de Genève.
Boutros-Ghali, B.,	ancien secrétaire général de l'Organisation des Nations Unies ; président du Curatorium de l'Académie de droit international de La Haye.
Cançado Trindade, A. A.,	Judge and Former President of the Inter-American Court of Human Rights ; Professor of International Law at the University of Brasilia.
Chemillier-Gendreau, M.,	professeur émérite de l'Université Denis-Diderot (Paris VII).
Condorelli, L.,	professeur émérite de l'Université de Genève.
Corell, H.,	Former Under-Secretary-General for Legal Affairs and the Legal Counsel of the United Nations.
Crawford, J.,	Whewell Professor of International Law, Director, Lauterpacht Centre for International Law, University of Cambridge.
Daudet, Y.,	professeur à l'Université Paris I (Panthéon-Sorbonne) ; Secrétaire général de l'Académie de droit international de La Haye.
El-Kosheri, A. S.,	professeur à l'Université du Caire.
Frowein, J. A.,	Director Max-Planck Institut, Heidelberg.
Glennon, M.,	Professor of International Law, Fletcher School of Law & Diplomacy, Tufts University.
Guillaume, G.,	ancien président de la Cour internationale de Justice.
Higgins, R.,	President of the International Court of Justice.
Kooijmans, P.,	Former Judge at the International Court of Justice.
Koskenniemi, M.,	Professor at the University of Helsinki.
Momtaz, D.,	professeur à l'Université de Téhéran.
Murase, S.,	Professor at Sophia University, Tokyo.
Ordzhonikidze, S.,	Director-General of the United Nations Office at Geneva.
Ortiz-Ahlf, L.,	Professor at the Iberoamericana University, Mexico.
Pellet, A.,	professeur à l'Université Paris X-Nanterre ; membre et ancien président de la Commission du droit international.
Pinto, M.,	professeur à l'Université de Buenos Aires.
Ronzitti, N.,	professeur à l'Université LUISS, Rome.

Schrijver, N.,	Professor of Public International Law, Academic Director, Grotius Centre for International Legal Studies, University of Leiden.
Skubiszewski, K.,	President of the Iran-United States Claims Tribunal.
Swinarski, C.,	professeur invité à l'Université Cardinal Stefan Wyszynski de Varsovie ; ancien conseiller juridique au Comité international de la Croix-Rouge.
Hout, T. van den,	secrétaire général de la Cour permanente d'arbitrage.
Venturini, G.,	professeur à l'Université de Milan.
Vereshchetin, V. S.,	Former Judge at the International Court of Justice.
Verhagen, M.,	ministre des Affaires étrangères du Royaume des Pays-Bas.
Verhoeven, J.,	professeur à l'Université Paris II (Panthéon-Assas).
Yee, S.,	Professor at Xi'an Jiaotong University.
Zacklin, R.,	Former Assistant Secretary-General for Legal Affairs, United Nations.

Coordinateur/Co-ordinator

Daudet, Y.,	professeur à l'Université Paris I (Panthéon-Sorbonne); Secrétaire général de l'Académie de droit international de La Haye.

TABLE DES MATIÈRES — CONTENTS

Troisième partie — Third Part

LA CONFÉRENCE DE LA HAYE ET LA RESTRICTION DE L'EMPLOI DE LA FORCE

THE HAGUE CONFERENCE AND RESTRICTIONS ON THE USE OF FORCE

I. Communications

Clôture du colloque — Closing of the workshop

Annexes

1. ACTES DE LA DEUXIÈME CONFÉRENCE DE LA PAIX (signés le 18 octobre 1907)

PRÉSENTATION

PRESENTATION

Y. DAUDET

En organisant ce colloque consacré à l'actualité de la Deuxième Conférence de la Paix, tenue à La Haye il y a juste un siècle, l'Académie poursuit une activité qui a fait l'objet de nombreux précédents depuis les manifestations mises en place par les anciens secrétaires généraux dont je salue la mémoire que furent René-Jean Dupuy puis Daniel Bardonnet. Toutefois, le dernier colloque remontait à 1994 et il n'était donc que temps de renouer avec ce qui était devenu et, je l'espère, demeurera une tradition de l'Académie.

Nous avons voulu ainsi que cette année 2007, année de notre réinstallation au Palais de la Paix dans un bâtiment flambant neuf, inauguré il y a quelques mois seulement par Sa Majesté la reine Béatrix, soit une étape marquante dans le développement de l'Académie. Pour ce faire, aucune entreprise ne saurait être mieux choisie qu'un colloque réunissant tant de personnalités. En effet, parmi d'autres activités de l'Académie, la tenue d'un colloque est encore un moyen d'atteindre son objectif: favoriser, par l'enseignement et la recherche, l'étude et la diffusion du droit international au service de la paix.

Le sujet retenu pour le présent colloque, «Actualité de la Conférence de La Haye de 1907, Deuxième Conférence de la Paix» est, en cette année du centenaire, à l'image de l'Académie qui relie un bâtiment moderne à celui du Palais de la Paix, l'incarnation de la dialectique de la tradition et de la modernité.

Si les juristes ont le légitime souci de l'actualité, il est important de ne pas perdre de vue les lignes de force, les grandes conquêtes du droit, celles qui traversent le temps et répondent probablement à la nécessité humaine. Cette réflexion permet de vérifier l'ossature de notre monde, de tester la charpente de la maison commune, afin de ne pas confondre des évolutions nécessaires de la règle de droit avec des abandons néfastes de celle-ci. Dans le monde d'aujourd'hui où l'actualité récente nous montre que les principes les mieux établis peuvent être mis à mal, que des conquêtes patientes peuvent être brutalement remises en cause, il n'est certainement pas inutile de nous interroger sur l'actualité de ces thèmes majeurs qui, souvent avec une grande prescience, avaient occupé, à La Haye il y a un siècle, les délégués des Etats de l'époque. Or les conquêtes du droit international doivent impérativement s'accompagner d'un effet de cliquet empêchant les retours en arrière. Les acquis fondamentaux doivent demeurer des socles insusceptibles d'être remis en question et sur lesquels, patiemment, année après année, se construisent les améliorations. La paix, la primauté de la règle de droit, le règlement pacifique des différends, les principes humanitaires ne sauraient connaître ni transgression ni régression.

Les travaux de ce colloque auront prioritairement pour objet de vérifier si les lignes de force établies il y a juste un siècle demeurent pertinentes ou si, au contraire, les exigences du monde actuel les ont affectées. Le monde d'il y a un siècle ne ressemble que de très loin à celui que nous vivons. Il est donc certainement légitime de se poser la question de savoir si les règles établies en 1907 répondent aux besoins de 2007. Certes, comment contester que l'exigence de paix, de droit, de règlement des différends, de principes humanitaires est toujours présente et plus forte encore qu'elle n'était. Mais face aux contraintes nouvelles auxquelles notre monde est confronté: terrorisme, dégradation de l'environnement, amplification du sous-développement de certains Etats, crises alimentaires et énergétiques, face aux déséquilibres nouveaux qui se dessinent autour des puissances émergentes, de nouvelles formes de développement, de l'omniprésence des nouvelles technologies, face à ces données nouvelles, le besoin de réforme est évident et doit être satisfait. La question est de savoir si, au nom de ces exigences, il est désormais possible de s'écarter de certains principes qui peuvent être regardés comme des conquêtes fondamentales. Tel est le cas de l'interdiction du recours à la force et du strict encadrement des conditions dans lesquelles il faut se résoudre à l'utiliser. Ainsi, la lutte contre le terrorisme ne doit pas conduire l'Etat victime à se comporter en Etat terroriste, au risque de faire le jeu du terrorisme lui-même et d'assurer sa victoire.

Dans quelle mesure, donc, les grandes conquêtes réalisées à l'aube du siècle dernier se maintiennent-elles au centre des règles applicables à celui qui commence, sans exclure les évolutions et réformes nécessaires dans un monde si différent de celui d'il y a un siècle ? Telle sera la question fondamentale à laquelle il sera tenté de répondre au cours de ces deux journées, en espérant qu'évolutions et réformes ne signifieront pas abandon des conquêtes et retours en arrière.

Yves DAUDET,
professeur à l'Université Paris I
(Panthéon-Sorbonne),
Secrétaire général de l'Académie
de droit international de La Haye.

In organizing this workshop devoted to the topicality of the Second Peace Conference, held in The Hague almost exactly a century ago, the Academy is pursuing an activity that has had numerous forerunners in the events organized by previous Secretaries-General, the late lamented René Jean Dupuy and Daniel Bardonnet. However, the most recent workshop was held in 1994, and the time is therefore more than ripe to revive what has become, and I hope will remain, one of the Academy's traditions.

We therefore wanted 2007, the year of our return to the Peace Palace in a brand new building, opened just a few months ago by Her Majesty Queen Beatrix, to mark a new stage in the development of the Academy. With this aim in mind, there can be no more appropriate event than a workshop bringing together so many eminent people. Indeed, the organization of a workshop is one more means, amongst the Academy's other activities, of achieving the Academy's objective, which is to promote, through teaching and research, the study and dissemination of international law in the service of peace.

The subject chosen for this workshop, "Topicality of the 1907 Hague Conference, the Second Peace Conference", is, in this centenary year, a reflection of the Academy itself, which combines a modern building with the Peace Palace building, an incarnation of the dialectic between tradition and innovation.

While jurists are legitimately concerned with topical issues, it is important not to lose sight of the fundamentals and of the great achievements of the law, which traverse the ages and probably respond to human needs. This process of reflection allows the underlying structure of our world to be verified and the foundations of our common home to be tested, in order not to confuse the necessary changes in the rule of law with harmful abandonments of the same rule. In today's world, where recent events have shown that the most well-established principles can be flouted and that patiently achieved victories can be brutally put into question, it is certainly not without interest to inquire into the topicality of those major themes that, often with great forethought, were the concern of the delegates of the States at the time, when they came to The Hague a century ago. In fact, it is essential for the achievements of international law to be accompanied by a locking mechanism to prevent any steps backward. The fundamental achievements of international law must remain foundations that can no longer be shaken, upon which, year after year, improvements are patiently constructed. Under no circumstances should there be allowed any infringement or regression of peace, the primacy of the rule of law, the peaceful settlement of disputes, or humanitarian principles.

The priority of this workshop will be to determine whether the fundamentals that were established exactly a century ago remain relevant or whether, on the contrary, they have been affected by the requirements of today's world. The world of a century ago only faintly resembles the world in which we now live, and it is therefore certainly legitimate to ask whether the rules laid down in 1907 respond to the needs of 2007. To be sure, how can it be disputed that the requirement for peace, law, the settlement of disputes, and humanitarian principles still exists, and even more emphatically than in the past? But given the new constraints with which our world is faced — terrorism, degradation of the environment, the exacerbation of under-development in certain States, and food and energy crises — and given the new imbalances that are appearing around the emerging powers, new forms of development, and the ubiquity of new technologies, given all these new factors, there is a clear need for reform, and that need must be satisfied. The question is whether, in the name of such requirements, it is now possible to depart from certain principles that can be viewed as fundamental achievements. Such is the case of the prohibition of the use of force and the strict framework regulating the circumstances in which a decision must be taken to use it. Thus, the fight against terrorism must not lead the victim State to act as if it were a terrorist State, with the risk of playing into the hands of terrorism itself and of ensuring its victory.

To what extent, therefore, do the great achievements dating from the dawn of the last century survive among the rules applicable to the century that is now beginning, without excluding the developments and reforms that are necessary in a world that is so different from the world as it was a century ago? This will be the fundamental question *that we will attempt to answer during these two days, in the hope that development and reform will not mean the abandonment of achievements or any backward steps.*

Yves DAUDET,
Professor at the University Paris I
(Panthéon-Sorbonne),
Secretary-General of the Hague Academy
of International Law.

OUVERTURE DU COLLOQUE

OPENING OF THE WORKSHOP

1. OUVERTURE DU COLLOQUE
PAR S. E. M. B. BOUTROS-GHALI [1]

Excellences,
Mesdames, Messieurs,
Chers Collègues et Amis,

C'est un grand honneur, en ma qualité de président du Curatorium de l'Académie de droit international, de présider ce colloque. Je souhaiterais, avant toute chose, remercier chaleureusement les personnalités qui ont accepté de participer à cette manifestation.

Je tiens à saluer, tout particulièrement, Mme Rosalyn Higgins, président de la Cour internationale de Justice, Son Excellence le ministre néerlandais des Affaires étrangères, le maire de La Haye et les éminents juristes qui, tous, par leur présence, confèrent à cet événement l'éclat et la solennité qu'il mérite.

Voilà cent ans, en 1907, se réunissaient les représentants de la Conférence de La Haye. Leur objectif n'était pas de mettre fin à la guerre, mais de prévenir l'éclatement de nouveaux conflits.

C'est ainsi que se fit jour le concept nouveau de prévention des conflits par la construction de la paix, et la reconstruction de la paix, une fois les hostilités terminées. Concept que j'ai développé dans mon « Agenda pour la paix », présenté aux Nations Unies en 1992.

La Conférence de La Haye de 1907, c'est aussi l'adoption de treize conventions et d'une déclaration qui constituent une étape essentielle au regard du développement des principes humanitaires du règlement pacifique des conflits internationaux.

En d'autres termes, la Conférence de La Haye a fait entrer la société internationale dans la modernité, en posant les jalons de l'architecture juridique et politique que nous avons vu se construire, se préciser, s'affirmer, au fil des années, tout en essayant de s'adapter aux évolutions du monde.

Nous avons tous, à l'esprit, les grandes étapes qui ont scandé cette évolution.

---

1. Ancien secrétaire général de l'Organisation des Nations Unies ; président du Curatorium de l'Académie de droit international de La Haye.

Qu'il s'agisse des Conventions de Genève de 1949 — emblématiques de l'événement du droit international humanitaire — qui montrent, désormais, dans une certaine mesure, leurs limites.

Qu'il s'agisse de la création de tribunaux internationaux qui ont contribué à l'élaboration progressive et au renforcement des règles du droit humanitaire.

Qu'il s'agisse de l'action du Conseil de sécurité de l'Organisation des Nations Unies en vue de faire respecter le droit international humanitaire dans les conflits dont il est saisi.

Pour autant, l'inadaptation de la réglementation du droit humanitaire s'est fait sentir, notamment, au regard de l'apparition de conflits d'un type nouveau : conflits à l'intérieur même des nations, conflits identitaires, conflits déstructurés.

Conflits qui affectent, avant tout, les populations civiles.

Conflits qui entraînent d'énormes mouvements de personnes déplacées ou de réfugiés.

Conflits qui s'accompagnent, parfois, de la disparition des structures étatiques, rendant très difficile toute action humanitaire indépendante, voire impossible toute intervention.

Conflits où disparaît la frontière entre actes de guerre et banditisme, entre civils et combattants.

Conflits où la valeur des emblèmes n'est plus respectée, transformant les intervenants humanitaires en cibles privilégiées des prédateurs de l'humanitaire.

Conflits où le droit international humanitaire n'est donc plus même en mesure de fournir des réponses appropriées.

Il faut ajouter à cette sommaire typologie, la « guerre contre le terrorisme », telle que les Etats-Unis d'Amérique et leurs alliés l'ont qualifiée après les attentats du 11 septembre 2001.

Cela étant, on ne peut pas transformer un crime de droit interne — en l'occurrence ces attentats — en un acte de guerre, établissant un état de guerre entre l'Etat agressé et le groupe terroriste. Bien plus, l'invocation du droit de guerre, ou du droit de légitime défense prévu par l'article 51 de la Charte des Nations Unies, n'autorise pas de mener une guerre préventive ou guerre générale hors frontières, dans laquelle toute distinction entre combattants et non-combattants est rendue impossible.

Je mentionnerais, enfin, un phénomène malheureusement en recrudescence ces dernières années. Je veux parler des mercenaires armés et payés par des sociétés privées qui passent des contrats avec certains Etats. Ce début de privatisation des forces armées confrontera, tôt ou tard, le droit international humanitaire à de nouveaux défis.

Beaucoup donc reste encore à conceptualiser et à mettre en œuvre pour renouveler et adapter les acquis de La Haye à la nouvelle conjoncture conflictuelle.

Comment mettre de l'ordre dans le désordre qui règne aujourd'hui dans les conflits internes?

Comment contrôler le commerce et le trafic d'armes légères dont la prolifération nourrit et attise ces conflits?

Comment rappeler que, dans les conflits asymétriques en termes de puissance aérienne et de puissance de feu, il ne reste aux insurgés du tiers-monde que la guérilla et le terrorisme?

Comment rappeler que les dommages collatéraux créés par les bombardements aériens font infiniment plus de victimes parmi les civils que ceux provoqués par la guérilla ou le terrorisme?

Comment obtenir l'attention et l'intervention des acteurs humanitaires pour mettre un terme à ces conflits barbares?

Je ne prétends pas détenir la réponse à toutes ces questions, mais j'ai la profonde conviction que nous devons plus que jamais réaffirmer haut et fort l'importance du droit international humanitaire. Car c'est en recherchant de nouvelles pistes de réflexion, en mobilisant les nouveaux acteurs humanitaires que nous pourrons poursuivre l'œuvre entreprise, il y a cent ans, à La Haye, même si nous savons bien que, des textes à la pratique, le chemin reste long et la pente ardue.

Cette conviction, je sais que vous la partagez pleinement. Et c'est donc sur une note d'espoir et d'optimisme que je voudrais conclure ce propos.

2. DISCOURS
DE S. E. M. M. VERHAGEN [1],

Excellences,
Mesdames, Messieurs,

Au nom du Gouvernement néerlandais, que je représente ici, je suis heureux de vous souhaiter la bienvenue à La Haye pour ce colloque célébrant le centenaire de la Deuxième Conférence de La Haye de 1907. Vous le savez, les Pays-Bas sont particulièrement attachés à la promotion du droit international. C'est pourquoi je suis très honoré de m'adresser à vous aujourd'hui.

Au terme de la Conférence de 1907, le ministre des Affaires étrangères des Etats-Unis d'Amérique, Elihu Root, qui fut plus tard le premier président de la Fondation Carnegie, déclara qu'il ne fallait pas évaluer seulement les acquis de chaque conférence de la paix, mais aussi les développements amorcés et les avancées.

Cent ans plus tard, nous pouvons conclure que la Deuxième Conférence de La Haye a été, dans l'optique de Root, un grand succès de par les changements enclenchés. Elle a même sans doute dépassé les attentes de ses participants. La Conférence a posé le fondement indispensable au développement du droit international et à la formation d'une communauté internationale. Elle a aussi attribué à La Haye et aux Pays-Bas un rôle nouveau sur la scène internationale, celui de capitale juridique du monde. Permettez-moi de développer ces deux points.

Il est bon de se rappeler une fois encore ce qui est difficilement concevable aujourd'hui: la Deuxième Conférence de La Haye a eu lieu à une époque où la guerre et la violence étaient des moyens légitimes de résoudre les conflits. Une époque où la loi du plus fort régissait les relations internationales.

L'ambition des conférences de La Haye était de brider cette loi du plus fort et d'établir des règles applicables aux conflits armés, le *jus in bello*. La particularité de ces deux conférences par rapport à celles qui les avaient précédées, c'est qu'elles ne visaient pas à mettre fin à

---

1. Ministre des Affaires étrangères du Royaume des Pays-Bas.

des conflits en cours : elles furent instituées pour prévenir les conflits et en limiter les conséquences atroces. La Première Conférence de 1899 donna l'impulsion. Celle de 1907 posa un fondement solide pour la résolution pacifique des conflits et le développement du droit humanitaire en temps de guerre. Ce sont, aujourd'hui encore, des piliers du droit international tel que nous le connaissons.

L'évolution qu'a connue le droit international de la guerre depuis le début du XXe siècle n'a, pour vous, pas de secrets ; je ne m'arrêterai donc pas sur ce sujet. Je reprends toutefois volontiers les mots de l'historien Eric Hobsbawm, qui qualifie le XXe siècle d'« âge des extrêmes ». Un siècle des extrêmes, il le fut certainement. Dès 1914, en effet, les efforts de la Deuxième Conférence de La Haye en faveur de la paix et de la sécurité internationales ont été contrariés par le grondement des canons. Deux guerres mondiales allaient fortement ébranler la communauté internationale naissante.

Ce sont pourtant ces deux conflits mondiaux qui ont relancé le développement du droit international et la création de nouvelles institutions. Les conventions de Genève de 1929 et de 1949 et les différentes conventions des droits de l'homme signées après 1945 formaient la réponse aux horreurs de ces deux guerres. On peut en dire autant de la Société des Nations, des Nations Unies et des Tribunaux de Nuremberg et de Tokyo.

La fin de la guerre froide a permis de sortir d'une bipolarité qui, de facto, ravalait souvent l'application du droit international au rang d'illusion. En revanche, de vieux conflits se sont ranimés et de nouveaux foyers de tension surgissent. Les plus fortes menaces ne proviennent plus de conflits classiques, interétatiques — comme au temps de la Deuxième Conférence de La Haye —, mais de conflits infraétatiques. Je pense notamment au conflit en ex-Yougoslavie, au génocide rwandais et, actuellement, à la situation au Darfour.

Je pense aussi aux réseaux et aux groupes terroristes sans attaches idéologiques ou géographiques uniques, et totalement étrangers à la notion d'ordre juridique international. Nous en avons vu les conséquences à New York, mais aussi à Madrid, à Londres et à Bali.

Voilà les défis qui se posent aujourd'hui à notre communauté internationale. Notre tâche est d'y trouver des réponses appropriées, tout comme nos prédécesseurs, il y a cent ans, ont essayé de faire face aux défis d'alors. Comment allons-nous par exemple faire front aux crimes de guerre, aux violations massives de droits de l'homme, aux génocides et aux crimes contre l'humanité ? Quel est le rapport du droit humanitaire en temps de guerre à la lutte contre le terrorisme? Le droit international actuel fournit-il suffisamment de moyens pour s'attaquer aux organisations criminelles internationales? Si nous voulons perpétuer l'esprit de la Deuxième Conférence de La Haye au XXIe siècle, nous ne pouvons pas éluder ces questions.

Les Pays-Bas ont des idées bien arrêtées sur certaines de ces questions. Le Gouvernement néerlandais estime ainsi que l'urgence humanitaire peut justifier moralement et politiquement l'intervention militaire. L'absence de base juridique claire n'exclut pas que, dans des cas exceptionnels et dans des conditions strictes, l'intervention humanitaire soit admise comme issue de secours. Pour ce qui est de la lutte contre le terrorisme, les Pays-Bas considèrent qu'elle doit impérativement s'inscrire dans les limites du droit. Les droits de l'homme s'appliquent à tous et en tout temps.

Mais, cela ne répond évidemment pas à toutes les interrogations que je viens de soulever. Il est manifeste que ces questions appellent une discussion et un examen plus approfondis. Et, en tant que spécialistes du droit international, vous pouvez apporter une éminente contribution à cette réflexion.

Je saisis l'occasion de notre réunion aujourd'hui à La Haye pour évoquer rapidement la position spéciale des Pays-Bas à l'égard du droit international. La Deuxième Conférence de La Haye a confirmé notre rôle d'hôte des institutions et des réunions internationales. Les Pays-Bas se sont acquittés avec conviction de cette mission, qu'ils ont sans cesse étendue. L'installation d'instituts renommés comme l'Académie de La Haye a fait de cette ville un centre important de l'étude du droit international. Et la venue de la Cour permanente d'arbitrage, de la Cour internationale de Justice, du Tribunal pénal pour l'ex-Yougoslavie et, naturellement, de la Cour pénale internationale ont définitivement consacré La Haye capitale juridique du monde. Comment aurions-nous pu imaginer, au début des années quatre-vingt-dix, que des criminels de guerre congolais, ougandais et yougoslaves seraient jugés ici? Tout le monde comprend désormais ce que veut dire «être envoyé à La Haye», et j'en suis fier.

Comme vous le savez, le Secrétaire général de l'Organisation des Nations Unies, Ban Ki-Moon, nous a récemment demandé d'accueillir aux Pays-Bas le Tribunal spécial pour le Liban. Le Gouvernement néerlandais est honoré qu'il soit une fois de plus fait appel à lui, et il a répondu favorablement à la demande du Secrétaire général. Une délégation des Nations Unies est venue la semaine dernière aux Pays-Bas pour examiner les questions telles que le site, les modalités financières et l'exécution des jugements.

La contribution des Pays-Bas à l'application du droit international procède de la conviction qu'un ordre juridique solide est une des conditions de l'équité, de la prospérité et de la sécurité dans le monde. Un monde où la liberté, la démocratie et la dignité humaine sont protégées. Un monde où la promotion, l'application et le respect des droits de l'homme sont des principes directeurs non négociables. Un monde qui combat l'impunité.

Cet engagement constitue l'un des piliers de mon action politique. Ce faisant, nous devons garder à l'esprit que l'ordre juridique international profite finalement aux individus. Les mots de l'homme d'Etat grec Périclès sont ici de circonstance : « Ce que nous laissons derrière n'est pas ce qui est gravé dans les monuments de pierre, mais ce qui a touché la vie des autres. »

C'est dans cette perspective que je voudrais placer les acquis de la Deuxième Conférence de La Haye. Pour que nous gardions à l'esprit, durant ce séminaire de commémoration, que l'héritage majeur de la Deuxième Conférence de La Haye est que des dizaines de différends internationaux ont été réglés pacifiquement, épargnant selon toute vraisemblance un conflit armé à de nombreuses personnes. C'est aussi que, depuis la seconde guerre mondiale, beaucoup d'autres personnes se sont vu reconnaître des droits en temps de guerre. Et c'est encore que l'on peut de plus en plus souvent réclamer justice après un conflit armé.

Espérons que l'Histoire aura sur nos efforts un jugement aussi positif que celui que nous portons aujourd'hui même sur la Deuxième Conférence de La Haye.

3. ADDRESS
BY H.E. S. A. ORDZHONIKIDZE [1]

Mr. Secretary-General of the Academy,
Excellencies,
Ladies and Gentlemen,

It is a great pleasure to be with you to mark the 100th anniversary of the 1907 Hague Conference. It is a distinct privilege to join such eminent personalities and distinguished legal experts at the podium. Esteemed colleagues from the United Nations will speak to the historical trajectory leading from the Hague Conferences, via the League of Nations, to the present-day United Nations and the ideas that underpin our Organization.

For my part, I should like to touch on an area where there were high hopes that the Second Peace Conference would significantly advance international peace and security, but it was unable to do so: namely, a reduction in armaments. The 1907 Hague Conference may not have produced substantive arms control measures, but it nevertheless remains important as one of the first conferences on what we today call disarmament, and in this sense it laid down the ground rules for subsequent initiatives on arms limitation. In my capacity as Secretary-General of the Conference on Disarmament — the world's only multilateral negotiating body dedicated to strategic disarmament and non-proliferation — I should like to share with you a few thoughts on this longer-term impact of the 1907 Hague Conference, and on the lessons that I believe we may apply in today's disarmament and non-proliferation efforts.

The United Nations Secretary-General, Mr. Ban Ki-moon, has highlighted disarmament and non-proliferation as essential dimensions of the maintenance of international peace and security, and he has placed emphasis on the connection between disarmament and development. He has done so against a background of rising global military spending and decreasing development aid. According to the

---

1. United Nations Under-Secretary-General, Director-General of the United Nations Office at Geneva.

Stockholm International Peace Research Institute, world military expenditure reached 1.2 trillion US dollars in 2006. The same year — as calculated by the United Nations — developed countries spent only 103 billion US dollars on official overseas development assistance. Global military expenditure has gone up — in real terms — by 37 per cent over the past ten years. Official overseas development assistance — by comparison — declined by 1.8 per cent from 2005 to 2006. Both trends are likely to continue, unless addressed more resolutely.

Apart from a vague declaration to the effect that it was "eminently desirable that the Governments should resume the serious examination" of the issue of limitation of arms expenditure, references to specific arms control measures were most conspicuous by their absence in the Final Act of the 1907 Hague Conference. Paradoxically, maybe, but this is not all too different from the Outcome Document of the 2005 World Summit, where the Member States of the United Nations could not agree to devote a single sentence to disarmament and non-proliferation. What compounds this paradox is that both events took place in a context of growing military spending. Similarly, both meetings were set at a historical juncture of intensifying interaction among the nations of the world. Already in 1899, Baron de Staal — a fellow countryman of mine — who presided over the First Hague Peace Conference stressed that:

> "The ties, which bind the various branches of the great human family, are ever drawing them closer to each other. If a nation wished to remain isolated, it could not. . . . The effects of an international conflict in any quarter of the globe echo far and wide in every direction. These truths are not new, but they claim our attention more than ever at the present time."

These words may just as well have been spoken today in our age of globalization.

As we debate the topicality of the Second Hague Conference — and without over-emphasizing the parallels between the geopolitical realities then and now — what lessons can we draw for our continued disarmament and non-proliferation efforts?

First, we must recognize that despite their uncontested benefits, disarmament and non-proliferation remain highly sensitive issues, and closely connected with individual countries' wider security agendas and priorities. We must be realistic about what can be achieved, and pursue a pragmatic approach that balances carefully the legitimate, but differing — and sometimes maybe even conflicting — interests of States.

Second, despite the difficulties and the — at times — limited progress, we must persevere, and not allow disarmament and non-proliferation to become detached from wider peace, security and development efforts. We must pursue a long-term strategy. Building on the principles and norms agreed to at The Hague in 1907, countries have later put in place significant arms control and disarmament measures, such as the Nuclear Non-Proliferation Treaty, the Chemical Weapons Convention and the Biological Weapons Convention — to mention only a few developments in the weapons of mass destruction area. It is instructive to note that the word "disarmament" itself was not used in 1907 — and not even specified in the United Nations Charter of 1945 — but has entered and become entrenched in our peace and security vocabulary since then. Progress may have been slower, more acrimonious and more restricted than could have been wished for, but these instruments all represent incremental steps forward.

Third, disarmament and non-proliferation undertaken in multilateral frameworks is more credible and more effective. The 1907 Hague Conference stood out because of its relatively comprehensive participation of 44 countries, including representatives from South America and Asia. And while these States did not agree on concrete arms limitation initiatives, they did commit to the importance of pursuing arms control.

In 1907, the leaders of the day drew the conclusion from the Second Peace Conference that multilateral forums could not generate reliable and realistic arms control measures, and that in their absence, enhancing existing armaments was the only option. United States President Theodore Roosevelt, who had in the first instance proposed the Second Hague Conference and had strongly supported the inclusion of arms limitation items, summarized in his State of the Union address in December of 1907 this prevailing sentiment following the conclusion of the conference:

> "It is evident, therefore, that it is folly for this Nation to base any hope of securing peace on any international agreement as to the limitations of armaments. Such being the fact it would be most unwise for us to stop the upbuilding of our Navy."

President Roosevelt was not alone in his disillusionment and his subsequent policy prescriptions. The result of this continuing, collective arms build-up — fed by, and, in turn, exacerbating deep-seated political tensions — helped to lead the world further down the path towards the First World War.

Our shared challenge today is to confront the negative trends in the global security environment as a result of the ongoing stalemate in multilateral and bilateral disarmament and non-proliferation efforts, so as to not allow us to follow down that same path. We must continue our work based on a multilateral approach, with persistence and patience, with a long-term perspective, and in pursuit of a balanced agenda that takes into consideration the legitimate security concerns of all countries. Individually and collectively, States must show leadership to bring disarmament and non-proliferation into the international spotlight. I hope that this — together with an ever-more refined international legal and institutional framework — will be yet another part of the legacy of The Hague conferences. The disarmament challenge is as urgent today as it was then — and just as in 1907, it requires a robust response.

Let us rise to that challenge.

4. ADDRESS
BY S. BALDEWSINGH[1]

Your Excellencies,
Ladies and Gentlemen,

It is a great honour for me to be here today on behalf of the local government to welcome you to the city of The Hague.

I should like to address a special word of welcome to His Excellency, Mr. Boutros Boutros-Ghali, president of the Curatorium of the Hague Academy of International Law and former Secretary-General of the United Nations.

I am also very pleased to see here among us the Secretary-General of the Hague Academy of International Law, Professor Yves Daudet.

Lastly, I should like to warmly greet Her Excellency, Dame Rosalyn Higgins, President of the International Court of Justice.

Of course, I am also extremely gratified that so many of you, ladies and gentlemen, are present here today in this beautiful new building of the Hague Academy of International Law and the Library of the Peace Palace.

Exactly one hundred years ago the world was a guest in The Hague. Eight years after the First Peace Conference in 1899 the long-expected follow-up meeting took place at the initiative of President Theodore Roosevelt. This time with significantly more participants. For at the First Conference there were 100 delegates from 24 countries and at the 1907 Conference there were 250 delegates from 44 countries. Partly because of these numbers, the conference was held in the Ridderzaal or Knights' Hall and the other buildings around the Dutch Houses of Parliament, the Binnenhof, and not in the Huis ten Bosch Palace.

The Second Hague Peace Conference, and you will be devoting detailed attention to it today and tomorrow, did not produce the results that had been anticipated. Arthur Eyffinger rightly commented recently that, in contrast to the First Peace Conference, the second was, ultimately, not so much about peace as about war.

---

1. Alderman, The Hague.

The main results of 1907 after all were the agreements that were reached on the laws of war.

As far as that is concerned, looked at cynically, one could regard the Second Peace Conference as a rendezvous of the imperialist superpowers of the day who in reality had quite a few other things on their agendas than world peace. A painful example of this was the refusal to admit the Korean delegation to the conference. The Korean Yi Jun, who, together with two compatriots, on the fringes of the conference, tried to draw attention to the sorry state of his own country, died unexpectedly in a Hague hotel. The centenary of his death was commemorated here in The Hague in July in an impressive ceremony.

The calls for real peace, which could clearly be heard in the publications of Bertha von Suttner and William Stead, publisher of the *Courrier de la Conférence de la Paix*, were for the most part drowned out either by the roaring of guns or the rhetoric of war or by the sounds of revelry in and around the conference in the chic hotels of The Hague and Scheveningen.

Nevertheless the Second Peace Conference was an important step in the development of international law and a stimulus for the further development of The Hague as the city of peace, justice and security. During the conference, for example, the first stone was laid for the Peace Palace, the home of the Permanent Court of Arbitration and, after the Second World War, the International Court of Justice, the principal judicial organ of the United Nations. Did you know, by the way, that during the last war for some time the illegal newspaper *Je maintiendrai* was printed in the attic of the Palace? A voice for freedom coming from the palace of peace. What could be more appropriate?

Since the days of the Second Peace Conference The Hague has developed to become, in the words of Mr. Boutros Boutros-Ghali, the "legal capital of the world". But we have acquired this title not on our own merit but thanks to all those generations of lawyers, legal experts and academics from the past and present. They, after all, are the ones who, step by step, have created the framework of international law and international treaties that constitute the basis for the many organizations and courts that The Hague has the privilege of accommodating. The presence of so many legal institutions staffed by top legal experts from all over the world has turned The Hague into an international centre of legal knowledge. The municipal authority fully recognizes this and, of course, in conjunction with third parties, wants to do everything it can to expand and reinforce this knowledge economy.

The Hague is very proud to bear this honorary title conferred upon it by the former Secretary-General of the United Nations. But in our view this also entails responsibilities. Not alone to house the international community in The Hague as well as possible and to make amenities available, but also to actively propagate peace, justice and security. The Hague does this together with other towns and cities in a number of ways. Allow me to briefly explain.

Since 2006 Mayor Wim Deetman has been chairman of the Committee on City Diplomacy of the organization United Cities and Local Governments (UCLG). This committee focuses on the role that local authorities can play in areas where peace, democracy and human rights cannot be taken for granted. The contribution that local governments can make in building peace and creating good governance comes from the expertise that they automatically have in-house. Governing local communities on the basis of democratic principles.

Examples in the past years are the mission of Pax Christi, the Association of Netherlands Municipalities and Mayors in Europe, including Wim Deetman, to Colombia, to provide local politicians there with some moral support in the run-up to the local elections. The aim of the mission was to let local politicians know that they could count on the practical support of local authorities in other countries.

In addition, the international section of the Association of Netherlands Municipalities has helped with setting up an association of municipalities in Rwanda — extremely important work, because without a central organization which helps local populations in organizing local government, it is extremely difficult to build a democracy in that country.

Perhaps the most compelling project is the Municipal Alliance for Peace in the Middle East. In this project mayors in Palestinian and Israeli municipalities are working together to get concrete projects off the ground in conjunction with a foreign municipality. The Hague is playing a pioneering role in this project. The aim is to resolve practical problems together with The Hague in the role of mediator so that lasting relationships can be built between local populations on both sides.

A hundred years ago towns and cities were not concerned with matters of this kind. They had other things to think about and did not encroach upon the international domain which was the sole preserve of the superpowers. As far as that is concerned, much has changed in the past century. The Second Peace Conference in The Hague, despite all its shortcomings, marked an important step in the development of international law and international co-operation. The Hague is honoured that for so long now it has been able to play such an important role. And it is precisely because of this that we feel obliged, in the spirit of people like Bertha von Suttner, William Stead and Andrew Carnegie, to make a contribution to a more peaceful, more just and more secure world.

5. REMARKS
BY H.E. H. CORELL [1]

Mr. Foreign Minister,
Dr. Boutros-Ghali, President of the Curatorium of the Academy,
Professor Daudet, Secretary-General of the Academy,
Excellencies, Colleagues and Friends,

Allow me, first, to extend my warmest thanks to the Academy for inviting me to address you on this occasion.

Among the participants in this colloquium I recognize many friends from my years as the Legal Adviser of the Swedish Ministry for Foreign Affairs and, indeed, from my time as the Legal Counsel of the United Nations from 1994 to 2004. I would like to thank once again Dr. Boutros-Ghali for asking me to join his team when he was Secretary-General of the United Nations. I would also like to pay tribute to Ralph Zacklin, who was my deputy during my United Nations years.

Professor Daudet suggested that I reflect on my UN experience in connection with some of the aims of the Hague Conference. I will do that, although time allows only for some very brief remarks. But I will also reflect on the effectiveness of "the legal and political structure of today's world", to quote from the invitation to the colloquium.

For someone with his roots in a national judiciary it is natural to take as a point of departure one of the paragraphs in the preamble of the 1907 Convention for the Pacific Settlement of International Disputes: "Desirous of extending the empire of law and of strengthening the appreciation of international justice." Today we would of course refer to "the rule of law" rather than to "the empire of law".

Over the past hundred years we have seen an extraordinary development towards the establishment of the rule of law both at the national and international level. If we focus only on the few years that have passed since the Berlin Wall came down, several new instruments and institutions have been established.

---

1. Former Under-Secretary-General for Legal Affairs and the Legal Counsel of the United Nations.

Let me first mention the law of the sea; matters relating to the seas have great potential for disputes among States. When the UN Convention on the Law of the Sea entered into force in 1994, the Seabed Authority was established in Kingston, Jamaica, in the presence of the then UN Secretary-General Boutros Boutros-Ghali.

Two years later, the International Tribunal for the Law of the Sea was established. It was inaugurated in Hamburg in October 1996 also in the presence of Secretary-General Boutros-Ghali. I still remember him repeatedly asking why this new Court was not a UN institution. Without going into detail as to why it is not, suffice it to say that the Tribunal is closely linked to the United Nations through an agreement.

The last of the three institutions established by the UN Convention on the Law of the Sea — the Commission on the Limits of the Continental Shelf — held its first meeting in New York in June 1997. This Commission, serviced by the UN Secretariat, will be of great importance in the years to come. There are presently several applications pending before it. Of particular interest in this context is the development in the Arctic, where the melting of the sea ice results in sea areas opening up for navigation and for exploitation of mineral resources.

I venture to suggest that the UN Convention on the Law of the Sea is one of the greatest contributions to international peace and security that have been created under the auspices of the Organization.

Let me now focus on international criminal law. This law is closely linked to the general topic of the 1907 Conference, namely humanitarian law and the efforts to create peace among nations.

It is fair to say that we have seen a remarkable development in the field of international criminal law over the past few years. It started with an initiative in the Sixth Committee of the UN General Assembly in 1989 to revitalize the work towards the creation of an international criminal court. Many contributed to the work leading up to the successful 1998 Rome Conference. I would like to mention, in particular, the work of the International Law Commission and its working group under the chairmanship of Professor James Crawford, who is with us today. But also Adrian Bos, Philippe Kirsch and many others should be remembered.

However, it goes without saying that this work may not have been so successful if we had not in parallel experienced the development in the former Yugoslavia and Rwanda. In 1993 and 1994, respectively, international tribunals for those regions were established by the Security Council. They are still in operation with jurisdiction over genocide, war crimes, and crimes against humanity. But the question we should ask today is how the mighty Security Council can allow itself to be embarrassed by the fact that two of the main suspects — Radovan Karadzić and Radko Mladić — are still at large.

The Statute of the International Criminal Court was adopted on 17 July 1998. It was ratified in record time and entered into force on 1 July 2002, only four years after its adoption. In the meantime an agreement on the Special Court for Sierra Leone had been negotiated between the United Nations and that country. It was signed on 16 January 2002. Today the Special Court is in full operation. A former Head of State is on trial before the Court, which for this case is not sitting in Freetown but here in The Hague.

The most recent among these institutions are the Extraordinary Chambers within the national courts of Cambodia. The task of these Chambers is to try the senior Khmer Rouge leaders. The agreement between the United Nations and Cambodia was signed on 6 June 2003 after several years of painstaking negotiations. The Chambers have only recently started to operate and it is yet too early to say how this effort will develop.

All these institutions should be seen as necessary corollaries to the courts that already existed when this development started, not only to the Permanent Court of Arbitration and the International Court of Justice, the principal judicial organ of the United Nations, but also to the existing regional courts.

I would like to see these institutions and the many international agreements, in particular the agreements in the field of human rights, as extremely important parts of "the legal and political structure of today's world". Over the years we have also seen great steps towards democracy and the rule of law. And yet, there is so much more to be done. As a matter of fact, the development in later years gives reason for concern unless States change their behaviour.

One of the initiators of the Second Peace Conference and indeed also one of the supporters of this Academy was the United States Secretary of State at the time, Elihu Root. You may recall that he was awarded the Nobel Peace Prize for the year 1912. In his lecture delivered in acceptance of the prize he spoke of causes of war — among them race, local prejudice and national "amour propre" — and added:

"With these go the popular assumption, often arrogant, often ignorant, that the extreme claims of one's own country are always right and are to be rigidly insisted upon as a point of national honour. With them go intolerance of temperate discussion, of kindly consideration, and of reasonable concession."

Unfortunately, this remarkable statement is just as relevant today as it was a hundred years ago. The only difference is that the challenges that humanity is facing today are even greater than at that time.

On 1 December 2004, the High-level Panel on Threats, Challenges and Change presented its recommendations to then UN Secretary-General, Kofi Annan. The Panel maintained that any event or process that leads to large-scale death or lessening of life chances and undermines States as the basic unit of the international system is a threat to international security. Against the background of this definition the Panel identified six clusters of threats with which the world must be concerned now and in the decades ahead:

— economic and social threats, including poverty, infectious diseases and environmental degradation;
— inter-State conflict;
— internal conflict, including civil war, genocide and other large-scale atrocities;
— nuclear, radiological, chemical and biological weapons;
— terrorism; and
— transnational organized crime.

A common denominator in addressing these threats is a well-functioning system of collective security. Such a system was established through the Charter of the United Nations. However, a precondition for making this system work as it was intended is that the Members of the Organization respect the Charter.

And this is where I felt the greatest sadness when I left the United Nations in March 2004. I came to the United Nations with a very positive opinion of the Organization and also inspired by Dag Hammarskjöld's thinking on the role of the international civil servant. I witnessed remarkable efforts by the Organization, and I also saw individual staff members making extraordinary contributions to its work. As in every organization, there are also the odd ones who do not live up to the standards and must be dealt with accordingly.

But, perhaps more importantly, I witnessed how States behaved. Some are stalwart defenders of the UN ideals. But I also saw some of them acting in flagrant violation of the Charter. Among them were the obvious ones. But among them were also States for which I had great respect. I had expected those States to be in the lead, setting the example. The question to be asked is: Why are the lessons from the past, including the experiences of two world wars, so quickly forgotten?

Never before has the need for an international society based on the rule of law been so great. The challenges ahead are tremendous. The six clusters of threats are a clear indication.

Without going into detail with respect to the causes, global warming must now be seen not only as an environmental issue but also in the context of international peace and security. At the same time we are witnessing an enormous geopolitical shift. The economic realities will change dramatically over the next few years. In parallel, the world population of some 6.5 billion today is expected to rise by 40 per cent by mid-century — to 9.1 billion!

Certainly, "the legal and political structure of today's world" is influenced by the result of the Hague conferences. Some suggest that this structure will be different in tomorrow's world. Maybe, but I certainly do not see an alternative to the nation State. The problem is rather that too many nation States are too weak. States with a deficit when it comes to democracy and rule of law constitute a threat to international peace and security.

But also States that claim to be democracies under the rule of law must take a serious look at themselves and ask whether they meet the standards that humanity is entitled to expect.

We must strengthen our efforts to establish democracy and the rule of law. In this work also civil society must engage just as it did when it initiated the Second Peace Conference. At the moment we are trying to organize a global rule of law movement. Time does not allow me to go into detail. But I am sure that you will soon hear more about the efforts of the International Bar Association, the American Bar Association, the International Legal Assistance Consortium, the Hague Institute for Internationalization of Law, and many others engaged in this work.

It is said about Elihu Root that he believed that international law, along with its accompanying machinery, represented mankind's best chance to achieve world peace. But he also understood that it would take much time to implement it effectively. The question is how much progress we have really made in a hundred years. I wonder what Elihu Root would have said, had he been with us today.

Finally, as lawyers we must be realistic and rational and act accordingly. But let us for a moment attempt to view the situation through the mind of a poet.

When I joined the United Nations in 1994 it struck me that some of the poetry by the Scottish poet Robert Burns reflects the ideals of the United Nations. I once ventured to suggest that his poem "To a Mouse" is really about the little people that the United Nations is trying to assist.

When the poet's plough has destroyed the little mouse's house — that little heap of leaves and stubble — Burns says to the mouse:

> "Still thou art blest, compar'd wi' me:
> The present only toucheth thee:
> But och! I backward cast my e'e,
>   On prospects drear!
> An' forward, tho' I canna see,
>   I guess an' fear!"

Now, if we cast our eyes backwards, what do we see? I suggest we see millions and millions of years. And not until we come to the very last fraction of this time do we see the human being appearing on this earth. And what if we look forward and guess? I suggest we see many more millions of years. The question is now: For how long will this species that has the audacity to call itself homo sapiens remain on earth?

Judging from the history of the earth we must realize that the day will come when — for reasons over which we may have no control — the conditions may be such that homo sapiens can no longer exist. What will be the verdict over this species when the most high sits in judgment? Will it be that at long last this species realized that it had to create conditions under which all human beings could live in peace and dignity — or?

May I close on the note that we must never ever give up striving for peace and security. But we will never reach this goal if we do not remember the lessons of the past.

LA CONFÉRENCE DE LA HAYE DE 1907 : ORIGINES ET PERSPECTIVES

Sous la présidence de
Boutros BOUTROS-GHALI

FIRST PART

THE 1907 HAGUE CONFERENCE : ORIGINS AND PROSPECTS

Boutros BOUTROS-GHALI,
presiding

I. COMMUNICATIONS

1. THE 1907 HAGUE PEACE CONFERENCE AS A MILESTONE IN THE DEVELOPMENT OF INTERNATIONAL LAW

H.E. Judge R. HIGGINS [1]

This is a marvellous occasion for the organization of which the Hague Academy is to be warmly congratulated. My modest contribution is to set the scene in a rather general sense for how we may today see the 1907 Hague Peace Conference as a milestone in the development of international law.

The 1907 Conference did not achieve all that it set out to do, but that which it did accomplish was remarkable and has proved significant.

Before looking a little more at this balance sheet, we should note at the outset that the achievements of the 1907 Hague Peace Conference are all the more extraordinary given the atmosphere prevailing at that time. In the years since the 1899 Hague Peace Conference, there had been the Boer War (1899-1902), the Russo-Japanese War (1904-1905), and the related Dogger Bank incident (1904). Indeed, the impetus for the 1907 Conference came not from a State, but from one of the flourishing peace movements. In 1904, the Inter-Parliamentary Union, which had long been supportive of the development of international arbitration, called for the conference. President Theodore Roosevelt consulted with the Russian Government and others, and it was decided that Tsar Nicholas II would convene a Second Peace Conference.

Looking back, it is remarkable that the Conference took place at all, let alone that it produced a declaration on the principle of obligatory arbitration and 13 conventions, 3 of which were revisions to conventions adopted in 1899 and 10 of which were entirely new.

When Tsar Nicolas II first called for the holding of a Peace Conference in 1899, he had intended primarily to seek agreement to obtain a reduction of military budgets through restrictions on armaments and to reduce the suffering of war, especially by members of

---

1. President of the International Court of Justice.

the armed forces. His subsidiary aim was to improve the prospects for the peaceful settlement of international disputes. These aims remained in place for the 1907 Conference. Little specific commitments were then made in the area of arms control, though the door was opened for a topic that still remains a "work in progress". At the same time, the 1907 Conference elevated the development of mechanisms of international dispute resolution to new prominence and also made great progress in developing and codifying the laws of war. It equally left a procedural legacy that still shapes the codification of international law today. I shall make some remarks on each of these three elements.

*

Throughout the nineteenth century some major disputes had been settled by arbitration. Such arbitrations were undertaken on an *ad hoc* basis. There was no general obligation to have recourse to arbitration to settle disputes and when recourse was made, there were no fixed rules of procedure. The Institut de droit international, as one of its first projects, had adopted a code for arbitral procedure in 1875, but this lacked the status of an international convention[2]. The 1907 Conference attempted to build on the work of the Institut and of the 1899 Conference by concluding a universal treaty providing for general obligatory arbitration and standard rules of procedure. While the Conference did not succeed in reaching a binding agreement on obligatory arbitration, the Final Act included a declaration "admitting" the principle of obligatory arbitration, in particular for disputes relating to the interpretation and application of the provisions of international agreements[3].

The Hague Convention I of 1907 revised and extended the Convention for the Pacific Settlement of International Disputes prepared in 1899 by developing the regulations for international commissions of inquiry and revising the rules on arbitration in the light of the four cases that had been brought before the Permanent Court of Arbitration. Convention I has a remarkable scope, covering good

---

2. Shabtai Rosenne, "Introduction", in *The Hague Peace Conferences of 1899 and 1907 and International Arbitration: Reports and Documents*, Shabtai Rosenne (ed.), pp. xiii-xxix, at p. xvi.
3. Final Act of the Second International Peace Conference, 1907, Declarations 1 and 2.

offices and mediation, commissions of inquiry, and setting out 39 articles on arbitral procedure.

The Convention marked a milestone in the commitment to the peaceful settlement of disputes between States. It was followed by the 1928 General Act for the Pacific Settlement of International Disputes, a revised version of which was adopted by the General Assembly in resolution 268 A (III) of 1949 [4]. The Revised Act, among other things, allowed a wider range of States to accede to it. Non-treaty modalities also picked up the theme of the peaceful settlement of disputes, such as the 1970 Declaration on the Principles of Friendly Relations [5] and the 1982 Manila Declaration [6]. Most strikingly, we see the lasting impact of the Hague Convention I in Article 1 of the UN Charter's statement of the very purposes of the United Nations, namely

> "to bring about by peaceful means, and in conformity with the principles of justice and international law, adjustment or settlement of international disputes or situations which might lead to a breach of the peace".

The methods of dispute settlement set out in Convention I of 1907 are reflected in contemporary instruments. Part XV of the UN Convention on the Law of the Sea embodies the flexibility of means envisaged by Convention I of 1907. It establishes a sophisticated dispute settlement system under which the settlement of disputes is obligatory, but the particular procedure to be followed by the parties is largely a matter of choice. The approach of the Convention I of 1907 is also echoed in the means for the pacific settlement of disputes listed in Article 33 of the UN Charter, which all Member States are required to apply when involved in a dispute "the continuance of which is likely to endanger the maintenance of international peace and security". Regrettably, realism requires that we acknowledge that this is all too infrequently done. At the same time, one sees every day these very methods being employed, from the

---

4. Revised General Act for the Pacific Settlement of International Disputes, resolution 268 A (III), *Official Records of the General Assembly, Third Session*, Part II (A/900), p. 10, entry into force 20 September 1950.
5. General Assembly resolution 2625 (XXV), Declaration on Principles of International Law concerning Friendly Relations and Co-operation among States in accordance with the Charter of the United Nations, 24 October 1970.
6. General Assembly resolution 37/10, Peaceful Settlement of Disputes between States, 15 November 1982.

good offices of former Secretary-General Kofi Annan in Cyprus, East Timor, Iraq, Libya, Nigeria and Western Sahara, to the International Commission of Inquiry on Darfur headed by Professor Antonio Cassese, to the judicial settlement of disputes by the International Court of Justice (ICJ) and so on and so forth.

One of the principal innovations of the 1899 Hague Conference had been the establishment of the Permanent Court of Arbitration. At the 1907 Conference, the idea of a standing international court of justice was born. Although the delegates were unable to agree on the method of electing judges to such a Court, they did produce a Draft Convention for the Creation of a Court of Arbitral Justice.

The momentum towards the launching of an international court was interrupted by the First World War, but the founding of the Permanent Court of International Justice in 1922 and its legal continuation as the International Court of Justice in 1946, were clearly inspired by the ideas of 1907. Dispute settlement has assumed a greater and greater importance in the century since the 1907 Conference. Provision for judicial settlement is routinely included, in one form or another, in the vast majority of multilateral treaties. To take but one example, some 300 bilateral or multilateral treaties provide that disputes concerning the application or interpretation of the instrument may be referred to the ICJ for decision. During the Cold War years this form of dispute settlement was unacceptable to the Socialist countries, which could not then accept the idea of an impartial tribunal. Reservations to treaties were often made with respect to referral to the ICJ. But the ending of the Cold War has led to extraordinary changes. Many of these treaty reservations have been dropped. Such a clause is unproblematic in new treaties. In the 1990s, the ICJ saw its first intra-East European case[7]. Ukraine and Romania have a case pending before us, and Russia is supportive of positive references to the ICJ in key UN documents.

The past two decades has seen the burgeoning of international courts and tribunals equipped to deal with disputes that might arise under the growing reach of international law. The International Court is now joined by regional human rights courts, by international criminal courts and tribunals, by courts which are part of treaty systems for regional economic integration, by a Tribunal for the

---

7. *Gabcíkovo-Nagymaros Project (Hungary/Slovakia)*, Application filed by Hungary on 23 October 1992.

Law of the Sea, by decision-making panels on trade — and very many more. If in today's world the substance of inter-State disputes has become so varied and specialized, the desire to have them settled judicially surely finds it roots in the 1907 Conference.

Yet despite all the progress that has been made, there is still an area in which the settlement of international disputes remains under-developed. It is still accepted by States as a "given" that recourse to the International Court to settle their disputes must always continue to be based on consent. Although the Court does play a significant role in international judicial settlement — 79 States have engaged in Court proceedings in the past decade — the absence of a compulsory recourse to the Court falls short of what was hoped for one hundred years ago. It is also in stark contrast to the compulsory adjudication systems build in to most international treaties today. It is out of joint with the times. Perhaps this is something to be realised this new century?

*

The other area in which the 1907 Conference has had a lasting impact is the codification of the laws of war. The Conference built on certain preparatory works, including the Geneva Convention of 1864[8], the Brussels Declaration of 1874[9], and the Oxford Manual on the laws of war of 1880[10], which had been adopted by the Institut de droit international. The 1907 Conference resulted in Convention III on the Opening of Hostilities, Convention IV on the Laws and Customs of War, Conventions V and XIII on neutrality on land and at sea, and five Conventions on various aspects of the law of war at sea[11].

---

8. Amelioration of the Condition of the Wounded on the Field of Battle (Red Cross Convention), signed 22 August 1864; superseded by conventions of 6 July 1906, 27 July 1929 and 12 August 1949 as between contracting parties to the later conventions in each instance.

9. Project of an International Declaration concerning the Laws and Customs of War, 27 August 1874, 4 *Martens nouveau recueil* (Ser. 2) 219, 65 *Brit. Foreign & St. Papers* 1005 (1873-1874).

10. *The Laws of War on Land*, Manual published by the Institute of International Law ("Oxford Manual"), Adopted by the Institute of International Law at Oxford, 9 September 1880.

11. Convention II on the Limitation of Employment of Force for Recovery of Contract Debts; Convention III on the Opening of Hostilities; Convention IV on the Laws and Customs of War on Land; Convention V on the Rights and Duties of Neutral Powers and Persons in Case of War on Land; Convention VI on the

One of these Conventions, Convention VIII on the Laying of Automatic Submarine Contact Mines, featured in the very first Judgment decided by the International Court of Justice, the *Corfu Channel* case of 1948. The Applicant, the United Kingdom, complained that in 1946 two British destroyers were damaged with large loss of life by mines laid with the connivance or knowledge of the Albanian Government and that "the Albanian Government did not notify the existence of these mines as required by the Hague Convention VIII of 1907 in accordance with the general principles of international law and humanity". This Convention only applies in times of war, but the Court held that Albania was bound, not by the Convention as such, "but on certain general and well-recognized principles, namely: elementary considerations of humanity, even more exacting in peace than in war . . ." [12]. This conclusion was reiterated almost four decades later in the case concerning *Military and Paramilitary Activities in and against Nicaragua*:

> "[I]f a States lays mines in any waters whatever . . . and fails to give any warning or notification whatsoever, in disregard of the security of peaceful shipping, it commits a breach of the principles of humanitarian law underlying the specific provisions of Convention No. VIII of 1907." [13]

Thus the specific provisions of Convention VIII and the general obligations of international law were seamlessly merged by the Court. Indeed, much of the treaty provisions agreed upon in 1907 have passed into customary international law.

Of all the Conventions concluded by the 1907 Conference, the most significant has been Convention IV and its annexed Regulations. These so-called "Hague Regulations" were in 1946 held by the Nuremberg Military Tribunal to have become part of custo-

---

Status of Enemy Merchant Ships at the Outbreak of Hostilities; Convention VII on the Conversion of Merchant Ships into War-Ships; Convention VIII on the Laying of Automatic Submarine Contact Mines; Convention IX on Bombardment by Naval Forces in Time of War; Convention X on Adaptation to Maritime War of the Principles of the Geneva Convention; Convention XI on Certain Restrictions with Regard to the Exercise of the Right of Capture in Naval War; Convention XII on the Creation of an International Prize Court (not ratified); Convention XIII on the Rights and Duties of Neutral Powers in Naval War.

    12. *Corfu Channel (United Kingdom v. Albania), Merits, Judgment, ICJ Reports 1949*, p. 4 at p. 22.

    13. *Military and Paramilitary Activities in and against Nicaragua (Nicaragua v. United States of America), Merits, Judgment, ICJ Reports 1986*, p. 14 at p. 112, para. 215.

mary international law. This has been the designation used by the ICJ on several occasions, including in its Advisory Opinion on the *Legality of the Threat or Use of Nuclear Weapons*[14]. They have also been recognized as having passed into customary law by other UN entities. When the International Criminal Tribunal for the former Yugoslavia was being established in 1993, the Secretary-General stated that the tribunal "should apply rules of international humanitarian law which are beyond any doubt part of customary law" including the Hague Convention IV and its annexed Regulations[15].

As the Court observed in its *Nuclear Weapons* Advisory Opinion, the Hague Regulations "fixed the rights and duties of belligerents in their conduct of operations and limited the choice of methods and means of injuring the enemy in an international armed conflict"[16]. The Hague Regulations enshrined cardinal principles that constitute the "fabric of humanitarian law"[17]. They established the distinction between combatants and non-combatants, specifying that States must never make civilians the object of attack and must never use weapons that are incapable of distinguishing between civilian and military targets. The Regulations prohibited weapons that cause superfluous injury or are calculated to cause unnecessary suffering. In its 1996 *Nuclear Weapons* Advisory Opinion, the International Court unanimously held that the provisions of international humanitarian law apply to nuclear weapons despite the fact that existing legal principles had never imagined a weapon of such destructive power. The intrinsic complexities of the issues were deployed in detail — with all their uncertainties — and the Hague Regulations were throughout present in the thinking of the Court.

The law on belligerent occupation laid down in the Hague Regulations has been in issue in two recent cases before the International Court. In the case concerning *Armed Activities on the Territory of the Congo (Democratic Republic of the Congo* v. *Uganda)*[18], the Court referred to Article 42 of the Hague Regulations to determine whether Ugandan forces were occupying parts of

---

14. *Legality of the Threat or Use of Nuclear Weapons, Advisory Opinion, ICJ Reports 1996*, p. 226 at p. 258.

15. Report of Secretary-General pursuant to paragraph 2 of Security Council resolution 808 (1993), UN doc. S/25704, at para. 34.

16. *Legality of the Threat or Use of Nuclear Weapons, Advisory Opinion, ICJ Reports 1996*, p. 226 at p. 256.

17. *Ibid.*, p. 257, at para. 78.

18. *Merits, Judgment,* 19 December 2005.

the Democratic Republic of the Congo. In applying the Hague Regulations, the Court noted that it was not sufficient to prove that armed forces were stationed in a particular location; it had to be proved that these armed forces had substituted their own authority for that of the Congolese Government in that location. The Court concluded that Uganda established and exercised authority in the province of Ituri as an Occupying Power, but not in other areas in which Uganda forces were present[19]. As a result, the Court had to deal with two separate areas to which different legal regimes applied. In Ituri, Article 43 of the 1907 Hague Regulations imposed on Uganda a duty to restore and ensure public order and safety while respecting the laws of the Congo. Uganda could therefore be held responsible not only for its own acts and omissions in that region but also for any lack of vigilance in preventing violations of human rights and humanitarian law by other actors in that territory and more specifically rebel groups. The Court noted that it was irrelevant whether the armed forces were acting contrary to instructions or exceeded their authority because Article 3 of Hague Convention IV requires that a party to an armed conflict be responsible for *all* acts by persons forming part of its armed forces. Article 3 was one of the innovations of the 1907 Conference; no such provision had been included in Convention II of 1899.

The application of the Hague Regulations in the *Congo* v. *Uganda* case was on the one hand novel, but at the same time rather straightforward. By contrast, the Court's Advisory Opinion on the *Legal Consequences of the Construction of a Wall in the Occupied Palestinian Territory* might be said to highlight the need for further development of humanitarian law rules[20]. In the *Wall* case, participants invoked a wide range of alleged violations of the Hague Regulations and the Fourth Geneva Convention. Despite the great variety of provisions invoked, the Court found only two breaches of humanitarian law in determining the illegality of the Wall along its present line: a violation of Article 49 of the Fourth Geneva Convention with respect to the establishment of Israeli settlements in the Occupied Palestinian Territory; and violations of Articles 46 and 52 of the Hague Regulations and Article 53 of the Fourth Geneva Convention

---

19. *Merits, Judgment,* 19 December 2005, at paras. 178-180.
20. *Legal Consequences of the Construction of a Wall in the Occupied Palestinian Territory, Advisory Opinion, ICJ Reports 2004,* p. 136.

by the destruction or requisition of properties. The gap between the plethora of provisions invoked and the small number of violations found might tell us something about the disjunction between international humanitarian law rules and the reality of modern conflicts. As Professor Pellet has observed:

> "[The] development of the law of belligerent occupation occurred in the context of temporary situations, and, at the beginning of the century, no one imagined that such situations might endure for decades. When such is the case, numerous legal and practical problems can arise which the traditional rules, designed for times of war, may prove ill-adapted to resolve."[21]

It seems that the delegates to the 1907 Conference were aware that at least some of the rules they were codifying would need to adapt to changing conditions. When the delegates failed to agree on the issue of the status of civilians who took up arms against an occupying force, a clause was formulated by the Russian delegate at the 1899 Conference. This became known as the Martens Clause, and it was repeated in the preamble to the Conventions that emerged from the 1907 Conference:

> "Until a more complete code of the laws of war is issued, the High Contracting Parties think it right to declare that in cases not included in the Regulations adopted by them, inhabitants and belligerents remain under the protection and empire of the principles of the law of nations, as they result from the usages established between civilized nations, from the laws of humanity and the dictates of the public conscience."

The Martens Clause was relied on in the Nuremberg jurisprudence to establish the concept of crimes against humanity, it has been cited by the ICJ and human rights bodies, and has been reiterated in many humanitarian law treaties, including the 1949 Geneva Conventions and the 1977 Additional Protocols[22]. The significance of the Martens

---

21. Alain Pellet, "The Destruction of Troy Will Not Take Place", in *International Law and the Administration of Occupied Territories: Two Decades of Israeli Occupation of the West Bank and Gaza Strip*, Emma Playfair (ed.) (1992), pp. 169, 192.

22. T. Meron, "The Martens Clause, Principles of Humanity and Dictates of Public Conscience", 94 *American Journal of International Law* 78.

Clause was recognized by the ICJ in its *Nuclear Weapons* Advisory Opinion, where it stated that the Martens Clause was an affirmation that the principles and rules of humanitarian law apply to nuclear weapons and that it "has proved to be an effective means of addressing the rapid evolution of military technology"[23].

States in the nineteenth century widely believed that if right was on their side they were entitled to use force. 1907 marked the beginning of an era in which the purposes for which force was to be used could be more and more constrained. The Hague Convention II of 1907 on the Limitation on the Use of Force for the Recovery of Contract Debts was the first international convention aimed at restricting the use of armed force to obtain a legal entitlement[24].

The 1907 Conference also laid the foundation for future lawmaking in specific areas. The sections of the Hague Conventions IV and IX that dealt with the protection of historic and religious buildings provided the launching point for the 1954 Convention on the Protection of Cultural Property[25]. And the Hague Regulations set out some minimum protections for civilians such as the prohibition on bombardment of undefended dwellings and the prohibition on pillage that were then significantly expanded 70 years later in Additional Protocol I to the Geneva Conventions[26].

*

In addition to the achievements of the 1907 Conference in terms of substantive law, the Conference was a milestone in procedural terms too.

The 1907 Hague Conference, and its predecessor in 1899, were path-breaking in that, unlike earlier peace conferences, which were convened to terminate ongoing armed conflicts or to deal with their immediate aftermath, the Hague Conferences met in peacetime for

---

23. *Legality of the Threat or Use of Nuclear Weapons, Advisory Opinion, ICJ Reports 1996,* p. 226 at p. 257.

24. Shabtai Rosenne, "Introduction", in *The Hague Peace Conferences of 1899 and 1907 and International Arbitration: Reports and Documents,* Shabtai Rosenne (ed.), pp. xiii-xxix, at p. xxi.

25. Convention for the Protection of Cultural Property in the Event of Armed Conflict with Regulations for the Execution of the Convention 1954, opened for signature 14 May 1954, entered into force 7 August 1956.

26. Protocol Additional to the Geneva Conventions of 12 August 1949, and relating to the Protection of Victims of International Armed Conflicts (Protocol 1), adopted on 8 June 1977, entered into force on 7 December 1979.

the purpose of making law. This was a new, proactive approach to the progressive codification of international law that is today carried forward by multilateral conferences and bodies such as the International Law Commission.

It can be said that the Hague Conferences established the method of work for international diplomatic conferences. The 1907 Conference adopted formal "Regulations" (the equivalent of Rules of Procedure) according to which the work was divided between Commissions in which every delegation could be represented, and Sub-commissions, which were composed of smaller groups of delegates working in detail on specific issues. Each would report to the plenary, where final decisions were made. A Conference Drafting Committee centralized the drafts of the various Commissions [27]. This pattern is still employed in multilateral conferences today. Significantly, the Hague Conferences operated on the basis of the principle of sovereign equality — each national delegation had one vote. This was a major innovation at that time, and was later the underpinning principle of the both the League of Nations and the United Nations. While power politics will always play their role, international law has to an extent levelled the playing field of international relations, and has indeed been seen by the less strong as their main protection in the face of disparate power realities.

The hosting of the 1899 and 1907 Conferences by the Dutch Government established the Netherlands as a pioneer in its support for international peace — and for international dispute resolution mechanisms in particular — setting a commendable example for other nations. The Conferences helped create the identity of The Hague as a centre for peace and justice. The Hague is now home to more than 150 international legal organizations.

Indeed, the first stone for the Peace Palace, home to the International Court of Justice and the Permanent Court of Arbitration, was laid during the 1907 Hague Peace Conference.

*
* *

---

27. Shabtai Rosenne, "Introduction", in *The Hague Peace Conferences of 1899 and 1907 and International Arbitration: Reports and Documents*, Shabtai Rosenne (ed.), pp. xiii-xxix, at p. xix.

The 1907 Hague Peace Conference made little progress on restricting the mass production of weapons — Tsar Nicholas II's original motivation — and failed to prevent the outbreak of war seven years later. But it was nonetheless a milestone in the development of the law on the peaceful settlement of disputes and the regulation of armed conflict.

In the words of US Secretary of State (and the first president of the Carnegie Endowment for International Peace) Elihu Root:

> "Some of the resolutions adopted . . . do not seem to amount to very much by themselves, but each one marks on some line of progress the farthest point to which the world is yet willing to go. They are like cable ends buoyed in midocean, to be picked up hereafter by some other steamer, spliced and continued to shore." [28]

Since the 1907 Hague Peace Conference empires have disintegrated, two world wars have been fought, and dozens of new States have emerged. Yet many of the "cable ends" left by the 1907 Conference have been picked up and carried forward, and there are some others that may yet be taken up in the future.

The 1907 Hague Peace Conference was a remarkable event — not only for what was done, but also for *how* it was done. Its legacies are numerous, and should serve as inspiration for what more can yet be achieved.

---

28. Elihu Root, Prefatory Note to the *Texts of the Peace Conferences at The Hague, 1899 and 1907*, James Brown Scott (ed.), 1908, at p. iv.

2. SOME REFLECTIONS OF A RUSSIAN SCHOLAR ON THE LEGACY OF THE SECOND PEACE CONFERENCE

V. S. VERESHCHETIN [1]

I

After the excellent comprehensive report by President Higgins I will confine my intervention only to some points related to the legacy of the Second Hague Conference. However, at the outset I would like to say a few words about the recent commemoration in Moscow of the centenary of the Second Peace Conference. In July 2007 the Russian Association of International Law held the fiftieth annual meeting. Its agenda was largely devoted to the topic of our current colloquium. Because of the two jubilees (that of the Peace Conference and that of the establishment of the Russian Association) the meeting was attended not only by the fellow-members of the Association but also by a number of leading political figures of the State. Among them were the first Deputy Prime Minister, Mr. Medvedev (now President of the Russian Federation), two former Prime Ministers and others. A number of invited foreign guests also spoke at the meeting. I would like to mention in particular the Chairman of the Executive Council of the ILA, Lord Slynn of Hadley, the Vice-President of the ICJ, Judge Al-Khasawneh, and the President-elect of the American Society of International Law, Ms Lucy Reed. Their speeches were warmly welcomed by the participants.

The key-note report made by the former member of the Russian Constitutional Court, Professor O. Tiunov, was devoted to the role of the Second Peace Conference in the development of humanitarian law and the current problems of its further progress. Among other things, the speaker dealt with such issues as relationship between the Hague Law and the Geneva Law; the link between the law of armed

---

1. Professor of International Law (Moscow), former Judge of the International Court of Justice.

conflicts and humanitarian law, on the one hand, and human rights law, on the other. On this latter point, it is worth mentioning that the ICJ in a number of its recent judgments and opinions stressed the existence of such a link and the operation of human rights law also in time of armed conflict and occupation[2].

In his report Judge Tiunov also touched upon some problems related to the changes which have to be introduced into the Russian national legislation for the full implementation of a number of provisions of humanitarian law and of the Rome Statute, if the latter were to be ratified by the Russian Federation. Amendments and supplements have to be made in the Penal Code, the Code of Criminal Procedure, the constitutional law "On the Judicial System of the Russian Federation" and in a number of federal laws. It is estimated, for example, that only in the Penal Code will it be necessary to add about 50 elements of war crimes. The review of the Rome Statute in the light of the Russian Constitution has revealed a number of collisions. To mention just one of them, the Russian Constitution (Art. 47, part 2) establishes the right of every person accused of committing a crime to have his (her) case examined by a court with the participation of a jury, while the Rome Statute does not envisage such a procedure[3].

II

Turning now to the substance of my presentation today, I would like to focus it mainly on two aspects: first, the Hague Conference and the development of international adjudication; second, the Conference as a precursor of global international organizations and of the development of universal international law.

As is known, the immediate reaction of many contemporaneous commentators as to the results of the Second Conference, in contrast to the first one, was not enthusiastic, to say the least. However now, with hindsight, we see that the Second Conference was a very important event in the development of international law and its

---

2. See, for example, *Armed Activities on the Territory of the Congo (Democratic Republic of the Congo v. Uganda)*, Order for Provisional Measures of 1 July 2000 and Judgment of 19 December 2005. *Legal Consequences of the Construction of a Wall in the Occupied Palestinian Territory*, Advisory Opinion of 9 July 2004.

3. The proceedings of the Moscow Conference will be published in the *Russian Yearbook of International Law*.

results preserved their significance even one hundred years later. As the legal historian, Arthur Eyffinger, has rightly observed, "in 1907 the pace was set for the next century"[4].

Naturally, the contemporaries of the Conference expected that a peace conference, by definition, would deal with such a problem as reduction of armaments, the problem which already at that time was very topical. Therefore the mere fact that disarmament could not even be included in the agenda was met with great disappointment and criticism. No less disappointing was the failure to make the recourse to inter-State arbitration obligatory. The maximum that could be achieved on the matter of arbitration was the provision in Article 38 of the Convention for the Pacific Settlement of International Disputes which stipulates that

> "In questions of legal nature, and especially in the interpretation or application of international conventions, arbitration is recognized by the contracting Powers as the most effective, and, at the same time, the most equitable means of settling disputes which diplomacy has failed to settle. Consequently it would be desirable that in disputes about the above-mentioned questions, the contracting Powers should, if the case arose, have recourse to arbitration, in so far as the circumstances permit."

This is a far cry from obligatory arbitration. But as is common knowledge even nowadays, one hundred years later, with all the progress of international adjudication and multiplication of international courts and tribunals, prior consent, unfortunately, remains the basic principle of international adjudication. Nevertheless, it should be emphasized that in the field of judicial settlement of international disputes the two Hague conventions for pacific settlement of international disputes and the establishment of the Permanent Court of Arbitration paved the way for the institutionalization of international adjudication which eventually found its expression in the creation of the Permanent Court of International Justice, of the International Court of Justice, and over the past decades of many other international courts and tribunals.

Yet, in spite of this tremendous progress in international judica-

---

4. Arthur Eyffinger, *The Hague — International Centre of Justice and Peace*, 2003, p. 23. See also his well-researched account of the Second Peace Conference, in *The 1907 Hague Peace Conference: The Conscience of the Civilized World*, 2007.

ture, even today the situation of international relations and of international law is such that, as we all know, it would be a great delusion to suppose that with the sole help of a court of law or arbitration it would be possible, once and for all, to put an end to war and other armed conflicts, as some had expected at the time of the Hague Peace Conferences.

Bearing in mind this circumstance and also realizing that the International Court of Justice is but one of the fora available for the peaceful settlement of disputes, I would like to note that the contribution of the ICJ to the prevention and resolution of international conflicts involving the use of force has become so visible, especially in the two past decades, that some authors even speak of an evident "revolution" in the character of cases brought before the Court[5].

I will not task your patience with citing examples of well-known cases recently heard by the Court, but rather will merely mention that a distinction can be drawn between two categories of case: those in which the matters directly resolved by the Court concerned not the armed conflict as such but the territorial or other claims which lay at the origin of the conflict, and those cases in which the legality of the use or the threat of the use of force were at the very core of the dispute. Of particular complexity, both from political and fact-finding perspectives, are the cases that have to be examined by the Court while the armed conflict is still going on. In view of the special role played by the Security Council in the resolution of such disputes it is sometimes wondered whether the Court should accept such cases at all. This objection is usually dismissed by the Court, without in the least encroaching upon the prerogatives of the Security Council, on the ground that the Security Council's special role does not preclude the Court from exercising its *judicial* function when dealing with such cases[6].

The current multiplication and specialization of international adjudicative bodies gave rise to another issue much discussed nowadays. This is the lack of any co-ordination or harmonization in their work, let alone of any coherent international judicial system or of any hierarchy among diverse courts and tribunals.

---

5. Christine Gray, "The Use and Abuse of the International Court of Justice: Cases concerning the Use of Force after Nicaragua", in *EJIL*, 2003, Vol. 14, No. 5, pp. 867-905.

6. See *Military and Paramilitary Activities in and against Nicaragua (Nicaragua* v. *United States of America), ICJ Reports 1984*, p. 392, at paras. 91-98.

One may argue whether this situation has already created or potentially may create inconsistency among their decisions, their interpretation of the same legal norms and the ensuing fragmentation of international law. It is also arguable whether any corrective measures are realistically feasible already now. Proposals to this effect have already been advanced in literature, in the United Nations and other fora[7]. In any case, it can hardly be doubted that more profound study of this topic is very desirable for the sake of preservation of the unity and effectiveness of international law.

III

I would like to turn now to the second subject of my comments — the role of the Hague Conference as a precursor of world peace organizations and of the universalization of international law.

A number of features of both Hague Conferences contributed to the further institutionalization of inter-State relations in the political field which finally led to the establishment of the League of Nations and after the Second World War of the United Nations. Already at the First Conference in 1899 it was envisaged to hold another conference within a few years. Its convocation was delayed due to the prevailing international situation. At the Second Conference the US representative, General Porter, proposed to convene such conferences on a regular basis. The preparation of an agenda for a third conference, already started by the Dutch Government, but aborted by the outbreak of the First World War, included the topic of institutionalization of the Hague Peace Conferences[8].

The Hague Conferences can be seen as the first attempt to manage political relations among States in a number of important areas on a regular universal basis. Professor F. Martens, in accordance with his theory of international community, considered the Hague Conferences as essential organs of international administration, as an attempt of the Governments to organize and regulate the relations among the peoples with the aim of peaceful and amicable cohabitation[9].

---

7. See on this matter, Tulio Treves, "Judicial Lawmaking in the Era of 'Proliferation' of International Courts and Tribunals: Development or Fragmentation of International Law", in Rüdiger Wolfrum and Volker Röben (eds.), *Developments of International Law in Treaty Making*, Springer, 2005, pp. 587-620.

8. *Netherlands International Law Review*, 1996, Vol. XLIII, Issue 2, p. 220.

9. V. Poustogarov, *Au service de la paix. F. de Martens, juriste et diplomate russe*, Geneva, 1999, p. 260.

Some procedural principles of the Hague Conferences also proved to be useful for the construction of the future world peace organizations. These principles included quasi-universal participation of sovereign States, the equality of the participants reflected in the rule "one State one vote", the method of work in commissions and plenary.

The existence of binding universal rules of international law is, naturally, of great importance for the functioning of global organizations having as their main objective the maintenance of peace and security on the basis of respect for law.

The Second Hague Conference marked an important step forward in the direction of the universalization of international law. It manifested itself in what would be nowadays designated as "codification and progressive development" of international law and in the participation in this process of the broadest possible number of States.

The Conference brought together about 250 delegates coming from 44 States, out of 57 States claiming independence at that time. It was a big leap forward compared to the First Conference where only 24 States were represented. Regrettably, African and some Asian delegates were not invited, but Latin America was represented at the Second Conference by 17 States which actively promoted on the global level their regional legal doctrine related to the limitation on the use of force in international relations [10].

IV

Thus, the Hague Conferences gave a great impetus for further consolidation and development of universal international law, as a system, universal both in the geographical and the substantive sense. Certainly genuinely universal, from the geographical point of view, could international law become only after the world ceased to be divided into so-called "civilized" and "non-civilized" nations, that is to say after the complete decolonization.

As to the substance of international law, in the course of history its content has radically changed and become enriched in particular due to the prohibition of the use of force, the recognition of the principle of self-determination and the advent of the law of international

---

10. Convention II, adopted at the Conference, dealt with the limitation on the employment of force for the recovery of contract debts.

human rights. The adoption of the UN Charter and the work of the UN International Law Commission played a singular role in the universalization of international law.

At the same time, the significantly increased number of the members of the international community different in their cultures, religions, political histories and the level of economic development gave rise to the debate as to whether international law, predominantly European by its origin, could continue to perform its universal function in the new political setting. The growth of the density, specialization and diversification of the norms of international law further complicated this debate, and the globalization with its multiple and diverse actors in the world arena and the complexity of transborder activities added to it a new dimension. Globalization provoked the revival of the ideas of so-called "legal pluralism" which sometimes challenge not only the unity of international law, as a system, but the very nature of law and its distinctive role among other normative orders in social life.

Among the manifestations of the recent revival of these concepts, rooted in the century-old anthropological and sociological theories of law, I would like to mention the theory which proposes the shift in focus from international law to "law and globalization". This theory blurs the boundary between public and private international law, legal and non-legal norms and emphasizes the role of non-State or private actors in the process of "transnational" norm development and application[11].

The universality of general international law and its basic principles is also challenged, sometimes with the best of intentions, by the proposition that general international law is or should be divided into two categories, types or forms: one is the law for international courts and tribunals, whose sources can be found in Article 38 of

---

11. See Paul Schiff Berman, "From International Law to Law and Globalization", 43 *Colum. J. Transnat'l L.*, pp. 485-556, stating among other things the following:

"This article obviously takes a broad view of what counts as law, including within its purview not only official norms articulated by state sanctioned regulatory bodies and courts, but also 'non-official' legal norms that often bind sub-national, transnational, or international communities." (P. 552.)

The author, however, does not explain why these "non-official" norms, which undoubtedly play an increasing role in regulating transnational relations, should also be called "legal".

the ICJ Statute, the other is the law regulating the conduct of States. Thus, Professor W. Michael Reisman, advocating this perception of the law-making and law-applying process in international law, designates the law applied in international courts and other formal institutions of international law as "State-made law", and the other category (the law generally regulating the conduct of States) as "media-made law", which takes the name from the channels through which most diverse "non-State actors [transmit] their prescriptive endeavors"[12].

Another proponent of the division of general international law into two categories, Professor Onuma Yasuaki, takes the view that the law as defined in Article 38 of the ICJ Statute reflects "west-centric preconceptions and judicial centrism", which is alien for non-Western countries. Therefore Professor Onuma Yasuaki proposes, for the establishment of "transcivilizational global legal order", to elaborate a theory "based on the recognition that ordinary norms of conduct in international law can be identified independently of Article 38 of the ICJ Statute"[13]. The author does not clearly define the sources of these norms. An exception is made for the resolutions of the UN General Assembly and of other international organizations which, not without hesitation, he refers to as possible sources of norms of conduct.

Professor Onuma Yasuaki considers that the new norms which he is proposing should be more flexible, less binding, and hence more appropriate for overcoming "west-centric preconceptions", "judicial centrism", and "positivism". They may be formulated, interpreted and applied by a large number of different actors "in order to justify their claims and interests, and to negate the legitimacy of the claims made by their opponents"[14]. In the view of Onuma Yasuaki, "[t]through such 'political' use of international law, international law contributes

---

12. See W. Michael Reisman. "The Democratization of Contemporary International Law-Making Process and the Differentiation of Their Application", in Rüdiger Wolfrum and Volker Röben (eds), *Developments of International Law in Treaty Making*, Springer, 2005, pp. 15-30. For the critique of this theory see Georges Abi-Saab (defining the "media-made law" as "antithetical to the very concept of law"), "Comment", *ibid.*, pp. 31-37.
13. Onuma Yasuaki, "A Transcivilizational Perspective on Global Legal Order in the Twenty-first Century: A Way to Overcome West-centric and Judiciary-centric Deficits in International Legal Thoughts", in Ronald St. John MacDonald and Douglas M. Johnston (eds.), *Towards World Constitutionalism*, 2005, pp. 151-189.
14. *Ibid*, p. 186.

to various socially useful functions including legitimation through the process of conflicting justification" [15].

In my opinion, the universality of public international law, as a system of law, is its essential characteristic. Any undermining of the unity, or commonality, of the universal international law and of its major historically formed principles would be counter-productive and would diminish its role and authority as the basis of world legal order. As to the work of international adjudicative bodies, I do not see how they could render their judgments, if they had to do it on the basis of the norms differing from those which actually govern the relations between States [16].

I would also note, in passing, that the view that the judicial dispute-settlement is alien to non-Western countries runs counter to the clear practice to have recourse to international adjudication, including the International Court of Justice, pursued over two last decades by many countries of the world. It is also belied by the fact of the recent establishment of the African Court on Human and Peoples' Rights.

The concern about safeguarding the universality of international law, as a system of law applicable to all States in all spheres of their activities, should not be mistakenly understood as a denial of the importance of sociological or anthropological approach to the study of "living law" [17], as distinguished from the "law on the books", or of the increasing role of political and other rules in international relations, or of the gradual departure from purely "étatique" structure of international law or, for that matter, of the inevitable diversification and specialization of international law. The point is that the highly needed cross-cultural understanding and dialogue at all levels in the multicultural and multi-religious international community require not the abandonment of universal principles of international

---

15. Yasuaki, *op. cit.* For the critique of this theory see Christian Tomuschat (stating in particular that "if every state was free to formulate its own conception of international law without encountering the boundaries set by the case law of the ICJ, international law would inevitably fall apart"), "World Order Models, A Disputation with B. S. Chimni and Yasuaki Onuma", in *International Community Law Review* 8:71-79, 2006.

16. On this point see also Ch. Tomuschat, *International Law: Ensuring the Survival of Mankind on the Eve of a New Century,* 2001, p. 307.

17. The term was introduced at the beginning of the twentieth century by Eugen Ehrlich in his *Grundlegung der Soziologie des Rechts.* For the English translation of this book see Eugen Ehrlich, *Fundamental Principles of the Sociology of Law,* Cambridge, Massachusetts, 1936.

law which legally express common human values but rather their further strengthening.

However, as Sir Robert Jennings put it many years ago, it would be a "flawed universality" to present modern international law in a mono-cultural sense [18]. The traditions and concepts of non-Western nations have made a very important input to the development of international law practically from its outset and can significantly contribute to the modern discourse on the universality of international law.

*

* *

I would like to finish this presentation by paying tribute to Professor F. Martens. He was a man ahead of his time. Although his role at the Second Hague Conference was less visible and less appreciated than during the First Hague Conference, Professor Martens, who was rather ill at the time of the Second Conference (he died two years later), contributed a lot to the very possibility of its convening. With this purpose he performed "shuttle diplomacy", visiting the capitals of many European States. Martens played a very important role in the formulation of the programme and of the rules of this Conference, and headed one of its major commissions.

In regard to the Second Peace Conference, Martens wrote:

> "Je suis fier d'avoir contribué, autant que je le pouvais, à poser les jalons de la cohabitation entre les peuples. Je peux fermer les yeux sereinement. On se souviendra de moi, en Russie et dans le reste du monde, et l'on n'oubliera pas ce que j'ai fait pour le développement du droit international." [19]

I am happy that on the occasion of the commemoration of the First Peace Conference in 1999 a bust of Professor Martens was unveiled in the Peace Palace, the Palace whose very existence, to a large extent, is also due to the efforts of this great humanist and internationalist.

---

18. Robert Y. Jennings, "Universality of International Law in a Multicultural World", in *Liber Amicorum for the Rt. Hon. Lord Wilberforce* (1987), p. 48.

19. V. Poustogarov, *Au service de la paix. F. de Martens, juriste et diplomate russe*, Geneva, 1999, p. 285.

3. THE PRESENCE AND PARTICIPATION OF LATIN AMERICA AT THE SECOND HAGUE PEACE CONFERENCE OF 1907

A. A. CANÇADO TRINDADE[1]

I. Preliminary Considerations

It is a high distinction to contribute to this historical colloquium, whereto contemporary international law scholars come, and gather in the new premises of the Hague Academy of International Law, in order to review and reassess the work and outcome of the Second Hague Peace Conference of 1907, and to identify, in historical projection, its legacy and topicality, one century after it took place in this city. The world today is entirely different from that of 1907, but some human aspirations, which motivated the convening of the Second Hague Peace Conference and found expression therein, remain as topical and as vivid nowadays, in 2007, as they were in 1907: such is the case of the perennial human aspirations to the preservation of peace and the realization of justice.

The high relevance of the aims of this centennial colloquium stems also from the fact that a proper understanding of the *corpus juris* of international law, as it has evolved over this last century and as it stands today, and any attempted projection into the future, cannot make abstraction of the lessons from the past. International law is not formed, and does not operate, in a vacuum, and scholars of the discipline could hardly escape to bear always in mind the lessons from the past and the overriding importance of its general principles.

In the course of this last century, international law has evolved, faithful to its general principles, to respond to changing needs, and recurring aspirations, of the international community. International law has survived undue attempts of its deconstruction, on the part of irresponsible heralds of unilateralism and unwarranted use of force. International law has kept alive the awareness of the needed

---

1. Judge and former President of the Inter-American Court of Human Rights; Professor of International Law at the University of Brasilia.

prevalence of law over force. International law has devised more effective means of peaceful settlement of international disputes and has fostered sensible advances in the arbitral and judicial solutions.

The Second Hague Peace Conference of 1907 was a milestone to this effect, and its work and outcome are of relevance to all international law scholars concerned with the present state and the future of the discipline, as related to the fate of humankind as a whole. For the consideration of the general theme — the "Topicality of the Second Hague Peace Conference of 1907" — which gathers us together today and tomorrow (6 and 7 September 2007) — here at the Hague Academy of International Law, I have been entrusted with a particular topic, namely, that of the presence and participation of Latin American States at the aforementioned Conference of 1907.

For the purposes of my presentation, I shall address, at first, the presence of Latin American States at the 1907 Conference, by reviewing its historical antecedents relevant to international law itself, and by identifying the contributions of those States to the work and the outcome of the Second Hague Peace Conference. Attention will then be focused on four main points of the contributions of Latin American States to the Second Hague Peace Conference, namely: recourse to arbitration and non-use of force, the principle of the juridical equality of States, the strengthening of international jurisdiction, and the direct access of individuals to international justice.

Following that, I shall dwell upon the outcome of the 1907 Conference, in the light of the aforementioned Latin American contributions, singling out the fostering of codification of international law, the awakening and development of conscientization, and the formation of a new *opinio juris*. I shall then focus on the historical projection of the 1907 Conference in time. The way will at last be paved for the presentation of my final considerations on this process, in its moving towards what I perceive as the emergence of a new *jus gentium*, the International Law for Humankind.

II. Latin American States at the Second Hague Peace Conference

1. Historical Antecedents

Of the 26 States which participated in the First Hague Peace Conference of 1899, only one (Mexico) was from Latin America; in turn, of the 44 participating States at the Second Hague Peace

Conference of 1907, 18 were Latin American States — as acknow-ledged by its *Acte final*[2] — that is, almost half of the participants. Thus, in a time-span of 8 years, much progress was achieved towards universality in participation, from a Latin American perspective. This substantial change, in so far as Latin American participation was concerned, can nowadays, one century later, be understood and appreciated in historical perspective.

On the American continent, inter-State concertation had in fact begun one decade before the First Hague Peace Conference of 1899: the series of International Conferences of American States started in 1889, and, between the First and the Second Hague Peace Confer-ences (of 1899 and 1907), two such Conferences of American States took place, namely, the second of them in Mexico City in 1901, and the third of them in Rio de Janeiro in 1906[3]. In both of them the par-ticipating States displayed their preparedness in taking part in the work of systematization of international law also at universal level.

Thus, at the Second Conference of American States of Mexico City in 1901, Latin American States took note of the three Conven-tions adopted at the First Hague Peace Conference of 1899, particu-larly the one on Peaceful Settlement of International Disputes, and made theirs the principles underlying it[4]. Moreover, in order to enhance recourse to arbitration, Latin American States adopted at the aforementioned Mexico Conference a General Treaty on Arbitration, open to signature on 30 January 1902[5]. By pledging the same ideals of the States which had participated in the First Hague Peace

---

2. Those 18 States were: Argentina, Bolivia, Brazil, Chile, Colombia, Cuba, Dominican Republic, Ecuador, El Salvador, Guatemala, Haiti, Mexico, Nicaragua, Panama, Paraguay, Peru, Uruguay and Venezuela. Cf. *Deuxième Conférence internationale de la Paix — Actes et documents*, Vol. I, *Séances plé-nières de la Conférence*, La Haye, Ministère des Affaires étrangères, Imprimerie nationale, 1907, pp. 689-701.

3. The IV and V Conferences were held, respectively, in Buenos Aires in 1910 and in Santiago de Chile in 1923; and the sixth of them took place in Havana, in 1928, two decades after the Second Hague Peace Conference of 1907. For an account, cf., e.g., F. V. García Amador, *Sistema Interamericano a través de Tratados, Convenciones y Otros Documentos*, Vol. I, *Asuntos Jurídico-Políticos*, Washington DC, OAS General Secretariat, 1981, pp. 67 and 133-141; César Sepúlveda, *El Sistema Interamericano*, 2nd ed., Mexico, Ed. Porrúa, 1974, pp. 23-28.

4. As the 1899 Hague Conventions originally foresaw the accesion only of those States which had in fact participated in the First Hague Peace Conference.

5. F.-J. Urrutia, "La codification du droit international en Amérique", 22 *Recueil des cours de l'Académie de droit international de La Haye* (1928), p. 113, and cf. pp. 116-117.

Conference of 1899, Latin American States sent a clear message to these latter, to the effect that they were quite well prepared, and willing, to participate at the forthcoming Conference of the kind, the Second Hague Peace Conference of 1907.

To the same effect, Latin American States began to give expression to the principle of the prohibition of the use of force in inter-State relations also before the Second Hague Peace Conference of 1907. It may be recalled, in this connection, that the Drago doctrine had been formulated five years earlier, in reaction to an armed attack by three European powers (Germany, Great Britain and Italy) in Puerto Cabello against Venezuela; on 29 December 1902 the Foreign Minister of Argentina, exposed in a Note the doctrine named after him, whereby the coercitive recovery of public debt was declared inadmissible in Latin America. Although the Note had been sent by L. M. Drago to his Minister in Washington[6], it also repercuted elsewhere: Carlos Calvo, who lived in Paris and was the Argentine Minister before the French Government, translated the Note of L. M. Drago and, shortly before dying, circulated it in 1903 to some of the most distinguished European jusinternationalists, members of the Institut de Droit International; Drago's Note became well known in European juridical circles as well[7], four years before the Second Hague Peace Conference[8].

As the report of the Delegation of Colombia to the Second Hague Peace Conference of 1907 later recalled, the Drago doctrine was brought to the attention of the Third International Conference of

---

6. For his own account, cf. L. M. Drago, "La Cuestión de Venezuela", in *Anales de la Facultad de Derecho y Ciencias Sociales*, Vol. IV, Buenos Aires, Libr. Prudent Hermanos y Moetzel, 1903, pp. 50-59; L. M. Drago, "Nota del 29.12.1902 Enviada al Ministro Argentino en Washington (M. García Merou)", in A. A. Conil Paz, *Historia de la Doctrina Drago*, Buenos Aires, Abeledo-Perrot, 1975, pp. 125-131.

7. S. M. Lozada, "Carlos Calvo, la Doctrina Drago y la Deuda Externa", 4 *Revista de Derecho Público y Teoría del Estado* (1989), pp. 33-34, and cf. pp. 35-37.

8. Years earlier, Carlos Calvo himself called for juridical equality so as to put an end to rivalries in inter-State relations, and to foster the advances of international law so as "no longer to allow the sacrifice of the superior interests of humankind"; C. Calvo, *Manuel de droit international public et privé*, 3rd rev. ed., Paris, LNDJ/A, Rousseau Ed., 1892, p. 118, and cf. pp. 83 and 215. Still in the second half of the nineteenth century, Andres Bello also expressed similar aspirations; cf. A. Bello, *Principios de Derecho Internacional*, 3rd ed., Paris, Garnier, 1873, pp. 12-14. And, for an assessment of A. Bello's legal thinking, cf., e.g., A. de Avila Martel, "La Filosofía Jurídica de Andres Bello", in *Congreso Internacional "Andres Bello y el Derecho"*, Santiago, 1981, Editorial Jurídica de Chile, 1982, pp. 41-62.

American States held in Rio de Janeiro in 1906, but, since most of the Delegates to this latter were representatives of debtor States, they decided to defer discussion of the matter and to schedule it for the following year, at the aforementioned Second Hague Peace Conference[9], where it at last gained international recognition[10]. The Rio de Janeiro Conference of 1906 took two important decisions: first, to ratify the Convention of Mexico of 1902 (for pecuniary claims); and secondly, to submit to the forthcoming Second Hague Peace Conference of 1907 the topic of the recovery of public debts (whether the use of force would be admissible or not to that end)[11].

The way was paved, by the Latin American States themselves, for consideration of the matter at the Second Hague Peace Conference of 1907. The principle of the prohibition of the use of force or coercion in inter-State relations in effect found expression — with the support of Latin American States, more forcefully as from the 1907 Hague Peace Conference onwards — and was to exert, ever since, in the years to come, considerable influence on the evolution of international law in the following decades.

As the days of the Second Hague Peace Conference came closer (15 June to 18 October 1907), the decision had been taken that the Second Hague Conference was meant to be a "universal" Conference, and that Latin American States were to be invited, as they in fact were[12], 18 of them having participated in it. Latin American States had in fact earned their place in the concert of nations. Their presence itself at the Hague Conference in 1907 contributed to give concrete expression to another fundamental principle of international law, that of the juridical equality of States.

In fact, by the time they assembled at The Hague for the 1907 Peace Conference, Latin American States had already gathered experience in international concertation, besides having formed a sense

---

9. MRE, *Informes y Notas de la Delegación de Colombia en la II Conferencia de la Paz de La Haya (1907)*, Rotterdam, M. Wyt & Zonen Impr., 1908, pp. 38-39.

10. J. C. Arellano, "La Doctrina Drago y Su Importancia Americanista", 36 *Boletín de la Academia de Ciencias Políticas y Sociales*, Caracas, 1977, n. 71, p. 157, and cf. pp. 154-155. And, for a study, cf. L. M. Drago, *La República Argentina y el Caso de Venezuela*, Buenos Aires, Impr. Ed. Coni Hermanos, 1903, pp. 1-326; A. N. Vivot, *La Doctrina Drago*, Buenos Aires, Impr. Ed. Coni Hermanos, 1911, pp. 5-367.

11. I. Fabela, *Intervention*, Paris, Pedone, 1961, pp. 144-145.

12. D. Gaurier, *Histoire du droit international*, Rennes, Presses universitaires de Rennes, 2005, pp. 421-422.

of common solidarity among themselves. When they convened, with other States from distinct parts of the world, at the Second Hague Peace Conference of 1907, they were already imbued with this spirit. As aptly remarked by a legal commentator early in the twentieth century,

> "La solidarité continentale des républiques américaines procède d'un grand nombre d'éléments d'ordre moral et matériel : elle est étrangère à toute espèce d'hégémonie et se fonde sur les principes démocratiques et l'égalité juridique des Etats." [13]

2. Contributions to the Conference

The contributions of Latin American States to the work and outcome of the Second Hague Peace Conference of 1907 and to developments thereafter focused mainly on four issues, namely : recourse to arbitration and non-use of force, the basic principle of the juridical equality of States, the strengthening of international jurisdiction, and the direct access of individuals to international justice. It is thus all too proper to review each of them on this occasion.

(a) *Recourse to arbitration and non-use of force*

During the consideration by the Second Hague Peace Conference of 1907 of the issue of peaceful recovery of contract debts, the Porter proposal — of prior recourse to arbitration — represented a significant advance towards international peace, but much was owed to the Drago doctrine, which did not admit, in any circumstance whatsoever, "armed aggression" for the recovery of international contract debts [14]. Intervening at the First Commission of the Hague

---

13. F.-J. Urrutia, "La codification du droit international en Amérique", *op. cit. supra* footnote 5, p. 120, and cf. pp. 116-117. Thus, for example, bearing in mind that the First Hague Peace Conference of 1899 had sought in vain to obtain the adoption of compulsory arbitration, the 1906 Rio de Janeiro Conference of American States adopted a resolution on the "principle of arbitration", and recommended to the Delegations of Latin American States to the forthcoming Second Hague Peace Conference of 1907 to endeavour to obtain therein the adoption of a General Convention on Arbitration, that could be put into practice by all States. In this way,

> "les délégations américaines à la Seconde Conférence de La Haye se sont non seulement conformées aux vœux de la Conférence de Rio de Janeiro, mais ont encore manifesté, par l'unanimité et la fermeté de leurs opinions dans ce domaine de l'arbitrage, une politique de continuité qui leur fait grand honneur" ; *ibid.*, pp. 133-134.

14. S. Pérez Triana and W. T. Stead (intr.), *Doctrina Drago — Colección de Documentos*, London, Impr. Wertheimer, Lea & Co., 1908, pp. lxxiv and xliv.

Peace Conference on 16 July 1907, H. Porter himself stated that one of the significant aspects of the Conference was that at The Hague the "creditor and debtor nations of the world" were amicably working together to draft a general treaty on peaceful recovery of contract debts that would serve "the true interests of peace in the world" [15]. Two days later (18 July 1907), the Delegate of Colombia (S. Pérez Triana) warned that forced recovery was "a danger for peace in the world", this being the reason for discarding the "use of force" [16]. Days later (on 23 July 1907), the Delegate of Uruguay (J. P. Castro), further warned that "the sacrifice of the principles established by the law of nations would be too high a price for the advantages sought sometimes by daring businessmen" [17].

The Chilean Delegate (A. Matte) also supported recourse to arbitration for the settlement of pecuniary claims; and the Delegate of the Dominican Republic (Henriquez y Carvajal) expressed (on 23 July 1907) the belief of his Delegation that it was convenient, in order to improve inter-State relations,

> "and to give greater value and brilliance to international justice and greater confidence to small States, to submit, without exception, all controversies of pecuniary nature to the decision of arbitration" [18].

The Delegate of Haiti (P. Hudicourt) added (on 27 July 1907) that his Delegation was prepared thereby to contribute to the "progress of international law" [19]. The Delegation of the Dominican Republic further argued, at the First Commission of the 1907 Conference, that the principle of non-use of force should be erected by the Second Hague Peace Conference, as a

> "règle de conduite internationale, ... dans le but de poser la première pierre du droit des gens contemporain et futur, et d'empêcher par tous les moyens qui soient à leur portée les actes de force, toujours funestes et affreux" [20].

In its report, of 19 October 1907, to the Argentine Foreign Office,

---

15. In S. Pérez Triana and W. T. Stead, *op. cit. supra* footnote 14, p. 100.
16. In *ibid.*, p. 117.
17. In *ibid.*, p. 120.
18. In *ibid.*, pp. 125 and 127 (my own translation).
19. In *ibid.*, p. 148.
20. In *Deuxième Conférence internationale de la Paix — Actes et documents* (1907), Vol. II, *Première Commission, op. cit. infra* footnote 37, p. 922.

the Argentine Delegation to the Second Hague Peace Conference (R. Saenz Peña, L. M. Drago and C. Rodríguez Larreta) indicated that there was initially, as to the issue of recourse to arbitration for recovery of contract debts, a "fundamental dissent" between the original proposal of the United States and the Argentine position based on the Drago doctrine. With the Porter amendment, Argentina voted in favour of the project (of the resulting Convention) with reservations (as to the eventual possibility of residual corrective measures), yet the vote in favour was "in tribute to the application of the principle of [recourse to] arbitration"[21].

Moreover, in the discussions in plenary of the proposed recourse to arbitration so as to avoid the use of force for the recovery of contract debts, Latin American States supported resort to arbitration in the present context, and the following Delegations of Latin American States went even further, in expressing their reservations (already made in the First Commission of the Second Hague Peace Conference) even as to eventual and residual recourse to force (failing arbitration): Argentina, Colombia, Dominican Republic, Ecuador, El Salvador, Guatemala, Nicaragua, Paraguay, Peru, Venezuela and Uruguay[22]. The participation of Latin American States in the Conference debates repercuted in public opinion of those times[23].

---

21. [MRE,] *La República Argentina en la II Conferencia Internacional de la Paz — Haya 1907*, Buenos Aires, Impr. A. Pech, 1908, pp. 6-7. And, for a subsequent account of the participation of the Argentine Delegation at the Second Hague Peace Conference, cf., e.g., Carlos Alberto Silva, *La Política Internacional de la Nación Argentina*, Buenos Aires, Impr. Cámara de Diputados, 1946, pp. 255-261. It may be recalled that the Drago doctrine totally discarded the use of force for the recovery of public debts. The Porter proposal or amendment distorted the Drago doctrine by leaving the door open for an eventual or residual use of force in case of failure of arbitration; although not wholly adopted by the Second Hague Peace Conference of 1907, the Drago doctrine contributed to put an end to old methods of coercion. It was not surprising that Argentina presented a reservation to the Porter proposal, while supporting arbitration; cf. J.-M. Yepes, "La contribution de l'Amérique latine . . .", *op. cit. infra* footnote 30, pp. 737-739 and 743-744.

22. In *Deuxième Conférence internationale de la Paix — Actes et documents* (La Haye — 15 juin/18 octobre 1907), vol. I, *Séances plénières de la Conférence*, La Haye, Ministère des Affaires étrangères, Imprimerie nationale, 1907, pp. 337-338.

23. The *Courrier de la Conférence* of 19 July 1907 took due account of their contribution to the debates, and the *Daily News* of London of 21 October 1907 reckoned the "solid and positive achievement" of the incorporation of the "essence of the Drago doctrine" in the solution at last adopted of prior recourse to arbitration for the recovery of contractual debts; cf. S. Pérez Triana and W. T. Stead (intr.), *Doctrina Drago — Colección de Documentos, op. cit. supra* footnote 14, pp. 205 and 236.

It is significant that, at the Second Hague Peace Conference of 1907, the project on compulsory arbitration was supported by *all* American States participating in the Conference; in fact, while none of their Delegations were squarely opposed to it, each of them sought to accept it with greater or lesser reservations or limitations, and in this way it was at last approved on 15 October 1907[24]. As to the principle of non-use of force, the Drago doctrine (on absolute prohibition of the use of force), even with the Porter amendment (rendering such use only residual, in case of refusal or failure of arbitration), represented a sensible advance towards recourse to arbitration and abandonment of "measures of violence"; furthermore — it was realized in those days —

> "comme l'a démontré l'expérience, et comme l'a compris la Conférence de La Haye, le problème présente, par sa nature même, un caractère universel, et ne peut être envisagé comme intéressant un groupe de pays seulement"[25].

At the close of the Second Hague Peace Conference of 1907, its *Acte final* included, at the end, a statement of "principles" that the Conference considered as having been "unanimously recognized", namely, firstly, "the principle of compulsory arbitration", and, secondly, the declaration that "certains différends, et notamment ceux relatifs à l'interprétation et à l'application des stipulations conventionnelles internationales, sont susceptibles d'être soumis à l'arbitrage obligatoire sans aucune restriction". And it added, significantly, that the Conference was unanimous

> "à proclamer que, s'il n'a pas été donné de conclure dès maintenant une convention en ce sens, les divergences d'opinion qui se sont manifestées n'ont pas dépassé les limites d'une controverse juridique, et qu'en travaillant ici ensemble pendant quatre mois, toutes les Puissances du monde, non seulement ont appris à se comprendre et à se rapprocher davantage, mais ont su dégager, au cours de cette longue collaboration, un sentiment très élevé du *bien commun de l'humanité*"[26].

Finally, the *Acte final* of the Conference included a Resolution,

---

24. F.-J. Urrutia, "La codification du droit international en Amérique", *op. cit. supra* footnote 5, pp. 134-135.
25. *Ibid.*, p. 137.
26. *Ibid.*, p. 700 (emphasis added).

adopted by unanimity, whereby the 1907 Hague Peace Conference urged States to retake the study of the "limitation of military expenditures", and expressed the *vœux* of the adoption of a Convention for the establishment of an Arbitral Court of Justice, of control of military expenditures, of observance of the principles on the laws and customs of war, of peaceful settlement of inter-State disputes, and of convening a Third Hague Peace Conference in the future[27].

Although the projected Third Peace Conference never took place, two decades after the Second Peace Conference, already in the course of the League of Nations era, the 1928 General Treaty for the Renunciation of War as an Instrument of National Policy (the so-called Briand-Kellogg Pact, in force as from 24 July 1929) was concluded and became of almost universal application. It was followed, in Latin America, by the 1933 Saavedra Lamas Pact (the so-called Anti-War Pact, adopted at the Seventh Conference of American States in Montevideo)[28], amidst constant reassertions of the principle of prohibition of the use of force in successive regional Conferences of American States (e.g., of Havana in 1928, of Montevideo in 1933, of Buenos Aires in 1936, of Lima in 1938, and of Mexico in 1945)[29].

As I had the occasion to recall in my General Course on Public International Law at the Hague Academy of International Law in 2005, the cumulative effect of the 1928 Briand-Kellogg Pact and the 1933 Saavedra Lamas Pact was that of

> "crystallizing a customary norm of condemnation of illegality of the use of armed force as instrument of national policy. The prohibition of war in International Law had become *opinio juris communis.* Three decades after the historical II Hague Peace Conference, the *principle of the non-use of force* found eloquent expression, in the American continent, in the Declaration of Principles adopted by the Inter-American Conference of Lima of 1938[30]. Shortly afterwards, that principle

---

27. F.-J. Urrutia, *op. cit. supra* footnote 5, pp. 700-701.
28. Cf. Carlos Saavedra Lamas, *Por la Paz de las Américas*, Buenos Aires, M. Gleizer Ed., 1937, pp. 91-134.
29. Cf., e.g., H. Accioly, *Tratado de Direito Internacional Público*, 2nd ed., Vol. I, Rio de Janeiro, [MRE], 1956, pp. 266-268; L. A. Podestá Costa and J. M. Ruda, *Derecho Internacional Público*, Vol. II, Buenos Aires, Tip. Ed. Argentina, 1985, pp. 221-224.
30. Followed by the Declaration adopted in Mexico by the Inter-American Conference on Problems of War and Peace of 1945. Cf. J.-M. Yepes, "La contri-

transcended that regional ambit to reach the universal one, set forth as it was in Article 2 (4) of the United Nations Charter[31], in culmination of a long and dense evolution of consolidation of the prohibition of the threat or use of force."[32]

The historical roots of this remarkable evolution are found in the First and Second Hague Peace Conferences (1899 and 1907, respectively). Whatever doubts may have subsisted as to the prohibition of measures "short of war", the fact remains that the 1928 Briand-Kellogg Pact became the point of no return to traditional international law and the no longer warranted *jus ad bellum*, heralding the advent of the new *jus contra bellum* ever since[33]. And Latin American States gave their valuable contribution to this effect, as stressed by the subsequent Saavedra Lamas Pact, followed by their overwhelming support to the adoption of Artice 2 (4) of the United Nations Charter. The preservation of peace has ever since become and remained the "centre explicatif" of the purposes and evolution of the United Nations, oriented "towards the imperative *pax est servanda*"[34].

(b) *The principle of the juridical equality of States*

The convening of the Second Hague Peace Conference of 1907, with the presence of Latin American States, gave concrete expression to the principle of the juridical equality of States, grouping

---

bution de l'Amérique latine au développement du droit international public et privé", 32 *Recueil des cours de l'Académie de droit international de La Haye* (1930), pp. 744-747; and J. C. Puig, *Les principes du droit international public américain*, Paris, Pedone, 1954, pp. 23-25.

31. The prohibition of war was, thus, in fact, formulated in Europe, where, notwithstanding, it regrettably kept on being practised, with millions of murdered persons. The Latin-American countries, in their turn, kept on condemning intervention and the use of force (short of war), which often victimized them, to the point of contributing successfully to set forth the principles of non-intervention and non-use of force both in the 1945 UN Charter (Art. 2 (4)) and in the 1948 OAS Charter (Art. 18). G. Arangio-Ruiz, *The United Nations Declaration on Friendly Relations and the System of the Sources of International Law*, Alphen aan den Rijn, Sijthoff/Noordhoff, 1979, pp. 118-120.

32. A. A. Cançado Trindade, "International Law for Humankind: Towards a New *Jus Gentium*. General Course on Public International Law: Part I", 316 *Recueil des cours de l'Académie de droit international de La Haye* (2005), pp. 124-125.

33. Cf. R. Kolb, *Ius contra bellum — Le droit international relatif au maintien de la paix*, Bâle/Bruxelles, Helbing & Lichtenhahn/Bruylant, 2003, pp. 39-47.

34. D. Sidjanski, "L'ONU et la norme *pax est servanda*", 8 *Revue hellénique de droit international* (1955), p. 3, and cf. pp. 4-29.

together the most powerful and the more fragile or vulnerable States of the world. It was regarded as constituting an advance in international law: since one of the intentions was to put an end to the increase in armaments, and another one to regulate the conduct of war, the "most hideous cause of grief and misery", there was awareness of the need to increase, as much as possible, the number of participating States, united in juridical equality[35]. In the reflection of S. Pérez Triana, in an account published in 1908,

> "in the matter of regulation of war, very little weight can have the word of the Latin American continent, beside the voice of the exclusively military nations, as almost all of Europe are, while the recognition of the juridical equality in such a clear and so explicit way was, indeed, of an invaluable and beneficial scope for the Latin nations of America"[36].

The principle of the *juridical equality of States* was consistently relied upon by the Delegations of Latin American States in the course of the debates and work of the First Commission of the Second Hague Peace Conference of 1907. The Venezuelan Delegation, for example, while reckoning that the projected creation of an international tribunal such as the projected International Prize Court was due to a manifestation of "the juridical conscience of the entire world", complained that the envisaged procedure for the nomination of judges was "in evident contradiction with the principle of equal representation of States"[37]. The Mexican Delegation, likewise, finding the project, in this respect, "contrary to the equality of nations", appealed to "a spirit of justice and of equity" to overcome that deadlock[38]. In a long intervention to the same effect, the Brazilian Delegation insisted that

> "chaque Etat, quelle qu'en soit la condition matérielle, ... ait une représentation égale au tribunal, ... Il y a, sans doute, entre les Etats, comme entre les individus, des diversités de culture, ... de richesse et de force. Mais est-ce qu'il en résulte une dif-

---

35. S. Pérez Triana and W. T. Stead (intr.), *Doctrina Drago — Colección de Documentos, op. cit. supra* footnote 14, pp. x, xii-xiii, xvi, xviii and xxiii.

36. In *ibid.*, p. xxvii (my own translation).

37. In *Deuxième Conférence internationale de la Paix — Actes et documents* (La Haye — 15 juin/18 octobre 1907), Vol. II, *Première Commission*, La Haye, Ministère des Affaires étrangères, Imprimerie nationale, 1907, pp. 20-21.

38. In *ibid.*, p. 145.

férence quelconque en ce qui regarde leurs droits essentiels ? ...
La souveraineté est le droit élémentaire par excellence des
Etats constitués et indépendants. Or, souveraineté veut dire égalité. ... La distribution juridictionnelle du droit est une branche
de la souveraineté. Donc, s'il doit y avoir entre les Etats un
organe commun de la justice, nécessairement tous les Etats y
doivent avoir une représentation équivalente." [39]

The Delegate of Brazil (Ruy Barbosa) added that the principle of
the equality of States should be taken into account in the composition of projected international courts and tribunals, as that principle
was "la condition primordiale de la paix entre les nations"; observance of that principle was a matter of "conscience", and the "diffé-
rences de grandeur entre les pays d'Europe et ceux d'Amérique sont
bien accidentelles" [40]. He further recalled that the principle of the
juridical equality of States was already underlying the initiative of
establishment of a Court of Arbitration proposed at the First Hague
Peace Conference of 1899, and one could not step backwards in
respect of that principle eight years later, then at the Second
Hague Peace Conference of 1907; in the words of Ruy Barbosa,

> "Il faut ajouter que la Conférence de 1899 se trouvait en face
> du droit international comme devant une agglomération
> immense d'idées pour la plupart en état d'abstraction, de théo-
> rie, telles qu'elles se rencontrent dans la doctrine, ou de précé-
> dents épars, tels qu'ils paraissent dans les événements ou dans
> les traités internationaux. Alors du fond de cette masse en éla-
> boration, inconsistante et contradictoire, elle a pris certaines
> notions, les plus urgentes, les plus larges, les plus fondamen-
> tales, les plus universellement reconnues, et en a fait des
> normes consacrées. Celle de l'égalité des Etats dans la consti-
> tution de la Cour d'arbitrage commune à toutes les nations est
> de ce nombre. Elle est dans la Convention de 1899, qui y donne
> à chaque Etat une place égale à celle des autres." [41]

Ruy Barbosa insisted on compliance with the principle of the juridical equality of States, in particular in relation to "the organization
of international arbitration" so as to

---

39. In *op. cit. supra* footnote 37, pp. 150-151.
40. In *ibid.*, pp. 153-155, and cf. pp. 618 and 688.
41. In *ibid.*, p. 625.

"rétablir l'équilibre de la justice entre les faibles et les forts. ... Dans cette forteresse d'un droit égal pour tous, et également inviolable, inaliénable, indiscutable, chaque Etat, grand ou petit, se sentait si maître de lui-même et si sûr *vis-à-vis* des autres, que le citoyen libre entre les murs de sa maison"[42].

The Second Hague Peace Conference of 1907 was, thus, seen by Latin American Delegations as the proper occasion to consolidate the principle of the juridical equality of States, without making any concessions which would amount to steps backwards on the matter[43].

Moreover, in the course of the work of the 1907 Hague Peace Conference, that principle was also invoked in the debates on the proposed Convention on Recourse to Arbitration for the Recovery of Contract Debts: the principle of the juridical equality of States was thus directly related to that of the non-use of force (cf. *supra*).

While the Second Hague Peace Conference of 1907 sought, from the start, to consolidate and expand the achievements of the earlier First Conference of 1899[44], yet such expansion was met with some resistance aiming at putting into practice the principle of the juridical equality of States. Thus, for example, although the idea of a permanent Court of Arbitration met with general acceptance, no agreement was reached as to the organization of the proposed Court. Among others, the Argentine Delegation, for example, expressed its reservations on the particular issue of election of judges and constitution of the Court, invoking "the principle of the equality of

---

42. *Deuxième Conférence de la Paix, Actes et discours de M. Ruy Barbosa*, La Haye, W. P. van Stockum et fils, 1907, pp. 209 and 212, and cf. pp. 209, 117-118, 214-215, 217-218 and 319-321. For further interventions by Ruy Barbosa, throughout the debates of the Second Hague Peace Conference, in support of the principle of the juridical equality of States, cf. *Obras Completas de Rui Barbosa*, Vol. XXXIV-II *(A Segunda Conferência da Paz, 1907)*, Rio de Janeiro, MEC, 1966, pp. 49-50, 163-164, 252-258, 327 and 343. R. Barbosa's contribution to the work of the Second Hague Peace Conference has been generally recognized, and a parallel has been drawn, in historical perspective, between him and Andres Bello, given "the diversity of his intellectual activity"; A. Truyol y Serra, *Histoire du droit international*, Paris, Economica, 1995, p. 129.

43. In this respect, on the "eloquent and forceful" contribution by Ruy Barbosa, during the Second Hague Peace Conference of 1907, to the prevalence of the principle of the juridical equality of States, cf. R. P. Anand, "Sovereign Equality of States in International Law", 197 *Recueil des cours de l'Académie de droit international de La Haye* (1986), pp. 73-74.

44. By inviting, at its first session, the countries which had not participated in this latter, to subscribe to its *Acte final*.

nations"[45]. Likewise, the proposed International Prize Court, though regarded as an "undoubted progress" in "eliminating a cause of conflicts among nations", gave rise to reservations of the same kind, bearing in mind the principle of juridical equality of States[46].

During the voting, in plenary session, of the Draft Convention on the Establishment of an International Prize Court, the following Delegations of Latin American States also expressed their reservations in particular as to the proposed system of appointment of judges: Chile, Colombia, Cuba, Ecuador, El Salvador, Haiti and Uruguay[47]. The Delegation of Brazil was the only one to have gone as far as to vote against the project, having clarified that it did so for the same reason, the "injustice" in the method of its composition, although it had "applauded", in support, the "principle" and the setting up of the International Prize Court[48]. The work of the Second Hague Peace Conference of 1907 heralded the general acknowledgment of the basic principle of the juridical equality of States[49], as a

45. MRE, *La República Argentina en la II Conferencia Internacional de la Paz — Haya 1907*, Buenos Aires, Impr. A. Pech, 1908, pp. 4 and 8-9.

46. *Ibid.*, p. 9.

47. In *Deuxième Conférence internationale de la Paix — Actes et documents* (La Haye — 15 juin/18 octobre 1907), vol. I, *Séances plénières de la Conférence*, La Haye, Ministère des Affaires étrangères, Imprimerie nationale, 1907, p. 168.

48. *Ibid.*, p. 168. Brazil criticized, in the projected International Prize Court and the proposed new Court of Arbitral Justice, the inequality of representation in their composition (without prejudice to their creation), in the appointment of judges; Brazil defended compliance herein with the principle of the juridical equality of States, in order to avoid distinct "categories of sovereignty" (unduly benefiting some), and insisted on the juridical equality of States "in theory and in practice", as "the primordial condition of peace among nations"; João Cabral, *Evolução do Direito Internacional, op. cit. infra* footnote 117, pp. 109-111, 284-285, 293 and 297; Clovis Bevilaqua, *Direito Público Internacional — A Synthese dos Principios e a Contribuição do Brasil*, 2nd ed., Vol. II, Rio de Janeiro, Livr. Ed. Freitas Bastos, 1939, pp. 169-170.

49. It may be summed up that, just as the international Permanent Court of Arbitration (PCA) had resulted from the work of the First Hague Peace Conference (1899), the Second Hague Peace Conference (1907) embarked on the organization of the Arbitral Court of Justice, so as to render arbitration more effective, but there was no agreement on the appointment or election of judges of such Arbitral Court; in the discussions on this issue, Latin American States firmly sustained the principle of the juridical equality of States, and were unanimous in their determination "to defend this equality"; F.-J. Urrutia, "La codification du droit international en Amérique", *op. cit. supra* footnote 5, pp. 138 and 140. Subsequently, the consistent support of Latin American States to the principle of non-intervention (in inter-State relations) and the juridical equality of States repercuted in distinct chapters of international law (e.g., *inter alia*, recognition of Governments); cf. L. A. Podestá Costa and J. M. Ruda, *Derecho Internacional Público*, Vol. I, Buenos Aires, Tip. Ed. Argentina, 1988, pp. 162-165; César Sepúlveda, *Derecho Internacional*, 15th ed., Mexico, Ed. Porrúa, 1986, pp. 265-270.

manifestation of the incoming democratization of international law[50].

(c) *Strengthening of international jurisdiction*

Reference has already been made to the general support, expressed at the Second Hague Peace Conference of 1907 (also on the part of the participating Latin American States), for the initiative of creation of a permanent Court of Arbitration and an International Prize Court (whereto individuals would be granted direct access); difficulties — which proved insurmountable in those days — subsisted as to the *organization* of those Courts, and, in particular, the appointment of their judges *(supra)*.

Despite the fact that the proposed permanent Court of Arbitration[51] and the International Prize Court, which were object, both of them, of much debate at the Second Hague Peace Conference of 1907, did not see the light of the day, as envisaged in the original proposals, there were, however, manifestations of recognition of the need to enhance international jurisdiction in the years to come. Latin American States were among those which took such a stand at the 1907 Conference, and their position should here be recalled.

In fact, in the course of the debates of the First Commission of the

---

50. Cf., on this issue, e.g., H. Valladão, *Democratização e Socialização do Direito Internacional — Os Impactos Latino-Americano e Afro-Asiático*, Rio de Janeiro, Livr. J. Olympio Ed., 1961, pp. 48-98.

51. The First Hague Peace Conference had set up optional arbitration, and an institution to oversee the arbitral process, the Permanent Court of Abitration (PCA); it was, however, "a bit of a misnomer, since it really was not 'permanent' nor really a 'court'"; thus, the Second Hague Peace Conference attempted to create a truly *permanent* Court of Arbitral Justice, to operate continuously and develop its own jurisdiction and jurisprudence, but there was no agreement on its composition (the appointment of judges); D. J. Bederman, "The Hague Peace Conferences of 1899 and 1907", in *International Courts for the Twenty-First Century* (ed. M. W. Janis), Dordrecht, Nijhoff, 1992, pp. 10-11. The idea was, however, to flourish later on (cf. *infra*). But in those days, of the two Hague Peace Conferences, the PCA was "not a 'court' in the conventional understanding of that term, but an administrative organization with the object of having permanent and readily available means to serve as the registry for purposes of international arbitration and other related procedures, including commissions of enquiry and conciliation, if the States concerned agreed to have recourse to such means"; S. Rosenne, "Introduction", in PCA, *The Hague Peace Conferences of 1899 and 1907 . . .*, *op. cit. infra* footnote 67, p. xxi. Yet, the PCA represented the first institutionalization of the arbitral solution, which began to be resorted to in 1902; the initiative received a further impulse at the 1907 Hague Peace Conference; D. Spielmann, "Il y a cent ans, La Haye devenait la capitale du monde (à propos de la Iʳᵉ Conférence de la Paix de 1899)", 9 *Annales du droit luxembourgeois* (1999), pp. 15 and 17-20.

Second Hague Peace Conference of 1907, there was support among Delegations of Latin American States for the idea of compulsory arbitration, to the extent that it enhanced the principle of non-use of force. Reference can be made, in this respect, to the statements of the Delegations of Chile and Peru, to the proposals of the Delegations of Uruguay and the Dominican Republic, and to the declarations of the Delegations of Venezuela, El Salvador and Mexico[52]. Moreover, recourse to arbitration, in the view of the Delegation of Brazil, would pave the way also for judicial settlement, bringing to the fore the ideal of international justice[53].

The proposed International Prize Court, in the observation of the Delegation of Argentina, would be a first significant initiative to that effect[54]. Yet, for international justice hopefully to advance, added the Delegation of Uruguay, it should be a joint enterprise of the whole "association of nations", and not of a group of more powerful States only[55]. Reference to the right of direct access to the projected International Prize Court was also made by the Delegation of Cuba[56].

On its part, the Mexican Delegation to the Second Hague Peace Conference reported to the Mexican Foreign Office, on 19 October 1907, singling out the importance of the work of the First Commission of the Hague Conference, in particular in relation to the topics of arbitration and of the proposed International Prize Court. It referred to Mexico's support for arbitration (having evoked at the Conference the Treaty on Arbitration signed in Mexico on 30 January 1902). As for the proposal of establishment of a permanent Court of Arbitration, the Mexican Delegation insisted on the need of observance of the principle of the "juridical equality of States", and reported on the "vigorous opposition" on the part of the "main Latin American Delegations" to the non-observance of that principle in the composition of the projected Court[57].

This led to a motion to approve only the "rules pertaining to the operation of the permanent Court" and the procedures before it,

---

52. In *Deuxième Conférence internationale de la Paix — Actes et documents* (La Haye — 15 juin/18 octobre 1907), vol. II, *Première Commission*, La Haye, Ministère des Affaires étrangères, Imprimerie nationale, 1907, pp. 356, 915, 918-921 and 924-925.
53. *Ibid.*, p. 659.
54. *Ibid.*, pp. 13-14.
55. *Ibid.*, p. 915.
56. *Ibid.*, p. 791.
57. Secretaría de Relaciones Exteriores (SRE)/[Archivo Diplomático], *Informe a la SRE de la Delegación de México a la II Conferencia de Paz de La Haya,*

leaving open for subsequent deliberation the form of the constitution itself of the new international organism. Mexico gave support specifically to the "rules of procedure" before the newly proposed Court, bearing in mind the principle of the "juridical equality of States"[58]. The pacifist ideals of Latin American States propounded at the Second Hague Peace Conference of 1907[59] contributed to the growing acceptance of of international arbitration; the Delegation of the Dominican Republic was the first one to propose therein compulsory arbitration as a means of settlement of all possible inter-State disputes[60]. According to an account of the memorable debates on the matter, of 5 October 1907, of the Second Hague Peace Conference,

> "ce furent encore les 18 délégations latino-américaines, qui, à la mémorable séance du 5 octobre 1907, par leur unanimité, assurèrent le triomphe du principe de l'arbitrage pour résoudre les conflits internationaux d'ordre juridique. Et il est intéressant de rappeler que ce principe fut accepté par une majorité de 35 voix, dont 18 latino-américaines, sur un total de 44 votants. Si la Deuxième Conférence de La Haye peut être considérée comme un pas en avant dans le chemin qui conduit à l'adoption de l'arbitrage, c'est donc grâce à l'appui décidé, efficace, enthousiaste de l'Amérique latine. L'action de l'Amérique latine à la Deuxième Conférence de La Haye mérite d'être rappelée aussi en raison de l'influence qu'elle exerça sur la conception d'une notion juridique inconnue jusqu'alors: celle du *devoir international*. Les délégations du Pérou et du Chili proposèrent, en effet, 'd'accorder à chacune des Puissances en conflit le droit de faire connaître au Bureau international de La Haye leur volonté de se soumettre à l'arbitrage, le Bureau devant porter immédiatement cette déclaration à la connaissance de l'autre Puissance'. Moyennant cette proposition latino-

---

of 19 October 1907, pp. 1, 3, 9, 13-15 and 17 (internal circulation — document provided to the author of the present study by the SRE/Archivo Diplomático in Mexico City, on 26 March 2007).

58. *Ibid.*, pp. 14-15.

59. To recall another example, in the discussions on a project on the use of automatic mines, the Delegate of Colombia (Pérez Triana) proposed a "humanitarian amendment" on the prohibition of such mines, given their destructive effects, thus expressing one of the Latin American ideals in this domain; J.-M. Yepes, "La contribution de l'Amérique latine . . .", *op. cit. infra* footnote 61, pp. 741-742 and 764-765.

60. *Ibid.*, pp. 764-765.

américaine, reproduite dans l'article 48 de la Convention pour le règlement pacifique des conflits internationaux, l'application de l'arbitrage fut considérablement facilitée, en même temps que fut amplifié le devoir international — que l'article 27 de la Convention de 1899 avait imposé aux Etats neutres — de rappeler aux Puissances en conflit la faculté qu'elles ont de recourir à la Cour permanente d'arbitrage."[61]

Although by the end of the Second Hague Peace Conference of 1907 recourse to arbitration[62] had been made — or remained — optional[63], the ideal of compulsory arbitration had already marked its presence at the Conference, and remained alive in the years to come[64]. It exerted influence on the chapter of peaceful settlement of international disputes as a whole[65], and in particular also on judicial settlement, as the "clause Raul Fernandes" (Art. 36 (2)) — the optional clause of compulsory jurisdiction — of the Statute of the Permanent Court of International Justice (PCIJ), and, later, of the International Court of Justice (ICJ), was to bear witness from 1920 and 1945 onwards, respectively. That clause came to be acclaimed as a Latin American contribution to the foundation of international jurisdiction[66].

The proposal for a permanent Court of Arbitral Justice as a whole

---

61. J.-M. Yepes, "La contribution de l'Amérique latine au développement du droit international public et privé", 32 *Recueil des cours de l'Académie de droit international de La Haye* (1930), p. 765.

62. I.e., to the Permanent Court of Arbitration (PCA).

63. D. Gaurier, *Histoire du droit international*, op. cit. supra footnote 12, p. 429.

64. C. Wilfred Jenks, *The World beyond the Charter*, London, G. Allen & Unwin, 1969, pp. 42-43.

65. The debates of the 1907 Hague Peace Conference are acknowledged as having been notable for advances in the development of institutions and procedures to resolve international conflicts peacefully; the adopted Convention on the Peaceful Settlement of International Disputes "still exerts a powerful influence for reason and restraint in international relations"; D. J. Bederman, "The Hague Peace Conferences of 1899 and 1907", op. cit. supra footnote 51, p. 11. And cf., on the international commissions of inquiry, e.g., C. Bevilaqua, *Direito Público Internacional . . .*, op. cit. supra footnote 48, pp. 163-164.

66. For a personal account of its original drafting in 1920, the purpose aimed at, and the bearing in mind of the principle of the juridical equality of States therein, cf. Raul Fernandes, *Nonagésimo Aniversário — Conferências e Trabalhos Esparsos*, Vol. I, Rio de Janeiro, MRE, 1967, pp. 174-175. And, for a recent reassessment, cf. A. A. Cançado Trindade, "The Relevance of International Adjudication Revisited: Reflections on the Need and Quest for International Compulsory Jurisdiction", in *Towards World Constitutionalism — Issues in the Legal Ordering of the World Community* (eds. R. St. J. Macdonald and D. M. Johnston), Leiden, Nijhoff, 2005, pp. 515-542.

was to project itself on the advent of judicial solution itself at international level. It formed the "principal model" for the Statute of the PCIJ in 1920. Several of its provisions were to reappear, either unchanged or altered, and subsequently (in 1945) also in the Statute of the ICJ[67]. The strengthening of international jurisdiction, propounded and supported at the Second Hague Peace Conference of 1907 by Latin American Delegations[68], was thus later on to see the light of day.

In fact, shortly after the adoption of the PCIJ Statute in 1920, Raul Fernandes, evoking the unanimous support of Latin American States participating at the Second Hague Peace Conference to the principle of the juridical equality of States, remarked that this principle has relevance for the realization of justice at the international level[69]. Over three decades later, on the occasion of the fiftieth anniversary of the Second Hague Peace Conference, in 1957, it was again pointed out that international justice required the juridical equality of States, and, just as the "universal juridical conscience" called for putting an end to war, it had succeeded in giving expression to the principle of the juridical equality of all member States as proclaimed in Article 2 (1) of the UN Charter, to the benefit of humankind[70].

(d) *Direct access of individuals to international justice*

Although the projected International Prize Court, set forth in the [XII] Convention on the Establishment of an International Prize Court, was never created, the Convention, though not having entered into force, presented issues of relevance for the evolution of international law, namely: firstly, it foresaw the establishment of a jurisdic-

---

67. S. Rosenne, "Introduction", in PCA, *The Hague Peace Conferences of 1899 and 1907 and International Arbitration — Reports and Documents* (ed. S. Rosenne), The Hague, T.M.C. Asser Press, 2001, p. xxi. And cf. also A. Eyffinger, "A Highly Critical Moment: Role and Record of the 1907 Hague Peace Conference", 54 *Netherlands International Law Review* (2007), n. 2, pp. 217 and 227.

68. Cf. A. Truyol y Serra, *Histoire du droit international public, op. cit. supra* footnote 42, p. 113.

69. Raul Fernandes, *Le principe de l'égalité juridique des Etats dans l'activité internationale de l'après-guerre*, Geneva, Impr. A. Kundig, 1921, pp. 18-22 and 33.

70. I. Penna Marinho, "A Atuação de Rui Barbosa na Haia e Sua Influência sobre a Evolução do Direito Internacional", 24 *Boletim da Sociedade Brasileira de Direito Internacional* (1958), n. 27/28, pp. 11-13, 16 and 18, and cf. pp. 5 and 19.

tion above national jurisdictions to decide on last appeal on maritime prizes; secondly, it provided, for example, in such circumstances, for the access of individuals directly to international jurisdiction; thirdly, it envisaged a type of international compulsory jurisdiction; and fourthly, it admitted the proposed Court's free authority to decide *(compétence de la compétence)*[71].

The initiative of the aforementioned Convention further indicated that, already one century ago, there was awareness that "the individual is not without standing in modern international law"[72]. At the Second Hague Peace Conference of 1907, the discussions on the projected International Prize Court (international jurisdiction on appeal on prizes) focused on the recognition, for the first time by an international diplomatic Conference, of the right of petition by individuals against other States (so as to avoid direct intervention by their own States); although there was no unanimity on the issue, most participants deemed that it would be in the interests of the States — particularly the small or weaker ones — to avoid giving to this kind of cases the character of inter-State disputes: "les litiges nés des prises garderaient ... le caractère qu'ils avaient en première instance ..., affaires regardant d'un côté l'Etat capteur et de l'autre les particuliers"[73].

The majority of participants felt that it would be "unjust" to deprive the injured individuals to appear before the projected International Prize Court; and, after all, it was in line with the evolution of international law to enable individuals to have direct access to the international jurisdiction in order to obtain redress, without the intervention of their State. The debates of the 1907 Hague Peace Conference led to the prevailing view of allowing individuals, in the context at issue, to bring "personally" their complaints before the projected International Prize Court[74].

---

71. João Cabral, *Evolução do Direito Internacional, op. cit. infra* footnote 117, pp. 97-98. On the evolution of this last point (the *compétence de la compétence* of international tribunals), cf., generally, I. F. I. Shihata, *The Power of the International Court to Determine Its Own Jurisdiction (Compétence de la Compétence)*, The Hague, Nijhoff, 1965, pp. 1-304.

72. James Brown Scott, "The Work of the Second Hague Peace Conference", 2 *American Journal of International Law* (1908), p. 22.

73. S. Séfériadès, "Le problème de l'accès des particuliers à des juridictions internationales", 51 *Recueil des cours de l'Académie de droit international de La Haye* (1935), pp. 38-40.

74. *Ibid.*, pp. 40-41. It was decided at the Second Hague Peace Conference that, in order to avoid undue delays, resort could be made to the projected

The following initiative, in the same line, occurred still in the year of 1907. On the last day of the Central American Peace Conference, convened in Washington from 14 November to 20 December 1907, five Central American States (Costa Rica, El Salvador, Guatemala, Honduras and Nicaragua) adopted the Convention for the Establishment of a Permanent Central American Court of Justice[75], endowed with jurisdiction extended not only to inter-State disputes but also to disputes opposing individuals to the States Parties. As I had the occasion to point out, in the seventieth anniversary of the Second Hague Peace Conference of 1907, in its ten years of existence

> "the Central American Court became the first international *judicial* organ in modern history, endowed with continuing functions, to grant procedural status and direct access to individuals; at a time when States would normally resort to arbitration, the Court was open to individuals who could apply for the finding or administration of a judicial remedy"[76].

In its decade of operation, the Court was seised of 10 cases, 5 lodged with it by individuals and 5 inter-State cases[77]. Thus, under the impulse of the Second Hague Peace Conference of 1907, the Central American States promptly succeeded in establishing an international tribunal with a wide jurisdictional basis, truly pioneering in granting direct access not only to States but also to individuals, thus contributing to the acknowledgment of these latter as subjects of international law[78]. Gradually it became recognized — as pointed out three

---

International Prize Court, if national tribunals failed to render a definitive decision within two years from the date of capture; the XII Hague Convention on the Establishment of the International Prize Court thus granted direct appeal to individuals, and acknowledged the primacy of the public interest over the private one, further acknowledging the new tendencies in favour of human rights protection. S. Séfériadès, *op. cit. supra* footnote 73, pp. 75 and 90.

75. Promptly ratified, by March 1908, by the five signatory States.

76. A. A. Cançado Trindade, "Exhaustion of Local Remedies in International Law Experiments Granting Procedural Status to Individuals in the First Half of the Twentieth Century", 24 *Netherlands International Law Review / Nederlands Tijdschrift voor international Recht* (1977), p. 376.

77. Cf. *ibid.*, pp. 376-377; and cf. F. A. von der Heydte, "L'individu et les tribunaux internationaux", 107 *Recueil des cours de l'Académie de droit international de La Haye* (1962), p. 321.

78. Carlos José Gutiérrez, *La Corte de Justicia Centroamericana*, San José de Costa Rica, Edit. Juricentro, 1978, pp. 42, 106, 150-152. Its judges worked as "representatives" of the "Central American conscience", and during the ten years of its operation the rule of law prevailed, as well as the peaceful juridical settlement of Central American controversies; *ibid.*, pp. 154 and 157-158.

decades after the 1907 Hague Conference — that the ideal whereto humankind should orient itself was that of securing to human beings direct access to international jurisdiction[79].

III. The Outcome: Codification, Conscientization and Opinio Juris

In a relatively short time (15 June to 18 October 1907), the Second Hague Peace Conference adopted 13 Conventions. Some of them contained the seeds for further development of international law. Thus, to recall but a couple of examples, the [I] Convention for the Pacific Settlement of International Disputes dealt with — in its Part III — International Commissions of Inquiry, a means of peaceful settlement which was sensibly developed; the [IV] Convention Respecting the Laws and Customs of War on Land contained the "Martens Clause", with its reference to "public conscience"; the [XII] Convention on the Creation of an International Prize Court was relevant to the issue of the individual's direct access to international justice[80]. And the Convention on the Limitation of the Employment of Force for the Recovery of Contract Debts (the so-called Drago-Porter Convention) contributed decisively to enhancing recourse to arbitration as a means to put an end to coercitive means and the use of force.

By and large, the two Hague Peace Conferences of 1899 and 1907 served clear purposes[81] — forming the *opinio juris comunis* — and projected their influence in time, through the decades that followed them. Firstly, they sought to find ways to avoid war by the development of methods of peaceful settlement of international disputes; secondly, they sought "to humanize war through the development of humanitarian law so as to spare all belligerents some of the horrors of war"[82]; thirdly, they sought to encourage the codification of inter-

---

79. S. Séfériadès, "Le problème de l'accès des particuliers . . .", *op. cit supra* footnote 73, p. 66, and cf. p. 42. And, for a recent reassessment, cf. A. A. Cançado Trindade, *El Acceso Directo del Individuo a los Tribunales Internacionales de Derechos Humanos*, Bilbao, Universidad de Deusto, 2001, pp. 9-104.
80. João Cabral, *Evolução do Direito Internacional*, *op. cit. infra* footnote 117, pp. 85, 89 and 92.
81. For a *vue d'ensemble* of their results, cf. Louis Renault (ed.), *Les deux Conférences de la Paix 1899 et 1907 — Recueil des textes*, Paris, A. Rousseau Ed., 1908, pp. 1-215.
82. S. Rosenne, "Third-Party Dispute Settlement at the Turn of the Century: Some Old Problems Revisited and Some New Problems Not Foreseen at The Hague in 1899/1907, or in the Statutes of the PCIJ and the ICJ — Introductory

national law so as to preserve international peace and to develop progressively the discipline at the universal level.

The Second Hague Peace Conference of 1907 fostered the work of codification of international law, also at the regional level, in Latin America. In the years following it, projects of codification of international law flourished in Latin America — such as those of, for example, Epitacio Pessôa[83], Lafayette Rodrigues Pereira[84], Alejandro Álvarez[85] — and the work of Gustavo Guerrero[86]. Whether undertaken at the global or regional level, the work of codification, by apprehending fundamental general principles, which are universal, was to have the same character and was meant to be also universal. Such exercise of codification, and the evolution itself of international law in general, were recognizably moved ahead by the universal juridical conscience:

> "La conscience universelle se pénètre chaque jour davantage de l'idée qu'une justice supérieure impose, aux Etats comme aux hommes, des devoirs que la communauté internationale doit défendre et sauvegarder, et que, spécialement en cas de différends, ce sont non pas les intérêts des Etats, mais les principes et les lois de cette justice, qui doivent régir les rapports internationaux."[87]

Reference has already been made to a Resolution, included in the *Acte final* of the Second Hague Peace Conference, adopted by

Statement", in United Nations, *International Law as a Language for International Relations — Proceedings of the U.N. Congress on Public International Law*, New York, March 1995, United Nations/Kluwer, The Hague, 1996, pp. 479-480; and cf. also E. Jiménez de Aréchaga, *El Derecho Internacional Contemporáneo*, Madrid, Tecnos, 1980, p. 108.

83. Epitacio Pessôa, *Projecto de Código de Direito Internacional Público*, Rio de Janeiro, Imprensa Nacional, 1911, pp. 5-323.

84. Lafayette Rodrigues Pereira, *Princípios de Direito Internacional*, Vols. I-II, Rio de Janeiro, J. Ribeiro dos Santos Ed., 1902-1903, pp. 1 *et seq.*

85. F.-J. Urrutia, "La codification du droit international en Amérique", *op. cit.*, *supra* footnote 5, pp. 162-163. Furthermore, the search for international compulsory jurisdiction was again to find expression in the drafting, in 1920, by a Committee of Jurists, of the Statute of the Permanent Court of International Justice, and in particular in the adoption therein of the "clause Raul Fernandes"; *ibid.*, p. 148.

86. Cf. G. Guerrero, *La codification du droit international*, Paris, Pedone, 1930, pp. 9-10, 13, 24, 27 and 150, and cf. pp. 182 and 175, on the assertion by the "universal conscience" of the ideal of a "universal justice"; and cf. also A. A. Cançado Trindade and A. Martínez Moreno, *Doctrina Latinoamericana del Derecho Internacional*, Vol. I, San José of Costa Rica, Inter-American Court of Human Rights, 2003, pp. 5-64.

87. *Ibid.*, p. 175, and cf. p. 182.

unanimity, whereby the 1907 Hague Conference urged States to reconsider the needed "limitation of military expenditures" (cf. *supra*). Such Resolution, inserted into the *Acte final* of the 1907 Conference, between the 13 adopted Conventions (and declarations) and the final *vœux* (and recommendations), belongs — as held decades later by Jorge Castañeda — to the category of international resolutions which are *declaratory* of international law, their basic content being "customary rules or general principles of law", which thereby become more precise and clarified in "their terms and scope"[88]. There was the seed to disarmament.

The work of codification of international law — such as the one undertaken, for example, at the Second Hague Peace Conference of 1907 — seems to assume the conscientization as to its need. As we know it today, that work owes much to the influence of the German "historical school" in the nineteenth century (Savigny and others), in its building of the normative order emanating from the *juridical conscience* (then conceived as the *Volksgeist*, *l'esprit du peuple*), and perfected through the social evolution[89]. Somewhat distinctly, attention is turned today, in my view, to the conscience of the international community as a whole (rather than of each people), to the *universal juridical conscience*, as the ultimate material source of universalized international law[90].

Codification of international law has already evolved in a long journey, of over a century, *pari passu* with the progressive development of the discipline. There are those who identify the two Hague Peace Conferences (of 1899 and 1907) as "the first modern codification Conferences"[91]. One century after the Second Hague Peace

---

88. Jorge Castañeda, *Legal Effects of United Nations Resolutions*, New York, Columbia University Press, 1969, pp. 168-169, and cf. pp. 166-167; and cf. Jorge Castañeda, *Obras Completas — I: Naciones Unidas*, Mexico City, El Colegio de México/SRE, 1995, pp. 461-465.

89. G. Abi-Saab, "La Commission du droit international, la codification et le processus de formation de droit international", in United Nations, *Making Better International Law: The International Law Commission at 50 — Proceedings of the U.N. Colloquium on Progressive Development and Codification of International Law*, New York, October 1997, New York, United Nations, 1998, p. 186.

90. A. A. Cançado Trindade, "International Law for Humankind: Towards a New *Jus Gentium*. General Course on Public International Law: Part I", 316 *Recueil des cours de l'Académie de droit international de La Haye* (2005), Chap. VI, pp. 177-202.

91. Intervention by S. Rosenne, in United Nations, *Making Better International Law . . .*, *op. cit. supra* footnote 89, p. 127; and cf. F. Münch, "La codification inachevée", in *Le droit international à l'heure de sa codification — Etudes en l'honneur de Roberto Ago*, Vol. I, Milan, Giuffrè, 1987, p. 376.

Conference, codification and progressive development of international law are nowadays undertaken by a multiplicity of organs, at universal as well as regional levels, and by means of treaties as well as resolutions, in a much more complex way, to fulfil the current normative needs of the international community as a whole.

Underlying this process is "the primacy of international law in international relations", as propounded, for example, over a century ago, by one of the promoters of the two Hague Peace Conferences (of 1899 and 1907), the Russian jurist F. F. de Martens[92]. In our days, the work of codification and progressive development of international law purports to give expression of the *opinio juris* of the international community as a whole[93]. In a thoughtful essay on the matter, it was pondered that the codification of public international law

> "nous conduit, en effet, à l'essence du droit, à ses conditions vitales, à l'art d'exprimer en une langue professionnelle des projections intérieures, à une prise de conscience dans un domaine qui, de par sa nature même, appartient à l'invisible et est destiné à y rester en dépit des symboles de notre écriture"[94].

The work of codification of international law, undertaken nowadays at the universal level, appears as a manifestation of the juridical conscience[95]. The work of codification purports to strengthen the international legal order, to secure the primacy of international law; it ensues from a spontaneous *prise de conscience* of the members of

---

92. Y. M. Kolosov, "Overview of the International Law-Making Process and the Role of the International Law Commission", in United Nations, *Making Better International Law . . .*, *op. cit. supra* footnote 89, p. 203.

93. E. Suy, "Développement progressif et codification du droit international : Le rôle de l'Assemblée générale revisité", in United Nations, *International Law as a Language for International Relations — Proceedings of the U.N. Congress on Public International Law*, New York, March 1995, United Nations/Kluwer, The Hague, 1996, p. 216; and cf. K. Zemanek, "Does Codification Lead to Wider Acceptance ?", in *ibid.*, p. 228; K. Zemanek, "Codification of International Law : Salvation or Dead End ?", in *Le droit international à l'heure de sa codification — Etudes en l'honneur de Roberto Ago*, Vol. I, Milan, Giuffrè, 1987, p. 601.

94. M. Bos, "Aspects phénoménologiques de la codification du droit international public", in *Le droit international à l'heure de sa codification — Etudes en l'honneur de Roberto Ago*, Vol. I, Milan, Giuffrè, 1987, p. 142.

95. A. Mahiou, "Rapport général", in *La codification du droit international* (Colloque d'Aix-en-Provence de la Société française pour le droit international), Paris, Pedone, 1999, pp. 30, 41-42 and 45.

the international community to respond to its normative needs[96]. The relationship between conscience and the formulation of general principles and the codification of international law marked presence in Latin American doctrine throughout the twentieth century.

Thus, in his writings during the Second World War, the Chilean jurist Alejandro Álvarez, for example, sustained (in 1944) that the principles of law and the precepts of international justice emanated spontaneously from the international juridical conscience[97]. In his view, it was natural law thinking which best captured that conscience, wherefrom the principles of law emanate, including such "new principles" as the condemnation of genocide and "the condemnation of war as a crime against humanity"[98]. He further recalled the reference to conscience (as a source of applicable legal rules in the absence of express conventional provisions) found in the preamble of the [IV] 1907 Hague Convention on the Laws and Customs of War on Land (the well-known "Martens Clause"), in acknowledgment of the presence of conscience in the work of codification, such as the one undertaken at the two Hague Peace Conferences (of 1899 and 1907) in the regulation of war and neutrality[99].

IV. Projection of the Peace Conference of 1907 in Time

The Second Hague Conference of 1907 took place in a time of presentiments, of apprehensions, of fears of what could happen.

---

96. Roberto Ago, "Nouvelles réflexions sur la codification du droit international", in *International Law at a Time of Perplexity — Essays in Honour of S. Rosenne* (eds. Y. Dinstein and M. Tabory), Dordrecht, Nijhoff, 1989, pp. 2 and 22.

97. A. Álvarez, *La Reconstrucción del Derecho de Gentes — El Nuevo Orden y la Renovación Social*, Santiago de Chile, Ed. Nascimento, 1944, pp. 19-21, 24-25 and 86-87.

98. A. Álvarez, *El Nuevo Derecho Internacional en Sus Relaciones con la Vida Actual de los Pueblos*, Santiago, Editorial Jurídica de Chile, 1961, pp. 155-157 and 304.

99. Cf. *ibid.*, pp. 156 and 356-357. A. Álvarez's outlook did not pass unnoticed to some of his contemporaries; cf., e.g., J.-M. Yepes, "Les problèmes fondamentaux du droit des gens en Amérique", 47 *Recueil des cours de l'Académie de droit international de La Haye* (1934), p. 8. In 1947, in a report submitted to the Institut de Droit International (1947 Lausanne session), A. Álvarez, amidst the "grave crisis" faced by international law, reiterated his view that international justice was a manifestation of the international juridical conscience, to which the precepts of the law of nations owed their formation; A. Álvarez, "Méthodes de la codification du droit international public — Rapport", in *Annuaire de l'Institut de droit international* (1947), pp. 38 and 46-47, and cf. pp. 50-51, 54, 64 and 69. He added that the general interests of the international community

Hence the concern with the prevalence of peace, in view of the risks of the practice of alliances, and of the fact that arbitration had become no longer resorted to for certain major conflicts[100]; participating States were thus engaged in securing the prevalence of peace and of the existing international *ordre public*; they succeeded in achieving a fairly advanced codification of the law of armed conflicts and neutrality, besides some advances on the procedures of conciliation and arbitration which States might deem fit to resort to[101].

It became clear that the endeavours of the 1907 Peace Conference marked only the beginning of a long journey at universal level, and not only in relation to the principle of juridical equality of States. If one takes, for example, the principle of the prohibition of the use of force in the relations among States, the underlying situation was even more dramatic. As the question of the limitation of armaments did not form part of the agenda of the Second Hague Peace Conference, some Delegations reserved the faculty to submit it to its deliberation. They did so in vain; the "security of failure" led to the unanimous adoption of a wishful declaration, confirming another one of the kind adopted by the First Hague Peace Conference, concerning the limitation of military expenditure, declaring it to be "highly desirable" for Governments "to study seriously this question"[102].

There were those who were concerned that the Second Hague Peace Conference could not offer the definition of "war" requested in some of its debates[103].

The aforementioned resolution of 1907 was unanimously adopted by the Second Hague Conference after this latter had acknowledged that military expenditure had considerably increased "in almost all countries" since the earlier resolution of the same kind had been adopted by the 1899 First Hague Peace Conference[104]. More than a clear warning, it sounded as a premonition. As governmental action

---

should "model" the "rights of States and individuals" and guide the work of reconstruction of international law; *op. cit.*, pp. 44-45 and 68-69, and cf. p. 70.
    100. R. Ferrero, *Derecho Internacional*, Vol. I, Lima, Ed. Peruanas, 1966, p. 39.
    101. *Ibid.*, pp. 39-40.
    102. As reported in MRE, *La República Argentina en la II Conferencia Internacional de la Paz — Haya 1907*, Buenos Aires, Impr. A. Pech, 1908, p. 12.
    103. Marqués de Olivart, *[Prólogo:] Acta Final de la II Conferencia de Paz y Convenciones Anexas a la Misma (Haya 1907)*, Madrid, Ed. Rev. de Derecho Internacional y Política Exterior, 1908, p. VIII.
    104. *Ibid.*, p. 8.

was not in accordance with principle, the seeds of war were already being spread.

The envisaged Third Hague Peace Conference never took place. Seven years later, Europe was engulfed in a major war, the devastating consequences of which affected the whole world. Political blindness had ruined all faith that social progress would accompany technical and material progress, and had spread a pathological mistrust of all towards all; reason was betrayed, and much of human dignity was from then onwards lost along the twentieth century marked by successive atrocities [105]. States learned the disasters they were bound to experience by not abiding by the basic principles of international law. The seeds of peace, on the other hand, had also been spread by the First and Second Hague Peace Conferences, of 1899 and 1907, and they were to leave the indelible mark in the history of contemporary international law, leaving hope that not all was lost.

One decade after the Second Hague Peace Conference of 1907, when the world was already drowned in war, the former Brazilian Delegate to the 1907 Hague Conference (Ruy Barbosa), in his personal recollection of it in a guest lecture at the Faculty of Law and Social Sciences in Buenos Aires, singled out the consciousness and the spirit of "solidarity in Law" and "impartiality in Justice" which led to the adoption of the Conventions therein. Some of their provisions were already "customary law", and were duly systematized; in signing those Conventions, he added, there was a general feeling that the participating States became jointly responsible for compliance with them, aware that they had "the right and the duty to constitute a tribunal of conscience, an instance of opinion, a moral jurisdiction on the States in war, to judge their acts and reproach their excesses" [106].

He ascribed particular importance to the prevalence, in the work of the Conference, of the principle of the juridical equality of States, not only for the solemn adoption of the Conventions therein, but also for the failure to agree on the *organization* of the projected perma-

---

105. Stefan Zweig, *O Mundo que Eu Vi (Die Welt von Gestern)*, Rio de Janeiro, Ed. Record, 1999 [reed.], pp. 160, 467, 488-489 and 500.

106. Ruy Barbosa, *Conceptos Modernos del Derecho Internacional* (Conferencia Pronunciada el 14.07.1916 en la Facultad de Derecho y Ciencias Sociales de Buenos Aires), Buenos Aires, Impr. Coni Hermanos, 1916, p. 63, and cf. pp. 58 and 65.

nent Court of Arbitral Justice, precisely for not faithfully reflecting, in the view of several Delegations (including the Latin American ones), the principle of the juridical equality of States[107]. Such principle had become part of the conceptual universe of modern international law.

In his turn, the former Cuban Delegate to the 1907 Hague Conference (Antonio Bustamante y Sirvén), in his assessment of the historical event singled out that the 1907 Conference at least attempted to give expression to the aspiration to disarmament, in, for example, acknowledging that in principle force could not be resorted to for the recovery of contractual debts, whatever the amounts concerned might be (which could never be sufficiently important to put at risk peace in the world). What powerful States did not do in their relations *inter se*, they could not do with fragile or weaker States, and international law could not be invoked or applied as a means to sanction through procedures "only applicable among countries of unequal force"[108].

V. *Final Considerations: Towards a New* Jus Gentium, *the International Law for Humankind*

A most significant result of the Second Hague Peace Conference of 1907 was the codification it achieved of the law of war and neutrality, aiming "to humanize" the methods of combat, despite recurring claims of State sovereignty; a true *jus in bello* had taken shape and the idea of "humanization" has survived ever since. More than that, it has kept on aiming to go much further[109], towards the creation of a true *jus contra bellum* in our days[110], one century later.

---

107. Ruy Barbosa, *op. cit. supra* footnote 106, p. 47, and cf. p. 55. In fact, in the years following the Second Hague Peace Conference, and until his death in 1923, Ruy Barbosa constantly recalled the common support of all Latin American Delegations at the 1907 Conference to the principle of the juridical equality of all States, and insisted on the consolidation of the much-needed *jus contra bellum*, for the sake of humankind; R. Barbosa, *Os Conceitos Modernos do Direito Internacional*, Rio de Janeiro, FCRB, 1983 [reed.], pp. 44, 33 and 62-63.

108. Antonio S. de Bustamante y Sirvén, *La Segunda Conferencia de la Paz Reunida en La Haya en 1907*, Vol. I, Madrid, Libr. Gen. de V. Suárez, 1908, pp. 43 and 80-81. He recalled that, on 16 October 1907, all articles pertaining to Commissions of Inquiry were read and unanimously approved, without any modification or difficulty; this was not an original creation, but an improvement and development of what already existed; *ibid.*, p. 96.

109. D. Gaurier, *Histoire du droit international, op. cit. supra* footnote 12, pp. 428, 430 and 432-433.

110. Cf. footnotes 33 and 34, *supra*.

Looking back in time, in his assessment of the Second Hague Peace Conference, the former Delegate of Cuba, Antonio Bustamante y Sirvén, pondered that the 1907 Conference contributed to developing further humanitarian principles and propitiated a greater acceptance of previous international instruments towards universal international law, a "common law of humankind"; in his vision, the wider participation that the 1907 Conference counted on, with contributions of States from different continents and with distinct cultures, enabled the Second Hague Peace Conference to behold the advent of a world "juridical community" and to bear in mind the "unity of humankind"[111].

Although the 1907 Conference did not achieve disarmament or the limitation of armaments[112], the prevention and avoidance of international conflicts, and the suppression of the multiple causes of discord that caused turmoil in the world one century ago, yet — added A. S. Bustamante y Sirvén — the principles which found expression therein contributed to the "progress of International Law" and the "human welfare", and left the legacy of the acknowledgment of the much-needed compliance with the "duties of humanity", even when they do not form part of positive law[113]. It is highly significant that, at the time of the convening of the 1907 Hague Peace Conference, when legal positivism was still at its height, with its characteristic and invariable subservience to power, a new outlook of international law was being formed, shifting attention from the will of individual States to the fulfilment of the needs and aspirations of humankind.

There was already consciousness of the pitfalls of the positivist-voluntarist conception of international law, as, if it was by their will

---

111. A. S. de Bustamante y Sirvén, *La Segunda Conferencia de la Paz Reunida en el Haya en 1907*, Vol. II, Madrid, Libr. Gen. de V. Suárez, 1908, pp. 137 and 139-141.

112. The failure of participating States to limit the burden of armaments had likewise negatively marked the outcome of the First Hague Peace Conference of 1899; cf. UNITAR, *The Centennial of the I International Peace Conference [The Hague, 1899] — Reports and Conclusions* (ed. F. Kalshoven), The Hague, Kluwer, 2000, p. 46.

113. A. S. de Bustamante y Sirvén, *La Segunda Conferencia de la Paz . . .*, *op. cit. supra* footnote 111, pp. 157-159, and cf. pp. 133 and 147. In his forecast, the principles which found expression at the Second Hague Peace Conference would become "world law", therefrom emerging "the definitive and necessary codification of International Law"; *ibid.*, pp. 157-158. He further regarded, as one of the greatest achievements of the 1907 Hague Conference, the acknowledgment of the principle of the juridical equality of States; *ibid.*, p. 145.

that States allegedly created international law, it was also by their will that States violated it, and such voluntarist conception revolved in a vicious circle, wholly incapable of explaining the formation and evolution of the norms of international law[114]. The danger of increasing armaments and the threat of war awakened the general awareness that, in order to preserve international peace, it was imperative to replace *Realpolitik* by the pursuance by all of the common good, well beyond the interests of individual States. It had become, in sum, imperative to reckon that conscience stood well above the will.

Thus, by the end of the Second Hague Peace Conference of 1907 the universalist outlook of international law had gained considerable ground. The betrayal of its ideals engulfed the world in the tragedy of two wars of devastating and catastrophic dimension, with millions of victims. But the seed of universalism, to secure peace and justice, and going well beyond the insufficient inter-State dimension of the past, had already been planted. From time to time it was again recalled, up to our days, at this beginning of the twenty-first century.

In historical retrospect, Latin American international law commentators, already in the years following the Second Hague Peace Conference of 1907, credited to the wider participation in that historical Conference — encompassing several Latin American States and a few Asian States — the paving of the way for a "universal juridical organization" aimed at by international peace conferences of the kind[115]; peaceful settlement of disputes was enhanced, and there was recognition of the pressing need of evolution of international jurisdiction, and of the direct access of individuals thereto, all this as "a demand of the universal juridical conscience"[116].

As is known, the proposed International Prize Court did not, after all, come into being as a result of the Second Hague Peace Conference, but in the same year of 1907, the decision was taken in the American continent to establish the Central American Court of Justice, granting direct access to individuals thereto (cf. *supra*). It was not surprising that the ideal of "compulsory international arbi-

114. A. A. Cançado Trindade, "The Voluntarist Conception of International Law: A Re-Assessment", 59 *Revue de droit international de sciences diplomatiques et politiques* (Sottile), Geneva, 1981, pp. 201-240.
115. Alberto Ulloa, *Derecho Internacional Público*, Vol. II, 4th ed., Madrid, Edic. Iberoamericanas, 1957, p. 398.
116. Philadelpho Azevedo, *A Justiça Internacional*, Rio de Janeiro, MRE, 1949, pp. 24 and 26, and cf. pp. 9-10.

tration" was enhanced, as such, at the Second Hague Peace Conference of 1907, and that the *Acte final* of the Conference acknowledged that the participating States learned to understand better each other, and displayed "a very high feeling of the common good of humankind"[117].

In the days of the Second Hague Peace Conference, jurists who participated in it as Delegates of their respective countries found time to reflect on the historical significance of the 1907 Conference; as they were not in those days distracted by television nor by internet, they had more time to think, and some of them wrote not only their reports to their respective Foreign Ministries, but also their personal recollections of the event and its projections into the future of international law, to the ultimate benefit of succeeding generations of scholars of the discipline.

Non-use of force and recourse to arbitration and other means of peaceful settlement of international disputes, respect for the juridical equality of States, international jurisdiction strengthened, and direct access of individuals to international justice, such were the contributions of Latin American States to the work and outcome of the Second Hague Peace Conference of 1907, and to the evolution of international law ever since. Such contributions became part and parcel of contemporary international law. One cannot nowadays pretend to face new challenges to international peace and security by simply making abstraction of one century of evolution of international law. Such challenges are to be faced within the law, the international rule of law, keeping in mind the lessons of the past and the sufferings of succeeding generations throughout the twentieth century and this beginning of the twenty-first century.

In effect, one century after the convening of the 1907 Conference, we keep in mind what the perceptions of the Delegates to the Second Hague Peace Conference were, of the times in which they were living, their apprehensions as well as their ideals, as Delegates of their countries but also as jurists and human beings. The world has changed much ever since, but their aspirations for peace and justice among nations remain the same. Some of them had already a sense of the need for a new *jus gentium*, an international law for humankind — an outlook I allowed myself to develop in my

---

117. João Cabral, *Evolução do Direito Internacional*, Rio de Janeiro, Typ. Rodrigues & Cia., 1908, pp. 77 and 81-82.

General Course on Public International Law at the Hague Academy of International Law in 2005 [118].

There was general recognition that the participation of Latin American States at the Second Hague Peace Conference of 1907 [119] was a remarkable feature of this latter, which contributed to the *modification* of existing international law in its attempt "to humanize" the hardships of war and to replace it with resort to peaceful settlement of international disputes, codifying a "common law to international law" pursuant to an *"appeal to reason and justice"* [120]. The Second Hague Peace Conference of 1907 provided invaluable elements for the challenges it faced in its time, which remain valid and relevant also for the formidable task before us nowadays, one century later: that of the reconstruction of the *jus gentium*, in consonance with the *recta ratio*, as a new and truly *universal law for humankind*, turned more directly to the identification and pursuance of superior common values and goals — such as the preservation of peace and realization of justice — in order to fulfil the needs and aspirations of humankind as a whole.

---

118. A. A. Cançado Trindade, "International Law for Humankind: Towards a New *Jus Gentium*. General Course on Public International Law: Part I", 316 *Recueil des cours de l'Académie de droit international de La Haye* (2005), pp. 31-439; A. A. Cançado Trindade, "International Law for Humankind: Towards a New *Jus Gentium*. General Course on Public International Law: Part II", 317 *Recueil des cours de l'Académie de droit international de La Haye* (2005), pp. 19-312.

119. Formally invited to it on 14 June 1907.

120. This was the assessment, e.g., of James Brown Scott, who further recalled that, moreover, the Institut de Droit International had been created in 1873 precisely to advance the discipline by "an appeal to reason"; J. Brown Scott, "Introduction", in *Texts of the Peace Conferences at The Hague, 1899 and 1907* (ed. J. Brown Scott), Boston/London, International School of Peace/Ginn & Co., 1908, pp. ix, xi-xiii, xv, xxi and xxix. However, he added, "the friends of peace regarded the failure to limit the burden of armaments as a misfortune", and the "greater task" thus remained "to remove the causes of war" and to keep on developing peaceful settlement; *ibid.*, pp. xxxi and xxxiii-xxxiv; J. Brown Scott, "The Work of the Second Hague Peace Conference", *op. cit. supra* footnote 72, pp. 25 and 28, and cf. pp. 1 and 13-14.

4. THE PRESENCE OF ASIA
AT THE 1907 HAGUE CONFERENCE [1]

S. MURASE [2]

At the Second Hague Conference, Asia was represented by the same four Governments that attended the Conference in 1899, namely, China, Japan, Persia and Siam. Following Dr. Eyffinger's standard as set in his voluminous book on the First Hague Conference [3], I do not include Turkey as an Asian country. In any event, Asian representation was low, as compared to the 53 Asian countries that are members of the United Nations today. Apart from those four countries, the rest of Asia was wholly absent. Moreover, it can be said that the contribution to the work of the Conference by those four countries was markedly insignificant [4]. This is even more apparent when compared to the splendid accomplishment achieved by the Latin American countries at the same Conference [5].

---

1. The present writer wishes to thank Professor Lee Keun Gwan of Seoul National University, Dr. Choi Seon Ho, Lecturer at Hosei University, Tokyo, and Mr. Seo Hyunkoo, Graduate Student at Hosei University, for supplying the Korean language material, and also Dr. Boris Dmitrievich Park of the Russian Academy of Science, Institute of Oriental Studies, for the valuable information on Yi Wi-Jong and his family in Russia. The writer also wishes to thank Rhoda and Peter Trooboff for their thoughtful advice and suggestions on the manuscript. Appreciation should also be expressed to Joseph Altham for his insightful comments on the paper. The writer wishes to thank him for allowing to read his unpublished paper, Joseph Altham, "The Summoning of the Hague Conference: An Episode in Russian Foreign Policy", 2004.
2. Professor at Sofia University, Tokyo.

3. Arthur Eyffinger, *The 1899 Hague Peace Conference: The Parliament of Man, the Federation of the World*, Kluwer Law International, 2001, p. 451.

4. See in general, Shabtai Rosenne, ed., *The Hague Peace Conferences of 1899 and 1907 and International Arbitration: Reports and Documents*, T.M.C. Asser Press, 2001.

5. See Antonio Cançado Trindade, "Presence of Latin America at the Second Hague Peace Conference", p. 51, *supra*. It may be noted that, while the First Conference had been held by the Russian initiative, the Second Conference was predominantly the "American project" led by President Theodore Roosevelt whose Government wished to exert as much influence as possible over Latin America. Calvin D. Davis, *The United States and the Second Hague Peace Conference: American Diplomacy and International Organization 1899-1914*, Duke University Press, 1976.

In this presentation, I want to explore the reasons for this situation regarding Asia and focus particularly on the treatment of the Korean Delegation by the Conference since that story has lessons for all of us to this day.

I think that this episode tells us a great deal about early twentieth-century aspirations for self-determination and the barriers that subjugated peoples faced in pursuing recognition of their national identity.

First, why did Asian countries play such a minor role in the 1907 Conference?

To begin with, China under the Ch'ing dynasty was on the verge of collapse in 1907. China proved unable to resist the aggression, first of the Western powers and, then, of Japan. At a time when Chinese internal affairs were in disarray, China's foreign policy was in such a state of paralysis that the Chinese representatives were unable to make any positive contribution to the work of the Conference.

The same might be said of Persia, a powerful but troubled empire in the West Asian region whose internal affairs at that time were going through the constitutional revolution. It may be recalled that this year is also the centennial of the 1907 Anglo-Russian entente, and that the centrepiece of that agreement, signed on 31 August 1907, was the division of Persia into spheres of influence by the two imperial powers[6].

Some may wonder why Siam was selected to participate. Siam was certainly not a power at that time. Yet it was an important buffer State between the various colonial powers that were vying for influence and possessions in South East Asia. As an old, peace-loving kingdom which had never been colonized, Siam carefully held the balance of power in the region at that time[7]. Moreover, Siam was accredited to the court of the Tsar in St. Petersburg, and

---

6. A. J. P. Taylor, *The Struggle for Mastery in Europe*, Oxford, 1954, pp. 443-445; Harold Nicolson, *Sir Arthur Nicolson, First Lord Carnock: A Study in the Old Diplomacy*, London, Constable and Co., 1930, pp. 240-242, pp. 251-252; Fruz Kazemzadeh, *Russia and Britain in Persia, 1864-1914*, Yale Univ. Press, 1968.

7. With regard to Siam's insistence on inserting an arbitration clause in the 1897 Treaty of Friendship and Commerce with Japan, see Yasuo Ishimoto, "Meijiki ni okeru Chusai-saiban" (Arbitration in the Meiji Era), in *Kokusaiho no Kozo-tenkan* (Structural Change of International Law), Yushindo, 1998, pp. 305-306 (in Japanese).

close personal ties existed between the Siamese royal family and the Russian imperial family [8].

It appears, at least from the records, that these Asian delegations generally regarded their invitation to the Conference as more symbolic than substantive.

Japan was emerging as a new power in Asia after its victory over Russia in the war of 1904-1905. The outlook of Japan at the Second Conference, however, differed markedly from what it had been at the First. The Japanese delegates in 1899 are described by Dr. Eyffinger as

> "keenly sensible of their importance and ensuing responsibility . . ., [and] coming to The Hague, [they were] excellently prepared and most keen indeed to make a full contribution on behalf of the Asian Continent" [9].

Yet in 1907, Japan showed itself to be more preoccupied with attaining recognition of its equal status with the countries of the West [10].

In 1899, for instance, Japan was quite enthusiastic about the conclusion of the Hague Convention I on the Pacific Settlement of Disputes and the ensuing establishment of the Permanent Court of Arbitration (PCA). And once it was established, the Japanese were very keen to make use of the PCA in order to demonstrate their country's willingness to submit disputes to arbitration. Thus in 1902 Japan referred the *Japanese House Tax* case [11] to the PCA as soon as

---

8. Vitit Muntarbhorn, "The 1899 Hague Peace Conference and the Development of the Laws of War: Asia's Contribution to the Quest for Humanitarianism?", in Timothy L. H. McCormack *et al.*, eds., *A Century of War and Peace: Asia-Pacific Perspectives on the Century of the 1899 Hague Peace Conference*, Kluwer Law International, 2001, p. 113.

9. Eyffinger, *op. cit. supra* footnote 3, pp. 160-161.

10. Klaus Schlichtmann, "Japan and the Two Hague Peace Conferences, 1899 and 1907", http://www.ne.jp/asahi/peace/unitednationsreform2007/hague_peace_and_japan.

11. The *Japanese House Tax* case concerned the conflict between the right of British, French and German nationals to the perpetual lease of land and the right of the Japanese municipal governments to levy tax on buildings standing on such leased land. The decision of the tribunal, pronounced on 22 May 1905, held that the house tax exemption should continue even after the revision of the unequal treaties. *RIAA*, Vol. II (1961), pp. 41-58; Shigeki Miyazaki, "Japanese House Tax Arbitration", in R. Bernhardt, ed., *Encyclopedia of Public International Law*, Vol. III, pp. 2-3.

While all the experts in Japan of that period were convinced of their victory in the case, it would be fair to say, in retrospect, that Japan's contentions had some

it was established, in order to be registered as the first nation to bring a case before it. The Japanese international lawyers were very disappointed to learn that their case was not to be the first but only the second, because the *Pious Fund of the Californias* case had been submitted a few months earlier by the United States and Mexico. Although they did not win the submission race, the Japanese lawyers and officials nevertheless felt sure that they would win their case. Thus for instance Tsunejiro Miyaoka, who acted as agent for Japan, declared in a grand gesture that, should the judgment go against Japan, he would be willing to perform *hara-kiri* in the traditional *samurai* fashion.

When the tribunal rendered its decision against Japan on 22 May 1905, the Japanese were deeply disappointed and disillusioned[12]. Because of their unduly high expectations, the Japanese complainants did not accept the PCA decision. Instead, they aired their unjustifiable accusation that PCA was unfair to non-white peoples. Thus, at the Second Peace Conference in 1907, Japan was eager to block the proposal for a compulsory system of arbitration[13]. One may see here a sudden change of attitude on the part of the Japanese

---

weakness from a juridical point of view, and were not entirely persuasive. Kisaburo Yokota, "Kokusai Saiban to Nihon" (International Adjudication and Japan), in *Kokusaiho Ronshu* (Treatises on International Law), Yuhikaku, 1976, pp. 183-185). Thus, the Japanese experts may have unfairly attributed their loss to prejudice and drawn the wrong conclusion about arbitration from the outcome.

In any event, due to the bitter experience of this case, Japan abstained for many years from referring international disputes to international adjudication.

12. Mr. Miyaoka, as expected, did not perform *hara-kiri* after the judgment. It may be interesting to compare him with the Thai army captain described by Judge Jessup:

> "after the Court's decision in the *Temple* case, the Thai government ordered its small detachment, which was stationed on the Temple promontory, to withdraw. There is a story ... which relates that the captain commanding the detachment declared that he would never pull down the Thai flag flying over Thai territory — as he considered it to be. So he ordered his men to dig up the flagpole and they carried the pole, flag still flying, off the disputed ground." (Philip C. Jessup, *The Price of International Justice*, Columbia University Press, 1971, p. 20).

13. The original instruction from the Japanese Government was that the delegates should vote, in support of Germany, against the proposal for obligatory arbitration, but Ambassador Tsudzuki, head of the Japanese delegation, abstained in the final vote at the end of conference's fifth session (Commission I) on 5 October 1907, "in order that [the] country might have further time for reflection" (James Brown Scott, *The Hague Peace Conferences of 1899 and 1907*, John Hopkins Press, 1909, Vol. 2, p. 160).

Government around 1905, especially after the Russo-Japanese War. Once Japan had itself become an imperialist power, its foreign policy tended to rely more on force than law [14].

In any event, there is little in the 1907 Conference that could be described as "The *Presence* of Asia". I would rather speak of "The *Non-Presence* of Asia". In fact, the Peace Conference was indifferent, perhaps even hostile, to the legitimate aspirations and outcry of Asian peoples, which I would like to highlight this afternoon. In so doing, I will focus particularly on the episode of the three Korean envoys who came to The Hague in June 1907 demanding to be represented, only for the Conference to refuse them [15].

Korea was deprived of its right of diplomatic representation under the treaty of protectorate with Japan concluded in 1905, immediately after the end of the Russo-Japanese War. Emperor Ko-Jong of Korea had taken every opportunity to send messages abroad to protest against the treaty, while Japanese officials tried to prevent the Korean Emperor from having any contact with foreign Governments. Learning about the Hague Peace Conference, the Emperor thought that he saw his chance of at last striking a blow for freedom [16]. He believed that, despite its defeat in the war with Japan, Russia would

---

14. Shinya Murase, "The Most-Favored-Nation Treatment in Japan's Treaty Practice 1854-1905", *American Journal of International Law*, Vol. 70, 1976, pp. 273-297; Shinya Murase, "Japan and International Law", *The Japan Foundation Newsletter*, Vol. XXV, No. 4, 1997, pp. 1-5.

15. See in general, Shinya Murase, "1907 Hague Peace Conference Revisited: Envoys of the Korean Emperor", *Gaiko Forum* (Diplomatic Forum), No. 227 (June 2007), pp. 56-63; No. 228 (July 2007), pp. 70-77 (in Japanese); translated in part into Korean in the *Monthly Chosun*, July 2007, pp. 192-203.
Korea was included in the original list of 47 countries to be invited to the Second Hague Conference in a diplomatic note sent by Russia to these countries in October 1905 (before Korea's concluding the protectorate treaty with Japan). In a note from the Russian ambassador in Washington, DC, to the US Secretary of State dated 12 April 1906, it was stated that Panama had declined the invitation, that Korea had not returned the reply, and that Ethiopia had accepted the invitation. Panama eventually accepted the invitation and was represented at the Conference (probably at the strong insistence of the United States). Japan apparently opposed Korea's participation, stating that there should be no more new members except the Latin American countries. As a result of a by-blow, Ethiopia, which might have become the first African country to participate in an international peace conference, was not represented. James Brown Scott, *The Hague Peace Conferences*, Vol. II, The Johns Hopkins Press, 1909, pp. 178-180.

16. F. A. McKenzie, *Korea's Fight for Freedom*, Fleming H. Revell & Co., 1920, pp. 122-123; H. Hilary Conroy, *The Japanese Seizure of Korea: 1868-1910*, Univ. of Penn. Press, 1960, pp. 345-350; Eric Yong-Joong Lee, "Early Development of Modern International Law in East Asia: With Special Reference to China, Japan and Korea", *Journal of the History of International Law*, Vol. 4, 2002, pp. 51-52.

not recognize Japan's arbitrary rule over Korea. He also believed that neither the United States nor Great Britain would permit Korea to die before their eyes without extending their hands to help. He appeared optimistic that the Conference would come to the rescue and liberate his country from Japanese domination. Thus, with utmost secrecy, the Emperor Ko-Jong arranged to send his delegates to The Hague to participate in the Conference, in order to denounce Japan's brutal subjugation of his country.

The three Korean delegates arrived in The Hague on 25 June 1907, ten days after the opening of the Conference. The delegates were Yi Sang-Sol, former member of the Prime Minister's Council; Yi Jun, former preliminary judge of the Supreme Court; and Yi Wi-Jong, former Secretary at the Korean Legation at St. Petersburg, Russia. Yi Wi-Jong was only 20 years old. The son of a high-ranking diplomat, and educated in Europe from the age of seven, Yi was said to have spoken seven languages. He thus served in The Hague as spokesman of the Korean delegation.

Unfortunately, Emperor Ko-Jong's optimism bore little relation to the way the Great Powers really viewed Korea. In a secret agreement signed on 29 July 1905, the United States Secretary of War Taft had assured Japanese Prime Minister Katsura that the United States would recognize Japanese rule over Korea. This recognition was given in exchange for Japan's support of the US administration of the Philippines. Similar assurances were given to Japan by Great Britain (12 August 1905) and by France (10 June 1907).

Russia was also changing its policy toward Japan. While Russia had accepted Japan's right to "guide, protect and administer Korea" in the peace treaty of 1905, Russia began soon afterwards to evade the implications of the undertaking it had given in an attempt to regain its influence on the Korean Peninsula. However, by early 1907 when Count Izvolskii became Foreign Minister, Russia had shifted from its previous "confrontational" strategy towards Japan to a "conciliatory" policy. Thus, on 30 July 1907, an agreement was signed between the two countries to the effect that Russia would no longer intervene in Japanese-Korean relations. This concession was made in exchange for Japan's acknowledgment of Russia's special interests in Mongolia. Imperialism was in full swing in those days.

It is unclear whether the three Korean envoys knew of these developments when they arrived late for the Conference in The Hague. They seemed as optimistic about their project as Emperor Ko-Jong.

Three Delegates from Korea

Yi Sang-Sol (1870-1917). Having studied English, French and Modern Literature, he was Professor and President of the National Confucian Academy. In 1905, he resigned from his position as Councillor of the Prime Minister's Office in protest at the Treaty of Protectorate with Japan. In 1906, he defected to Vladivostok, Russia, where he founded a school to educate Korean youths for the struggle against Japan. He was Emperor Ko-Jong's chief delegate at The Hague in 1907. During his last ten years, he devoted himself to restoring Korea's independence, working on the establishment of the Yi Jun Yi Sang-Sol Yi Wi-Jong government in exile.

Yi Jun (1859-1907). Being a lawyer, political activist and pious Christian, he was the founder of the Red Cross, YMCA and Christian mission schools in Korea. He studied law, including international law, at the Legal Training Institute in 1895, and also at Waseda University, Tokyo, in 1896-1898. He resigned from his position as preliminary judge of the Supreme Court in protest at the 1905 Treaty of Protectorate, and led the anti-Japanese struggle afterwards. He died of sudden illness on 14 July 1907 at Hotel "De Jong", located at Wagenstraat 124a, The Hague, which has now become the "Yi Jun Peace Museum". The cause of his death was long debated, as the Korean newspapers had publicized it sensationally as a "suicide in protest". However, as the local Dutch newspapers as well as the *Courrier de la Conférence* reported, the fact was that Yi Jun had an abscess on his cheek which had been removed by an operation, causing erysipelas.

Yi Wi-Jong (1887-1920s ?). As a son of Yi Bong-Jing, former Minister of Korea in St. Petersburg, he lived with his father in the various European capitals from childhood, and he was therefore able to speak seven languages. After graduating from Janson de Sailly School in Paris, he was trained at the Saint-Cyr Military Academy. He served as secretary at the Korean Legation in St. Petersburg, until 1905 when it was ordered to be closed as a result of the Treaty with Japan. He was only 20 years old when he acted as spokesman of the Korean delegation to The Hague in 1907. His wife, Elizaveta Valerianovna Norken, was a daughter of Baron Karlofskii-Norken, a Russian aristocrat of Swedish origin and Governor of the Province of Tobolsk, Russia. He fought battles against the Japanese forces as an officer in command of a partisan unit in Siberia. He later joined the Bolshevik revolution in St. Petersburg, and it is believed that he served as an officer in the Russian Red Army and that he was killed in action at some point, leaving behind his wife and three daughters.

They were "secret delegates" when appointed by the Emperor, but after they had checked in at their hotel, Hotel de Jong, which is located near the railway station, they proudly put up the Korean national flag in their window to show that their activities were open and official.

On the day after their arrival, 26 June, they contacted Count Nelidov, the Russian representative who served as President of the Conference. Ambassador Nelidov refused to see them, rejecting their request to attend the Conference on the grounds that no delegates were to be accepted other than those invited by the Government of the Netherlands. The Dutch Foreign Minister also refused to see them. He said that they could not participate in the Conference because for the previous two years Korea had not enjoyed diplomatic relations with foreign countries. Only the American Ambassador, Joseph Choate, received them in person and with sympathy. However, his official response was the same.

This universal response to their presence was naturally experienced by the Korean delegates as a terrible disappointment. The reaction of the young spokesman, Yi Wi-Jong, was quoted in the *New York Times*: "Mr. Nelidof's refusal to receive us was astonishing and painful, as our relations with Russia, as well as with America, are so good that we thought they could not refuse to assist us." [17]

The envoys thereafter paid visits to the various delegations, including the British, French and German, to ask for help. On each occasion they were coldly rebuffed. For obvious reasons, the Japanese Ambassador, Keiroku Tsudzuki, had probably cautioned in advance the major delegations of the participating States to ignore the Korean request. Finally, the Korean group approached the Chinese delegation, hoping that it might render assistance to them as fellow Asians. This request was also declined. As I mentioned, on the eve of the Chinese revolution, the Chinese diplomats had their own fate in mind.

The only Japanese who met the three Korean delegates was a journalist named Shingoro Takaishi. He later became President of Mainichi Newspapers and, as a member of the International Olympic Committee, he would be instrumental in the 1960s and 1970s in bringing the Olympic Games to Tokyo and Sapporo. In 1907, he was 29 years old, and the only reporter despatched to The Hague from

---

17. *New York Times*, 30 June 1907.

Japan. Mr. Takaishi seems to have been a thoughtful, open-minded person. His memoir reveals in detail how the Korean delegates spent their three weeks that summer at The Hague. At the request of the Japanese ambassador, he delivered a message summoning the Korean delegation to a meeting with the Japanese envoy. The delegates replied that they would see Mr. Takaishi because he was a journalist, but that it was not necessary to see the officials of the Japanese Government. Mr. Takaishi saw the delegates almost every day. Observing that they appeared to be in dire straits financially, he was nonetheless deeply impressed by their sincerity, earnest patriotism, and determination to sacrifice their personal interests for the sake of their country [18].

Within a few days after their arrival at The Hague, it was clear that the attempt of the Korean delegates to attend the Conference had been thwarted. They distributed their statement, written in French, to the participants of the Conference and arranged for its publication in the *Courrier de la Conférence*, on 27 June 1907. It stated, *inter alia,* first, that the Korea-Japan protectorate treaty of 1905 had not been signed by the Emperor of Korea and therefore had no validity; second, that Japan had employed armed forces in order to achieve its goal; and third, that Japan had acted in contravention of the laws and customs of Korea. The Korean delegates requested that the representatives of the participating States should make an impartial examination as to whether these points were violations of international law and should render assistance to enable them to attend the Conference [19].

---

18. Shingoro Takaishi's Biography Publication Group, *Takaishi-san*, 1969, pp. 47-54 (in Japanese); Shingoro Takaishi, "Korean King's Secret Mission: The Important Role I Played", *Osaka Mainichi Shinbun*, 22 January 1930 (in Japanese).

19. *Courrier de la Conférence*, La Haye, le 27 Juin, 1907:

« Yi-Sang-Sul, ex-vice-premier ministre, Yj-Tjoune, ex-juge d'instruction de la Cour suprême de la justice de la Corée et Yi-Oui-Tjyong ex-secrétaire de la Légation de Corée à Saint-Pétersbourg, Envoyé de Sa Majesté l'Empereur de la Corée en qualité de délégué à la Conférence de la Paix à La Haye, ont l'honneur d'informer Leurs Excellences que l'indépendance de notre pays a été garantie et reconnue en 1884 par toutes les puissances. En outre notre indépendance est reconnue jusqu'à présent dans vos pays.

En 1905, le 17 novembre, Yi Sang-Sul étant vice-premier ministre a été témoin des agissements du Japon qui, au mépris de tout droit international et par force armée nous ont contraint à rompre les relations diplomatiques amicales qui existaient entre nos pays respectifs jusqu'à ce jour. En vue de cela je me permets de porter à la connaissance de Leurs Excellences les procédés employés par les Japonais qui, pour arriver à ce résultat, n'ont pas

An English journalist, William Stead, the editor of the *Courrier de la Conférence,* was sympathetic toward the Korean delegates. He organized a semi-public gathering for them to make their appeal. When the plan was announced, the Japanese ambassador was furious and pressed Stead to stop anything detrimental to Japanese interests from occurring at the meeting. Ambassador Tsudzuki reported to the Foreign Ministry that he believed he "had fairly succeeded in preventing Stead from becoming anti-Japanese"[20].

Yi Wi-Jong, the youngest member of the Korean delegation, was already quite popular among the journalists covering the Hague Conference. Educated in Paris and trained at the Saint-Cyr Military Academy, he was the son of Yi Bong-Jing, former Minister of Korea at St. Petersburg. He was raised in an aristocratic environment. His

---

hésité à employer les menaces de violence et à violer les droits et les lois du pays. Pour plus de clarté je diviserai nos griefs en trois cas séparés:

1. Les Japonais ont agi sans le consentement de Sa Majesté l'Empereur.
2. Pour arriver à leur but, les Japonais ont employé contre le Gouvernement impérial la force armée.
3. Les Japonais ont agi au mépris de toutes les lois et coutumes du pays.

L'impartialité de Leurs Excellences appréciera si les trois paragraphes ci-dessus ne sont pas une violation directe des Conventions internationales.

Pouvons-nous comme pays indépendant permettre que la ruse du Japon vienne détruire les relations amicales et diplomatiques qui ont existé jusqu'à présent entre nous et les autres pays et devienne une menace constante pour la paix en Extrême-Orient?

Je regrette infiniment d'être privé de la possibilité d'assister à la Conférence de La Haye, quoique délégué par S. M. l'Empereur dans ce but, par le fait même de cette violation de nos droits par les Japonais.

Nous joignons à cette lettre un résumé de tous les procédés employés et des actes commis par les Japonais jusqu'au jour de mon départ et vous prie de bien vouloir porter votre bienveillante attention sur cette question si vitale pour mon pays. Dans le cas où vous auriez besoin de renseignements complémentaires ou que vous désiriez vous assurer des pleins pouvoirs qui nous ont été conférés par Sa Majesté l'Empereur de Corée veuillez bien nous en informer; nous aurions l'honneur de nous mettre à l'entière disposition de Leurs Excellences.

Vu que les relations diplomatiques entre la Corée et les autres pays n'ont pas été rompues de par la volonté de la Corée elle-même, mais bien par suite de la violation de nos droits par le Japon, nous avons l'honneur de nous adresser à Leurs Excellences en les priant de bien vouloir nous assister à la Conférence de La Haye et y défendre nos droits en exposant les procédés des Japonais.

Veuillez agréer Leurs Excellences avec mes remerciements anticipés, l'assurance de notre très haute considération.

(Signé) Yi Sang-Sul, Yi-Tjoune, Yi-Oui-Tjyong.

20. Telegram from Ambassador Tsudzuki to Foreign Minister Hayashi on 9 July 1907. Ministry for Foreign Affairs, *Nippon Gaiko Bunsho* (Diplomatic Archives of Japan), Vol. 40, No. 1, pp. 436-437.

wife, Elizaveta Valerianovna Norken, was a daughter of Baron Karlofskii-Norken, a Russian aristocrat of Swedish origin and Governor
of the Russian Province of Tobolsk. This background explains why
the Conference journalists had already nicknamed him "the Prince".

Yi Wi-Jong was the speaker at this meeting, held by the
"Federation of Internationalism" on the evening of 8 July, with
William Stead presiding. The Japanese Ambassador reported the gist
of Stead's opening speech as follows:

> "Although he feels sympathy for the Koreans, he must
> remind them that a mouse which is already in a cat's jaws must
> not further enrage the cat. Neither the Conference nor the
> Arbitration Court is open to them [the Koreans]. The Dutch
> Government acted correctly in refusing them. He and the others
> assembled could do nothing but protest, and he would be happy
> if that protestation did not accelerate the final annexation of
> Korea. The burden of responsibility would rest entirely with the
> Prince [Yi Wi-Jong] should he decide to take that risk." [21]

Thus Stead exerted tremendous pressure on the 20-year-old Yi Wi-
Jong, implying that whatever the Prince Yi said would determine the
fate of his country. Almost anyone in his position would have been
terrified and shaken by such an overbearing introduction. Yi Wi-
Jong, however, remained calm. In a dignified manner, he delivered
his speech entitled "A Plea for Korea". (At this point I realized that
he was truly a hero whose courage and efforts deserved more recognition.) Mr. Takaishi, the journalist from Japan, attended the session. Based on his information, Ambassador Tsudzuki reported to
the Foreign Ministry, as follows:

> "Yi Wi-Jong addressed a rather crowded assembly in the
> semi-public meeting last night. He spoke eloquently in French
> for about an hour and vehemently attacked Japan's Korea
> policy." [22]

Yi Wi-Jong was straightforward, direct, and provocative. There
was no sign of East-Asian indirection or court-diplomacy elegance
in his speech. He spoke more like a revolutionary than a diplomat.

The audience was composed mostly of journalists who appeared

---

21. *Op. cit. supra* footnote 20.
22. *Ibid.*

deeply moved by Yi Wi-Jong's passionate appeal. One of them stood up after the speech, proposing a resolution that sympathized with the Koreans and criticized the Japanese. Stead and others opposed the criticism of the Japanese. In the end, a resolution was unanimously adopted confining itself to an expression of sympathy with the Koreans. The resolution included a paragraph "wishing that at some future time an international tribunal might be established for examining and adjudging such cases in order to find out truths and to administer justice all around"[23].

This occasion was the high point for the Korean delegates and for the young Yi Wi-Jong. Nevertheless, it was all that they achieved in The Hague. By this time, Emperor Ko-Jong in Seoul had been severely interrogated by the Japanese Resident-General, the Marquis Hirobumi Ito, and accused of betrayal. The Emperor claimed that he was innocent of the charge by arguing that he had had no knowledge of the so-called "secret envoys", who must have been "imposters". Asked about the Emperor's remark, Yi Wi-Jong replied to a reporter for the *New York Times* that he hoped the world would not blame Emperor Ko-Jong for acting under duress in repudiating their presence at The Hague. "To have admitted that he instructed us to represent him at The Hague would perhaps have meant his being dethroned, or even murdered."[24]

Tragically, the Deputy Chief of the Korean delegation, Yi Jun, died at his hotel in The Hague only six days later on Sunday, 14 July 1907, in despair and indignation. (The Hotel De Jong, located at Wagenstraat 124a, has now become the "Yi Jun Peace Museum" in his memory.) The cause of his death was long debated. Korean newspapers gave it sensational coverage, describing it as a "suicide in protest"[25].

---

23. *Op. cit. supra* footnote 20. See also *Haagesche Courant*, 10 July 1907, which reported the full detail of the meeting.

24. *New York Times,* 7 July 1907.

25. *Hwang Sung Shinmun* (The Imperial Palace News) and *Daehan Maeil Shinbo* (The Korea Daily News), Extra editions, 18 July 1907. The "suicide" theory was long supported by many in Korea. After a thorough examination by experts, the Government of the Republic of Korea (South Korea) pronounced in 1962 that the cause of Yi Jun's death had been erysipelas.

An extreme example of fabrication of the historical event may be cited as follows: The Postal Service of the Democratic People's Republic of Korea (North Korea) issued a postage stamp in July 2007 commemorating the centennial of Yi Jun's death, which shows the supposedly magnificent performance of Yi Jun in the conference room, with his left hand pointing at the dignitaries in fierce condemnation and with his right hand thrusting a sword into his stomach. (*Korean*

However, as the local Dutch newspapers[26] and the *Courrier de la Conférence*[27] reported, in fact Yi Jun had had an abscess on his cheek which was removed by an operation, causing erysipelas[28].

Yi Sang-Sol, the chief Korean delegate, returned to Vladivostok, Russia, where he devoted his life to educating Korean youths for the anti-Japanese struggle, to the movement for Korean independence, and to the establishment of the Korean government-in-exile. He died in the Maritime Province of Russia in 1917[29]. Both Yi Sang-Sol and Yi Jun are now remembered as heroes and their graves lie in the national cemetery in Seoul. There are a number of articles and books written about them in Korea.

By contrast, there is virtually no record about the subsequent life of Yi Wi-Jong, despite the fact that he was the most popular of the three Korean envoys in The Hague in 1907. I believe that Yi Wi-Jong deserves to be recognized for his contribution. Indeed, I regard his life after the Hague Conference as both fascinating and inspiring. So let me conclude with just a few words about his life after the Conference.

After 1908, Yi Wi-Jong fought against Japanese forces as an officer in command of a Russian partisan unit in Siberia. As a graduate of Saint-Cyr, he appeared to be an impressive commander on the battlefield. His father, Yi Bong-Jing, committed suicide in 1911 in protest at the treaty annexing Korea to Japan. Yi Wi-Jong gave away all of his father's property, valued at around 12,000 roubles, to various American and Russian organizations devoted to the Korean independence movement. He worked for a time as a railway station clerk. When the First World War began in 1914, he joined the Vladimir

---

Central News Agency, 6 July 2007, quoted in *Chosun News*, 11 July 2007). On this occasion, the following comment was given by the *Agency*:

> "The historical lesson to be learned from the blood spilled by Yi Jun at the Peace Conference is that a nation's independence had to be attained not by 'appeals' or 'diplomacy' but by the force of the people which was the only way to chase out the aggressors."

26. *Haagesche Courant*, 17 July 1907; *De Telegraaf*, 17 July 1907.
27. *Courrier de la Conférence*, 17 July 1907; Shingoro Takaishi also reported more than a week before Yi Jun's death that he had been seriously ill, and that the other two colleagues looked deeply concerned.
28. See further, Lee Sun-Jun, *A Biography of Yi Jun*, Eulchi Publishers, 1994, pp. 235, 237-238 (in Korean).
29. See B. S. Yoon, *Biography of Yi Sang-Sol*, 3rd ed., Ilchogak Publishers, 1998 (in Korean); Igor Saveliev, "Militant Diaspora: Korean Immigrants and Guerrillas in Early Twentieth Century Russia", *Forum of International Development Studies*, 26, 2004, pp. 147 *et seq.*

S. Murase

Military Academy where he completed his training in 1916, and later joined the Russian army as an officer [30]. At the start of the Russian Revolution, he joined the Bolsheviks and the Red Army. It has generally been assumed in Korea that he was killed in 1920 in a battle in Siberia against the invading Japanese army.

However, we have recently found documentary evidence indicating that in 1925 he was still alive and a resident of St. Petersburg, where he taught at the Korean Branch of the International Officers Academy of the Communist Party [31]. It is likely, therefore, that he was killed in action at some point in the late 1920s, leaving behind his wife [32] and three daughters [33]. Perhaps his association with Communism explains why so little has been written about his life after the Second Hague Conference, a state of neglect which, I believe, undervalues his character and his patriotism.

Returning to the 1907 "gate-crashing" incident of the three delegates in The Hague, the cost for Korea was disastrously high. The incident was naturally a great embarrassment to Japan. Taking advantage of the situation, the Japanese Foreign Minister, Kaoru Hayashi, rushed to the Korean capital on 18 July 1907, to demand the abdication of the Emperor of Korea. Coerced and intimidated,

---

30. Dr. Boris Dmitrievich Park of the Russian Academy of Science, Oriental History Division, has kindly informed the present writer that there was no record found as to where Yi Wi-Jong was posted after graduation from the Military Academy in 1916. However, Dr. Park has discovered that, in the letter dated on 6 October 1917, from Deputy Foreign Minister Neratov to the Minister of Finance Bernatskii, Yi Bong-Jing's and Yi Wi-Jong's merits in strengthening the Russian-Korean relations and the protection of the new fatherland were recognized. According to Dr. Park, there is a document certifying that Yi Wi-Jong was on the battlefield for two years between August 1917 and August 1919, but no further details are known. The writer wishes to thank Mr. Ryu Jae Hoon of the Hankyoreh Daily who provided the contact details of Dr. Park and Liudmila Vasil'evna Efimova (see footnote 32 below).

31. Yi Wi-Jong was listed as one of the "dangerous activists living in Europe" in the 1925 record of the Police Office of the Japanese Colonial Government (Chosen Sotokufu); he and his group published a Korean language journal, *Word and Sword*, whose office was listed as located in the Second Artillery School, Leningrad (St. Petersburg).

32. Yi Wi-Jong's wife, Elizaveta Valerianovna Norken, died in 1943 during the siege of Leningrad.

33. The three daughters were Vera (who died very young), Nina (who died in the 1940s) and Evgenia (who died in 1986). The present writer was able to get in contact with Liudmila Vasil'evna Efimova (Nina Vladimirovna Korolyova's daughter, i.e., Yi Wi-Jong's granddaughter, born in 1936) who lives in Moscow. Tatiana Proyaeva and Julia Piskulóva are Liudmila's daughters, i.e., Wi-Jong's great granddaughters. I would like to thank Dr. Svetlana Vassiliouk of Hosei University, Tokyo, for translating the telephone conversation on 14 September 2007.

the Emperor eventually agreed to resign from the throne, at two o'clock in the morning on 19 July. Hayashi only left the Korean capital after he had concluded the third Japan-Korea Agreement on 24 July 1907, by which Korea was virtually annexed to Japan. The formal annexation came three years later, in 1910[34]. Ironically, Foreign Minister Hayashi had headed the Japanese delegation at the First Hague Conference in 1899.

From the point of view of international law today, such acts ought undoubtedly to be judged as impermissible. I do not intend to justify them. However, I believe that we should assess historical events on the basis of a *contemporaneous perspective*, that is, in the context of the social and political climate and events of their day. The following editorial in the *New York Tribune* of 20 July 1907, probably reflect the mood that was widespread among the leading nations at that time.

"For years Korea has betrayed deplorable insufficiency for independent self-Government. For centuries it acknowledged the suzerainty of China. Rescued from that condition by Japan it became thereafter a voluntary shuttlecock between Japan and Russia and now the end comes, and the impartial judgment of the world will welcome the end. Saved by Japan from Russian conquest Korea agreed to be guided by Japanese advice on fiscal and other administrative matters and to conduct its foreign affairs through the Japanese Government. In return Japan was to guarantee her territorial integrity and the safety of her dynasty. This arrangement was recognized by all the world. The gravity of the offence of the Emperor of Korea sending a delegation to The Hague unknown to Japan may be estimated if we imagine the Emir of Bokhara sending one too as an intervention between him and the Tzar or the Annamese King

---

34. For many years after the end of the Second World War, the Republic of Korea asserted that the treaties and conventions concluded with Japan before 1910 were null and void *ab initio* because they had been concluded under duress, while Japan considered that they had been properly concluded and therefore been effective, admitting that they *now* have no validity. As a compromise, Article 2 of the Treaty on the Basic Relations between the two countries concluded in 1965 stipulated: "It is confirmed that all treaties or agreements concluded between the Empire of Japan and the Empire of Korea on or before 22 August 1910 are *already* null and void" (emphasis added). It is said that the ambiguous word "already" was inserted to express that the parties "agreed to disagree" after the decade-long, difficult negotiations.

against France or some Indian Maharajah asking The Hague to expel British rule from Hindustan. The title of Japan to deal with Korea, as she has done, is at least as good as that of Russia, France, England or any other power to deal with the subject nations as they have done. The subject nations are now so closely bound together that the state of one inevitably affects the others." [35]

Under the circumstances, the attempt of the three Korean delegates to participate in the 1907 Conference proved unsuccessful. Their actions were seized on in order to justify Japan's swift annexation of Korea. But were their efforts and sacrifice really a failure? I do not think so. The delegates appealed to the world in a most dignified manner. The Hague was the last such chance for them, which they tried to employ as best they could. Through the heroic acts of these delegates, the Korean people took a firm stand during the hard days of colonial rule. One might even say that Korea has become great today in large measure through the memory and example of such heroes, who have long been a source of pride for their people. It should be noted that the current UN Secretary-General, Mr. Ban Ki-Moon, is from Korea.

When the Second Hague Conference adjourned on 18 October 1907, it was agreed that the Third Peace Conference would be held seven years later, in 1914. However, the outbreak of world war destroyed all opportunities for such a conference. The next Peace Conference was held after the War, in 1919 at Versailles. It established the League of Nations and the Permanent Court of International Justice. The Versailles Conference was thus essentially the Third Peace Conference.

At Versailles in 1919, Ho Chi Minh and his group acted in much the same way as the Korean envoys had acted in 1907, demanding representation at the conference in order to denounce the French colonization of Vietnam and to restore Vietnam's independence [36]. History repeats itself. Perhaps it also moves forward step by step.

---

35. *New York Tribune*, Editorial, 20 July 1907.
36. Ho Chi Minh in Paris published, in his pseudonym Nguyen Ai Quoc (Nguyen the Patriot), "The Demands of the Vietnamese People" in a brief article on page 3 of the socialist newspaper *L'Humanité* of 18 June 1919, calling on victorious great powers to honour their promise of a new era of "law and justice" for subject peoples, and demanded to participate in the Peace Conference. Sophie Quinn-Judge, *Ho Chi Minh: The Missing Years, 1919-1941*, University of California Press, 2002, pp. 11-28.

The act of the Korean delegates has been a source of inspiration and encouragement for peoples fighting for freedom all over the world. The delegates are a noble example of self-sacrifice in the lofty causes of justice, honour and humanity. That is precisely what is so moving about the three Korean delegates: they left behind a valuable legacy which goes beyond time and national boundaries.

Significant achievements notwithstanding, the Second Hague Conference betrayed the aspirations of Asian peoples, a fact which we should not forget at this occasion of its centennial commemoration. From the Asian perspective, the centennial of the Second Hague Conference is not something to be *celebrated*. At best, it should simply be *commemorated*[37].

---

37. Cf. Muntarbhorn, *op. cit. supra* footnote 8.

II. COMPTE RENDU DES DÉBATS

SUMMING UP

M. KOSKENNIEMI : Je n'ai malheureusement pas de questions à poser mais quelques commentaires à faire et que peut-être les orateurs peuvent commenter à leur tour. I am going to do this in English.

It is of course customary to point out that the 1907 Conference was attended in a more universal way than the 1899 Conference and we have heard the speakers mention that in 1899 there were 26 delegations, while there were 44 in 1907. Nevertheless, examining those numbers does not give a clear sense of this matter. We have also heard two presentations from two parts of what then was doubtless the periphery, Latin America and Asia, and their level of representation. I would like to put my comments in a more abstract way. First "universality" is a difficult notion. We never quite know where "the universal" is and, in particular, who or what might be its real or authentic representative. For everybody tends to speak in the voice of "the universal". The 17 or 18 Latin-American delegations which were present here in The Hague at the time did in some respects, as numbers, represent something of a turn towards universality in the international law community at the time. Nevertheless Professor Trindade left unmentioned the role played by the United States in pushing for the increased representation of the Latin Americans in The Hague and elsewhere. The very important legal co-operation which emerged between the United States and the Latin American States already in the 1890s was in part motivated by a desire for pacification of the hemisphere, in part for enlisting at the international level support for various US projects and initiatives. The imaginative application of the Monroe Doctrine meant, among other things, the intensification of legal collaboration and legal thinking between the United States and its Latin American neighbours. I do not claim that the Latin American countries would not have appreciated this. Nevertheless, towards the end of the nineteenth century and the beginning of the twentieth century, the importance, from a policy perspective, of engaging the Latin American nations in a hemisphere-wide system of legal arrangements became an acute priority of US foreign politics. This occurred not at least due to the two Secretaries of State, John Hay and Elihu Root, both of whom were lawyers, were interested in arbitration and keen to implement of McKinley's activist Latin American policy. McKinley was assassinated in 1901 and succeeded by Theodore Roosevelt who had a rather similar agenda. In 1902, he faced the Venezuelan debt crisis when European gunboats were sailing outside Venezuela. Something had to be done quickly to ensure that Europeans would not set foot on Latin American soil. Through a series of diplomatic manœuvres, Roosevelt finally managed to persuade the Europeans to arbitrate in The Hague rather than to occupy Venezuelan territory in violation of the Monroe Doctrine. This led to an intensive effort on the part of the Roosevelt administration to create a series of legal arrangements including the pan-American conferences that could be used to co-ordinate and perhaps control Latin American countries. The intensity of this was not diminished by the fact that the United States started building the Panama Canal in 1902 as the United States was extremely worried that the poor relations between Central American States would disturb commerce and the administration of the canal territory. Therefore Roosevelt despatched his Secretary of State Elihu Root to South America. The first issue of the *American Journal of International Law* in 1907 celebrates Elihu Root's successful tour around the hemisphere, persuading the Latin Americans to become part of the Hague arrangement and to build the Central American Court of Justice. The intention from a US perspective was to keep the Panama Canal zone pacific. My point is not that in all of this, the Latin Americans acted slavishly in US interest. Throughout the first decade of the twentieth century, they obviously had their own legal agenda and were able to use American support for their purposes. My point is that the role of the United States and the interest of the United States in getting the Latin Americans in, in co-ordinating them and in conversing with them, was an extremely important part of their engagement of that periphery in the centre. If the Latin Americans contributed to the increased "universality" of the Second Hague Conference — and thereby of international law — they simultaneously contributed to that "universal" being manifested in a turn to US predominance in world diplomacy.

Let me add one comment to Shinya Murase's excellent presentation. As Professor Murase said, the Americans at The Hague were aware of the fact that the Asians held their representation here in The Hague as largely symbolic. Because of this, the Americans persuaded those delegations to co-opt American Foreign Service officials. Hence in the Chinese delegation John Watson became the delegation's voice behind the scene together with his son, being no minor a figure than John Foster Dulles. The Japanese delegation received advice from Mr. W. H. Davidson who had been posted in Japan as an advisor on foreign legal matters for a long time. When at one point things became desperate, the Americans even found a Princeton Ph.D. candidate who was present in The Hague to help the rest of the Asians in reacting to the proposals. This complicates the vision of the universality of the Second Hague Peace Conference; it is true that 44 delegations are different from 26 delegations. Nevertheless once you look at how those delegations behaved, how they used their voice, what kind of activity was behind it, we can see that the world was perhaps changing in a universal way, but that it was also doing this in a very particular way.

A. S. EL-KOSHERI: Monsieur le président, les interventions entendues cet après-midi sont fort intéressantes. Mais nous sommes face à un oubli: il s'agit de l'Afrique. Si l'Asie avait trois ou quatre représentants en 1907, l'Afrique n'en avait aucun. Le nom «Afrique» n'était pas inscrit sur la carte politique de l'époque. Je saisis cette occasion pour vous dire que cette absence revêt une signification très importante aujourd'hui, dans le monde de 2007. Pour moi, s'il y avait eu une voix de l'Afrique à l'époque de la Conférence de La Haye, peut-être que la situation ne serait pas aussi mauvaise qu'elle ne l'est actuellement. Bien sûr l'Afrique a été colonisée, en partie par la Grande-Bretagne et par la France, mais le peuple de l'Afrique ne possédait aucune voix propre permettant au continent noir de s'exprimer. Cela a contribué, au moins partiellement, à défaut d'une éducation civique appropriée, à ne pas apprécier l'importance de l'intégration dans l'universalisme voulu. Ainsi, un siècle plus tard, l'existence de certaines tendances subversives et terroristes sur le sol africain pourrait avoir pour origine l'exclusion du continent du processus aboutissant à l'élaboration du système mondial universel. C'est l'une des raisons de la situation actuelle, me semble-t-il, mais on ne peut éviter l'héritage du passé et il convient plutôt de se tourner vers l'avenir.

Je suis parmi ceux qui sont convaincus que l'éducation, notamment l'éducation juridique, permettrait de lutter véritablement contre les mouvements et les idées subversives. S'il pouvait exister un ouvrage de droit international écrit par de nombreux auteurs, comme Sørensen a essayé de le faire à l'époque héroïque d'Hammarskjöld, ainsi qu'un enseignement de droit international digne de ce nom, cela permettrait dans une grande mesure de faire acquérir aux gens de cette partie du monde la connaissance du droit international dans une perspective universaliste. Un tel ouvrage offrirait des réponses aux problèmes de pauvreté, de développement, d'environnement, de droits de l'homme, comme des autres maux dont on souffre dans le monde actuel. Je crois que le rôle de l'Académie de droit international, le rôle de ceux qui sont vraiment les juristes du monde moderne, c'est d'essayer, dans notre partie du monde, je parle particulièrement du monde arabe, du monde musulman et des pays d'Afrique, de leur fournir les éléments intellectuels et juridiques nécessaires pour empêcher l'expansion des idées étranges, telles que le retour au Jihad dans le sens de la guerre sainte, l'intolérance, surtout la lutte contre tous ceux qui ne sont pas des nôtres et qui sont perçus en tant qu'ennemis. De telles tendances subversives ne peuvent être éliminées du monde sauf par l'éducation. Nous, en tant que juristes, devons agir au niveau des universités, auprès des étudiants en droit, afin qu'ils aient en main une connaissance suffisante d'un droit international à vocation universaliste qui nourrisse leur esprit d'une façon qui permette leur formation pour devenir des éléments constructifs dans la vie internationale qui englobe tous les citoyens du monde, sans distinction entre races, religions ou genres. Une telle ouverture est nécessaire pour dresser un bilan positif du progrès achevé durant le dernier siècle. Je souhaite terminer en rappelant mon expérience personnelle. C'est au sein de cette Académie, en 1964, sous la direction de mon regretté cher maître René-Jean Dupuy, dans le cadre du Centre de recherche, que j'ai soumis un rapport sur la «fonction publique internationale», qui m'a guidé l'année dernière (2006) en tant que membre du panel des Nations Unies pour la réforme de la justice interne aux Nations Unies. Les jalons ont été posés deux ans après par cette Académie en 1966 sous la direction d'un autre regretté maître, P. Francescakis, en me permettant d'aborder l'étude des problèmes relatifs aux investissements dans les pays du tiers-monde devant les juridictions transnationales (ce qui m'a permis vingt ans après de devenir l'un des dix membres sur la liste des arbitres choisis par le président de la Banque mondiale), et d'être l'un des cinq rapporteurs au premier colloque de l'Académie en 1968, avant de donner un cours durant l'été 1975. Ainsi ma carrière a-t-elle été façonnée ici, à La Haye. En d'autres mots, je suis le produit de cette Académie, et je saisis l'occasion aujourd'hui devant cette illustre assemblée pour reconnaître publiquement ma dette à l'égard de l'Académie, en souhaitant que beaucoup d'autres, dans les générations futures puissent bénéficier de ce que j'ai appris ici dans un esprit d'universalisme ouvert faisant barrage aux particularismes étranges répandus au cours des dernières décennies.

D. MOMTAZ: J'aimerais revenir sur la communication de M. Murase et son assertion selon laquelle le rôle des Etats asiatiques à la Deuxième Conférence de Paix était plutôt symbolique. Pour l'orateur, les problèmes d'ordre interne auxquels ces Etats étaient confrontés étaient à l'origine de leur participation réduite aux travaux de la Conférence. Je ne saurais évidemment nier l'existence de telles difficultés. Pour ce qui est de la Perse, comme il a été rappelé, elle était en proie aux convoitises et à la rivalité des empires britannique et russe, qui finirent par s'entendre le 31 août 1907, alors même que la Conférence siégeait, pour partager le pays en zones d'influence. De même, c'est au cours de cette même période que l'intégrité du territoire perse a été violée par l'Empire ottoman, fait que la délégation de ce pays à la Conférence n'avait pas manqué de relater auprès des journalistes qui couvraient ses travaux. Je me réfère ici au n° 70 du *Courrier de la Conférence* en date du mercredi 4 septembre 1907.

Ces difficultés, loin d'avoir freiné ou réduit le rôle de la Perse à la Conférence ont été au contraire à l'origine d'une prise de conscience de sa faiblesse face aux puissances qu'elle devait confronter et de la nécessité de miser sur le droit international. Les interventions de Samad Khan Momtaz-os-Saltaneh en faveur de l'arbitrage obligatoire constituent la preuve d'une telle prise de conscience. Le 27 juillet 1907, il affirmait devant la Première Commission de la Conférence qu'il fallait extirper de notre vocabulaire l'expression *Si vis pacem, para bellum*, cela ne pouvant se faire que si on s'accorde sur la nécessité de recourir à l'arbitrage obligatoire pour régler les différends qui opposent les Etats. Le 24 août 1907, lors de la discussion sur la composition de la Cour permanente, il insistait sur l'impératif de respecter le principe de l'égalité juridique entre les Etats, estimant que la Perse, en raison de son passé historique et culturel, méritait un meilleur traitement que celui qui lui avait été réservé dans le projet soumis.

L'importance des travaux de la Conférence était telle pour la Perse que sa délégation avait eu recours au service de deux juristes étrangers : un Belge, en la personne de M. Hennebicq, qui travaillait au ministère perse des Affaires étrangères à Téhéran, et un Britannique, M. Oppenheim, consul honoraire de Perse à La Haye.

A. A. CANÇADO TRINDADE: May I thank Martti Koskenniemi for his remarks, which give me the opportunity to make my own comments on the points raised. My subject was the presence and participation of Latin America at the Second Hague Peace Conference of 1907, so I based my research on the *Official Records* of the Conference as well as on the diplomatic archives of the Latin American countries which participated in it, and on other Latin American sources. It was not my intention to focus on the entire history of the Second Hague Peace Conference, but what Professor Koskenniemi said about United States foreign policy could be added. For example, President Theodore Roosevelt, and the diplomacy of Elihu Root, played an important role, as widely known, in the invitation to Latin American States, which was formalized on 14 June 1907, but we could also bring in other elements besides the influence of President T. Roosevelt. For example, the role of Mexico as the intermediary was important as well, because Mexico had been the only Latin American country which had participated in the First Hague Peace Conference, from where it became a spokesman for the Latin American States. Parallel to that, the first Conference of American States took place in Washington in 1889, the second in Mexico City in 1901, and the third in Rio de Janeiro in 1906. From the time when they celebrated the Treaty on Arbitration in Mexico City in 1902, Mexico in fact acted as the spokesman for an approximation of Latin American States with the United States and the other countries that had been invited to, and participated in, the First Hague Conference of 1899. The *Official Records* state that there were 26 States represented at the First Hague Peace Conference, and 44 at the Second Hague Peace Conference. There was one Latin American State represented at the First Hague Conference (Mexico), but there were 18 delegations of Latin American States present at the Second Hague Conference. Of course the Monroe Doctrine had a role to play, which was until then a positive role, but not so later on. As decades passed, the Monroe Doctrine became a rather divisive factor, but until then it had played a very positive role.

As to the second point that Professor Koskenniemi raised, I would like to make a distinction between universality in participation on the one hand, and universality in outlook on the other. I agree that as far as Latin American nations were concerned, there was universality or near-universality in participation, because two countries, which had been invited to the 1907 Hague Conference could not come: Honduras and Costa Rica. In this respect, I thank Professor Koskenniemi for giving me the opportunity to address matters on which I did research, but had no time to discuss during my presentation. I see it fit now to emphasize that the universality in outlook was already very much deep-rooted among Latin American countries, even before the Second Hague Peace Conference convened. I would like to give a couple of examples, because this is a very important point: such universality in outlook was not only the work of statesmen, not only the work of diplomats; it was also the work of jurists. We both, Koskenniemi and I, like to study the work of jurists, we both like to read the classics, both you and I, so I would like to give you an example of how it worked among jurists at that time. Carlos Calvo used to live in Paris, not in Buenos Aires; he was the Minister of Argentina in Paris, and as soon as he received the copy of the note of December 1902 by the Argentine Foreign Minister L.-M. Drago which had been sent to the Argentine Minister in Washington, what did he do? He translated it into French, and circulated it to his *confrères* of the Institut de Droit International. So, his *confrères* of the Institut, mostly European, became quite familiar with the Drago doctrine as from 1904, three years before the Second Hague Peace Conference took place. C. Calvo died shortly after translating and distributing the aforementioned note by Drago, but some years before this happened, he had propounded the same ideas that were in the Drago note of 1902 in a book he wrote, titled *Manuel de droit international public et privé*, published in its 3rd edition in Paris in 1892, as he used to publish in French rather than in Spanish. Even before that, in 1873, Andres Bello also published in Paris, but in Spanish, also the 3rd edition of his *Principios de Derecho Internacional*, a classic work in Latin American doctrine, in which A. Bello also propounded the outlook of a universal international law. So, I would say that, besides universality in participation (at the 1907 Conference), that was very much — and more significantly — Latin American universality in outlook. And here I allow myself to take exception from the expression "periphery" or "peripheral States" used by Professor Koskenniemi. To my mind, "peripheral States" is an expression for political scientists, not for jurists. In my understanding, it is the principles and norms, the rights and obligations, rather than the interests and strategies that are the proper concern of jurists. Moreover, as the earth is round, depending on where you look from at the *mappa mundi*, all the regions of the world may appear peripheral. We who live in Latin America may sense, by looking at it, that Europe, or northern Europe, looks a bit "peripheral". The idea at the 1907 Conference was precisely to overcome the Eurocentric outlook of the international legal order, which until then had prevailed. I am aware of the source you indicated, the issue of the *American Journal of International Law* of 1907. Shortly afterwards, an outstanding article by James Brown Scott was published, in 1908, brilliantly recognizing the genuine doctrinal contribution of Latin American delegations to the work of the Second Hague Peace Conference; in his monograph, covering the work of both the 1899 and the 1907 Hague Peace Conferences, J. Brown Scott gave due credit to the Latin American doctrine expounded at the Second Hague Peace Conference of 1907. So, I think that I have hereby responded to the remarks by Professor Koskenniemi, thanking him again for having made them and given me the occasion for these additional comments; may I finalize with a reference to the thematic course which F.-J. Urrutia delivered here, at our beloved Hague Academy of International Law, in 1928 (Vol. 22 of the *Recueil des cours*), wherein he made precisely the same point, namely, that universality for Latin Americans meant not only universality in participation in international conferences, but also and mainly universality in the outlook of international law. Thank you very much.

S. MURASE: First I would like to refer to Professor El-Kosheri's remark about the participation by an African State. There was a possibility that Ethiopia might have participated in the 1907 Conference. In April 1906, the Russian ambassador in Washington DC sent a letter to the US Secretary of State, stating that Korea had not replied about its possible participation while Ethiopia had accepted the invitation. Presumably the same information was forwarded to Japan. Apart from the Latin American countries, the Japanese Government opposed any new participants being added to the conference, and so, as a result of a by-blow, Ethiopia, which might have been the first African country to participate in the international conference, was not represented, which I wanted to supply just as a footnote. As to Professor Momtaz's comment, I agree with him completely because his grandfather, Mirza Samad Khan Momtas-es-Saltaneh, was the head of the Persian delegation in 1907. When I said "symbolic participation", I meant that all the basic drafts had been prepared by the European and American experts: the delegates of other countries, particularly the Asian countries, might have supported, opposed or made reservations, but their contribution was generally quite passive, as I judge from reading the records of the conference.

I would also like to thank Professor Koskenniemi for commenting on my paper, to which I just have one remark: he referred to Denison, but the role he played as legal adviser to the Japanese delegation at the 1907 Conference did not appear to be as great as that when he attended the 1899 Conference in the same capacity. What I want to stress, nonetheless, is that Denison was more loyal to Japan, even more than ordinary Japanese. He was deeply committed to the Japanese cause and after having served the Japanese Foreign Ministry for 34 long years, he was buried in the cemetery of Tokyo, and was succeeded by Thomas Baty soon afterwards. In any event, I do not think there was any possibility at all of the American influence exerted through Mr. Denison who acted as a most loyal legal advisor to Japan. Thank you.

B. BOUTROS-GHALI: Je voudrais faire une remarque sur ce que vient de dire le professeur Koskenniemi. Toutes les conférences internationales se situent sur deux niveaux. Vous vous êtes intéressé à montrer les dessous de la Conférence en posant la question de savoir quels étaient les intérêts immédiats de certains Etats. Quant à nous, nous avons choisi de retenir de la Conférence de 1907 les principes généraux de droit international qui y ont été adoptés. En réalité, ces deux niveaux d'analyse sont présents dans toutes les conférences internationales: les Etats participent, ont des contacts indirects ou des contacts bilatéraux, ils cherchent à protéger des intérêts particuliers, parfois avec succès, d'autres fois sans y parvenir, mais sans que cela ait un rapport direct avec le résultat de la conférence.

Ici, pour fêter le centième anniversaire de la Conférence de La Haye, nous privilégions l'analyse des résultats relatifs aux principes du droit international en écartant celle des intérêts réels ou immédiats des Etats qui ont provoqué cette conférence. Je ne vois donc pas d'incompatibilité entre les deux analyses, qui sont différentes l'une de l'autre.

A. S. EL-KOSHERI: Je voudrais revenir sur ma proposition et la formuler de manière plus précise: je serais très heureux avant de quitter ce monde de voir réaliser un manuel de droit international écrit par des auteurs provenant de différents horizons du globe. Ce pourrait être le même manuel enseigné dans un pays comme l'Arabie saoudite aussi bien que dans les pays européens, en évitant ainsi les fausses impressions attribuées à tort au droit international islamique. Ce que j'envisage est un programme d'éducation consacré à tous les futurs juristes dans les différents pays du monde et qui auront des postes de responsabilité dans leur pays. C'est la tentative déjà mentionnée, en passant, de l'ouvrage rédigé par le professeur Sørensen et certains autres, qui ont fourni, il y a quatre décennies, un exemple très important. Peut-être cette expérience pourrait-elle être reprise par l'Académie, ou bien par une autre organisation pour publier un manuel traduit en différentes langues qui couvrirait tous les aspects du droit international contemporain. Je vous assure que cela serait vraiment une contribution formidable pour l'humanisation et l'universalisation du droit international public aussi bien que privé.

A. PELLET: Je voulais faire une remarque sur la première intervention de M. El-Kosheri et souligner que, en regardant la liste des participants à ce colloque, on se dit que, décidément, l'Afrique, surtout au sud du Sahara, est encore bien périphérique.

La deuxième remarque de M. El-Kosheri me conduit à donner une information. Cette année, durant la session de la Commission du droit international, j'ai suggéré qu'au lieu de ne faire que des travaux de codification traditionnelle, la CDI essaie de se lancer dans la rédaction d'un «Restatement of International Law». Ce serait une façon aussi de répondre à cette préoccupation d'avoir un ouvrage collectif, préparé par des juristes d'horizons différents et qui présente le droit international dans son ensemble. Cette initiative a été reçue avec un intérêt poli mais je ne désespère pas qu'elle débouche sur quelque chose.

Permettez-moi de poser deux questions.

La première s'adresse à M. Cançado Trindade: il faut que je prépare mon intervention de demain et je lui serais reconnaissant de me donner des idées... Vous avez à juste titre insisté sur la convention Drago-Porter, qui est un peu passée à pertes et profits de cette conférence de 1907 alors que je suis convaincu qu'il s'est agit d'un texte tout à fait extraordinaire et visionnaire. J'ai l'habitude de présenter la convention Drago-Porter à mes étudiants comme la première étape de l'interdiction juridique du recours à la force dans les relations internationales. Je dois dire que je me demande si cela est tout à fait exact, et si il y a vraiment un continuum entre Drago/Porter d'une part et les « étapes » suivantes : le Pacte de la Société des Nations, le Pacte Briand-Kellog et la Charte des Nations Unies. Je serais intéressé par votre point de vue à ce sujet.

Ma seconde question s'adresse à M. Boutros-Ghali au sujet de quelque chose qu'il a dit ce matin : il nous a invités à ne pas être diplomatique ; comme je ne suis pas très bon en diplomatie, cela tombe bien ! D'une façon générale, son intervention n'a pas été très « politically correct » et je dois dire que je l'en félicite très vivement. J'ai tendance à être d'accord avec lui à peu près sur tout ce qu'il a dit sauf sur un point. Vous avez dit, Monsieur le Secrétaire général, que l'attentat du 11 septembre était un problème interne, je dois dire que je vous serais reconnaissant si vous pouviez élaborer sur ce point, car bien que j'éprouve moi-même des doutes sur l'expression « guerre contre le terrorisme » je ne pense pas que l'on puisse dire que cet attentat est l'affaire des seuls Etats-Unis.

J'ai été un peu exaspéré par les réactions après le 11 septembre, j'avais même commis un article dans le journal *Le Monde* intitulé : « Non, ce n'est pas la guerre. » Mais de là à dénier à l'attentat du 11 septembre tout caractère international me paraît très excessif. Si l'on soutient cela, je vois mal comment on peut expliquer la résolution 1368, et d'ailleurs toutes celles qui ont suivi. Je crains qu'en fait cette thèse, pour laquelle je reconnais avoir eu une tentation, mais c'était plutôt de l'exaspération politique que du raisonnement juridique, risque d'avoir des effets boomerang assez fâcheux : en interdisant toute intervention du Conseil de sécurité dans ce genre d'affaires, on encourage du même coup des réponses unilatérales, qui seraient infiniment plus contestables à mes yeux que des opérations contrôlées au moins par le Conseil de sécurité.

A. A. CANÇADO TRINDADE : May I thank you very much, Professor Alain Pellet, for your question. Before I reply, I would like to say that I very much sympathize with the second observation made by Dr. El-Kosheri, and would just like to recall the somewhat pioneering initiative of the *Manual of Public International Law* edited by Max Sørensen in 1968, which contained among the contributions one by the distinguished Latin American scholar Eduardo Jiménez de Aréchaga, on international responsibility ; that collective work was of much avail to the next generation of international lawyers. It was translated into Spanish and widely circulated in Latin America. Besides that, I would like to pay tribute to some initiatives of Unesco, such as the two-volume work *Droit international — bilan et perspectives*, edited by Mohammed Bedjaoui in 1991, which likewise contained contributions by international lawyers from different continents. These are examples in the line of the suggestion made by Dr. El-Kosheri, with which I sympathize.

Turning to the question raised by Professor Alain Pellet, I would like to make a further comment in relation to the Drago-Porter Convention in historical projection. I think it is fair to say, as quite aptly pointed out by Professor Pellet, that it was a "first stage" or "first step". But then we can ask: why? Because Latin Americans came to the conclusion, at the 1907 Hague Conference, that there was no option but to accept the Porter amendment, otherwise the Drago doctrine would not be accepted; so L. M. Drago himself made a statement at the First Commission of the Conference to the effect that he would accept the amendment so as to render his doctrine acceptable at the universal level. Shortly afterwards, the Latin American delegations at the 1907 Conference, including the Argentine delegation, indicated that they had accepted the Convention on Recourse to Arbitration for Recovery of Contract Debts, but that they nevertheless reserved their position as to a residual possibility of an eventual use of force, should arbitration fail. So, the Drago-Porter Convention was a "first step", it was *only* a first step, and here the position of Latin America was different from the position of Europe, as it became clear years later. In 1928 the Briand-Kellogg Pact was concluded, as a General Treaty for the Renunciation of War as an Instrument of National Policy. This was not sufficient to us, Latin Americans; we were very much concerned also with measures short of war. But Latin American States, of course, acceded to the Briand-Kellogg Pact, which became of nearly universal application at the time, and has not been technically abrogated. However, the Saavedra Lamas Pact of 1933 was much more concerned with measures short of war, because of interventions in Latin America, in addition to the prohibition of war, which Latin American States took for granted. In the same line of thinking were the Declarations of Principles adopted at the Conferences of Lima in 1938, and of Mexico in 1945, paving the way for the adoption of Article 2 (4) of the United Nations Charter, with the strong support of Latin

American States. So, I think that your point is correct, Professor Pellet, the Drago-Porter Convention was the "first step", as Latin Americans, as you know, from the start opposed even a residual possibility of an eventual recourse to force, should arbitration fail. To the Latin American delegations at the 1907 Conference, the prohibition of the use or threat of force in inter-State relations was absolute, and this is the position which they hold until nowadays, one century later. The Saavedra Lamas Pact was much more concerned with measures short of war, such as intervention, and an evidence of that can be found in classic doctrinal works on the matter, such as the book by Isidro Fabela entitled *Intervention*, published in 1961. Ultimately, it amounted to upholding the primacy of law over force. May I thank you, Professor Pellet, for having raised the issue and having given me the occasion to make these additional comments on the matter. Thank you very much.

V. S. VERESHCHETIN: The clarification of the notion of universality of international law and of the use of the terms "universal" and "universality" in international law generally is, in my view, very important. Professor Koskenniemi rightly observed in his comments that "it is pretty obscure what real universality is". International scholars, judges and lawyers use a number of notions and terms (some of them being fundamental for our discipline) while we all well know that there exists no agreement on their meanings in modern or so-called postmodern legal theory and philosophy. Even the notions of "law" and "legal", as distinct from non-legal, are being attacked in some quarters.

But let us turn to international law proper and its doctrine. Do we have a shared understanding of the term "general international law" or for that matter of the difference, if any, between general international law and universal international law? I certainly know that for the mainstream doctrine general international law is a synonym of customary international law or rather general customary international law. But there also exists a different school of thought for which it is unacceptable to view general international law at the dawn of the twenty-first century as excluding the UN Charter or some other practically universal treaties.

This brings me back to the difficult issue of universality. I understand universality of international law in the sense that, as a system of law, there is only one international law and its basic principles and rules are applicable to all subjects of international law and in all spheres of their activity. This certainly requires further clarification of the term "subjects of international law" which for now I will not pursue. On the other hand, universality of a multilateral treaty can be evaluated not only in terms of initial participation (which is certainly a very important element of evaluation), but also in terms of its object and purpose, its effect on the development of international law generally or of its certain field. In this sense, universality seems to be not a static but rather a dynamic notion which should be seen as a process.

Looking at the 1907 Conference from this perspective, we should not judge it with modern yardsticks. Forty-four States represented there constituted the vast majority of the States that could, according to the standards of the time, have an independent voice in the world arena. From this point of view, it was a quasi-universal participation, although undoubtedly it is deplorable that only so-called "civilized" nations could participate. It is also deplorable that the term "civilized" nations was used even after the Second World War in the Statute of the International Court of Justice (Art. 38). What is most important in terms of the substantive results of the 1907 Conference is the message it sent to the future in regard to a number of important fields of international law.

In conclusion, I would like to support the idea advanced by Professor El-Kosheri, namely to write a manual of international law prepared, to use his words, "par des gens de différents horizons du monde". Indeed it would be a very important contribution of the scholars to the shared understanding and teaching of modern international law. I would think, however, that the accomplishment of such a project will require, among other things, a prior agreement or at least a kind of working consensus among the participants on the meaning of the basic legal terms and notions used in such a manual.

B. BOUTROS-GHALI: Je voudrais répondre à la question du professeur Pellet.

Me situant dans le cadre du droit international, j'observe que l'attaque du 11 septembre n'est pas le fait d'un Etat, mais d'une nébuleuse ou de quelque chose d'assez inconnu. Par conséquent, si ce n'est pas une attaque « internationale », de quoi s'agit-il ? C'est une attaque interne perpétrée par une autorité, que l'on peut qualifier de *sui generis*, qui n'est pas un Etat. Mais si l'on considère qu'il s'agit

d'une agression, soit nous sommes face à une agression interétatique, et la Charte ne vise que les Etats, soit c'est une agression d'un
autre ordre. Si la qualification d'«interne» vous gêne, je ne vois pas
d'inconvénient à employer un autre terme mais il est clair qu'il ne
s'agit pas d'une «agression» conformément à la définition du terme
«agression» en droit international.

N. RONZITTI: I would like to make a comment on the question of
universality. My intention is not to define universality; I merely want
to bring this notion to the attention of those who employ the term in
various ways. In the field of disarmament and humanitarian law —
but also in a number of other fields — if a multilateral treaty is not
universal and not subject to widespread ratification, its purpose is
missed. For instance the Conventions on Bacteriological Weapons
and Chemical Weapons are universal treaties even though there are a
few States that are not party to them.

For the sake of argument, I will assume that the universality refers
to a principle of general customary international law or a principle
embedded in a treaty supported by unanimity or by a vast majority
of States. This line of reasoning emerged from the intervention of
Judge Vereshchetin. Universality has to be understood historically
because, when the Hague Conventions were drafted in 1907, only a
few States, then representing almost all members of the international
community, took part in the negotiation. Afterwards, however, those
principles were embedded in customary international law or provided the basic elements that were inserted in other conventions in
which almost all States took part.

I would like to give an example which was raised by the President
of the International Court of Justice on the law of occupation. This
body of law, as it was codified by the regulations appended to the
Hague Convention IV, is now customary international law. On this
point we may cite the Nuremberg Tribunal judgment as well as the
judgments and the advisory opinions of the International Court of
Justice. Hence, even though the law of occupation was drafted and
elaborated upon by a small number of States, it is now universal.
Subsequent codification in relation to those principles has taken
place, especially through the IV Geneva Convention and Protocol I
additional to it. Indeed, the diplomatic conference which drafted the
Protocols was attended by almost all States of the international community. I would like to refer to two principles which are very impor-

tant for the law of occupation and which were inspired by African and Asian countries, namely the principles of self-determination and of permanent sovereignty of States over their natural resources. The human rights principles and the human rights provisions as spelled out by the International Court of Justice have also inspired the law of occupation. Recently, ICJ judgments and the Advisory Opinion on the Wall in Palestine stated that the occupying power is obliged to apply, not only the law of occupation, but also international humanitarian law.

One can also look at the practice of the Security Council, although this is, of course, not universal, as it does not reflect the will of all States of the international community even though it is a UN body. The Security Council incorporated those principles in its resolutions, for instance when it enacted resolution 1483 on Iraq. It stated that the occupying powers should abide by the law of occupation and by the new principles which have become customary international law. My conclusion is that universality should be understood and seen as a historical process and only if we consider it in this way can we understand the true legacy of the 1907 Conference.

M. GLENNON: I teach at the Fletcher School of Law and Diplomacy in the United States. I was a bit perplexed by the response that you, Secretary-General Boutros-Ghali, gave to Professor Pellet's question a moment ago so I would like to seek further clarification. It seemed almost as though you were suggesting that the inherent right to self-defence recognized in Article 51 of the Charter does not embrace the use of defensive force against a non-State actor. Is that the view you were expressing? Is it your view that the United States is not permitted under Article 51 to respond with the use of force to an attack by Al-Qaeda and the Taliban on the United States? It is not part of the inherent right to self-defence? That would be just extraordinary, I think.

B. BOUTROS-GHALI: Non, cela ne relève pas de la légitime défense au sens de l'article 51 de la Charte. Cette disposition vise en effet l'hypothèse d'une agression armée d'un Etat contre un autre Etat, lequel est alors autorisé à recourir à la légitime défense. Certes, les termes de l'article 51 peuvent être jugés peu précis dans la mesure où il n'est pas expressément dit que l'agression armée doit émaner d'un Etat. Néanmoins, il convient de se référer aux règles générales d'interprétation des traités et, à cet égard, on ne peut contester que le système de la Charte est fondé sur les Etats : les Nations Unies sont une organisation interétatique qui vise à établir des relations pacifiques entre Etats et à prévenir et à mettre fin à des rapports conflictuels entre Etats. Un texte tel que la résolution 3314 (XXIX) du 14 décembre 1974 sur la définition de l'agression repose d'ailleurs clairement sur cette logique interétatique, en particulier dans la rédaction de son article 3, alinéa *g)*, auquel la Cour internationale de Justice a expressément reconnu une valeur coutumière dans son arrêt du 26 novembre 1984, rendu dans l'affaire des *Activités militaires et paramilitaires au Nicaragua et contre celui-ci (CIJ Recueil 1986,* p. 14), dans laquelle elle a jugé qu'une action militaire menée par des forces irrégulières pouvait constituer une agression armée si ces éléments étaient envoyés par l'Etat ou au nom de celui-ci (*CIJ Recueil 1986*, p.104, par. 195). C'est encore l'Etat, et non un quelconque groupement, nébuleuse, organisation non gouvernementale ou mouvement terroriste qui ne lui serait pas rattaché, qui se trouve au centre du dispositif dans le passage bref mais non équivoque de l'avis consultatif du 9 juillet 2004, *Conséquences juridiques de l'édification d'un mur dans le territoire palestinien occupé*, où la Cour internationale de Justice précise expressément et sans équivoque que « l'article 51 de la Charte reconnaît ainsi l'existence d'un droit naturel de légitime défense en cas d'agression armée par un Etat contre un autre Etat » (*CIJ Recueil*, p. 194, par. 139).

Par conséquent, pour répondre clairement au professeur Glennon, j'estime que les Etats-Unis pouvaient répliquer à l'attaque terroriste perpétrée le 11 septembre mais sans pouvoir fonder leur action sur l'article 51 de la Charte des Nations Unies, faute d'agression armée préalable émanant d'un Etat.

H. CORELL : I have been wrestling with this question tremendously in the United Nations. There are two elements to it ; the first one was 9/11, which I observed from my windows in the UN Secretariat, and the other one was Iraq. With regard to Afghanistan, 9/11 was an attack launched from the territory of a State, which obviously could not keep its territory free from terrorists or was maybe even collaborating with them. I have given much thought to this : if a State is not able to keep order within its borders, and if attacks are launched from the territory of that State while you plead with that State, saying "you have to put a stop to this" and they do not, then I do not think there is any other choice than to apply the rule of self-defence. You are allowed to attack. We discussed this action at a seminar in Salzburg over the last few days. On the contrary, when you come to Iraq, there I have a very firm opinion: when I observed the attack on Iraq, my heart sank. This was a clear violation of international law and we are now seeing the results of that.

When I initially asked for the floor, it was really to comment on Professor Vereshchetin's observations. I have also been wrestling with the term "civilized nations" and I decided to solve the problem in a very simple manner. I simply put the word "civilized" between quotation marks. The same way as I do with "rogue" States. They are also in quotation marks. Who is a "civilized" State? Who is a "rogue" State? Thank you.

A. A. CANÇADO TRINDADE: I would like just to propose a foot-note to what Dr. Hans Corell said before. I think we could sustain, one century after the holding of the Second Hague Peace Conference of 1907, that "civilized States" nowadays are those which abide by international law.

DEUXIÈME PARTIE

LA CONFÉRENCE DE LA HAYE ET LA JURIDICTIONNALISATION DU RÈGLEMENT DES DIFFÉRENDS

Sous la présidence de
T. van den HOUT

SECOND PART

THE HAGUE CONFERENCE AND GROWTH IN ADJUDICATION FOR THE SETTLEMENT OF DISPUTES

T. van den HOUT,
presiding

I. COMMUNICATIONS

1. THE IDEOLOGY OF INTERNATIONAL ADJUDICATION AND THE 1907 HAGUE CONFERENCE

M. KOSKENNIEMI[1]

I. Introduction — Adjudication as Ideology

We live in an era of international adjudication. The past years have seen an unprecedented increase in the number of international courts and tribunals — *ad hoc* war crimes tribunals, the International Criminal Court, the Law of the Sea Tribunal, the Appellate Body of the WTO, and a huge number of regional judicial bodies. A recent study lists 20 permanent courts and around 70 other bodies with judicial or quasi-judicial functions[2]. But no new theory accompanies them. We continue to think about international adjudication in view of ideas and proposals dating back to around the turn of the twentieth century, the time between the Arbitral Award in the *Alabama* case of 1872 and the establishment of the Permanent Court of International Justice (PCIJ) in 1921. The view of international courts and tribunals as instruments of peace and progress is an idea with a history, an idea of the nineteenth century that grew up in the twentieth. I have been requested to examine it as ideology.

To do so, there is no better place to begin than by quoting the editor-in-chief of the *American Journal of International Law* in 1921, as the League Assembly had decided upon the establishment of the PCIJ: "We should . . . fall upon our knees and thank God that the hope of ages is in process of realization."[3]

Scott was not a recent convert to this religion. In the first issue of the *American Journal of International Law* 15 years earlier he had complained about there being no "supreme court of nations" in

---

1. Professor at the University of Helsinki.

2. PICT list. November 2004. See www.pict-pcti.org/publications/synoptic_chart.html.

3. James Brown Scott, "Editorial Comment", 15 *AJIL* (1921), 55.

which "dispute[s] may be litigated"[4]. In 1920 he had gone to The Hague to correct that state of affairs by assisting his former chief, Elihu Root, the US member of the Advisory Committee that drafted the PCIJ Statute. Their collaboration had begun already in 1906 when Root, as US Secretary of State, appointed Scott as solicitor (legal adviser) in the State Department. The following year Root sent him to the Second Hague Peace Conference and enlisted his help in pushing 24 arbitration treaties through the Senate[5]. Scott and Root were also among the founders of the American Society of International Law a century ago and while Root was appointed the organization's first president, Scott became the Editor-in-Chief of its Journal — a position he preserved until 1924. Together they succeeded in bringing Latin American countries into the Hague System and created a Central American Court of Justice. Root's instructions to the US delegation at the Second Hague Peace Conference insisted on a permanent international tribunal as the country's single most important objective.

It is impossible to think of international adjudication without thinking of these two men. Root had begun his career as a New York corporate lawyer, turned later into a leader of the Republican Party, he was a conservative who both spoke highly of the public opinion and feared the masses; as such he was, a recent discussion suggests, "deeply representative of elite lawyers of the late nineteenth and early twentieth centuries"[6]. As Secretary of State, he became Theodore Roosevelt's "most trusted advisor"[7], chairing over the turn in US policy to imperial concerns, reorganizing the military, quelling the revolution in the Philippines and drafting the constitution of Cuba that made it a virtual vassal of the United States[8]. Scott had

---

4. James Brown Scott, "The Legal Nature of International Law", 1 *AJIL* (1907), 831.

5. See Calvin DeArmond Davis, *The United States and the Second Hague Peace Conference. American Diplomacy and International Organization 1899-1914*, Duke University Press, 1975, pp. 297-300.

6. Jonathan Zasloff, "Law and the Shaping of American Foreign Policy: From the Gilded Age to the New Era", 78 *NYUL Rev.* (2003), 245. On Root's inheritance and career before President McKinley appointed him Secretary of War in 1899, see Richard W. Leopold, *Elihu Root and the Conservative Tradition*, Boston, Little & Brown, 1954, pp. 10-23. Root's conservatism is always remarked upon. But sometimes it is thought to include also a racist streak. See George E. Mowry, *The Era of Theodore Roosevelt 1900-1912*, London, Hamish, 1958, pp. 43, 93, 165-166.

7. Mowry, *The Era of Theodore Roosevelt, supra* footnote 6, p. 125.

8. For biography, see Philip C. Jessup, *Elihu Root*, 2 vols., New York, Mead 1938.

studied international law in Paris and Heidelberg and been Dean of the law schools at the Universities of Southern California and Illinois before he joined the State Department from the position of Professor of Law at Columbia University. If he — unlike Root — had little flamboyance as a foreign policy operator, he was indispensable as expert on arbitration and adjudication. He was also a kind of international law visionary who admired the early Catholic tradition in international law and, after leaving the State Department in 1910, became trustee and secretary of the Carnegie Endowment for International Peace until 1940, including director of its division of international law and responsible for its influential publication activities[9].

To study the ideology of an institution is to examine where it comes from and what it is expected to achieve. International adjudication was an American project. True, philosophers, peace activists, lawyers and diplomats from many countries supported arbitration and judicial settlement in the nineteenth and early twentieth centuries. But only the United States adopted it as an aspect of its foreign policy. Only American lawyers possessed recent domestic experience of how to settle jurisdictional disputes by referring them to a Supreme Court. Their arguments and writings at this time were full of analogies between that domestic experience and expectations about the coming international court. Their influence is an aspect of the turn from Europe's "old diplomacy" to the "American century" in which the assumptions of US foreign policy elite would set the agenda for international reform[10].

This is an elite of lawyers. Contributions to the recent centennial of the American Society of International Law have highlighted the stunning coincidence between officials of the Society and American foreign policy leadership. Root and Scott are only the most striking examples — a Secretary of State and his legal advisor. They were no anomalies, however. Between 1889 and 1945, *all* US Secretaries of State were lawyers, and most of them were associated with the ASIL since its establishment. As one recent overview suggests:

"The various officers of the society were part of an inter-

---

9. See especially Christopher R. Rossi, *Broken Chain of Being: James Brown Scott and the Origins of Modern International Law*, London etc., Kluwer, 1998.

10. Aspects of this turn have been provocatively but not incorrectly laid out in Carl Schmitt, *Der Nomos der Erde im Völkerrecht des Jus publicum europaeum*, 3rd ed., Berlin, Duncker & Humblot, 1988, pp. 111-185.

locking directorate of the US legal and international relations establishment, and very much part of what has been described as a new American 'Gentry' class."[11]

This class was internationally active but reluctant to think of itself in the language of European diplomacy. It was keen to rule the world but in a new way — like the United States itself was ruled. Many non-Americans saw no reason to object. On the strength of his mediatory role in the Russo-Japanese war and for his successful direction of the Venezuelan claims dispute to Permanent Court of Arbitration Roosevelt received the Nobel Peace Prize in 1906. Root received the Prize for these and his various other activities in support of international law and adjudication in 1912. It was then perfectly appropriate that at the ceremony held 100 years ago to lay the corner-stone of the Peace Palace — donated by the American millionaire Andrew Carnegie — two flags were flown: those of the Netherlands and the United States, marking the special relationship between the Court and those two countries[12].

II. United States and International Arbitration until 1907

The nineteenth-century peace movement was overall dominated by Anglo-Americans but this was especially the case of its emphasis on arbitration towards the end of the century. The first influential formulations of the idea of an international court as the way for peace were made by utilitarian philosophers Jeremy Bentham and James Mill. According to the former, "between the interests of nations, there is nowhere any real conflict; if they appear repugnant anywhere it is only in proportion as they are misunderstood". "Establish a common tribunal" — he continued — "[and] the necessity for war no longer follows from difference of opinion. Just or unjust, the decision of the arbiter will save the credit of the contenting party."[13] His argument for courts was analogous to his argument

---

11. Carl Landauer, "The Ambivalences of Power: Launching the *American Journal of International Law* in an Era of Empire and Globalization", 20 *Leiden Journal of International Law* (2007), 327. See also David Bederman, "Appraising a Century of Scholarship in the *American Journal of International Law*", 100 *AJIL* (2006), especially pp. 25-31.

12. Davis, *United States, supra* footnote 5, p. 259.

13. Jeremy Bentham, quoted in F. H. Hinsley, *Power and the Pursuit of Peace*, Cambridge University Press, 1963, pp. 83, 85.

for free trade. Both substitute a utilitarian *reason* for the obscure political goals and selfish passion of politicians and Governments.

This idea was taken up by Bentham's disciple, James Mill in an article in the *Encyclopaedia Britannica* of 1825 on "The Law of Nations".

From his utilitarian premises, Mill drew two techniques for world peace: freedom of commerce and an international code enforced by an international tribunal. For, he wrote, "it is well-known that laws, however carefully or accurately constructed, would be of little avail . . . if there was not some organ, by means of which it might be determined when individuals had acted in conformity with them" — and then he went on to discuss its composition and jurisdiction[14]. Unlike their continental colleagues, neither Bentham nor Mill spoke for World Government. In fact, they distrusted government and their stress on courts and Mill's insistence of public opinion as the means of enforcing their judgments emerged as off-shoots of this distrust. Even though Bentham and Mill were British, their influence in the United States was enormous[15]. Their utilitarianism represented an anti-government ethos and commercialism that buttressed the sense of American modernity vis-à-vis a Europe fomented by revolutionary strife. The American view of law was also strongly influenced by the expansive jurisprudence by the United States Supreme Court on international matters and the image of a similar type of World Court routinely included in the proposals by US peace societies.

The early peace movement culminated in the series of Universal Peace Congresses in 1843-1850 and was completely dominated by Anglo-American Quakers, pacifists and other activists:

> "The Congresses were all organised by the Anglo-American Societies; and at the congresses, it was Anglo-American plans — for disarmament, arbitration and a Congress of Nations — that were always tabled. At the first Universal Peace Congress in London in 1843 there were only 6 delegates from Europe

---

14. James Mill, "Law of Nations", reprinted from the *Supplement to the Encyclopaedia Britannica*, 1825, p. 28.

15. It is not for nothing that Mark Janis began his recent history of the "American Tradition in International Law" by a Chapter on the legacy of Benthamite thought. Mark Janis, *The American Tradition of International Law. Great Expectations 1798-1914*, Oxford University Press, 2004, pp. 11-24.

when 292 attended from the United Kingdom and 26 from the
United States." [16]

By contrast, the meetings were treated by indifference or hostility
in most parts of Europe where peace activists were speaking about
World Government, which in practice mostly meant European
federalism. Arbitration seemed too technical and modest for continental activists many of whom had been revolutionaries but always
built upon the seventeenth- and eighteenth-century utopian proposals
that had European unity as their objective [17].

On the basis of ideas by men such as William Ladd and Richard
Cobden, the early peace movement built on three key themes: free
trade, an international court and public opinion as securing the
implementation of both. After the precedent of the *Alabama* affair in
1872, the second wave of peace movements — equally dominated by
Anglo-Americans — now began to include lawyers as well.
Compulsory arbitration became the principal proposal and, this time
around, the intention was to involve Governments as well. For that
purpose, the British Reform League produced an "Outline of a Plan
for the Establishment of a High Court of Nations" in 1871 and some
years later Hodgson Pratt set up an "International Arbitration and
Peace Society" [18]. US lawyers such as David Dudley Field and John
Noble and activists such as Elihu Burritt travelled in Europe and at
home to propagate compulsory arbitration [19]. As part of this activity,
the Institut de droit international and the Association for the Reform
and Codification of the Law of Nations, later dubbed International
Law Association were set up, both advocating arbitration [20]. Even as
Europeans usually followed suit, the Anglo-Americans were often
critical of the tendency of the Europeans to exempt matters of
"honour" and "vital interests" from any compulsory third party settlement [21]. The main bone of contention in the many proposals that
were made on compulsory arbitration towards the end of the century,
however, was what matters would have to be excluded from its
scope.

---

16. Hinsley, *Power and the Pursuit of Peace*, *supra* footnote 13, pp. 100-101.
17. *Ibid.*, pp. 100-109.
18. *Ibid.*, pp. 124, 130.
19. Janis, *American Tradition*, *supra* footnote 15, pp. 103-116.
20. See especially the *Projet de règlement pour la procédure arbitrale internationale*, 28 August 1875, IDI Annuaire, Session de La Haye, 1875.
21. Hinsley, *Power and the Pursuit of Peace*, *supra* footnote 13, p. 128.

Nor was this only an activity of private individuals. At least since 1851, the Congress had repeatedly called for the settlement of international disputes by arbitration[22]. But already since the Jay Treaty of 1794, the United States and Britain had been by far the most frequent users of arbitration. La Fontaine's *Pasicrisie internationale* lists altogether 177 arbitrations between 1794 and 1900. Out of these 126 involved either Britain or the United States as parties — often against each other. The predominance of the United States is highlighted by the fact that out of the following 10 countries in the list, 6 were South Americans and, as President Taft proudly remarked, they had been persuaded to use arbitration by the United States[23].

Sometimes — as in pursuit of the Treaty of Ghent of 1812 and then again after the 1870s — the cases submitted to arbitration concerned important aspects of British-American relations. The United States Government was, in fact, never more interested in arbitration than in the 1890s — a time also of war and expansion. These included the Bering Sea Fur dispute and the Guiana-Venezuela Boundary dispute — "two of the decade's most serious Anglo-American controversies"[24]. In the first Pan-American Conference in 1889-1890, Secretary of State James Blaine hailed the hemispheric arbitration agreements "as a new 'Magna Charta' abolishing war in the Americas".[25] American statesmen routinely declared their attachment to arbitration and proposals for an Arbitral Tribunal between Britain and the United States were circulated at governmental levels and ended in a general arbitration treaty, the Olney-Pauncefote Treaty of 1897, to which US President McKinley referred to in his inaugural speech in March of that same year as follows:

> "Arbitration is the true method of settlement of international as well as local or individual differences [and the Olney-

---

22. See Frederick W. Holls, *The Peace Conference of The Hague and Its Bearing on International Law and Policy*, New York, Macmillan, 1901, pp. 232-236. See also *Arbitration and the United States*, World Peace Foundation Pamphlets, Vol. IX/Nos. 6-7, 1926, pp. 488-492, and Jackson H. Ralston, *International Arbitration from Athens to Locarno*, Stanford University Press, 1929, pp. 128-132.
23. H. La Fontaine, *Pasicrisie internationale 1794-1900. Histoire documentaire des arbitrages internationaux*, Preface by Pierre-Michel Eisemann, The Hague, Nijhoff, 1997, [1902]), pp. xii-xiii. *Addresses of President Taft*, Washington, 1911, pp. 27-28.
24. Davis, *United States*, *supra* footnote 5, p. 19.
25. *Ibid.*

Pauncefote treaty was a] glorious example of reason and peace
. . . I cannot but consider it fortunate that it was reserved to the
United States to have the leadership in so grand a work." [26]

Sadly, but inaugurating a pattern that was to become familiar later,
the treaty failed to receive the Senate's advice and consent owing
to the Congress's traditional fear for entanglement in foreign
alliances [27].

The nineteenth-century activity peaked of course in the First
Hague Conference of 1899. McKinley reacted to the Russian
Emperor's invitation to The Hague with enthusiasm: "Why, of
course we will accept it." [28] Failure to proceed with disarmament
directed attention to the laws of war, on the one hand, and compulsory arbitration and international court on the other. The proposal in
the Russian note concerning arbitration awoke great interest in US
peace societies and the instructions drawn up by Secretary of State
John Hay called on the US delegation to "concentrate the attention of
the world upon a definite plan for the promotion of international justice by the establishment of an international court" [29]. The delegation
itself, though divided on other matters, was eminently in favour of
arbitration and brought to The Hague a draft proposal drawn up by
the Bar Association of the New York State [30]. One of the members of
the delegation noted that it was the only one with "anything like a
full and carefully adjusted plan for a court of arbitration" [31]. At the
Conference itself, the proposal for a tribunal was laid out by Lord
Pauncefote of Britain, supported by the US delegation of which one
of the members — Holls — was instrumental in persuading the
German delegation to back down from its initial rejection of the
idea [32]. Even as the Convention on the Peaceful Settlement of
International Disputes fell short of the US goal of a permanent tribu-

---

26. Holls, *The Peace Conference*, *supra* footnote 22, p. 335 n.
27. Davis, *United States*, *supra* footnote 5, p. 20.
28. *Ibid.*, p. 7.
29. Quoted in Clarence Leighton, *International Arbitration and the Influence
of the United States at the Hague Conferences* (mimeo, 1916), p. 3.
30. Davis, *United States*, *supra* footnote 5, p. 22; Leighton, *International
Arbitration*, *supra* footnote 29, p. 6.
31. Andrew D. White, as quoted in *Arbitration and the United States*, World
Peace Fopundation Pamphlets, Vol IX/Nos. 6-7, 1926, p. 465.
32. The story of the "arbitration crisis" is told in many places, most recently
in Arthur Eyffinger, *The 1899 Hague Peace Conference. The Parliament of Man,
the Federation of the World*, The Hague, Kluwer, 1999, pp. 374-376.

nal plus general arbitration treaty, the Permanent Court of Arbitration was still seen as a "step towards a world court"[33].

The 1899 Conference was still a European affair: among the "true leaders of the Conference", Eyffinger's history lists only continental Europeans[34]. As Theodore Roosevelt began his presidency in 1901, however, things had changed. Both of his Secretaries of State, Hay and Root, were advocates of international adjudication. And so was he, at least when that suited the more general objectives of his "imperial presidency". In 1902 he allowed himself to be persuaded by the French Parlamentarian and activist Baron d'Estournelle de Constant that the Permanent Court of Arbitration set up at The Hague needed a case to get going and instructed the submission of the *Pious Fund* case with Mexico to it[35]. In the following year, he concluded an agreement with Britain on arbitrating the *Alaska Boundary* case and mediated to push Europeans to bring their grievances against Venezuela to The Hague (*Venezuelan Claims* case, Award 24 February 1904)[36]. In late 1904, Roosevelt, like his predecessor, took steps to secure the conclusion of arbitration treaties with a number of countries. The effort failed owing to Senate's insistence that every individual *compromis* would also need to have the Senate's consent[37]. Furious, Roosevelt withdrew the treaties from the Senate. One historian of the Second Peace Conference summarizes that at the run-up to the presidential election of 1904: "it seemed as though the United States government had signed up for membership in the American Peace Society and a half dozen other such organizations"[38].

But Roosevelt was also the man who presided over United States becoming a world power with an imperial agenda. If this was to be a different empire, then perhaps law — especially a court — might bring about that difference.

III. The 1907 Peace Conference, an American Event

In 1904 a world fair was to be held in Saint Louis. This prompted Congressman Richard Bartholdt from Saint Louis to suggest that the

---

33. Davis, *United States*, *supra* footnote 5, p. 33.
34. Eyffinger, *The 1899 Hague Peace Conference, supra* footnote 32, p. 360.
35. Davis, *United States*, *supra* footnote 5, pp. 57-61.
36. *Ibid.*, pp. 73-90.
37. *Ibid.*, pp. 116-118.
38. *Ibid.*, p. 92.

meeting of the Inter-Parliamentary Union of that same year might take place in connection with the event. Bartholdt had been one among the many American visitors to the 1899 Hague Peace Conference and had been impressed by what he had witnessed there. On that same trip he had joined the Inter-Parliamentary Union that, since its establishment 10 years before, had concentrated on propagating arbitration[39]. The invitation was enthusiastically accepted, and Bartholdt began immediately to consider the practical arrangements, receiving Roosevelt's support also for the setting up of an Arbitration Group among his colleagues on Capitol Hill that ensured rapid acceptance of the invitation by the Congress.

Bartholdt seized upon the fact that the 1899 Conference had left a number of matters connected with arbitration and the laws of war unsettled and prepared a draft resolution that would call on the US President to summon another peace conference[40]. The resolution was eventually passed and stressed that disputes between nations should be dealt with "in the same manner as disputes between individuals are adjudicated, namely by the arbitrament of courts in accordance with general principles of law"[41]. Bartholdt who had meanwhile been elected President of the Inter-Parliamentary Union then led a deputation to Washington on 24 September to present the request to Roosevelt. To the surprise of even the delegation, Roosevelt immediately acceded to the request, promising that he

---

39. Of all this activity, the most important was perhaps the establishment in Paris in 1888 of the Inter-Parliamentary Conference on International Arbitration — what later came to call itself the Inter-Parliamentary Union. This began as a meeting of 9 British and 25 French parliamentarians; the most important item was to advocate arbitration between France, Britain and the United States. In the 1890s, this activity was based on a Report by Philip Stanhope, Lord Weardale, a close friend of Gladstone's who himself had pronounced himself in favour of "a central European Tribunal". Auguste Schou, *Histoire de l'internationalisme*, Oslo, 1963, p. 397. Although at this time the role of Americans in this was relatively small, this was to change later.

40. Davis, *United States*, *supra* footnote 5, pp. 103-107.

41. It invited Governments to send representatives to a conference — the date and time of which ought to be decided later — to deal with three sets of issues:

> "(1) the questions for the consideration of which the conference at The Hague expressed a wish that further conference be called;
> (2) the negotiation of arbitration treaties between the nations represented at the conference to be convened;
> (3) the advisability of establishing an international congress, to convene periodically for the discussion of international questions". *Union interparlementaire pour l'arbitrage international. Session de 1904. Compte rendu de la XIIe Conférence à Saint-Louis, Missouri, du 12 au 14 septembre 1904*, Washington, Impremerie nationale, 1905, p. 60.

"shall at an early date ask the other nations to join in a second congress at The Hague"[42].

Roosevelt understood the value of peace initiatives towards the end of a presidential campaign — the election would be held in November 1904 — and despatched Hay to draft a circular to propose both the conclusion of arbitration treaties with other Governments and the convening of a second conference to carry out the work left over from 1899. The response was positive. Many States accepted the proposal to conclude arbitration treaties and no opposition to the idea of the conference was expressed. The arbitration treaties, as pointed out above, were withdrawn, however, owing to the Senate's awkward proposals and action on the Conference was deferred owing to the on-going Russo-Japanese war and the Morocco crisis both of which were finally settled with involvement by the United States. In regard to the formal invitation to The Hague, Roosevelt yielded to Russian wishes, prompted by domestic Russian concerns, ironically remarking to Root that this showed that in the end, "Kings and such-like are fundamentally just as funny as American politicians"[43].

At the preparatory meeting of the US delegation in Washington in April 1907 Root held obligatory arbitration and a permanent court as the most important objective to be attained from the Conference[44]. In his final instructions he wrote:

> "It should be your effort to bring about in the Second Conference a development of The Hague Tribunal into a permanent tribunal composed of judges who are judicial officers and nothing else, who are paid adequate salaries, who have no other occupation, and who will devote their entire time to the trial and decision of international causes by judicial methods and under a sense of judicial responsibility."[45]

It was important for Root that the judges should not be diplomats — one alternative was for the members to be chosen by the Supreme

---

42. *Op. cit. supra* footnote 41, p. 61.
43. Davis, *United States, supra* footnote 5, p. 123.
44. Kuehl, *Seeking World Order: The United States and International Organization to 1920*, Nashville, Vanderbilt University Press, 1969, p. 102 (noting that the Head of the US delegation Joseph H. Choate was convinced that President Roosevelt himself considered a general treaty on arbitration as its most important goal).
45. *Arbitration and the United States, supra* footnote 22, p. 473.

Courts of the various nations. No detailed plan was put forward, however, and the delegation was instructed to react to proposals on the spot. Root was of course aware of the Senate's reservations — the wish to exclude matters having to do with "honour" and "vital interests" — and he requested the delegation to keep this is mind. He stressed that he saw the Conference as only one step in a "process" that would continue and eventually lead into compulsory adjudication and a permanent court.

At the Conference itself, the United States made its proposal — prepared by Hill and Scott in The Hague — for compulsory arbitration and a permanent tribunal immediately after Russia. The US proposal was taken as the basis of the debate. Root had to remind the delegation about the position of the Senate, and so the proposal was equipped by the "honour" and "vital interests" reservation[46]. As the Commission began its work on 1 August 1907, the US delegates stressed the firmness of US commitment to the court. They emphasized that it should be a real court and not just an arbitral body and in all manner "wanted the new court to make decisions in a manner like that of American courts"[47]. And indeed, in the commentary to the proposal prepared by Scott, the precedent of the US Supreme Court figures prominently. The proposal failed in the end owing to lack of agreement on how the judges should be chosen, and, especially, what would be the relative representation of small and great powers. The same fate was encountered by the proposal on general and compulsory arbitration. The US delegation was to such degree disappointed about this outcome that it even refused to participate in the vote for the *vœu* that endorsed the principles of obligatory arbitration proposed that the matter be taken up at a later conference[48]. Nevertheless, low intensity negotiations under US leadership for the proposed Court of Arbitral Justice continued still after 1907 and, although they did not succeed in breaking the deadlock, by 1914 "there was general conviction that a new judicial institution of this kind was really needed"[49].

Soon after the Conference, Root took up the proposal for arbitration treaties that had been frozen by Roosevelt's withdrawal of them from the senate in 1905. This time around, the treaties were drafted

---

46. Davis, *United States*, *supra* footnote 5, pp. 251-255.
47. *Ibid.*, p. 261.
48. *Ibid.*, p. 284.
49. Eyffinger, *The 1899 Hague Peace Conference*, *supra* footnote 32, p. 458.

so as to honour the Senate's position, including by attaching to them the reservation of "vital interests, honour and independence". Altogether 24 treaties were concluded and Root found himself celebrated in the United States as a real hero of its peace movement[50].

*

Such are the facts. As summarized by a 1926 study carried out by the United-States-based World Peace Foundation:

> "The United States both through its public officials and its citizenry has throughout its history expressed itself more in quantity and quality in favour of arbitration than any other country."[51]

The Second Peace Conference was from the beginning to the end, with the brief Russian interlude, an American affair. Although US political leadership was not always consistent, and tensions between the executive and the Senate undermined the country's ability to take on international commitments, a wider spectrum of the political elite than elsewhere applied a legalistic mindset to thinking about international affairs[52]. This did not stop in 1907. For example, in 1910 Root, Scott, former President Taft, Andrew Carnegie and many other dignitaries set up an International Conference of the American Society for Judicial Settlement of International Disputes that met annually with great publicity to push the idea of arbitration and a permanent court into the agenda of the projected Third Hague Conference[53].

Instead of dressing its position as the new leading world power in the traditional rhetoric of diplomacy, empire and the balance of power, the United States thought of itself as *different*. As the former Secretary of State Richard Olney put it to the ASIL in 1907, where the Concert of Europe had practically taken over the affairs of

---

50. *Arbitration and the United States*, *supra* footnote 22, pp. 521-523; Kuehl, *Seeking World Order*, *supra* footnote 44, p. 114.

51. *Arbitration and the United States*, *supra* footnote 22, p. 477.

52. Manley Hudson of Harvard Law School claimed, however, that the standard view of the United States as the principal supporter of international arbitration was exaggerated. See his *By Pacific Means. The Implementation of Article Two of the Pact of Paris*, Yale University Press, 1935, pp. 96-100. His critique was, however, simply a prologue for his own pleading for more US involvement in the League.

53. See Janis, *Great Expectations*, *supra* footnote 15, pp. 152-154.

sovereign States — "the United States . . . has never undertaken and does not now undertake anything of the sort." [54] It was not engaged in world-wide effort to grasp new territories. Its was a spiritual mission that combined democracy, free trade and the rule of law — if necessary (as in the case of the "open door policy" in the Far East) by military intervention. Roosevelt's support for arbitration and the Hague system are part of that novel ethos. And yet it was also unabashedly nationalist ethos, carrying with it the supposition that only American activity — indeed activism — buttressed by American economic and military power could bring about those new conditions. Already in 1900 Roosevelt had noted the way the United States might be needed to support Britain in upholding the balance of power in Europe, simultaneously recognizing that "we ourselves are becoming, owing to our strength and geographical situation, more and more the balance of power of the whole globe" [55]. Roosevelt's speeches were notable by their stress on the universal benefits derived from US strength, graphically illustrated by his advocacy of a navy that would be able to control the maritime routes and thus secure the inviolability of private property in the seas, the single most important objective of his naval policy, reflected also in his opposition to European rules of maritime neutrality and contraband [56].

Roosevelt's successor, William Taft, also a lawyer, was no less keen on arbitration and the world court and gave innumerable addresses suggesting that *all* disputes that could not be settled by negotiation — irrespectively of whether they were felt to deal with "honour, independence or vital interests" — were to be submitted to arbitration. For, as he put in a speech of 1911, when everyone will have accepted compulsory arbitration and the international court, then "the motive for armament will disappear" [57]. The theory was that once a country submits a claim to the other one no longer will it use force because it will immediately appear as an aggressor in

---

54. Olney, "The Development of International Law", 1 *AJIL* (1907), p. 423.

55. George E. Mowry, *The Era of Theodore Roosevelt 1900-1912*, London, Hamish, 1958, p. 148.

56. When, for example, former Secretary of State Olney justified the US policy in support of the creation of the State of Panama he did by reference to the needs of all "civilized states". Olney, 'The Development', *supra* footnote 54, p. 426.

57. "Address to the Pennsylvania Society", *Addresses of President Taft*, Washington, 1911, p. 17.

front of world opinion. Consequently, Taft despatched his Secretary of State, Mr. Knox, to conclude general arbitration treaties without any reservations with Britain and France. They failed to pass the Senate, however. Thereafter, the same was attempted in 1913 by President Wilson whose treaties — the so-called Bryan Treaties — were less about adjudication than inquiry and a cooling-off period. They failed to cool anything, however, and the project was dropped as the war began[58].

IV. The Permanent Court of International Justice, 1920

The influence of US lawyers remained great in the process of setting up of the Permanent Court of International Justice although the country itself failed to join the League and even at the outset refused to join the Protocol for the Court. In 1915 former President Taft, for example, addressed a "World Court Congress" held at Cleveland by a long contemplation of the reasons that had persuaded the drafters of the Federal Constitution to include provision for a Supreme Court to deal with jurisdictional and other controversies between the member States. "The analogy", he noted, "between the function of the Supreme Court in deciding controversies between States and that of an international tribunal sitting to decide a cause between sovereign nations is very close."[59] There would have to be, he noted, in the future a Peace League with a commission of conciliation, a conference to agree on principles of international law and "a court which would be given jurisdiction by the consent of all the members of the League to consider and decide justiciable disputes between them"[60].

The proposal for such a court was included in the first drafts of the League Covenant prepared by Colonel House to President Wilson and were taken from there to the Hurst-Miller draft on which the Covenant was based. It had come there from the pen of Root himself[61]. And as Root's biographer notes, "the most constant and absorbing of Root's interests in the interwar years was the

---

58. For acerbic comments, see Sir Alfred Zimmern, *The League of Nations and the Rule of Law*, pp. 128-133.
59. William Howard Taft, "The US Supreme Court — The Prototype of a World Court", *Proceedings in Judicial Settlement of International Disputes*, No. 21, American Society of Judicial Settlement of International Disputes, Baltimore, 1915, pp. 6-7.
60. *Ibid.*, p. 18.
61. Scott, *The Project*, *supra* footnote 74, p. 103.

Permanent Court of International Justice"[62]. In 1920 Root travelled
to The Hague with his assistant James Brown Scott to sit as one of
the 10 members of the Advisory Committee of Jurists that had been
established by the League Council to draft the Statute of the Court.
Root was one of the most active members of the Committee broker-
ing, for example, the agreement that broke the deadlock on the
system of the election of the judges. In fact so much of the Statute
was based on the so-called Root-Phillimore plan, prepared by Root
together with his British colleague, Lord Phillimore, that in later
correspondence with the latter, Root referred to the institution as
"your and my Court of International Justice"[63].

In his letters, Root sometimes referred to a gap between the
Anglo-Saxons and the continental lawyers in the Committee visible
for example in the Anglo-Americans' insistence that judges should
come from the ranks of the domestic judiciary, not from among academics of jurisconsultants[64]. To ensure impartiality he insisted that
the judges be not nominated by Governments. Instead, they were to
be nominated by national groups, with the appointment made jointly
by the League Assembly and Council — a compromise formula to
ensure influence of small and great powers that corresponded to the
appointment of US judges by the two houses of the Congress[65].
Unlike his European colleagues, Root also stressed the permanency
of the appointments and the need for the institution to develop into a
real Court and not just into another temporary arrangement for the
settlement of occasional grievances between States. Both Root and
Scott made constant reference to the US Supreme Court in drafting
the Statute. Scott even wrote that the "Supreme Court [was] not only
a prototype, but is in fact a Permanent Court of International Justice,
administering in regular course the law of nations"[66].

Consistent with the US policy, Root favoured compulsory settlement and thought that this can be attained only if the Court is closely
prevented from venturing outside the application of legal rules. This

---

62. Leopold, *Elihu Root, supra* footnote 6, p. 161. Root's own views about the
post-war legal system, with emphasis on sanctions connected with an international court, is available in his "The Outlook fort International Law", 10 *AJIL*
(1916), 1-11.
63. Jessup, *Elihu Root*, Vol II, *supra* footnote 8, p. 422.
64. Scott, *The Project, supra* footnote 74, p. 51.
65. Jessup *Elihu Root*, Vol. II, *supra* footnote 8, pp. 420-421; Scott, *The
Project, supra* footnote 74, pp. 27-48.
66. Scott, *The Project, supra* footnote 74, p. 102.

tended to limit the Court's jurisdiction quite dramatically, owing to the relative lack of codified, black-letter international law. In his speeches to the American Society of International Law he pointed out that one of the benefits of codification would precisely be the extension of the Court's jurisdiction. Root was initially opposed to the proposal by Baron Descamps from Belgium that the Court ought to have a gap-filling function by recourse to large international law "principles". In the end he consented however, as the formulation took the US Supreme Court language and referred to "general principles of law recognized by civilized nations"[67]. Like the US Judge John Bassett Moore in the Court later, Root was also apprehensive of the Court's advisory jurisdiction — especially because he feared that the Senate would see this as a legislative function and that it would thus lead to the United States staying indefinitely outside the Court. The importance that American lawyers attached to the Court was reflected in the appointment of judges: Moore was followed by two former Secretaries of States, Charles Evans Hughes and F. B. Kellogg.

V. Conclusion: The Ideology of International Adjudication

International adjudication emerged as a significant institutional and diplomatic project around the turn of the twentieth century in connection with a change from a Eurocentric, Vattelian perception of the international world to one ideologically dominated by the United States. If the 1899 Peace Conference was still a European affair, the 1907 Conference was held in a new environment. Without the influence of American lawyers in the formulation of US foreign policy, the project for a permanent Supreme Court of the world would not have become a reality.

This is not to say that adjudication would not have had many supporters or that it would not have been supported from many perspectives. Several people may sleep in the same bed but dream different dreams. As a matter of official foreign policy, however, it was part of the new international agenda of the United States. And this was so independently of the legal-theoretical views of its staunchest supporters — Scott a natural lawyer, Root a "classic positivist legalist"[68].

---

67. Ole Spiermann, *International Legal Argument in the Permanent Court of International Justice*, Cambridge University Press, 2005, pp. 58-60, 165-167.
68. Anne-Marie Slaughter, "The Legacy of Elihu Root", *ASIL Proc. 2006*, p. 208.

Their support for a permanent international court followed from their shared cultural sense that for law to play a beneficial role in the world of States, it must be conceived in common law terms and in accordance with the American perception of the relations of courts to the surrounding society. This ideology may be characterized from four perspectives.

1. Against Government

First, it emerges from an anti-government ethos, transposed into international law. Philosophers like Bentham and Mill and internationalists like Ladd and Cobden took international problems to emerge principally from nationalist agitation, governmental pursuit of "irrational" objectives such as glory, prestige, or domination. For these men, as for the lawyers who followed them, States were no original collectivities. As Scott put it in 1907:

> "A state is nothing but a political body or corporation existing for the benefit of its corporate members, subjects and citizens; and the state has no right in its individual or corporate capacity." [69]

The very point of Root's insistence that the judges in the PCIJ be not appointed by Governments but by the national groups of the Permanent Court of Arbitration was precisely to keep Governments away from the process and to transfer dealing with disputes from diplomats and Governments to independent, impartial, objective and reasonable judges. Governments were perhaps a necessary evil, but it was the task of effective internationalism to limit their power, and this could be done as it had been done within the United States itself — by a system of courts whose judgments would, as Root and his compatriot, another winner of the Nobel Prize, Nicholas Murray Butler, insisted, be enforced by world public opinion against egotistic Governments. Root's first address as Secretary of State to the American Society of International Law emphasized the need for lawyers to educate the public in international legal matters for, as he put it: "the true basis of the peace and order in which we live is not fear of the policeman; it is the self-restraint of the thousands of

---

69. James Brown Scott, "The Legal Nature of International Law", *supra* footnote 4, pp. 849-850.

people who make up the community"[70]. Root specifically saw the task of the Advisory Committee that drafted the PCIJ Statute to "pass beyond the rights of sovereignty" while he held that it was the task of the future court "to render judgment limiting the rights of nations"[71]. Where future generations of US lawyers would highlight the role of international law as an instrument of policy, Root and Scott saw it rather as a *limit* to policy, an impartial set of principles growing spontaneously from international practices[72].

Of course, the US Senate was not equally committed to setting aside national priorities, insisting that the reservation of "vital interests, honour and independence" be inserted in arbitration treaties — a suggestion that the US delegation in The Hague in 1907 accepted reluctantly as part of its proposal for a permanent court. Nevertheless, this matter remained contested and President Taft expressly insisted that he did not "see any more reason why matters of honour should not be referred to a court of arbitration any more than matters of national proprietorship"[73]. Root also accepted the distinction between justiciable and non-justiciable disputes — after all, the very terminology was Anglo-American — but suggested that the proposed series of further conferences would in due course lead to further law-making treaties so that in the end the area of non-justiciability would be reduced to a minimum. As Scott put it in regard to the PCIJ: "year after year, and generation after generation, [it would] be exercising continuously enlarging jurisdiction"[74].

2. Against World Federalism

A second, related aspect of this ideology is its predilection against world federalism. Already William Ladd's famous 1840 proposal was for the institution of a "Congress of Nations" and "Court of Nations" — the former an instrument of negotiations between (Christian) nations, the latter a place of settlement for issues for

---

70. Elihu Root, "The Need of Popular Understanding of International Law", 1 *AJIL* (1907), 2.

71. Scott, *The Project, supra* footnote 74, pp. 33, 33-35.

72. For a summary, see Richard H. Steinberg and Jonathan M. Zasloff, "Power and International Law", 100 *AJIL* (2006), 65-69.

73. *Addresses of President Taft*, Washington, 1911, p. 5.

74. James Brown Scott, *The Project of a Permanent Court of International Justice*, Washington, Carnegie Endowment for International Peace: 35, 1920, p. 106.

which no result had been attained by negotiation[75]. Any proposal for
world government was conspicuously absent. The proposal — a
conference and a court, but no government — was made by President Taft in 1915, and endorsed by no less a legal authority than Sir
Frederick Pollock before an audience of American lawyers. Pollock,
perhaps the most important theorist of common law, endorsed this particularly against federalist proposals "framed by speculative writers
who have no experience in the conduct even of ordinary business"[76].

None of the US lawyers spoke the language of world
government. In fact some of the most furious infighting in the nineteenth-century peace movement took place between the proponents
of world government — these were Europeans — and the supporters
of arbitration and a permanent court[77]. In the end, the latter won
because they could enlist the political support of England and the
United States. A recent discussion of the first years of the *American
Journal of International Law* (1907-1914) finds there:

> "an overall importance of always complete dedication to explor-
> ing the virtues and possibilities of international arbitration, the
> wisdom of international legislation on the laws of war and the
> essential nature of international law itself"[78].

The society saw itself as a continuation of the late nineteenth-
century arbitration movement — seeing the international problem as
the problem of war, and seeking its resolution though arbitration by
reference to principles outside governmental diplomacy so as to turn
it to a peaceful direction, not to abolish it. When Scott, for instance,
examined the recommendation of the Second Hague Peace Conference to call a third conference in the future, he specifically rejected
that this would have meant "a first step to a confederation". This
was a matter of "dreamers" whereas for "the man of affairs" national
independence was too important to be given up in this way[79]. Root's
addresses and writings on international law always presupposed a
system of international adjudication premised upon the existence of
separate, independent Governments between which disputes would

---

75. Schou, *Histoire*, *supra* footnote 39, pp. 82-88.
76. Frederick Pollock, "Cosmopolitan Custom and International Law", xxix
Harvard Law Review (1916), 578.
77. See Hinsley, *Power and Pursuit of Peace*, *supra* footnote 13, pp. 100-106.
78. Bederman, "Appraising a Century", *supra* footnote 11, p. 26.
79. James Brown Scott, "Recommendation for a Third Peace Conference at
the Hague", 2 *AJIL* (1908), 821-822.

be settled. In a 1925 report he submitted to the Inter-Parliamentary Union, for example, Root spoke only of the need to develop conciliation, arbitration and adjudication. There is no reference whatsoever to any need of developing international institutions and even less anything resembling world government[80]. None of the influential US peace activists, and later lawyers, proposed merging the United States in some world government scheme — although there was of course many that saw it the manifest destiny of the United States to become a world leader. In some minds, no doubt, the two may even have entailed each other.

The rejection of world federalism was supported by the analogy Root, Scott and others made between the development of international law and their common law experience[81]. After all, had not Pollock himself declared that law "does not depend on legislation or upon the express will of any defined authority". It was, instead, above all "custom of the realm" — not of the King but of the Kingdom[82]. Scott never thought one needed world government to accompany a world court or to ensure the enforcement of its judgments. In a programmatic article in the first volume of his journal, he sketched the development of international law in fully common law terms. International law developed, he wrote, as a "common law of nations", not something dictated by sovereign Governments. It was a "growth of usage and custom" that emerged independently of the sovereign[83]. This was Root's ideology, too. For him, "[t]he real force of law . . . is derived from the assent of the people" and not from governmental enforcement[84]. In his addresses to the American

---

80. Elihu Root, "The Codification of International Law" (Report Submitted to the 23rd Conference of the Interparliamentary Union, Washington DC, 3 October 1925, 19 *AJIL* (1925), 675-684.

81. For a particularly striking example, see Elihu Root, "The Relations between International Tribunals of Arbitration and the Jurisdiction of National Courts", 3 *AJIL* (1909), 524, 534-536. See also R. Floyd Clark, "A Permanent Tribunal of International Arbitration: Its Nature and Value", 1 *AJIL* 1907, 351-360.

82. Frederick Pollock, "The Continuity of the Common Law", xi *Harvard Law Review* (1898), 430.

83. Scott, "The Legal Nature", *supra* footnote 4, p. 851. He continued: "as clearly and surely as the common customs and usages of England became the common law of that realm".

84. Quoted in Zasloff, "Law and the Shaping of American Foreign Policy", *supra* footnote 6, p. 262. The point that international law is enforced by public opinion — that is, "not so much by the governments as by the people of each country" — is forcefully made in Elihu Root, "The Sanction of International Law", 2 *AJIL* (1908), 456, 451-457.

Society, he constantly stressed the popular and customary basis of the law and its independence from governmental dictates and, as president of the American Law Institute, was instrumental in pushing forward the Restatements project that manifested this belief[85].

3. *Private Rights and World Peace*

Third, the idea of adjudication as a way to world peace was premised on the perception that in a world of expanding international contacts, the violation of private rights by foreign Governments was becoming an increasingly significant cause of war. Think of the *Venezuelan Claims* case, for example, and the role played by Teddy Roosevelt in persuading Europeans to arbitrate their grievances, or of the US proposal at the Second Hague Conference that ended up in the Porter convention against the enforcement of contracts by force.

The cases of arbitration in the nineteenth century — and certainly of arbitrations involving the United States — were almost all cases of injury to a private alien travelling or doing business in non-European or non-United States territory. As Philip Jessup suggests, "[t]he history of the development of the international law of responsibility of states for injuries to aliens was thus an aspect of the history of 'imperialism' or 'dollar diplomacy' "[86]. Indeed, the vast majority of cases reported in the very influential six-volume *History and Digest of International Arbitrations to which the US has been a Party* of 1898 by John Bassett Moore were property cases. It became the point of the emerging doctrine of State responsibility to compel non-European States to abide by European and US legal standards, somewhat like consular jurisdiction and mixed tribunals had done, articulated in a doctrine of "international standards" against the typically Latin American appeals to a domestic standard. Even Scott wrote in his commentary to the PCIJ Statute that "the cases will be largely, if not always, claims [of a State's] citizen or subjects" — giving the examples of commercial matters and questions of treatment of minorities[87]. A solid system of private rights, enforceable by impartial tribunals would guarantee the stability of international exchanges and bind the hands of suspect or weak Governments

---

85. Zasloff, "Law and the Shaping of American Foreign Policy", *supra* footnote 6, p. 277.

86. Philip Jessup, *A Modern Law of Nations*, New York, Macmillan, 1958, p. 96 and generally pp. 94-122.

87. Scott, *The Project*, *supra* footnote 74, pp. 94-96.

reneging on their commitments to foreign individuals and commercial operators.

Here the United States had a special interest, having been the most significant party in international litigation and as by far most of this litigation had concerned the violation of the private rights of Americans in connection with internal disturbances and changes of government especially in Latin America. State responsibility for injuries to aliens was really an American topic; to dispose of it what were needed were international tribunals that could deal justice to Governments trespassing on the rights of innocent foreigners carrying out business in their territories. In fact, the point of the Senate reservation of disputes concerning "honour, independence and vital interests" may be understood as an effort to limit adjudication precisely to those kinds of disputes.

International adjudication — in this American version — is based on the assumption that international problems are caused by Governments and experienced by individuals as violations of rights. A system of rules and tribunals will stabilize and protect those rights, enabling individuals and commercial operators to plan their activities and use the opportunities of enrichment available in the international world by interacting with each other through private contracts. Rules and tribunals are particularly indispensable for the enforcement of contracts. They are thus a part of a project of an international world in which something like an international civil society will gradually emerge from private trade and wealth-seeking against war and the egotistic diplomacy of States.

There is a cosmopolitanism embedded in the project of international adjudication. The keenness with which Root, Scott and others insisted on compulsory arbitration and a permanent tribunal was part of gradualist view of how the world would and should develop. For each backlash, they always wrote an article pointing out that progress is slow and gradual and that one cannot have everything at once. Root thought the acceptance of periodic meetings after 1907 as perhaps the conference's most significant achievement. And Scott held that it made the eventual establishment of a permanent jurisdiction a virtual certainty[88]. But this was not a project of cosmopolitan

---

88. Kuehl, *Seeking World Order, supra* footnote 44, pp. 104-105, and James Brown Scott, "The Work of the Second Hague Conference", 5 *International Conciliation* (1908), 105.

federation, it was a project for what may be called "empire of civil society" — a global system of enforcement of private rights against public power.

4. *Impartiality and Reasonableness as Cultural Dispositions*

The legalism of Root, Scott or indeed John Bassett Moore was not simply an offshoot of what US legal historians have called "classical legal thought" — that is, a faith in objective and determinate rules and their automatic application through legal technique[89]. Although Root did think codification important, for him as well as for the whole US delegation in The Hague, it was still more important to seek to bind the States to a court. This may perhaps reflect their common law background and when Root argued for increased legislation he did this so as to argue for the extension of the jurisdiction of an international court: his legalism was less a legalism of rules than of a sensibility about courts and the legal process[90]. Instead of a legalism of rules, theirs is more a legalism of cultural and professional sensibility, a disposition, faith in the reasonableness of the legal class, its ability to rise above sectarianism and to take a view on disputes that will enable disposing them in an enlightened and reasonable fashion. Thus, for example, unlike their continental colleagues, Anglo-American lawyers rarely made a principled distinction between arbitration and adjudication. Of course, they were aware of that difference — but they saw that difference manifested above all in the fact of one being temporary and the other permanent[91]. They did sometimes note that whereas one was more inclined to seeking a diplomatic adjustment, the other was more bound to apply strict law. But that distinction was consistently played down. The arbitration movement transformed itself practically without anybody noticing, into a movement for a permanent tribunal. Although Root did highlight the need eventually for an international code that a tribunal would apply, he never thought that this was a *sine qua non* for such a tribunal. After all, the Anglo-Americans were in their domestic systems accustomed to judge-made law. In the twentieth century, this approach peaked in the work of Hersch Lauterpacht for

---

89. Zasloff, for example, in his important essay (*supra* footnote 6) on the whole exaggerates the formalism of Root and the conservative legal class.

90. Elihu Root, "The Outlook for International Law", 10 *AJIL* (1916), 1-11.

91. Scott, *The Project, supra* footnote 74, p. 99.

whom it was the task of international judges not only to apply existing law but — perhaps above all — to develop international law in
order to protect individual rights and thus work towards a particular
kind of cosmopolitan world[92].

In other words, the ideology of international adjudication was not
constituted of a blind faith in rules. It relied, instead, in the "reasonableness and good temper" of men participating in negotiation and
arbitration[93] — their sense of justice and their spirit or "calling" in
defence of private rights against government, the enforcement of
contracts in view of reasonable conditions, and their view of progress as a global society of individuals that would, ultimately, be like
the domestic society of the United States. Even as Root appealed to
public opinion, he was, as conservative, also deeply distrustful of the
masses, seeing the "mindset for war" strengthened by the "con-
tinually advancing democratic control over foreign affairs". For him,
both the public and the press were "apt to see only one side of [a]
controversy [and] to assume that their own country is completely
right; and to regard any concession bestown by their government as
a betrayal"[94]. The work of international law was, as Zasloff has
noted, a work of "civilization"[95].

VI. Epilogue

Is this all there is to be said about the ideology of international
adjudication? That it was an aspect of American imperialist thinking
from 1900 to 1907 and slightly beyond? Well, no. In the first place,
the proposal was always made in general terms; even if there was a
policy of national strength behind it, its point was not to support
American power but American ideals — understood as the proper
ideals of everyone. In the second place, there were always many
Non-Americans, from Europe and elsewhere, who supported it for
varying reasons. As I have already intimated, its most important
twentieth-century representative was a Galician Jew who had been
educated in Vienna and found home in Cambridge, United Kingdom,

---

92. See Martti Koskenniemi, "Hersch Lauterpacht 1897-1960", in Jack
Beatson and Reinhard Zimmermann, *Jurists Uprooted. German-Speaking
Emigré Lawyers in Twentieth-Century Britain*, Oxford University Press, 2004,
pp. 601-662.
93. Root, "Popular Understanding", *supra* footnote 70, p. 2.
94. Elihu Root, "The Codification of International Law", 19 *AJIL* (1925), 677.
95. Jonathan Zasloff, "The Legacy of Elihu Root", *ASIL Proc. 2006*, p. 214.

Hersch Lauterpacht. And third, there is no necessary reason why US preferences would always or necessarily lie with international adjudication. Indeed, those preferences may often appear to clash with it. I wonder what Scott or Root would have said about the contracts whereby the United States sought to immunize itself from the jurisdiction of the International Criminal Court. It is in the nature of ideologies to rise and fall with changing circumstances. For Marx, ideologies were "false consciousness", defined by their opposition to "truth". In a post-Marxist era, the distinction between "truth" and "falsity" is no longer clear-cut and neither epithet can any longer be automatically attached to an idea or project. If international adjudication still sounds like "ideology", this is not necessarily pejorative but indicates the close relationship of that institutional project with a number of associated ideas about the nature of the international political world and what ought to be done to govern or contest it. But whatever its pedigree, it is high time that "international adjudication" were made the object of critical analysis instead of religious faith.

2. THE INSTITUTION OF PERMANENT ADJUDICATORY BODIES AND RECOURSE TO *AD HOC* TRIBUNALS

J. CRAWFORD[1] and N. SCHRIJVER[2]

"What then is this court whose members do not even know one another? The Court of 1899 is but an idea which occasionally assumes shape and then again disappears. This is why the Russian delegation submitted its project, in order . . . to bring about an exchange of views with regard to the matter of the Permanent Court . . ."[3]

1. Introduction

Studying the 1899-1907 discussions from the perspective of international dispute settlement takes one back to a different era. However forward-looking the delegates to the Hague Peace Conferences might have been and however thought-provoking their debates, no delegate could have foreseen the enormous increase in the number of international courts and tribunals during the twentieth century, and especially during the period since 1989. At the turn of the century, war was a regular way of resolving or suppressing conflicts; international organizations were limited to the functional domain of posts, telecommunications, and river navigation; experience with inter-State arbitrations, let alone international judicial settlement, was confined to *ad hoc* tribunals or to references to another head of State; international criminal courts for the prosecution and adjudication of international crimes would not have been contemplated.

Yet, in retrospect the Hague Peace Conferences can be viewed as

---

1. Whewell Professor of International Law, Director, Lauterpacht Centre for International Law, University of Cambridge.
2. Professor of Public International Law, Academic Director, Grotius Centre for International Legal Studies, University of Leiden.
Our thanks to Francesco Messineo, LCIL, for his assistance in the preparation of this paper.
3. F. F. Martens (Russia), 9th meeting, First Commission: First Sub-Commission, 1 August 1907, in J. B. Scott (ed.), *The Proceedings of the Hague Peace Conferences. The Conference of 1907*, Vol. II, New York, Oxford University Press, 1921, p. 327.

a milestone in the emergence of the contemporary "system" of international dispute settlement, as substantively recorded in Article 33 of the UN Charter and in dispute settlement clauses of other treaties, and institutionally reflected in the multiplicity of international courts, arbitral tribunals, panels and commissions, now numbering in their dozens.

In this chapter we will first discuss the issues at the 1907 Conference from the perspective of international dispute settlement. What was the *acquis* of 1899, what was the experience with arbitration following the 1899 Conference, what were the ideas of systemic justice in 1907, which Governments were the main protagonists and which the major opponents?

In the second part, we will discuss the issues of 1907 from the perspective of 2007. How to assess the evolution of international courts, tribunals and other dispute settlement mechanisms over a period of 100 years? What went well, what went wrong? How to view the now 100-year-old dichotomy between arbitration and judicial settlement and between *ad hoc* and permanent? Are diversity of approaches and pluriformity of institutions signs of failure or hallmarks of success in international dispute settlement?

2. The Issues at the 1907 Hague Peace Conference

The Second Hague Peace Conference built largely on the First[4]. The 1899 crown jewel was the Convention on the Pacific Settlement of International Disputes[5]. At the time, this Convention was called the "Magna Carta of international law" and "the keystone of the arch of international justice"[6]. According to Tryon, "the chief feature of the convention . . . was the establishment of a Permanent Court of Arbitration, the forerunner of the Court to which the dreamers of the early days had always looked forward"[7]. It is true that the 26 participating States agreed on nothing more than the principle of voluntary arbitration. Obligatory arbitration was considered both impos-

---

4. For a general account, see A. Eyffinger, "A Highly Critical Moment: Role and Record of the 1907 Hague Peace Conference", 54 *Netherlands International Law Review* (2007), p. 197.

5. 91 *BFSP* 970; 2 *US Treaties* 2016; 187 *CTS* 410; 26 *Martens NRG*, 2nd ser. 920; 23 *Hertslet* 509; *USTS* 392; 1 *AJIL Supp.* (1907), 107.

6. W. I. Hull, *The Two Hague Conferences and Their Contributions to International Law*, Boston, Ginn & Co., 1908, p. 471.

7. J. L. Tryon, "The Hague Conferences", 20 *Yale LJ* (1911), 475.

sible and undesirable under prevailing circumstances. Nevertheless, the Rapporteur (Descamps of Belgium) could state in his final report "that arbitration belongs *par excellence* to the organic institutions of juristic peace between nations"[8]. As the German delegate Baron Marschall von Bieberstein stated:

> "it would be an error . . . to believe that a general arbitrational agreement concluded between two states can serve purely and simply as a model or, so to speak, a formulary for a world treaty. The matter is very different in the two cases . . . If we raise before the world the flag of obligatory arbitration, we must surely have an arbitrational agreement which would do honour to this flag and define clearly and precisely the character of the obligation."[9]

Apart from arbitration, the First Hague Peace Conference also sought to facilitate through the PCA, "before an appeal is made to arms", the good offices or mediation of one or more friendly powers, but qualified by two main clauses: "in case of serious disputes or conflict" and "as far as circumstances permit". Furthermore, such good offices and mediation would have exclusively the character of advice and would never be binding. Here one was building on the achievements of the 1856 Treaty of Paris[10] and the 1885 Act of Berlin[11].

The PCA had not been an immediate success. The brief period 1899-1907 saw various armed conflicts — the Anglo-Boer war, the blockade and bombardment of Venezuelan ports by European powers, the Boxer Revolt in China, Japan's annexation of Korea and the Japanese-Russian war (to general astonishment won by Japan), to mention only the main ones[12].

---

8. Hull, *supra* footnote 6, p. 300.
9. Quoted in Hull, *supra* footnote 6, p. 313.
10. General Treaty between Great Britain, Austria, France, Prussia, Russia, Sardinia and Turkey for Re-establishment of Peace, Paris, 30 March 1856, 114 *CTS* 409, 46 *BFSP* 12, 10 *Hertslet* 533, Art. VIII.
11. General Act of the Berlin Conference regarding Africa; 26 February 1885, 165 *CTS* 485, 10 *Martens NRG*, 2nd ser. 414, 76 *BFSP* 4, 17 *Hertslet* 62, Arts. 8, 12.
12. See, e.g., B. Nasson, "Waging Total War in South Africa: Some Centenary Writings on the Anglo-Boer War, 1899-1902", 66 *The Journal of Military History* (2002), 813; B. S. McBeth, *Gunboats, Corruption, and Claims: Foreign Intervention in Venezuela, 1899-1908*, Westport, Conn., Greenwood Press, 2001; V. Purcell, *The Boxer Uprising. A Background Study*, Cambridge,

At the same time, many new arbitration treaties were concluded on both sides of the Atlantic. Quite a number of these provided for either obligatory arbitration without restriction or obligatory arbitration of certain classes of cases. The *Dogger Bank* incident in 1904 raised immediate passions but was ultimately resolved by a Commission of Inquiry under the auspices of the PCA[13]. During the early years of the twentieth century considerable thought was given, both in government circles and in the context of international associations such as the Inter-Parliamentary Union, the Pan-American Movement, the American Peace Society, the Institut de droit international and the International Law Association, on how to build upon the international dispute settlement arrangements of 1899. It led to proposals to activate the Hague Court, to establish an International Prize Court or to supplement the PCA with a Court of Arbitral Justice or even an International High Court of Justice[14].

In 1907, the commission dealing with international dispute settlement (arbitration and international commissions of inquiry) was again, as in 1899, chaired by Léon Bourgeois from France[15]. The many meetings of his First Commission[16], convened in the *Salle des Trèves* (where now the weekly Dutch cabinet meetings take place), resulted in:

— a revision of the 1899 Convention;
— a declaration on obligatory arbitration;
— a *vœu* in the Final Act for the adoption of an annexed draft convention for the creation of a Court of Arbitral Justice;

Cambridge University Press, 1963; D. Preston, *A Brief History of the Boxer Rebellion: China's War on Foreigners, 1900*, London, Robinson, 2002; P. Duus, *The Abacus and the Sword: The Japanese Penetration of Korea, 1895-1910*, Berkeley, London, University of California Press, 1995; J. W. Steinberg and D. Wolff (eds.), *The Russo-Japanese War in Global Perspective: World War Zero*, Leiden, Brill, 2005-2007

13. See A. P. Higgins, *The Hague Peace Conferences and Other International Conferences concerning the Laws and Usages of War: Texts of Conventions with Commentaries,* Cambridge, Cambridge University Press, 1909, pp. 167-169.

14. J. L. Tryon, "The Proposed High Court of Nations", 19 *Yale LJ* (1910), 145.

15. L. Bourgeois had served as the president of the Third Commission on "arbitration" of the 1899 Conference, which had become the First Commission of the 1907 Conference.

16. The First Commission held ten sessions, between 22 June and 11 October 1907; its first sub-commission (revision 1899 Convention) and its various sub-committees met 47 times; and its second sub-commission (maritime prizes) and sub-committees met six times.

— Convention XII on the establishment of an International Prize Court.

The 1899 Convention underwent considerable revision. An extensive new part was added, Articles 9-36 on International Commissions on Inquiry to replace the six articles on this in the 1899 Convention. The opening article, Article 9, demonstrates the sensitivities involved and is worth quoting in full:

> "In disputes of an international nature *involving neither honor nor vital interests*, and arising from a difference of opinion on points of fact, the Contracting Powers deem it expedient *and desirable* that the parties who have not been able to come on an agreement by means of diplomacy, should, *as far as circumstances allow*, institute an International Commission of Inquiry, to facilitate a solution of these disputes by elucidating the facts by means of an impartial and conscientious investigation." [17]

No doubt encouraged by the experience with the 1904 Dogger Bank Commission, Martens had submitted various proposals to expand the competence of the commissions beyond mere inquiry, for example by giving them the power to determine responsibility. But this and other proposals were not adopted [18]. Moreover, the 1907 Conference maintained the purely voluntary character of international commissions of inquiry and continued to hedge them with conditional phrases as to honour, essential interest, etc.

Equally challenging were the negotiations on the revision of the Part on International Arbitration. France and Great Britain advocated a general arbitration treaty and even favoured general obligatory arbitration. For many States — most notably Germany and Austria — this was a bridge too far [19]. Subsequently, proposals were put forward, especially by Portugal, to list categories of dispute which would be fit for obligatory arbitration, but ultimately no agreement could be reached. There was some progress compared with 1899 in

---

17. Convention for the Pacific Settlement of International Disputes, as adopted in 1899 and amended in 1907, Art. 9 (emphasis added), in Higgins, *supra* footnote 13, p. 107.

18. See Higgins, *supra* footnote 13, p. 169.

19. J. H. Choate, *The Two Hague Conferences*, Princeton, Princeton University Press, and London, Oxford University Press, 1913, p. 36; F. W. Holls, *The Peace Conference at The Hague*, New York and London, Macmillan, 1900; reprinted 1914, pp. 246-248.

that in 1907 many States expressed support for the principle of restricted obligatory arbitration in some form[20]. Article 38 (1899) referred to arbitration as "the most effective and, at the same time, the most equitable, means of settling disputes" on questions of a legal character, and especially on the interpretation or application of treaties. In 1907, on the proposal of the Austro-Hungarian delegation, a clause was added declaring resort to arbitration actually desirable[21]. But praise was not the same thing as commitment: as Elliott concluded in 1908, proposals for a Court of Arbitral Justice and for a system of compulsory arbitration were "interred among the pious wishes"[22]; T. E. Holland in 1908 referred to them as "Cloud-cuckootown"[23]. Apart from this, the Conference adopted a Declaration in the Final Act which merely provided that obligatory arbitration was "permitted" in principle[24].

The Part on International Arbitration also included various minor revisions as to the role of the PCA, including a further procedure for appointing party arbitrators (Art. 45), a procedure for gently communicating to parties in dispute the availability of the PCA to assist (Art. 48), an extensive list of elements to be contained in the *compromis* (Art. 52) and a facility for a summary procedure of arbitration (Arts. 86-90)[25].

From the proceedings it can be seen that many delegations perceived the weakness of the PCA as neither a court nor permanent. It is interesting to note that two major powers, the United States and Russia, came forward with drafts for a permanent body under various names — a Court of Arbitral Justice, a Judicial Arbitral Court or even an International High Court of Justice. The proposals by Russia left the concept of the PCA intact and sought to strengthen

---

20. Hull reports that the American proposition of obligatory arbitration for judicial disputes and those relating to the interpretation and application of treaties secured an affirmative vote of 35 to 9; the Portuguese proposition of obligatory arbitration for some list of cases 33 to 11; and obligatory arbitration for the proposed list of specific cases 31 to 13. Hull, *supra* footnote 6, pp. 345 and 462.

21. "Consequently, it would be desirable that, in disputes about the above-mentioned questions, the contracting powers should, if the case arose, have recourse to arbitration, in so far as circumstances permit."

22. E. G. Elliott, "The Development of International Law by the Second Hague Conference", 8 *Colum. LR* (1908), 96, 98.

23. T. E. Holland, "The Hague Conference of 1907", 24 *LQR* (1908), 76, 78.

24. First *vœu* of the Final Declaration of the Second Hague Conference, Higgins, *supra* footnote 13, pp. 67, 82-85.

25. *Ibid.*, pp. 129, 133.

it. The American proposals (later in revised form jointly presented with Britain) went considerably further and essentially sought to establish nothing less than a permanent International Court of Justice. The concept met with remarkably little opposition but ultimately stranded on the criteria for selecting and appointing judges, especially as regards permanent seats for great powers. The Latin American countries led by Barbosa from Brazil insisted on the principle of equality among sovereign nations and put a stop to the project[26]. One was left with a Court but without judges[27]. Thus it had no effect on the Convention on Pacific Settlement. Nonetheless the text of the Draft Convention for the Creation of a Court of Arbitral Justice — effectively the first draft of the Statute of the Permanent Court of International Justice of 1922 — was attached to *vœu* No. 1 in the Final Act[28].

By contrast Convention XII on the Creation of an International Prize Court was very much a German project. It was agreed that it would exercise merely complementary jurisdiction to national prize courts. Nevertheless, as Choate commented in 1913, it had advanced features of permanency and compulsory arbitration[29]. Agreement could also be reached on a Court of 15 judges (Art. 14), but the allocation of 8 of these 15 seats to the then 8 great powers (Art. 15) met with considerable opposition. Upon signing Convention XII, several States registered reservations to Article 15[30]. As a result of a lack of

---

26. On the Latin American perspective at the conference, see De Bustamante y Sirvén, *La Cour Permanente de Justice Internationale*, The Hague, M. Nijhoff, 1923, pp. 4-5.

27. For a comprehensive account of the proceedings of the Conference with regards to the issue of a permanent court, see H. Wehberg, *The Problem of an International Court of Justice*, Vol. II of *The Work of the Hague*, Oxford, Clarendon Press for the Carnegie Endowment for International Peace, 1918, English translation of *Das Problem eines internationalen Staatengerichtshofes*, Vol. II of *Das Werk vom Haag*, Munich, Leipzig, Duncker & Humblot, 1912, pp. 172-197. On the American proposal, see Higgins, *supra* footnote 13, pp. 509-517; Holls, *supra* footnote 19; J. B. Scott, "The Evolution of a Permanent International Judiciary", 6 *AJIL* (1912), 316.

28. The text of the draft Convention is in Higgins, *supra* footnote 13, pp. 498-509.

29. Choate, *supra* footnote 19, pp. 65-73.

30. On the International Prize Court, see H. B. Brown, "The Proposed International Prize Court", 2 *AJIL* (1908), 476; C. N. Gregory, "The Proposed International Prize Court and Some of Its Difficulties", 2 *AJIL* (1908), 458; W. Schücking, *The International Union of the Hague Conferences*, Vol. I of *The Work of the Hague*, Carnegie Endowment for International Peace, Oxford, Clarendon Press, 1918, English translation of *Der Staatenverband der Haager Konferenzen*, Vol. I of *Das Werk vom Haag*, Munich, Leipzig, Duncker & Humblot, 1912; Wehberg, *supra* footnote 27, pp. 159 *et seq.*

ratifications the International Prize Court never came into being —
and indeed the law of prize itself was soon obsolescent. What could
have become the first truly permanent international court did not
materialize.

The records of the Hague Peace Conferences show the extent to
which the delegates were struggling to institutionalize international
arbitration. In 1899 this effort had crystallized in the establishment
of the Permanent Court of Arbitration, which was in truth a secretariat or registry rather than a court. In 1907 the delegates aimed to
take international dispute settlement further by seeking to establish
forms of compulsory international arbitration, by contemplating a
full-fledged international court and by seeking to institutionalize
non-judicial procedures for dispute settlement such as inquiry,
mediation and conciliation. In key respects the 1907 Conference
utterly failed; not only did it not help prevent the outbreak of the
Great War seven years later; it was not even seen as *relevant* to its
prevention. But on a fairer assessment the 1907 Conference made a
contribution by a substantial improvement to the 1899 Convention
for the Pacific Settlement of Disputes and by developing recognizable schemes for what after the war became the Permanent Court
for International Justice.

On a conceptual level, 1907 involved early discussions of permanent versus *ad hoc* tribunals, of obligatory versus optional procedures, of the coherence of decisions of dispute settlement bodies
and of their integration into wider political schemes for international
co-operation. These themes are still with us 100 years later.

In this way the two Conferences contributed to the evolution and
the advancement of international law. Many delegates considered a
permanent international tribunal somehow historically inevitable[31].
As two commentators put it:

> "Lente et réfléchie, patiente et sage, l'œuvre de La Haye
> n'est pas la décevante chimère d'un jour, ou la capricieuse utopie
> d'un moment: c'est, d'époque en époque, et d'étape en
> étape, l'inlassable poursuite de l'Idéal juridique à travers les
> temps."[32]

---

31. J. B. Scott, "The Evolution of a Permanent International Judiciary", 6
AJIL (1912), 316, 319.
32. A. G. De Lapradelle and N. Politis, "La Deuxième Conférence de La Paix
— Origine. Convocation. Organisation", 16 *RGDIP* (1909), 385, 388.

Others — including British commentators — were more scepti-cal[33]. But whatever one's attitude to the 1907 agenda, key aspects of the agenda remain, and the issues are still debated.

3. The Issues of 1907 Seen in 2007

At the start of the twenty-first century we still seek to find ways to address the pros and cons of permanent versus *ad hoc* courts and tribunals, to define the characteristics of permanent courts and to assess the merits of the diversity of approaches in international arbi-tration and adjudication.

3.1. Permanence — an inherently ambiguous concept

One hundred years after the Second Hague Conference, there are so many international tribunals and adjudicatory bodies of all kinds that authors propose a separate branch of the discipline, dealing with the "international judiciary"[34]. The proliferation — a current and somewhat over-used term — of courts and tribunals prompts reflec-tion on some old terminological problems, and perhaps even a re-thinking of categories such as "permanent" and *"ad hoc"*.

The list of international adjudicatory bodies which came into exis-tence since 1899 reveals the difficulty of classification. For example, is it appropriate to consider the International Criminal Tribunal for the Former Yugoslavia an *ad hoc* institution — as is commonly done — when it is effectively a permanent court with full-time judges, more than 1,100 staff members[35], a specific competence *ratione materiae* but (so far) indefinite competence *ratione temporis*? It is true that an "exit strategy" is being discussed and that the intention is to close down the ICTY sooner rather than later. But it has been in operation for well over a decade: the Permanent Court of Inter-national Justice (on any view a "permanent" court) operated in substance for less than two decades. In human affairs nothing is per-

---

33. See e.g. T. E. Holland, "The Hague Conference of 1907", 24 *LQR* (1908), 76; see also the scoffing remarks of two French authors: L. Le Fur, "La paix perpétuelle et l'arbitrage international", 16 *RGDIP* (1909), 437; A. Pillet, *La cause de la paix et les deux conférences de La Haye*, Paris, J. Dumoulin, 1908.

34. C. Romano, "The Proliferation of International Judicial Bodies: The Pieces of the Puzzle", (1999) 31 *NYUJILP* 709, 749.

35. See "ICTY at a Glance: General Information", <http://www.un.org/icty/glance-e/index.htm> (accessed 17 September 2007).

manent, not even a permanent court. Compare also the Iran-United States Claims Tribunal, an institution often referred to as an *"ad hoc"* court despite its 27-year history, exclusive jurisdiction, standing composition and thousands of claims decided[36]. Although the Tribunal is limited in its jurisdiction both *ratione materiae* and *ratione temporis*, one cannot necessarily conclude that it is an *ad hoc* tribunal.

One reason for this confusion might lie in the interaction between States and individuals as parties to international proceedings. While the Iran-United States Claims Tribunal is an *ad hoc* institution from the point of view of potential litigation between the two States (because its establishment was the result of a classically arbitral "post-crisis" settlement of a dispute), from the point of view of individual claimants the Tribunal was a permanent one in the sense that *(a)* they had no choice as to the judges, *(b)* they had no choice as to the extent of the court's jurisdiction, and *(c)* the court pre-existed individual claims (though many had already been presented elsewhere). On the other hand, while all individual claims "had to be filed with the Tribunal by 19 January 1982, and their number is therefore finite"[37], no time limit was set with regards to "disputes between the two Governments concerning the interpretation of the Algiers Declarations" — and, it has to be said, there seems to be no end in the Tribunal's handling of these disputes, a fact by no means exclusively the fault of the Tribunal[38].

These two examples show that a categorical either/or approach to the distinction between permanent and *ad hoc* tribunals may be misleading. Setting aside the issue of international criminal courts — which may require different treatment taking into account their special purpose — we may think of permanency in international civil jurisdiction as a set of characteristics, not all of which are present at all times in all bodies. The two extremes of the spectrum are, on one hand, the project of a permanent international court of justice with

---

36. E. A. Posner and J. C. Yoo, "A Theory of International Adjudication", (2004) *Boalt Working Papers in Public Law*, Paper 36, <http://repositories. cdlib.org/boaltwp/36> (accessed 17 September 2007). According to the authors, despite its long life and the number of cases decided by it, the tribunal is an *ad hoc* system of arbitration, whose mandate is clearly delimited and whose judges were chosen with the classic scheme of one third by each party and a third neutral: "In sum, the Tribunal is highly dependent" (*ibid.*, p. 30).

37. *Ibid.*

38. *Ibid.*

universal compulsory jurisdiction over all legal disputes among States and other international legal persons; on the other hand, the *ex post facto ad hoc* arbitration tribunal instituted by a bilateral arbitral convention between the two parties signed after a dispute has arose, with its composition settled only after the event.

Writing in 1912, Hans Wehberg described the former ideal. He argued that:

> "The following marks [should be] characteristic of an international court of justice: (1) No diplomats, but judges by profession; (2) The exclusion of national judges; (3) A truly permanent court of justice; (4) The exclusion of members appointed by the contending parties and above all by the states; (5) A direct right of action; (6) The creation of a right of appeal." [39]

This project was rejected in 1907, in 1922 and again in 1945, and one can only imagine the circumstances in which it would even now be accepted. Subject to that obvious point, all existing international judicial tribunals lie somewhere between the two extremes.

3.2. Characteristics of permanent courts

Approaches to the distinction between *ad hoc* and permanent tribunals will vary according to one's preference either for "dependent" or "independent" jurisdictions [40]. On one view the dominant question is one of simple efficiency and the advantage lies with the *ad hoc* tribunals, since they will be more responsive to the parties. Thus Posner and Yoo advocate the most dependent tribunals:

> "[T]ribunals are simple problem-solving devices. They do not transform the interests of states; nor do they cause states to ignore their own interest for the sake of a transnational ideal. [I]ndependent tribunals pose a danger to international cooperation because independent tribunals can render decisions that violate the interests of state parties." [41]

On this view, which for example underlies some criticisms of the

---

39. Wehberg, *supra* footnote 27, p. 156.
40. The terminology employed by Posner and Yoo, *supra* footnote 36, pp. 5-6.
41. *Ibid.*

WTO Appellate Body, Wehberg's value of the "development of international law" is synonymous with unaccountable decision-making going beyond the original mandate of the States parties. On another and more refined view, it is the *ad hoc* tribunals — barely existent even at the time they function — which are unaccountable. In any event, discussion of some of characteristics of permanent or *ad hoc* tribunals helps to identify the issues at stake.

(a) *Composition*

According to Wehberg, "the chief element of a judicial system is that the court of justice shall be composed of jurists and not of diplomats"[42]. The more professionalized the judges, the more the court is likely to be permanent in character[43]. Underlying this assumption is the view that:

> "Since the international court has for its object not only the settlement of international disputes, but also the development of international law, it is necessarily the agent of the family of nations, and not merely the agent of the parties who make use of it in a particular case."[44]

A permanent court has effectively the same composition from case to case. Mere lists of available arbitrators who "do not even know one another"[45], including procedurally pre-defined systems such as the WTO panels, do not give rise to permanent adjudication but to ad hoc jurisdiction.

(b) *Date of establishment*

In general terms, a court formed *ex post facto* will most probably be an *ad litem* court — or even, as recently some of the criminal tribunals, an *ad hominem* one[46]. This is the most obvious identifier of

---

42. Wehberg, *supra* footnote 27, p. 53.
43. J. H. Ralston, "Some Suggestions as to the Permanent Court of Arbitration", 1 *AJIL* (1907), 321, 322-324.
44. *Ibid.*, p. 61.
45. See Martens, *supra* footnote 3.
46. Or, rather, *ad crimen*: the mixed domestic-international Special Tribunal for Lebanon was established solely "to prosecute persons responsible for the attack of 14 February 2005 resulting in the death of former Lebanese Prime Minister Rafiq Hariri and in the death or injury of other persons" (Art. 1, Agreement between the United Nations and the Lebanese Republic on the establishment of a Special Tribunal for Lebanon, annexed to UNSCR 1757/2007 of 30 May 2007).

an *ad hoc* jurisdiction. As we have seen, the Iran-United States Claims Tribunal was established after the events on which it was called to adjudicate, but before many of the claims were formulated by the individual parties involved. Similar consideration might lead to the qualification of the UN Compensation Commission established in 1991 as a permanent institution rather than an *ad hoc* one.

On the other hand, the fact of being established in advance is usually a good indicator that the court is permanent in character.

(c) *Intended duration*

As we saw earlier, to be permanent a court does not need to "last indefinitely without change"[47]. It is true that a court which is "designed to continue or last indefinitely" will be a permanent one. But the actual number of years a court remains in operation is immaterial to its classification. What does count is how long a court was designed to last for, not how long it survived in practice.

(d) *Determinate rules of procedure*

Usually, permanent courts have a predetermined set of rules of procedure, which States have to follow to act in front of them. *Ad hoc* tribunals may not, although in some cases their constituent instrument may contain rather detailed procedures on particular points. Normally procedural rules are incorporated by reference, sometimes after the event and not always appropriately — as for example with the UNCITRAL Rules of 1976 which were drafted with contractual, commercial disputes in mind but have been applied to a wide range of non-commercial cases.

(e) *Application of precedent*

The more a court makes use of its own precedents to rule, the more it is said to be permanent. However, this may simply be the obvious result of the fact that a permanent court will hear multiple hearings and have a case law that *ad hoc* jurisdictions by definition lack[48].

---

47. "Permanent", *Oxford English Dictionary*, 2nd ed., 1989.
48. Wehberg, *supra* footnote 27, p. 67.

(f) *Compulsory jurisdiction*

The issue of compulsory jurisdiction is often associated to the concept of a permanent court, because the latter was often considered to entail the former[49]. However, compulsory jurisdiction is not an essential feature of a permanent court — indeed that may be one of the lessons learnt, or linkages broken, by the 1907 Conference[50]. Permanent courts exist with a mix of compulsory and voluntary jurisdiction (such as the PCIJ and now the ICJ).

(g) *Scope of jurisdiction*

That a court is limited in its jurisdiction *ratione materiae* is not an indication of the *ad hoc* or permanent status of the court, unless the competence is so restricted as to equal an *ad litem* jurisdiction. The great majority of the almost 30 regional and universal permanent courts which came into existence since 1899 have had a limited jurisdiction *ratione materiae*.

Similar considerations apply to jurisdiction *ratione personae* and *ratione temporis*. As for the latter, the fact that a court is only called to adjudicate facts occurred during a certain span of time does not *per se* qualify the court as *ad hoc*, albeit it may be a relevant factor (in conjunction with establishment *ex post facto* and/or for a defined and predetermined set of disputes).

3.3. *A select list of tribunals*

Bearing in mind the difficulties inherent in this classification, we may tentatively list and classify a selection of international tribunals and dispute settlement bodies which became operational since 1899. The list catalogues also the most relevant regional institutions, but not criminal courts. Bodies are included in chronological order of establishment[51].

---

49. See e.g. H. Lammasch, "Compulsory Arbitration at the Second Hague Conference", 4 *AJIL* (1910), 83; Le Fur, *supra* footnote 33.

50. Wehberg recognized this, noting also that the wide practice of voluntary arbitration by States rendered the issues of compulsory jurisdiction and of supra-national enforcement of decisions less crucial: *supra* footnote 27, p. 106.

51. All dates of establishment are taken from C. Romano, "The International Judiciary in Context", synoptic chart published by the Project on International Courts and Tribunals, 2004, available at <http://www.pict-pcti.org/publications/synoptic_chart.html> (accessed 17 September 2007).

Name	Type	Estab-lished	Termi-nated	Notes
Permanent Court of Arbitration	*Ad hoc (each individual tribunal)*	1899		
Central American Court of Justice	Permanent	1908	1918	*"Cortes de Justicia Centro-americana"*; see below for *"Corte Centroamericana de Justicia"*
Upper Silesia Arbitral Tribunal	*Ad hoc*	1922	1937	
Permanent Court of International Justice	Permanent	1922	1946	
Bank for International Settlements Arbitral Tribunal	Permanent	1930	2003	Judges appointed in 2001 pursuant to Article XV of the agreement of The Hague of 20 January 1930[52] and acting within the framework of the Permanent Court of Arbitration. Final award rendered 19 September 2003[53].
International Court of Justice	Permanent	1946		
Court of Justice of the European Communities	Permanent	1952		
European Court of Human Rights	Permanent	1959		
International Centre for the Settlement of Investment Disputes	*Ad hoc (each individual tribunal)*	1966		
East African Community Court of Appeal	Permanent	1967	1977	
East African Community Common Market Tribunal	Permanent	1967	1977	
Benelux Economic Union Court of Justice	Permanent	1974		
Economic Community of West African States Tribunal	Permanent	1975	1991	
Inter-American Court of Human Rights	Permanent	1979		
Iran-United States Claims Tribunal	Permanent	1980		
Court of Justice of the Andean Community	Permanent	1984		
Court of First Instance of the European Communities	Permanent	1988		
United Nations Compensation Commission	*Ad hoc*	1991		
Economic Court of the Commonwealth of Independent States	Permanent	1993		Operational and hears cases since 1994[54]
Court of Justice of the European Free Trade Agreement	Permanent	1994		Operational and hears cases since 1994[55]
Central American Court of Justice	Permanent	1994		*"Corte Centroamericana de Justicia"* — Operational and hears cases since 1994[56]
NAFTA Dispute Settlement Panels	*Ad hoc*	1994		
World Intellectual Property Organization Arbitration and Mediation Centre	*Ad hoc*	1994		
WTO Dispute Settlement Body:		1995		
— *Panels*	*Ad hoc*			
— *Appellate Body*	Permanent			

Name	Type	Estab-lished	Termi-nated	Notes
International Tribunal for the Law of the Sea	Permanent	1996		
Court of Justice of the West African Economic and Monetary Union	Permanent	1996		
Court of Justice of the Organization for the Harmonization of African Business Law	Permanent	1995		Operational since 1996; heard more than 200 cases so far [57]
Court of Justice of the Common Market for Eastern and Southern Africa	Permanent	1998		Operational since 1998; heard more than 4 cases so far [58]
African Court on Human and Peoples' Rights	Permanent	1998		Operational since 2007 — no cases so far [59]
Court of Justice of the Central African Economic and Monetary Community	Permanent	1999		Operational since 2000 — more than 27 decisions so far [60]
Eritrea-Ethiopia Boundary Commission	*Ad hoc*	2000	2007	On 30 November 2007 the Commission reported that its mandate can be regarded as fulfilled
Eritrea-Ethiopia Claims Commission	*Ad hoc*	2000		
Southern Africa Development Community Tribunal	Permanent	2000		Operational since 2005 [61]
Court of Justice of the Economic Community of West African States	Permanent	2001		Operational since 2002 — heard 10 cases so far [62]
Court of Justice of the East African Community	Permanent	2001		Operational since 2001 — first judgment 2007 [63]
Caribbean Court of Justice	Permanent	2003		Operational April 2005 — first judgment October 2005 [64]
Total				**37 (of which 30 are still functioning)**
— permanent				**27 (of which 22 are still functioning)**
— *ad hoc*				**10 (of which 8 are still functioning)**

52. Agreement regarding the Complete and Final Settlement of the Question of Reparations from Germany, and Annexes I-XII, The Hague, 20 January 1930, entered into force on 17 May 1930, 104 *LNTS* 243, also available at <http://www.pca-cpa.org/upload/files/hague1930.pdf> (accessed 17 September 2007).

53. According to the agreement of 1930, which established the tribunal, the judges were to be appointed for a fixed term of five years, and subsequently reappointed, making the arbitral tribunal semi permanent. In practice, the tribunal was probably an *ad hoc* institution, albeit the three private parties which submitted claims had no choice over the composition of the court. See <http://www.pca-cpa.org/showpage.asp?pag_id=1157> (accessed 17 September 2007).

54. See G. M. Danilenko, "The Economic Court of The Commonwealth of Independent States", (1999) 31 *NYUJILP* 893.

55. See <http://www.eftacourt.lu/> (accessed 17 September 2007).

56. See <http://www.ccj.org.ni/> (accessed 17 September 2007).

57. See <http://www.aict-ctia.org/> (accessed 17 September 2007).

58. See <http://www.worldlii.org/int/other/PICTRes/2004/14.html> (accessed 17 September 2007).

59. See <http://www.aict-ctia.org/courts_conti/achpr/achpr_news.html> (accessed 17 September 2007).

60. See <http://www.aict-ctia.org/> (accessed 17 September 2007).

61. *Ibid.*

62. *Ibid.*

63. *Ibid.*

64. See <http://www.caribbeancourtofjustice.org/> (accessed 17 September 2007).

The table calls for some observations.

First of all, total numbers are not very revealing, given that the bulk of international arbitration occurring within the various *ad hoc* institutions (and outside them) is hardly quantifiable, and certainly higher than the proportion of one *ad hoc* institution to almost three permanent ones. However, the fact of 22 permanent courts and tribunals for the settlement of civil international disputes currently functioning is remarkable[65].

Secondly, the phenomenon of "regionalization" of international law is mirrored in the number of courts which exercise within regional international organizations functions analogous to the European Court of Justice and the European Court of Human Rights. In this respect, the model of professionalized, independent adjudicatory bodies seems to be alive and well.

Thirdly, settlement of international disputes of a purely economic character between States and private individuals or organizations, such as investment disputes, are for the most part resolved through *ad hoc* institutions. This includes, in the case of ICSID, *ad hoc* annulment — something which might be thought a contradiction in terms but which has been defended as "the least worst" system, given institutional and other constraints[66].

3.4. Incidence of arbitration/judicial settlement

From the point of view of the practice of States, judicial settlement is a relatively new phenomenon, with the establishment of most permanent courts after 1945. By contrast arbitration has been resorted to for millennia[67]. Stuyt's *Survey of International Arbitration*[68],

---

65. See, e.g., J. C. Charney, "The Impact on the International Legal System of the Growth of International Courts and Tribunals", 31 *NYUJILP* (1999), 697, 698:

> "Recent developments are changing the international environment as a result of the establishment of more permanent tribunals and, perhaps, the use of fewer *ad hoc* tribunals. In very recent years, the rate of change from *ad hoc* to permanent tribunals appears to be increasing dramatically."

66. See E. Gaillard and Y. Banifatemi (eds.), *Annulment of ICSID Awards*, Huntington, NY, Juris Publishing, 2004; C. Schreuer, "ICSID Annulment Revisited", 30 *LIEI* (2003), 103.

67. See S. Ager, *Interstate Arbitrations in the Greek World 337-90 BC*, Berkeley, London, University of California Press, 1996, who lists 171 cases.

68. A. M. Stuyt, *Survey of International Arbitrations: 1794-1989*, 3rd updated edition, Dordrecht, Boston, London, M. Nijhoff, 1990.

which surveys the period from the Jay Treaty of 1794 to 1989, shows that in the nineteenth century arbitration was already intensively practised. The following table makes the point [69].

	Number of arbitral agreements of treaties conventions, signed	*... of these disputes, those eventually settled by conventions, agreements, protocols or procès-verbaux*	*... those not settled, or settled through other means, or about which no information is available*	*... those which gave rise to one or more known arbitral awards*	*Total number of arbitral claims decided (estimate)*
1794 (Jay Treaty-1899 (until First Hague Conference)					
Inter-State **227**	34	32	**161**	*6,117*
Between States and other entities 1			1	
1899-1922 (after First Hague Conference until establishment of PCIJ)					
Inter-State **125**	6	22	**97**	*266 (many more are unaccounted for)*
Between States and other entities 6			6	
1923-1989					
Inter-State **195**	1	12	182	*309 (many are unaccounted for, including all Iran-US claim tribunal awards)*
Between States and other entities 84	3	9	72	*76*

69. All data elaborated from the entries provided in Stuyt, *supra* footnote 68. It should be noted that the three total numbers of interstate claims decided are not comparable one with the other. The first very high number can be explained because the Jay Treaty of 1794 alone gave rise to 537 awards; in 1871-1876 a Mexico-United States mutual claims commission decided 2,015 awards; in 1880-1884 a France-United States mutual claims commission decided 745 cases, and so on. However, it is not clear when each claim was settled through a separate award (as under the Jay Treaty) or if there were one or more cumulative awards (as it may be the case in the Mexico-United States and France-United States arbitrations mentioned above). Furthermore, while the author provides detailed numbers of claims for most pre-1899 awards, the same detailed information is not available for the following periods, about which we are only informed when there were multiple awards rather than a single one. Thus, the more recent figures are most probably much higher, especially considering the thousands of Iran-United States claims decided.

In sum, the difference in the number of arbitral treaties signed between the nineteenth and the twentieth centuries is not particularly significant, especially considering the increase in inter-State co-operation after 1899. States often resorted to arbitration, and have increasingly done so, but arbitration was not born with the Permanent Court of Arbitration, albeit the first 20 years of the twentieth century saw a miniboom in arbitral agreements.

3.5. Are ad hoc institutions preferable?

The question is often posed as to which method should in principle be preferred, if a judicial settlement by a permanent court or an arbitration by an *ad hoc* institution. In itself, the question is indeterminate, because the practice of states adapts to reality and employs different methods for different purposes.

An international symposium in 1972 tried to address this problem. In his report, Bindschedler identified some advantages and disadvantages of *ad hoc* institutions[70]. Among other advantages, he mentioned:

— the "autonomy of the parties", i.e. "the possibility of taking their wishes and interests into account"[71]. This in turn would render compliance more likely;
— "flexibility", i.e. the possibility of selecting "the most appropriate body" (or number of bodies) and "exclude less suitable ones", something which "cannot be done in the case of permanent courts"[72];
— "the freedom to choose the appropriate persons" as adjudicators, not only for obvious political reasons, but also to include "experts and specialists in particular fields of law"[73].

---

70. R. L. Bindschedler, "Report" on "Subject III — To Which Extent and for Which Questions Is It Advisable to Provide for the Settlement of International Legal Disputes by Other Organs than Permanent Courts?", in Max Planck Institute for Comparative Public Law and International Law (eds.), *Judicial Settlement of International Disputes: International Court of Justice, Other Courts and Tribunals, Arbitration and Conciliation; An International Symposium*, Berlin, Heidelberg, New York, Springer, 1974, pp. 133-146.
71. *Ibid.*, p. 135.
72. *Ibid.*, p. 136.
73. *Ibid.*, p. 136. See also A. Boyle, "The Proliferation of International Jurisdictions and Its Implications for the Court", in D. W. Bowett *et al.*, *The International Court of Justice: Process, Practice and Procedure*, London, British Institute of International and Comparative Law, 1997, p. 124; Charney, *supra* footnote 65, p. 698.

— "simple and quicker" proceedings, because "the parties are fully at liberty to agree on details of the procedure" and even to "keep the proceedings secret" so as to avoid embarrassment [74].
— the fact that "non-judicial bodies are better suited to cases to be decided *ex aequo et bono*" [75], especially given the liberty of choice of the arbitrators;
— the circumstance that "no indeterminate commitment has to be undertaken", because "states are not obliged to commit themselves vis-à-vis a large number of partners without knowing what disputes may eventually arise or what matters may be at issue in them. The undertaking remains a concrete one, and its effects are foreseeable" [76];
— the fact that decisions can also be "non-binding", i.e. "compromises" [77];
— the smaller "precedent effect", "because the procedure is less spectacular. Consequently, the resolution of the conflict leaves greater room for manœuvre in the future" [78].

Furthermore, according to the author, "a general argument in favour of non-judicial bodies is the preponderance of concrete facts and norms in international law over typical, general, abstract ones" [79].

However, *ad hoc* institution suffer also from some drawbacks. First and foremost, they are not compulsory:

> "Non-judicial bodies are more dependent than courts on the consent and benevolency of the opposing party. They are therefore unlikely to serve as the basis for a watertight system for the settlement of disputes." [80]

---

74. Bindschedler, *supra* footnote 70, p. 136. See also Boyle, *supra* footnote 73, 124; I. Brownlie, "The Peaceful Settlement of International Disputes in Practice — The *Blaine Sloan Lecture*", (1995) 7 *Pace ILR* 257, 276; G. Hafner, "Should one fear the proliferation of mechanisms for the peaceful settlement of disputes?", in L. Caflisch (ed.), *Règlement pacifique des différends entre Etats: perspectives universelle et européenne; The Peaceful Settlement of Disputes between States: Universal and European Perspectives*, The Hague, London, Kluwer Law International, 1998, pp. 25-41, 32.
75. Bindschedler, *supra* footnote 70, p. 137.
76. *Ibid.*, p. 138.
77. *Ibid.*
78. *Ibid.*, p. 139.
79. *Ibid.*, p. 140.
80. *Ibid.*

Also, as Brownlie has pointed out, *ad hoc* arbitration can be quite expensive for small States[81].

Finally, Bindschedler underlines that the "non-uniformity of the decisions reached" might constitute a problem:

> "The large numbers of deciding bodies may result in a fragmentation of international law and in differences in its interpretation and application. . . . The fact that such bodies do not set very firm precedents, and that their authority may be weaker, diminishes their ability to contribute to the development of international law."[82]

In his view this problem was more theoretical than practical, because there are important precedents set by non-permanent, non-judicial courts while the ICJ at times is inconsistent[83].

Despite this, "in theory, and from the purely legal standpoint, permanent courts are preferable", because

> "[t]hey ensure:
>
> — continuity and uniformity of case law;
> — greater legal certainty;
> — the continued development of international law;
> — independence of judges;
> — immediate availability;
> — little or no opportunity to sabotage the proceedings;
> — final and binding settlement of the dispute"[84].

Nonetheless:

> "[P]ermanent courts require a degree of homogeneity among nations which is either non-existent or limited in scope, confined to particular areas or to particular spheres of interest. Accordingly, the political foundations for a comprehensive system of permanent adjudication are lacking; as always, considerations of sovereignty and nationalism are the dominant poli-

---

81. Brownlie, *supra* footnote 74, p. 276.
82. Bindschedler, *supra* footnote 70, p. 140. See also T. Buergenthal, "Proliferation of International Courts and Tribunals: Is It Good or Bad?", 14 *LJIL* (2001), 267, 272; G. Guillaume, "Editorial Comments on the Proliferation of International Courts — Advantages and Risks of Proliferation: A Blueprint for Action", 2 *JICJ* (2004), 300.
83. Bindschedler, *supra* footnote 70, p. 141.
84. *Ibid.*, p. 142.

tical factors. To this must be added the fact that the dynamics of life, the lack of contentment of certain countries and the unsolved problem of 'peaceful change', all have repercussions on the settlement of conflicts. On the one hand, States want new law, or at least the adaptation of the old law to new situations; they demand that courts should not operate in too formalistic or too legalistic a fashion. On the other hand, the function of the courts is a predominantly conservative and static one. Decisions creating new law are only possible within narrow limits in the settlement of international disputes by courts, if the latter are to continue to enjoy the confidence of States at all. This is the dilemma in which the permanent courts find themselves. On the one hand, they ought to abide by existing legislation if they are not to lose the confidence of parties and if the outcome of the proceedings is not to become wholly unpredictable; but on the other hand they are expected to provide solutions appropriate to new requirements. The case law of the International Court of Justice demonstrates this clearly. One of its characteristics is vacillation between strict conservatism and unexpected innovation. This is no doubt one of the principal reasons why governments are reluctant to submit disputes to it." [85]

4. Conclusions

In 1899 and 1907, no permanent world political organization such as the United Nations or the League or Nations was in place. Indeed, in the hearts and minds of international public opinion, international lawyers and other "Victorian gentlemen" [86], the Hague Peace Conferences were meant to be the first meeting of such a political organization devoted to peace, as well as the first world conference of States. The term "Parliament of man" finds its origins in these conferences [87].

No doubt the expectations which preceded the conference were

---

85. Bindschedler, *supra* footnote 70, p. 143.
86. Cf. M. Koskenniemi, "Lauterpacht: The Victorian Tradition in International Law", 8 *EJIL* (1997), 215.
87. See A. Eyffinger, *The 1899 Peace Conference: "The Parliament of Man, The Federation of the World"*, The Hague, Kluwer Law International, 1999, and *The 1907 Hague Peace Conference: "The Conscience of the Civilized World"*, The Hague, Judi Cap, 2007. Cf. Paul Kennedy, *The Parliament of Man: the United Nations and the Quest for World Government*, Penguin, 2005.

wholly misplaced[88]. But it remains true that the Second Hague Conference paved the way for the creation of what would in 1922 become the PCIJ, and later the ICJ. The ideas of compulsory arbitration, and of judicial settlement of disputes, slowly entered the language and the practice of international law. The institutionalized international courts and tribunals have contributed considerably to the consolidation and development of international law. One hundred years later, pluriformity is the main feature of the international settlement of disputes. This means that more disputes are settled by means of international law[89]. The increasing plurality of actors, including non-State entities, poses an additional challenge. The existence of such a variety of different adjudicatory bodies and plurality of actors should prompt reflection on the value of independence for the development of international law.

---

88. De Lapradelle and Politis, *supra* footnote 32; Pillet, *supra* footnote 33.

89. Brownlie, *supra* footnote 74, p. 276; Buergenthal, *supra* footnote 82, p. 271; Charney, *supra* footnote 65, p. 704; Hafner, *supra* footnote 74, p. 41; Romano, *supra* footnote 34, p. 750. See also F. Orrego Vicuna and M. C. W. Pinto, "Peaceful Settlement of Disputes: Prospects for the 21st Century", in F. Kalshoven (ed.), *The Centennial of the First International Peace Conference*, The Hague, Kluwer Law International, 2000, p. 261.

3. ÉVOLUTIONS DANS LE RÈGLEMENT PACIFIQUE DES DIFFÉRENDS ÉCONOMIQUES DEPUIS LA CONVENTION DRAGO-PORTER

G. ABI-SAAB[1]

I. Introduction

Le sujet que l'Académie m'a demandé de traiter dans ce colloque célébrant le centenaire de la Deuxième Conférence de la Paix de 1907 porte sur les «Evolutions dans le règlement pacifique des différends économiques depuis la convention Drago-Porter»; en d'autres termes, il s'agit de retracer un siècle d'évolution. Projet ambitieux, puisqu'il recouvre plusieurs périodes fortement contrastées d'un siècle non seulement entrecoupé par les deux guerres mondiales, mais traversé aussi par plusieurs crises profondes ou points de rupture, telles la révolution bolchévique de 1917 et la grande crise économique *(the Great Depression)* de 1929, sans oublier l'avènement et l'évanouissement de la guerre froide.

Projet ambitieux également car il porte sur une matière qui se branche sur trois flux économiques distincts, à savoir: *a)* des flux de commerce et d'échange de biens et de services; *b)* des flux de capitaux sous forme d'investissements; et *c)* des flux financiers et monétaires pour les besoins de paiements (ou de la spéculation). Ces flux n'ont pas toujours, et même pas fréquemment, suivi le même cheminement quant au règlement des différends qu'ils auraient pu susciter.

Par ailleurs, la forme et l'évolution des mécanismes et des procédures de règlement des différends auxquels ces flux ont donné lieu ne peuvent se comprendre sans remonter, pour chacune de ces catégories, en amont vers le droit applicable et même, au-delà, vers la pensée et les politiques économiques dominantes, qui ont suscité l'évolution de ce droit. Ce qui revient à dire que pour chaque période ou chaque tournant je dois utiliser une grille d'analyse à neuf

---

1. Professeur honoraire, Institut universitaire de hautes études internationales (IUHEI), Genève; membre de l'Organe d'appel de l'Organisation mondiale du commerce (OMC). Je tiens à remercier, pour son aide précieuse à ma recherche, M. Fouad Zarbiev, assistant à l'IUHEI.

variables; chacun de ces trois flux devant être examiné à trois niveaux d'analyse: celui des idées et des politiques économiques dominantes; celui de leur traduction dans le droit applicable, et enfin celui du recours aux mécanismes et procédures de règlement des différends qui appliqueraient ce droit.

Vaste programme, qui dépasse de loin les dimensions de cette présentation. Je me bornerai donc à en brosser un tableau schématique, en forme de carte topographique sur l'échelle temps.

II. La Deuxième Conférence de la Paix de 1907

La Deuxième Conférence de la Paix de 1907 comporte deux ajouts essentiels par rapport à la première, ajouts particulièrement pertinents pour notre sujet. Le premier ajout réside dans la poussée vers l'universalisme, ou sa «vocation universaliste», dans le sens d'une participation plus large et plus représentative de la communauté internationale des Etats de l'époque. Rappelons que la Première Conférence avait réuni 26 pays, dont 19 européens (y compris la Bulgarie qui n'était pas encore indépendante!); 2 américains, les Etats-Unis d'Amérique et le Mexique; et 5 asiatiques: la Turquie (l'Empire ottoman), la Chine, le Japon, la Perse et le Siam.

En comparaison, la Deuxième Conférence a réuni 44 pays, une participation en forte augmentation de 18 Etats, soit deux tiers de plus que la Première Conférence. S'y trouvent les mêmes 19 Etats européens, devenus 20 (la Norvège s'étant séparée de la Suède), les mêmes 5 Etats asiatiques; mais l'élargissement vient de l'hémisphère occidental, reflet sans doute du rôle pivot joué par les Etats-Unis dans la convocation de la Deuxième Conférence, car, à côté des Etats-Unis et du Mexique, viennent s'ajouter 17 nouveaux participants: Haïti et 16 républiques d'Amérique latine; l'Amérique latine, constituant à cette époque le tiers-monde avant la lettre; ce qui est un fait important au regard de notre sujet.

Le second ajout, ou la seconde contribution substantielle pour notre sujet de la Conférence est la convention n° 2 (dite Drago-Porter) qu'elle a adoptée, et dont le titre officiel est «Convention concernant la limitation de l'emploi de la force pour le recouvrement des dettes contractuelles» («réclamées au Gouvernement d'un pays par le Gouvernement d'un autre pays comme dues à ses nationaux», selon l'article 1).

La grande signification de cette convention pour le droit international en général est qu'elle constituait un premier pas, bien timide il est vrai, d'un tournant crucial dans l'évolution de ce droit, remontant de l'abysse de la «théorie de l'indifférence». Cette théorie marquait l'apogée de l'école positiviste volontariste, qui prédominait au XIXe siècle, surtout en Allemagne, et qui considérait que le droit international est «indifférent» à la question de recours à la guerre, en l'absence d'une règle limitant la liberté des Etats en la matière qu'ils auraient acceptée expressément ou implicitement. Ce qui revient à dire que le recours à la guerre était exclu du domaine de la réglementation juridique, et qu'il n'y avait pas de *jus ad bellum* réglementé, ou plutôt qu'il était sans limite.

Advient alors la convention Drago-Porter pour introduire une petite entrave ou limite à cette liberté débridée; premier pas dans un processus qui trouvera son aboutissement dans l'article 2, paragraphe 4, de la Charte des Nations Unies.

En ce qui concerne plus particulièrement les conflits économiques, la convention Drago-Porter était une conséquence directe, ou plutôt une réaction à l'intervention armée de la Grande-Bretagne, de l'Italie et de l'Allemagne en 1902-1903, par le bombardement des ports vénézuéliens et leur blocus maritime, pour cause de cessation de paiement des dettes; et cela jusqu'à ce que le Gouvernement du Venezuela accepte de régler le contentieux en le soumettant à des commissions arbitrales mixtes.

C'est au cours de cette crise, que Luis Drago, ministre des Affaires étrangères de l'Argentine, adresse une lettre au secrétaire d'Etat américain, protestant contre cette intervention, en invoquant la «doctrine Monroe», tout en formulant la proposition qui est devenue la «doctrine Drago», à savoir l'impermissibilité de recouvrement des dettes contractuelles par la force.

Cependant, la convention Drago-Porter diverge de la doctrine Drago sur certains points essentiels. Il est vrai que la convention suit la doctrine Drago en interdisant le recours à la force, et non pas seulement à la guerre (car les interventions musclées pour le recouvrement des dettes, comme les prétendues «interventions humanitaires», étaient considérées comme des «mesures en deçà de la guerre», *«measures short of war»*). Mais chez Drago, cette interdiction était absolue, alors que dans la convention elle était conditionnée à l'acceptation par l'Etat débiteur de recourir à l'arbitrage et de ne pas l'entraver. En revanche, selon Calvo, le recours à l'arbitrage ne se justifiait qu'en cas de déni de justice, et par conséquent était limité à ce cas. Ce qui exigeait au préalable l'épuisement des recours internes; par respect de la souveraineté de l'Etat, puisqu'on lui accorde la possibilité de remédier aux éventuels manquements avant de passer au niveau international; condition ou limite qui ne figurait pas dans la convention. Ce qui explique les réserves formulées par Drago lui-même à propos de cette convention dont on s'obstine à lui attribuer la paternité.

III. *Première période: le XIXe siècle finissant jusqu'à la première guerre mondiale*

Situer la convention Drago-Porter dans son temps nous amène à la première période à examiner.

Le grand historien allemand du droit international, Wilhelm Grewe, dans son maître livre *The Epochs of International Law*[2], dit que le nadir de l'arbitrage international, c'est-à-dire le point le plus bas de son histoire, était la période qui a suivi la paix de Westphalie[3]. Pourquoi? Parce que les princes, ayant réussi à asseoir leur souveraineté, c'est-à-dire le droit d'avoir le dernier mot, comme clef de répartition du pouvoir dans le nouveau système émergeant du droit international, ne voulaient pas donner de la main gauche ce qu'ils avaient chèrement acquis de la droite. Ils étaient donc réfractaires à se soumettre à la décision d'un tiers, même si cela devait être un juge, qui trancherait leur différend en application du droit international auquel ils devaient soumission. Cette situation se prolonge jusqu'au dernier quart du XIXe siècle.

Grewe écrit aussi[4] que l'arbitrage a connu trois périodes florissantes: la première entre les cités Etats de la Grèce antique; la seconde au bas Moyen Age; et la troisième à la fin du XIXe et au début du XXe siècle, qui est la période qui nous intéresse ici. La première période est trop lointaine. Mais qu'y a-t-il de commun entre les deux dernières? En fait, les deux périodes se situent au tournant de deux vagues ou poussées vers la «mondialisation». La première coïncide avec la Renaissance, le *Quatro Cento*, l'âge des découvertes, la révolution copernicienne; en d'autres termes, l'explosion de la vision du monde étriquée, autocentrée et statique du Moyen

---

2. Traduction anglaise par Michael Byers, Gruyter, Berlin, New York, 2000.
3. *Ibid.*, p. 363.
4. *Ibid.*, p. 104.

Age, et l'ouverture vers des horizons presque illimités et des activités économiques qui s'ensuivent et fleurissent notamment sur les rives méditerranéennes de l'Europe, à Venise et ailleurs, où domine une frénésie de commerce et d'échanges, et où on invente des instruments juridiques pour les accompagner, tels les effets de commerce et l'institution bancaire.

Cependant, cette frénésie se tasse bientôt et son élan se casse et se transforme en une politique d'accaparement engendrant des luttes et des tentations de division du monde entre les puissants. Cela conduit à la première vague de colonialisme au plan politique, et au mercantilisme au plan économique. Il est à noter que parallèlement, pendant cette même période, alors que les pères fondateurs du droit international de l'école espagnole, tels Vitoria et Suárez, parlaient d'un droit des gens naturel et universel, s'appliquant à tout le genre humain, y compris aux Amérindiens, ils postulaient l'existence, au sein même de ce droit, d'un *jus communicationis*; un droit d'entrer en contact avec les autres peuples, de faire du commerce avec eux, ainsi que le libre passage et la libre circulation sur leur territoire; un droit qui peut être coercitivement appliqué, si son exercice est entravé arbitrairement, ce qui justifiait, selon eux, la *conquista* du nouveau monde.

De même, la troisième et dernière période de floraison de l'arbitrage, selon Grewe, à la fin du XIXe et au début du XXe siècle, qui commence approximativement avec l'arbitrage de l'*Alabama* en 1872, et dans laquelle se situe la convention Drago-Porter, est considérée aujourd'hui par les économistes comme celle de la première vague de mondialisation moderne, issue de la révolution industrielle. Révolution qui avait déjà déployé ses effets et démontré que l'échelle optimale des nouvelles activités économiques qu'elle a rendues possibles dépasse de loin l'assiette territoriale des Etats. Ce qui a conduit à la deuxième vague de colonialisme du XIXe siècle et à la ruée sur l'Afrique *(the scramble for Africa)*, considérée comme la dernière terre sans maître, et dont la Conférence de Berlin de 1884-1885 est l'épisode le plus marquant.

Paradoxalement, cependant, cette expansion coloniale au plan politique a favorisé, dans une certaine mesure, la conversion du mercantilisme vers le libéralisme au plan économique. Et ce libéralisme économique a coïncidé, et a peut-être même suscité, la floraison de l'arbitrage. Mais ce n'est pas tant dans leurs politiques économiques internes appliquées sur leur territoire métropolitain que les Etats

« européens » (qualificatif transformé en « occidentaux » avec l'avènement des Etats-Unis d'Amérique) ont opté pour le libéralisme, bien que la conversion de la Grande-Bretagne, le berceau de la révolution industrielle, du mercantilisme vers le libéralisme, grâce à la campagne héroïque de Richard Cobden (connue sous le nom de *Repeal of the corn laws*) soit une saga très intéressante. C'est surtout dans leurs relations économiques avec le reste du monde que les Etats occidentaux commencent à cette époque à se convertir au libéralisme économique, à des degrés différents, il est vrai.

Le reste du monde pouvait être divisé schématiquement en trois catégories de pays ou territoires : les colonies ou autres entités dépendantes des puissances occidentales ; les autres pays du vieux monde (essentiellement asiatiques, y compris l'Empire ottoman), qui sont restés formellement indépendants ; et les pays latino-américains.

Pour ce qui est des colonies ou autres territoires dépendants, une des raisons principales, si ce n'est la principale, de leur acquisition, pour les puissances coloniales, était d'étendre le champ exclusif de leurs activités économiques, en monopolisant l'accès aux ressources et aux marchés de ces territoires. Mais la compétition s'est aiguisée au cours du XIXᵉ siècle entre les puissances sur ce qui pouvait encore être colonisé, accroissant les tensions entre elles et menaçant de dégénérer en guerres coloniales (qui s'entendaient à cette époque comme guerres entre puissances sur les colonies plutôt que contre les pays à coloniser).

Pour réduire ces tensions et se prémunir contre ces menaces, certaines puissances coloniales ont prôné une reconversion vers une solution libérale dans leurs propres colonies ou zones d'influence par l'application de la politique de la « porte ouverte », politique qu'elles avaient auparavant essayé d'appliquer en l'imposant à certains pays de la seconde catégorie, celle des pays d'Orient et d'Extrême-Orient, telle la Chine.

Cette deuxième catégorie comprenait essentiellement les grands pays asiatiques, ceux-là mêmes qui ont participé aux deux Conférences de La Haye (la Chine, le Japon, la Perse, le Siam et l'Empire ottoman). Ils sont restés indépendants soit parce qu'ils étaient trop grands pour être contrôlés complètement (la Chine), mais surtout parce qu'ils étaient des Etats tampons (*buffer States*) entre les grands empires coloniaux. Dans l'ancienne littérature, on les appelait des pays « hors chrétienté », puis, au tournant du XXᵉ siècle, des pays « non civilisés » ou « semi civilisés », leur degré

de civilisation se mesurant en fonction de leurs attaches conventionnelles avec les puissances occidentales. En effet, ils étaient soumis à
la forte pression et à l'influence grandissante de ces derniers, qui
leur ont imposé, souvent par la force, le *jus communicationis*, c'est-
à-dire d'ouvrir leurs territoires et leurs marchés au commerce et aux
investissements occidentaux; et cela par des traités inégaux de capi-
tulation, établissant des régimes d'extraterritorialité et d'autres privilèges exorbitants en faveur des ressortissants de ces puissances occidentales.

Si ces puissances considéraient que les droits de leurs ressortissants étaient atteints, elles n'hésiteraient pas à recourir à la force, par
exemple pour le recouvrement des dettes; et parfois elles prenaient
également le contrôle direct des ressources financières de l'Etat territorial, telles ses douanes, ou même occupaient une partie de son
territoire. L'Egypte, par exemple, un pays que je connais bien, a
subi à la fin du XIXᵉ siècle le triple outrage *(triple jeopardy)* d'être
occupé militairement par la Grande-Bretagne, de voir ses finances
publiques soumises à un contrôle international, et son système judiciaire dédoublé par des tribunaux consulaires, puis remplacés par des
tribunaux mixtes, avec compétence exclusive sur tout différend ayant
pour partie un ressortissant étranger bénéficiant des capitulations. La
compétition parmi les puissances occidentales pour obtenir de tels
privilèges auprès de ces pays créa beaucoup de tensions entre elles,
tensions que certains ont essayé de dépasser par l'imposition à ces
pays, telle la Chine, d'une politique dite de la «porte ouverte», exigeant l'extension de tout privilège obtenu par une puissance occiden-
tale pour ses ressortissants aux ressortissants de toutes les autres
puissances occidentales; une sorte de clause de la nation la plus
favorisée ou de la non-discrimination dans les privilèges octroyés
aux étrangers occidentaux.

Ainsi, l'opinion dominante à cette première période semblait trouver dans la politique de la porte ouverte une meilleure solution alternative à la dangereuse compétition entre les puissances occidentales
dans leur quête des matières premières et des débouchés pour leurs
industries confirmées ou naissantes et pour leurs investissements.
Compétition qui se manifestait aussi bien dans la ruée coloniale que
dans leurs relations avec les pays d'Orient.

La politique de la porte ouverte a été appliquée unilatéralement
par certaines puissances coloniales dans leurs colonies. Elle a été
également garantie par certains traités multilatéraux, tels l'Acte

général de Berlin de 1885 et la Convention de Saint-Germain-en-Laye qui y renvoie (tous deux invoqués dans l'affaire *Oscar Chinn* devant la Cour permanente de Justice internationale[5]); l'Acte d'Algésiras de 1911 (également invoqué dans l'affaire des *Ressortissants des Etats-Unis au Maroc* devant la Cour internationale de Justice[6]); et même le Pacte de la Société des Nations, dans son article 22, concernant les territoires sous mandat.

Malgré cette pratique unilatérale et conventionnelle, la politique de la porte ouverte ne s'était pas consolidée en forme de principe ou règle de droit international général, n'ayant pas été suivie de manière conséquente par toutes les puissances concernées, car elle servait un intérêt médiat aux dépens d'intérêts plus évidents et immédiats.

La troisième catégorie des pays composant le « reste du monde » est celle des républiques latino-américaines, à propos desquelles on a écrit qu'elles ont acquis leur indépendance sous le double parapluie de la doctrine Monroe et de la flotte britannique. Ce qui les protégeait contre les visées de reconquête par la Sainte Alliance européenne, mais les livrait à l'hégémonie des Etats-Unis, qui y voyaient une zone d'expansion économique idéale à travers les activités de leurs citoyens et de leurs entreprises. Les controverses suscitées par ces activités ont constitué l'essentiel de la « pratique internationale » qui est à la base de l'élaboration des règles de la responsabilité internationale au tournant du siècle passé. Des règles qui ne pouvaient que refléter les rapports de force qui les sous-tendaient. Ce qui a fait dire au grand juriste américain, le juge Philip Jessup:

> « The history of the development of the international law on responsibility of States for injuries to aliens is thus an aspect of the history of "imperialism" or "dollar diplomacy" »[7]

C'est là l'ordre économique qui régnait au moment de la Deuxième Conférence de la Paix. Il reflétait un impérialisme triomphant, alliant le colonialisme politique à un libéralisme économique favorisant l'ouverture du reste du monde à l'expansion économique des puissances occidentales (leur *jus communicationis*), par des moyens coercitifs s'il le fallait; et cela en application d'un droit issu de ces idées et de ces pratiques.

---

5. *CPJI série A/B n° 63 (1934)*, p. 18.
6. *CIJ Recueil 1952*, p. 197.
7. Philip Jessup, *A Modern Law of Nations* (1946), p. 96.

Et cela coïncide avec le troisième âge d'or de l'arbitrage de l'histoire selon Grewe. Y a-t-il un lien ? Peut-être, à travers l'exemple de l'évolution des relations entre la France et la Grande-Bretagne, pouvons-nous entrevoir les éléments d'une réponse. Allant dans la compétition coloniale jusqu'aux bords de la confrontation militaire lors de l'incident de Fachoda au Soudan en 1899, celles-ci finirent par conclure un traité général d'arbitrage en 1903 (à la veille de l'Entente cordiale), prévoyant le recours à l'arbitrage pour résoudre tout différend qui n'aurait pas été réglé directement. Mais il s'agissait simplement d'introduire un cadre général et non pas d'instaurer l'arbitrage obligatoire, car il fallait encore conclure un compromis pour chaque différend.

Ce traité, largement considéré comme le premier du genre, a servi de modèle à d'autres traités bilatéraux conclus pendant cette période. De même, se multipliaient les clauses compromissoires dans les traités les plus divers, ainsi que les compromis d'arbitrage (après le fait).

Peut-on cependant déceler une tendance spécifique aux différends économiques, que ce soit dans la prévision du mode de règlement dans les traités, ou dans le recours effectif à l'arbitrage une fois le différend né ? Il est difficile de répondre avec précision à cette interrogation sans un examen empirique détaillé de la pratique ; ce qui dépasse les dimensions de cet exposé. Mais un recensement rapide des affaires figurant dans le *Recueil des sentences arbitrales* des Nations Unies peut fournir un échantillon représentatif des affaires réglées par arbitrage pendant cette période. Il en ressort que, mises à part les affaires concernant les frontières, l'essentiel de ces affaires ont un objet économique. Ce qui s'explique par le fait qu'elles relèvent en grande partie de la «protection diplomatique», ayant à leur base une réclamation individuelle pour atteinte à des intérêts privés.

Parmi celles-ci, il faut relever le grand nombre de sentences rendues par les commissions mixtes de réclamation, établies par des accords bilatéraux entre le Venezuela et plusieurs Etats à l'issue de la crise de 1902-1903 déjà mentionnée.

Il faut enfin ajouter, à propos du troisième flux, le flux monétaire, qu'apparemment il n'y a pas eu beaucoup de turbulences ou de revirements, la période s'étendant de la fin des guerres napoléoniennes à la première guerre mondiale étant l'«âge d'or» de l'«étalon or». Un étalon qui garantissait une stabilité monétaire absolue, en terme de parités fixes, au plan international. Car, si un Etat avait le loisir de manipuler sa monnaie, il pouvait affecter les deux autres flux de manière radicale. Mais cela était au prix d'une discipline sévère au plan interne ; prix se révélant exorbitant pour certains pays à économie fragile ou en phase de transition, tels l'Egypte et le Venezuela, les entraînant à la faillite et à la cessation de paiement, et les exposant ainsi à l'intervention armée, à l'occupation ou du moins à l'arbitrage forcé.

Pour conclure sur cette première période, on constate que malgré l'enthousiasme pour l'arbitrage, la prolifération des compromis, des clauses compromissoires et même des traités d'arbitrage, et le recours croissant à ce mode de règlement des différends, le recours à l'arbitrage est resté limité aux différends de seconde importance. Ainsi, l'arbitrage n'a pas réussi à atteindre les conflits intenses, avec leurs soubassements économiques, qui ont mené aux guerres majeures de cette période, telles la guerre entre les Etats-Unis et l'Espagne au tournant du siècle, la guerre russo-japonaise ou la guerre des Boers en Afrique du Sud, ni enfin et surtout la première guerre mondiale.

IV. Deuxième période : l'entre-deux-guerres

La deuxième période ou tournant commence avec l'éclatement de la première guerre mondiale. C'est une période de grande turbulence et de ruptures dans les faits ainsi qu'au plan des idées et des politiques générales ; plus particulièrement, et avec davantage d'intensité, dans le domaine économique.

La guerre a fourni le lit de la révolution d'Octobre et l'émergence d'une nouvelle puissance avec une idéologie et des politiques radicales et radicalement différentes de celles des puissances occidentales. Elle a surtout conduit à une redistribution fondamentale des cartes territoriales, les vaincus ayant perdu toutes leurs colonies en faveur des vainqueurs. Des empires se sont effondrés, et de nouveaux Etats sont apparus à leur place ; le Traité de Versailles a imposé, particulièrement à l'Allemagne, une paix économiquement draconienne, dénoncée par Lord Keynes dans son fameux essai *The Economic Consequences of Peace,* où il affirme que les vainqueurs allaient, avec ce traité, détruire à la fois l'économie allemande, le système monétaire et la paix. Economiquement parlant, cette affirmation s'est révélée tout à fait prophétique ; l'hyperinflation et l'hyperchômage en Allemagne ont conduit à l'effondrement de la République de Weimar, à la montée du totalitarisme et à la quête par Hitler du *Lebensraum*, et enfin à la seconde guerre mondiale.

Il est vrai de grands efforts ont été déployés en vue de recoller les morceaux et rétablir l'économie mondiale comme elle commençait à se profiler à la veille de la guerre. On a essayé, par exemple, de faire revivre la politique de la «porte ouverte» en l'insérant dans l'article 22 du Pacte de la Société des Nations (SDN), traitant des territoires sous mandat.

Mais la guerre n'avait pas seulement stoppé le fonctionnement des institutions de cette économie mondiale, elle les avait détruites. Et, de toute manière, les modestes résultats de ces efforts de reconstruction ont été engloutis par la grande crise de 1929, qui a achevé d'éroder ce qui restait des structures de l'économie mondiale. Les petits pays, comme les grands, se sont tournés vers une politique invertie de chacun pour soi, en s'enfonçant dans une spirale de dévaluations compétitives de leurs monnaies, tout en adoptant des politiques commerciales extrêmement protectionnistes; bref, la désastreuse *beggar thy neighbour policy*.

Paradoxalement, cette même période est celle qui a vu l'établissement de la première juridiction internationale permanente au plan universel, la Cour permanente de Justice internationale (CPJI). Elle a également hébergé une activité judiciaire et arbitrale abondante, traitant largement un contentieux économique. Cependant, on ne doit pas se laisser leurrer par les statistiques. Car l'essentiel de cette activité ne portait pas sur les conditions et les problèmes de cette période elle-même, mais sur les séquelles de la guerre. Cela s'applique particulièrement aux deux grandes innovations institutionnelles au plan du règlement des différends: la CPJI et les tribunaux arbitraux mixtes, avec accès direct des particuliers.

La Cour elle-même est l'héritage de la période précédente, car elle a été envisagée dès la Première Conférence de La Haye. Son établissement était prévu dans le Pacte de la SDN, qui faisait partie du Traité de Versailles. Et la seule raison pour ne pas l'avoir intégrée dans le Pacte était le rejet du Traité de Versailles par les Etats-Unis. Une bonne moitié des affaires décidées par la Cour pendant ses vingt ans d'existence effective trouvent leur titre de compétence dans les traités de paix; et c'est également la même proportion pour ce qui est des sujets sur lesquels portaient les avis consultatifs qu'on lui a demandés. Une bonne partie de ces affaires et de ces avis traitaient des garanties établies par les traités de paix; notamment pour les minorités ethniques dans les nouveaux Etats issus de la guerre. Un contentieux économique par excellence.

Il en est de même pour les tribunaux arbitraux mixtes, avec accès direct des particuliers; tribunaux établis par les traités de paix, mais ouverts exclusivement aux réclamations de dédommagement des ressortissants des pays vainqueurs (sauf pour la Turquie, qui était vaincue dans un premier temps, puis vainqueur dans un deuxième temps; ce qui lui a permis de conclure un deuxième traité de paix, ouvrant le for également à ses propres ressortissants).

Si les tribunaux arbitraux mixtes étaient imposés par les vainqueurs aux vaincus dans les traités de paix, d'autres mécanismes similaires ont été imposés par des puissances majeures à des pays plus faibles ou affaiblis par des circonstances particulières, telles les commissions arbitrales mixtes, établies entre le Mexique et les Etats-Unis et plusieurs puissances européennes, à l'issue de la «révolution mexicaine», qui a duré de 1910 à 1920.

Cependant, cette prolifération des moyens de règlement «pacifique» des différends par le recours à la justice et à l'arbitrage n'a pas eu un grand effet de «pacification», ou d'apaisement, car elle n'a pas touché aux racines des grands conflits économiques et politiques de cette deuxième période turbulente. On peut même dire que là où ces méthodes ont été par trop «imposées», cela a peut-être contribué à attiser les passions et les tensions. Car c'est la solution substantielle équitable qui peut apaiser les différends et non pas le simple fait de l'existence de procédures, ou de leur utilisation, aussi obligatoires qu'elles soient.

De sorte que les efforts déployés par la suite pour contenir la crise croissante par le recours à l'arbitrage ou à la Cour, telle par exemple la demande d'avis consultatif sur le *Régime douanier entre l'Allemagne et l'Autriche*[8], ne pouvaient être qu'un coup d'épée dans l'eau.

V. Troisième période: l'après-guerre

Cela nous amène à la période actuelle, celle de l'après-guerre, qui se divise à son tour en trois. Chacune de ces sous-périodes apporte des changements importants aux trois niveaux des idées et des poli-

---

8. *Série A/B n° 41 (1931).*

tiques, de l'évolution du droit, et enfin au niveau des instances et des procédures de règlement des différends économiques.

1) L'immédiat après-guerre (1945-1960): les efforts de reconstruction

Les Alliés avaient commencé à planifier pour l'après-guerre, bien avant la fin du conflit. Ils envisageaient de reconstruire le système international à partir de l'ancien modèle, mais de manière plus perfectionnée et plus sécurisée. Ce qui, au plan politique, conduisit à la Charte des Nations Unies avec son système de règlement pacifique des différends du chapitre VI et son système de sécurité collective du chapitre VII.

En matière économique, la reconstruction de l'économie mondiale était envisagée à travers une troïka d'organisations s'occupant respectivement des trois flux du commerce, des investissements, et monétaire. Deux ont été créés à Bretton Woods, en 1944, bien avant la fin de la guerre: Le Fonds monétaire international et la Banque internationale pour la reconstruction et le développement. La troisième, l'Organisation internationale du commerce, a dû attendre trois ans, pour être mort-née en 1947 à La Havane, bien qu'une partie ait survécu sous forme atténuée avec le General Agreement on Tariffs and Trade (GATT).

Les idées et les politiques dominantes étaient celles d'une évolution progressive vers un libéralisme policé par ces organisations, qui interviendraient également pour aider les Etats en difficulté, afin d'éviter les cassures du système.

Cependant, il ne faut pas oublier que ces idées et ces politiques n'étaient pas unanimement partagées. Car la guerre a énormément consolidé le statut de l'Union soviétique comme puissance mondiale, à la tête d'un «camp socialiste» bientôt en guerre froide avec les anciens alliés occidentaux, et qui n'est pas partie prenante à ces idées et politiques, ni à ces organisations ou aux arrangements économiques de l'après-guerre.

Les Etats socialistes rejettent le droit traditionnel en la matière, dont l'épitome se trouve dans les règles classiques de la responsabilité de l'Etat pour dommages subis par les étrangers sur son territoire. Ils rejettent aussi toute juridiction obligatoire consentie d'avance.

Se greffe sur ce conflit idéologico-juridique un autre conflit qui ressurgira dans les années cinquante, par la revendication de certains pays, bientôt appelés du tiers-monde, de reconquérir le contrôle sur leurs ressources naturelles et leurs richesses nationales.

Cela commence avec la nationalisation par l'Iran de l'Anglo-Iranian Oil Co., en 1951. Le Royaume-Uni porte l'affaire devant la Cour internationale de Justice (CIJ), dont l'Iran conteste la compétence, avec succès[9]. L'affaire trouve son issue dans un coup d'Etat instigué de l'extérieur contre le gouvernement nationaliste du Dr. Mossadegh.

Puis advient la nationalisation du Canal de Suez en 1956. L'Egypte avait inséré dans l'acte de nationalisation une déclaration d'acceptation de la juridiction obligatoire de la CIJ, conformément à l'article 36, paragraphe 2, du Statut de la Cour, pour tout différend concernant la liberté de passage dans le canal, selon la Convention de Constantinople; mais pas pour les autres aspects du différend. On connaît la suite: l'attaque tripartite des Anglais, des Français et des Israéliens contre l'Egypte, forcés de se retirer par l'ONU; le contentieux économique enfin réglé par l'entremise de la Banque mondiale.

Il n'y a pas beaucoup de cas de règlement judiciaire ou arbitral des différends économiques pendant cette période, sauf par les commissions mixtes issues du traité de paix avec l'Italie.

Les années cinquante s'achèvent avec des tensions montantes, ne favorisant pas le recours aux voies juridictionnelles.

2) La montée du tiers-monde: 1960-1980

1960 était l'année de l'Afrique aux Nations Unies, seize des dix-sept pays admis à l'Organisation cette année-là étant des Etats africains récemment indépendants. Le groupe afro-asiatique se transforme en groupe des non-alignés, puis en groupe des 77 avec la création de la CNUCED en 1964, englobant les pays latino-américains.

Ces Etats du tiers-monde, dit «en voie de développement» — ce que la plupart d'entre eux n'étaient pas en réalité, et c'est même la cause de leur grief — se mettent progressivement en rébellion contre le système économique international et luttent pour sa reconfiguration de manière à le rendre plus équitable et plus favorable à leurs besoins de développement.

---

9. Affaire de l'*Anglo-Iranian Oil Co. (compétence), CIJ Recueil 1952*, p. 93.

Cela se passe par plusieurs étapes, à commencer par l'établissement de la CNUCED en 1964 ; puis, après le premier choc pétrolier de 1973, par la «Déclaration concernant l'instauration d'un nouvel ordre économique international» [10], et la «Charte des droits et des devoirs économiques des Etats» [11], adoptées toutes deux par l'Assemblée générale des Nations Unies en 1974.

Des nationalisations pétrolières ont lieu, particulièrement en Libye, et mènent à une série d'arbitrages (les contrats de concession contenant des clauses compromissoires). Ce qui amène certains observateurs à dire que l'activité est passée de la CIJ à l'arbitrage. Une constatation qui n'est pas tout à fait exacte, car il ne s'agit pas de la même chose, ces arbitrages n'étant pas interétatiques mais entre parties privées et Etats.

Il est vrai cependant que prévalait à cette époque l'impression que la Cour manquait d'affaires et qu'elle traversait une crise que certains expliquaient par la méfiance des pays du tiers-monde à son égard, suite à son arrêt aberrant dans la deuxième phase des affaires du *Sud-Ouest Africain* [12]. Explication inexacte également, car il ne s'agissait pas de raison subjective, mais objective. En effet, ces pays avaient de sérieuses réserves à l'égard de certains aspects substantiels du droit existant. Il était donc logique, de leur point de vue, d'éviter de se soumettre volontairement à la juridiction d'une Cour qui est appelée, par sa constitution même, à appliquer fidèlement ce droit.

Cependant, alors qu'on attribuait tout le blâme aux pays du tiers-monde, les vrais problèmes sont venus d'ailleurs. Le système monétaire international établi à Bretton Woods cherchait à maintenir la stabilité monétaire en adoptant une version modifiée de l'«étalon or» dite de l'«étalon échange-or», en permettant de garder les réserves monétaires exigées des Etats membres, non pas en or mais en bons du trésor d'un pays dont la monnaie est convertible en or, à parité fixe. Ce pays était les Etats-Unis, qui ont drainé ainsi une bonne partie des réserves monétaires du reste du monde.

Or, en 1971, les Etats-Unis, en proie à de grandes difficultés économiques, empêtrés comme ils l'étaient dans la guerre du Vietnam, ont unilatéralement arrêté la convertibilité du dollar en or et rompu

---

10. Assemblée générale, résolution 3201 (S-IV), 1974.
11. Assemblée générale, résolution 3281 (XXIX), 1974.
12. *CIJ Recueil 1966*, p. 6.

le taux de conversion fixe entre eux, laissant flotter le prix de l'or, qui a quintuplé en quelques jours. Cela revient à une confiscation d'une grande partie de la valeur réelle des réserves monétaires mondiales ; sans compensation, évidemment ; en plus de la destruction du système monétaire international.

Mais, dans ce domaine, il n'y a aucun for compétent pour trancher juridictionnellement les différends. Le reste du monde a acquiescé, en entérinant le fait accompli dans le cadre du Fonds monétaire international (FMI).

Depuis lors, l'instabilité monétaire associée à la flottaison des taux de change est venue s'ajouter aux autres facteurs perturbateurs de l'économie mondiale.

3) La déferlante néolibérale : dès 1980

Avec l'accès au pouvoir de Margaret Thatcher en Grande-Bretagne et de Ronald Reagan aux Etats-Unis, une ère nouvelle commence dès le début des années quatre-vingt. Tous deux adoptent une politique néolibérale à tout va, démantelant autant que possible l'«Etat providence» à l'intérieur, et résistant farouchement à toute tentative de projection de telles idées au plan international. Ce qui revient à un rejet total de l'idée du nouvel ordre économique international, selon la vision tiers-mondiste. Une politique qui s'enhardit avec l'effondrement de l'Union soviétique et du bloc de l'Est, et la fin de la guerre froide.

La confrontation s'engage à l'occasion de deux crises financières aiguës, en Amérique latine d'abord, en Asie ensuite. Crises qui permettent de casser l'élan des revendications tiers-mondistes, et de faire plier les pays en difficulté aux nouvelles règles du jeu libérales, à travers les politiques d'ajustement structurel imposées par le Fonds monétaire, puis par la Banque mondiale.

La conversion de bon nombre de pays du tiers-monde, de gré ou de force, à un modèle néolibéral de développement les encourage à conclure avec les pays développés des milliers de traités bilatéraux d'investissement (TBI). Ces traités donnent des garanties aux investisseurs étrangers et surtout permettent de porter devant un tribunal arbitral du Centre international pour le règlement des différends relatifs aux investissements (CIRDI) les différends ayant trait aux investissements entre les citoyens du pays développé et l'Etat hôte.

Il faut encore ajouter que ces années sont aussi celles de la révolution dans les techniques d'information et de communication, techniques qui sont à la base de ce qu'on considère généralement comme la deuxième vague de mondialisation moderne, surtout la mondialisation économique et financière. Et, comme on l'a déjà vu, les vagues précédentes de mondialisation ont coïncidé avec l'âge d'or de l'arbitrage.

En effet, depuis une vingtaine d'années, un des thèmes favoris des internationalistes est celui de la prolifération des juridictions internationales. Période qui voit l'établissement de plusieurs organes juridictionnels de haute visibilité, qu'ils soient *ad hoc* ou permanents, tels les tribunaux pénaux internationaux *ad hoc*, suivis par la Cour pénale internationale, le Tribunal international du droit de la mer, et l'Organe d'appel de l'OMC.

Voyons dans quelle mesure ce phénomène s'est manifesté dans le domaine économique et plus particulièrement par rapport à chacun des trois flux économiques qui nous intéressent ; sans oublier pour autant les affaires qui peuvent être portées devant les autres juridictions non spécialisées exclusivement dans ce domaine, telles que la CIJ ou le Tribunal international du droit de la mer.

a) *Le commerce*

La grande transition dans ce domaine s'est faite par la conclusion, en 1994, des Accords de Marrakech et l'avènement de l'OMC avec son système élaboré de règlement des différends (par rapport au GATT), introduisant l'Organe d'appel comme juridiction permanente. Ce système est généralement considéré comme un grand succès. Au cours de ses douze ans d'existence, l'Organe d'appel a tranché quatre-vingt-quatre affaires, d'une complexité variable, mais toujours substantielle. Il a accumulé une jurisprudence importante, généralement perçue comme claire et équitable. Et si les pays en voie de développement demandent une plus grande prise en considération de la spécificité de leur condition, ils savent que cela ne peut se faire exclusivement par la jurisprudence, mais doit trouver une base dans les accords, qui sont toujours sur le métier dans le cadre de la «Ronde de Doha pour le développement». Il ne faut pas oublier, cependant, qu'une des raisons principales du succès du système de l'OMC réside dans sa juridiction obligatoire sur tous les différends relevant des accords ; ce qui n'est pas toujours le cas des autres juridictions.

Signalons également un certain nombre de systèmes régionaux de règlement de différends commerciaux (mais par l'arbitrage seulement), tels les systèmes de l'Accord de libre-échange nord-américain (ALENA) ou du Marché commun de l'Amérique du Sud (MERCOSUR).

b) *Les investissements*

Bien qu'il s'agisse du domaine le plus contentieux pendant la période précédente, et par conséquent pauvre en règlement juridictionnel, les choses tendent à changer au cours des années quatre-vingt: à commencer par l'établissement du Tribunal des réclamations Etats-Unis-Iran au début de la décennie, tribunal qui est toujours en fonction.

Mais c'est surtout la prolifération prodigieuse des traités bilatéraux d'investissement (TBI), à partir de la fin de cette décennie, qui donne une énorme impulsion à l'arbitrage au sein du Centre international pour le règlement des différends relatifs aux investissements de la Banque mondiale, Centre établi déjà en 1965, mais ayant fonctionné au ralenti jusque-là. Selon le rapport d'activités de 2006, le nombre total des affaires enregistrées par le Centre depuis sa création (jusqu'à la fin de 2006) a atteint deux cent dix, dont vingt-six pour la seule année 2006.

Le CIRDI fonctionne selon le système d'arbitrage institutionnalisé et, contrairement au système de l'OMC, qui est exclusivement interétatique, le contentieux CIRDI se déroule entre investisseur privé et Etat hôte.

Malgré ce succès quantitatif, des critiques acerbes se sont élevées dans les pays du tiers-monde contre la jurisprudence CIRDI, selon lesquelles le système arbitral ne produit pas une jurisprudence cohérente, que trop d'avocats d'affaires siègent comme arbitres. Les critiques soulignent surtout trois tendances dans cette jurisprudence, à savoir:

— de trouver un consentement à l'arbitrage là où il n'y en a pas, au point qu'on parle maintenant d'«arbitrage sans lien» *(arbitration without privity)* [13];
— d'interpréter l'«investissement» de manière trop extensive pour

---

13. Titre d'un fameux article de Jan Paulsson, *ICSID Review*, vol. 10, 1995, p. 232.

couvrir presque n'importe quelle activité qu'un étranger exerce sur le territoire de l'Etat;

— et enfin d'interpréter les obligations de l'Etat de la manière la plus large, au point (mais c'est une boutade que j'ai entendue plus d'une fois) de l'ériger en assureur non seulement de la nébuleuse juridique qu'est le «climat d'investissement», mais du climat tout court.

Indépendamment du bien-fondé de ces critiques, elles reflètent un malaise et un sens d'insatisfaction avec le droit applicable, ou du moins la manière dont il est appliqué; ce qui ne saurait être ignoré.

c) *La monnaie et la finance*

C'est le domaine qui comporte les plus grands dangers. Car l'effondrement du système initial de Bretton Woods et les avances technologiques dans l'information et la communication ont permis l'accumulation d'une somme colossale de capitaux financiers, tout à fait déconnectée de l'économie réelle, et largement spéculative, qui vagabonde d'un marché à l'autre en quête d'un gain boursier rapide, ou en spéculant sur les «futurs» ou sur les taux de change; tout en restant rebelle à tout contrôle national ou international. Il en est de même pour les manipulations des taux de change par les politiques monétaires des Etats, tel l'effondrement actuel du dollar face à l'euro et au yen.

Dans ce domaine, il n'y a plus de normes ou de régulation qui vaillent, ni d'agent régulateur efficace pour veiller à leur application (n'en déplaise au Fonds monétaire et à la Banque des règlements internationaux), ni enfin un for compétent pour régler les différends qui s'y rattachent. Et c'est là que réside le plus grand danger pour l'ensemble du système économique international.

En somme, nous vivons actuellement une période de floraison sans précédent du règlement juridictionnel des différends économiques; ce qui est une cause de satisfaction. Mais nous ne devons pas nous réjouir trop tôt, car il ne suffit pas d'avoir une pléthore de tribunaux et autres fors qui soient de plus en plus perfectionnés et performants; ceux-ci doivent encore aboutir à des solutions substantielles qui «vident» les différends tout en les réglant formellement. En d'autres termes des solutions perçues comme équitables de part et d'autre. Ce qui est également fonction du droit applicable par ces tribunaux, qui doit être acceptable pour tout le monde, et non pas un droit perçu par certains comme servant les intérêts des uns contre ceux des autres. Et, sur ce plan, il y a encore pas mal de chemin à faire ; sans oublier l'impossible tâche de brider juridiquement le Léviathan monétaire et financier qui hypothèque lourdement à la fois le commerce et les investissements.

II. COMPTE RENDU DES DÉBATS

SUMMING UP

G. GUILLAUME: J'ai beaucoup apprécié l'excellent exposé que nous a fait le professeur Koskenniemi sur l'idéologie du règlement juridictionnel des différends internationaux. J'ai été extrêmement intéressé par son propos concernant le développement de cette idéologie aux Etats-Unis et en Grande-Bretagne à l'époque des Conférences de La Haye.

Je souhaiterais cependant apporter deux compléments à l'exposé qui nous a été fait. Il convient en premier lieu de souligner que cette idéologie a trouvé son origine, dès le siècle des Lumières, dans la pensée de philosophes tels que Kant ou l'abbé de Saint-Pierre dont il aurait été utile de rappeler les œuvres.

En second lieu, je crois qu'à l'époque de la Conférence de La Haye il faut bien marquer la différence entre les positions prises par les tenants de l'idéologie du règlement juridictionnel des différends internationaux et les positions des gouvernements. Comme il nous a été bien montré, cette idéologie était très vivante du côté américain, mais cela n'a pas empêché le Sénat des Etats-Unis de se refuser à ratifier les traités d'arbitrage auxquels avait souscrit la délégation américaine, puis le Pacte de la Société des Nations, pas plus que cela n'a pas empêché l'impérialisme américain de se manifester à l'époque de Théodore Roosevelt en Amérique latine ou vis-à-vis de l'Espagne dans des conditions comparables à celles dans lesquelles l'impérialisme européen se déployait à l'époque dans d'autres régions du monde. En Europe également l'idéologie du règlement juridictionnel des différends internationaux était puissante, comme en témoigne par exemple la personne de Louis Renault qui fut jurisconsulte du Quai d'Orsay et prix Nobel de la paix et qui a sa statue ici même au Palais de la Paix. Mais les gouvernements, là encore, avaient leurs intérêts qui ne coïncidaient pas nécessairement avec le point de vue des penseurs. Aussi bien aux Etats-Unis qu'en Europe, il faut donc bien distinguer les positions des idéologues et celle des Etats qui entendaient réserver leur liberté d'action et n'aller devant les arbitres ou les juges qu'après avoir pesé leur décision au cas par cas.

L. BOISSON DE CHAZOURNES: Mon commentaire a trait à la belle fresque présentée par les professeurs James Crawford et Nico Schrijver. Restituant l'évolution du droit relatif au règlement des différends depuis cent ans, elle a été réalisée en deux teintes, celle des juridictions *ad hoc* et celle des juridictions permanentes. Cette présentation m'a conduit à me demander si, aux côtés de la tendance à la « permanence » des juridictions comme reflet de l'évolution qui s'est dessinée au cours du XXe siècle, on ne pouvait pas aussi identifier l'apparition d'une tendance en matière d'administration de la justice favorisant la création de mécanismes qui ne soient ni *ad hoc* ni permanents. Je pense, par exemple, à la Commission de compensation des Nations Unies et aux commissions mixtes. En outre, le droit international couvre désormais de très nombreuses sphères d'activités et il y a un très grand nombre d'acteurs intéressés par le règlement juridictionnel des différends à l'échelon international. Cette évolution donne une nouvelle coloration aux catégories de différends qui sont portés devant les instances internationales, à celles des mécanismes mis en place, comme à celles de leurs fonctions. Ces catégories quelles qu'elles soient ne répondent plus à celles de 1907. Les liens entre la gestion des intérêts privés et celle des intérêts publics sont de plus en plus étroits. Dans ce contexte, la nécessité s'est fait jour de prendre en compte tant les intérêts publics que privés dans le domaine économique, par exemple. Le recours aux commissions mixtes est révélateur de ce fait. Il est aussi à noter que l'exigence du respect du « due process » a pris beaucoup d'ampleur. La question est de savoir si les mécanismes de type *ad hoc* peuvent satisfaire à toutes les exigences qui en découlent. Les exigences découlant du « due process » favorisent d'ailleurs l'établissement d'autres catégories de procédures de type juridictionnel. Les demandes en faveur d'un mécanisme d'appel dans le domaine des investissements paraissent en découler. Le droit relatif à l'administration de la justice, on le constate, fait place à de nouveaux mécanismes de règlement des différends pour répondre à des préoccupations qui ont émergé au cours du XXe siècle.

J. CRAWFORD: The distinction between permanent and *ad hoc* tribunals is more complicated. There are a number of reasons for having institutions. One is to create a way of quarantining disputes from the general relations between the States for the purpose perhaps of resolving them, but at least for setting them aside. When two States are in dispute over a maritime boundary, or a small island, to the outside world it might seem a minor matter but it might have been there for 20 or more years causing considerable irritation between those two States. One way of resolving the issue could be to refer it to a tribunal, which can be *ad hoc* or permanent. Such a reference gets it out of the normal range of politics; therefore it has, as it were, an immediate effect. That is something which is seen as a virtue of dispute settlement in general but it seems to me probably more a virtue of a permanent institution than of an *ad hoc* one. As for due process, once again, one can think of *ad hoc* tribunals that have been immaculate in due process terms and permanent tribunals that may not have been. On one view the UNCC was set up with the aim of denying due process to one of the parties. It was obviously set up with a view to giving effect to a particular judgment, a judgment made by a political organ (though one cannot quibble with the content of the judgment) as to a breach of Article 2 (4) of the Charter. The point we make, however, is that where due process goes wrong in an *ad hoc* institution it can be much harder to fix, as we saw with the *Guinea Bissau/Senegal* case (*ICJ Reports 1991*, p. 53). Another example, which shall remain nameless, is that of an *ad hoc* tribunal in an inter-State matter which did not meet to deliberate on its award, because the members of the tribunal could not get together afterwards. That led to a somewhat unusual award which the parties had no choice but to accept. You would not find that form of violation of due process in a permanent tribunal. I agree entirely with Martti Koskenniemi that we should look at tribunals with a view to assessing their merits in relation to the particular reasons they are created. It is not a question of ultimate belief — at least not for me. But let us admit that there are some values of adjudication and process which are better guaranteed if you have an existing framework.

J. A. FROWEIN: Thank you very much Mr. Chairman, with your permission I would like to make two points. The first one is a rather technical one, but I think it is worth mentioning it. The arbitral tribunal for the Bank of International Settlements is mentioned as an *ad hoc* tribunal. I happen to be a member of that tribunal and if one looks into the 1930 Treaty, one will see that it is clearly a permanent arbitral tribunal. It was set up in 1930. When the matter arose in 2000 that the Bank of International Settlements excluded the private shareholders, cases where brought in three different jurisdictions and the Bank all of a sudden realized that there was full and exclusive jurisdiction with that arbitral tribunal. Of course all the members of the first generation had died. So a new arbitral tribunal had to be established but this is still in existence. It was not terminated in 2003 with the award concerning the exclusion. In fact the mandate of the judges has been prolonged. As of now only one important case namely the case concerning the exclusion of the private shareholders was decided in a published decision.

The second remark I would like to make concerns the ideology issue, where Professor Koskenniemi has so impressively made us familiar with this trend of thought, in particular in Anglo-American theory and thinking. The terrible thing is that you had counter-ideologies and for that, of course, Germany was unfortunately very prominent. Erich Kaufmann, who is still known at least with some experts of international law, wrote in his famous dissertation in 1912 on the *Clausula Rebus Sic Stantibus*, that war should be the final arbitrator in very serious international law disputes. He clearly put it that way. He was of Jewish origin, his life was saved in this country, the Netherlands, during the Second World War and he became Counsel to the German Federal Government again after the Second World War. But it is of some interest to mention this, because it was a view not limited to one individual. It was clearly a trend of intel-lectual thinking and it was not even limited to Germany, although it was most prominent there, and of course, it had terrible conse-quences.

M. KOSKENNIEMI: I thank Professor Frowein for mentioning Erich Kaufmann in this connection. Certainly Kaufmann is a repre-sentative of something one could call counter-ideology at the time. There were also some people from outside Germany who were advancing similar kinds of views, especially among the nationalist politicians at the time. They were a very small minority among the international lawyers, however. It was certainly very difficult to make a legally plausible point about war being the ultimate arbitra-tor among States. And although Kaufmann did this brilliantly, the political problems in making it were obvious. What I wanted to say, however, not by way of excusing myself in any sense, is that the notion that there exists a single or homogeneous "ideology" of inter-national adjudication is hugely problematic. This lecture title was thrust upon me by the Academy and as Yves Daudet knows very well at one point I tried to change the title, but then everything had gone into print already. The expression "ideology" is too fixed, too uniform to convey the meanings of international adjudication even at the period we are now discussing, let alone in a wider chronological vision. An "ideology" tends to suggest the presence of one single homogeneous block of thought, whereas, when one looks into what people were writing at that time, there were many more angles from which people looked at arbitration, adjudication and all that. In my presentation, I concentrated on and wanted to draw your attention to the striking fact that support for adjudication at the time had become an elite governmental position in the United States. These ideas received such a position nowhere else in the world. It was impossible for any European statesman to speak like president Taft did, or like president Roosevelt did, or to be in the position where Root was at the time when he operated. So, I was invited by the title to draw our attention to the political and cultural aspects of the turn to adjudication, the way it linked with parallel phenomena in a country that was only taking its place as the leading world power. But I hope everybody bears in mind that just like we in Finland had our own advocates of permanent courts and tribunals, the Germans certainly had theirs, as did the French. But the four ideas that I lay out as constituting the elements of the "ideology of international adjudication" were all key elements of the US position.

J. VERHOEVEN: C'est avec un grand intérêt que j'ai, comme chacun, écouté les exposés ou les commentaires des orateurs qui m'ont précédé, sans avoir à confesser de sérieux désaccords à leurs propos. Ce qui me frappe, toutefois, c'est que la spécificité du règlement juridictionnel n'y apparaît pas toujours clairement. Régler un litige, ce peut être d'évidence rétablir des relations « normales », cordiales, entre des personnes qui sont en conflit. C'est assurément très important, mais cela ne rend pas compte du rôle qui appartient au juge en cette matière, lequel est bien moins de rétablir des relations cordiales entre des personnes que de lever les incertitudes ou contestations qui entourent juridiquement la situation à propos de laquelle elles se divisent. L'objectif propre du règlement juridictionnel n'est pas de rétablir la concorde, mais de dire où est le droit... quitte à espérer que ce faisant il la rétablisse. Des époux qu'on divorce sont des époux dont la situation matrimoniale est réglée parce qu'ils ne sont plus mariés. Cela n'implique pas du tout qu'ils s'entendront bien par la suite... comme en témoignent par exemple les abondants contentieux relatifs au paiement de pensions alimentaires ou à la garde des enfants. Au moins faudrait-il pour que la concorde ou la discorde n'ait plus d'importance que le système juridique soit construit d'une manière telle qu'il assure à tous égards le respect du dit-pour-droit du juge. Ce n'est pas simple, même dans les droits internes. Il faut reconnaître que c'est particulièrement difficile en droit international, où l'exécution des décisions de justice demeure — comme l'a souligné James Crawford — particulièrement aléatoire. Cela explique sans doute que l'on paraisse souvent mettre exactement sur le même pied la conciliation, la médiation ou autres formules de règlement que l'on appelle diplomatiques et le règlement juridictionnel. Or, il n'en est rien. Le règlement diplomatique est en soi étranger au droit, en ce sens qu'il ne présuppose pas plus un différend en droit qu'il ne procure un règlement selon le droit. Il est possible que l'un et l'autre rétablissent une certaine paix entre ceux qui sont en litige, ce qui est peut-être plus important d'ailleurs. Cela ne saurait toutefois faire oublier que la recherche de cette « paix » n'est pas l'objet premier du règlement juridictionnel, qui est attentif au premier chef au respect de l'« intégrité » du droit. Ce qui ne peut avoir de sens qu'entre les membres d'un milieu (social) pour lesquels la « part » du droit est suffisamment développée... Il faut espérer qu'il en aille ainsi dans les relations internationales (interétatiques) comme ailleurs ; il n'est pas sûr que cela soit déjà le cas... ce qui explique une certaine marginalité persistante du règlement juridictionnel. Dans ces droits internes, la conciliation, la médiation, etc., sont des formules « alternatives » de règlement des différends dont les bienfaits par rapport à ce dernier sont de plus en plus — et souvent en vain — vantés ; dans le droit international, c'est le juge qui est la plupart du temps « alternatif »... en dépit des vertus qui lui sont — et souvent avec raison — reconnues. Les « progrès » actuels de la juridiction internationale ne sauraient le faire oublier.

La difficulté n'est pas tant à cet égard que les règles (ou les autorités) qui doivent garantir le respect et l'exécution de la justice font défaut. Ce qui est vrai pourtant. C'est aussi, et peut-être surtout, que les règles sur la base desquelles le règlement (juridictionnel) doit être obtenu sont ou paraissent défaillantes. Et comme elles le sont ou le paraissent, seuls les intérêts acquis ou espérés peuvent justifier les solutions retenues... ce qui explique sans peine le succès des politiques ou des diplomates. Cela dit, le problème n'est pas tant qu'il n'existe(rait) pas de règles. La pratique montre que l'on en a découvert sans trop de peine là où a priori on aurait cru ne jamais en trouver. Le standard minimum de justice fut par exemple affirmé, sans autre hésitation, il y a plus d'un siècle pour protéger les Etats (et leurs entreprises) qui exportaient leurs capitaux et leur personnel à l'étranger..., la jurisprudence CIRDI semblant d'ailleurs toujours faire preuve, un siècle et demi plus tard, d'une grande inventivité en cette matière. La difficulté est plutôt que la teneur normative de ces règles est souvent particulièrement réduite, ce qui conduit aisément hors du droit ceux qui les formulent et ceux qui les appliquent. En matière de délimitation maritime par exemple, la règle paraît bien être aujourd'hui que, hors la mer territoriale, les intéressés doivent par accord parvenir à une solution équitable. On est bien en peine de découvrir où est, en pareille hypothèse, le commandement du droit. Comme si l'on ne pouvait jamais trancher seul ce qui concerne plusieurs ou ambitionner de ne pas respecter l'équité... Le fait n'en est pas moins que cela n'a aucunement empêché les recours à un juge ou à un arbitre de se multiplier en la matière, avec apparemment un grand succès. On ne peut assurément que s'en réjouir. Cela ne devrait pas exagérément surprendre ceux qui connaissent l'importance que prennent les juges (souvent dits «de paix») dans le règlement des problèmes de bornage entre domaines limitrophes, particulièrement lorsque leurs propriétaires sont querelleurs. La différence est seulement que, dans les ordres internes, ce règlement est généralement adossé sur un ensemble complexe de règles et de pouvoirs... qui fait encore largement défaut dans l'ordre international. Ce qui n'en rend que plus méritoire sans doute la prétention du juge à juridifier des rapports sociaux en juridictionnalisant les différends qu'ils suscitent. Comme si avant le droit était le juge... ce qui est d'ailleurs largement vrai historiquement dans bien d'autres matières que le droit international.

A. A. CANÇADO TRINDADE : I would like to thank all the *rapporteurs* of this panel for their contributions, and would like to refer to a point made in the excellent presentation by Professor Georges Abi Saab, to which I attribute much importance. I quite agree with his assessment that the Drago-Porter Convention was endowed with great significance at the time (in 1907) when there was a prevalence of positivist thinking, for having acknowledged the need to place restraint on State voluntarism. I agree with Professor Abi Saab and I would allow myself to add another reflection in the same line of thinking. In the field of peaceful settlement of disputes, which was also addressed by Professor N. Schrijver, we have, in my view, and in the same line of thinking, another illustration of the awakening of conscience, so as to place restraint on State voluntarism. I refer to the project relating to the Permanent Court of Arbitral Justice discussed in the 1907 Hague Peace Conference, so as to enhance the corresponding initiative of the 1899 Conference. It is interesting to point out that all the participating States agreed with, and endorsed, the principle of juridical equality of States, although they interpreted that principle in a different way. That is very interesting and should not pass unnoticed here. For example, the most powerful States proposed in the 1907 Conference that all States might appoint a judge for the full period of the corresponding Convention, namely, 12 years, and those judges should sit for a longer or shorter period, according to a rotation system which was to be determined by the elements of population, industry and commerce (of the appointing States). This proposition, favoured by the powerful States, was, in their view, arguably in accordance with the principle of juridical equality of States, because all of them would have had the faculty of appointing judges. But the so-called small States, like the Latin American States in those days of the 1907 Conference, bitterly opposed this proposition. Ruy Barbosa could be mentioned here, but others as well, such as A. Bustamante y Sirvén. They argued that they shared the belief in the juridical equality of States, but they interpreted that principle in a different way. I have allowed myself to add this comment to Professor Abi Saab's presentation because, to my mind, this is another illustration of the awakening of conscience so as to put restraint on the free will of States, and also, ultimately, so as to construct a truly universal international law.

L. ORTIZ-AHLF: Chapter 19 of the North American Free Trade Agreement and the Dispute Resolutions under the World Trade Organization, for anti-dumping and countervailing duty, established that the parties in the dispute resolutions process are the States, but the real parties are the nationals, or residents of those States, because they are responsible for presenting their version of the facts, the memoranda and documents in the cases. The resolutions are binding for the involved parties, nationals or residents of the State, and the process of the panel is a substitute for judicial domestic review. These remedies don't give any compensation for the damage suffered, for the anti-dumping or countervailing duty, imposed to the goods that affect the nationals or residents of the other party. When the process is concluded the result is that justice has been denied to nationals or residents of the parties. What can we expect with the current evolution, the access to justice for natural persons or corporations, nationals or residents of the States, in this kind of mechanism?

G. ABI SAAB: I did not get your point exactly; do you mean that in the "contentieux", in the system of settlement of disputes in the WTO, there is no access for the individual, for private parties, is that the question?

L. ORTIZ-AHLF: Yes, the parties of the treaty are the States, but the process is organized by nationals or residents of the State, they provide the evidence, they contact the lawyers, they have to take care about all the procedural issues. However, those persons (natural or corporations) do not get reparation for the injuries they suffered. If the States do not comply with the decision of the panel, the only consequence for the aggrieved party is to suspend the application to the party complained against of the benefits of equivalent effect until such time as they have reached agreement on a resolution of the dispute. We are waiting for a direct access for the real parties in this case of arbitration.

G. ABI-SAAB: In every rule the final addressee is the individual. A great master, George Scelle, said a long time ago, in the 1930s, that the only subjects of law, whatever law it is, are the individuals. But of course, it is a question of social arrangements, and as far as the WTO Agreements go, which are really continuation of GATT, this was basically a system of continuous negotiation. It is a framework for negotiation. If you look at GATT, there are two articles, Articles 22 and 23, which do not really speak of settlement of disputes. They speak, in a very general way, of a right to consultation; if one party considers that the other party is not fulfilling its obligation, it has the right to ask for consultation. Then the second article states that the Contracting Parties, meaning the Plenary, can decide to allow one party to withdraw the concessions from the other party, if it persists in violation. So, the whole system has developed by practice, but it developed with the mentality that it is basically a forum for continuous negotiation to reduce obstacles to trade; in other words, to facilitate the trade flows. When we come to the WTO, GATT was transformed into something much more institutionalized and elaborate. But the ideology remained the same. As I wrote several times, it is really an ironical paradox that everybody attacks the WTO as the ruthless vehicle of marching triumphant globalization, whilst in its structure and modalities of functioning it is the most inter-State organization I know of. Even the trivial question, in my opinion, of *amicus curiae* briefs, is the subject of a great debate. I agree with you on the fact that private lobbies often move States to make claims. You call that individuals, but they can also be, and are more often than not, great economic interests. I agree, but I do not see how, if we leave out symbolism and rhetoric, we can consider certain phenomena, like access of individuals to the dispute settlement system of the WTO, by themselves as progress. Instead, we ought to examine in what ways they can improve the welfare of the individuals, etc., whether they would make any difference. I do not see where they would, in this respect, because the cases are based on interpretation of the Agreements and on how they work. Usually, to get to the level of the WTO, there is a kind of — not exhaustion of local remedies — but an internal procedure whereby the national of the State goes to a domestic institution with his complaint, saying for example: "Our competitors from abroad are dumping and you have to take measures against that." And it is the action of the State, in response to such a complaint, which is contested on the international level by the State against whose experts that action is taken. I can see how this procedure could be transformed. But in this case you have to separate this completely from the negotiating forum aspect of the Organization. It is a question of institutional arrangements, of social arrangements. In other words, it is not inherently necessary, in order for an international court to be considered "progressive", that it admits individuals to its forum. That is my answer to your question.

As to Professor Cançado Trindade, I thank him for adding to what I tried to demonstrate.

M. PINTO: La prise de conscience de l'épuisement de ressources humaines et matérielles que suppose la guerre est, peut-être, l'une des causes non négligeables de l'établissement des instances judiciaires ou quasi judiciaires internationales de caractère permanent pour le règlement des différends entre Etats.

Dans ce contexte, les Conférences de La Haye de 1899 et de 1907 ont fourni des cadres adéquats pour le développement des moyens alternatifs de règlement des différends. Toutefois, elles n'ont pas touché au droit des Etats de faire la guerre.

Depuis lors les efforts ont été concentrés plutôt sur les limites à l'emploi de la force armée par les Etats que sur les méthodes de solution des conflits qui les séparaient.

Ce cadre trouve une nouvelle approche dans l'ordre juridique et politique installé à partir de la Conférence de San Francisco en 1945 et l'entrée en vigueur de la Charte des Nations Unies.

Parmi d'autres nouveautés, la Cour internationale de Justice est établie en tant qu'organe judiciaire principal des Nations Unies. Au fur et à mesure que le XXe siècle avance, d'autres instances sont établies aux mêmes fins. Cette multiplication de tribunaux internationaux est un réflexe de la globalisation ou mondialisation de certains biens, tels que, notamment, les droits de l'homme, les investissements, le commerce, la mer.

Or, il semble que la recherche d'un niveau raisonnable de coexistence est l'un des buts qui guident l'établissement de ces instances — commissions, comités, tribunaux — internationales.

A un moment où le niveau du litige dans le droit interne est neutralisé par des moyens alternatifs, la communauté internationale tend à s'institutionnaliser par la voie judiciaire ou quasi judiciaire.

Pourtant, il ne s'agit pas de l'acquisition d'un pouvoir judiciaire *stricto sensu* mais, simplement, de la mise en place des instances — dont la procédure est réglée — afin de réduire les occasions pour les divergences graves.

Il se peut que la «fonction judiciaire» y ait un sens différent. Il ne s'agit pas seulement de «dire le droit» mais aussi d'œuvrer pour la paix, pour résoudre les conflits. Cela ne veux pas dire que la seule tâche des tribunaux internationaux est celle de faire la paix entre les parties en cause — c'est-à-dire le *peaceful settlement of disputes* — non plus qu'ils ne doivent agir seulement comme les opérateurs de ce qu'on connaît comme *adjucation of claims* à la façon des tribunaux de droit privé interne. La différence s'explique par une certaine dose d'ordre public ou de *global commons* qui vient s'immiscer dans la solution de certaines disputes. Que les atteintes contre cet ordre public s'expriment par l'emploi de la force, la violation systématique des droits de l'homme ou la pollution des mers, la fonction judiciaire reste importante.

Dans cet ordre d'idée, la Cour internationale de Justice a beaucoup réfléchi sur la «fonction judiciaire» et sur cette base elle a mené une politique judiciaire donnée, par exemple à l'égard des emplois de la force armée et des droits de l'homme.

La conception de cette fonction judiciaire tient compte d'autres éléments, notamment des traditions des tribunaux, des juges et du juge individuel. Par tradition, on entend la jurisprudence comme produit final du travail judiciaire et les motivations sous-jacentes. Bien que la jurisprudence ne soit, en général, obligatoire que pour le cas d'espèce, elle exerce une influence sur les politiques extérieures et même intérieures — dans des domaines tels que les droits de l'homme, par exemple — des Etats.

Les juges sont les opérateurs des règles de droit. Lorsqu'il s'agit des juges internationaux, il y a beaucoup à dire et à construire à propos des nominations, des critères suivis par les Etats pour choisir leurs candidats, des qualifications retenues tant pour la nomination que pour l'élection, des conditions d'exercice des mandats, des questions qui ont trait à ce que l'on appelle en anglais *the accountability*, notamment.

Finalement, il y a le juge individuel, son univers mental, sa capacité d'intégration du monde et du droit, ses perceptions du rôle à jouer par le droit international et par lui ou elle-même. Le nombre des juges internationaux, des femmes et des hommes qui ont la responsabilité de régler les différends du monde global n'est pas très élevé. Il n'est pas, par conséquent, trop égoïste de leur demander d'essayer de faire la différence avec le reste du monde et de ne pas rester dans la simple application déductive du droit.

Voilà certaines idées pour une plus large réflexion.

G. VENTURINI: I would like to address the issue of private rights, mentioned by Professor Koskenniemi among the elements of the "ideology" of the jurisdictional settlement of international disputes. I have in mind Article 3 of the Hague Convention (IV) of 1907, that was referred to by President Higgins as an important innovation, since no corresponding provision existed in the previous 1899 Convention (II) with respect to the laws and customs of war. Article 3 of the Hague Convention (IV) reads:

> "A belligerent party which violates the provisions of the said
> Regulations [i.e. the Regulations respecting the laws and
> customs of war on land, annexed to the Convention] shall, if
> the case demands, be liable to pay compensation. It shall be

responsible for all acts committed by persons forming part of its armed forces."

This is an early example of absolute State responsibility: a belligerent must assume responsibility for all acts of the members of its armed forces, including those performed in their private capacity. This rule was re-stated in Article 91 of Protocol I of 1977, additional to the Geneva Conventions of 1949. In the case concerning *Armed Activities on the Territory of the Congo* of 2005, the International Court of Justice has expressly recognized its customary nature.

The dominant opinion maintains that Article 3 relates to the responsibility of the States towards one another, excluding individuals from its field of application. This interpretation stems from the fact that the provision does not mention individual rights, and from the inter-State nature of international law at the outset of the twentieth century, as well. According to this view, the settlement of any indemnity in favour of individuals is to be set between (former) belligerent States. Yet, Article 3 was included in the Hague Convention (IV) following a proposal drafted by the German delegation. This was originally meant to make a belligerent liable to indemnify neutral persons which had suffered prejudice from a violation of the laws of war. Based on this draft is the interpretation of those who argue that the very purpose of the article was to grant individuals the right to claim compensation for war damages directly from the responsible State. It must be said that the subsequent State practice and the established trend of national jurisprudence heads for the denial of the individual right to compensation. More recently, however, some domestic courts (such as the Italian Court of Cassation in the *Ferrini* case, 2004) have recognized that individuals have the right to claim and receive compensation from the responsible State for violations of the laws of war.

Could we conclude that Article 3 of the Hague Convention (IV) is a wide open provision, leaving room for the progressive development of the right of individuals to demand compensation for damages and injury caused by the violations of the laws of war? I thank the Rapporteurs, and particularly Professor Koskenniemi, for expressing their opinion on this issue.

C. SWINARSKI: J'ai deux points qui concernent les présentations du professeur Koskenniemi et du professeur Abi-Saab. Durant la période précédant les Conventions de La Haye il s'est posé dans certains pays un problème relevant à la fois de la réforme du droit et d'un programme politique extrêmement important, relatif à la liquidation de ce qui restait en vigueur des mesures pénales pour dette en droit interne. Il s'agissait de la prison pour dettes, c'est-à-dire des moyens *jure imperii* du droit pénal permettant de garantir l'exécution des obligations de droit privé. C'était le cas en Autriche-Hongrie, d'où probablement la référence à Sir Hersch Lauterpacht, qui était originaire de cet espace de droit (d'ailleurs un de ses professeurs, Zygmunt Cybichowski, était très engagé contre la prison pour dettes). En Argentine il y avait le même problème — l'intervention de Monica Pinto m'en a rafraîchi le souvenir —, les socio-libéraux argentins l'étaient aussi. J'adresse cette question, ou plutôt cette information au professeur Abi-Saab.

Ma question au professeur Koskenniemi est la suivante : Are we speaking here about international law, about not only the judicial but also the juridical ideology or policies of juridical ideology, while at that time public law, and international law would have belonged for many, if not for all, to the same body of law? Could we not look for the measure to which these two issues, that is the use of coercion for debts in domestic law and State liabilities in case of international law, are related? Couldn't we analyse in that light the nature of debts, for instance in the Egyptian or the Dominican cases? Could we not speak, instead of a juridical ideology or public law ideology, of a relation between public and private law in general? I once discussed it with an eminent Argentine constitutionalist — and I'm grateful to Professor Abi-Saab for his so well taken and vast socio-historic background of the ideas underlying the Drago-Porter solution — for him political reasons of not ratifying the Drago-Porter by Argentina proceeded from the general attitude towards criminal measures for debts at the time, which has been transposed into international law, even if the issues were of different nature. Still, it remains that there were contracted debt elements and the use of public force elements versus the peaceful, e.g. non-violent settlement in both issues. These are my two points, and I would like to thank again both speakers for such a comprehensive way of placing the Drago-Porter within the larger scope of ideology of debt.

G. ABI-SAAB : As far as private rights go, I have no problem with individuals having direct access to an international forum, if the treaty which has created the forum, and which the forum applies, creates direct individual rights. It is natural, for example, for human rights treaties, when they are applied by tribunals or commissions, that the individual enjoys a right of access. Now, about the interpretation of Article 3, I have to plead the Fifth Amendment, I have not studied the Convention enough to give you a precise answer. But, in principle, of course we have to look at the law: law is a means of social regulation; applying it is part of that social regulation. If the law says "this is a right directly accorded to the indivudual", then the individual should be in the position to prosecute. As to my friend Swiniarski, I think what he said is a little bit what I have been trying to say, that the settlement of disputes is a means of application and enforcement of the law. However, law does not come from outside; it tries to translate the shared perceptions of what is needed to protect and promote the public good. Tom Franck one said, "law is congealed politics". This is a "racourci", but it has a grain of truth.

If there is a kind of consensus on a certain policy at a certain time, or a general recognition of a certain social interest or value that could be served in a certain way — if there is enough consensus, it can be congealed into law. Of course, the process of law creation, the transformation of this consensus into law, is not automatic. Every period secretes its law this way.

This brings me to the question why Calvo talked about denial of justice. Because the great problem with the United States, in its relations with the Latin American States, was that the United States considered the systems of internal justice of the latter to be below the international standard. They wanted to go directly to diplomatic protection, which means that the State Department representative comes to a weak Government in Latin America and says: "Listen, you have done this and that to our citizens", without even trying to look first at the contractual rights involved. The investor has signed a contract, like any other contract, but instead of going to a court which they claim won't deliver justice, they resort directly to political means. And if that did not work, they would use something stronger, a measure short of war, as was mentioned yesterday. Diplomatic protection with exhaustion of local remedies was a kind of protection from non-diplomatic protection. That was the reason, and not so much any ideological underpinnings, such as liberal reasons, etc. It was this: a reflection of self-protection.

M. KOSKENNIEMI: I think there were three questions to me, I do not have the time to explore all of them but I would like to give a brief response to each of them.

Professor Pinto pointed at the phenomenon of proliferation and I think that behind the question was the idea that through proliferation and specialization, our concept of what it is to be an international "judge" is going to change. We have very different kinds of judges today in different international law-applying bodies with different kinds of ideologies. At law school, students no longer want to be educated as international lawyers in the nineteenth-century sense; they want to be educated as technical specialists of this or that branch of the law, as human rights lawyers, environmental lawyers, trade lawyers, criminal lawyers etc. All of these specializations come with their own biases, embedded preferences and — in this sense — with their own ideologies. A classroom of human rights students is very different from a classroom of trade law students. Their political alignments and career expectations are far from homogeneous. That I think is a new situation. I have recently been rather obsessed by thinking about how legal education should be in today's conditions of fragmentation and deformalization. I believe it should at least move away from a very tight specialization into offering a more broad-ranging and more critical set of tools to appreciate the political and cultural significance of particular forms of the legal craft.

From Professor Venturini, I received a question about Article 3 of the Fourth Convention of 1907 with regard to individual rights. Did the participants of the 1907 Conference envisage the possibility of individual recourse before some institutions to claim rights violated in an international armed conflict or during war? I see no reason to think that such an idea would have occurred to them. They were living in a world where States were regarded as rather hermetic and impenetrable wholes; individuals could not have enjoyed an independent standing before international bodies. This is not to condemn that system, since it was, as Georges Abi-Saab said a moment ago, a social arrangement. That social arrangement was only beginning to be broken down through the kind of ideology that I tried to expunge in my talk in which globalization became a matter for individuals to fight out between themselves and for the courts to help in that process.

With regard to the last question from Professor Swinarski: do we really have an ideology of judges, a juridical ideology, or what do we see down there? I pose this question constantly to myself: what is the invisible but nevertheless quite tangible cloud behind the profession that makes the profession what it is, that gives it its particular political bent and supports the preferences which its members have, preferences we recognize in each other? I think ideology is a bad word, too rigid and all-encompassing, too arrogant in its suggestion that there is "truth" that can be juxtaposed to what people think as mere "ideology". Instead of "ideology", I would rather use the word "sensibility". There is shared *sensibility* which arose in the late nineteenth century and which is manifested in many of the aspects of the law of the period of the turn of the century. In a previous work which some of you know I am sure, I had tried to trace the Victorianism of the international law profession as it arose. When I look at Root and Scott, like when I think of Henry and William James, it is that kind of Bostonian, or East Coast, sensibility that is hard to put in few criteria, but which one recognizes when one sees it. We admire it and think that although it is sometimes perhaps a bit limited, there are nevertheless worse things in this world than it. This sensibility — or ideology, if you so wish — is the air we breathe as international lawyers.

M. CHEMILLIER-GENDREAU: Les réflexions qui suivent ne s'adressent pas spécialement à l'un des rapporteurs que nous avons entendus. Il s'agit plutôt d'une distance critique que je souhaiterais introduire par rapport à la ligne générale de cette rencontre. Il est vrai que nous sommes réunis dans un cadre académique. Mais cela doit-il nous conduire à une posture académique? Devons-nous étudier le droit d'une manière spéculative comme une science répondant à sa propre logique et nous en tenir là? Ce n'est pas ma conception du rôle des juristes. Le droit que nous étudions est une pratique sociale dotée d'une finalité. Tout examen de la norme juridique doit tenir compte de cette finalité. Alors il apparaît clairement que les normes auxquelles nous nous référons ici, à l'occasion de ce retour sur la Conférence de la Paix de 1907, ont été pensées pour encadrer les comportements des individus et des sujets du droit international en général de manière à éviter des situations de violence. Telle était clairement la préoccupation des initiateurs des conférences de la paix. Et les juridictions internationales, venues plus tard, ont été voulues pour régler les différends de manière à substituer une solution pacifique fondée sur le droit à une situation de tension ouvrant un risque de guerre.

Aussi sommes-nous ici pour tenter d'évaluer l'évolution du droit international en un siècle (et je crois que c'était bien là le but de cette rencontre). Si nous le faisons à l'aune des objectifs de cette époque : c'est-à-dire de poser des règles limitant le droit de la guerre et favorisant la paix, de faire avancer l'idée d'un règlement juridictionnel entre les Etats et de tendre vers un universalisme du droit international, alors nous sommes devant la situation de la bouteille à moitié vide ou à moitié pleine. On peut noter avec satisfaction les progrès accumulés en un siècle. On ne peut nier qu'il y a eu accumulation spectaculaire de conventions sur tous les sujets et multiplication des juridictions internationales. Mais nous ne pouvons ignorer pour autant que ces progrès du droit se situent pour l'essentiel dans un cadre contractuel, ce qui en limite considérablement la portée. Quant aux juridictions internationales, le volontarisme étatique qui domine en restreint à l'évidence le champ d'intervention. C'est ainsi que nous nous trouvons aujourd'hui, en 2007, devant des situations d'une violence effroyable. Dans la plupart des cas, ces situations sont l'objet de déni de justice. Or cela est inacceptable et nous ne pouvons pas nous cacher que l'effet de cette situation s'est aggravé en un siècle.

En 1945, après la tentative infructueuse de la SDN, un pas considérable sembla franchi parce que l'on quittait le terrain des tentatives pour limiter la guerre pour aller vers un droit nouveau pour interdire la guerre. Mais l'espoir ainsi ouvert s'est soldé par un échec avéré. Nous pouvons le constater en Palestine, en Irak, en Afghanistan, en Tchétchénie, au Darfour, etc. L'engagement des Etats à ne pas recourir à la force avait été accompagné avec sagesse dans la Charte par le devoir imposé au Conseil de sécurité, en vertu de l'article 26, de limiter les armements de manière « *à ne détourner vers eux que le minimum des ressources humaines et matérielles du monde* ». Aujourd'hui les mots de ce texte sonnent étrangement, comme un mensonge du droit, devant l'augmentation accélérée des dépenses d'armement. Il y a donc eu démission complète du Conseil de sécurité sur ce point.

En tant que juristes, deux routes s'ouvrent à nous : celle du positivisme formel qui conduit à commenter doctement les résolutions, les conventions, l'ensemble des textes, à discuter de leur validité supposée et de leur force obligatoire, à se féliciter de telle injonction du Conseil de sécurité appelant à un « cessez-le-feu immédiat » comme il l'a fait tant de fois, sans se préoccuper de l'application concrète de ces normes aux réalités qu'elles sont censées régir ; l'autre est celle des juristes qui considèrent le droit comme une pratique sociale par laquelle des institutions ayant la compétence nécessaire vont dire quelle est la norme, soit au niveau de son affirmation générale (par les institutions représentatives des Etats ou des organisations internationales), soit au niveau de son application à un cas concret (par les juridictions internationales). Ceux-là se préoccupent des effets de ces normes sur les rapports sociaux. A cet égard, les règles du droit international, comme celles du droit interne, ont pour but de substituer à l'expression d'un désaccord par la violence son règlement par l'application du droit. C'est à cette aune que, pour ma part, j'évalue le droit international. Je suis alors dans l'obligation de constater, devant l'ampleur prise par les violences déchaînées dans les conflits actuels, le cruel échec du droit.

Nous pouvons faire une longue liste des situations de violence où la vie humaine est méprisée, les droits de l'homme massivement violés et les responsabilités non établies. Chacun d'entre nous peut faire ce bilan. Pour ma part, je citerai ici deux exemples.

D'abord celui de la guerre faite au Liban par Israël en 2006 en riposte à des attaques du Hezbollah libanais. Devant l'ampleur des destructions occasionnées par les opérations militaires israéliennes, lorsque les combats cessèrent les Libanais se sont demandé avec perplexité comment ils pourraient obtenir réparation pour les dégâts causés sur leurs biens, leurs vies, leur environnement, par cette guerre. Mais la notion de réparations de guerre semble avoir disparu du paysage juridique, si l'on excepte la manière, éminemment contestable, dont le Conseil de sécurité a mené le dossier des réparations de la guerre du Koweït, en en faisant porter toute la charge à l'Irak et en laissant s'installer le laxisme sur les évaluations. A l'exception de ce cas, il est rare de voir posé le problème des responsabilités dans les opérations militaires. Et dans le cas du Liban une première conférence des « donateurs » a été réunie en Suède en août 2006 pour pourvoir aux fonds nécessaires à la reconstruction du Liban. Mais les sommes promises relevaient de démarches « caritatives » de pays non engagés directement dans ces combats et elles étaient très largement inférieures à l'évaluation des dommages. Et il n'a pas été question d'affirmer que le responsable des destructions menées au Liban, au mépris le plus souvent des règles du droit des conflits armés et du principe de proportionnalité de toute riposte militaire, à savoir l'Etat d'Israël, devait porter le poids des réparations.

Et il y un autre exemple, qui est très peu médiatisé, mais qui mérite de retenir notre attention. Or, il ne fait pas l'objet de beaucoup de commentaires dans la doctrine. Pourtant il résume toute la paralysie du droit international : ce sont les suites des déversements de dioxine opérés par l'armée américaine sur le Vietnam pendant dix ans de guerre (1961-1971). Quarante ans plus tard les sols sont imprégnés, ils le seront encore longtemps, parce que la décontamination est presque impossible dans certains secteurs et extrêmement onéreuse. On dénombre quatre cent mille victimes de pathologies indescriptibles et certaines sont héréditaires parce qu'il y a des atteintes au patrimoine génétique. Que dit le droit ? Que permet-il de faire ? Il est vrai que la Convention de 1925 sur les armes chimiques ne s'appliquait pas aux Etats-Unis pendant la période des faits parce qu'ils n'y avaient pas adhéré. La convention suivante, celle de 1993 sur les armes chimiques, est intervenue après les faits et elle ne concerne pas les herbicides, parce que l'on considère que les herbicides sont fabriqués pour nuire aux plantes et pas aux humains. Enfin du point de vue du règlement juridictionnel, ni la Cour internationale de Justice ni la Cour pénale internationale ne peuvent être saisies en raison des règles de compétence. Les victimes vietnamiennes démunies de tous secours restent entièrement à la charge de leurs familles. Elles ont tenté de se constituer en associations pour poursuivre devant les juridictions américaines non pas les responsables militaires et politiques américains de ces déversements, parce que ce n'est pas possible, mais les compagnies fabriquant ces produits. En première instance, le juge américain a dit que la demande était irrecevable, la dioxine de toute façon n'est pas interdite par le droit international. Les victimes ont fait appel devant la Cour de New York. Celle-ci a suivi sans nuances le jugement de première instance (arrêt du 22 février 2008).

Mais voir les victimes de ces déversements aujourd'hui, quarante ans après, dans les hôpitaux vietnamiens ou sur les photos produites par les associations, nous persuade que la clause Martens est restée lettre morte et que les processus de déshumanisation n'ont pas régressé. N'avait-on pas posé le principe que les civils devaient être épargnés ? Que les combattants ne devaient pas user de moyens disproportionnés à leurs objectifs ? Que les poisons étaient interdits ? La résolution de l'Assemblée générale de 2005, pour un droit au recours et à la réparation des victimes des violations graves des droits de l'homme et du droit humanitaire en cas de conflit armé, reste, nous le savons bien, de la « soft law » pendant que les guerres et les souffrances sont évidemment des « hard » guerres et des « hard » souffrances. Il me semble que ce sont ces situations qui doivent requérir toute notre attention et nos analyses doctrinales quand nous faisons un bilan d'un siècle de droit international.

Nous n'avons pas progressé du point de vue des effets du droit. Et cela est dû au durcissement de la souveraineté. Gardant son statut de principe central, elle permet que les normes soient à géométrie variable. Etant de nature contractuelle pour l'essentiel (puisqu'il faut la volonté de l'Etat « souverain » pour s'engager), les règles du droit international ne s'appliquent qu'à ceux qui y ont adhéré. Et nous savons bien que pour imposer les quelques règles de nature coutumière ou appartenant au droit impératif général qui sont considérées comme universelles, il faut l'autorité du juge. Mais on retombe sous les conséquences de la souveraineté. Un Etat peut refuser le prétoire et, de ce fait, échapper à l'application du droit.

Dire que l'ère des souverainetés doit finir, parce que cette notion porte aujourd'hui plus d'effets négatifs que positifs, est, me semble-t-il, l'impérieux devoir des juristes de notre temps.

LA CONFÉRENCE DE LA HAYE ET LA RESTRICTION DE L'EMPLOI DE LA FORCE

Sous la présidence de
M. BENNOUNA

THIRD PART

THE HAGUE CONFERENCE AND RESTRICTIONS ON THE USE OF FORCE

M. BENNOUNA,
presiding

I. COMMUNICATIONS

1. FORCE AND THE SETTLEMENT
OF POLITICAL DISPUTES : THE DEBATE

LA FORCE ET LE RÈGLEMENT
DES DIFFÉRENDS POLITIQUES : ARGUMENTS CROISÉS

M. GLENNON[1] et/and A. PELLET[2]

Michael J. Glennon

It's an honour to return to the Hague Academy today, all the more so to share the podium with my friend Alain Pellet. I first met Professor Pellet here in The Hague 23 years ago. He was a member of the legal team of Nicaragua in its action against the United States; I was a witness for Nicaragua. When I walk into the Peace Palace today, I am still reminded of its picture on a postcard written by Abe Chayes during the proceedings on the merits. The card was addressed to the State Department Legal Adviser, Abe Sofaer. It said simply : "Dear Abe : Having a great time. Wish you were here. Abe."

Some believe, of course, that the United States has too often been missing from the precincts of international law, gone, at least, from the regime governing use of force. Iraq, Kosovo, Grenada, Panama, Nicaragua, the Bay of Pigs — evidence, *arguendo*, is not lacking for their claim.

Yet evidence of transgression is broader than evidence of mere *American* transgression. The Secretary-General's High-Level Panel found violations of the Charter use-of-force rules so numerous as to defy quantification[3]. By one count, the Panel said, from 1945 to

---

1. Professor of International Law, Flechter School of Law and Diplomacy, Tufts University.

2. Professeur à l'Université Paris X-Nanterre; membre et ancien président de la Commission du droit international.

3. "[F]or the first 44 years of the United Nations", the Panel concluded, "Member States often violated [the Charter] rules and used military force literally hundreds of times, with a paralyzed Security Council passing very few Chapter VII resolutions and Article 51 rarely providing credible cover." "A More Secure World: Our Shared Responsibility", Report of the Secretary General's High-Level Panel on Threats, Challenges and Change (United Nations, 2004), at p. 62 <http://www.un.org/secureworld/report.pdf>.

1989 "force was employed 200 times, and by another count, 680 times"[4]. Other studies have reported similar results[5].

The central question today is this: what is the juridical significance of this deviant practice? Professor, now Judge, Rosalyn Higgins has observed that "what one identifies as international law will be closely dependent upon what one believes is the basis of legal obligation"[6]. Legal obligation is the core issue: how does repeated and widespread violation of a rule by many States over an extended period of time affect States' legal obligation to obey it?

One answer commonly given is that violation has no effect on obligation. This answer often rests, at least implicitly, upon the supposition that there is a moral obligation to obey treaty rules, and perhaps a special obligation to obey rules prohibiting aggression[7]. But whether there is a moral obligation to obey any law can be answered, if at all, only by a moral system, not by a legal system. Lawmakers create legal obligations, not moral obligations. As the Court reminded us in the *South West Africa* case, a court of law "can take account of moral principles only in so far as these are given sufficient expression in legal form"[8].

At the other end of the spectrum, some respond that violation *vitiates* obligation — that in a voluntarist legal system, a State is

---

4. *Op. cit. supra* footnote 3, at p. 140, n. 104.

5. See, e.g., Arthur M. Weisburd, *Use of Force: The Practice of States Since World War II* (1997). Weisburd counted 100 inter-State wars between 1945 and 1997. Franck counted the same number in 1970. See footnote 27 *infra*. K. J. Holsti counted 38 between 1945 and 1995. K. J. Holsti, *The State, War, and the State of War* 24 (1996). The Correlates of War Project has counted 23 between 1945 and 1997. Meredith Reid Sarkees, "The Correlates of War on War: An Update to 1997", 18 *Conflict Management and Peace Science* 123-144 (2000). Herbert K. Tillema counted 690 overt foreign military interventions between 1945 and 1996. Herbert K. Tillema, *Risks of Battle and the Deadliness of War: International Armed Conflicts: 1945-1991* (paper presented to International Studies Association, San Diego, 16-29 April 1996) quoted in "New Actors, New Issues, New Actions", in *International Intervention: New Norms in the Post-Cold War Era?*, Peter Wallensteen, ed., 1997. A report of the Carter Center in February, 1998 identified 30 "major ongoing wars". The Carter Center, "Conflict Resolution Update: Update on World Conflicts," 9 February 1998. See generally Michael J. Glennon, *Limits of Law, Prerogatives of Power: Interventionism after Kosovo* (2001).

6. Rosalyn Higgins, "The Identity of International Law", in *International Law: Teaching and Practice* 32 (Bin Cheng, ed., 1982).

7. This seems to have been the Panel's conviction, urging the Security Council, as it did, to adopt just war principles. See Michael J. Glennon, "Platonism, Adaptivism, and Illusion in UN Reform", 6 *Chicago Journal of International Law* 613 (Winter, 2006).

8. *South West Africa (Second Phase)*.

obliged to honour only those rules to which it consents, and that violation signifies objection to a rule. This answer gets closer to the truth, recognizing as it does the positivist underpinnings of the contemporary international legal order. Few today would contend that states have *no* control over the rules by which they are bound, that there is a "brooding omnipresence in the sky" that somehow imposes legal rules on States notwithstanding their objection.

Yet this "pure" consent-based view of obligation, like its opposite, misses the mark. It presupposes an international legal order devoid of "informal" sources of coercion. States' discretion is in fact circumscribed all the time — coercively — not only by governmental or quasi-governmental authority, but also by other States. It is unthinkable, for example, that one member State of the European Union would use force against another, not because of any specific treaty commitment but because informal, regional coercive forces are as powerful as they are. Whether such coercion creates legal obligations — whether there is a causal relationship between norm and conduct — is a another question for another day[9]. But it won't do to dismiss a rule as "not law" merely because coercion does not flow from the top. A norm can be obligatory — policymakers within a State can feel "obliged" to honour it — even if the State has not freely consented to it.

How can this be so? Why do States do things that they do not want to do? Professor Pellet has provided a succinct and persuasive answer.

"The short answer", he has written, "is because they need to. Not only because they need money, technical assistance, urgent food help, and so on. But also because they feel very strongly the absolute necessity to 'participate'. And this holds true not

---

9. We know that obligation alone does not create law. Social norms such as queuing are obligatory; one sometimes feels "obliged" to stand in line. But no law compels it. The harmonies as well as the pathologies of the international system often are idiopathic; comity, convenience, and coincidence can create an illusion of compliance with a legalist norm when in reality the "felt needs" of the community — the reasons for ostensibly compliant conduct — are in fact quite different. That is why the International Court has rightly insisted upon a causal relationship between practice and *opinio juris. North Sea Continental Shelf* cases *(Federal Republic of Germany* v. *Denmark; Federal Republic of Germany* v. *Netherlands), ICJ Reports 1969*, p. 4 at pp. 44-45 ("There is no evidence that they so acted because they felt legally compelled . . . by a rule of customary international law obliging them to do so").

only for treaties but, more generally, for international law, whatever its form." [10]

States have, in other words, a *practical obligation* to comply with certain norms [11], an obligation generated by what Holmes called "the felt necessities of the times" [12] and by States' drives to meet those necessities. States are thus "obliged" to do certain things — "obliged" to comply with certain norms — not because they freely consent, but because the benefits of compliance, in light of States' needs, outweigh the costs of non-compliance.

Conversely, Professor Pellet's account also provides a cogent answer to the question of why some States decline to comply with some norms. The short answer is, because they don't need to. States weigh costs against benefits and conclude that they don't need whatever it is that they have to give up because of their violation — money, allies, reputation, whatever. They don't feel a need to "participate". This holds true for treaties as well as custom. States do not, in other words, feel "obliged" to carry out rules if the net benefits of compliance don't meet their needs. That is why 19 NATO States representing 780 million people felt free to wage war in flagrant violation [13] of the use-of-force rules of the Charter. They did not feel obliged to honour the Charter's most fundamental rules.

This needs-based approach to law places Professor Pellet in good

---

10. Alain Pellet, "The Normative Dilemma: Will and Consent in International Law-Making", 12 *Australian YBIL* 22, 43 (1988-1889) (hereinafter "The Normative Dilemma").

11. See Michael J. Glennon, "How International Rules Die", 93 *Georgetown LJ* 939 (2005).

12. "The life of the law", Holmes famously wrote, "has not been logic: it has been experience. The felt necessities of the time, the prevalent moral and political theories, intuitions of public policy, avowed or unconscious, even the prejudices which judges share with their fellow-men, have had a good deal more to do than the syllogism in determining the rules by which men should be governed." Oliver Wendell Holmes, *The Common Law*, p. 173 (M. Howe, ed., 1963).

13. The assessment of Bruno Simma is widely shared. He wrote:

"[I]t may be concluded that the NATO threats of air strikes against the FRY, not having been authorized by the Security Council, are not in conformity with the UN Charter. In this regard, it makes little difference that the threat had not been carried out until now because Article 2 (4) prohibits such threats in precisely the same way as it does the actual use of armed force. . . . [T]here is no denying the fact that a requirement of Charter law has been breached." Bruno Simma, "Kosovo: A Thin Red Line", *European Journal of International Law* 10, No. 1 (1999) available at http://www.ejil.org/journal/Vol10/No1/ab1-2.html#Heading2 (visited 2 August 2007).

company, at least from an American perspective. His analysis parallels Justice Holmes's famous "bad man" theory.

> "If you want to know the law and nothing else", Holmes wrote, "you must look at it as a bad man, who cares only for the material consequences which such knowledge enables him to predict, not as a good one, who finds his reasons for conduct . . . in the vaguer sanctions of conscience."[14]

Professor Pellet's insight is similar. In his words, "those who hold the most power and influence" shape international law to guide social conduct in their interest — not in the interest of "all members of society"[15]. States inevitably "take the existence and relative power of other countries into consideration". The needs of the powerful are different from the needs of the weak; the powerful don't need to be concerned about penalties for violation that might dissuade the weak. Obligation is therefore a function of power and influence. A rule that "obliges" the weak may not oblige the powerful — even though the powerful may miscalculate and flout that rule to their peril.

That, in a nutshell, is how legal obligation emerges and also how legal obligation fades: States engage in a hard-headed, cold-blooded calculus, weighing the costs of violation against the benefits of compliance with an international norm. International norms are thus not irrelevant to State policy-making processes; norms probably are *a* factor in many if not most of the cases that present facts situations to which they apply. Norms pervade the international system and provide constant incentives and disincentives for compliance. When norms generate a sufficient measure of compliance, we call them "law". But legal norms that are obligatory, like sub-legal norms that are not, are not are the *only* things that affect States' needs and policy-makers' decisions. The quality of a State's leadership, the power of domestic constituencies, the structure of the international system, the State's relative military and economic power, its "soft power" and myriad other factors all contribute to States' needs and all influence policy-makers' assessment whether they need to violate or comply with the norm in question.

---

14. Oliver Wendell Holmes, "The Path of the Law", 10 *Harv. L. Rev.* 457, 459 (1897).
15. "The Normative Dilemma", *supra* footnote 10, at p. 46.

Now, the question arises whether consent to a rule, once given, can be withdrawn. The argument is made that "once a state . . . has entered into a treaty, the trap closes; its will is bound and will be freed only through processes in which the will of an individual State will have little or nothing to do"[16]. This is Professor Pellet's claim. He writes that "[w]hen they want to terminate the treaty, the parties must act together. 'All states' must express the same will . . ."[17] Why is this so? Because, he suggests, States have consented to this rule: this is the "clear result"[18] of the Vienna Convention.

The problem with this argument is that its logic is circular. Professor Pellet suggests that States have individually willed a rule to the effect that they cannot individually withdraw their will to a rule[19]. But what is the source of this rule? Professor Pellet's insistence that a State cannot will that its will be withdrawn was refuted long ago by Humphrey Waldock in his rejoinder to the argument for *pacta sunt servanda*, demonstrating that that rule — like Professor Pellet's corollary — is grounded upon an infinite regress[20]. For bindingness, Professor Pellet's rule relies upon its own bindingness. It's turtles all the way down.

I'm a bit baffled by this argument because Professor Pellet elsewhere recognizes that "treaty-law changes . . .". It "lives", he writes, "as does any part of law, either through an informal evolution (mainly thanks to interpretation), or formally"[21]. But, of course, change implies the possibility of termination. When a treaty rule takes on a new and different meaning, the old rule terminates and a new rule takes its place. Adaptation and termination both involve ending an old rule. Both presuppose a new rule different from an original rule that no longer exists.

So let us not confuse semantics with substance: it is not true that "whatever its will, a State must abide by the law it entered into"[22]. Treaty-law lives, as does any part of law. Treaty law dies, as does any other part of law. And when treaty law dies, it may die not with

---

16. "The Normative Dilemma", *supra* footnote 10, at p. 35.
17. *Ibid.,* at p. 34.
18. *Ibid.*
19. *Ibid.*
20. J. L. Brierly, *The Origins of International Law in The Law of Nations: An Introduction to the International Law of Peace,* 6th ed., Sir Humphrey Waldock, ed., Cambridge, 1984, p. 57.
21. The Normative Dilemma, *supra* footnote 10, at p. 33.
22. *Ibid.*

a bang but with a whimper. When a significant number of States over an extended period of time engage in a substantial number of violations of a treaty norm — or a customary norm — it is no longer law. It has been allowed to fall into desuetude.

After up to 680 violations, that, I submit, is the fate of the obligation of Article 2 (4) of the United Nations Charter. Article 2 (4) has fallen into desuetude.

Here I disagree with Professor Pellet, whom I gather would continue to call this provision "law". The issue is not morality, as he contended in his oral remarks in this colloquium. The issue is simple analytic clarity. To Professor Pellet, law includes norms that are not obligatory[23]. To me, and to many others, law must oblige. Oscar Schachter, for example, wrote that law "is in essence a system based on a set of rules and obligations. They must in some degree be binding . . ."[24] Rules that nobody cares to heed, Christian Tomuschat said in his 1999 Hague lectures, are not rules[25]. The view that a minimal level of effectiveness is a requirement for legal validity makes sense. As Hans Kelsen put it, "The validity of the law presupposes a minimum efficacy of the law."[26] Roscoe Pound thus distinguished "working rules" that oblige from "paper rules" that do not[27]. Treaty rules as well as customary rules fall into desuetude when they change from working rules to paper rules. Clarity of analysis is not advanced by confusing the two; paper rules may still in some circumstances generate compliance — but not often enough to qualify as law, for the key element of obligation is missing[28].

That is what has happened to the UN Charter's use-of-force rules. There is nothing innovative or novel in this conclusion. In 1970 Tom Franck forcefully announced the "demise of Article 2 (4)"[29]. Jean

---

23. "[A]s long as it influences or guides", he writes, "it is nonetheless a legal norm." *Ibid.*, at p. 38.

24. Oscar Schachter, "International Law in Theory and Practice. General Course in Public International Law", 178 *Recueil des cours* 25 (1982).

25. Christian Tomuschat, "International Law: Ensuring the Survival of Mankind on the Eve of a New Century. General Course on Public International Law", 281 *Recueil des cours* 447, para. 31 (1999).

26. Hans Kelsen, "Law and Peace in International Relations", p. 16 (1942).

27. Roscoe Pound, "Law in Books and Law in Action", 44 *Am. L. Rev.* 12 (1910).

28. The argument has been made that this difference is more semantic than substantive. See Glanville Williams, "International Law and the Controversy Concerning the Word 'Law'", 22 *BYIL* 146, 151 (1945).

29. Thomas M. Franck, "Who Killed Article 2 (4)?", 64 *Am. J. Int'l L.* 809, 809 (1970). "The practice of these States has so severely shattered [mutual

Combacau[30], Anthony Arend[31], Richard Falk[32] and others have expressed similar views.

Others assert that Article 51 has not disappeared but has merely "evolved". One view is that the scope of its prohibition has narrowed and that Article 51 now permits the use of defensive force in response to an "imminent" threat of attack. But this argument is unconvincing. The premise on which it rests is no different than the premise on which desuetude analysis rests: the premise of both approaches is that practice inconsistent with a treaty rule changes the rule. If incongruent practice can change a treaty rule a little, it can

---

confidence in] . . . the precepts of Article 2 (4) that . . . only the words remain . . . In the twenty-five years since the San Francisco Conference, there have been some one hundred separate outbreaks of hostilities between states. . . ." Franck, *op. cit.* footnote 29, *supra*, at pp. 810-811. "What killed Article 2 (4) was the wide disparity between the norms it sought to establish and the practical goals that nations are pursuing in defense of their national interest." Thomas M. Franck, "Who Killed Article 2 (4)?", 64 *Am. J. Int'l L.* 809, 837 (1970). Twenty years later Article 2 (4) in Franck's view remained dead:

> "[T]he extensive body of international 'law' which forbids direct or indirect intervention by one state in the domestic affairs of another [and] precludes the aggressive use of force by one state against another . . . simply, if sadly, is not predictive of the ways of the world." Thomas M. Franck, *The Power of Legitimacy among Nations* 32 (1990).

In 2003, following the U.S. invasion of Iraq, Franck concluded that Article 2 (4) "has died again, and, this time, perhaps for good". Thomas M. Franck, "Future Implications of the Iraq Conflict: What Happens Now? The United Nations after Iraq", 97 *AJIL* 607, 610 (July 2003).

30. Reviewing practice under the Charter through 1986, Combacau concluded that

> "the international community no longer believes in the system of the Charter . . . [and] is in fact back where it was in 1945: in the state of nature . . ." Jean Combacau, "The Exception of Self-Defense in United Nations Practice", in *The Current Legal Regulation of the Use of Force*, pp. 9, 32 (A. Cassese, ed., 1986).

31. "[T]hrough customary practice", Arend observed, "states have withdrawn their consent" from Article 2 (4); the argument that it is still in force denies "the dynamic nature of international law". Anthony Clark Arend, *Legal Rules and International Society* 75 (1999).

32. Falk has opined that

> "the [Charter's] formalized . . . renunciation of nondefensive claims to use force . . . provide little assured restraint upon state action. The decline of normative restraint can be seen in the broadening of the definition of self-defense and in the increasing resort to unilateral force by sovereign states. A consequence of this is to convert the rules of behavior embedded in the United Nations Charter into aspirational norms." Richard Falk, *Revitalizing International Law*, p. 96 (1989).

"The conclusion", for Falk, "is that the legal effort to regulate recourse to force in international relations has virtually collapsed in state-to-state relations." *Ibid.*, at pp. 96-97.

change it a lot, and if it can change a rule a lot, it can eviscerate the rule altogether. There is no conceptual difference between a process that creates a different rule and a process that creates a *laissez-faire* rule. What State practice supports the conclusion that the speeding sled of desuetude stopped abruptly three-fourths of the way down the hill but not at the bottom ? Recall the reminder of the *Lotus* Court that the burden of persuasion is on he who advocates restrictions on States' freedom to act, not upon advocates of freedom[33]. Recall too the reminder of the Court in the *Nicaragua* case : "The mere fact that States declare their recognition of certain rules is not sufficient", it said. "The Court must satisfy itself that the existence of the rule in the *opinio juris* is confirmed by practice." Ask yourself : what has been State practice ? How many States have declined to use armed force in response to a serious and probable threat because they believed that that threat was not yet imminent ?

The question of course answers itself : there is no such practice, and there is no such practice for the obvious reason that as a matter of political reality, the so-called "imminence" requirement is a formula for national suicide. It would forbid a State from using *any* amount of force — even *de minimis* force against a *serious* and *likely* threat — until that threat has become imminent. In real-world practice, the gravity of a threat and the probability of its occurrence weigh far more heavily than a threat's imminence. If a nation is faced with a threat from some rogue State or terrorist group that is both grave and probable, what real-world decision-maker would delay acting until that threat is immediate — until there are no alternatives — until it may be impossible for the State to defend itself ?

Others argue, conversely, that Article 51 has evolved in the opposite direction. They insist that Article 51 has become more restrictive. They claim that Article 51 now *prohibits* a State from defending itself with armed force *even if that State has been subject to an actual armed attack* unless the Security Council has given its prior approval. Professor Pellet himself argued that the action taken by the United States against the Taliban and Al-Qaeda in Afghanistan was unlawful because it was undertaken without prior authorization by the Security Council. Three weeks after the 11 September attacks —

---

33. "The rules of law binding upon states . . . emanate from their own free will as expressed in conventions . . . . [R]estrictions upon the independence of states therefore cannot be presumed." *Lotus, [1927] PCIJ, Ser. A, No. 10*, at p. 18.

before the United States had taken or announced any military action in response — Professor Pellet was concerned about the United States "reflex for vengeance". He wrote the following:

> "It would be contrary to the letter as much as to the spirit of Article 51 that the United States, alone or with other states, were to by-pass the Council and proceed, alone and without its endorsement, with an armed response."[34]

I ask again: what State practice supports this his new rule? How many States that have been subjected to an *actual armed attack* have waited for Security Council approval before defending themselves? The question, again, answers itself — there is no such practice.

Boutros Boutros-Ghali has taken Professor Pellet's argument a step further. The former Secretary-General insisted on 6 September at this colloquium that, under the Charter, self-defence may be exercised only against an attack by a State, not against a non-State actor like Al-Qaeda. "Article 51 is talking about an aggression from a state against another state", he asserted. "It is very clear . . . The concept of non-state actors is a new concept which has existed only for the last 5 or 10 years." The United States therefore was not permitted under Article 51 to respond with the use of force to the attack by Al-Qaeda and the Taliban on the United States; it was not, he opined, part of the inherent right of self-defence.

It is mercifully understated, in my view, to suggest that this contention has no support in international law. Set aside considerations concerning consent, obligation, and desuetude, sketched out earlier. Assume that the United Nations Charter is still good law. The Charter in plain terms recognizes the "inherent right" of States to use armed force in response to an armed attack. Nowhere does it say that the attack in question must come from a State. The Security Council itself on 12 September 2001 underscored its recognition of that inherent right in unanimously adopting resolution 1368, in which it "unequivocally condemn[ed]" the previous day's attacks as an act of

---

34. Alain Pellet, "No, This is Not War!", *European Journal of International Law*, Discussion Forum, "The Attack on the World Trade Center: Legal Responses, 3 October 2001", available at http://www.ejil.org/forum_WTC/ny-pellet.html#fn (visited 13 August 2007). "One can understand the United States' reflex for vengeance", Professor Pellet continued. "But to understand is not to approve." *Ibid.* The action taken by the United States against the Taliban and Al-Qaeda in Afghanistan was not, in his view, lawful because the United States did not seek the Security Council's approval.

"international terrorism" that was a "threat to international peace and security"[35]. How can it be, therefore, that the right to use force against an attacker encompasses only attacking *States*? Were the United States and Britain both wrong when they concluded in 1838, after *The Caroline* incident[36], that force could lawfully be used against non-State actors (who had used the boat to support insurgents)? When did these and other States consent to a new, different rule that is at odds with the one that they accepted in the United Nations Charter?

I know that some will respond, as Professor Pellet did in his oral remarks, that all this is just another argument that might makes right. I beg to differ. I make no claim that the law as I have described it today is "right" in any moral sense. My account of the law is *de*scriptive, not *pre*scriptive. I describe the law as it is, not the law as it should be. I look to the deeds of those who make that law, not to the words of those who would like to. Rules that work — the law as it is — are made by States, not by law professors. Rules created by States capture the complexity of the real world more fully — and therefore work better — than rules imagined by publicists. Rules that work are made by State policy-makers whose lives are grounded in geopolitical give-and-take, in power and weakness, in confusion and uncertainty, in conflicting cultures and clashing personalities. It is too easy for the professoriate to imagine a different world, too easy to create simplistic "models" that leave out what really matters, too easy to build castles in the sky grounded on logic but not experience[37]. This well-intentioned but misguided moralism is worse than pointless — it is ultimately destructive of the legalist ends that it seeks to achieve, for fanciful rules undermine real rules. They create the illusion that all international rules are merely hortatory and can be violated with impunity. "Laws, like houses, lean on one another"[38], as Burke put it. What would the international system actually look like, hobbled with this new utopian purity? Would it

---

35. Sec. res. 1368, 12 September 2001.
36. See Daniel Webster, Letter to Henry Fox, British Minister in Washington (24 April 1841) in Kenneth Bourne and D. Cameron Watt, eds., 1 *British Documents on Foreign Affairs: Reports and Papers from the Foreign Office*, Part I, Series C, at p. 153 (1986).
37. See Holmes, *supra* footnote 12.
38. Edmund Burke, *Tracts Relating to Popery Laws,* Chap. 3, Part. 1 (1765; reprinted in *The Writings and Speeches of Edmund Burke,* Vol. 9, ed. by Paul Langford, 1991.

attract the States that, the moralists say, should participate more fully in the international legal system? What tools would their Kantian system wield to confront the very real crises that loom over humanity in this turbulent century — terrorism and genocide and climate change? The answer, one fears, is hinted in Charles Péguy's remark to the effect that Kant's ethics has clean hands — but it has no hands.

The challenge faced by the international legal order today is not to devise purer rules untainted by the of *sturm und drang* of geopolitics — rules that would be based, ultimately, upon values that the world does not share. "[T]here is grave danger", Henry Cabot Lodge said, "in an unshared idealism."[39] The challenge is to remember that States make international rules governing use of force for one overriding purpose — to enhance their security — and that rules that stand in the way of States' security wind up on the back shelves of archives, gathering dust. The challenge is to assess States' capacities before assessing their obligations — to ground legal discourse upon empiricism, not metaphysics — to begin our analysis with *descrip*tion, not *pre*scription.

I conclude with the words of someone who similarly *de*scribed the law. He described the effect of widespread violation of a regime intended to "enforce peace by providing security from and a deterrent against aggression . . ."[40]. I trust that no one seriously would contend that he was making a veiled argument that might makes right. He wrote as follows:

> "The frustration of [its] overriding object . . . has gone so far that it is no longer merely a political fact constituting a regrettable departure from the law. That failure has now become part of the law; . . . [I]ts impotence when repeated, tolerated and willed, must tell in the end; its continued futility ceases to be a disappointment of legitimate expectations . . . [T]here has disappeared a vital condition of the obligation of collective security."[41]

---

39. Senator Henry Cabot Lodge, Address in Washington D.C. (12 August 1919), available online at <http://www.firstworldwar.com/source/lodge_leagueofnations.htm> (visited 18 September 2005).

40. Hersch Lauterpacht, Address to the Cambridge University League of Nations Union, 16 November 1938, reprinted in *International Law, Being the Collected Papers of Hersch Lauterpacht*, E. Lauterpacht, ed., Vol. 3, p. 576 (1977).

41. *Ibid.,* at p. 576, 578.

These are not the words a "denier" of international law or of some mindless mouthpiece of hegemonic power. They are the words of Hersch Lauterpacht, spoken in November 1938. He was referring to Article 10 of the League of Nations Covenant — the provision, he said, that had been "repeatedly described by leading lawyers as the backbone of the Covenant"[42]. His conclusion was that in light of its non-observance, the obligation of Article 10 had, as he put it, "been allowed to fall into desuetude"[43].

The question that we confront today is a simple one, and the question is this: was Hersch Lauterpacht wrong — and if not, why does the same conclusion not apply to the use-of-force rules in the UN Charter, which have been violated even *more* times by even *more* States from even *more* regions for even *more* years?

Alain Pellet

Outre l'honneur que je ressens à avoir été convié à cette conférence commémorative de l'un des actes fondateurs du droit international contemporain, je suis heureux de cette occasion de croiser, non pas le fer mais des «arguments», avec mon vieil ami Michael Glennon, que j'ai, naguère, connu moins anxieux d'excuser les violations du droit au nom de la puissance. Car, bien qu'il ait, cet après-midi, fait (relativement) patte de velours et manifesté plus de retenue dans son acharnement à défendre la «politique juridique» (ou antijuridique?) de l'actuelle administration des Etats-Unis), je n'arrive pas, malgré ses protestations, à interpréter sa fort stimulante intervention autrement que comme un hymne au «might is right» ou, si l'on préfère, un remarquable exercice de pompier pyromane; car, en gros, et malgré l'adresse de sa présentation — à laquelle je rends hommage —, son message me paraît être le suivant: les violations du droit international deviennent règles de droit lorsqu'elles sont commises par les plus puissants; les Etats-Unis (et quelques autres moindres seigneurs — car je concède volontiers qu'ils ne sont pas les seuls à passer outre, mais leur plus grande puissance les investit d'une responsabilité plus grande) ont détruit le principe de l'interdiction du recours à la force dans les relations internationales conformément à la Charte des Nations Unies; comme l'absence de règles est un grand mal pour

---

42. Lauterpacht, *op. cit.* footnote 40, *supra*, at p. 577.
43. *Ibid.*

les faibles, remplaçons-le par des principes nouveaux permettant... aux Etats-Unis d'intervenir en fonction de leur meilleur intérêt.

Tel, à mes yeux, ne saurait être le droit. Cela étant, je n'ai pas l'intention de me placer sur le terrain très abstrait sur lequel mon contradicteur et ami s'est lui-même situé pour présenter mes propres vues — infiniment moins hétérodoxes, et donc, je le crains, moins amusantes (ou... effrayantes) — sur la question qui nous a été posée. Pour y répondre, je procéderai par « propositions successives » dont j'essaierai d'illustrer le bien-fondé sur la base de raisonnements qui n'ont aucune prétention à l'originalité.

Au préalable, je souhaite tout de même faire trois remarques liminaires :

En premier lieu, il m'apparaît que, même si elle est vaste, la question qui nous est posée l'est moins que Michael Glennon l'a envisagé : il ne s'agit pas de disserter, d'une manière générale, sur le recours à la force en ce début du XXIᵉ siècle, moins encore sur la vie et la mort des règles de droit international ou sur l'essence de celui-ci, mais de déterminer dans quelle mesure le recours à la force demeure un moyen licite de règlement des différends.

En deuxième lieu, avec tout le respect que je dois aux organisateurs de notre conférence, je ne crois pas qu'il existe des « différends politiques » par opposition aux « différends juridiques » ; comme l'a dit la Cour internationale de Justice dans son arrêt de 1980 dans l'affaire des otages :

« Nul n'a ... jamais prétendu que, parce qu'un différend juridique soumis à la Cour ne constitue qu'un aspect d'un différend politique, la Cour doit se refuser à résoudre dans l'intérêt des parties les questions juridiques qui les opposent »[44] ;

l'inverse est tout aussi exact : tout différend comporte des aspects juridiques et des aspects politiques et c'est, en définitive, le moyen retenu pour le régler qui constitue le meilleur — peut-être le seul — critère permettant de le qualifier[45] : le fait d'utiliser la force pour

---

44. Arrêt du 24 mai 1980, *Personnel diplomatique et consulaire des Etats-Unis à Téhéran, CIJ Recueil 1980*, p. 20, par. 37.

45. En ce sens, voir R. Higgins, « Policy Considerations and the International Judicial Process », *International and Comparative Law Quarterly*, vol. 17, 1968, p. 74, ou A. Pellet, « Le glaive et la balance — Remarques sur le rôle de la CIJ en matière de maintien de la paix et de la sécurité internationales », *International Law at a Time of Perplexity — Essays in Honour of Shabtai Rosenne*, Nijhoff, Dordrecht, Boston, Londres, 1989, pp. 551-559.

régler un différend le rend «politique» — mais ce caractère n'est pas «inscrit dans les gênes» de catégories de litiges prédéterminés.

En troisième lieu, et enfin, bien que je sois le premier à considérer qu'une telle limitation est, par elle-même, discutable, par souci d'aller à l'essentiel, je m'en tiendrai, à la force armée sans me poser la question de l'utilisation d'autres moyens de coercition, parfois tout aussi redoutables et, dans certaines circonstances, sans doute tout aussi illicites, que le recours à la coercition militaire.

Au bénéfice de ces remarques, mes propositions, au nombre de quatre, sont les suivantes:

1) dans la société internationale contemporaine, les relations entre règlement des différends et recours à la force sont paradoxales;
2) les règles de la Charte relatives au recours à la force conservent aujourd'hui toute leur valeur et toute leur force juridique obligatoire, mais
3) elles doivent être interprétées à la lumière des évolutions que le droit international a connues depuis 1945; il n'en reste pas moins que,
4) en aucun cas, le recours à la force ne peut constituer un moyen licite de régler les différends entre Etats et les seules exceptions au principe de l'interdiction du recours à la force sont celles qui permettent de faire prévaloir les intérêts communautaires sur les intérêts individuels des Etats.

Première proposition: Dans la société internationale contemporaine, les relations entre règlement des différends et recours à la force sont paradoxales

Dans la société westphalienne traditionnelle, le recours à la force constituait un moyen licite et, aussi monstrueux que ceci nous paraisse aujourd'hui, normal, de régler les différends entre Etats — il en résultait notamment que, dans ce contexte,

> «[e]n droit, la notion de légitime défense n'[avait] alors guère de sens. Pour que la légitime défense soit légitime, il faut que l'attaque soit illégitime!»[46]

---

46. Emile Giraud, «La théorie de la légitime défense», *Recueil des cours*, tome 49 (1934), p. 692; dans le même sens, Robert Kolb, «La légitime défense des Etats au XIXe siècle et pendant l'époque de la Société des Nations», dans Rahim Kherad (dir. publ.), *Légitimes défenses*, LGDJ, Paris, 2007, p. 27.

Les Conférences de la Paix de 1899 et de 1907 ont porté un premier coup à ce qui, jusqu'alors, avait toujours semblé aller de soi. Mais elles l'ont fait l'une et l'autre en mettant l'accent sur la nécessité de rechercher un règlement pacifique des différends et en en facilitant la possibilité, sans pour autant prohiber le recours à la force, qui est réglementée mais pas interdite — sous une réserve (marginale mais symbolique) cependant: la Convention II de 1907, dite «Drago-Porter» qui, à la suite de l'indignation suscitée en Amérique latine par le blocus des ports vénézuéliens, exclut le recours à la force pour le recouvrement des dettes contractuelles à condition que la partie défaillante se prête à un arbitrage. La suite est connue:

— le Pacte de la SDN accentue et la tendance à la limitation du recours à la force (tout en n'y offrant aucune alternative crédible) et l'obligation — encore relative — de la recherche de règlements pacifiques des différends;
— dans l'esprit du Protocole de Genève de 1924 (qui n'est jamais entré en vigueur), par le Pacte Briand-Kellog de 1928 les parties «condamnent le recours à la guerre pour le règlement des différends internationaux» et

> «reconnaissent que le règlement ou la solution de tous les différends ou conflits, de quelque nature ou de quelque origine qu'ils puissent être, qui pourront surgir entre elles, ne devra jamais être recherché que par des moyens pacifiques»[47];

oh! certes, comme Michael Glennon l'a relevé à l'envi, le «Traité général de renonciation à la guerre comme instrument de politique nationale» n'a pas empêché la seconde guerre mondiale; mais il me paraît difficile d'en nier la juridicité et le jugement de Nuremberg en atteste:

> «la renonciation solennelle à la guerre comme instrument de politique nationale implique que la guerre ainsi prévue est, en droit international, illégitime. Ceux qui la préparent ou la dirigent, déterminant par là ses inévitables et terribles conséquences, commettent un crime»[48];

---

47. Art. 1.
48. Jugement du Tribunal militaire international, 1er octobre 1946, *Procès des grands criminels de guerre devant le Tribunal militaire international, Nuremberg, 14 novembre 1945-1er octobre 1946*, Nuremberg, 1947, t. I, p. 232.

— adopté la même année, l'Acte général d'arbitrage renforce l'obligation de règlement pacifique mais n'offre pas davantage d'alternative réelle au recours à la force en cas de blocage ;
— c'est avec la Charte des Nations Unies que l'optique change. Essentiellement de deux manières. En premier lieu, l'obsession du règlement pacifique est abandonnée. Sans doute, l'article 2, paragraphe 3, et l'article 33 en maintiennent-ils le principe, mais pas d'une manière générale ; seulement si la prolongation du différend « est susceptible de menacer le maintien de la paix et de la sécurité internationales ». Comme on l'a écrit,

> « il est relativement indifférent à la Charte que les Etats trouvent une solution à leurs différends : ce qui lui importe, c'est que ces différends ne s'enveniment pas au point de les conduire à les régler par la force »[49].

Le règlement pacifique des différends est subordonné par la Charte au maintien de la paix — et cela constitue, me semble-t-il, un premier et fort argument en faveur de l'illicéité du recours à la force pour régler les litiges entre Etats : le but premier, le but ultime de la Charte, c'est le maintien de la paix ; il ne peut évidemment être atteint par le recours à la force armée, qui est le contraire de la paix. Permettez-moi de souligner que, pour établir cela, il n'est besoin d'interpréter ni l'article 2, paragraphe 4, ni l'article 51 ; les dispositions concernant le seul règlement des différends — que Michael Glennon n'a pas mentionnées — y suffisent. Il reste que, en second lieu, la Charte est tout de même aussi à l'origine d'une autre et considérable mutation : contrairement, ici encore, aux affirmations de mon savant contradicteur (et comme l'a rappelé, par exemple, Anne-Marie Slaughter au cours d'un autre dialogue avec lui — dans la revue *Foreign Affairs* en 2003[50]), la Charte, loin d'être animée par un esprit légaliste ou idéaliste est, dans ce domaine, fondamentalement pragmatique : en confiant la « responsabilité principale » du maintien de la paix au Conseil de sécurité, elle prend acte de la nécessité de l'accord des Puissances ; en prévoyant, dans son article 42, la possibilité d'opérations nécessaires au maintien de la paix et de

---

49. J. Charpentier et B. Sierpinski, « Commentaire de l'article 2, paragraphe 3 », dans J.-P. Cot, A. Pellet et M. Forteau (dir. publ.), *La Charte des Nations Unies — Commentaire article par article*, Economica, 2005, p. 429.
50. « Misreading the Record », *Foreign Affairs*, 2003, p. 203.

la sécurité internationales exécutées «par des forces aériennes, navales ou terrestres *de Membres des Nations Unies*», elle reconnaît que les instruments de la puissance militaire demeurent aux mains des Etats; et, en rappelant, dans son article 51, le droit «inhérent de légitime défense individuelle ou collective», elle fait preuve du plus grand (et du plus nécessaire...) des réalismes.

Il reste — et j'en reviens à mon paradoxe initial — que ce réalisme, contrairement au vieux cynisme d'avant le Pacte de la SDN, qui admettait que les différends puissent être réglés par la force des armes, n'exclut pas totalement l'usage de la force armée (en droit comme en fait), ni ne prévoit de mécanisme garantissant que tout différend sera réglé, d'une manière ou d'une autre. Mais cela n'est évidemment pas la fin de la question.

Deuxième proposition: Les règles de la Charte relatives au recours à la force conservent aujourd'hui toute leur valeur et toute leur force juridique obligatoire

Comme Michael Glennon, je suis tout à fait convaincu que, quand bien même elles sont énoncées dans le traité le plus solennel qui soit, les règles de droit évoluent (et doivent évoluer) en fonction des situations sous-jacentes et des rapports de forces — des «infrastructures», même si ce vocabulaire marxisant n'est plus à la mode. Non seulement, elles doivent être interprétées à la lumière des évolutions que le droit a ultérieurement connues, mais je conviens en outre bien volontiers que, toutes conventionnelles qu'elles soient, elles peuvent être modifiées ou abrogées par des règles coutumières contraires ou différentes. Mais cette constatation qu'aucun internationaliste ne devrait, je pense, contester, est soumise à deux *caveat* importants:

— en premier lieu, on ne saurait conclure légèrement au changement ou à la désuétude de règles qui constituent le fondement même de la société internationale depuis plus de soixante ans, et dont on peut, à mon avis légitimement, soutenir qu'elles ont le caractère de normes impératives du droit international général — même si le *jus cogens* lui-même n'est pas immuable;
— en second lieu, il ne faut pas confondre la modification de la règle avec sa violation; sans doute est-il exact que toute modification coutumière d'une règle existante suppose au départ sa vio-

lation; mais l'alchimie compliquée de la formation coutumière du droit ne saurait se satisfaire de la simple addition de violations — même si celles-ci sont nombreuses; même si elles sont imputables à plusieurs Etats; même si la puissance dominante du moment est à l'origine des violations les plus graves et les plus nombreuses de ces règles fondamentales (pour l'excellente raison que c'est elle qui a les moyens de les violer le plus «efficacement» car impunément); ce n'est pas parce que des meurtres, des viols, des rapts sont commis quotidiennement qu'ils cessent d'être des crimes — passibles d'engager la responsabilité de leurs auteurs, quand bien même ceux-ci ne sont pas forcément punis effectivement.

Aujourd'hui comme hier, on ne saurait voir dans l'utilisation unilatérale de la force armée que la manifestation d'une politique de puissance

> «qui, dans le passé, a donné lieu aux abus les plus graves et qui ne saurait, quelles que soient les déficiences présentes de l'organisation internationale, trouver aucune place dans le droit international»[51].

Sans doute, cette célèbre formule remonte-t-elle à 1949, mais je ne trouve dans la démonstration brillante de Michael Glennon aucun élément de nature à la remettre en question.

Comme l'a dit très justement la Cour, si les Etats

> «traitent eux-mêmes les comportements non conformes à la règle en question comme des violations de celle-ci et non pas comme des manifestations de la reconnaissance d'une règle nouvelle»

ou

> «[s]i un Etat agit d'une manière apparemment inconciliable avec une règle reconnue, mais défend sa conduite en invoquant des exceptions ou justifications contenues dans la règle elle-même, il en résulte une confirmation plutôt qu'un affaiblissement de la règle...»[52]

---

51. CIJ, arrêt du 9 avril 1949, *Détroit de Corfou (fond)*, *CIJ Recueil 1949*, p. 35. Ce *dictum* célèbre concerne «le prétendu droit d'intervention».
52. Arrêt du 27 juin 1986, *Activités militaires et paramilitaires au Nicaragua et contre celui-ci*, *CIJ Recueil 1986*, p. 98, par. 186.

Or, n'en déplaise à mon contradicteur, je ne connais aucun exemple de recours unilatéral à la force dont la conformité à la Charte faisait problème, dont l'auteur n'ait pas tenté de justifier son action en invoquant les hypothèses dans lesquelles les règles de San Francisco admettent une exception à l'interdiction. Même l'URSS les a invoquées lorsqu'elle a envahi l'Afghanistan[53]; et la France lors de ses interventions en Afrique; et les Etats-Unis eux-mêmes pour justifier leur agression contre l'Irak en 2005 ou — et de manière particulièrement nette — dans leurs plaidoiries orales devant la CIJ dans l'affaire des *Plates-formes pétrolières*[54]. Quant aux réactions des autres Etats, il faut un tropisme singulier pour y voir des applaudissements à la violation et des « manifestations de la reconnaissance d'une règle nouvelle »; il est significatif que même l'intervention de l'OTAN au Kosovo (dont, à mes yeux, la légitimité — à défaut de la licéité — n'était pas douteuse) ait été condamnée par ceux-là mêmes dont, pour d'autres raisons, on aurait pu s'attendre à ce qu'ils l'approuvent[55].

Le principe de l'interdiction du recours à la force contrairement à la Charte conserve — et j'allais dire « conserve évidemment » — toute sa valeur juridique. Ce n'est pas à dire qu'il soit, dans sa substance, demeuré immuable.

Troisième proposition: Le principe de l'interdiction du recours à la force doit, bien entendu, être interprété à la lumière des évolutions que la société internationale a connues depuis 1945

Je serai rapide sur ce point car, pour importante qu'elle soit dans l'absolu, cette troisième proposition n'a, en réalité, qu'un intérêt limité pour le thème qui nous occupe: la force *et* le règlement des différends.

Disons, pour faire court, que « l'évolution que le droit a ultérieu-

---

53. Voir, par exemple, S/PV.2186, 5 janvier 1980, par. 19 (déclaration de M. Troyanovsky au nom de l'URSS).

54. Voir notamment CR 2003/12, 28 février 2003, par. 18.42-18.61 (M. Matheson).

55. Pour une présentation remarquablement argumentée (mais, à mes yeux, trop rigide et catégorique) de la thèse diamétralement opposée à celle soutenue par M. Glennon, voir Olivier Corten, *Le droit contre la guerre*, Paris, Pedone, 2008, notamment pp. 352-390, 536-594, 630-669, 685-704 ou 779-804, où l'auteur montre que, dans la pratique, l'opposition à l'abandon des règles posées en 1945 a toujours été dominante.

rement connue [dans ce domaine] grâce à la Charte des Nations Unies et à la coutume»[56] conduit à faire les constatations (non exhaustives) suivantes:

i) en cas de blocage du Conseil de sécurité, qui a, en la matière, une responsabilité *principale* (mais non exclusive), l'Assemblée générale, à défaut de pouvoir obliger les Etats à recourir à la force armée, peut les y autoriser; telle est la principale conséquence, malheureusement sous-utilisée à mes yeux, de la résolution «Union pour le maintien de la paix», dont la CIJ a validé la pratique dans son avis sur les *Conséquences juridiques de l'édification d'un mur dans le territoire palestinien* de 2004[57];

ii) le droit naturel de légitime défense peut être exercé dans l'hypothèse d'une attaque armée imminente et prouvée[58]; et

iii) il peut être invoqué dans le cas d'une agression par un ou des groupes non étatiques et, en tout cas, dans l'hypothèse d'une action terroriste massive comme celle du 11 septembre 2001 ainsi que cela résulte des résolutions 1368 (2001) et 1373 (2001) des 12 et 28 septembre 2001[59];

iv) la notion de menace contre la paix n'est pas limitée à des conflits interétatiques (en admettant qu'elle l'ait jamais été) et de multiples hypothèses justifient que le Conseil de sécurité en tire les conséquences dans le cadre du chapitre VII, y compris en cas de «catastrophe humanitaire»; cela ressort clairement, par

---

56. Cf. CIJ, avis consultatifs des 21 juin 1971, *Conséquences juridiques pour les Etats de la présence continue de l'Afrique du Sud en Namibie (Sud-Ouest africain) nonobstant la résolution 276 (1970) du Conseil de sécurité, CIJ Recueil 1971*, p. 31, par. 53, et 16 octobre 1975, *Sahara occidental, CIJ Recueil 1975*, p. 32, par. 56.

57. 9 juillet 2004, *Conséquences juridiques de l'édification d'un mur dans le territoire palestinien occupé, CIJ Recueil 2004*, pp. 150-151, par. 29-30.

58. Voir le rapport du Secrétaire général, *Dans une liberté plus grande: développement, sécurité et respect des droits de l'homme pour tous*:

«Les menaces imminentes sont pleinement couvertes par l'article 51 de la Charte, qui garantit le droit naturel de légitime défense de tout Etat souverain, dans le cas où il est l'objet d'une agression armée. Les juristes ont depuis longtemps établi que cette disposition couvre les attaques imminentes, ainsi que celles qui ont déjà eu lieu» (A/59/2005, par. 124);

contra: Olivier Corten, «Le débat sur la légitime défense préventive à l'occasion des 60 ans de l'ONU: Nouvelles revendications, oppositions persistantes» (dans R. Kherad (dir. publ.), *op. cit. supra* note 46, pp. 217-232) et *op. cit. supra* note 55, pp. 630-669, qui analyse les opinions contraires exprimées par les Etats.

59. Sur ce point, je partage l'opinion exprimée par M. Glennon lors de nos discussions du 6 septembre 2007.

exemple du rapport de 2004 du groupe des personnalités de haut
niveau sur les menaces, les défis et les changements:

> « Tout événement ou phénomène meurtrier ou qui compro-
> met la survie et sape les fondements de l'Etat en tant qu'élé-
> ment de base du système international constitue une menace
> contre la sécurité internationale. » [60]

Il s'agit là de précisions d'importance, mais elles ne sont pas de
nature à remettre en cause les dispositions de la Charte, dont le
Sommet mondial de 2005 a estimé qu'elles étaient « suffisantes pour
faire face à l'ensemble des menaces contre la paix et la sécurité
internationales » [61]. Au surplus, comme je l'ai dit, j'éprouve quelque
difficulté à voir comment elles influent sur la réponse à apporter à la
question qui nous a été posée. Il me semble en effet, en guise de
conclusion, qu'elles laissent intact le principe selon lequel:

*Quatrième et dernière proposition: Le recours à la force ne peut
   constituer un moyen licite de régler les différends entre Etats,
   étant entendu que les seules exceptions au principe de l'interdiction du recours à la force sont celles qui permettent de faire prévaloir les intérêts communautaires sur les intérêts individuels des
   Etats*

En réalité, aucune des précisions (des modifications si l'on y
tient) apportées par la pratique des soixante dernières années à la
portée et aux modalités de mise en œuvre du principe de l'interdiction du recours à la force ne me paraît avoir d'incidence directe sur
le principe fondamental selon lequel les Etats n'ont pas l'obligation
absolue de régler leurs différends mais ont, en revanche, s'ils les
règlent, celle de ne jamais les régler par la force.

Le recours à la force, lorsqu'il est autorisé par la Charte, ne vise
jamais et en aucune manière à régler un différend, mais à mettre fin
à une situation dans laquelle la paix est rompue ou menacée, ou à
empêcher qu'elle le soit. On pourrait, dans une perspective académique, invoquer ici la célèbre et délicate distinction entre « différends » et « situations ». Mais ce détour me paraît inutile: il suffit

---

60. Rapport du groupe de personnalités de haut niveau sur les menaces, les
défis et les changements, *Un monde plus sûr: notre affaire à tous*, A/59/565,
p. 12 et p. 26.
61. Document final du Sommet mondial de 2005, A/60/1, par. 79.

bien plutôt de constater que les seules hypothèses dans lesquelles l'usage de la force demeure licite en vertu de la Charte et des évolutions qu'elle a connues sont celles dans lesquelles les intérêts de la communauté internationale dans son ensemble sont en cause — et, d'abord, celui qui demeure au centre des préoccupations des Etats — de tous les Etats : le maintien de la paix et de la sécurité internationales.

Si une évolution a eu lieu depuis 1945, elle a consisté à affirmer l'idée, en germe dans la Charte cependant[62], que la paix et la sécurité internationales ne sont pas mises en danger seulement par le recours à la force armée ou sa menace, mais qu'elles le sont aussi, pour reprendre l'expression du rapport «Evans/Sahnoun» sur *La responsabilité de protéger*, par les situations «manifestement «attentatoire[s] à la conscience de l'humanité»[63]. Mais, dans ces circonstances exceptionnelles, si les mots ont un sens, il ne s'agit plus de régler un différend entre Etats, mais de faire prévaloir l'«intérêt de tous les Etats à maintenir un ordre international stable»[64]. Le préambule de la Charte ne dit d'ailleurs pas autre chose lorsque les «peuples des Nations Unies» s'y déclarent résolus

> «à accepter des principes et instituer des méthodes garantissant qu'il ne sera pas fait usage de la force des armes, *sauf dans l'intérêt commun*».

Alors que la conviction que le recours à la force contrairement à la Charte est interdit demeure fermement ancrée dans les esprits (pas dans celui de Michael Glennon, il est vrai...), c'est sans doute l'idée que l'on se fait de cet «intérêt commun» qui a le plus évolué depuis 1945. Au sortir de la guerre, la paix apparaissait comme le bien suprême, un but presque exclusif, en tout cas premier, en comparaison duquel les autres objectifs des Nations Unies étaient rabaissés au rang de moyens[65]. Aujourd'hui, on assiste sûrement à la concurrence de principes, considérés comme également éminents et qu'il n'est pas toujours aisé de concilier. L'exemple topique en est donné par le dilemme qui peut exister entre l'interdiction du recours à la force et

---

62. Cf. surtout le préambule et l'article 1, paragraphe 1.
63. Cf. le rapport de la Commission internationale de l'intervention et de la souveraineté des Etats, *La responsabilité de protéger*, par. 4.13.
64. *Ibid.*
65. Voir l'article 55 de la Charte et le commentaire de A. Pellet dans J.-P. Cot, A. Pellet et M. Forteau (dir. publ.), *La Charte des Nations Unies — Commentaire article par article*, Economica, Paris, 2005, pp. 1451-1480.

celle du génocide : si un génocide ou des crimes massifs contre l'humanité sont commis, en Bosnie-Herzégovine, au Rwanda, au Darfour ou ailleurs, faut-il, en l'absence d'une autorisation du Conseil de sécurité, se croiser les bras et laisser les massacres se perpétrer, ou intervenir, au besoin par la force, au mépris de l'article 2, paragraphe 4, de la Charte ?

Dans ses articles sur la « Responsabilité de l'Etat pour fait internationalement illicites », la Commission du droit international a privilégié la première solution : en précisant, dans l'article 50, que

> « les contre-mesures ne peuvent porter aucune atteinte : *a)* à l'obligation de ne pas recourir à la menace ou à l'emploi de la force telle qu'elle est énoncée dans la Charte des Nations Unies »,

et en insistant, dans l'article 54, sur le fait que, si un Etat autre qu'un Etat lésé est en droit de « prendre des mesures » à l'encontre d'un Etat responsable de

> « violations d'obligations essentielles pour la protection de l'intérêt collectif ou d'obligations envers la communauté internationale dans son ensemble »[66],

ces mesures doivent être « licites »[67] — ce qui exclut tout recours à la force armée. A l'inverse et paradoxalement, l'analyse de Michael Glennon, pour cynique et froidement réaliste qu'elle soit, permettrait, dans un cas de ce genre, à tout Etat tiers d'intervenir pour empêcher que se perpétue ou se produise le crime des crimes qu'est le génocide.

Mais cela ne saurait être le mot de la fin. Ce serait, à nouveau, s'en remettre à la seule politique de puissance, car seuls les puissants, ceux qui ont les moyens d'agir, pourraient décider « du bien ou du mal » — et déterminer si les intérêts de la communauté internatio-

---

66. Selon l'expression du paragraphe 7 du commentaire de l'article 54 (*Rapport de la Commission du droit international*, cinquante-troisième session, 2001, Assemblée générale, *Documents officiels, cinquante-sixième session*, A/56/10, p. 382.

67. Le texte complet de l'article 54 (« Mesures prises par des Etats autres qu'un Etat lésé ») se lit ainsi :

> « Le présent chapitre est sans préjudice du droit de tout Etat [autre qu'un Etat lésé], habilité en vertu du paragraphe 1 de l'article 48 à invoquer la responsabilité d'un autre Etat, de prendre des mesures licites à l'encontre de ce dernier afin d'assurer la cessation de la violation ainsi que la réparation dans l'intérêt de l'Etat lésé ou des bénéficiaires de l'obligation violée. »

nale ont pris le relais de ceux des Etats parties à un différend; rien ne peut, assurément, garantir que ces intérêts collectifs prévaudront sur ceux d'un ou de quelques Etats puissants à l'origine de la décision d'intervenir. Dans ce cas, ni la société internationale, ni le «collège invisible des internationalistes» si bien représenté ici, ni moi, n'avons de «recette»: si des Etats, se prévalant de «valeurs» supérieures, interviennent par la force pour trancher un différend auxquels ils ne sont pas parties, il faut admettre que le droit est violé — et que, face à la paralysie du Conseil de sécurité, cette violation peut, dans certains cas, être préférable à un honteux Munich. Je crains qu'il faille s'accommoder de cette réponse juridiquement décevante. C'est l'honneur des juristes de dénoncer ces violations plutôt que de se ranger aux côtés du violateur (fût-il bien intentionné) au nom d'un réalisme qui risque de n'être qu'à courte vue.

2. THE HAGUE CONFERENCE AND RESTRICTIONS ON THE USE OF FORCE
THE QUESTION OF THE USE OF FORCE TODAY
THE POINT OF VIEW OF THE UNITED NATIONS

R. ZACKLIN [1]

1. I am grateful to the Academy for this invitation to participate in this colloquium which marks not only the centenary of the 1907 Hague Conference but also celebrates the opening of the Academy's magnificent new buildings. Like countless students of public international law, the Hague Academy was my first true exposure to the wonderful and exhilarating universe that is international law. I vividly recall the first general course that I attended given by Charles Chaumont in 1970 and the realization that there was a diversity of thought that transcended national boundaries and which this institution has done so much to develop.

2. My thoughts today go particularly to the memory of René-Jean Dupuy who served as the inspirational Secretary-General of the Academy from 1966 to 1985. René-Jean was a remarkable personality. Erudite in the true sense of the word he conveyed an enthusiasm to his students that was in many cases career-forming. There are legions of teachers and practitioners all over the world who are in his debt.

3. I have been asked to speak about the question of the use of force today from the point of view of the United Nations. Although I do not consider myself as expressing the point of view of the United Nations as an Organization, in the light of my lengthy career in the service of the United Nations I certainly feel free to express a point of view from the United Nations. Any discussion of this topic quite obviously is dominated by the UN Charter provisions with which we are all familiar and need no elaboration: Article 2 (4) and (5); Article 2 (7); Chapter VII, particularly Article 42 and Article 51; and Chapter VIII on regional arrangements.

---

1. Former Assistant Secretary-General for Legal Affairs, United Nations.

4. These provisions represented a compact achieved by the powers gathered at Dumbarton Oaks in 1944 and were designed to address inter-State conflicts which twice in the preceding years had produced catastrophic world wars. That compact envisaged a collective security system which under the management of the Security Council of the future United Nations Organization, particularly its permanent members, would centralize collective security.

5. As may be seen from these references my remarks will focus on the use of armed force and do not address the use of Chapter VII enforcement powers either in the sense of Article 41 or in the expanding use of Chapter VII in UN peace-keeping.

6. The use of force and the United Nations in this perspective is the history of the failure of a principle (that is the principle of the non-use of force in international relations in the language of Article 2 (4), some might say an ideal), and more particularly of the collective security system that was intended to implement it.

7. The failure of the principle on its own is not too surprising. The Charter provisions were a break with the past but depended for their efficacy on being coupled with a workable and credible collective security system as well as an effective and reliable mechanism for dispute settlement which never fully materialized. The principle alone could not prevent armed conflict as we know from the scores of conflicts in the post-Charter twentieth century described by one leading British historian as "the most murderous century of which we have record by the scale, frequency and length of warfare which filled it"[2]. Will the twenty-first century be any better?

8. Looking at the implementation or failure to implement the Charter provisions on the use of force from 1945 to the present we can identify a number of key developments which have brought us to where we are today:

   (i) the Cold War which effectively paralyzed the collective security machinery for more than 40 years;

  (ii) the short-lived attempt to shift power from the Security Council to the General Assembly through the Uniting for Peace resolution (377 V);

 (iii) the introduction of peace-keeping;

---

2. Eric J. Hobsbawm, *The Age of Extremes: A History of the World, 1914-1991*, Michael Joseph, London, 1994.

(iv) the "promise" of collective security in the post-Cold War period and the Agenda for Peace;

(v) the Gulf War and its aftermath (especially Security Council resolution 687) which flattered only to ultimately deceive;

(vi) the tragedies of Bosnia and Rwanda;

(vii) the emerging doctrine of humanitarian intervention as applied in Kosovo and East Timor;

(viii) the Iraq war which exposed the limits of collective security; and

(ix) the High Level Panel report and the missed opportunity of the 2005 World Summit.

9. Almost from the beginning of the United Nations existence "coalitions of the willing" replaced the standing army and the Security Council resorted to "authorizing" use of force by individual member States as in Korea, the Gulf War and Kosovo. Although this practice has prompted some legal questions as to the authority of the Security Council to "contract out" that is not the main problem. The main problem lies in the fact that in doing so the Security Council has failed to retain its authority over such operations: it cannot exercise control over the choice and use of weapons; it cannot ensure that the means are proportionate to the ends; and above all it cannot bring them to a halt. Furthermore it must be said that on occasion the Security Council has been willing to authorize too broadly when acting in the heat of the moment (post 9/11 for example) rather than in a deliberate and thoughtful manner.

10. To overcome the obstacles to the full implementation of the collective security system the United Nations has sought to compensate by the introduction of peace-keeping which has become for better or worse emblematic of the United Nations. The once well-established and understood division between peace-keeping and peace-enforcement has been significantly blurred by the attribution of very robust rules of engagement. Some member States, including some of the P5, have also actively promoted the doctrine of humanitarian intervention or what is now referred to as the responsibility to protect. This has received a somewhat mixed reception, not surprisingly, since it is normatively weak and has been shown to be highly subjective in its application.

11. Following the Iraq war in 2003 many feared for the future of the Charter principles on use of force, the collective security system

and the future of the United Nations as a viable and effective organization. A period of introspection and internal examination followed:
had the Charter reached the end of its useful shelf-life; were its
principles out-dated; could the Security Council ever be reformed;
should the United Nations be consigned to history and be replaced
by a new organization based on different values and if so what
should those values be?

12. Crisis can bring opportunity and there is no doubt that since
the Iraq war the United Nations has been in crisis although it should
be noted that this is not the first time by any means that the Organization has been written off as irrelevant or worse. Paradoxically,
however, at the very moment when many commentators and pundits
believed that the United Nations and the Security Council in particular had demonstrated their incapacity by failing to avert war
in Iraq, the refusal of the Security Council to authorize use of force
through a second resolution demonstrated that the Charter principles on use of force were alive and well, condemning the coalition
of the willing to unilateral action which could only be described as
unlawful.

13. Although the word "watershed "is frequently over-used, the
events of 2003 do seem to fit the definition as far as the United
Nations is concerned. Questions regarding the use of force had been
mounting steadily for some time through the Bosnian and Kosovan
years in the 1990s and in the very protracted and very public run-up
to the Iraq war.

14. The United Nations itself was in shock if not in awe by the
end of 2003. It was a time for re-appraisal and possibly reform. The
60th anniversary of the Organization seemed to present the ideal
opportunity. The Secretary-General established a High Level Panel
on Threats, Challenges and Change to assess the security challenges
and to recommend measures for ensuring effective collective action.
The Panel reported in 2004 and the Secretary-General in his own
report to the General Assembly ("In Larger Freedom") endorsed its
core arguments [3].

15. The High Level Panel report is everything that one would
expect from such an exercise. It is a lucid and cogent update of the
collective security issues 60 years on from San Francisco. Its recom-

---

3. *In Larger Freedom. Towards Development, Security and Human Rights for
All*, Doc. A/59/2005.21, March 2005.

mendations are modest and balanced and for the most part reasonable. From the point of view of the Charter as a constitutional instrument adopted in 1945 two of the Panel's conclusions are most striking. The first is that in any new security consensus "the frontline actors . . . continue to be individual sovereign states . . .". The second is that both in situations in which a State is posing a threat to others outside its borders and in situations in which the threat is primarily internal

> "the Charter properly understood and applied is equal to the task: Article 51 needs neither extension nor restriction of its long-understood scope, and Chapter VII fully empowers the Security Council to deal with every kind of threat that States may confront. The task is not to find alternatives to the Security Council as a source of authority but to make it work better than it has."[4]

16. For purposes of this colloquium and this topic, however, it is the Panel's attempt to come to grips with the question of the legality and legitimacy of the use of force that is most interesting. As the report states:

> "in deciding whether or not to authorize the use of force, the Council should adopt and systematically address a set of agreed guidelines, going directly not to whether force can be legally used but whether, as a matter of good conscience and good sense, it should be used"[5].

The Panel proposed five basic criteria of legitimacy: seriousness of threat; proper purpose; last resort; proportional means; and balance of consequences and proposed that these guidelines should be embodied in declaratory resolutions of the Security Council and the General Assembly.

17. High level panels and reports by Secretaries-General containing proposals for reform of the United Nations litter the international landscape. Only the incurably optimistic, which would probably include a large number of international lawyers, would expect such efforts to achieve concrete results. But in 2004-2005 the expectations

---

4. *A More Secure World: Our Shared Responsibility*, Report of the Secretary-General's High-level Panel on Threats, Challenges and Change, 2004.
5. *Ibid.*, para. 205.

seemed to be more than usually justified. The 2005 Summit did indeed, in the words of Kofi Annan, appear to represent a once in a lifetime opportunity. Sadly, it was an opportunity that was missed. The Summit process fell victim to the politics as usual syndrome of the United Nations and fell far short of expectations.

18. The Summit document reaffirms the commitment to the purposes and principles of the Charter and international law, multilateralism, the rule of law and human rights. It could hardly do otherwise. On the use of force under the Charter it specifically re-affirms the non-use of force principle of Article 2 (4) and following the High Level Panel reaffirms that the relevant provisions of the Charter are sufficient to address the full range of threats to international peace and security.

But the Summit document did not take up the issue of legitimacy which had been highlighted by the Panel nor did it follow up on the suggestions for guidelines on the authorization of the use of force. The Panel's suggestions and recommendations regarding the reform of the Security Council are reduced to a bland statement of support for

> "early reform of the Security Council as an essential element of an overall effort to reform the United Nations in order to make it more broadly representative, efficient and transparent and thus to further enhance its effectiveness and the legitimacy of its decisions"[6].

Finally, even with regard to its widely proclaimed signature achievement on the responsibility to protect, a close reading of paragraphs 138-139 reveals that the language is hedged about by so many qualifications that it promises more than it actually delivers.

19. The document is long on rhetoric but short on substance. Member States signally failed to seize the opportunity to effect change. The vision peeps through the mist from time to time but the political will is lacking. This is not the failure of any one State or group of States but a collective failure. Until strong, effective and credible political leadership in both the north and the south is exercised the United Nations would seem to be condemned to the status quo.

20. Is this necessarily a bad thing? In my view probably not.

---

6. General Assembly, doc. A/60/L1, para. 153, of 20 September 2005.

Aside from changes in the composition and working methods of the Security Council there is not a great deal wrong with the Charter that cannot be repaired through practice and *de facto* amendment. The world can do without a better mouse-trap. What it really needs is a better mouse.

3. ARTICULATION ENTRE LE DROIT DE LA HAYE ET LE DROIT DE GENÈVE AU LENDEMAIN DES CONFÉRENCES DE 1906 ET DE 1907

Ch. SWINARSKI[1]

Le thème, parmi tous les autres, apparaît certainement au centre de la commémoration du centenaire de la Conférence de 1907, puisqu'elle a eu pour objectif principal de «diminuer les maux de la guerre autant que les nécessités militaires le permettent» par les dispositions de droit «destinées à servir de règle générale de conduite aux belligérants dans leurs rapports entre eux et avec les populations»[2], c'est-à-dire d'établir la trame normative, fondatrice de ce qu'on entend aujourd'hui par le droit international humanitaire.

Aborder en détails tous les aspects de l'ensemble de l'impact de la Conférence sur les lendemains de ce droit pour ce qui est de ces deux volets — dits respectivement «droit de La Haye» et «droit de Genève» — déborderait largement le cadre de ce colloque. Dès lors, ces réflexions ne peuvent avoir pour propos qu'une tentative de cerner les contours de l'empreinte que l'œuvre de la Conférence a durablement laissé sur le devenir de ce droit, en ce qui est de sa substance conventionnelle et coutumière, ainsi que de sa texture normative.

I. Cadre conventionnel

Dans ce cadre il convient tout d'abord de situer, par rapport à l'œuvre normative de la Conférence de 1907, celle qui avait été réalisée, une année auparavant, par la conférence de révision de la Convention de Genève de 1864[3]. Cette conférence, dont plusieurs

---

1. Professeur invité à l'Université Cardinal Stefan Wyszynski de Varsovie; ancien conseiller juridique au Comité international de la Croix-Rouge (CICR).

2. Préambule de la Convention IV concernant les lois et les coutumes de la guerre sur terre, alinéa 5 *in fine,* voir aussi alinéa 3, selon J. Brown Scott, «Les Conférences de la Paix de La Haye de 1899 et 1907», Paris, Pedone, 1927, appendice, p. 58.

3. Texte de la Convention dans P. Des Gouttes, *La Convention de Genève pour l'Amélioration du sort des blessés et malades dans les armées en cam-*

initiatives antérieures ont été frustrées par des raisons politiques et à cause de difficultés diplomatiques, s'était tenue à Genève, du 8 juin au 6 juillet 1906, pour se terminer par l'adoption d'un élargissement du traité de 1864 (en trente-trois articles en comparaison aux dix articles de 1864).

On l'a essentiellement élargi pour y introduire le régime de protection des blessés et des malades de la guerre sur terre aux marins et au personnel et matériel sanitaires d'un conflit armé sur mer, explicitant sans plus, dans ses cinq premiers articles, certaines dispositions générales de la première convention[4]. Cette deuxième, en date, Convention «de Genève» procédait directement d'un vœu exprès de la Conférence de la Paix de 1899[5].

La transformation normative de la Convention consistait à adapter les règles de Genève de 1864 à la réglementation de La Haye de 1899; à son tour, la Conférence de 1907 a repris ces règles dans la Convention (X) pour l'adaptation à la guerre maritime des principes des conventions de Genève[6], ce qui a permis de dire, dans la doctrine de l'époque, que c'étaient les instruments de La Haye de 1899 et de 1907 qui réglaient en fait le statut des blessés et malades dans la situation de guerre maritime[7]. Ainsi, voit-on que déjà dans la perception des premiers régimes de protection conventionnelle multilatérale, celle dite «de La Haye» et celle dite «de Genève» se sont vues déjà organiquement confondues, malgré leurs origines formellement distinctes. Il faut ajouter que ni la Convention de 1864 ni celle de 1906 n'ont été qualifiées, dans leurs titres respectifs, comme étant «de Genève»; ce fut en effet pour la première fois le cas de la convention suivante sur les blessés et malades de 1929[8]. Pourtant, la Conférence de 1929 ne l'avait pas accordé au «Code de prisonniers de guerre», un nouveau traité élaboré en même temps. D'ailleurs,

---

pagne du 27 juillet 1929, «Commentaire», Genève, CICR, 1930 pp. XXIII XL (en tableau synoptique) avec le texte de la Convention de Genève de 1929; voir également *ibid.,* «Introduction», p. 2, et, en général, J. Brown Scott, *op. cit.,* pp. 511-523; J. Pictet, *Development and Principles of International Humanitarian Law,* Dordrecht, Boston, Lancaster, Genève, Martinus Nijhoff, Henry Dunant Institute, 1985, pp. 34-35; L. Renault, «Convention for the Adaptation of the Principles of the Geneva Convention to Maritime Warfare», *AJIL,* vol. 2, n° 2, 1908, pp. 295-306.

4. J. Brown Scott, *op. cit.,* p. 512.
5. Texte dans J. Brown Scott, *op. cit.,* appendice, p. 6.
6. *Ibid.,* pp. 79-84.
7. J. Brown Scott, *op. cit.,* p. 514.
8. P. Des Gouttes, *op. cit.,* pp. 9-10.

d'autres traités de l'époque, comme le fameux Protocole de Genève de 1925 sur les gaz asphyxiants et les toxines ou la Convention sur l'opium de 1927, ont été connus sous la même dénomination, même si cette dernière n'avait nullement été considérée comme relevant du droit humanitaire. La troisième révision de la Convention de Genève sur les blessés et malades a reconduit tous les principes des conventions précédentes, celles de Genève de 1864 et de 1906 et des Conventions de La Haye de 1899 et de 1907. La doctrine de l'époque met cette filiation en relief[9].

Il convient de mentionner encore que l'une des innovations de la troisième révision consistait à introduire dans le droit conventionnel «de Genève» une disposition sur l'éventualité d'instituer une procédure de sanction internationale relative aux violations de la Convention[10], interpretée dans la doctrine de l'époque comme «un contrecoup» de l'œuvre de la Conférence de La Haye de 1907[11]. Ce «contrecoup» à envisager, longtemps avant l'admission de la responsabilité pénale internationale en vigueur de nos jours, dans le système de la sanction de droit humanitaire, ne présageait-il pas, un tout premier signe prémonitoire, en droit conventionnel, des développements normatifs à venir après la seconde guerre mondiale? En effet, on pourrait bien se poser la question de savoir si le contrecoup de 1929 n'était pas simplement — comme l'estime Christopher Greenwood — indicatif du fait que

«bien que les Conventions de 1899 et de 1907 n'aient pas contenu de disposition expresse sur la responsabilité pénale ... les violations des lois et coutumes de la guerre entérinées par le Règlement de La Haye ont été traitées comme des délits...»[12]

Quant à la nouvelle convention adoptée à Genève en 1929, sur les prisonniers de guerre, elle reconduisait l'ensemble du module normatif de fond du fameux Règlement de La Haye sur les lois et cou-

---

9. Cf. L. Renault, «Rapport général présenté à la Conférence de 1906 au nom du Comité de rédaction», *Actes de la Conférence de révision réunie à Genève du 11 juin au 6 juillet 1906*, Genève, 1906, pp. 243-268, pour 1864; J. Brown Scott, *op. cit.*, pp. 1-4, pour 1899 et 1907.
10. Art. 30.
11. P. Des Gouttes, *op. cit.*, pp. 213-219.
12. Ch. Greenwood, «International Humanitarian Law (Laws of War)», dans F. Kalshoven (dir. publ.), *The Centennial of the First International Peace Conference*, La Haye, Londres, Boston, Kluwer, 2000, p. 253 (la traduction est de nous).

tumes de la guerre. Une centaine de ses articles n'ont en réalité fait que réajuster son champ et ses modalités d'application, suite aux défis de protection de la première guerre mondiale[13].

A cet égard, pourrait-on parler des lendemains de l'impact du Règlement qui se prolongent jusqu'à nos jours. La résurgence actuelle du débat autour du statut de combattant, tout autant que du statut et du traitement des prisonniers de guerre n'est-elle pas la continuation de ce même débat normatif, lequel s'est poursuivi à travers des développements conventionnels ultérieurs, tels les cent quarante-trois articles de la troisième Convention de Genève et les seize articles y afférents du Protocole additionnel I de 1977? Cela donne raison au principal commentariste des deux traités, Jean de Preux, d'affirmer que «les règles de comportement entre combattants ... sont essentiellement celles qui figurent aux articles 22 et 23 (b, c, d, e, f) du Règlement de La Haye»[14]. Point n'est besoin aujourd'hui de souligner le poids de cette question dans le débat sur l'avenir du droit humanitaire, voire du droit international tout entier.

En corollaire, les premières règles fondamentales «de Genève» sur la protection des civils sont ancrées en toute occurrence dans le même cadre des règles de La Haye[15].

Enfin, rappelons que la dernière, en date, Convention universelle «de Genève» sur la guerre maritime, la IIe de 1949, a été toujours et encore entreprise afin de «développer les principes qui ont inspiré les Conventions internationales de La Haye»[16].

---

13. Cf. *inter alia* J. Pictet, *Development and Principles of International Humanitarian Law*, Dordrecht, Boston, Lancaster, Genève, M. Nijhoff, Henry Dunant Institute, 1985, pp. 35-37 et p. 51; R. J. Wilhelm: «Quelques considérations générales sur l'évolution du droit international humanitaire», dans A. J. M. Delissen et G. J. Tanja (dir. publ.), *Humanitarian Law of Armed Conflict: Challenges Ahead; in Honour of F. Kalshoven*, Dordrecht, Boston, Londres, M. Nijhoff, 1991, pp. 46 ss.

14. J. de Preux, dans Y. Sandoz, Ch. Swinarski, D. Zimmermann (dir. publ.), «Commentaire des Protocoles additionnels du 8 juin 1977», CICR, M. Nijhoff, Genève, 1986, par. 1366; voir aussi M. Bothe, K. J. Partsch et W. A. Solf, «New Rules for Victims of Armed Conflicts», Dordrecht, Boston, Lancaster, M. Nijhoff, 1982, pp. 184-185.

15. Cf. J. Pictet (dir. publ.), *Commentaire de la IVe Convention de Genève*, CICR, Genève, 1956, p. 7; voir aussi M. Bothe, K. J. Partsch et W. A. Solf, *op. cit.*, pp. 274 ss.; Y. Sandoz, Ch. Swinarski, et B. Zimmermann (dir. publ.), *op. cit.*, par. 1817-1818, et observations de E. P. Syquia, «Non-Combatant Immunity in Armed Conflict», dans A. A. Cançado Trindade et Ch. Swinarski (dir. publ.), *Hector Gros Espiell Amicorum Liber*, Bruylant, Bruxelles, 1997, t. II, pp. 1549-1550.

16. Préambule de la IIe Convention de 1949; cf. aussi J. Pictet (dir. publ.), *Commentaire de la IIe Convention de Genève*, Genève, CICR, 1959, pp. 3-23.

II. Cadre coutumier

Pour ce qui est de la coutume de droit humanitaire, la récente étude des règles qui en relèveraient, faite sur l'initiative et sous l'égide du CICR, a identifié cent soixante et une normes de ce droit comme étant de nature coutumière[17]. Cette étude procède d'un mandat constitué pour le CICR par la XXVIᵉ Conférence internationale de la Croix-Rouge et du Croissant-Rouge, réunie à Genève en 1998, à savoir juste à la veille du centenaire de la Première Conférence de la Paix de 1899. Aux termes de ce mandat, le CICR fut chargé de :

> «préparer, avec l'assistance des experts en droit humanitaire, représentants différentes régions géographiques et systèmes juridiques, en consultation avec des experts des gouvernements et des organisations internationales, un rapport sur les règles coutumières de droit international humanitaire applicable dans les conflits internationaux et non internationaux»[18].

Après sept ans de travail, le rapport a vu le jour avec l'ambition de recenser, d'une manière exhaustive, l'ensemble des règles susceptibles d'être considérées comme coutumières, pour les présenter aux gouvernements. La méthodologie de l'approche reposait sur l'examen sélectif de la pratique étatique et sur son évaluation dans la jurisprudence internationale et nationale ainsi que par la doctrine (cent vingt experts du monde entier ont pris part aux travaux du CICR), y compris celle provenant des organisations internationales[19]. Les travaux ont abouti à établir un catalogue de la coutume du droit humanitaire en vigueur.

Vu sous l'angle de l'impact de la Conférence de La Haye de 1907 sur la formation de la coutume humanitaire, ce catalogue démontre que la plupart des règles y figurant trouvent leurs racines dans l'œuvre de 1907. Elles s'y répartissent en trois catégories :

---

17. J.-M. Henckaerts et L. Doswald-Beck, *Customary International Humanitarian Law*, Cambridge University Press, Cambridge, 3 t., 2005.
18. J. Kellenberger, «Foreword», *ibid.*, p. IX (la traduction est de nous). Qu'on se souvienne que les résolutions proviennent des organismes du Mouvement de la Croix-Rouge et du Croissant-Rouge ainsi que de tous les Etats parties aux Conventions de Genève de 1949.
19. *Ibid.*, t. I, p. II ; cf. aussi J. M. Henckaerts, «Etude sur le droit international coutumier. Une contribution à la compréhension et au respect du droit international des conflits armés», *Revue internationale de la Croix-Rouge*, vol. 87, 2005, pp. 289-314.

a) les règles à contenu expressément formulé ou reconduit dans les instruments issus de la Conférence[20] ;

b) les règles reconfirmant, entièrement ou partiellement, le contenu desdits instruments[21], et

c) les règles ayant ces instruments en filigrane normatif de leur contenu à un titre ou à un autre[22].

Environ trois quarts des règles font parties de l'une ou l'autre de ces catégories, de sorte que l'on peut affirmer que l'œuvre de la Conférence non seulement a marqué tout le processus de formation, mais demeure jusqu'à nos jours le moule formateur du contenu de la coutume humanitaire, tant en ce qui est de sa substance de « La Haye », qu'en ce qui relève de celle de « Genève ».

Par ailleurs — comme on le sait —, les règles conventionnelles élaborées en 1907 applicables dans les conflits armés revêtaient, tout au moins pour celles demeurant encore à ce titre en vigueur, le caractère coutumier à partir de la fin de la première guerre mondiale. Preuve en est, en plus de l'absence de leur ratification par les nouveaux membres de la communauté internationale à partir de cette période[23], pour la IVe Convention de La Haye et son Règlement — d'où la grande majorité des règles en question est issue — le jugement de Nuremberg, où en 1946, il fut statué que

> « les règles de la guerre sur terre exprimées dans cette convention, lesquelles étaient sans doute en avance sur le droit international existant à l'époque ... ont été reconnues, déjà en 1939, par toutes les nations civilisées et considérées déclaratoires des lois et coutumes de la guerre »[24].

Ce rapide inventaire de l'état de la matière normative du droit de Genève permet de conclure que, sur ce plan, bien davantage que de la simple interaction entre le droit de protection « de Genève » et celui « de La Haye », il s'agissait, dès l'origine et d'une manière

---

20. Cf. par exemple règle n° 1, J.-M. Henckaerts et L. Doswald-Beck, *op. cit.*, pp. 5 ss.

21. Cf. par exemple règle n° 7, *ibid.*, pp. 25 ss.

22. Cf. par exemple règle n° 82, *ibid.*, pp. 283 ss.

23. A part les Conventions IV et V, les autres (Conventions VI à XIV) de 1907 portant sur la situation de la guerre maritime sont pratiquement tombées en désuétude pour la plupart de leurs dispositions opératives. Cf. N. Ronzitti, « The Crisis of the Traditional Law Regulating International Armed Conflicts at Sea and the Need for its Revision », dans N. Ronzitti (dir. publ.), *The Law of Naval Warfare*, Dordrecht, Boston, Londres, M. Nijhoff, 1988, pp. 1-58.

24. Texte dans *AJIL*, vol. 41 (1947), pp. 248-249 (la traduction est de nous).

continue, d'une véritable interdépendance entre les deux volets, ayant tous les deux comme point de départ l'acquis de la Conférence de 1907. La IVe Convention et avant tout le Règlement avec — dans une moindre mesure — la Ve ont ainsi fourni la charpente, pour ne pas dire construit le «gros œuvre» de ce qu'on appelle aujourd'hui le droit international humanitaire.

Comme on peut le constater, ce n'est donc pas dans leur substance et leurs fonctions normatives qu'il convient de rechercher des raisons pour la distinction entre le «droit de La Haye» et le «droit de Genève».

III. Cadre systémique

La définition classique de la configuration normative du droit international humanitaire en droit international se sert de deux corps de règles matériellement distincts; celui visant la conduite des hostilités, c'est-à-dire les méthodes et les moyens de la guerre — dénommés, depuis les deux Conférences de la Paix, «le droit de La Haye» — et celui sur la condition des victimes de la guerre, connu, à partir de la Convention de 1864, sous le nom de «droit de Genève». Les deux corps forment ce qui est convenu représenter l'ensemble de ce droit en tant que *jus in bello*, lui-même une partie du plus encore classique concept du droit international: le droit de la guerre. Bien entendu, l'appellation donnée aux règles de conduite des hostilités s'est fixée à la suite des codifications des deux Conférences de la Paix, même si — comme le remarque pertinemment F. Kalshoven — c'est à Washington («Code Lieber») et à Saint-Petersbourg (Déclaration de 1868) qu'il faudrait en rechercher le véritable berceau[25]. Toujours en est-il qu'une telle définition reste jusqu'à nos jours bien présente dans l'enseignement et dans la diffusion du droit humanitaire[26].

Dans la doctrine contemporaine, pour certains, la relation entre les deux corps se conçoit dans les termes de «perspectives» ou d'«aspects». Pour eux,

---

25. F. Kalshoven et L. Zegfeld, *Constraints on the Waging of War*, CICR, Genève, 2001, p. 19.
26. Pour les plus populaires manuels académiques français, cf., *inter alia*, P. Reuter, *Droit international public*, PUF, 1968, pp. 396-310; Ch. Rousseau, *Droit international public*, Dalloz, Paris, 1970, pp. 335-336; P.-M. Dupuy, *Droit international public*, Dalloz, 1992, pp. 412-413; pour la diffusion, par exemple, C. de Rover, *To Serve and to Protect*, CICR, Genève, 1998, pp. 164-166.

«on peut dire que le «droit de La Haye» se concentre sur ceux qui «agissent», alors que le «droit de Genève» se concentre sur ceux qui «subissent». Certes, les limitations à l'action opérées par le droit de La Haye bénéficie aussi aux victimes potentielles : il y a donc un aspect humanitaire.»[27]

D'autres, en parlant de la «confluence» actuelle de deux branches en question, les considèrent comme des «courants» du processus de la formation de l'ensemble du droit humanitaire[28].

Dans la vision classique, l'on définit ce droit toujours au moyen de deux volets, considérant la distinction entre les deux toujours valable[29], quoique moins démarquée depuis l'adoption du Protocole additionnel I en 1977[30], tout en préconisant son maintien, car «elle se fonde sur l'essentielle différence du genre»[31] entre les deux.

Enfin, pour d'autres encore, le développement du droit international humanitaire se serait poursuivi en filiation directe depuis les Conventions de La Haye de 1899 et de 1907 jusqu'aux Conventions de Genève de 1949 et de leurs Protocoles additionnels de 1977 ; ces derniers ne seraient alors, par rapport aux premières, que leur développement postérieur[32].

Qu'en était-il dans la période de l'entre-deux-guerres, lorsque cette sémantique s'est installée dans la doctrine et dans le conceptuel systémique du droit international ?

En fait, la distinction entre le «droit de La Haye» et «droit de Genève» y est née pour des raisons politiques. Il s'agissait, face aux

---

27. R. Kolb, *Jus in bello*, Helbing et Lichtenhahn, Bruylant, Bâle, Genève, Munich, Bruxelles, 2003, pp. 28-29.

28. F. Kalshoven et L. Zegfeld, *op. cit.*, pp. 18-29.

29. Cf., *inter alia*, J. Pictet, "International Humanitarian Law: Definitions", *International Dimensions of Humanitarian Law*, UNESCO, Henry Dunant Institute, M. Nijhoff, Paris, Genève, Dordrecht, Boston, Londres, pp. XIX-XXII.

30. Cf. R. Abi-Saab, *Droit humanitaire et conflits armés*, Institut Henry-Dunant, Paris, Pedone, Genève, p. 13 :

«La distinction traditionnelle entre le droit de Genève» et le «droit de La Haye» n'a plus une grande valeur aujourd'hui dans la mesure, où, dès 1929, les Conventions de Genève ont progressivement englobé les matières qui faisaient originairement parties du «droit de La Haye»...»

31. J. Pictet, «International Humanitarian Law; Definitions», *op. cit.*, p. XX (la traduction est de nous).

32. Notamment dans la doctrine postsoviétique, cf., *inter alia*, J. M. Kolasov et V. I. Kuznetzov (dir. publ.), *Mezdunorodnoye Prawo*, Ed. Mezdunarodnoye Otnoshenya, Moscou, 1998, p. 346 ; L. K. Bakaev, *Specyalnyj Kurs Mezdunarodnovo Gumanitarnovo Prawa*, Académie des sciences de la République de Kazakhstan, Almatyi, 1998, pp. 23-30.

espoirs de la première période de l'époque de la Société des Nations, de départager la matière normative qui continuait à relever de la compétence des Etats, dans le domaine de la limitation et de l'interdiction des moyens de la guerre, «exercée dorénavant de concert dans un système de sécurité collective à vocation universelle», des règles visant à soumettre au droit international le régime de protection des victimes de la guerre, c'est-à-dire des civils et des personnes «hors de combat». En d'autres termes, l'idée avait pour but de sauvegarder, dans les nouvelles structures de la société internationale, ce qui devait demeurer du domaine de l'humanitaire, de ce qui restait de la gestion des Etats, afin de protéger ce domaine contre les interférences d'intérêts politiques. Un tel souci de sauvegarde est bien présent dans les propos d'une des personnalités dont le prestige et l'autorité, à la fois en droit humanitaire et en droit international, était alors des plus incontestables ; Max Huber, déjà en pleine seconde guerre mondiale, affirmait en effet que dans cette période

> «la guerre contre la guerre ne devait plus revêtir la forme de combat entre les adversaires ayant des droits égaux ; au lieu de cela il devrait y avoir dorénavant un système de défense collective contre toutes les effractions à la paix des nations. Ainsi les lois de la guerre déjà adoptées — auxquelles la Convention de Genève a été *incorporée*, tout comme l'institution de la neutralité ... se sont pour la première fois trouvées contestées en tant que principes.»[33]

Cette préoccupation n'est pas sans rappeler celle qui était à la base du concept lancé dans les années quatre-vingt-dix, lui aussi de vocation éminemment politique, qui prônait le besoin de la démarcation entre l'«espace humanitaire» et l'«espace politique» dans la société internationale[34].

Or, pour le droit humanitaire la dualité présentait aussi un danger de taille dans la mesure où seul «le droit de La Haye» demeurait

---

33. M. Huber, «The Red Cross as a National and International Reality», Conférence du 22 novembre 1940, dans *The Red Cross*, CICR, 1943, p. 164-165 (la traduction et l'italique sont de nous). Cf. aussi, du même auteur, *The Red Cross and the Recent Development of International Law*, pp. 10-20, aussi publié en français dans la *Revue internationale de la Croix-Rouge*, n° 121, 1929, pp. 8-18.

34. Cf., *inter alia*, C. Sommaruga, «L'action humanitaire et l'action politico-militaire : Pour une complémentarité dans la gestion des conflits», *Boutros Boutros-Ghali amicorum discipulorumque liber*, Bruxelles, Bruylant, 1998, pp. 739-749 ; du même auteur, «Action humanitaire et opérations de mantien de la paix», *Revue internationale de la Croix-Rouge*, n° 824, avril 1997, pp. 189-198.

partie intégrante du droit international général, alors que celui «de Genève» — parfois dénommé aussi «le droit de la Croix-Rouge»[35] — apparaissait pour d'aucuns comme un système normatif subsidiaire, fondé à cheval des contraintes de la règle de droit positif et des préceptes de bonne conduite d'inspiration morale[36]. Ce danger se fait déjà pressentir à La Haye en 1907, sans y avoir heureusement eu d'influence décisive sur le parachèvement de l'œuvre normative de la Conférence[37].

Voilà pourquoi dans la rétrospective du centenaire on peut dire que la figure de la dualité systémique semble bien correspondre, en ce qui concerne le droit humanitaire, aux récents propos sur la fragmentation du droit international de Martti Koskenniemi : elle

> «a émergé de l'activité informelle des juristes, des diplomates et des groupes de pression, davantage en tant que résultat des modifications de la culture juridique pour répondre aux besoins pratiques de spécialisation, plutôt que d'actes conscients de la création d'un régime juridique»[38].

IV. *Texture normative : Clause de Martens*

On ne saurait dans ces observations omettre l'un des acquis les plus fertiles pour le droit humanitaire de la Conférence de 1907.

Bien que «la clause de Martens» — évoquée ici par le juge V. S. Vereshchtetin[39] — fût apparue déjà en 1899, sa reconduction en 1907 rehaussa son rang normatif, en ouvrant la voie de sa trajectoire vers un principe général de l'ensemble du système de protection de l'individu en situations de conflits armés[40]. De cette manière elle a

---

35. Cf. par exemple P. Fauchille et N. Politis, *Manuel de la Croix-Rouge*, Société française d'imprimerie et de librairie, Paris, 1908.

36. Cf., pour le développement, Ch. Swinarski, *A Norma e A Guerra*, SaFe, Porto Alegre, 1991, pp. 11-12 ; aussi, du même auteur, «Aux contours des fondements du droit international humanitaire», dans J. Makarczyk (dir. publ.), *Theory of International Law at the Threshold of The 21st Century, in Honour of Krzysztof Skubiszewski*, 1996, pp. 967-968.

37. Cf. F. Kalshoven, «The Soldier and His Clubs», dans Ch. Swinarski (dir. publ.), *Etudes et essais sur le droit international humanitaire et sur les principes de la Croix-Rouge en honneur de Jean Pictet*, Genève, La Haye, CICR, M. Nijhoff, pp. 369-385.

38. M. Koskenniemi, «Fragmentation of International Law: Difficulties Arising from the Diversification and Expansion of International Law», Nations Unies, doc. A/CN.4/L.682, avril 2006, p. 84 (la traduction est de nous).

39. *Supra* p. 45.

40. La littérature sur la clause est abondante. En général, M. Strebel, «Martens Clause», *Encyclopedia of Public International Law*, 1982, instalment 3,

pu façonner les développements postérieurs du droit international humanitaire conventionnel, en tant qu'une disposition clé des mécanismes d'applicabilité des Conventions de Genève de 1949[41], pour devenir ensuite la clause charnière du Protocole additionnel I[42] et même trouver sa place, de façon naturellement plus sommaire, au Protocole II de 1977[43].

Dans ce droit, la clause, d'une part, garantit la cohérence entre les exigences de la conscience publique et les principes de l'humanité, constituant un lien indispensable de l'interdépendance intrinsèque entre la légalité de la protection de l'individu et sa légitimité[44], et, de l'autre, consacre le postulat que personne ne devrait se trouver dépourvu de la protection de ce droit, c'est-à-dire la portée universelle de son champ d'application *ratione personae* — condition *sine qua non* de son effectivité[45].

En outre, elle représente d'ores et déjà un mécanisme commun à tous les systèmes de protection internationale de l'individu, en tant qu'un pivot précieux pour la dynamique des rapports entre le droit international humanitaire et la normative des droits de l'homme.

Sans entrer ici dans le fond de la genèse de la subjectivité de l'individu en droit international, il est généralement admis que le droit humanitaire

> « a toujours eu pour l'un de ses principaux objectifs la protection des victimes individuelles des conflits armés, des combat-

pp. 252-253 ; F. Munch, *Die Marten'sche Klausel und die Grundlagen des Völkerrechts,* vol. 36, 1976, pp. 347-373 ; S. Miyazaki, « The Martens Clause and International Humanitarian Law », *Etudes et essais en l'honneur de Jean Pictet, op. cit.,* pp. 433-444 ; R. Penna : « Customary International Law and Protocol I », *ibid.,* pp. 201-207. Cf. aussi, sur Martens et son œuvre, V. V. Pustogarov, *Fiodor Fiodorovitch Martens: jurist i diplomat,* Ed. Mezdunarodnoye Otonoshenya, Moscou, 1996 (en russe), et, du même auteur, « Un humaniste des temps modernes : Fiodor Fiodorovitch Martens », *Revue internationale de la Croix-Rouge,* n° 819, mai-juin 1996, pp. 322-338.

41. Articles 63/I, 62/II, 142/III, et 158/IV des Conventions de Genève de 1949.

42. Article 1, paragraphe 2, du Protocole additionnel I de 1977. Cf. aussi B. Zimmermann, *Commentaire des Protocoles additionnels, op. cit.,* par. 54-56.

43. Préambule, considérant IV du Protocole additionnel II de 1977. Cf. aussi S. S. Junod, *Commentaire...,* par. 32-44.

44. Cf. Th. Meron, « The Martens Clause, Principles of Humanity and Dictates of Public Conscience », *AJIL,* 2000, pp. 78-89 ; R. Kolb, *op. cit.,* p. 228 ; voir aussi Ch. Swinarski, *Principales Nociones e Institutos del Derecho Internacional Humanitario como Sistema de Protección de la Persona Humana,* IIDH, San José de Costa Rica, p. 20. Aussi du même auteur, « Nasledenye F. F. Martensa i Sovremennoye Mezdunardnoye Gumanitarnoye Prawo », dans V. V. Pustogarov, *op. cit.* (en russe), pp. VII-VIII.

45. Cf. Ch. Swinarski, *A Norma e A Guerra, op. cit.,* p. 16.

tants malades et blessés, des prisonniers de guerre, et des civils »[46].

Même si les tenants des théories positivistes de la personnalité juridique internationale sont réticents à voir dans l'œuvre de La Haye des éléments constitutifs de la personnalité de l'individu, ils acceptent néanmoins d'en reconnaître l'existence en ce qui concerne les destinataires non étatiques de certains droits de la Convention IV de 1907, leur accordant la qualité de « sujets de droit des gens »[47].

Dans la doctrine contemporaine des droits de l'homme l'affirmation de l'existence d'une telle personnalité est bien plus résolue[48], sans toutefois être unanime[49].

Il n'en demeure pas moins que le débat sur la relation entre le droit des droits de l'homme et le droit humanitaire a été *ab initio* conditionné par la question de la qualité de sujet de l'individu en droit international, avec la clause de Martens comme son fil conducteur, régulateur de la préservation de l'acquis normatif de La Haye en matière de protection, fût-elle d'origine conventionnelle ou coutumière[50].

Georges Abi-Saab a mis ce processus bien en évidence, l'analysant comme l'une des caractéristiques spécifiques du développement du droit humanitaire tout entier :

> « les nouveaux instruments contiennent habituellement un article les mettant en relation aux instruments précédents. Ces articles stipulent parfois une application cumulative, où l'instrument précédent est censé s'étendre au suivant... ou, plus souvent, substituer l'ancien instrument par le nouveau... Ces dispositions préservent l'applicabilité continue entre les Etats parties,

---

46. G. H. Aldrich, « Individuals as Subjects of International Humanitarian Law », *Essays in Honour of Krzysztof Skubiszewski*, *op. cit.*, p. 851 (la traduction est de nous).

47. Cf. J. A. Barberis, « Nouvelles questions concernant la personnalité juridique internationale », *Recueil des cours*, tome 179 (1983).

48. Cf. A. A. Cançado Trindade, *Tratado do Direito Internacional dos Direitos Humanos*, SaFe, Porto Alegre, 2003, t. III, pp. 506-509. Cf. aussi une analyse de l'ensemble du problème, *ibid.*, pp. 448-537, et du même auteur « International Law for Humankind : Towards a New Jus Gentium », *Recueil des cours*, tome 316 (2005), pp. 310-359.

49. Cf. R. Provost, *International Human Rights and Humanitarian Law*, Cambridge University Press, Cambridge, 2002, pp. 116-117.

50. Cf. R. Kolb, « Relations entre le droit international humanitaire et les droits de l'homme », *Revue internationale de la Croix-Rouge*, septembre 1998, pp. 437-447, et aussi Ch. Swinarski, *Principales nociones...*, *op. cit.*, pp. 82-83.

autant pour ceux qui n'auraient pas accédé au nouvel instrument, qu'entre eux et ceux qui y avaient accédé.»[51]

Dans le même cadre, il faut noter encore la part que la clause a récemment pris dans la jurisprudence de la Cour internationale de Justice sur la portée et le contenu juridique des «principes de l'humanité», tout dernièrement dans son avis consultatif sur la licéité des armes nucléaires[52].

Finalement, son caractère coutumier *juris cogentis* et ses effets *erga omnes* paraissent aujourd'hui indiscutables[53].

En prenant la mesure de l'apport de La Haye de 1907 à l'occasion de son centenaire, force est de constater que la clause a servi de matrice, à la fois simple et efficace, de la dynamique des développements et de la mise en œuvre non seulement du droit humanitaire, mais aussi de tout le système de la protection internationale par le droit de la personne humaine. En tout cas, au regard du droit humanitaire, elle a ainsi pleinement répondu à l'un des postulats recteurs des travaux de la Conférence, celui notamment d'arriver — dans les termes de son concepteur même —, à ce que

«la société internationale réserve à tout être humain le droit de rechercher la réalisation de ses besoins vitaux et juridiques, partout dans l'espace des relations internationales»[54].

En guise d'observation finale à ces réflexions, en droit international humanitaire l'on a toutes les raisons — pour paraphraser la conclusion de Shinya Murase[55] — non pas seulement de commémorer, mais vraiment de célébrer le centenaire de la Conférence de 1907.

---

51. G. Abi-Saab, «The Specifities of Humanitarian Law», *Etudes et essays en l'honneur de J. Pictet, op. cit.*, pp. 275-276 (la traduction est de nous).
52. Cf. R. Ticehurst, «La clause de Martens et le droit des conflits armés», *Revue internationale de la Croix-Rouge*, n° 824, mars-avril, 1997, pp. 133-142.
53. A. A. Cançado Trindade, *Tratado dos Direitos Humanos, op. cit.*, p. 509; voir aussi G. Abi-Saab, «The Specifities of Humanitarian Law», *op. cit.*, pp. 271-273.
54. F. F. Martens, *Droit contemporain des nations civilisées*, t. I, Saint-Pétersbourg, p. 327.
55. *Supra* p. 101.

II. COMPTE RENDU DES DÉBATS

SUMMING UP

G. ABI-SAAB: J'ai beaucoup apprécié la discussion d'aujourd'hui. Mes remarques, très brèves, sont adressées surtout au professeur Glennon, et je les ferai en anglais.

I would like to make a very short remark about the concept of practice and its effect on the evolution of rules. As you have cited my old and regretted friend Abe Chayes, I would start by another quotation from Abe Chayes, who once ironically said: "Other states violate international law, the United States create precedents." I believe that in many ways this is a prevalent attitude among our colleagues from the United States. This attitude is also, in my view, characterized by a simplistic concept of practice. For them, practice is what a State does; that is practice. But in fact, the legally significant practice is an interaction between what a State does and how this action is perceived and received by the rest of the international community. If the rest of the international community considers, even if it is a new pattern, that this is an acceptable interpretation or adaptation of the rule to social conditions, then it can make a precedent. If the others consider it a violation, even it it is repeated hundred times, but every time it is done, the reaction of the international community is "it is a violation", then it remains a violation and it does not become a precedent, even if the international community can do nothing about it. This is what transforms an action into a precedent, or keeps it as violation, which I think is very important as far as the use of force is considered.

I would like to make a second comment about the effect and the impact of violations on rules. This morning, I cited Tom Franck, who once said that "law is congealed politics". I think that if law is not written, if it is of a customary nature, then it is a kind of crystallization of patterns, which are being accepted. But crystals are very different; a crystal of salt can be dissolved by two or three rain showers. But there are other crystals, for example diamonds, which cannot be dissolved very easily; and the rules of *jus cogens* are the diamonds in international law. It is not enough to violate them once or twice, or even a hundred times, to undo them. People play with numbers; there is even a Penguin book called "How to lie with statistics". The people who claim that there are 600 violations of the rules, where did they get this number from? However, I repeat, even if you have 600 violations, if every time or most of the times the reaction of the international community is to say "it is a violation", then this would not really dissolve the rules.

M. GLENNON: Let me start with his final question concerning *jus cogens*.

I do not think there is such a thing as a peremptory norm. I do not think there is any practice to support the proposition that some principles of customary law cannot be changed in the same way that all other principles of customary international law are changed.

I understand that a lot of people regard the prohibition against aggression as *jus cogens* and they regard the use of force rules generally in the United Nations Charter as *jus cogens*. But why weren't the use of force rules in the League Covenant *jus cogens*? Why weren't the use of force rules in the Kellogg-Briand peace pact *jus cogens*? Who seriously would contend that the fact that these treaties were violated only once or twice or three times meant that they had not fallen into desuetude — as Hersh Lauterpacht concluded they had?

In fact, if you believe in *jus cogens*, the strongest case to be made is that the doctrine was created as a matter of progressive development in the Vienna Convention on the Law of Treaties — which does not apply to treaties that precede it, and hence it has no application to the United Nations Charter. If therefore the contention is that the use of force rules in the United Nations Charter are *jus cogens*, the Vienna Convention itself denies that fact, because the Convention says it has no application to the United Nations Charter.

So, when did the Charter rules suddenly become *jus cogens,* peremptory norms that trump everything else which may compete with them? Why are these rules *jus cogens* — rather than, for example, the principle for which Nato fought in 1998, the principle that intra-State ethnic cleansing can be stopped through external intervention? This principle seems pretty close to the "responsibility to protect" principle; you can make a pretty strong case that that principle is also *jus cogens*. Hence you have one peremptory norm conflicting with another peremptory norm. Which one prevails? How do you know which is the peremptory norm? The answer is: this is all really a continuation of politics by other means. *Jus cogens* is wishful thinking, and I think it has no place in modern treaty law.

My second comment relates to the question as to what the international community has in a fact consented to. Professor Pellet pointed out that Abe Chayes, in the *Nicaragua* case, made an argument a few feet from here — which the court accepted — to the effect that explicit repudiation of a rule is required. The presumption, the Court said, is that when a State argues that its conduct is in fact consistent with a rule, this argument has the effect of reinforcing the rule rather than undercutting it.

My first question is this: where is the practice to support this rule? Where in the *Nicaragua* case does the Court show us why this is a rule? The answer is: there is no practice to support this rule. The Court simply made it up out of thin air. States have never insisted that principles of customary law must have been explicitly repudiated.

Moreover, I hate to point this out — it is not something I take glee in — but I am asked: when did the United States ever explicitly repudiate the principles that I am talking about? With all respect, one has to have not been reading newspapers for the last few years to have missed some rather important statements made by American political officials. Let me just refer you to two or three of them.

Powell, 2003, quote: "We continue to reserve our sovereign right to take military action against Iraq alone or in a coalition of the willing." Our sovereign rights? I thought that the United States had in the United Nations Charter restricted its sovereign right to take military action.

Bush, 2003: "The course of this nation does not depend on the decisions of others." It does not? I had thought the decisions of the Security Council were regarded by member States as binding.

Bush, 2004: "America will never seek a permission slip to defend the security of our country." Of course the whole point of the United Nations Charter is that you need a permission slip from the Security Council to wage war unless it is for defensive purposes.

Now, if these and other statements like them do not explicit repudiation, what are we waiting for? You got to have your head buried in the sand to miss the fact that the United States has, in Tom Franck's words, "boldly proclaimed a new policy that openly repudiates the article 2.4 obligation". That is the reality.

On the broader point that was just raised, I will conclude. The question is, in a consent-based system, what evidence is probative of the rule to which a State has consented? Words are probative, conduct that constitutes acquiescence is probative, but you have to weigh all kinds of evidence in determining what it is that the international law system has posited, in this positivist legal order, as the rules. If you want to understand whether the international system has really created binding rules, look at whether the international law system has caused the costs of violation to outweigh the benefits of violation. If States had done that, if they had really intended for the rules to be binding, there would not be up to 680 violations of the United Nations Charter. Words and actions sometimes conflict, but when they do one has to be realistic, and, unfortunately, the actions of States speak much more loudly than their words.

L. CONDORELLI: J'entends présenter rapidement quelques remarques au sujet de la pratique internationale, ou plutôt de la conception de « pratique internationale » sur laquelle se base le professeur Glennon pour prétendre que les principes relatifs à l'interdiction de la menace et de l'emploi de la force, tels qu'inscrits dans la Charte des Nations Unies, ne sont pas ou plus en vigueur. Je tiens à indiquer préliminairement que je partage l'observation faite tout à l'heure par le professeur Abi-Saab, quand il a souligné qu'afin d'évaluer la pratique il ne suffit pas d'observer ce que les Etats font : il faut prendre en considération aussi comment les autres réagissent. Mais ce n'est pas tout : d'autres objections sont à mon avis à soulever quant à la thèse que le professeur Glennon nous a illustrée.

Le point de départ de son analyse est que, depuis la seconde guerre mondiale, des centaines et centaines de fois la force armée a été utilisée dans les relations internationales (plus de six cents fois, nous dit-il). Une telle pratique imposante suffit, d'après lui, pour démontrer que l'interdiction proclamée dans la Charte est tombée en désuétude.

Ma première objection est la suivante. Même en admettant que le calcul soit juste, il ne faut pas raisonner de façon simpliste : le seul nombre brut de fois où la force a été employée ne saurait être significatif en soi, sans savoir de manière précise par qui, contre qui, dans quel contexte et pourquoi. La Charte — nous le savons bien — n'est pas un instrument « pacifiste » : il y est établi, en effet, que dans certaines situations l'emploi de la force est parfaitement légitime. Il s'ensuit que les cas où la force a été utilisée en observant les principes de la Charte doivent être comptés au sein de la pratique en faveur de l'existence et de la vigueur des principes en question, et non pas le contraire.

Certes, il est impossible de penser que la force ait pu être employée de façon légitime des deux côtés. On pourrait donc soutenir que, s'il y a eu depuis 1945 six cents conflits armés, ce nombre devrait comporter très en gros un calcul d'après lequel — pour simplifier — six cents parties à ces divers conflits violaient la Charte, alors que leurs six cents adversaires la respectaient: le nombre de violations serait toujours écrasant, nous dira le professeur Glennon. Toutefois, il faut souligner que le poids de chaque situation peut être extrêmement différent. Raisonnons ainsi, par exemple sur l'opération *Desert Storm*: un Etat se rend responsable d'une agression contre un autre, suite à quoi une coalition d'Etats réagit au nom et en application des principes de la Charte sur la légitime défense collective et conformément à une autorisation onusienne. Ici non seulement nous avons la pratique de plusieurs Etats utilisant la force de manière qui confirme la Charte contre un autre qui l'a violée, mais nous avons une crise qui dans son ensemble doit être analysée comme une preuve formidable que sont en vigueur — non pas en désuétude — les principes en question. Autrement dit, quand on évalue l'affaire tout entière, la violation par l'Irak de la Charte apparaît comme l'un des éléments d'un épisode saillant de la pratique internationale qui est à compter *in toto* parmi les confirmations les plus remarquables, et non parmi les infirmations de principes. En somme, chaque situation doit être jaugée de manière spécifique pour savoir de quel côté ranger son poids.

Prenons comme autre exemple la seconde guerre mondiale. Il est courant de dire qu'elle constitue la preuve la plus évidente qui soit de l'échec de la Société des Nations. C'est indiscutable, mais ce n'est pas tout. La seconde guerre mondiale démontre aussi quelque chose d'autre: elle s'analyse en effet comme une réaction par les «Nations Unies» dans la guerre contre les multiples agressions des puissances de l'Axe, au nom de principes qui ont été finalement incorporés dans la Charte. N'oublions pas que la Charte a été construite sur la base de cette expérience: il serait donc bien hâtif de prétendre que ce qui s'est passé, en fait d'emploi de la force, pendant ce cataclysme mondial, n'est pas globalement en ligne avec le régime de l'emploi de la force consacré dans la Charte des Nations Unies.

Mais même si l'on analyse la pratique internationale par une méthode plus appropriée et plus fine, il n'en reste pas moins que les violations des principes de la Charte ont été indiscutablement très nombreuses. Toutefois, voilà alors ma seconde objection: pourquoi, afin de vérifier la vigueur persistante d'une règle de droit, devrait-on réputer dignes d'être prises en compte, en tant qu'éléments de la pratique internationale, seulement les violations de cette règle, et non pas les comportement respectueux? N'est-ce pas de la véritable myopie intellectuelle que de se polariser sur les seuls rejets de la règle en oubliant de regarder en même temps tout ce qui les entoure? La pratique contraire pourrait être gagnante seulement dans la mesure où elle justifierait la constatation que la norme violée n'est plus suivie d'une manière générale, c'est-à-dire n'a plus d'assise sociale réelle. En d'autres termes, il ne suffit pas, pour ainsi dire, de dénombrer et peser les violations: il faut aussi dénombrer et peser les attitudes et comportements respectueux (puisque ceux-ci, tout en étant évidemment bien moins visibles, font également partie, et à plein titre, de la pratique internationale), puis comparer les résultats des deux calculs pour vérifier si par hasard la balance ne penche pas nettement du côté indiquant la persistante emprise sociale de la norme, ce dont témoignerait le fait qu'elle est par ailleurs généralement suivie et continue de l'être.

Il y a certes une difficulté majeure, que l'on oppose normalement contre celui qui avance ce genre d'argument: comment identifier et peser la pratique conforme? Est-ce significatif d'observer, par exemple, que ces derniers temps l'Italie, qui a pourtant des différends l'opposant à plusieurs Etats, ne leur a pas fait la guerre pour les régler? Peut-on sérieusement calculer une telle abstention au titre de la pratique favorable à l'existence de la règle? A mon avis, il s'agit d'une objection bien trop superficielle: ce qui est proposé n'est pas de se contenter de dénombrer les cas de non-emploi de la force, mais de mener une recherche empirique sur la conduite des Etats pour répondre à la question que posait magistralement un maître américain, le professeur Louis Henkin, dans le titre même de son ouvrage célèbre: *How Nations Behave*. La question est: peut-on dire ou non que la grande majorité des Etats dans la grande majorité des cas respectent la grande majorité des règles internationales? Et peut-on dire cela pour les règles dont nous discutons maintenant? Si une analyse empirique de ce genre donne lieu — comme je le pense — à une réponse positive, force est alors de conclure que la pratique internationale témoigne que les règles en question ont une assise sociale réelle en tant que droit en vigueur, et ce même si elles subissent par-ci par-là d'importantes et fréquentes violations.

K. SKUBISZEWSKI: It seems that the course the discussion has taken warrants a few words to recall the basic rules on the use of military force by States (I shall not deal with the use of force by international organizations).

The principle embodied in Article 2, paragraph 4, of the United Nations Charter refers to "the threat or use of force" and not to "war" or "resort to war". Thus the Charter avoids the difficulties which arose under the Covenant of the League of Nations (1919) and the Treaty for the Renunciation of War (Briand-Kellogg Pact, 1928) in connection with the meaning of the term "war". The Charter clearly encompasses also the use of armed force short of war. The notion of "war on terrorism" (particularly in use by the United States) does not cover inter-State relations alone; its ingredients are both political and legal. It means something else than war conceived as absence of peace between two or more States.

Let me raise briefly three problems: self-defence; use of force in self-help and similar situations; and armed intervention.

The first problem — self-defence — involves the interpretation of Article 51 of the Charter. The interpretation to which I agree is that a State may act in individual self-defence or in defence of another State only if an armed attack occurred or if a threatened attack is imminent or proximate, "no other means would deflect it and the action is proportionate"[1]. The latter possibility is that of a pre-emptive action in self-defence[2]. Such action must be distinguished from preventive action. Preventive action, when the threat is not imminent yet exists, is within the competence of the United Nations Security Council which then acts under Chapter VIII of the Charter. Also the General Assembly can make recommendations in accordance with the Uniting for Peace Resolution.

It may be added that the notion of collective self-defence in Article 51 goes further than mere application, on a collective plane, of individual self-defence (hence I spoke above of action in defence of another State). This view finds support in the preparatory work on the Charter at the San Francisco Conference in 1945 and, what is

---

1. "A More Secure World: Our Shared Responsibility", Report of the High-level Panel on Threats, Challenges and Change (hereafter: Report), United Nations, 2004, p. 63, para. 188.

2. My earlier views on self-defence were more restrictive, i.e., I did not regard pre-emptive action as constituting self-defence. I have found support for my earlier view in some practice of the UN Security Council. See, *inter alia*, Chapter 12 in M. Sørensen (ed.), *Manual of Public International Law*, Macmillan, London-Melbourne-Toronto, and St. Martin's Press, New York, 1968, pp. 767-768. On pre-emptive action in self-defence, see Y. Dinstein, *War, Aggression and Self-Defence*, 4th ed., Cambridge University Press, 2005, pp. 187-192.

particularly important, in the subsequent practice of the Members of the United Nations. The lawfulness of their bilateral or multilateral mutual defence treaties could not be and was not questioned by the United Nations, international courts and tribunals or — barring some political propaganda arguments — State practice. Strictly speaking, one should refer here to collective defence of another State rather than collective *self*-defence.

The second problem I wish to address is those categories of use of force by States which might be similar to self-defence or contain some elements of it. The labels are various: self-preservation, self-protection, self-help and necessity. The history of international relations, including that of the nineteenth and twentieth centuries, abounds in examples of forcible action when those pleas were invoked. The practice of States which developed when war was still a lawful means of settlement does not allow for any clear-cut distinctions between these categories. They have been and are still used interchangeably in diplomatic language and, contrary to the developed systems of municipal and particularly criminal law, no effort has been made to distinguish one category from the other or from each and self-defence.

The answer appears to be that the United Nations Charter has eliminated the admissibility of forcible measures based *exclusively* on the above pleas as understood by the State resorting to them. In the *Corfu Channel* case between the United Kingdom and Albania the International Court of Justice said in the context of "self-protection or self-help" that "[b]etween independent States, respect for territorial sovereignty is an essential foundation of international relations"[3]. States seeking protection of their interests or rights are under a duty to submit to peaceful procedures of settlement. These procedures, no doubt, may prove, as they often do, lengthy, ineffective or inconclusive and the State's interests may suffer before it receives satisfaction of one kind or another. But it remains the paramount interest of the international community that force is not used unilaterally, when States invoke general reasons for their armed action and when, at the same time, the party at which such action is aimed has not yet attacked another State by force of arms or is not preparing an imminent attack. In fact, the latter possibility, i.e., the lawfulness of pre-emptive action in self-defence, is what today remains of the

---

3. *ICJ Reports 1949*, at p. 35.

past justification of the use of force by one country against another in self-preservation, self-protection, self-help or necessity. Recent experience, i.e., the Iraq war, illustrates some fundamental legal difficulties that arise when individual States or their groups invoke those or similar pleas and apply force.

My third and last problem is the contemporary discussion on humanitarian intervention. The prohibition to resort to threat or use of force covers armed intervention. This follows from Article 2, paragraph 4, of the Charter. Under another paragraph of the same Article, viz., paragraph 7, the Organization is not authorized "to intervene in matters which are essentially within the domestic jurisdiction of any State". However, that principle did not prove a bar for the United Nations to take up matters that traditionally belonged to the internal sphere of the State. It seems that UN practice could not have been different as international regulation has become and continues to be broader and deeper, especially with the inclusion of human rights and fundamental freedoms into the scope and range of international law.

The place of humanitarian intervention in international law has always been controversial. Some States regarded intervention to be permissible when a State was guilty of cruelties against, and persecution of, its nationals or foreign nationals residing in its territory. Before the First World War, European powers resorted to humanitarian intervention in their relations with the Ottoman Empire and certain non-European States. As a tool of policy in the hands of individual States, and particularly the great powers, humanitarian intervention frequently led to abuses. For often the intervening party did not restrict its activity only to preventing the State guilty of carrying out inhuman policies to continue, but also fostered its own interests. Under the law of the UN Charter and decolonization humanitarian intervention might be held to have fallen into desuetude[4] because it was disregarded in practice.

Yet, when at the end of the twentieth century and the beginning of the twenty-first century several large-scale humanitarian disasters occurred[5], the question arose whether they gave the law a new turn. These tragic facts have begun to influence the development, interpre-

---

4. The use of this term implies that humanitarian intervention was based on law, and not only on practice of the great powers. But that was a debatable point.
5. E.g., Somalia, Bosnia and Herzegovina, Rwanda and Darfur in Sudan. Cf. Report, paras. 199-203.

tation and implementation of law; for could the prohibition of intervention apply to genocide or large-scale humanitarian disasters? In such situations there is room for the concept of international responsibility to protect and if, for whatever reason, there is no collective exercise of that responsibility by the United Nations, individual States or groups thereof can act within the limits of what is absolutely necessary to save human lives and health, when other measures have failed.

While some elements of the law on the foregoing subject may still be unclear or in the process of crystallization, the approach of the International Court of Justice should be noted. In the case of *Military and Paramilitary Activities in and against Nicaragua (Nicaragua v. United States of America), Merits*, the Court said:

> "There can be no doubt that the provision of strictly humanitarian aid to persons or forces in another country, whatever their political affiliations or objectives, cannot be regarded as unlawful intervention, or as in any other way contrary to international law. The characteristics of such aid were indicated in the first and second of the fundamental principles declared by the Twentieth International Conference of the Red Cross, that
>
>> 'The Red Cross, born of a desire to bring assistance without discrimination to the wounded on the battlefield, endeavours — in its international and national capacity — to prevent and alleviate human suffering wherever it may be found. Its purpose is to protect life and health and to ensure respect for the human being. It promotes mutual understanding, friendship, co-operation and lasting peace amongst all peoples'
>
> and that
>
>> 'It makes no discrimination as to nationality, race, religious beliefs, class or political opinions. It endeavours only to relieve suffering, giving priority to the most urgent cases of distress.'[6]
>
> . . . .
>
> In the view of the Court, if the provision of 'humanitarian assistance' is to escape condemnation as an intervention in the

---

6. *ICJ Reports 1986*, at pp. 124-125, para. 242.

internal affairs of Nicaragua, not only must it be limited to the purposes hallowed in the practice of the Red Cross, namely 'to prevent and alleviate human suffering', and 'to protect life and health and to ensure respect for the human being'; it must also, and above all, be given without discrimination to all in need in Nicaragua, not merely to the *contras* and their dependents."[7]

The subjects I have discussed have been today covered in particular by the paper read by my friend and colleague Dr. Zacklin. I find his approach both realistic and reasonable.

Time permitting, I would appreciate comments from the panel on the three problems I have considered.

To conclude, and to generally answer Professor Glennon's opinion on permissible State action, I wish to quote Pope John Paul II who emphasized that in view of the contemporary "temptation to appeal to the *law of force* rather than to the *force of law*" respect for the rule *pacta sunt servanda* is paramount[8]. As we all realize this is the critical issue when States decide to use force.

N. RONZITTI: I have a comment on what has been said on the principle of prohibiting the use of force. I am familiar with the ideas of Michael Glennon, since we have had other occasions to debate the question of the prohibition of the use of force in international relations. I am convinced of the permanent validity of Article 2 (4) of the Charter of the United Nations, which embodies a principle of international law that is obligatory for all States within the international community. What is the nature of Article 2 (4)? It has a triple nature.

First, it is treaty law. It is difficult to find subsequent practice abrogating treaty law, even if one is leaving aside the Vienna Convention on the Law of Treaties, since this Convention applies only to treaties concluded after its entry into force.

The second nature of Article 2 (4) is customary international law and the previous speakers have established that there is no practice or even *opinio juris* which certifies that this rule has fallen into desuetude.

---

7. *ICJ Reports 1986*, p. 125, para. 243.
8. John Paul II, Message for the 2004 World Day of Peace, para. 5; Pontifical Council for Justice and Peace, *Compendium of the Social Doctrine of the Church*, Libreria Editrice Vaticana, 2004, para. 437.

The third argument is a logical argument about *jus cogens* of which the core of Article 2 (4) is a part. It is true that this notion of international law is still controversial for a few authors. However, not only regional and *ad hoc* criminal tribunals, but for the first time also the International Court of Justice in the case of *Armed Activities on the Territory of the Congo* has referred to *jus cogens* as a positive concept of international law. In my opinion, not all of Article 2 (4) is covered by the notion of *jus cogens* but its core is, for instance the prohibition of aggression. Logically, it is difficult to conceive of a violation of the prohibition of aggression resulting in the abrogation of this fundamental rule of international law.

With regard to the second argument about the permanent validity of Article 2 (4), there are numerous judgments and advisory opinions of the International Court of Justice on this matter. Since the *Corfu Channel* case, the International Court of Justice has maintained that the prohibition on the use of force and on the policy of intervention is a paramount rule of international law, even though there is an imperfection with regard to international organization (say, the United Nations). Thus the validity of this rule does not depend on the functioning of the Security Council. Also, one cannot distinguish the different meanings of the rule on self-defence, if there is no rule which prohibits the use of the force. One can only construe self-defence as an exception to this rule. This was said, for instance, by Professor Ago in his report on State responsibility. Moreover, there is quasi-unanimity on the doctrine of international law on the permanent validity of the rule forbidding the use of force. The doctrine of international law is a subsidiary means for determining the rules of international law.

When speaking about the rule on the prohibition of the use of force in international law, we also have to interpret Article 51 as an exception to this rule. The reason why there is currently a wider interpretation of the rule of self-defence is because the opinion that self-defence can only apply if an armed attack has occurred is no longer tenable. Nowadays, it is very difficult and controversial to follow this interpretation, and part of the doctrine on the Continent says that in the imminence of an armed attack you can intervene in self-defence. The same doctrine rightfully states that self-defence is not available in case of a latent threat. If there is a latent threat, the job falls upon the Security Council. It may grant permission to intervene; otherwise intervention is not permitted. Practice shows that the Security Council will in general not control the use of force, which is carried out by the States, but the principle is that authorization by the Security Council is required.

What about self-defence? I support the doctrine according to which you can intervene in self-defence against a non-State actor. Moreover, I would like to point out that although the International Court of Justice has not yet clearly endorsed this doctrine, there are a number of separate opinions stating that self-defence can also be exercised against non-State actors.

P. D'ARGENT: Nous sommes les témoins d'un fascinant débat entre Michael Glennon et Alain Pellet. Au-delà des questions un peu techniques qu'il soulève et sur lesquelles nous avons tous des choses à dire, ce qui me paraît particulièrement intéressant, c'est que ce débat nous ramène à une question d'éthique professionnelle des professeurs. Alain Pellet y a fait allusion en disant que «l'honneur des internationalistes, c'est de dénoncer les violations pour ce qu'elles sont». On ne peut qu'être d'accord avec lui sur ce point. Cela dit, contrairement à ce que l'on pourrait a priori penser, la position de Michael Glennon me paraît également témoigner d'une certaine éthique professionnelle. Sans pour autant me rallier à la position juridique de Michael Glennon ni apporter de l'eau au moulin de son argumentation technique, il me semble en effet que l'honneur des internationalistes c'est aussi — et parfois, c'est plutôt —, de dire que l'on se ment en prétendant que le droit que l'on proclame protège effectivement. Beaucoup d'entre nous sont assurément choqués, voire révoltés, par la position doctrinale de Michael Glennon. Et en dénonçant ses faiblesses techniques, nous avons sans doute aussi le sentiment de combattre une position que nous avons rapidement tendance à considérer comme immorale, la vigueur de nos contre-arguments «positivistes» étant d'ailleurs attisée par ce sentiment.

Cependant, je pense qu'il faut pouvoir reconnaître l'éthique professionnelle qui se cache derrière sa démonstration, même si l'on peut demeurer en parfait désaccord avec lui sur le fond du droit. Peut-on vraiment dire que le droit que l'on proclame protège effectivement? Ne se berce-t-on pas d'illusions en continuant à être les grands prêtres d'une religion évanescente? Ces questions, qui nous secouent un peu, n'ont rien d'immoral et témoignent d'une éthique professionnelle tout aussi digne de considération.

S. YEE: I have two questions and they are both very short.

The first one is for Professor Swinarski. I am wondering whether this is the right time for us to reconsider some of the issues relating to applying humanitarian law equally to both sides in an armed conflict. What I have in mind is the question of military necessity: whether we should in some clear cases not allow the benefit of military necessity to one of the parties. For example, if there is a clear aggressor, should the aggressor still have military necessity as a kind of benefit?

The second question I have is for Professor Glennon and Professor Pellet. It is a very simple idea. Let us for example consider the war in Iraq. When the United States said that they were looking for weapons of mass destruction, it turned out to be incorrect. Assuming for the sake of argument that in the very beginning, what the United States did was reasonable while now it turned out to be incorrect. How do we consider the responsibility that may ensue? The idea was that this all happened in a case of self-defence, but when you start to behave in self-defence, it may be reasonable to you, but then, when opposing factors are evaluated, it turns out to be incorrect. How do we allocate State responsibility?

A. PELLET: D'une façon générale, je me félicite de ce qui a été dit, à l'exception toutefois de l'intervention de Pierre d'Argent avec lequel je crois être en profond désaccord. Il a affirmé, en évoquant la question de savoir si le droit est, effectivement, protecteur, que l'on « se berce d'illusions en continuant à être les grands prêtres d'une religion évanescente ». Je trouve honnêtement que c'est un peu léger ; en un certain sens, c'est poser en principe que ce droit, auquel je suis attaché, est inefficace et qu'il faut s'accommoder du mépris dans lequel certains le tiennent. Or, à mes yeux, c'est précisément l'honneur de la doctrine et des internationalistes de savoir dire non quand il faut dire non. Je crois à la responsabilité des clercs, dont je fais partie (même si je suis aussi quelquefois un « mercenaire » — lorsque je fais mon autre métier, celui d'avocat...). Je pense cependant qu'il faut savoir prendre ses responsabilités et, en tant que clerc, ne pas hésiter à utiliser l'arme dont nous disposons pour dénoncer les violations du droit : la parole.

Ça m'amène à dire quand même un ou deux mots sur ce qu'a dit Michael Glennon en particulier sur cette façon, que je trouve personnellement cynique et discutable, d'évaluer les coûts et avantages de la violation de la règle au départ. J'ai la ferme conviction que l'on ne peut pas raisonner comme cela, au cas par cas, Etat par Etat, situation par situation. Il faut raisonner globalement. Ce n'est pas parce qu'une grande puissance à un moment particulier, dans une situation spéciale, peut considérer qu'il est meilleur pour elle de violer le droit qu'on peut dire pour autant que cela est la bonne manière d'appréhender le droit.

Tout à l'heure, Michael Glennon m'a fait un peu de publicité, qu'il voulait perfide, en disant qu'après tout j'avais moi-même écrit qu'une règle de droit était quelque chose qui répondait à un besoin. Je suis à vrai dire une espèce d'objectiviste, vaguement scellien, un peu plus cynique que Georges Scelle. Je considère en effet que le droit répond à un besoin social et que les règles de droit ne se justifient que de cette manière. Je pense aussi que le critère du droit est l'*opinio juris* généralisée — mais pas l'*opinio juris* de tel Etat, à tel moment.

Ce qui me paraît assez affolant dans la doctrine qu'a défendue Michael Glennon tout à l'heure, c'est cette façon de dire que c'est à chaque Etat individuellement de décider. Je ne peux adhérer à cette idée, je ne suis pas un volontariste, je ne suis pas un positiviste, je suis convaincu que cette manière de raisonner aboutit à la négation absolue du droit. On peut penser que mon indignation est peut-être un peu facile ou démagogique mais c'est chez moi vraiment très profond, je crois véritablement que ce genre de thèse finit par détruire la branche même sur laquelle nous sommes assis, et je ne parle pas tellement de nous en tant qu'universitaires, en tant que professeurs, mais de nous en tant que société internationale contemporaine.

Deux petits points rapides, Michael Glennon nous dit : mais lisez donc ce qu'a raconté M. Powell, ce qu'a raconté M. Bush, et vous saurez ce qu'est le droit ; je ne suis pas d'accord. Pourquoi donc ce que disent les dirigeants américains serait le droit ? Est-ce que, sous prétexte que M. Powell ou M. Bush ont cyniquement annoncé que leur pays allait violer le droit en vigueur, je dois m'incliner et voir dans leur propos le reflet du droit international nouveau ? Au nom de quoi ?

Dernier point pour, répondre au professeur Yee sur la responsabilité. J'ai écrit des choses très désagréables sur ce que je considère avoir été et être l'agression des Etats-Unis et des pays qui sont intervenus auprès d'eux en Irak. Je considère qu'il y avait là une agression pure et simple et la postérité de l'intervention américaine semble m'avoir donné raison. Je suis convaincu qu'il s'est toujours agi d'une guerre de menteurs, que les Américains savaient parfaitement qu'il n'y avait pas d'armes chimiques et d'armes de destruction massive en Irak; une intervention construite sur un mensonge ne peut pas être justifiée.

M. GLENNON: A number of questions have been put to me and regrettably I do not have time to answer all of them, for which I apologise.

I will begin with a couple of very penetrating observations made by Professor Condorelli. First, he rightly points out that there is a methodological problem in simply counting supposed violations. As he suggests, all violations are not equal; there is a commensurability problem. One might count as "one violation", for example, the events that Madeleine Albright has referred to as Africa's First World War. This would be one violation involving nine African States that were engaged for five years in inter-State violence, resulting in the death of 3.5 million people. Does this one violation count the same as x, y or z? I do not suggest there is any easy answer to this question; the bottom-line, however, is one that every individual and organization that has studied this problem agrees that however the violations are quantified, the number of violations is enormous.

Number two, in every one of those instances, one State has been violating the United Nations charter: it is impossible for both States in a conflict to be engaged simultaneously in an act of self-defence. One State has to be acting in violation of the Charter.

Third, I am asked, why not look at confirming evidence, rather than simply at disconfirming evidence? That is a good point. My thesis concerning desuetude does rely upon falsification. I falsify the rule by adducing disconfirming evidence. I do not refer to confirming evidence, because confirming evidence of a prohibition is not probative; the reason that it is not probative is that one cannot thereby empirically establish causation. It is true that yesterday the Netherlands did not invade Guatemala, so yesterday the Netherlands complied with Article 2, paragraph 4, of the United Nations Charter. It is possible that that inaction was caused by the Charter. It is also possible, however, that the costs of invasion, deterrence, or seventeen hundred other factors were causative. So, the element of causation that is required to establish a customary rule — underscored by the Court in the *North Sea Continental Shelf* case — is very difficult to establish with respect to confirming evidence. In contrast, disconfirming evidence falsifies the rule; you know for a certainty that, when the rule is violated, the States intended to engage in that violation.

I do want to express a little disappointment that I feel in this meeting. The disappointment is this: we have not focused at all on where we go from here; we have not focused at all on how the system regulating the use of force under the United Nations Charter can be improved. I suppose that if one really believes — as a number of people have suggested that they do — that the Charter is working just fine, that no changes are necessary, as the High Level Panel seems to have concluded, then there really is no reason to ask how it can be fixed. But from my perspective I consider fixing it to be an urgent consideration; indeed, I was rather hoping that someone would ask me the question which I get asked all the time: okay, you do not think that it works, so what is your solution?

I am going to give a different answer to that which I have given in the past, because the earlier answer is no longer satisfactory as it pre-supposed there is no real fix. My view was that a fundamental reintegration of the international legal order occurs only once in several generations, because it takes the kind of calamity that occurred in the Thirty Years War, in the Napoleonic War, in the First and Second World Wars, to bring humanity to the point where it says "never again" and makes those words stick with new rules, rules that it tries seriously to make work. My view is that we may be approaching another one of those moments of potential calamity because of the confluence of the debacle in Iraq and the threat posed by international terrorism. As a consequence, a potential opening of this window of opportunity may be about to occur — in which we can really do something productive. One solution in my view may be to do what the former Secretary-General Boutros Boutros-Ghali recommended 15 years ago. In "The Agenda for Peace," he proposed an idea the time of which may come again over the next few years.

What if we had a Third Hague Peace Conference in which the participants agreed upon the broad outlines of special agreements to be negotiated with the Security Council under which they would provide land, naval and air forces for stand-by contingents to be made available to the Security Council in meeting crises of the sort that have arisen in Darfur or Kosovo or Rwanda? What if members of the Security Council then faced the pressure of knowing that the community of nations was in broad agreement — that they are willing to make the Charter work as it was intended? It is not, after all, the Charter that has failed — what has failed is a bastardized version of the United Nations that is vastly different from what was contemplated in 1945. The reason that the Charter has not worked is that its rules are not backed by force. Why not create the missing piece? Maybe what I am describing is not politically feasible, but what do we lose by trying? The worst that can happen is we will end up right where we are today.

C. SWINARSKI: The question was whether this would be the right time to adapt the fundamental rules of 1907 to the situations of protection in today's wars. My answer: I don't think it is.

These rules seem to me sufficient and adequate, as are the related rules on combatants whose very status can be only defined through law. Combat circumstances have been certainly changing, but did they not change during the First World War? Did they not change several times before now, for instance since the appearance of the threat of weapons of mass destruction? Of course they did. The real issue is how they can still measure up to the definitions of the Hague law. Military necessity existed, exists and will exist. The overall relationship of any given context of military necessity, in so far as warfare produces victims — that is people in need of protection in light of the proportions qualified by law — is rather being constant. Indeed, there is a not so variable correspondence between these factors, and it does not seem to have presently reached the point of requiring the revision of principles and general rules of the Hague law, more than ever before.

Therefore, the concept of so-called illegal combatants is somewhat aberrant to me, both as a lawyer and as a person who happened to have had some direct insight into the practice of armed conflicts. Illegal combat may be legitimate or not, but who is a combatant or not is always to be determined only by law. Eventually, the Hague rules are presumed to be apt enough to provide us with such a legal definition of a combatant. The question of legitimacy of combat is about something else; re-appraising which means and methods of warfare may be legitimate or not sets us back to the definitely old problematic of a just or unjust war, even beyond the one of legal or illegal war. That is why my answer would be "no" on revising the existing law, except, perhaps, for some adjustment of its technical rules. To me, the Regulations of the Hague 1907 — as Madam

President Higgins pointed out yesterday — remain still valid and operative, so the problem is not about the rules of protection, it lies with the means and methods of warfare, with legal or illegal weaponry employed, and, above all, with compliance with the legal means of preventing wars, which was of course the focal point of this session. It does not concern the legal framework of protection in the Hague law, and thus neither the fundamental rules of protection of Geneva law, as issued from the Hague law.

CLÔTURE DU COLLOQUE

CLOSING OF THE WORKSHOP

CLOSING ADDRESS
BY P. H. KOOIJMANS[1]

We have come to the close of a highly interesting and thought-provoking colloquium. Although I am not able to draw final conclusions from what has been said during the last two days at this early stage, allow me to give some comments on its subject "Topicality of the 1907 Hague Peace Conference" from my own perspective.

It is a platitude to say that much has changed since 1907. From a legal point of view the international scene has become much more crowded. International organizations, transnational corporations, insurgent movements, non-governmental organizations, and — last but not least — the individual human being have entered the legal scene and have found their place, both in the field of norm-setting and of norm-implementation. Gradually they have been empowered in some instances to claim directly their rights under international law whereas they are also directly obligated by that law. The State as indispensable intermediary between the international legal system and these other actors has lost its exclusive character. Nevertheless this system has remained mainly State-centred and this is a remarkable phenomenon in an era which we characterize with the concept of globalization, whatever may be understood by that term.

It reflects, however, the awareness that the interests of the citizens of the world have obtained a global dimension whereas the dangers which threaten them are also global in character.

The main question, therefore, is whether a State-centred legal system, which was logical and necessary in 1899 and 1907 as the starting point for a better organized and more disciplined world society, even if it dramatically failed to achieve the goals it set itself, can in the twenty-first century even dream of providing its citizens with the protection that the State itself is no longer able to guarantee on its own; in short: is increased and sustained inter-State co-operation a reliable and effective solution for the needs and problems of this globalized world?

---

1. Former Judge at the International Court of Justice.

The problem is that no alternative for the State as a viable public institution has presented itself or at least has been given a fair chance. And I am not talking here about breathtaking constructions like a world State or a world federation for the simple reason that these constructions — unrealizable though they always may have been — are (or rather were) nevertheless modelled on the State and this made them into unworkable behemoths.

But just as in 1899 and 1907 conference diplomacy and the establishment of a permanent body for dispute settlement paved the way for a State-based international organization, the first two decades after the Second World War saw some equally innovative suggestions to transcend a State-focused model for the management of world affairs.

I am thinking here, for instance, of the 1946 Baruch Plan for the management of atomic energy under supranational control by an International Atomic Development Authority without veto power of the permanent members of the Security Council. This plan was formally submitted by the United States to the United Nations but was torpedoed by the Soviet Union for being an infringement upon the principle of national sovereignty — which it exactly intended to be, both for the Soviet Union and the United States, as well as for any other State.

Equally innovative was the idea, launched in the 1960s, to place the seabed beyond national jurisdiction under a transnational authority as the common heritage of mankind. Even if this idea survived to a small extent in the Seabed Authority of the 1982 Convention on the Law of the Sea, its essence was defeated as the result of a new wave of sea-grabbing by coastal States which recently reached its pinnacle in the planting of the Russian flag on the bed of the polar sea.

The only but partial success on a non-global scale of this innovative thinking was the establishment of the European Coal and Steel Community in 1952. But the 1958 communities were already less supranational than their older sibling and as their membership increased the commitment to a truly supranational character decreased. Is it not ironical that it is hailed as a triumph that in the *compromis* that has been reached on the thorny question of the Constitutional Treaty during the June 2007 meeting of the Heads of State and Government the role of the *national* parliaments has been strengthened? But still, the European Union is the only international organization which is based on a pattern which is not exclusively or mainly inter-governmental.

It is therefore not a lack of imagination but a lack of political enthusiasm — or should we say a lack of political foresight? — that is responsible for the failure of efforts to lay the foundation of a more functionally organized international system which is based on the awareness that the interests of mankind are best served by public institutions that are less State-centred without, however, trying to replace the State. The Bernard Baruchs, Arvid Pardos and Jean Monnets were no starry-eyed utopians but visionary realists. States and their corollary, State sovereignty, however, have turned out to be tough cookies.

There is another phenomenon which has to be mentioned. It is strange and even seems contradictory that in an increasingly interdependent and interconnected world people are nowadays more than in previous decades inclined to look to the State for the protection of their well-being. An unmanageable and therefore dangerous world is seemingly thought best to be taken care of by the familiar and supposedly reliable functions of the State. But that is less an indication of the effectiveness of the protection provided by the State than of the absence of alternative systems which are seen as better equipped to serve that purpose. Globalization has not led to a transfer of allegiance from the State to another entity; even in the relatively secure and limited European context there is no allegiance to a European identity since there is no awareness of belonging to a European entity. The notion of European citizenship contained in the Treaty of Maastricht has remained a paper concept. Even less has the undeniable reality of the global village brought with it an awareness of global citizenship since there is nothing to visualize that village. Inter-State organizations evidently no longer qualify as such. As Dominique Moïsi put it:

> "In the post cold war global age, the state's legitimacy and competence appeared to be waning. Caught between the emergence of civil society and the growing power of transnational corporations, the state appeared to be fighting a rearguard battle. Now, with security a priority, it is back with a vengeance."[2]

---

2. Dominique Moïsi, "Early Winners and Losers in a Time of War", *Financial Times* (US ed.), 19 November 2001, p. 15.

If, however, we look at the formation process and the content of the substantive norms that together constitute the international legal system the picture is slightly different. The development of these norms can in my view no longer realistically be caught in terms of necessarily relying on explicit or implicit State authorization. Of course, State consent continues to play an important role as far as treaty law and State practice-based customary law is concerned. But the process of norm development is in reality much more multi-faceted as it increasingly takes place via what have been called inchoate legal networks which lead to the growth of a legal conscious-ness that transcends the traditional categories of the consent-based sources of law. Of course, the category of "general principles of international law recognized by civilized nations" always comes in handy, but does it always reflect the real situation?

In its Judgment in the *Gabčíkovo-Nagymaros* case of 25 September 1997 the ICJ by way of a general statement referred to "new norms and standards, set forth in a great number of instruments during the last two decades, which have to be taken into considera-tion not only when States contemplate new activities but also when continuing with activities begun in the past" (in the case in hand the particular treaty was concluded 20 years earlier). And the Court continued: "This need to reconcile economic development with pro-tection of the environment is aptly expressed in the *concept* of sus-tainable development."[3] Mind you, the Court does not refer to a legal *principle* of sustainable development. The Court further on refers for the future relations between the parties to the case to a norm in a general treaty which had been adopted by the General Assembly barely five months before. Everything is worded cautiously and with care, but does this statement fit in smoothly with the official mechanisms of law creation? Elsewhere I have called this statement a felicitous example of a pro-active judicial policy. And it certainly can be characterized as an approach which

> "while duly deciding the case in hand, with the necessary sup-porting reasoning, and while not unduly straying outside the four corners of the case, utilize[s] those aspects of it which have a wider interest or connotation, in order to make general

---

3. Case concerning the *Gabčíkovo-Nagymaros Project (Hungary/Slovakia)*, *ICJ Reports 1997*, pp. 74-75, para. 140.

pronouncements of law and principle that may enrich and develop the law",

to use Sir Gerald Fitzmaurice's famous citation[4].

Other developments also may be mentioned. The concept of jurisdiction which always has been closely linked to that of territorial sovereignty has become much more fluid in an era in which the internet establishes a truly global connection-system. As one learned author puts it:

> "[P]hysical location seems increasingly unimportant as a way of determining whether a given act or actor should fall within the dominion of a particular community. As a result, we see courts around the world struggling to develop jurisdictional models to account for the fact that people enter relationships and cause harms without regard to the territorial boundaries of the Westphalian nation-state system."[5]

Another noticeable phenomenon is an increasing interplay between international tribunals and local courts. Local courts are more and more confronted with cases transcending national jurisdictions and national legal rules; they may look for guidance to international tribunals but their decisions sometimes will also be of relevance for those international tribunals themselves and it is too simple to explain this away with a reference to national judicial decisions as State practice. The Pinochet decisions of the House of Lords are a case in point.

I cannot deal with these and other issues in depth; I have mentioned them in order to illustrate that in the practice of law the effects of globalization in the sense of an intensification of global interconnectedness are very real and have to be taken care of in an imaginative way, often bypassing traditional frames of reference. Dispute settlement mechanisms, whether international or national, can play a tremendously significant role in this respect.

From an organizational point of view, however, the international community has not kept pace with these developments. It is still more or less exclusively organized on the pattern of formally inde-

---

4. Sir Gerald Fitzmaurice, *The Law and Procedure of the International Court of Justice*, Vol. II, 1986, pp. 647-648.
5. Paul Schiff Berman, "From International Law to Law and Globalization", *Columbia Journal of Transnational Law* 43 (2005), p. 530.

pendent territorial units which steadfastly refuse to cede and transfer powers to a higher authority where such higher authority is direly needed. Let me add that such higher authority would not necessarily have to be the same or structured in an identical pattern in all fields, like for instance those of the protection of the environment or of human rights, of the provision of energy or of arms control or counter-terrorism. What is needed, however, is imaginative thinking supported by political enthusiasm which translates itself into political will. For how long will the statesmen of this world think they can solve the pressing problems of this planet satisfactorily by inter-governmental co-operation only?

Thirteen years from now, in 2020, colloquia and seminars will in all probability be organized to commemorate the fact that a century earlier the League of Nations was established, the first universal inter-governmental organization of a general character. I wonder what the comments will be on those occasions on the theme of "the topicality of the establishment of the League of Nations". Will the conclusion be that the world is still primarily organized on a State-centred basis? Or will it be possible to spot some elements of a more diverse world order?

1. ACTES
DE LA DEUXIÈME CONFÉRENCE
DE LA PAIX

(Signés le 18 octobre 1907)

I. CONVENTION POUR LE RÈGLEMENT PACIFIQUE DES CONFLITS INTERNATIONAUX

Sa Majesté l'Empereur d'Allemagne, Roi de Prusse ; le Président des Etats-Unis d'Amérique ; le Président de la République Argentine ; Sa Majesté l'Empereur d'Autriche, Roi de Bohême, etc., et Roi apostolique de Hongrie ; Sa Majesté le Roi des Belges ; le Président de la République de Bolivie ; le Président de la République des Etats-Unis du Brésil ; Son Altesse Royale le Prince de Bulgarie ; le Président de la République de Chili ; Sa Majesté l'Empereur de Chine ; le Président de la République de Colombie ; le Gouverneur provisoire de la République de Cuba ; Sa Majesté le Roi de Danemark ; le Président de la République Dominicaine ; le Président de la République de l'Equateur ; Sa Majesté le Roi d'Espagne ; le Président de la République française ; Sa Majesté le Roi du Royaume-Uni de Grande-Bretagne et d'Irlande et des Territoires britanniques au-delà des mers, Empereur des Indes ; Sa Majesté le Roi des Hellènes ; le Président de la République de Guatemala ; le Président de la République d'Haïti ; Sa Majesté le Roi d'Italie ; Sa Majesté l'Empereur du Japon ; Son Altesse Royale le Grand-Duc de Luxembourg, Duc de Nassau ; le Président des Etats-Unis mexicains ; Son Altesse Royale le Prince de Monténégro ; Sa Majesté le Roi de Norvège ; le Président de la République de Panama ; le Président de la République du Paraguay : Sa Majesté la Reine des Pays-Bas ; le Président de la République du Pérou ; Sa Majesté impériale le Schah de Perse ; Sa Majesté le Roi de Portugal et des Algarves, etc. ; Sa Majesté le Roi de Roumanie ; Sa Majesté l'Empereur de toutes les Russies ; le Président de la République du Salvador, Sa Majesté le Roi de Serbie ; Sa Majesté le Roi de Siam ; Sa Majesté le Roi de Suède ; le Conseil fédéral suisse ; Sa Majesté l'Empereur des Ottomans ; le Président de la République orientale de l'Uruguay ; le Président des Etats-Unis de Venezuela,

Animés de la ferme volonté de concourir au maintien de la paix générale ;

Résolus à favoriser de tous leurs efforts le règlement amiable des conflits internationaux ;

Reconnaissant la solidarité qui unit les membres de la société des nations civilisées ;

Voulant étendre l'empire du droit et fortifier le sentiment de la Justice internationale ;

Convaincus que l'institution permanente d'une juridiction arbitrale accessible à tous, au sein des Puissances indépendantes, peut contribuer efficacement à ce résultat ;

Considérant les avantages d'une organisation générale et régulière de la procédure arbitrale ;

Estimant avec l'Auguste Initiateur de la Conférence internationale de la

Paix qu'il importe de consacrer dans un accord international les principes d'équité et de droit sur lesquels reposent la sécurité des Etats et le bien-être des peuples;

Désireux, dans ce but, de mieux assurer le fonctionnement pratique des Commissions d'enquête et des tribunaux d'arbitrage et de faciliter le recours à la justice arbitrale lorsqu'il s'agit de litiges de nature à comporter une procédure sommaire;

Ont jugé nécessaire de reviser sur certains points et de compléter l'œuvre de la Première Conférence de la Paix pour le règlement pacifique des conflits internationaux;

Les Hautes Parties contractantes ont résolu de conclure une nouvelle Convention à cet effet et ont nommé pour Leurs Plénipotentiaires, savoir:

[Dénomination des plénipotentiaires]

Lesquels, après avoir déposé leurs pleins pouvoirs, trouvés en bonne et due forme, sont convenus de ce qui suit:

Titre I. Du maintien de la paix générale

Article premier

En vue de prévenir autant que possible le recours à la force dans les rapports entre les Etats, les Puissances contractantes conviennent d'employer tous leurs efforts pour assurer le règlement pacifique des différends internationaux.

Titre II. Des bons offices et de la médiation

Article 2

En cas de dissentiment grave ou de conflit, avant d'en appeler aux armes, les Puissances contractantes conviennent d'avoir recours, en tant que les circonstances le permettront, aux bons offices ou à la médiation d'une ou de plusieurs Puissances amies.

Article 3

Indépendamment de ce recours, les Puissances contractantes jugent utile et désirable qu'une ou plusieurs Puissances étrangères au conflit offrent de leur propre initiative, en tant que les circonstances s'y prêtent, leurs bons offices ou leur médiation aux Etats en conflit.

Le droit d'offrir les bons offices ou la médiation appartient aux Puissances étrangères au conflit, même pendant le cours des hostilités.

L'exercice de ce droit ne peut jamais être considéré par l'une ou l'autre des Parties en litige comme un acte peu amical.

Article 4

Le rôle du médiateur consiste à concilier les prétentions opposées et à apaiser les ressentiments qui peuvent s'être produits entre les Etats en conflit.

Article 5

Les fonctions du médiateur cessent du moment où il est constaté, soit par l'une des Parties en litige, soit par le médiateur lui-même, que les moyens de conciliation proposés par lui ne sont pas acceptés.

Article 6

Les bons offices et la médiation, soit sur le recours des Parties en conflit, soit sur l'initiative des Puissances étrangères au conflit, ont exclusivement le caractère de conseil et n'ont jamais force obligatoire.

Article 7

L'acceptation de la médiation ne peut avoir pour effet, sauf convention contraire, d'interrompre, de retarder ou d'entraver la mobilisation et autres mesures préparatoires à la guerre.

Si elle intervient après l'ouverture des hostilités, elle n'interrompt pas, sauf convention contraire, les opérations militaires en cours.

Article 8

Les Puissances contractantes sont d'accord pour recommander l'application, dans les circonstances qui le permettent, d'une médiation spéciale sous la forme suivante.

En cas de différend grave compromettant la paix, les Etats en conflit choisissent respectivement une Puissance à laquelle ils confient la mission d'entrer en rapport direct avec la Puissance choisie d'autre part, à l'effet de prévenir la rupture des relations pacifiques.

Pendant la durée de ce mandat dont le terme, sauf stipulation contraire, ne peut excéder trente jours, les Etats en litige cessent tout rapport direct au sujet du conflit, lequel est considéré comme déféré exclusivement aux Puissances médiatrices. Celles-ci doivent appliquer tous leurs efforts à régler le différend.

En cas de rupture effective des relations pacifiques, ces Puissances demeurent chargées de la mission commune de profiter de toute occasion pour rétablir la paix.

TITRE III. DES COMMISSIONS INTERNATIONALES D'ENQUÊTE

Article 9

Dans les litiges d'ordre international n'engageant ni l'honneur ni des intérêts essentiels et provenant d'une divergence d'appréciation sur des points de fait, les Puissances contractantes jugent utile et désirable que les Parties qui n'auraient pu se mettre d'accord par les voies diplomatiques instituent, en tant que les circonstances le permettront, une Commission internationale d'enquête chargée de faciliter la solution de ces litiges en éclaircissant, par un examen impartial et consciencieux, les questions de fait.

Article 10

Les Commissions internationales d'enquête sont constituées par convention spéciale entre les Parties en litige.

La convention d'enquête précise les faits à examiner; elle détermine le mode et le délai de formation de la Commission et l'étendue des pouvoirs des commissaires.

Elle détermine également, s'il y a lieu, le siège de la Commission et la faculté de se déplacer, la langue dont la Commission fera usage et celles dont l'emploi sera autorisé devant elle, ainsi que la date à laquelle chaque Partie devra déposer son exposé des faits, et généralement toutes les conditions dont les Parties sont convenues.

Si les Parties jugent nécessaire de nommer des assesseurs, la convention d'enquête détermine le mode de leur désignation et l'étendue de leurs pouvoirs.

Article 11

Si la convention d'enquête n'a pas désigné le siège de la Commission, celle-ci siégera à La Haye.

Le siège une fois fixé ne peut être changé par la Commission qu'avec l'assentiment des Parties.

Si la convention d'enquête n'a pas déterminé les langues à employer, il en est décidé par la Commission.

Article 12

Sauf stipulation contraire, les Commissions d'enquête sont formées de la manière déterminée par les articles 45 et 57 de la présente Convention.

Article 13

En cas de décès, de démission ou d'empêchement, pour quelque cause que ce soit, de l'un des commissaires, ou éventuellement de l'un des assesseurs, il est pourvu à son remplacement selon le mode fixé pour sa nomination.

Article 14

Les Parties ont le droit de nommer auprès de la Commission d'enquête des agents spéciaux avec la mission de les représenter et de servir d'intermédiaires entre Elles et la Commission.

Elles sont, en outre, autorisées à charger des conseils ou avocats nommés par elle, d'exposer et de soutenir leurs intérêts devant la Commission.

Article 15

Le Bureau international de la Cour permanente d'arbitrage sert de greffe aux Commissions qui siègent à La Haye, et mettra ses locaux et son organisation à la disposition des Puissances contractantes pour le fonctionnement de la Commission d'enquête.

Article 16

Si la Commission siège ailleurs qu'à La Haye, elle nomme un Secrétaire général dont le bureau lui sert de greffe.

Le greffe est chargé, sous l'autorité du Président, de l'organisation matérielle des séances de la Commission, de la rédaction des procès-verbaux et, pendant le temps de l'enquête, de la garde des archives qui seront ensuite versées au Bureau international de La Haye.

Article 17

En vue de faciliter l'institution et le fonctionnement des Commissions d'enquête, les Puissances contractantes recommandent les règles suivantes qui seront applicables à la procédure d'enquête en tant que les Parties n'adopteront pas d'autres règles.

Article 18

La Commission réglera les détails de la procédure non prévus dans la convention spéciale d'enquête ou dans la présente Convention, et procédera à toutes les formalités que comporte l'administration des preuves.

Article 19

L'enquête a lieu contradictoirement.

Aux dates prévues, chaque Partie communique à la Commission et à l'autre Partie les exposés des faits, s'il y a lieu, et, dans tous les cas, les actes, pièces et documents qu'elle juge utiles à la découverte de la vérité, ainsi que la liste des témoins et des experts qu'elle désire faire entendre.

Article 20

La Commission a la faculté, avec l'assentiment des Parties, de se transporter momentanément sur les lieux où elle juge utile de recourir à ce moyen d'information, ou d'y déléguer un ou plusieurs de ses membres. L'autorisation de l'Etat sur le territoire duquel il doit être procédé à cette information devra être obtenue.

Article 21

Toutes constatations matérielles et toutes visites des lieux doivent être faites en présence des agents et conseils des Parties ou eux dûment appelés.

Article 22

La Commission a le droit de solliciter de l'une ou l'autre Partie telles explications ou informations qu'elle juge utiles.

Article 23

Les Parties s'engagent à fournir à la Commission d'enquête, dans la plus large mesure qu'elles jugeront possible, tous les moyens et toutes les facilités nécessaires pour la connaissance complète et l'appréciation exacte des faits en question.

Elles s'engagent à user des moyens dont elles disposent d'après leur législation intérieure, pour assurer la comparution des témoins ou des experts se trouvant sur leur territoire et cités devant la Commission.

Si ceux-ci ne peuvent comparaître devant la Commission, elles feront procéder à leur audition devant leurs autorités compétentes.

Article 24

Pour toutes les notifications que la Commission aurait à faire sur le territoire d'une tierce Puissance contractante, la Commission s'adressera directement au Gouvernement de cette Puissance. Il en sera de même s'il s'agit de faire procéder sur place à l'établissement de tous moyens de preuve.

Les requêtes adressées à cet effet seront exécutées suivant les moyens dont la Puissance requise dispose d'après sa législation intérieure. Elles ne peuvent être refusées que si cette Puissance les juge de nature à porter atteinte à sa souveraineté ou à sa sécurité.

La Commission aura aussi toujours la faculté de recourir à l'intermédiaire de la Puissance sur le territoire de laquelle elle a son siège.

Article 25

Les témoins et les experts sont appelés à la requête des Parties ou d'office par la Commission, et, dans tous les cas, par l'intermédiaire du Gouvernement de l'Etat sur le territoire duquel ils se trouvent.

Les témoins sont entendus, successivement et séparément, en présence des agents et des conseils et dans un ordre à fixer par la Commission.

Article 26

L'interrogatoire des témoins est conduit par le Président.

Les membres de la Commission peuvent néanmoins poser à chaque témoin les questions qu'ils croient convenables pour éclaircir ou compléter sa déposition, ou pour se renseigner sur tout ce qui concerne le témoin dans les limites nécessaires à la manifestation de la vérité.

Les agents et les conseils des Parties ne peuvent interrompre le témoin dans sa déposition, ni lui faire aucune interpellation directe, mais peuvent demander au Président de poser au témoin telles questions complémentaires qu'ils jugent utiles.

Article 27

Le témoin doit déposer sans qu'il lui soit permis de lire aucun projet écrit. Toutefois, il peut être autorisé par le Président à s'aider de notes ou documents si la nature des faits rapportés en nécessite l'emploi.

Article 28

Procès-verbal de la déposition du témoin est dressé séance tenante et lecture en est donnée au témoin. Le témoin peut y faire tels changements et additions que bon lui semble et qui seront consignés à la suite de sa déposition.

Lecture faite au témoin de l'ensemble de sa déposition, le témoin est requis de signer.

Article 29

Les agents sont autorisés, au cours ou à la fin de l'enquête, à présenter par écrit à la Commission et à l'autre Partie tels dires, réquisitions ou résumés de fait, qu'ils jugent utiles à la découverte de la vérité.

Article 30

Les délibérations de la Commission ont lieu à huis clos et restent secrètes.
Toute décision est prise à la majorité des membres de la Commission.
Le refus d'un membre de prendre part au vote doit être constaté dans le procès-verbal.

Article 31

Les séances de la Commission ne sont publiques et les procès-verbaux et documents de l'enquête ne sont rendus publics qu'en vertu d'une décision de la Commission, prise avec l'assentiment des Parties.

Article 32

Les Parties ayant présenté tous les éclaircissements et preuves, tous les témoins ayant été entendus, le Président prononce la clôture de l'enquête et la Commission s'ajourne pour délibérer et rédiger son rapport.

Article 33

Le rapport est signé par tous les membres de la Commission.
Si un des membres refuse de signer, mention en est faite; le rapport reste néanmoins valable.

Article 34

Le rapport de la Commission est lu en séance publique, les agents et conseils des Parties présents ou dûment appelés.
Un exemplaire du rapport est remis à chaque Partie.

Article 35

Le rapport de la Commission, limité à la constatation des faits, n'a nullement le caractère d'une sentence arbitrale. Il laisse aux Parties une entière liberté pour la suite à donner à cette constatation.

Article 36

Chaque Partie supporte ses propres frais et une part égale des frais de la Commission.

Titre IV. De l'arbitrage international

Chapitre I. De la justice arbitrale

Article 37

L'arbitrage international a pour objet le règlement de litiges entre les Etats par des juges de leur choix et sur la base du respect du droit.
Le recours à l'arbitrage implique l'engagement de se soumettre de bonne foi à la sentence.

Article 38

Dans les questions d'ordre juridique, et en premier lieu, dans les questions d'interprétation ou d'application des Conventions internationales, l'arbitrage est reconnu par les Puissances contractantes comme le moyen le plus efficace et en même temps le plus équitable de régler les litiges qui n'ont pas été résolus par les voies diplomatiques.

En conséquence, il serait désirable que, dans les litiges sur les questions susmentionnées, les Puissances contractantes eussent, le cas échéant, recours à l'arbitrage, en tant que les circonstances le permettraient.

Article 39

La Convention d'arbitrage est conclue pour des contestations déjà nées ou pour des contestations éventuelles.

Elle peut concerner tout litige ou seulement les litiges d'une catégorie déterminée.

Article 40

Indépendamment des Traités généraux ou particuliers qui stipulent actuellement l'obligation du recours à l'arbitrage pour les Puissances contractantes, ces Puissances se réservent de conclure des accords nouveaux, généraux ou particuliers, en vue d'étendre l'arbitrage obligatoire à tous les cas qu'elles jugeront possible de lui soumettre.

Chapitre II. De la Cour permanente d'arbitrage

Article 41

Dans le but de faciliter le recours immédiat à l'arbitrage pour les différends internationaux qui n'ont pu être réglés par la voie diplomatique, les Puissances contractantes s'engagent à maintenir, telle qu'elle a été établie par la Première Conférence de la Paix, la Cour permanente d'arbitrage, accessible en tout temps et fonctionnant, sauf stipulation contraire des Parties, conformément aux règles de procédure insérées dans la présente Convention.

Article 42

La Cour permanente est compétente pour tous les cas d'arbitrage, à moins qu'il n'y ait entente entre les Parties pour l'établissement d'une juridiction spéciale.

Article 43

La Cour permanente a son siège à La Haye.

Un Bureau international sert de greffe à la Cour; il est l'intermédiaire des communications relatives aux réunions de celle-ci; il a la garde des archives et la gestion de toutes les affaires administratives.

Les Puissances signataires s'engagent à communiquer au Bureau, aussitôt que possible, une copie certifiée conforme de toute stipulation d'arbitrage intervenue entre elles et de toute sentence arbitrale les concernant et rendue par des juridictions spéciales.

Elles s'engagent à communiquer de même au Bureau les lois, règlements et documents constatant éventuellement l'exécution des sentences rendues par la Cour.

Article 44

Chaque Puissance contractante désigne quatre personnes au plus, d'une compétence reconnue dans les questions de droit international, jouissant de la plus haute considération morale et disposées à accepter les fonctions d'arbitre.

Les personnes ainsi désignées sont inscrites, au titre de Membres de la Cour, sur une liste qui sera notifiée à toutes les Puissances contractantes par les soins du Bureau.

Toute modification à la liste des arbitres est portée, par les soins du Bureau, à la connaissance des Puissances contractantes.

Deux ou plusieurs Puissances peuvent s'entendre pour la désignation en commun d'un ou de plusieurs Membres.

La même personne peut être désignée par des Puissances différentes.

Les Membres de la Cour sont nommés pour un terme de six ans. Leur mandat peut être renouvelé.

En cas de décès ou de retraite d'un Membre de la Cour, il est pourvu à son remplacement selon le mode fixé pour sa nomination, et pour une nouvelle période de six ans.

Article 45

Lorsque les Puissances contractantes veulent s'adresser à la Cour permanente pour le règlement d'un différend survenu entre elles, le choix des arbitres appelés à former le Tribunal compétent pour statuer sur ce différend doit être fait dans la liste générale des Membres de la Cour.

A défaut de constitution du Tribunal arbitral par l'accord des Parties, il est procédé de la manière suivante :

Chaque Partie nomme deux arbitres, dont un seulement peut être son national ou choisi parmi ceux qui ont été désignés par elle comme Membres de la Cour permanente. Ces arbitres choisissent ensemble un surarbitre.

En cas de partage des voix, le choix du surarbitre est confié à une Puissance tierce, désignée de commun accord par des Parties.

Si l'accord ne s'établit pas à ce sujet, chaque Partie désigne une Puissance différente et le choix du surarbitre est fait de concert par les Puissances ainsi désignées.

Si, dans un délai de deux mois, ces deux Puissances n'ont pu tomber d'accord, chacune d'elles présente deux candidats pris sur la liste des Membres de la Cour permanente, en dehors des Membres désignés par les Parties et n'étant les nationaux d'aucune d'elles. Le sort détermine lequel des candidats ainsi présentés sera le surarbitre.

Article 46

Dès que le Tribunal est composé, les Parties notifient au Bureau leur décision de s'adresser à la Cour, le texte de leur compromis, et les noms des arbitres.

Le Bureau communique sans délai à chaque arbitre le compromis et les noms des autres membres du Tribunal.

Le Tribunal se réunit à la date fixée par les Parties. Le Bureau pourvoit à son installation.

Les membres du Tribunal, dans l'exercice de leurs fonctions et en dehors de leur pays, jouissent des privilèges et immunités diplomatiques.

Article 47

Le Bureau est autorisé à mettre ses locaux et son organisation à la disposition des Puissances contractantes pour le fonctionnement de toute juridiction spéciale d'arbitrage.

La juridiction de la Cour permanente peut être étendue, dans les conditions prescrites par les règlements, aux litiges existant entre des Puissances non contractantes ou entre des Puissances contractantes et des Puissances non contractantes, si les Parties sont convenues de recourir à cette juridiction.

Article 48

Les Puissances contractantes considèrent comme un devoir, dans le cas où un conflit aigu menacerait d'éclater entre deux ou plusieurs d'entre elles, de rappeler à celles-ci que la Cour permanente leur est ouverte.

En conséquence, elles déclarent que le fait de rappeler aux Parties en conflit les dispositions de la présente Convention, et le conseil donné, dans l'intérêt supérieur de la paix, de s'adresser à la Cour permanente, ne peuvent être considérés que comme actes de bons offices.

En cas de conflit entre deux Puissances, l'une d'elles pourra toujours adresser au Bureau international une note contenant sa déclaration qu'elle serait disposée à soumettre le différend à un arbitrage.

Le Bureau devra porter aussitôt la déclaration à la connaissance de l'autre Puissance.

Article 49

Le Conseil administratif permanent, composé des Représentants diplomatiques des Puissances contractantes accrédités à La Haye et du Ministre des Affaires étrangères des Pays-Bas, qui remplit les fonctions de Président, a la direction et le contrôle du Bureau international.

Le Conseil arrête son règlement d'ordre ainsi que tous autres règlements nécessaires.

Il décide toutes les questions administratives qui pourraient surgir touchant le fonctionnement de la Cour.

Il a tout pouvoir quant a la nomination, la suspension ou la révocation des fonctionnaires et employés du Bureau.

Il fixe les traitements et salaires, et contrôle la dépense générale.

La présence de neuf membres dans les réunions dûment convoquées suffit pour permettre au Conseil de délibérer valablement. Les décisions sont prises à la majorité des voix.

Le Conseil communique sans délai aux Puissances contractantes les règlements adoptés par lui. Il leur présente chaque année un rapport sur les travaux de la Cour, sur le fonctionnement des services administratifs et sur les dépenses. Le rapport contient également un résumé du contenu essentiel des documents communiqués au Bureau par les Puissances en vertu de l'article 43, alinéas 3 et 4.

Article 50

Les frais du Bureau seront supportés par les Puissances contractantes dans la proportion établie pour le Bureau international de l'Union postale universelle.

Les frais à la charge des Puissances adhérentes seront comptés à partir du jour où leur adhésion produit ses effets.

Chapitre III. De la procédure arbitrale

Article 51

En vue de favoriser le développement de l'arbitrage, les Puissances contractantes ont arrêté les règles suivantes qui sont applicables à la procédure arbitrale, en tant que les Parties ne sont pas convenues d'autres règles.

Article 52

Les Puissances qui recourent à l'arbitrage signent un compromis dans lequel sont déterminés l'objet du litige, le délai de nomination des arbitres, la forme, l'ordre et les délais dans lesquels la communication visée par l'article 63 devra être faite, et le montant de la somme que chaque Partie aura à déposer à titre d'avance pour les frais.

Le compromis détermine également, s'il y a lieu, le mode de nomination des arbitres, tous pouvoirs spéciaux éventuels du Tribunal, son siège, la langue dont il fera usage et celles dont l'emploi sera autorisé devant lui, et généralement toutes les conditions dont les Parties sont convenues.

Article 53

La Cour permanente est compétente pour l'établissement du compromis, si les Parties sont d'accord pour s'en remettre à elle.

Elle est également compétente, même si la demande est faite seulement par l'une des Parties, après qu'un accord par la voie diplomatique a été vainement essayé, quand il s'agit:

1) D'un différend rentrant dans un Traité d'arbitrage général conclu ou renouvelé après la mise en vigueur de cette Convention et qui prévoit pour chaque différend un compromis et n'exclut pour l'établissement de ce dernier ni explicitement ni implicitement la compétence de la Cour. Toutefois, le recours à la Cour n'a pas lieu si l'autre Partie déclare qu'à son avis le différend n'appartient pas à la catégorie des différends à soumettre à un arbitrage obligatoire, à moins que le Traité d'arbitrage ne confère au Tribunal arbitral le pouvoir de décider cette question préalable;

2) D'un différend provenant de dettes contractuelles réclamées à une Puissance par une autre Puissance comme dues à ses nationaux, et pour la solution duquel l'offre d'arbitrage a été acceptée. Cette disposition n'est pas applicable si l'acceptation a été subordonnée à la condition que le compromis soit établi selon un autre mode.

Article 54

Dans les cas prévus par l'article précédent, le compromis sera établi par une commission composée de cinq membres désignés de la manière prévue à l'article 45, alinéas 3 à 6.

Le cinquième membre est de droit Président de la commission.

Article 55

Les fonctions arbitrales peuvent être conférées à un arbitre unique ou à plusieurs arbitres désignés par les Parties à leur gré, ou choisis par Elles parmi les membres de la Cour permanente d'arbitrage établie par la présente Convention.

A défaut de constitution du Tribunal par l'accord des Parties, il est procédé de la manière indiquée à l'art. 45, al. 3 à 6.

Article 56

Lorsqu'un Souverain ou un Chef d'Etat est choisi pour arbitre, la procédure arbitrale est réglée par lui.

Article 57

Le surarbitre est de droit Président du Tribunal.

Lorsque le Tribunal ne comprend pas de surarbitre, il nomme lui-même son Président.

Article 58

En cas d'établissement du compromis par une commission, telle qu'elle est visée à l'article 54, et sauf stipulation contraire, la commission elle-même formera le Tribunal d'arbitrage.

Article 59

En cas de décès, de démission ou d'empêchement, pour quelque cause que ce soit, de l'un des arbitres, il est pourvu à son remplacement selon le mode fixé pour sa nomination.

Article 60

A défaut de désignation par les Parties, le Tribunal siège à La Haye.

Le Tribunal ne peut siéger sur le territoire d'une tierce Puissance qu'avec l'assentiment de celle-ci.

Le siège une fois fixé ne peut être changé par le Tribunal qu'avec l'assentiment des Parties.

Article 61

Si le compromis n'a pas déterminé les langues à employer, il en est décidé par le Tribunal.

Article 62

Les Parties ont le droit de nommer auprès du Tribunal des agents spéciaux, avec la mission de servir d'intermédiaires entre elles et le Tribunal.

Elles sont en outre autorisées à charger de la défense de leurs droits et intérêts devant le Tribunal, des conseils ou avocats nommés par elles à cet effet.

Les Membres de la Cour permanente ne peuvent exercer les fonctions d'agents, conseils ou avocats, qu'en faveur de la Puissance qui les a nommés membres de la Cour.

Article 63

La procédure arbitrale comprend en règle générale deux phases distinctes : l'instruction écrite et les débats.

L'instruction écrite consiste dans la communication faite par les agents respectifs, aux membres du Tribunal et à la Partie adverse, des mémoires, des contre-mémoires et, au besoin, des répliques ; les Parties y joignent toutes pièces et documents invoqués dans la cause. Cette communication aura lieu, directement ou par l'intermédiaire du Bureau international, dans l'ordre et dans les délais déterminés par le compromis.

Les délais fixés par le compromis pourront être prolongés de commun accord par les Parties, ou par le Tribunal quand il le juge nécessaire pour arriver à une décision juste.

Les débats consistent dans le développement oral des moyens des Parties devant le Tribunal.

Article 64

Toute pièce produite par l'une des Parties doit être communiquée, en copie certifiée conforme, à l'autre Partie.

Article 65

A moins de circonstances spéciales, le Tribunal ne se réunit qu'après la clôture de l'instruction.

Article 66

Les débats sont dirigés par le Président.

Ils ne sont publics qu'en vertu d'une décision du Tribunal, prise avec l'assentiment des Parties.

Ils sont consignés dans des procès-verbaux rédigés par des secrétaires que nomme le Président. Ces procès-verbaux sont signés par le Président et par un des secrétaires ; ils ont seuls caractère authentique.

Article 67

L'instruction étant close, le Tribunal a le droit d'écarter du débat tous actes ou documents nouveaux qu'une des Parties voudrait lui soumettre sans le consentement de l'autre.

Article 68

Le Tribunal demeure libre de prendre en considération les actes ou documents nouveaux sur lesquels les agents ou conseils des Parties appelleraient son attention.

En ce cas, le Tribunal a le droit de requérir la production de ces actes ou documents, sauf l'obligation d'en donner connaissance à la Partie adverse.

Article 69

Le Tribunal peut, en outre, requérir des agents des Parties la production de tous actes et demander toutes explications nécessaires. En cas de refus, le Tribunal en prend acte.

Article 70

Les agents et les conseils des Parties sont autorisés à présenter oralement au Tribunal tous les moyens qu'ils jugent utiles à la défense de leur cause.

Article 71

Ils ont le droit de soulever des exceptions et des incidents. Les décisions du Tribunal sur ces points sont définitives et ne peuvent donner lieu à aucune discussion ultérieure.

Article 72

Les membres du Tribunal ont le droit de poser des questions aux agents et aux conseils des Parties et de leur demander des éclaircissements sur les points douteux.

Ni les questions posées, ni les observations faites par les membres du Tribunal pendant le cours des débats ne peuvent être regardées comme l'expression des opinions du Tribunal en général ou de ses membres en particulier.

Article 73

Le Tribunal est autorisé à déterminer sa compétence en interprétant le compromis ainsi que les autres actes et documents qui peuvent être invoqués dans la matière, et en appliquant les principes du droit.

Article 74

Le Tribunal a le droit de rendre des ordonnances de procédure pour la direction du procès, de déterminer les formes, l'ordre et les délais dans lesquels chaque Partie devra prendre ses conclusions finales, et de procéder à toutes les formalités que comporte l'administration des preuves.

Article 75

Les Parties s'engagent à fournir au Tribunal, dans la plus large mesure qu'elles jugeront possible, tous les moyens nécessaires pour la décision du litige.

Article 76

Pour toutes les notifications que le Tribunal aurait à faire sur le territoire d'une tierce Puissance contractante, le Tribunal s'adressera directement au Gouvernement de cette Puissance. Il en sera de même s'il s'agit de faire procéder sur place à l'établissement de tous moyens de preuve.

Les requêtes adressées à cet effet seront exécutées suivant les moyens dont la Puissance requise dispose d'après sa législation intérieure. Elles ne peuvent être refusées que si cette Puissance les juge de nature à porter atteinte à sa souveraineté ou à sa sécurité.

Le Tribunal aura aussi toujours la faculté de recourir à l'intermédiaire de la Puissance sur le territoire de laquelle il a son siège.

Article 77

Les agents et les conseils des Parties ayant présenté tous les éclaircissements et preuves à l'appui de leur cause, le Président prononce la clôture des débats.

Article 78

Les délibérations du Tribunal ont lieu à huis clos et restent secrètes.

Toute décision est prise à la majorité de ses membres.

Article 79

La sentence arbitrale est motivée. Elle mentionne les noms des arbitres ; elle est signée par le Président et par le greffier ou le secrétaire faisant fonctions de greffier.

Article 80

La sentence est lue en séance publique, les agents et les conseils des Parties présents ou dûment appelés.

Article 81

La sentence, dûment prononcée et notifiée aux agents des Parties, décide définitivement et sans appel la contestation.

Article 82

Tout différend qui pourrait surgir entre les Parties, concernant l'interprétation et l'exécution de la sentence, sera, sauf stipulation contraire, soumis au jugement du Tribunal qui l'a rendue.

Article 83

Les Parties peuvent se réserver dans le compromis de demander la révision de la sentence arbitrale.

Dans ce cas, et sauf stipulation contraire, la demande doit être adressée au Tribunal qui a rendu la sentence. Elle ne peut être motivée que par la découverte d'un fait nouveau qui eût été de nature à exercer une influence décisive sur la sentence et qui, lors de la clôture des débats, était inconnu du Tribunal lui-même et de la Partie qui a demandé la révision.

La procédure de révision ne peut être ouverte que par une décision du Tribunal constatant expressément l'existence du fait nouveau, lui reconnaissant les caractères prévus par le paragraphe précédent et déclarant à ce titre la demande recevable.

Le compromis détermine le délai dans lequel la demande de révision doit être formée.

Article 84

La sentence arbitrale n'est obligatoire que pour les Parties en litige.

Lorsqu'il s'agit de l'interprétation d'une convention à laquelle ont participé d'autres Puissances que les Parties en litige, celles-ci avertissent en temps utile toutes les Puissances signataires. Chacune de ces Puissances a le droit d'intervenir au procès. Si une ou plusieurs d'entre elles ont profité de cette faculté, l'interprétation contenue dans la sentence est également obligatoire à leur égard.

Article 85

Chaque Partie supporte ses propres frais et une part égale des frais du Tribunal.

Chapitre IV. De la procédure sommaire d'arbitrage

Article 86

En vue de faciliter le fonctionnement de la justice arbitrale, lorsqu'il s'agit de litiges de nature à comporter une procédure sommaire, les Puissances contractantes arrêtent les règles ci-après qui seront suivies en l'absence de stipulations différentes, et sous réserve, le cas échéant, de l'application des dispositions du chapitre III qui ne seraient pas contraires.

Article 87

Chacune des Parties en litige nomme un arbitre. Les deux arbitres ainsi désignés choisissent un surarbitre. S'ils ne tombent pas d'accord à ce sujet, chacun présente deux candidats pris sur la liste générale des membres de la Cour permanente en dehors des Membres indiqués par chacune des Parties elles-mêmes et n'étant les nationaux d'aucune d'Elles; le sort détermine lequel des candidats ainsi présentés sera le sur-arbitre.

Le surarbitre préside le Tribunal, qui rend ses décisions à la majorité des voix.

Article 88

A défaut d'accord préalable, le Tribunal fixe, dès qu'il est constitué, le délai dans lequel les deux Parties devront lui soumettre leurs mémoires respectifs.

Article 89

Chaque Partie est représentée devant le Tribunal par un agent qui sert d'intermédiaire entre le Tribunal et le Gouvernement qui l'a désigné.

Article 90

La procédure a lieu exclusivement par écrit. Toutefois, chaque Partie a le droit de demander la comparution de témoins et d'experts. Le Tribunal a, de son côté, la faculté de demander des explications orales aux agents des deux Parties, ainsi qu'aux experts et aux témoins dont il juge la comparution utile.

Titre V. Dispositions finales

Article 91

La présente Convention dûment ratifiée remplacera, dans les rapports entre les Puissances contractantes, la Convention pour le règlement pacifique des conflits internationaux du 29 juillet 1899.

Article 92

La présente Convention sera ratifiée aussitôt que possible.

Les ratifications seront déposées à La Haye.

Le premier dépôt de ratifications sera constaté par un procès-verbal signé par les représentants des Puissances qui y prennent part et par le Ministre des Affaires étrangères des Pays-Bas.

Les dépôts ultérieurs de ratifications se feront au moyen d'une notification écrite, adressée au Gouvernement des Pays-Bas et accompagnée de l'instrument de ratification.

Copie certifiée conforme du procès-verbal relatif au premier dépôt de ratifications, des notifications mentionnées à l'alinéa précédent, ainsi que des instruments de ratification, sera immédiatement remise, par les soins du Gouvernement des Pays-Bas et par la voie diplomatique, aux Puissances conviées à la Deuxième Conférence de la Paix, ainsi qu'aux autres Puissances qui auront adhéré à la Convention. Dans les cas visés par l'alinéa précédent, ledit Gouvernement leur fera connaître en même temps la date à laquelle il a reçu la notification.

Article 93

Les Puissances non signataires qui ont été conviées à la Deuxième Conférence de la Paix pourront adhérer à la présente Convention.

La Puissance qui désire adhérer notifie par écrit son intention au Gouvernement des Pays-Bas en lui transmettant l'acte d'adhésion qui sera déposé dans les archives dudit Gouvernement.

Ce Gouvernement transmettra immédiatement à toutes les autres Puissances conviées à la Deuxième Conférence de la Paix copie certifiée conforme de la notification ainsi que de l'acte d'adhésion, en indiquant la date à laquelle il a reçu la notification.

Article 94

Les conditions auxquelles les Puissances qui n'ont pas été conviées à la Deuxième Conférence de la Paix pourront adhérer à la présente Convention, formeront l'objet d'une entente ultérieure entre les Puissances contractantes.

Article 95

La présente Convention produira effet, pour les Puissances qui auront participé au premier dépôt de ratifications, soixante jours après la date du procès-verbal de ce dépôt et, pour les Puissances qui ratifieront ultérieure-ment ou qui adhéreront, soixante jours après que la notification de leur ratification ou de leur adhésion aura été reçue par le Gouvernement des Pays-Bas.

Article 96

S'il arrivait qu'une des Puissances contractantes voulût dénoncer la présente Convention, la dénonciation sera notifiée par écrit au Gouvernement des Pays-Bas, qui communiquera immédiatement copie certifiée conforme de la notification à toutes les autres Puissances en leur faisant savoir la date à laquelle il l'a reçue.

La dénonciation ne produira ses effets qu'à l'égard de la Puissance qui l'aura notifiée et un an après que la notification en sera parvenue au Gouvernement des Pays-Bas.

Article 97

Un registre tenu par le Ministère des Affaires étrangères des Pays-Bas indiquera la date du dépôt de ratifications effectué en vertu de l'article 92, alinéas 3 et 4, ainsi que la date à laquelle auront été reçues les notifications d'adhésion (art. 93, al. 2) ou de dénonciation (art. 96, al. 1).

Chaque Puissance contractante est admise à prendre connaissance de ce registre et à en demander des extraits certifiés conformes.

En foi de quoi, les Plénipotentiaires ont revêtu la présente Convention de leurs signatures.

Fait à La Haye, le dix-huit octobre mil neuf cent sept, en un seul exemplaire qui restera déposé dans les archives du Gouvernement des Pays-Bas et dont des copies certifiées conformes seront remises par la voie diplomatique aux Puissances contractantes.

II. CONVENTION CONCERNANT LA LIMITATION DE L'EMPLOI DE LA FORCE POUR LE RECOUVREMENT DES DETTES CONTRACTUELLES

[Pour les Etats parties, voir convention I, supra, p. 305]

Désireux d'éviter entre les nations des conflits armés d'une origine pécu-niaire, provenant de dettes contractuelles, réclamées au Gouvernement d'un pays par le Gouvernement d'un autre pays comme dues à ses nationaux,

Ont résolu de conclure une Convention à cet effet et ont nommé pour leurs Plénipotentiaires, savoir:

[Dénomination des plénipotentiaires]

Lesquels, après avoir déposé leurs pleins pouvoirs trouvés en bonne et due forme, sont convenus des dispositions suivantes:

Article premier

Les Puissances contractantes sont convenues de ne pas avoir recours à la force armée pour le recouvrement de dettes contractuelles réclamées au Gouvernement d'un pays par le Gouvernement d'un autre pays comme dues à ses nationaux.

Tourefois, cette stipulation ne pourra être appliquée quand l'Etat débiteur refuse ou laisse sans réponse une offre d'arbitrage, ou, en cas d'acceptation, rend impossible l'établissement du compromis, ou, après l'arbitrage, man-que de se conformer à la sentence rendue.

Article 2

Il est de plus convenu que l'arbitrage, mentionné dans l'alinéa 2 de l'ar-ticle précédent, sera soumis à la procédure prévue par le titre IV chapitre 3 de la Convention de La Haye pour le règlement pacifique des conflits inter-nationaux. Le jugement arbitral détermine, sauf les arrangements particu-liers des Parties, le bien-fondé de la réclamation, le montant de la dette, le temps et le mode de paiement.

Article 3

La présente Convention sera ratifiée aussitôt que possible.

Les ratifications seront déposées à La Haye.

Le premier dépôt de ratifications sera constaté par un procès-verbal signé par les représentants des Puissances qui y prennent part et par le Ministre des Affaires étrangères des Pays-Bas.

Les dépôts ultérieurs de ratifications se feront au moyen d'une notifica-tion écrite, adressée au Gouvernement des Pays-Bas et accompagnée de l'instrument de ratification.

Copie certifiée conforme du procès-verbal relatif au premier dépôt de ratifications, des notifications mentionnées à l'alinéa précédent, ainsi que des instruments de ratification, sera immédiatement remise, par les soins du Gouvernement des Pays-Bas et par la voie diplomatique, aux Puissances conviées à 1a Deuxième Conférence de la Paix, ainsi qu'aux autres Puissances qui auront adhéré à la Convention. Dans les cas visés par l'alinéa précédent, ledit Gouvernement leur fera connaître en même temps la date à laquelle il a reçu la notification.

Article 4

Les Puissances non signataires sont admises à adhérer à la présente Convention.

La Puissance qui désire adhérer notifie par écrit son intention au Gouvernement des Pays-Bas en lui transmettant l'acte d'adhésion qui sera déposé dans les archives dudit Gouvernement.

Ce Gouvernement transmettra immédiatement à toutes les autres Puissances conviées à la Deuxième Conférence de la Paix copie certifiée conforme de la notification ainsi que de l'acte d'adhésion, en indiquant la date à laquelle il a reçu la notification.

Article 5

La présente Convention produira effet, pour les Puissances qui auront participé au premier dépôt de ratifications, soixante jours après 1a date du procès-verbal de ce dépôt et, pour les Puissances qui ratifieront ultérieurement ou qui adhéreront, soixante jours après que 1a notification de leur ratification, ou de leur adhésion aura été reçue par le Gouvernement des Pays-Bas.

Article 6

S'il arrivait qu'une des Puissances contractantes voulût dénoncer 1a présente Convention, la dénonciation sera notifiée par écrit au Gouvernement des Pays-Bas qui communiquera immédiatement copie certifiée conforme de la notification à toutes les autres Puissances en leur faisant savoir la date à laquelle il l'a reçue.

La dénonciation ne produira ses effets qu'à l'égard de la Puissance qui l'aura notifiée et un an après que la notification en sera parvenue au Gouvernement des Pays-Bas.

Article 7

Un registre tenu par le Ministère des Affaires étrangères des Pays-Bas indiquera la date du dépôt de ratifications effectué en vertu de l'article 3, alinéas 3 et 4, ainsi que la date à laquelle auront été reçues les notifications d'adhésion (article 4, alinéa 2) ou de dénonciation (article 6, alinéa 1).

Chaque Puissance contractante est admise à prendre connaissance de ce registre et à en demander des extraits certifiés conformes.

En foi de quoi, les Plénipotentiaires ont revêtu la présente Convention de leurs signatures.

Fait à La Haye, le dix-huit octobre mil neuf cent sept, en un seul exemplaire qui restera déposé dans les archives du Gouvernement des Pays-Bas et dont des copies certifiées conformes seront remises par la voie diplomatique aux Puissances contractantes.

III. CONVENTION RELATIVE À L'OUVERTURE DES HOSTILITÉS

[Pour les Etats parties, voir convention I, supra, p. 305]

Considérant que, pour la sécurité des relations pacifiques, il importe que les hostilités ne commencent pas sans un avertissement préalable;

Qu'il importe, de même, que l'état de guerre soit notifié sans retard aux Puissances neutres;

Désirant conclure une Convention à cet effet, ont nommé pour leurs Plénipotentiaires, savoir:

[Dénomination des plénipotentiaires]

Lesquels, après avoir déposé leurs pleins pouvoirs, trouvés en bonne et due forme, sont convenus des dispositions suivantes:

Article premier

Les Puissances contractantes reconnaissent que les hostilités entre elles ne doivent pas commencer sans un avertissement préalable et non équivoque, qui aura, soit la forme d'une déclaration de guerre motivée, soit celle d'un ultimatum avec déclaration de guerre conditionnelle.

Article 2

L'état de guerre devra être notifié sans retard aux Puissances neutres et ne produira effet à leur égard qu'après réception d'une notification qui pourra être faite même par voie télégraphique. Toutefois les Puissances neutres ne pourraient invoquer l'absence de notification, s'il était établi d'une manière non douteuse qu'en fait elles connaissaient l'état de guerre.

Article 3

L'article 1 de la présente Convention produira effet en cas de guerre entre deux ou plusieurs des Puissances contractantes.

L'article 2 est obligatoire dans les rapports entre un belligérant contractant et les Puissances neutres également contractantes.

Article 4

La présente Convention sera ratifiée aussitôt que possible.

Les ratifications seront déposées à La Haye.

Le premier dépôt de ratifications sera constaté par un procès-verbal signé par les représentants des Puissances qui y prennent part et par le Ministre des Affaires étrangères des Pays-Bas.

Les dépôts ultérieurs de ratifications se feront au moyen d'une notification écrite adressée au Gouvernement des Pays-Bas et accompagnée de l'instrument de ratification.

Copie certifiée conforme du procès-verbal relatif au premier dépôt de ratifications, des notifications mentionnées à l'alinéa précédent ainsi que des instruments de ratification, sera immédiatement remise par les soins du Gouvernement des Pays-Bas et par la voie diplomatique aux Puissances conviées à la Deuxième Conférence de la Paix, ainsi qu'aux autres Puissances qui auront adhéré à la Convention. Dans les cas visés par l'alinéa précédent, ledit Gouvernement leur fera connaître en même temps la date à laquelle il a reçu la notification.

Article 5

Les Puissances non signataires sont admises à adhérer à la présente Convention.

La Puissance qui désire adhérer notifie par écrit son intention au Gouvernement des Pays-Bas en lui transmettant l'acte d'adhésion qui sera déposé dans les archives dudit Gouvernement.

Ce Gouvernement transmettra immédiatement à toutes les autres Puissances copie certifiée conforme de la notification ainsi que de l'acte d'adhésion, en indiquant la date à laquelle il a reçu la notification.

Article 6

La présente Convention produira effet, pour les Puissances qui auront participé au premier dépôt de ratifications, soixante jours après la date du procès-verbal de ce dépôt, et, pour les Puissances qui ratifieront ultérieurement ou qui adhéreront, soixante jours après que la notification de leur ratification ou de leur adhésion aura été reçue par le Gouvernement des Pays-Bas.

Article 7

S'il arrivait qu'une des Hautes Parties contractantes voulût dénoncer la présente Convention, la dénonciation sera notifiée par écrit au Gouvernement des Pays-Bas qui communiquera immédiatement copie certifiée conforme de la notification à toutes les autres Puissances en leur faisant savoir la date à laquelle il l'a reçue.

La dénonciation ne produira ses effets qu'à l'égard de la Puissance qui l'aura notifiée et un an après que la notification en sera parvenue au Gouvernement des Pays-Bas.

Article 8

Un registre tenu par le Ministère des Affaires étrangères des Pays-Bas indiquera la date du dépôt de ratifications effectué en vertu de l'article 4, alinéas 3 et 4, ainsi que la date à laquelle auront été reçues les notifications d'adhésion (article 5, alinéa 2) ou de dénonciation (article 7, alinéa 1).

Chaque Puissance contractante est admise à prendre connaissance de ce registre et à en demander des extraits certifiés conformes.

En foi de quoi, les Plénipotentiaires ont revêtu la présente Convention de leurs signatures.

Fait à La Haye, le dix-huit octobre mil neuf cent sept, en un seul exemplaire qui restera déposé dans les archives du Gouvernement des Pays-Bas et dont des copies, certifiées conformes, seront remises par la voie diplomatique aux Puissances qui ont été conviées à la Deuxième Conférence de la Paix.

IV. CONVENTION CONCERNANT LES LOIS ET COUTUMES DE LA GUERRE SUR TERRE

[Pour les Etats parties, voir convention I, supra, *p. 305]*

Considérant que, tout en recherchant les moyens de sauvegarder la paix et de prévenir les conflits armés entre les nations, il importe de se préoccuper également du cas où l'appel aux armes serait amené par des événements que leur sollicitude n'aurait pu détourner ;

Animés du désir de servir encore, dans cette hypothèse extrême, les intérêts de l'humanité et les exigences toujours progressives de la civilisation ;

Estimant qu'il importe, à cette fin, de réviser les lois et coutumes générales de la guerre, soit dans le but de les définir avec plus de précision, soit afin d'y tracer certaines limites destinées à en restreindre autant que possible les rigueurs ;

Ont jugé nécessaire de compléter et de préciser sur certains points l'œuvre de la Première Conférence de la Paix qui, s'inspirant, à la suite de la Conférence de Bruxelles de 1874, de ces idées recommandées par une sage et généreuse prévoyance, a adopté des dispositions ayant pour objet de définir et de régler les usages de la guerre sur terre.

Selon les vues des Hautes Parties contractantes, ces dispositions, dont la rédaction a été inspirée par le désir de diminuer les maux de la guerre, autant que les nécessités militaires le permettent, sont destinées à servir de règle générale de conduite aux belligérants, dans leurs rapports entre eux et avec les populations.

Il n'a pas été possible toutefois de concerter dès maintenant des stipulations s'étendant à toutes les circonstances qui se présentent dans la pratique ;

D'autre part, il ne pouvait entrer dans les intentions des Hautes Parties contractantes que les cas non prévus fussent, faute de stipulation écrite, laissées à l'appréciation arbitraire de ceux qui dirigent les armées.

En attendant qu'un Code plus complet des lois de la guerre puisse être édicté, les Hautes Parties contractantes jugent opportun de constater que, dans les cas non compris dans les dispositions réglementaires adoptées par Elles, les populations et les belligérants restent sous la sauvegarde et sous l'empire des principes du droit des gens, tels qu'ils résultent des usages établis entre nations civilisées, des lois de l'humanité et des exigences de la conscience publique.

Elles déclarent que c'est dans ce sens que doivent s'entendre notamment les articles 1 et 2 du Règlement adopté.

Les Hautes Parties contractantes, désirant conclure une nouvelle Convention à cet effet, ont nommé pour leurs Plénipotentiaires, savoir :

[Dénomination des plénipotentiaires]

Lesquels, après avoir déposé leurs pleins pouvoirs, trouvés en bonne et due forme, sont convenus de ce qui suit :

Article premier

Les Puissances contractantes donneront à leurs forces armées de terre des instructions qui seront conformes au Règlement concernant les lois et coutumes de la guerre sur terre, annexé à la présente Convention.

Article 2

Les dispositions contenues dans le Règlement visé à l'article premier ainsi que dans la présente Convention, ne sont applicables qu'entre les Puissances contractantes et seulement si les belligérants sont tous parties à la Convention.

Article 3

La Partie belligérante qui violerait les dispositions dudit Règlement sera tenue à indemnité, s'il y a lieu. Elle sera responsable de tous actes commis par les personnes faisant partie de sa force armée.

Article 4

La présente Convention dûment ratifiée remplacera, dans les rapports entre les Puissances contractantes, la Convention du 29 juillet 1899 concernant les lois et coutumes de la guerre sur terre.

La Convention de 1899 reste en vigueur dans les rapports entre les Puissances qui l'ont signée et qui ne ratifieraient pas également la présente Convention.

Article 5

La présente Convention sera ratifiée aussitôt que possible.

Les ratifications seront déposées à La Haye.

Le premier dépôt de ratifications sera constaté par un procès-verbal signé par les représentants des Puissances qui y prennent part et par le Ministre des Affaires étrangères des Pays-Bas.

Les dépôts ultérieurs de ratifications se feront au moyen d'une notification écrite adressée au Gouvernement des Pays-Bas et accompagnée de l'instrument de ratification.

Copie certifiée conforme du procès-verbal relatif au premier dépôt de ratifications, des notifications mentionnées à l'alinéa précédent ainsi que des instruments de ratification, sera immédiatement remise par les soins du Gouvernement des Pays-Bas et par la voie diplomatique aux Puissances conviées à la Deuxième Conférence de la Paix, ainsi qu'aux autres Puissances qui auront adhéré à la Convention. Dans les cas visés par l'alinéa précédent, ledit Gouvernement leur fera connaître en même temps la date à laquelle il a reçu la notification.

Article 6

Les Puissances non signataires sont admises à adhérer à la présente Convention.

La Puissance qui désire adhérer notifie par écrit son intention au Gouvernement des Pays-Bas en lui transmettant l'acte d'adhésion qui sera déposé dans les archives dudit Gouvernement.

Ce Gouvernement transmettra immédiatement à toutes les autres Puissances copie certifiée conforme de la notification ainsi que de l'acte d'adhésion, en indiquant la date à laquelle il a reçu la notification.

Article 7

La présente Convention produira effet, pour les Puissances qui auront participé au premier dépôt de ratifications, soixante jours après la date du procès-verbal de ce dépôt et, pour les Puissances qui ratifieront ultérieurement ou qui adhéreront, soixante jours après que la notification de leur ratification ou de leur adhésion aura été reçue par le Gouvernement des Pays-Bas.

Article 8

S'il arrivait qu'une des Puissances contractantes voulût dénoncer la présente Convention, la dénonciation sera notifiée par écrit au Gouvernement des Pays-Bas qui communiquera immédiatement copie certifiée conforme de la notification à toutes les autres Puissances en leur faisant savoir la date à laquelle il l'a reçue.

La dénonciation ne produira ses effets qu'à l'égard de la Puissance qui l'aura notifiée et un an après que la notification en sera parvenue au Gouvernement des Pays-Bas.

Article 9

Un registre tenu par le Ministère des Affaires étrangères des Pays-Bas indiquera la date du dépôt de ratifications effectué en vertu de l'article 5, alinéas 3 et 4 ainsi que la date à laquelle auront été reçues les notifications d'adhésion (article 6, alinéa 2) ou de dénonciation (article 8, alinéa 1).

Chaque Puissance contractante est admise à prendre connaissance de ce registre et à en demander des extraits certifiés conformes.

En foi de quoi, les Plénipotentiaires ont revêtu la présente Convention de leurs signatures.

Fait à La Haye, le dix-huit octobre mil neuf cent sept, en un seul exemplaire qui restera déposé dans les archives du Gouvernement des Pays-Bas et dont des copies, certifiées conformes, seront remises par la voie diplomatique aux Puissances qui ont été conviées à la Deuxième Conférence de la Paix.

Annexe à la Convention

RÈGLEMENT CONCERNANT LES LOIS ET COUTUMES DE LA GUERRE SUR TERRE

SECTION I. DES BELLIGÉRANTS

Chapitre I. De la qualité de belligérant

Article premier

Les lois, les droits et les devoirs de la guerre ne s'appliquent pas seulement à l'armée, mais encore aux milices et aux corps de volontaires réunissant les conditions suivantes:

1) d'avoir à leur tête une personne responsable pour ses subordonnés;
2) d'avoir un signe distinctif fixe et reconnaissable à distance;
3) de porter les armes ouvertement et
4) de se conformer dans leurs opérations aux lois et coutumes de la guerre.

Dans les pays où les milices ou des corps de volontaires constituent l'armée ou en font partie, ils sont compris sous la dénomination d'*armée*.

Article 2

La population d'un territoire non occupé qui, à l'approche de l'ennemi, prend spontanément les armes pour combattre les troupes d'invasion sans avoir eu le temps de s'organiser conformément à l'article premier, sera considérée comme belligérante si elle porte les armes ouvertement et si elle respecte les lois et coutumes de la guerre.

Article 3

Les forces armées des Parties belligérantes peuvent se composer de combattants et de non-combattants. En cas de capture par l'ennemi, les uns et les autres ont droit au traitement des prisonniers de guerre.

Chapitre II. Des prisonniers de guerre.

Article 4

Les prisonniers de guerre sont au pouvoir du Gouvernement ennemi, mais non des individus ou des corps qui les ont capturés.
Ils doivent être traités avec humanité.
Tout ce qui leur appartient personnellement, excepté les armes, les chevaux et les papiers militaires, reste leur propriété.

Article 5

Les prisonniers de guerre peuvent être assujettis à l'internement dans une ville, forteresse, camp ou localité quelconque, avec obligation de ne pas s'en éloigner au-delà de certaines limites déterminées; mais ils ne peuvent être enfermés que par mesure de sûreté indispensable, et seulement pendant la durée des circonstances qui nécessitent cette mesure.

Article 6

L'Etat peut employer, comme travailleurs, les prisonniers de guerre, selon leur grade et leurs aptitudes, à l'exception des officiers. Ces travaux ne seront pas excessifs et n'auront aucun rapport avec les opérations de la guerre.

Les prisonniers peuvent être autorisés à travailler pour le compte d'administrations publiques ou de particuliers, ou pour leur propre compte.

Les travaux faits pour l'Etat sont payés d'après les tarifs en vigueur pour les militaires de l'armée nationale exécutant les mêmes travaux, ou, s'il n'en existe pas, d'après un tarif en rapport avec les travaux exécutés.

Lorsque les travaux ont lieu pour le compte d'autres administrations publiques ou pour des particuliers, les conditions en sont réglées d'accord avec l'autorité militaire.

Le salaire des prisonniers contribuera à adoucir leur position, et le surplus leur sera compté au moment de leur libération, sauf défalcation des frais d'entretien.

Article 7

Le Gouvernement au pouvoir duquel se trouvent les prisonniers de guerre est chargé de leur entretien.

A défaut d'une entente spéciale entre les belligérants, les prisonniers de guerre seront traités pour la nourriture, le couchage et l'habillement, sur le même pied que les troupes du Gouvernement qui les aura capturés.

Article 8

Les prisonniers de guerre seront soumis aux lois, règlements et ordres en vigueur dans l'armée de l'Etat au pouvoir duquel ils se trouvent. Tout acte d'insubordination autorise, à leur égard, les mesures de rigueur nécessaires.

Les prisonniers évadés, qui seraient repris avant d'avoir pu rejoindre leur armée ou avant de quitter le territoire occupé par l'armée qui les aura capturés, sont passibles de peines disciplinaires.

Les prisonniers qui, après avoir réussi à s'évader, sont de nouveau faits prisonniers, ne sont passibles d'aucune peine pour la fuite antérieure.

Article 9

Chaque prisonnier de guerre est tenu de déclarer, s'il est interrogé à ce sujet, ses véritables noms et grade et, dans le cas où il enfreindrait cette règle, il s'exposerait à une restriction des avantages accordés aux prisonniers de guerre de sa catégorie.

Article 10

Les prisonniers de guerre peuvent être mis en liberté sur parole, si les lois de leur pays les y autorisent, et, en pareil cas, ils sont obligés, sous la garantie de leur honneur personnel, de remplir scrupuleusement, tant vis-à-vis de leur propre Gouvernement que vis-à-vis de celui qui les a faits prisonniers, les engagements qu'ils auraient contractés.

Dans le même cas, leur propre Gouvernement est tenu de n'exiger ni accepter d'eux aucun service contraire à la parole donnée.

Article 11

Un prisonnier de guerre ne peut être contraint d'accepter sa liberté sur parole ; de même le Gouvernement ennemi n'est pas obligé d'accéder à la demande du prisonnier réclamant sa mise en liberté sur parole.

Article 12

Tout prisonnier de guerre, libéré sur parole et repris portant les armes contre le Gouvernement envers lequel il s'était engagé d'honneur, ou contre les alliés de celui-ci, perd le droit au traitement des prisonniers de guerre et peut être traduit devant les tribunaux.

Article 13

Les individus qui suivent une armée sans en faire directement partie, tels que les correspondants et les reporters de journaux, les vivandiers, les fournisseurs, qui tombent au pouvoir de l'ennemi et que celui-ci juge utile de détenir, ont droit au traitement des prisonniers de guerre, à condition qu'ils soient munis d'une légitimation de l'autorité militaire de l'armée qu'ils accompagnaient.

Article 14

Il est constitué, dès le début des hostilités, dans chacun des Etats belligérants, et, le cas échéant, dans les pays neutres qui auront recueilli des belligérants sur leur territoire, un bureau de renseignements sur les prisonniers de guerre. Ce bureau, chargé de répondre à toutes les demandes qui les concernent, reçoit des divers services compétents toutes les indications relatives aux internements et aux mutations, aux mises en liberté sur parole, aux échanges, aux évasions, aux entrées dans les hôpitaux, aux décès, ainsi que les autres renseignements nécessaires pour établir et tenir à jour une fiche individuelle pour chaque prisonnier de guerre. Le bureau devra porter sur cette fiche le numéro matricule, les nom et prénom, l'âge, le lieu d'origine, le grade, le corps de troupe, les blessures, la date et le lieu de la capture, de l'internement, des blessures et de la mort, ainsi que toutes les observations particulières. La fiche individuelle sera remise au Gouvernement de l'autre belligérant après la conclusion de la paix.

Le bureau de renseignements est également chargé de recueillir et de centraliser tous les objets d'un usage personnel, valeurs, lettres etc., qui seront trouvés sur les champs de bataille ou délaissés par des prisonniers libérés sur parole, échangés, évadés ou décédés dans les hôpitaux et ambulances, et de les transmettre aux intéressés.

Article 15

Les sociétés de secours pour les prisonniers de guerre, régulièrement constituées selon la loi de leur pays et ayant pour objet d'être les intermédiaires de l'action charitable, recevront, de la part des belligérants, pour elles et pour leurs agents dûment accrédités, toute facilité, dans les limites tracées par les nécessités militaires et les règles administratives, pour accomplir efficacement leur tâche d'humanité. Les délégués de ces sociétés pourront être admis à distribuer des secours dans les dépôts d'internement, ainsi qu'aux lieux d'étape des prisonniers rapatriés, moyennant une permission personnelle délivrée par l'autorité militaire, et en prenant l'engagement par écrit de se soumettre à toutes les mesures d'ordre et de police que celle-ci prescrirait.

Article 16

Les bureaux de renseignements jouissent de la franchise de port. Les lettres, mandats et articles d'argent, ainsi que les colis postaux destinés aux prisonniers de guerre ou expédiés par eux, seront affranchis de toutes les taxes postales, aussi bien dans les pays d'origine et de destination que dans les pays intermédiaires.

Les dons et secours en nature destinés aux prisonniers de guerre seront admis en franchise de tous droits d'entrée et autres, ainsi que des taxes de transport sur les chemins de fer exploités par l'Etat.

Article 17

Les officiers prisonniers recevront la solde à laquelle ont droit les officiers de même grade du pays où ils sont retenus, à charge de remboursement par leur Gouvernement.

Article 18

Toute latitude est laissée aux prisonniers de guerre pour l'exercice de leur religion, y compris l'assistance aux offices de leur culte, à la seule condition de se conformer aux mesures d'ordre et de police prescrites par l'autorité militaire.

Article 19

Les testaments des prisonniers de guerre sont reçus ou dressés dans les mêmes conditions que pour les militaires de l'armée nationale.

On suivra également les mêmes règles en ce qui concerne les pièces relatives à la constatation des décès, ainsi que pour l'inhumation des prisonniers de guerre, en tenant compte de leur grade et de leur rang.

Article 20

Après la conclusion de la paix, le rapatriement des prisonniers de guerre s'effectuera dans le plus bref délai possible.

Chapitre III. Des malades et blessés

Article 21

Les obligations des belligérants concernant le service des malades et des blessés sont régies par la Convention de Genève.

SECTION II. DES HOSTILITÉS

Chapitre I. Des moyens de nuire à l'ennemi, des sièges et des bombardements

Article 22

Les belligérants n'ont pas un droit illimité quant au choix des moyens de nuire à l'ennemi.

Article 23

Outre les prohibitions établies par des conventions spéciales, il est notamment interdit :

a) d'employer du poison ou des armes empoisonnées ;
b) de tuer ou de blesser par trahison des individus appartenant à la nation ou à l'armée ennemie ;
c) de tuer ou de blesser un ennemi qui, ayant mis bas les armes ou n'ayant plus les moyens de se défendre, s'est rendu à discrétion ;
d) de déclarer qu'il ne sera pas fait de quartier ;
e) d'employer des armes, des projectiles ou des matières propres à causer des maux superflus ;
f) d'user indûment du pavillon parlementaire, du pavillon national ou des insignes militaires et de l'uniforme de l'ennemi, ainsi que des signes distinctifs de la Convention de Genève ;
g) de détruire ou de saisir des propriétés ennemies, sauf les cas où ces destructions ou ces saisies seraient impérieusement commandées par les nécessités de la guerre ;
h) de déclarer éteints, suspendus ou non recevables en justice, les droits et actions des nationaux de la Partie adverse.

Il est également interdit à un belligérant de forcer les nationaux de la Partie adverse à prendre part aux opérations de guerre dirigées contre leur pays, même dans le cas où ils auraient été à son service avant le commencement de la guerre.

Article 24

Les ruses de guerre et l'emploi des moyens nécessaires pour se procurer des renseignements sur l'ennemi et sur le terrain sont considérés comme licites.

Article 25

Il est interdit d'attaquer ou de bombarder, par quelque moyen que ce soit, des villes, villages, habitations ou bâtiments qui ne sont pas défendus.

Article 26

Le commandant des troupes assaillantes, avant d'entreprendre le bombardement, et sauf le cas d'attaque de vive force, devra faire tout ce qui dépend de lui pour en avertir les autorités.

Article 27

Dans les sièges et bombardements, toutes les mesures nécessaires doivent être prises pour épargner, autant que possible, les édifices consacrés aux cultes, aux arts, aux sciences et à la bienfaisance, les monuments historiques, les hôpitaux et les lieux de rassemblement de malades et de blessés, à condition qu'ils ne soient pas employés en même temps à un but militaire.

Le devoir des assiégés est de désigner ces édifices ou lieux de rassemblement par des signes visibles spéciaux qui seront notifiés d'avance à l'assiégeant.

Article 28

Il est interdit de livrer au pillage une ville ou localité même prise d'assaut.

Chapitre II. Des espions

Article 29

Ne peut être considéré comme espion que l'individu qui, agissant clandestinement ou sous de faux prétextes, recueille ou cherche à recueillir des informations dans la zone d'opérations d'un belligérant, avec l'intention de les communiquer à la Partie adverse.

Ainsi les militaires non déguisés qui ont pénétré dans la zone d'opérations de l'armée ennemie, à l'effet de recueillir des informations, ne sont pas considérés comme espions. De même, ne sont pas considérés comme espions : les militaires et les non-militaires, accomplissant ouvertement leur mission, chargés de transmettre des dépêches destinées, soit à leur propre armée, soit à l'armée ennemie. A cette catégorie appartiennent également les individus envoyés en ballon pour transmettre les dépêches, et, en général, pour entretenir les communications entre les diverses parties d'une armée ou d'un territoire.

Article 30

L'espion pris sur le fait ne pourra être puni sans jugement préalable.

Article 31

L'espion qui, ayant rejoint l'armée à laquelle il appartient, est capturé plus tard par l'ennemi, est traité comme prisonnier de guerre et n'encourt aucune responsabilité pour ses actes d'espionnage antérieurs.

Chapitre III. Des parlementaires

Article 32

Est considéré comme parlementaire l'individu autorisé par l'un des belligérants à entrer en pourparlers avec l'autre et se présentant avec le drapeau blanc. Il a droit à l'inviolabilité ainsi que le trompette, clairon ou tambour, le porte-drapeau et l'interprète qui l'accompagneraient.

Article 33

Le chef auquel un parlementaire est expédié n'est pas obligé de le recevoir en toutes circonstances.

Il peut prendre toutes les mesures nécessaires afin d'empêcher le parlementaire de profiter de sa mission pour se renseigner.

Il a le droit, en cas d'abus, de retenir temporairement le parlementaire.

Article 34

Le parlementaire perd ses droits d'inviolabilité, s'il est prouvé, d'une manière positive et irrécusable, qu'il a profité de sa position privilégiée pour provoquer ou commettre un acte de trahison.

Chapitre IV. Des capitulations.

Article 35

Les capitulations arrêtées entre les Parties contractantes doivent tenir compte des règles de l'honneur militaire.

Une fois fixées, elles doivent être scrupuleusement observées par les deux Parties.

Chapitre V. De l'armistice

Article 36

L'armistice suspend les opérations de guerre par un accord mutuel des Parties belligérantes. Si la durée n'en est pas déterminée, les Parties belligérantes peuvent reprendre en tout temps les opérations, pourvu toutefois que l'ennemi soit averti en temps convenu, conformément aux conditions de l'armistice.

Article 37

L'armistice peut être général ou local. Le premier suspend partout les opérations de guerre des Etats belligérants; le second, seulement entre certaines fractions des armées belligérantes et dans un rayon déterminé.

Article 38

L'armistice doit être notifié officiellement et en temps utile aux autorités compétentes et aux troupes. Les hostilités sont suspendues immédiatement après la notification ou au terme fixé.

Article 39

Il dépend des Parties contractantes de fixer, dans les clauses de l'armistice, les rapports qui pourraient avoir lieu, sur le théâtre de la guerre, avec les populations et entre elles.

Article 40

Toute violation grave de l'armistice, par l'une des Parties, donne à l'autre le droit de le dénoncer et même, en cas d'urgence, de reprendre immédiatement les hostilités.

Article 41

La violation des clauses de l'armistice, par des particuliers agissant de leur propre initiative, donne droit seulement à réclamer la punition des coupables et, s'il y a lieu, une indemnité pour les pertes éprouvées.

SECTION III. - DE L'AUTORITÉ MILITAIRE
SUR LE TERRITOIRE DE L'ETAT ENNEMI

Article 42

Un territoire est considéré comme occupé lorsqu'il se trouve placé de fait sous l'autorité de l'armée ennemie.

L'occupation ne s'étend qu'aux territoires où cette autorité est établie et en mesure de s'exercer.

Article 43

L'autorité du pouvoir légal ayant passé de fait entre les mains de l'occupant, celui-ci prendra toutes les mesures qui dépendent de lui en vue de rétablir et d'assurer, autant qu'il est possible, l'ordre et la vie publics en respectant, sauf empêchement absolu, les lois en vigueur dans le pays.

Article 44

Il est interdit à un belligérant de forcer la population d'un territoire occupé à donner des renseignements sur l'armée de l'autre belligérant ou sur ses moyens de défense.

Article 45

Il est interdit de contraindre la population d'un territoire occupé à prêter serment à la Puissance ennemie.

Article 46

L'honneur et les droits de la famille, la vie des individus et la propriété privée, ainsi que les convictions religieuses et l'exercice des cultes, doivent être respectés.

La propriété privée ne peut pas être confisquée.

Article 47

Le pillage est formellement interdit.

Article 48

Si l'occupant prélève, dans le territoire occupé, les impôts, droits et péages établis au profit de l'Etat, il le fera, autant que possible, d'après les règles de l'assiette et de la répartition en vigueur, et il en résultera pour lui l'obligation de pourvoir aux frais de l'administration du territoire occupé dans la mesure où le Gouvernement légal y était tenu.

Article 49

Si, en dehors des impôts visés à l'article précédent, l'occupant prélève d'autres contributions en argent dans le territoire occupé, ce ne pourra être que pour les besoins de l'armée ou de l'administration de ce territoire.

Article 50

Aucune peine collective, pécuniaire ou autre, ne pourra être édictée contre les populations à raison de faits individuels dont elles ne pourraient être considérées comme solidairement responsables.

Article 51

Aucune contribution ne sera perçue qu'en vertu d'un ordre écrit et sous la responsabilité d'un général en chef.

Il ne sera procédé, autant que possible, à cette perception que d'après les règles de l'assiette et de la répartition des impôts en vigueur.

Pour toute contribution, un reçu sera délivré aux contribuables.

Article 52

Des réquisitions en nature et des services ne pourront être réclamés des communes ou des habitants, que pour les besoins de l'armée d'occupation. Ils seront en rapport avec les ressources du pays et de telle nature qu'ils n'impliquent pas pour les populations l'obligation de prendre part aux opérations de la guerre contre leur patrie.

Ces réquisitions et ces services ne seront réclamés qu'avec l'autorisation du commandant dans la localité occupée.

Les prestations en nature seront, autant que possible, payées au comptant; sinon, elles seront constatées par des reçus, et le paiement des sommes dues sera effectué le plus tôt possible.

Article 53

L'armée qui occupe un territoire ne pourra saisir que le numéraire, les fonds et les valeurs exigibles appartenant en propre à l'Etat, les dépôts d'armes, moyens de transport, magasins et approvisionnements et, en général, toute propriété mobilière de l'Etat de nature à servir aux opérations de la guerre.

Tous les moyens affectés sur terre, sur mer et dans les airs à la transmission des nouvelles, au transport des personnes ou des choses, en dehors des cas régis par le droit maritime, les dépôts d'armes et, en général, toute espèce de munitions de guerre, peuvent être saisis, même s'ils appartiennent à des personnes privées, mais devront être restitués et les indemnités seront réglées à la paix.

Article 54

Les câbles sous-marins reliant un territoire occupé à un territoire neutre ne seront saisis ou détruits que dans le cas d'une nécessité absolue. Ils devront également être restitués et les indemnités seront réglées à la paix.

Article 55

L'Etat occupant ne se considérera que comme administrateur et usu-
fruitier des édifices publics, immeubles, forêts et exploitations agricoles
appartenant à l'Etat ennemi et se trouvant dans le pays occupé. Il devra
sauvegarder le fonds de ces propriétés et les administrer conformément
aux règles de l'usufruit.

Article 56

Les biens des communes, ceux des établissements consacrés aux cultes, à
la charité et à l'instruction, aux arts et aux sciences, même appartenant à
l'Etat, seront traités comme la propriété privée.

Toute saisie, destruction ou dégradation intentionnelle de semblables établissements, de monuments historiques, d'œuvres d'art et de science, est
interdite et doit être poursuivie.

V. CONVENTION CONCERNANT LES DROITS ET LES DEVOIRS DES PUISSANCES ET DES PERSONNES NEUTRES EN CAS DE GUERRE SUR TERRE

[Pour les Etats parties, voir convention I, supra, *p. 305]*

En vue de mieux préciser les droits et les devoirs des Puissances neutres en cas de guerre sur terre et de régler la situation des belligérants réfugiés en territoire neutre ;

Désirant également définir la qualité de neutre en attendant qu'il soit possible de régler dans son ensemble la situation des particuliers neutres dans leurs rapports avec les belligérants ;

Ont résolu de conclure une Convention à cet effet et ont, en conséquence, nommé pour Leurs Plénipotentiaires savoir :

[Désignation des plénipotentiaires]

Lesquels, après avoir déposé leurs pleins pouvoirs, trouvés en bonne et due forme, sont convenus des dispositions suivantes :

Chapitre I. Des droits et des devoirs des Puissances neutres

Article premier

Le territoire des Puissances neutres est inviolable.

Article 2

Il est interdit aux belligérants de faire passer à travers le territoire d'une Puissance neutre des troupes ou des convois, soit de munitions, soit d'approvisionnements.

Article 3

Il est également interdit aux belligérants :

a) d'installer sur le territoire d'une Puissance neutre une station radiotélégraphique ou tout appareil destiné à servir comme moyen de communication avec des forces belligérantes sur terre ou sur mer ;

b) d'utiliser toute installation de ce genre établie par eux avant la guerre sur le territoire de la Puissance neutre dans un but exclusivement militaire, et qui n'a pas été ouverte au service de la correspondance publique.

Article 4

Des corps de combattants ne peuvent être formés, ni des bureaux d'enrôlement ouverts, sur le territoire d'une Puissance neutre au profit des belligérants.

Article 5

Une Puissance neutre ne doit tolérer sur son territoire aucun des actes visés par les articles 2 à 4.

Elle n'est tenue de punir des actes contraires à la neutralité que si ces actes ont été commis sur son propre territoire.

Article 6

La responsabilité d'une Puissance neutre n'est pas engagée par le fait que des individus passent isolément la frontière pour se mettre au service de l'un des belligérants.

Article 7

Une Puissance neutre n'est pas tenue d'empêcher l'exportation ou le transit, pour le compte de l'un ou de l'autre des belligérants, d'armes, de munitions, et, en général, de tout ce qui peut être utile à une armée ou à une flotte.

Article 8

Une Puissance neutre n'est pas tenue d'interdire ou de restreindre l'usage, pour les belligérants, des câbles télégraphiques ou téléphoniques, ainsi que des appareils de télégraphie sans fil, qui sont, soit sa propriété, soit celle de compagnies ou de particuliers.

Article 9

Toutes mesures restrictives ou prohibitives prises par une Puissance neutre à l'égard des matières visées par les articles 7 et 8 devront être uniformément appliquées par elle aux belligérants.

La Puissance neutre veillera au respect de la même obligation par les compagnies ou particuliers propriétaires de câbles télégraphiques ou téléphoniques ou d'appareils de télégraphie sans fil.

Article 10

Ne peut être considéré comme un acte hostile le fait, par une Puissance neutre, de repousser, même par la force, les atteintes à sa neutralité.

Chapitre II. Des belligérants internés et des blessés soignés chez les neutres

Article 11

La Puissance neutre qui reçoit sur son territoire des troupes appartenant aux armées belligérantes, les internera, autant que possible, loin du théâtre de la guerre.

Elle pourra les garder dans des camps, et même les enfermer dans des forteresses ou dans des lieux appropriés à cet effet.

Elle décidera si les officiers peuvent être laissés libres en prenant l'engagement sur parole de ne pas quitter le territoire neutre sans autorisation.

Article 12

A défaut de convention spéciale, la Puissance neutre fournira aux internés les vivres, les habillements et les secours commandés par l'humanité.

Bonification sera faite, à la paix, des frais occasionnés par l'internement.

Article 13

La Puissance neutre qui reçoit des prisonniers de guerre évadés les laissera en liberté. Si elle tolère leur séjour sur son territoire, elle peut leur assigner une résidence.

La même disposition est applicable aux prisonniers de guerre amenés par des troupes se réfugiant sur le territoire de la Puissance neutre.

Article 14

Une Puissance neutre pourra autoriser le passage sur son territoire des blessés ou malades appartenant aux armées belligérantes, sous la réserve que les trains qui les amèneront ne transporteront ni personnel, ni matériel de guerre. En pareil cas, la Puissance neutre est tenue de prendre les mesures de sûreté et de contrôle nécessaires à cet effet.

Les blessés ou malades amenés dans ces conditions sur le territoire neutre par un des belligérants, et qui appartiendraient à la partie adverse, devront être gardés par la Puissance neutre de manière qu'ils ne puissent de nouveau prendre part aux opérations de la guerre. Cette Puissance aura les mêmes devoirs quant aux blessés ou malades de l'autre armée qui lui seraient confiés.

Article 15

La Convention de Genève s'applique aux malades et aux blessés internés sur territoire neutre.

Chapitre III. Des personnes neutres

Article 16

Sont considérés comme neutres les nationaux d'un Etat qui ne prend pas part à la guerre.

Article 17

Un neutre ne peut pas se prévaloir de sa neutralité :

a) s'il commet des actes hostiles contre un belligérant ;
b) s'il commet des actes en faveur d'un belligérant, notamment s'il prend volontairement du service dans les rangs de la force armée de l'une des Parties.

En pareil cas, le neutre ne sera pas traité plus rigoureusement par le belligérant contre lequel il s'est départi de la neutralité que ne pourrait l'être, à raison du même fait, un national de l'autre Etat belligérant.

Article 18

Ne seront pas considérés comme actes commis en faveur d'un des belligérants, dans le sens de l'article 17, lettre *b)* :

a) les fournitures faites ou les emprunts consentis à l'un des belligérants, pourvu que le fournisseur ou le prêteur n'habite ni le territoire de l'autre Partie, ni le territoire occupé par elle, et que les fournitures ne proviennent pas de ces territoires;

b) les services rendus en matière de police ou d'administration civile.

Chapitre IV. Du matériel des chemins de fer

Article 19

Le matériel des chemins de fer provenant du territoire de Puissances neutres, qu'il appartienne à ces Puissances ou à des sociétés ou personnes privées, et reconnaissable comme tel, ne pourra être réquisitionné et utilisé par un belligérant que dans le cas et la mesure où l'exige une impérieuse nécessité. Il sera renvoyé aussitôt que possible dans le pays d'origine.

La Puissance neutre pourra de même, en cas de nécessité, retenir et utiliser, jusqu'à due concurrence, le matériel provenant du territoire de la Puissance belligérante.

Une indemnité sera payée de part et d'autre, en proportion du matériel utilisé et de la durée de l'utilisation.

Chapitre V. Dispositions finales

Article 20

Les dispositions de la présente Convention ne sont applicables qu'entre les Puissances contractantes et seulement si les belligérants sont tous parties à la Convention.

Article 23

La présente Convention sera ratifiée aussitôt que possible.

Les ratifications seront déposées à La Haye.

Le premier dépôt de ratifications sera constaté par un procès-verbal signé par les représentants des Puissances qui y prennent part et par le Ministre des Affaires étrangères des Pays-Bas.

Les dépôts ultérieurs de ratifications se feront au moyen d'une notification écrite, adressée au Gouvernement des Pays-Bas et accompagnée de l'instrument de ratification.

Copie certifiée conforme du procès-verbal relatif au premier dépôt de ratifications, des notifications mentionnées à l'alinéa précédent, ainsi que des instruments de ratification sera immédiatement remise, par les soins du Gouvernement des Pays-Bas et par la voie diplomatique, aux Puissances conviées à la Deuxième Conférence de la Paix, ainsi qu'aux autres Puissances qui auront adhéré à la Convention. Dans les cas visés par l'alinéa précédent, ledit Gouvernement leur fera connaître en même temps la date à laquelle il a reçu la notification.

Article 22

Les Puissances non signataires sont admises à adhérer à la présente Convention.

La Puissance qui désire adhérer notifie par écrit son intention au Gouvernement des Pays-Bas en lui transmettant l'acte d'adhésion qui sera déposé dans les archives dudit Gouvernement.

Ce Gouvernement transmettra immédiatement à toutes les autres Puissances copie certifiée conforme de la notification ainsi que de l'acte d'adhésion, en indiquant la date à laquelle il a reçu la notification.

Article 23

La présente Convention produira effet, pour les Puissances qui auront participé au premier dépôt de ratifications, soixante jours après la date du procès-verbal de ce dépôt et, pour les Puissances qui ratifieront ultérieurement ou qui adhéreront, soixante jours après que la notification de leur ratification ou de leur adhésion aura été reçue par le Gouvernement des Pays-Bas.

Article 24

S'il arrivait qu'une des Puissances contractantes voulût dénoncer la présente Convention, la dénonciation sera notifiée par écrit au Gouvernement des Pays-Bas, qui communiquera immédiatement copie certifiée conforme de la notification à toutes les autres Puissances, en leur faisant savoir la date à laquelle il l'a reçue.

La dénonciation ne produira ses effets qu'à l'égard de la Puissance qui l'aura notifiée et un an après que la notification en sera parvenue au Gouvernement des Pays-Bas.

Article 25

Un registre tenu par le Ministère des Affaires étrangères des Pays-Bas indiquera la date du dépôt des ratifications effectué en vertu de l'article 21 alinéas 3 et 4, ainsi que la date à laquelle auront été reçues les notifications d'adhésion (article 22, alinéa 2) ou de dénonciation (article 24, alinéa 1).

Chaque Puissance contractante est admise à prendre connaissance de ce registre et à en demander des extraits certifiés conformes.

En foi de quoi, les Plénipotentiaires ont revêtu la présente Convention de leurs signatures.

Fait à La Haye, le dix-huit octobre mil neuf cent sept, en un seul exemplaire qui restera déposé dans les archives du Gouvernement des Pays-Bas et dont des copies, certifiées conformes, seront remises par la voie diplomatique aux Puissances qui ont été conviées à la Deuxième Conférence de la Paix.

VI. CONVENTION RELATIVE AU RÉGIME DES NAVIRES DE COMMERCE ENNEMIS AU DÉBUT DES HOSTILITÉS

[Pour les Etats parties, voir convention I, supra, p. 305]

Désireux de garantir la sécurité du commerce international contre les surprises de la guerre et voulant, conformément à la pratique moderne, protéger autant que possible les opérations engagées de bonne foi et en cours d'exécution avant le début des hostilités;

Ont résolu de conclure une Convention à cet effet et ont nommé pour leurs Plénipotentiaires, savoir:

[Dénomination des plénipotentiaires]

Lesquels, après avoir déposé leurs pleins pouvoirs trouvés en bonne et due forme, sont convenus des dispositions suivantes:

Article premier

Lorsqu'un navire de commerce relevant d'une des Puissances belligérantes se trouve, au début des hostilités, dans un port ennemi, il est désirable qu'il lui soit permis de sortir librement, immédiatement ou après un délai de faveur suffisant, et de gagner directement, après avoir été muni d'un laissez-passer, son port de destination ou tel autre port qui lui sera désigné.

Il en est de même du navire ayant quitté son dernier port de départ avant le commencement de la guerre et entrant dans un port ennemi sans connaître les hostilités.

Article 2

Le navire de commerce qui, par suite de circonstances de force majeure, n'aurait pu quitter le port ennemi pendant le délai visé à l'article précédent, ou auquel la sortie n'aurait pas été accordée, ne peut être confisqué.

Le belligérant peut seulement le saisir moyennant l'obligation de le restituer après la guerre sans indemnité, ou le réquisitionner moyennant indemnité.

Article 3

Les navires de commerce ennemis, qui ont quitté leur dernier port de départ avant le commencement de la guerre et qui sont rencontrés en mer ignorants des hostilités, ne peuvent être confisqués. Ils sont seulement sujets à être saisis, moyennant l'obligation de les restituer après la guerre sans indemnité, ou à être réquisitionnés, ou même à être détruits, à charge d'indemnité et sous l'obligation de pourvoir à la sécurité des personnes ainsi qu'à la conservation des papiers de bord.

Après avoir touché à un port de leur pays ou à un port neutre, ces navires sont soumis aux lois et coutumes de la guerre maritime.

Article 4

Les marchandises ennemies se trouvant à bord des navires visés aux articles 1 et 2 sont également sujettes à être saisies et restituées après la guerre sans indemnité, ou à être réquisitionnées moyennant indemnité, conjointement avec le navire ou séparément.

Il en est de même des marchandises se trouvant à bord des navires visés à l'article 3.

Article 5

La présente Convention ne vise pas les navires de commerce dont la construction indique qu'ils sont destinés à être transformés en bâtiments de guerre.

Article 6

Les dispositions de la présente Convention ne sont applicables qu'entre les Puissances contractantes et seulement si les belligérants sont tous parties à la Convention.

Article 7

La présente Convention sera ratifiée aussitôt que possible.

Les ratifications seront déposées à La Haye.

Le premier dépôt de ratifications sera constaté par un procès-verbal signé par les représentants des Puissances qui y prennent part et par le Ministre des Affaires étrangères des Pays-Bas.

Les dépôts ultérieurs de ratifications se feront au moyen d'une notification écrite, adressée au Gouvernement des Pays-Bas et accompagnée de l'instrument de ratification.

Copie certifiée conforme du procès-verbal relatif au premier dépôt de ratifications, des notifications mentionnées à l'alinéa précédent, ainsi que des instruments de ratifications, sera immédiatement remise par les soins du Gouvernement des Pays-Bas et par la voie diplomatique aux Puissances conviées à la Deuxième Conférence de la Paix, ainsi qu'aux autres Puissances qui auront adhéré à la Convention. Dans les cas visés par l'alinéa précédent, ledit Gouvernement leur fera connaître en même temps la date à laquelle il a reçu la notification.

Article 8

Les Puissances non signataires sont admises à adhérer à la présente Convention.

La Puissance qui désire adhérer notifie par écrit son intention au Gouvernement des Pays-Bas en lui transmettant l'acte d'adhésion qui sera déposé dans les archives dudit Gouvernement.

Ce Gouvernement transmettra immédiatement à toutes les autres Puissances copie certifiée conforme de la notification ainsi que de l'acte d'adhésion, en indiquant la date à laquelle il a reçu la notification.

Article 9

La présente Convention produira effet, pour les Puissances qui auront participé au premier dépôt de ratifications, soixante jours après la date du procès-verbal de ce dépôt et, pour les Puissances qui ratifieront ultérieurement ou qui adhéreront, soixante jours après que la notification de leur ratification ou de leur adhésion aura été reçue par le Gouvernement des Pays-Bas.

Article 10

S'il arrivait qu'une des Puissances contractantes voulût dénoncer la présente Convention, la dénonciation sera notifiée par écrit au Gouvernement des Pays-Bas qui communiquera immédiatement copie certifiée conforme de la notification à toutes les autres Puissances en leur faisant savoir la date à laquelle il l'a reçue.

La dénonciation ne produira ses effets qu'à l'égard de la Puissance qui l'aura notifiée et un an après que la notification en sera parvenue au Gouvernement des Pays-Bas.

Article 11

Un registre tenu par le Ministère des Affaires étrangères des Pays-Bas indiquera la date du dépôt de ratifications effectué en vertu de l'article 7, alinéas 3 et 4, ainsi que la date à laquelle auront été reçues les notifications d'adhésion (article 8, alinéa 2) ou de dénonciation (article 10, alinéa 1).

Chaque Puissance contractante est admise à prendre connaissance de ce registre et à en demander des extraits certifiés conformes.

En foi de quoi, les Plénipotentiaires ont revêtu la présente Convention de leurs signatures.

Fait à La Haye, le dix-huit octobre mil neuf cent sept, en un seul exemplaire qui restera déposé dans les archives du Gouvernement des Pays-Bas et dont des copies, certifiées conformes, seront remises par la voie diplomatique aux Puissances qui ont été conviées à la Deuxième Conférence de la Paix.

VII. CONVENTION RELATIVE À LA TRANSFORMATION DES NAVIRES DE COMMERCE EN BÂTIMENTS DE GUERRE

[Pour les Etats parties, voir convention I, supra, p. 305]

Considérant qu'en vue de l'incorporation en temps de guerre de navires de la marine marchande dans les flottes de combat, il est désirable de définir les conditions dans lesquelles cette opération pourra être effectuée ;

Que, toutefois, les Puissances contractantes n'ayant pu se mettre d'accord sur la question de savoir si la transformation d'un navire de commerce en bâtiment de guerre peut avoir lieu en pleine mer, il est entendu que la question du lieu de transformation reste hors de cause et n'est nullement visée par les règles ci-dessous ;

Désirant conclure une Convention à cet effet, ont nommé pour leurs Plénipotentiaires, savoir :

[Dénomination des plénipotentiaires]

Lesquels, après avoir déposé leurs pleins pouvoirs, trouvés en bonne et due forme, sont convenus des dispositions suivantes :

Article premier

Aucun navire de commerce transformé en bâtiment de guerre ne peut avoir les droits et les obligations attachés à cette qualité, s'il n'est placé sous l'autorité directe, le contrôle immédiat et la responsabilité de la Puissance dont il porte le pavillon.

Article 2

Les navires de commerce transformés en bâtiments de guerre doivent porter les signes extérieurs distinctifs des bâtiments de guerre de leur nationalité.

Article 3

Le commandant doit être au service de l'Etat et dûment commissionné par les autorités compétentes. Son nom doit figurer sur la liste des officiers de la flotte militaire.

Article 4

L'équipage doit être soumis aux règles de la discipline militaire.

Article 5

Tout navire de commerce transformé en bâtiment de guerre est tenu d'observer dans ses opérations, les lois et coutumes de la guerre.

Article 6

Le belligérant, qui transforme un navire de commerce en bâtiment de guerre, doit, le plus tôt possible, mentionner cette transformation sur la liste des bâtiments de sa flotte militaire.

Article 7

Les dispositions de la présente Convention ne sont applicables qu'entre les Puissances contractantes et seulement si les belligérants sont tous parties à la Convention.

Article 8

La présente Convention sera ratifiée aussitôt que possible.

Les ratifications seront déposées à La Haye.

Le premier dépôt de ratifications sera constaté par un procès-verbal signé par les représentants des Puissances qui y prennent part et par le Ministre des Affaires étrangères des Pays-Bas.

Les dépôts ultérieurs de ratifications se feront au moyen d'une notification écrite, adressée au Gouvernement des Pays-Bas et accompagnée de l'instrument de ratification.

Copie certifiée conforme du procès-verbal relatif au premier dépôt de ratifications, des notifications mentionnées à l'alinéa précédent, ainsi que des instruments de ratification, sera immédiatement remise, par les soins du Gouvernement des Pays-Bas, et par la voie diplomatique, aux Puissances conviées à la Deuxième Conférence de la Paix, ainsi qu'aux autres Puissances qui auront adhéré à la Convention. Dans les cas visés par l'alinéa précédent, ledit Gouvernement leur fera connaître en même temps la date à laquelle il a reçu la notification.

Article 9

Les Puissances non signataires sont admises à adhérer à la présente Convention.

La Puissance qui désire adhérer notifie par écrit son intention au Gouvernement des Pays-Bas en lui transmettant l'acte d'adhésion qui sera déposé dans les archives dudit Gouvernement.

Ce Gouvernement transmettra immédiatement à toutes les autres Puissances copie certifiée conforme de la notification ainsi que de l'acte d'adhésion, en indiquant la date à laquelle il a reçu la notification.

Article 10

La présente Convention produira effet, pour les Puissances qui auront participé au premier dépôt de ratifications, soixante jours après la date du procès-verbal de ce dépôt et, pour les Puissances qui ratifieront ultérieurement ou qui adhèreront, soixante jours après que la notification de leur ratification ou de leur adhésion aura été reçue par le Gouvernement des Pays-Bas.

Article 11

S'il arrivait qu'une des Puissances contractantes voulût dénoncer la présente Convention, la dénonciation sera notifiée par écrit au Gouvernement des Pays-Bas qui communiquera immédiatement copie certifiée conforme de la notification à toutes les autres Puissances en leur faisant savoir la date à laquelle il l'a reçue.

La dénonciation ne produira ses effets qu'à l'égard de la Puissance qui l'aura notifiée et un an après que la notification en sera parvenue au Gouvernement des Pays-Bas.

Article 12

Un registre tenu par le Ministère des Affaires étrangères des Pays-Bas indiquera la date du dépôt de ratifications effectué en vertu de l'article 8, alinéas 3 et 4, ainsi que la date à laquelle auront été reçues les notifications d'adhésion (article 9, alinéa 2) ou de dénonciation (article 11, alinéa 1).

Chaque Puissance contractante est admise à prendre connaissance de ce registre et à en demander des extraits certifiés conformes.

En foi de quoi, les Plénipotentiaires ont revêtu la présente Convention de leurs signatures.

Fait à La Haye, le dix-huit octobre mil neuf cent sept, en un seul exemplaire qui restera déposé dans les archives du Gouvernement des Pays-Bas, et dont des copies, certifiées conformes, seront remises par la voie diplomatique aux Puissances qui ont été conviées à la Deuxième Conférence de la Paix.

VIII. CONVENTION RELATIVE À LA POSE
DE MINES SOUS-MARINES AUTOMATIQUES DE CONTACT

[Pour les Etats parties, voir convention I, supra, p. 305]

S'inspirant du principe de la liberté des voies maritimes, ouvertes à toutes les nations;

Considérant que, si dans l'état actuel des choses, on ne peut interdire l'emploi de mines sous-marines automatiques de contact, il importe d'en limiter et réglementer l'usage, afin de restreindre les rigueurs de la guerre et de donner, autant que faire se peut, à la navigation pacifique la sécurité à laquelle elle a droit de prétendre, malgré l'existence d'une guerre;

En attendant qu'il soit possible de régler la matière d'une façon qui donne aux intérêts engagés toutes les garanties désirables;

Ont résolu de conclure une Convention à cet effet et ont nommé pour leurs Plénipotentiaires, savoir:

[Dénomination des plénipotentiaires]

Lesquels, après avoir déposé leurs pleins pouvoirs trouvés en bonne et due forme, sont convenus des dispositions suivantes:

Article premier

Il est interdit:

1) de placer des mines automatiques de contact non amarrées, à moins qu'elles ne soient construites de manière à devenir inoffensives une heure au maximum après que celui qui les a placées en aura perdu le contrôle;
2) de placer des mines automatiques de contact amarrées, qui ne deviennent pas inoffensives dès qu'elles auront rompu leurs amarres;
3) d'employer des torpilles, qui ne deviennent pas inoffensives lorsqu'elles auront manqué leur but.

Article 2

Il est interdit de placer des mines automatiques de contact devant les côtes et les ports de l'adversaire, dans le seul but d'intercepter la navigation de commerce.

Article 3

Lorsque les mines automatiques de contact amarrées sont employées, toutes les précautions possibles doivent être prises pour la sécurité de la navigation pacifique.

Les belligérants s'engagent à pourvoir, dans la mesure du possible, à ce que ces mines deviennent inoffensives après un laps de temps limité, et, dans

le cas où elles cesseraient d'être surveillées, à signaler les régions dange-
reuses, aussitôt que les exigences militaires le permettront, par un avis à la
navigation, qui devra être aussi communiqué aux Gouvernements par la voie
diplomatique.

Article 4

Toute Puissance neutre qui place des mines automatiques de contact
devant ses côtes, doit observer les mêmes règles et prendre les mêmes précautions que celles qui sont imposées aux belligérants.

La Puissance neutre doit faire connaître à la navigation, par un avis préalable, les régions où seront mouillées des mines automatiques de contact.
Cet avis devra être communiqué d'urgence aux Gouvernements par voie
diplomatique.

Article 5

A la fin de la guerre, les Puissances contractantes s'engagent à faire tout
ce qui dépend d'elles pour enlever, chacune de son côté, les mines qu'elles
ont placées.

Quant aux mines automatiques de contact amarrées, que l'un des belligérants aurait posées le long des côtes de l'autre, l'emplacement en sera notifié à l'autre partie par la Puissance qui les a posées et chaque Puissance
devra procéder dans le plus bref délai à l'enlèvement des mines qui se trouvent dans ses eaux.

Article 6

Les Puissances contractantes, qui ne disposent pas encore de mines
perfectionnées telles qu'elles sont prévues dans la présente Convention, et
qui, par conséquent, ne sauraient actuellement se conformer aux règles
établies dans les articles 1 et 3, s'engagent à transformer, aussitôt que possible, leur matériel de mines, afin qu'il réponde aux prescriptions susmentionnées.

Article 7

Les dispositions de la présente Convention ne sont applicables qu'entre
les Puissances contractantes et seulement si les belligérants sont tous parties
à la Convention.

Article 8

La présente Convention sera ratifiée aussitôt que possible.

Les ratifications seront déposées à La Haye.

Le premier dépôt de ratifications sera constaté par un procès-verbal signé
par les représentants des Puissances qui y prennent part et par le Ministre
des Affaires étrangères des Pays-Bas.

Les dépôts ultérieurs de ratifications se feront au moyen d'une notification écrite, adressée au Gouvernement des Pays-Bas et accompagnée de
l'instrument de ratification.

Copie certifiée conforme du procès-verbal relatif au premier dépôt de ratifications, des notifications mentionnées à l'alinéa précédent, ainsi que des instruments de ratification, sera immédiatement remise, par les soins du Gouvernement des Pays-Bas et par la voie diplomatique, aux Puissances conviées à la Deuxième Conférence de la Paix, ainsi qu'aux autres Puissances qui auront adhéré à la Convention. Dans les cas visés par l'alinéa précédent, ledit Gouvernement leur fera connaître en même temps la date à laquelle il a reçu la notification.

Article 9

Les Puissances non signataires sont admises à adhérer à la présente Convention.

La Puissance qui désire adhérer notifie par écrit son intention au Gouvernement des Pays-Bas en lui transmettant l'acte d'adhésion qui sera déposé dans les archives dudit Gouvernement.

Ce Gouvernement transmettra immédiatement à toutes les autres Puissances copie certifiée conforme de la notification ainsi que de l'acte d'adhésion, en indiquant la date à laquelle il a reçu la notification.

Article 10

La présente Convention produira effet pour les Puissances qui auront participé au premier dépôt de ratifications, soixante jours après la date du procès-verbal de ce dépôt et, pour les Puissances qui ratifieront ultérieurement ou qui adhèreront, soixante jours après que la notification de leur ratification ou de leur adhésion aura été reçue par le Gouvernement des Pays-Bas.

Article 11

La présente Convention aura une durée de sept ans à partir du soixantième jour après la date du premier dépôt de ratifications.

Sauf dénonciation, elle continuera d'être en vigueur après l'expiration de ce délai.

La dénonciation sera notifiée par écrit au Gouvernement des Pays-Bas qui communiquera immédiatement copie certifiée conforme de la notification à toutes les Puissances, en leur faisant savoir la date à laquelle il l'a reçue.

La dénonciation ne produira ses effets qu'à l'égard de la Puissance qui l'aura notifiée et six mois après que la notification en sera parvenue au Gouvernement des Pays-Bas.

Article 12

Les Puissances contractantes s'engagent à reprendre la question de l'emploi des mines automatiques de contact six mois avant l'expiration du terme prévu par l'alinéa premier de l'article précédent, au cas où elle n'aurait pas été reprise et résolue à une date antérieure par la troisième Conférence de la Paix.

Si les Puissances contractantes concluent une nouvelle Convention relative à l'emploi des mines, dès son entrée en vigueur, la présente Convention cessera d'être applicable.

Article 13

Un registre tenu par le Ministère des Affaires étrangères des Pays-Bas indiquera la date du dépôt de ratifications effectué en vertu de l'article 8, alinéas 3 et 4, ainsi que la date à laquelle auront été reçues les notifications d'adhésion (article 9, alinéa 2) ou de dénonciation (article 11, alinéa 3).

Chaque Puissance contractante est admise à prendre connaissance de ce registre et à en demander des extraits certifiés conformes.

En foi de quoi, les Plénipotentiaires ont revêtu la présente Convention de leurs signatures.

Fait à La Haye, le dix-huit octobre mil neuf cent sept, en un seul exemplaire qui restera déposé dans les archives du Gouvernement des Pays-Bas et dont des copies, certifiées conformes, seront remises par la voie diplomatique aux Puissances qui ont été conviées à la Deuxième Conférence de la Paix.

IX. CONVENTION CONCERNANT LE BOMBARDEMENT PAR LES FORCES NAVALES EN TEMPS DE GUERRE

[Pour les Etats parties, voir convention I, supra, *p. 305]*

Animés du désir de réaliser le voeu exprimé par la Première Conférence de la Paix, concernant le bombardement, par des forces navales, de ports, villes et villages, non défendus;

Considérant qu'il importe de soumettre les bombardements par des forces navales à des dispositions générales qui garantissent les droits des habitants et assurent la conservation des principaux édifices, en étendant à cette opération de guerre, dans la mesure du possible, les principes du Règlement de 1899 sur les lois et coutumes de la guerre sur terre;

S'inspirant ainsi du désir de servir les intérêts de l'humanité et de diminuer les rigueurs et les désastres de la guerre;

Ont résolu de conclure une Convention à cet effet et ont, en conséquence, nommé pour leurs Plénipotentiaires, savoir:

[Dénomination des plénipotentiaires]

Lesquels, après avoir déposé leurs pleins pouvoirs, trouvés en bonne et due forme, sont convenus des dispositions suivantes:

Chapitre I. Du bombardement des ports, villes, villages, habitations ou bâtiments non défendus

Article premier

Il est interdit de bombarder, par des forces navales, des ports, villes, villages, habitations ou bâtiments, qui ne sont pas défendus.

Une localité ne peut pas être bombardée à raison du seul fait que, devant son port, se trouvent mouillées des mines sous-marines automatiques de contact.

Article 2

Toutefois, ne sont pas compris dans cette interdiction les ouvrages militaires, établissements militaires ou navals, dépôts d'armes ou de matériel de guerre, ateliers et installations propres à être utilisés pour les besoins de la flotte ou de l'armée ennemie, et les navires de guerre se trouvant dans le port. Le commandant d'une force navale pourra, après sommation avec délai raisonnable, les détruire par le canon, si tout autre moyen est impossible et lorsque les autorités locales n'auront pas procédé à cette destruction dans le délai fixé.

Il n'encourt aucune responsabilité dans ce cas pour les dommages involontaires, qui pourraient être occasionnés par le bombardement.

Si des nécessités militaires, exigeant une action immédiate, ne permettaient pas d'accorder de délai, il reste entendu que l'interdiction de bombarder la ville non défendue subsiste comme dans le cas énoncé dans l'alinéa 1 et que le commandant prendra toutes les dispositions voulues pour qu'il en résulte pour cette ville le moins d'inconvénients possible.

Article 3

Il peut, après notification expresse, être procédé au bombardement des ports, villes, villages, habitations ou bâtiments non défendus, si les autorités locales, mises en demeure par une sommation formelle, refusent d'obtempérer à des réquisitions de vivres ou d'approvisionnements nécessaires au besoin présent de la force navale qui se trouve devant la localité.

Ces réquisitions seront en rapport avec les ressources de la localité. Elles ne seront réclamées qu'avec l'autorisation du commandant de ladite force navale et elles seront, autant que possible, payées au comptant; sinon elles seront constatées par des reçus.

Article 4

Est interdit le bombardement, pour le non-paiement des contributions en argent, des ports, villes, villages, habitations ou bâtiments, non défendus.

Chapitre II. Dispositions générales

Article 5

Dans le bombardement par des forces navales, toutes les mesures nécessaires doivent être prises par le commandant pour épargner, autant que possible, les édifices consacrés aux cultes, aux arts, aux sciences et à la bienfaisance, les monuments historiques, les hôpitaux et les lieux de rassemblement de malades ou de blessés, à condition qu'ils ne soient pas employés en même temps à un but militaire.

Le devoir des habitants est de désigner ces monuments, ces édifices ou lieux de rassemblement, par des signes visibles, qui consisteront en grands panneaux rectangulaires rigides, partagés, suivant une des diagonales, en deux triangles de couleur, noire en haut et blanche en bas.

Article 6

Sauf le cas où les exigences militaires ne le permettraient pas, le commandant de la force navale assaillante doit, avant d'entreprendre le bombardement, faire tout ce qui dépend de lui pour avertir les autorités.

Article 7

Il est interdit de livrer au pillage une ville ou localité même prise d'assaut.

Chapitre III. Dispositions finales

Article 8

Les dispositions de la présente Convention ne sont applicables qu'entre les Puissances contractantes et seulement si les belligérants sont tous parties à la Convention.

Article 9

La présente Convention sera ratifiée aussitôt que possible.

Les ratifications seront déposées à La Haye.

Le premier dépôt de ratifications sera constaté par un procès-verbal signé par les représentants des Puissances qui y prennent part et par le Ministre des Affaires étrangères des Pays-Bas.

Les dépôts ultérieurs de ratifications se feront au moyen d'une notification écrite, adressée au Gouvernement des Pays-Bas et accompagnée de l'instrument de ratification.

Copie certifiée conforme du procès-verbal relatif au premier dépôt de ratifications, des notifications mentionnées à l'alinéa précédent, ainsi que des instruments de ratification, sera immédiatement remise, par les soins du Gouvernement des Pays-Bas et par la voie diplomatique, aux Puissances conviées à la Deuxième Conférence de la Paix, ainsi qu'aux autres Puissances qui auront adhéré à la Convention. Dans les cas visés par l'alinéa précédent, ledit Gouvernement leur fera connaître en même temps la date à laquelle il a reçu la notification.

Article 10

Les Puissances non signataires sont admises à adhérer à la présente Convention.

La Puissance qui désire adhérer notifie par écrit son intention au Gouvernement des Pays-Bas en lui transmettant l'acte d'adhésion qui sera déposé dans les archives dudit Gouvernement.

Ce Gouvernement transmettra immédiatement à toutes les autres Puissances copie certifiée conforme de la notification ainsi que de l'acte d'adhésion, en indiquant la date à laquelle il a reçu la notification.

Article 11

La présente Convention produira effet, pour les Puissances qui auront participé au premier dépôt de ratifications, soixante jours après la date du procès-verbal de ce dépôt et, pour les Puissances qui ratifieront ultérieurement ou qui adhèreront, soixante jours après que la notification de leur ratification ou de leur adhésion aura été reçue par le Gouvernement des Pays-Bas.

Article 12

S'il arrivait qu'une des Puissances contractantes voulût dénoncer la présente Convention, la dénonciation sera notifiée par écrit au Gouvernement des Pays-Bas qui communiquera immédiatement copie certifiée conforme de la notification à toutes les autres Puissances en leur faisant savoir la date à laquelle il l'a reçue.

La dénonciation ne produira ses effets qu'à l'égard de la Puissance qui l'aura notifiée et un an après que la notification en sera parvenue au Gouvernement des Pays-Bas.

Article 13

Un registre tenu par le Ministère des Affaires étrangères des Pays-Bas indiquera la date du dépôt de ratifications effectué en vertu de l'article 9, alinéas 3 et 4, ainsi que la date à laquelle auront été reçues les notifications d'adhésion (article 10, alinéa 2) ou de dénonciation (article 12, alinéa 1).

Chaque Puissance contractante est admise à prendre connaissance de ce registre et à en demander des extraits certifiés conformes.

En foi de quoi, les Plénipotentiaires ont revêtu la présente Convention de leurs signatures.

Fait à La Haye, le dix-huit octobre mil neuf cent sept, en un seul exemplaire qui restera déposé dans les archives du Gouvernement des Pays-Bas et dont des copies, certifiées conformes, seront remises par la voie diplomatique aux Puissances qui ont été conviées à la Deuxième Conférence de la Paix.

X. CONVENTION POUR L'ADAPTATION
À LA GUERRE MARITIME DES PRINCIPES
DE LA CONVENTION DE GENÈVE

[Pour les Etats parties, voir convention I, supra, p. 305]

Egalement animés du désir de diminuer, autant qu'il dépend d'eux, les maux inséparables de la guerre ;

Et voulant, dans ce but, adapter à la guerre maritime les principes de la Convention de Genève du 6 juillet 1906 ;

Ont résolu de conclure une Convention à l'effet de réviser la Convention du 29 juillet 1899 relative à la même matière et ont nommé pour leurs Plénipotentiaires, savoir :

[Dénomination des plénipotentiaires]

Lesquels, après avoir déposé leurs pleins pouvoirs, trouvés en bonne et due forme, sont convenus des dispositions suivantes :

Article premier

Les bâtiments-hôpitaux militaires, c'est-à-dire les bâtiments construits ou aménagés par les Etats spécialement et uniquement en vue de porter secours aux blessés, malades et naufragés, et dont les noms auront été communiqués, à l'ouverture ou au cours des hostilités, en tout cas avant toute mise en usage, aux Puissances belligérantes, sont respectés et ne peuvent être capturés pendant la durée des hostilités.

Ces bâtiments ne sont pas non plus assimilés aux navires de guerre au point de vue de leur séjour dans un port neutre.

Article 2

Les bâtiments hospitaliers, équipés en totalité ou en partie aux frais des particuliers ou des sociétés de secours officiellement reconnues, sont également respectés et exempts de capture, si la Puissance belligérante dont ils dépendent, leur a donné une commission officielle et en a notifié les noms à la Puissance adverse à l'ouverture ou au cours des hostilités, en tout cas avant toute mise en usage.

Ces navires doivent être porteurs d'un document de l'autorité compétente déclarant qu'ils ont été soumis à son contrôle pendant leur armement et à leur départ final.

Article 3

Les bâtiments hospitaliers, équipés en totalité ou en partie aux frais des particuliers ou des sociétés officiellement reconnues de pays neutres, sont respectés et exempts de capture, à condition qu'ils se soient mis sous la direction de l'un des belligérants, avec l'assentiment préalable de leur propre

Gouvernement et avec l'autorisation du belligérant lui-même et que ce dernier en ait notifié le nom à son adversaire dès l'ouverture ou dans le cours des hostilités, en tout cas, avant tout emploi.

Article 4

Les bâtiments qui sont mentionnés dans les articles 1, 2 et 3, porteront secours et assistance aux blessés, malades et naufragés des belligérants sans distinction de nationalité.

Les Gouvernements s'engagent à n'utiliser ces bâtiments pour aucun but militaire.

Ces bâtiments ne devront gêner en aucune manière les mouvements des combattants.

Pendant et après le combat, ils agiront à leurs risques et périls.

Les belligérants auront sur eux le droit de contrôle et de visite; ils pourront refuser leur concours, leur enjoindre de s'éloigner, leur imposer une direction déterminée et mettre à bord un commissaire, même les détenir, si la gravité des circonstances l'exigeait.

Autant que possible, les belligérants inscriront sur le journal de bord des bâtiments hospitaliers les ordres qu'ils leur donneront.

Article 5

Les bâtiments-hôpitaux militaires seront distingués par une peinture extérieure blanche avec une bande horizontale verte d'un mètre et demi de largeur environ.

Les bâtiments qui sont mentionnés dans les articles 2 et 3, seront distingués par une peinture extérieure blanche avec une bande horizontale rouge d'un mètre et demi de largeur environ.

Les embarcations des bâtiments qui viennent d'être mentionnés, comme les petits bâtiments qui pourront être affectés au service hospitalier, se distingueront par une peinture analogue.

Tous les bâtiments hospitaliers se feront reconnaître en hissant, avec leur pavillon national, le pavillon blanc à croix-rouge prévu par la Convention de Genève et, en outre, s'ils ressortissent à un Etat neutre, en arborant au grand mât le pavillon national du belligérant sous la direction duquel ils se sont placés.

Les bâtiments hospitaliers qui, dans les termes de l'article 4, sont détenus par l'ennemi, auront à rentrer le pavillon national du belligérant dont ils relèvent.

Les bâtiments et embarcations ci-dessus mentionnés, qui veulent s'assurer la nuit le respect auquel ils ont droit, ont, avec l'assentiment du belligérant qu'ils accompagnent, à prendre les mesures nécessaires pour que la peinture qui les caractérise soit suffisamment apparente.

Article 6

Les signes distinctifs prévus à l'article 5 ne pourront être employés, soit en temps de paix, soit en temps de guerre, que pour protéger ou désigner les bâtiments qui y sont mentionnés.

Article 7

Dans le cas d'un combat à bord d'un vaisseau de guerre, les infirmeries seront respectées et ménagées autant que faire se pourra.

Ces infirmeries et leur matériel demeurent soumis aux lois de la guerre, mais ne pourront être détournés de leur emploi, tant qu'ils seront nécessaires aux blessés et malades.

Toutefois le commandant, qui les a en son pouvoir, a la faculté d'en disposer, en cas de nécessité militaire importante, en assurant au préalable le sort des blessés et malades qui s'y trouvent.

Article 8

La protection due aux bâtiments hospitaliers et aux infirmeries des vaisseaux cesse si l'on en use pour commettre des actes nuisibles à l'ennemi.

N'est pas considéré comme étant de nature à justifier le retrait de la protection le fait que le personnel de ces bâtiments et infirmeries est armé pour le maintien de l'ordre et pour la défense des blessés ou malades, ainsi que le fait de la présence à bord d'une installation radio-télégraphique.

Article 9

Les belligérants pourront faire appel au zèle charitable des commandants de bâtiments de commerce, yachts ou embarcations neutres, pour prendre à bord et soigner des blessés ou des malades.

Les bâtiments qui auront répondu à cet appel ainsi que ceux qui spontanément auront recueilli des blessés, des malades ou des naufragés, jouiront d'une protection spéciale et de certaines immunités. En aucun cas, ils ne pourront être capturés pour le fait d'un tel transport; mais, sauf les promesses qui leur auraient été faites, ils restent exposés à la capture pour les violations de neutralité qu'ils pourraient avoir commises.

Article 10

Le personnel religieux, médical et hospitalier de tout bâtiment capturé est inviolable et ne peut être fait prisonnier de guerre. Il emporte, en quittant le navire, les objets et les instruments de chirurgie qui sont sa propriété particulière.

Ce personnel continuera à remplir ses fonctions tant que cela sera nécessaire et il pourra ensuite se retirer, lorsque le commandant en chef le jugera possible.

Les belligérants doivent assurer à ce personnel tombé entre leurs mains, les mêmes allocations et la même solde qu'au personnel des mêmes grades de leur propre marine.

Article 11

Les marins et les militaires embarqués, et les autres personnes officiellement attachées aux marines ou aux armées, blessés ou malades, à quelque nation qu'ils appartiennent, seront respectés et soignés par les capteurs.

Article 12

Tout vaisseau de guerre d'une Partie belligérante peut réclamer la remise des blessés, malades ou naufragés, qui sont à bord de bâtiments-hôpitaux militaires, de bâtiments hospitaliers de société de secours ou de particuliers, de navires de commerce, yachts et embarcations, quelle que soit la nationalité de ces bâtiments.

Article 13

Si des blessés, malades ou naufragés sont recueillis à bord d'un vaisseau de guerre neutre, il devra être pourvu, dans la mesure du possible, à ce qu'ils ne puissent pas de nouveau prendre part aux opérations de la guerre.

Article 14

Sont prisonniers de guerre les naufragés, blessés ou malades, d'un belligérant qui tombent au pouvoir de l'autre. Il appartient à celui-ci de décider, suivant les circonstances, s'il convient de les garder, de les diriger sur un port de sa nation, sur un port neutre ou même sur un port de l'adversaire. Dans ce dernier cas, les prisonniers ainsi rendus à leur pays ne pourront servir pendant la durée de la guerre.

Article 15

Les naufragés, blessés ou malades, qui sont débarqués dans un port neutre, du consentement de l'autorité locale, devront, à moins d'un arrangement contraire de l'Etat neutre avec les Etats belligérants, être gardés par l'Etat neutre de manière qu'ils ne puissent pas de nouveau prendre part aux opérations de la guerre.

Les frais d'hospitalisation et d'internement seront supportés par l'Etat dont relèvent les naufragés, blessés ou malades.

Article 16

Après chaque combat, les deux Parties belligérantes, en tant que les intérêts militaires le comportent, prendront des mesures pour rechercher les naufragés, les blessés et les malades et pour les faire protéger, ainsi que les morts, contre le pillage et les mauvais traitements.

Elles veilleront à ce que l'inhumation, l'immersion ou l'incinération des morts soit précédée d'un examen attentif de leurs cadavres.

Article 17

Chaque belligérant enverra, dès qu'il sera possible, aux autorités de leur pays, de leur marine ou de leur armée, les marques ou pièces militaires d'identité trouvées sur les morts et l'état nominatif des blessés ou malades recueillis par lui.

Les belligérants se tiendront réciproquement au courant des internements et des mutations, ainsi que des entrées dans les hôpitaux et des décès survenus parmi les blessés et malades en leur pouvoir. Ils recueilleront tous les objets d'un usage personnel, valeurs, lettres, etc. qui seront trouvés dans les vaisseaux capturés, ou délaissés par les blessés ou malades décédés dans les hôpitaux, pour les faire transmettre aux intéressés par les autorités de leur pays.

Article 18

Les dispositions de la présente Convention ne sont applicables qu'entre les Puissances contractantes et seulement si les belligérants sont tous parties à la Convention.

Article 19

Les commandants en chef des flottes des belligérants auront à pourvoir aux détails d'exécution des articles précédents, ainsi qu'aux cas non prévus, d'après les instructions de leurs Gouvernements respectifs et conformément aux principes généraux de la présente Convention.

Article 20

Les Puissances signataires prendront les mesures nécessaires pour instruire leurs marines, et spécialement le personnel protégé, des dispositions de la présente Convention et pour les porter à la connaissance des populations.

Article 21

Les Puissances signataires s'engagent également à prendre ou à proposer à leurs législatures, en cas d'insuffisance de leurs lois pénales, les mesures nécessaires pour réprimer en temps de guerre, les actes individuels de pillage et de mauvais traitements envers des blessés et malades des marines, ainsi que pour punir, comme usurpation d'insignes militaires, l'usage abusif des signes distinctifs désignés à l'article 5 par des bâtiments non protégés par la présente Convention.

Ils se communiqueront, par l'intermédiaire du Gouvernement des Pays-Bas, les dispositions relatives à cette répression, au plus tard dans les cinq ans de la ratification de la présente Convention.

Article 22

En cas d'opérations de guerre entre les forces de terre et de mer des belligérants, les dispositions de la présente Convention ne seront applicables qu'aux forces embarquées.

Article 23

La présente Convention sera ratifiée aussitôt que possible.

Les ratifications seront déposées à La Haye.

Le premier dépôt de ratifications sera constaté par un procès-verbal signé par les représentants des Puissances qui y prennent part et par le Ministre des Affaires étrangères des Pays-Bas.

Les dépôts ultérieurs de ratifications se feront au moyen d'une notification écrite, adressée au Gouvernement des Pays-Bas et accompagnée de l'instrument de ratification.

Copie certifiée conforme du procès-verbal relatif au premier dépôt de ratifications, des notifications mentionnées à l'alinéa précédent, ainsi que des instruments de ratification, sera immédiatement remise par les soins du Gouvernement des Pays-Bas et par la voie diplomatique aux Puissances conviées à la Deuxième Conférence de la Paix, ainsi qu'aux autres Puissances qui auront adhéré à la Convention. Dans les cas visés par l'alinéa précédent, ledit Gouvernement leur fera connaître en même temps la date à laquelle il a reçu la notification.

Article 24

Les Puissances non signataires qui auront accepté la Convention de Genève du 6 juillet 1906, sont admises à adhérer à la présente Convention.

La Puissance qui désire adhérer, notifie par écrit son intention au Gouvernement des Pays-Bas en lui transmettant l'acte d'adhésion qui sera déposé dans les archives dudit Gouvernement.

Ce Gouvernement transmettra immédiatement à toutes les autres Puissances copie certifiée conforme de la notification ainsi que de l'acte d'adhésion, en indiquant la date à laquelle il a reçu la notification.

Article 25

La présente Convention, dûment ratifiée, remplacera dans les rapports entre les Puissances contractantes, la Convention du 29 juillet 1899 pour l'adaptation à la guerre maritime des principes de la Convention de Genève.

La Convention de 1899 reste en vigueur dans les rapports entre les Puissances qui l'ont signée et qui ne ratifieraient pas également la présente Convention.

Article 26

La présente Convention produira effet, pour les Puissances qui auront participé au premier dépôt de ratifications, soixante jours après la date du procès-verbal de ce dépôt et, pour les Puissances qui ratifieront ultérieurement ou qui adhéreront, soixante jours après que la notification de leur ratification ou de leur adhésion aura été reçue par le Gouvernement des Pays-Bas.

Article 27

S'il arrivait qu'une des Puissances contractantes voulût dénoncer la présente Convention, la dénonciation sera notifiée par écrit au Gouvernement des Pays-Bas, qui communiquera immédiatement copie certifiée conforme de la notification à toutes les autres Puissances en leur faisant savoir la date à laquelle il l'a reçue.

La dénonciation ne produira ses effets qu'à l'égard de la Puissance qui l'aura notifiée et un an après que la notification en sera parvenue au Gouvernement des Pays-Bas.

Article 28

Un registre tenu par le Ministère des Affaires étrangères des Pays-Bas indiquera la date du dépôt des ratifications effectué en vertu de l'article 23, alinéas 3 et 4, ainsi que la date à laquelle auront été reçues les notifications d'adhésion (article 24, alinéa 2) ou de dénonciation (article 27, alinéa 1).

Chaque Puissance contractante est admise à prendre connaissance de ce registre et à en demander des extraits certifiés conformes.

En foi de quoi, les Plénipotentiaires ont revêtu la présente Convention de leurs signatures.

Fait à La Haye, le dix-huit octobre mil neuf cent sept, en un seul exemplaire qui restera déposé dans les archives du Gouvernement des Pays-Bas et dont des copies, certifiées conformes, seront remises par la voie diplomatique aux Puissances qui ont été conviées à la Deuxième Conférence de la Paix.

XI. CONVENTION RELATIVE À CERTAINES RESTRICTIONS À L'EXERCICE DU DROIT DE CAPTURE DANS LA GUERRE MARITIME

[Pour les Etats parties, voir convention I, supra, p. 305]

Reconnaissant la nécessité de mieux assurer que par le passé l'application équitable du droit aux relations maritimes internationales en temps de guerre;

Estimant que, pour y parvenir, il convient, en abandonnant ou en conciliant le cas échéant dans un intérêt commun certaines pratiques divergentes anciennes, d'entreprendre de codifier dans des règles communes les garanties dues au commerce pacifique et au travail inoffensif, ainsi que la conduite des hostilités sur mer; qu'il importe de fixer dans des engagements mutuels écrits les principes demeurés jusqu'ici dans le domaine incertain de la controverse ou laissés à l'arbitraire des Gouvernements;

Que, dès à présent, un certain nombre de règles peuvent être posées, sans qu'il soit porté atteinte au droit actuellement en vigueur concernant les matières qui n'y sont pas prévues;

Ont nommé pour leurs Plénipotentiaires, savoir:

[Dénomination des plénipotentiaires]

Lesquels, après avoir déposé leurs pleins pouvoirs, trouvés en bonne et due forme, sont convenus des dispositions suivantes:

Chapitre I. De la Correspondance postale

Article premier

La correspondance postale des neutres ou des belligérants, quel que soit son caractère officiel ou privé, trouvée en mer sur un navire neutre ou ennemi, est inviolable. S'il y a saisie du navire, elle est expédiée avec le moins de retard possible par le capteur.

Les dispositions de l'alinéa précédent ne s'appliquent pas, en cas de violation de blocus, à la correspondance qui est à destination ou en provenance du port bloqué.

Article 2

L'inviolabilité de la correspondance postale ne soustrait pas les paquebots-poste neutres aux lois et coutumes de la guerre sur mer concernant les navires de commerce neutres en général. Toutefois, la visite n'en doit être effectuée qu'en cas de nécessité, avec tous les ménagements et toute la célérité possibles.

Chapitre II. De l'exemption de capture pour certains bateaux

Article 3

Les bateaux exclusivement affectés à la pêche côtière ou à des services de petite navigation locale sont exempts de capture, ainsi que leurs engins, agrès, apparaux et chargement.

Cette exemption cesse de leur être applicable dès qu'ils participent d'une façon quelconque aux hostilités.

Les Puissances contractantes s'interdisent de profiter du caractère inoffensif desdits bateaux pour les employer dans un but militaire en leur conservant leur apparence pacifique.

Article 4

Sont également exempts de capture les navires chargés de missions religieuses, scientifiques ou philanthropiques.

Chapitre III. Du régime des équipages des navires de commerce ennemis capturés par un belligérant

Article 5

Lorsqu'un navire de commerce ennemi est capturé par un belligérant, les hommes de son équipage, nationaux d'un Etat neutre, ne sont pas faits prisonniers de guerre.

Il en est de même du capitaine et des officiers, également nationaux d'un Etat neutre, s'ils promettent formellement par écrit de ne pas servir sur un navire ennemi pendant la durée de la guerre.

Article 6

Le capitaine, les officiers et les membres de l'équipage, nationaux de l'Etat ennemi, ne sont pas faits prisonniers de guerre, à condition qu'ils s'engagent, sous la foi d'une promesse formelle écrite, à ne prendre, pendant la durée des hostilités, aucun service ayant rapport avec les opérations de la guerre.

Article 7

Les noms des individus laissés libres dans les conditions visées à l'article 5, alinéa 2, et à l'article 6, sont notifiés par le belligérant capteur à l'autre belligérant. Il est interdit à ce dernier d'employer sciemment lesdits individus.

Article 8

Les dispositions des trois articles précédents ne s'appliquent pas aux navires qui prennent part aux hostilités.

Chapitre IV. Dispositions finales

Article 9

Les dispositions de la présente Convention ne sont applicables qu'entre les Puissances contractantes et seulement si les belligérants sont tous parties à la Convention.

Article 10

La présente Convention sera ratifiée aussitôt que possible.

Les ratifications seront déposées à La Haye.

Le premier dépôt de ratifications sera constaté par un procès-verbal signé par les représentants des Puissances qui y prennent part et par le Ministre des Affaires étrangères des Pays-Bas.

Les dépôts ultérieurs de ratifications se feront au moyen d'une notification écrite adressée au Gouvernement des Pays-Bas et accompagnée de l'instrument de ratification.

Copie certifiée conforme du procès-verbal relatif au premier dépôt de ratifications, des notifications mentionnées à l'alinéa précédent, ainsi que des instruments de ratification, sera immédiatement remise par les soins du Gouvernement des Pays-Bas et par la voie diplomatique aux Puissances conviées à la Deuxième Conférence de la Paix, ainsi qu'aux autres Puissances qui auront adhéré à la Convention. Dans les cas visés par l'alinéa précédent, ledit Gouvernement leur fera connaître en même temps la date à laquelle il a reçu la notification.

Article 11

Les Puissances non signataires sont admises à adhérer à la présente Convention.

La Puissance qui désire adhérer notifie par écrit son intention au Gouvernement des Pays-Bas en lui transmettant l'acte d'adhésion qui sera déposé dans les archives dudit Gouvernement.

Ce Gouvernement transmettra immédiatement à toutes les autres Puissances copie certifiée conforme de la notification ainsi que de l'acte d'adhésion, en indiquant la date à laquelle il a reçu la notification.

Article 12

La présente Convention produira effet pour les Puissances qui auront participé au premier dépôt de ratifications, soixante jours après la date du procès-verbal de ce dépôt et, pour les Puissances qui ratifieront ultérieurement ou qui adhéreront, soixante jours après que la notification de leur ratification ou de leur adhésion aura été reçue par le Gouvernement des Pays-Bas.

Article 13

S'il arrivait qu'une des Puissances contractantes voulût dénoncer la présente Convention, la dénonciation sera notifiée par écrit au Gouvernement des Pays-Bas, qui communiquera immédiatement copie certifiée conforme de la notification à toutes les autres Puissances en leur faisant savoir la date à laquelle il l'a reçue.

La dénonciation ne produira ses effets qu'à l'égard de la Puissance qui l'aura notifiée et un an après que la notification en sera parvenue au Gouvernement des Pays-Bas.

Article 14

Un registre tenu par le Ministère des Affaires étrangères des Pays-Bas indiquera la date du dépôt des ratifications effectué en vertu de l'article 10 alinéas 3 et 4, ainsi que la date à laquelle auront été reçues les notifications d'adhésion (article 11, alinéa 2) ou de dénonciation (article 13, alinéa 1).

Chaque Puissance contractante est admise à prendre connaissance de ce registre et à en demander des extraits certifiés conformes.

En foi de quoi, les Plénipotentiaires ont revêtu la présente Convention de leurs signatures.

Fait à La Haye, le dix-huit octobre mil neuf cent sept, en un seul exemplaire qui restera déposé dans les archives du Gouvernement des Pays-Bas et dont des copies, certifiées conformes, seront remises par la voie diplomatique aux Puissances qui ont été conviées à la Deuxième Conférence de la Paix.

XII. CONVENTION RELATIVE À L'ÉTABLISSEMENT D'UNE COUR INTERNATIONALE DE PRISES *

[Pour les Etats parties, voir convention I, supra, p. 305]

Animés du désir de régler d'une manière équitable les différends qui s'élèvent, parfois, en cas de guerre maritime, à propos des décisions des tribunaux de prises nationaux ;

Estimant que, si ces tribunaux doivent continuer à statuer suivant les formes prescrites par leur législation, il importe que, dans des cas déterminés, un recours puisse être formé sous des conditions qui concilient, dans la mesure du possible, les intérêts publics et les intérêts privés engagés dans toute affaire de prises ;

Considérant, d'autre part, que l'institution d'une Cour internationale, dont la compétence et la procédure seraient soigneusement réglées, a paru le meilleur moyen d'atteindre ce but ;

Persuadés, enfin, que de cette façon les conséquences rigoureuses d'une guerre maritime pourront être atténuées ; que notamment les bons rapports entre les belligérants et les neutres auront plus de chance d'être maintenus et qu'ainsi la conservation de la paix sera mieux assurée ;

Désirant conclure une Convention à cet effet, ont nommé pour leurs Plénipotentiaires, savoir :

[Dénomination des plénipotentiaires]

Lesquels, après avoir déposé leurs pleins pouvoirs, trouvés en bonne et due forme, sont convenus des dispositions suivantes :

TITRE I. DISPOSITIONS GÉNÉRALES

Article premier

La validité de la capture d'un navire de commerce ou de sa cargaison est, s'il s'agit de propriétés neutres ou ennemies, établie devant une juridiction des prises conformément à la présente Convention.

Article 2

La juridiction des prises est exercée d'abord par les tribunaux de prises du belligérant capteur.

Les décisions de ces tribunaux sont prononcées en séance publique ou notifiées d'office aux parties neutres ou ennemies.

---

* Non entrée en vigueur.

Article 3

Les décisions des tribunaux de prises nationaux peuvent être l'objet d'un recours devant la Cour internationale des prises:

1° lorsque la décision des tribunaux nationaux concerne les propriétés d'une Puissance ou d'un particulier neutres;

2° lorsque ladite décision concerne des propriétés ennemies et qu'il s'agit:

  a) de marchandises chargées sur un navire neutre,
  b) d'un navire ennemi, qui aurait été capturé dans les eaux territoriales d'une Puissance neutre, dans le cas où cette Puissance n'aurait pas fait de cette capture l'objet d'une réclamation diplomatique,
  c) d'une réclamation fondée sur l'allégation que la capture aurait été effectuée en violation, soit d'une disposition conventionnelle en vigueur entre les Puissances belligérantes, soit d'une disposition légale édictée par le belligérant capteur.

Le recours contre la décision des tribunaux nationaux peut être fondé sur ce que cette décision ne serait pas justifiée, soit en fait, soit en droit.

Article 4

Le recours peut être exercé:

1° par une Puissance neutre, si la décision des tribunaux nationaux a porté atteinte à ses propriétés ou à celles de ses ressortissants (article 3, 1°) ou s'il est allégué que la capture d'un navire ennemi a eu lieu dans les eaux territoriales de cette Puissance (article 3, 2° b));

2° par un particulier neutre, si la décision des tribunaux nationaux a porté atteinte à ses propriétés (article 3, 1°), sous réserve toutefois du droit de la Puissance dont il relève de lui interdire l'accès de la Cour ou d'y agir elle-même en ses lieu et place;

3° par un particulier relevant de la Puissance ennemie, si la décision des tribunaux nationaux a porté atteinte à ses propriétés dans les conditions visées à l'article 3, 2°, à l'exception du cas prévu par l'alinéa b)).

Article 5

Le recours peut aussi être exercé, dans les mêmes conditions qu'à l'article précédent, par les ayants-droit, neutres ou ennemis, du particulier auquel le recours est accordé, et qui sont intervenus devant la juridiction nationale. Ces ayants-droit peuvent exercer individuellement le recours dans la mesure de leur intérêt.

Il en est de même des ayants-droit, neutres ou ennemis, de la Puissance neutre dont la propriété est en cause.

Article 6

Lorsque, conformément à l'article 3 ci-dessus, la Cour internationale est compétente, le droit de juridiction des tribunaux nationaux ne peut être exercé à plus de deux degrés. Il appartient à la législation du belligérant capteur de décider si le recours est ouvert après la décision rendue en premier ressort ou seulement après la décision rendue en appel ou en cassation.

Faute par les tribunaux nationaux d'avoir rendu une décision définitive dans les deux ans à compter du jour de la capture, la Cour peut être saisie directement.

Article 7

Si la question de droit à résoudre est prévue par une Convention en vigueur entre le belligérant capteur et la Puissance qui est elle-même partie au litige ou dont le ressortissant est partie au litige, la Cour se conforme aux stipulations de ladite Convention.

A défaut de telles stipulations, la Cour applique les règles du droit international. Si des règles généralement reconnues n'existent pas, la Cour statue d'après les principes généraux de la justice et de l'équité.

Les dispositions ci-dessus sont également applicables en ce qui concerne l'ordre des preuves ainsi que les moyens qui peuvent être employés.

Si, conformément à l'article 3, 2° c)), le recours est fondé sur la violation d'une disposition légale édictée par le belligérant capteur, la Cour applique cette disposition.

La Cour peut ne pas tenir compte des déchéances de procédure édictées par la législation du belligérant capteur, dans les cas où elle estime que les conséquences en sont contraires à la justice et à l'équité.

Article 8

Si la Cour prononce la validité de la capture du navire ou de la cargaison, il en sera disposé conformément aux lois du belligérant capteur.

Si la nullité de la capture est prononcée, la Cour ordonne la restitution du navire ou de la cargaison et fixe, s'il y a lieu, le montant des dommages-intérêts. Si le navire ou la cargaison ont été vendus ou détruits, la Cour détermine l'indemnité à accorder de ce chef au propriétaire.

Si la nullité de la capture avait été prononcée par la juridiction nationale, la Cour n'est appelée à statuer que sur les dommages et intérêts.

Article 9

Les Puissances contractantes s'engagent à se soumettre de bonne foi aux décisions de la Cour internationale des prises et à les exécuter dans le plus bref délai possible.

TITRE II. ORGANISATION DE LA COUR INTERNATIONALE DES PRISES

Article 10

La Cour internationale des prises se compose de juges et de juges suppléants, nommés par les Puissances contractantes et qui tous devront être des jurisconsultes d'une compétence reconnue dans les questions de droit international maritime et jouissant de la plus haute considération morale.

La nomination de ces juges et juges suppléants sera faite dans les six mois qui suivront la ratification de la présente Convention.

Article 11

Les juges et juges suppléants sont nommés pour une période de six ans, à compter de la date où la notification de leur nomination aura été reçue par le Conseil administratif institué par la Convention pour le règlement pacifique des conflits internationaux du 29 juillet 1899. Leur mandat peut être renouvelé.

En cas de décès ou de démission d'un juge ou d'un juge suppléant, il est pourvu à son remplacement selon le mode fixé pour sa nomination. Dans ce cas, la nomination est faite pour une nouvelle période de six ans.

Article 12

Les juges de la Cour internationale des prises sont égaux entre eux et prennent rang d'après la date où la notification de leur nomination aura été reçue (article 11, alinéa 1), et, s'ils siègent à tour de rôle (article 15, alinéa 2), d'après la date de leur entrée en fonctions. La préséance appartient au plus âgé, au cas où la date est la même.

Les juges suppléants sont, dans l'exercice de leurs fonctions, assimilés aux juges titulaires. Toutefois ils prennent rang après ceux-ci.

Article 13

Les juges jouissent des privilèges et immunités diplomatiques dans l'exercice de leurs fonctions et en dehors de leur pays.

Avant de prendre possession de leur siège, les juges doivent, devant le Conseil administratif, prêter serment ou faire une affirmation solennelle d'exercer leurs fonctions avec impartialité et en toute conscience.

Article 14

La Cour fonctionne au nombre de quinze juges ; neuf juges constituent le quorum nécessaire.

Le juge absent ou empêché est remplacé par le suppléant.

Article 15

Les juges nommés par les Puissances contractantes dont les noms suivent : l'Allemagne, les Etats-Unis d'Amérique, l'Autriche-Hongrie, la France, la Grande-Bretagne, l'Italie, le Japon et la Russie sont toujours appelés à siéger.

Les juges et les juges suppléants nommés par les autres Puissances contractantes siègent à tour de rôle d'après le tableau annexé* à la présente Convention ; leurs fonctions peuvent être exercées successivement par la même personne. Le même juge peut être nommé par plusieurs desdites Puissances.

Article 16

Si une Puissance belligérante n'a pas, d'après le tour de rôle, un juge siégeant dans la Cour, elle peut demander que le juge nommé par elle prenne part au jugement de toutes les affaires provenant de la guerre. Dans ce cas,

---

* Non reproduit.

le sort détermine lequel des juges siégeant en vertu du tour de rôle doit s'abstenir. Cette exclusion ne saurait s'appliquer au juge nommé par l'autre belligérant.

Article 17

Ne peut siéger le juge qui, à un titre quelconque, aura concouru à la décision des tribunaux nationaux ou aura figuré dans l'instance comme conseil ou avocat d'une partie.

Aucun juge, titulaire ou suppléant, ne peut intervenir comme agent ou comme avocat devant la Cour internationale des prises ni y agir pour une partie en quelque qualité que ce soit, pendant toute la durée de ses fonctions.

Article 18

Le belligérant capteur a le droit de désigner un officier de marine d'un grade élevé qui siégera en qualité d'assesseur avec voix consultative. La même faculté appartient à la Puissance neutre, qui est elle-même partie au litige, ou à la Puissance dont le ressortissant est partie au litige; s'il y a, par application de cette dernière disposition, plusieurs Puissances intéressées, elles doivent se concerter, au besoin par le sort, sur l'officier à désigner.

Article 19

La Cour élit son Président et son Vice-Président à la majorité absolue des suffrages exprimés. Après deux tours de scrutin, l'élection se fait à la majorité relative et, en cas de partage des voix, le sort décide.

Article 20

Les juges de la Cour internationale des prises touchent une indemnité de voyage fixée d'après les règlements de leur pays et reçoivent, en outre, pendant la session ou pendant l'exercice de fonctions conférées par la Cour, une somme de cent florins néerlandais par jour.

Ces allocations, comprises dans les frais généraux de la Cour prévus par l'article 47, sont versées par l'entremise du Bureau international institué par la Convention du 29 juillet 1899.

Les juges ne peuvent recevoir de leur propre Gouvernement ou de celui d'une autre Puissance aucune rémunération comme membres de la Cour.

Article 21

La Cour internationale des prises a son siège à La Haye et ne peut, sauf le cas de force majeure, le transporter ailleurs qu'avec l'assentiment des Parties belligérantes.

Article 22

Le Conseil administratif, dans lequel ne figurent que les représentants des Puissances contractantes, remplit, à l'égard de la Cour internationale des prises, les fonctions qu'il remplit à l'égard de la Cour permanente d'arbitrage.

Article 23

Le Bureau international sert de greffe à la Cour internationale des prises et doit mettre ses locaux et son organisation à la disposition de la Cour. Il a la garde des archives et la gestion des affaires administratives.

Le Secrétaire général du Bureau international remplit les fonctions de greffier.

Les secrétaires adjoints au greffier, les traducteurs et les sténographes nécessaires sont désignés et assermentés par la Cour.

Article 24

La Cour décide du choix de la langue dont elle fera usage et des langues dont l'emploi sera autorisé devant elle.

Dans tous les cas, la langue officielle des tribunaux nationaux qui ont connu de l'affaire, peut être employée devant la Cour.

Article 25

Les Puissances intéressées ont le droit de nommer des agents spéciaux ayant mission de servir d'intermédiaires entre elles et la Cour. Elles sont, en outre, autorisées à charger des conseils ou avocats de la défense de leurs droits et intérêts.

Article 26

Le particulier intéressé sera représenté devant la Cour par un mandataire qui doit être soit un avocat autorisé à plaider devant une Cour d'appel ou une Cour suprême de l'un des Pays contractants, soit un avoué exerçant sa profession auprès d'une telle Cour, soit enfin un professeur de droit à une école d'enseignement supérieur d'un de ces pays.

Article 27

Pour toutes les notifications à faire, notamment aux parties, aux témoins et aux experts, la Cour peut s'adresser directement au Gouvernement de la Puissance sur le territoire de laquelle la notification doit être effectuée. Il en est de même s'il s'agit de faire procéder à l'établissement de tout moyen de preuve.

Les requêtes adressées à cet effet seront exécutées suivant les moyens dont la Puissance requise dispose d'après sa législation intérieure. Elles ne peuvent être refusées que si cette Puissance les juge de nature à porter atteinte à sa souveraineté ou à sa sécurité. S'il est donné suite à la requête, les frais ne comprennent que les dépenses d'exécution réellement effectuées.

La Cour a également la faculté de recourir à l'intermédiaire de la Puissance sur le territoire de laquelle elle a son siège.

Les notifications à faire aux parties dans le lieu où siège la Cour peuvent être exécutées par le Bureau international.

Titre III. Procédure devant la Cour internationale des prises

Article 28

Le recours devant la Cour internationale des prises est formé au moyen d'une déclaration écrite, faite devant le tribunal national qui a statué, ou adressée au Bureau international; celui-ci peut être saisi même par télégramme.

Le délai du recours est fixé à cent vingt jours à dater du jour où la décision a été prononcée ou notifiée (article 2, alinéa 2).

Article 29

Si la déclaration de recours est faite devant le tribunal national, celui-ci, sans examiner si le délai a été observé, fait, dans les sept jours qui suivent, expédier le dossier de l'affaire au Bureau international.

Si la déclaration de recours est adressée au Bureau international, celui-ci en prévient directement le tribunal national, par télégramme s'il est possible. Le tribunal transmettra le dossier comme il est dit à l'alinéa précédent.

Lorsque le recours est formé par un particulier neutre, le Bureau international en avise immédiatement par télégramme la Puissance dont relève le particulier, pour permettre à cette Puissance de faire valoir le droit que lui reconnaît l'article 4, 2°.

Article 30

Dans le cas prévu à l'article 6, alinéa 2, le recours ne peut être adressé qu'au Bureau international. Il doit être introduit dans les trente jours qui suivent l'expiration du délai de deux ans.

Article 31

Faute d'avoir formé son recours dans le délai fixé à l'article 28 ou à l'article 30, la partie sera, sans débats, déclarée non recevable.

Toutefois, si elle justifie d'un empêchement de force majeure et si elle a formé son recours dans les soixante jours qui ont suivi la cessation de cet empêchement, elle peut être relevée de la déchéance encourue, la partie adverse ayant été dûment entendue.

Article 32

Si le recours a été formé en temps utile, la Cour notifie d'office et sans délai à la partie adverse une copie certifiée conforme de la déclaration.

Article 33

Si, en dehors des parties qui se sont pourvues devant la Cour, il y a d'autres intéressés ayant le droit d'exercer le recours, ou si, dans le cas prévu à l'article 29, alinéa 3, la Puissance qui a été avisée, n'a pas fait connaître sa résolution, la Cour attend, pour se saisir de l'affaire, que les délais prévus à l'article 28 ou à l'article 30 soient expirés.

Article 34

La procédure devant la Cour internationale comprend deux phases distinctes: l'instruction écrite et les débats oraux.

L'instruction écrite consiste dans le dépôt et l'échange d'exposés, de contre-exposés et, au besoin, de répliques dont l'ordre et les délais sont fixés par la Cour. Les parties y joignent toutes pièces et documents dont elles comptent se servir.

Toute pièce, produite par une partie, doit être communiquée en copie certifiée conforme à l'autre partie par l'intermédiaire de la Cour.

Article 35

L'instruction écrite étant terminée, il y a lieu à une audience publique, dont le jour est fixé par la Cour.

Dans cette audience, les parties exposent l'état de l'affaire en fait et en droit.

La Cour peut, en tout état de cause, suspendre les plaidoiries, soit à la demande d'une des parties, soit d'office, pour procéder à une information complémentaire.

Article 36

La Cour internationale peut ordonner que l'information complémentaire aura lieu, soit conformément aux dispositions de l'article 27, soit directement devant elle ou devant un ou plusieurs de ses membres, en tant que cela peut se faire sans moyen coercitif ou comminatoire.

Si des mesures d'information doivent être prises par des membres de la Cour en dehors du territoire où elle a son siège, l'assentiment du Gouvernement étranger doit être obtenu.

Article 37

Les parties sont appelées à assister à toutes mesures d'instruction. Elles reçoivent une copie certifiée conforme des procès-verbaux.

Article 38

Les débats sont dirigés par le Président ou le Vice-Président et, en cas d'absence ou d'empêchement de l'un et de l'autre, par le plus ancien des juges présents.

Le juge nommé par une Partie belligérante ne peut siéger comme Président.

Article 39

Les débats sont publics, sauf le droit pour une Puissance en litige de demander qu'il y soit procédé à huis clos.

Ils sont consignés dans des procès-verbaux, que signent le Président et le greffier et qui seuls ont caractère authentique.

Article 40

En cas de non comparution d'une des parties, bien que régulièrement citée, ou faute par elle d'agir dans les délais fixés par la Cour, il est procédé sans elle et la Cour décide d'après les éléments d'appréciation qu'elle a à sa disposition.

Article 41

La Cour notifie d'office aux parties toutes décisions ou ordonnances prises en leur absence.

Article 42

La Cour apprécie librement l'ensemble des actes, preuves et déclarations orales.

Article 43

Les délibérations de la Cour ont lieu à huis clos et restent secrètes.

Toute décision est prise à la majorité des juges présents. Si la Cour siège en nombre pair et qu'il y ait partage des voix, la voix du dernier des juges, dans l'ordre de préséance établi d'après l'article 12, alinéa 1, n'est pas comptée.

Article 44

L'arrêt de la Cour doit être motivé. Il mentionne les noms des juges qui y ont participé, ainsi que les noms des assesseurs, s'il y a lieu; il est signé par le Président et par le greffier.

Article 45

L'arrêt est prononcé en séance publique, les parties présentes ou dûment appelées; il est notifié d'office aux parties.

Cette notification une fois faite, la Cour fait parvenir au tribunal national des prises le dossier de l'affaire, en y joignant une expédition des diverses décisions intervenues, ainsi qu'une copie des procès-verbaux de l'instruction.

Article 46

Chaque partie supporte les frais occasionnés par sa propre défense.

La partie qui succombe supporte, en outre, les frais causés par la procédure. Elle doit, de plus, verser un centième de la valeur de l'objet litigieux à titre de contribution aux frais généraux de la Cour internationale. Le montant de ces versements est déterminé par l'arrêt de la Cour.

Si le recours est exercé par un particulier, celui-ci fournit au Bureau international un cautionnement dont le montant est fixé par la Cour et qui est destiné à garantir l'exécution éventuelle des deux obligations mentionnées dans l'alinéa précédent. La Cour peut subordonner l'ouverture de la procédure au versement du cautionnement.

Article 47

Les frais généraux de la Cour internationale des prises sont supportés par les Puissances contractantes dans la proportion de leur participation au fonctionnement de la Cour, telle qu'elle est prévue par l'article 15 et par le tableau y annexé. La désignation des juges suppléants ne donne pas lieu à contribution.

Le Conseil administratif s'adresse aux Puissances pour obtenir les fonds nécessaires au fonctionnement de la Cour.

Article 48

Quand la Cour n'est pas en session, les fonctions qui lui sont conférées par l'article 32, l'article 34, alinéas 2 et 3, l'article 35, alinéa 1, et l'article 46, alinéa 3, sont exercées par une Délégation de trois juges désignés par la Cour. Cette Délégation décide à la majorité des voix.

Article 49

La Cour fait elle-même son règlement d'ordre intérieur, qui doit être communiqué aux Puissances contractantes.

Dans l'année de la ratification de la présente Convention, elle se réunira pour élaborer ce règlement.

Article 50

La Cour peut proposer des modifications à apporter aux dispositions de la présente Convention qui concernent la procédure. Ces propositions sont communiquées, par l'intermédiaire du Gouvernement des Pays-Bas, aux Puissances contractantes qui se concerteront sur la suite à y donner.

Titre IV. Dispositions finales

Article 51

La présente Convention ne s'applique de plein droit que si les Puissances belligérantes sont toutes parties à la Convention.

Il est entendu, en outre, que le recours devant la Cour internationale des prises ne peut être exercé que par une Puissance contractante ou le ressortissant d'une Puissance contractante.

Dans les cas de l'article 5, le recours n'est admis que si le propriétaire et l'ayant-droit sont également des Puissances contractantes ou des ressortissants de Puissances contractantes.

Article 52

La présente Convention sera ratifiée et les ratifications en seront déposées à La Haye dès que toutes les Puissances désignées à l'article 15 et dans son annexe seront en mesure de le faire.

Le dépôt des ratifications aura lieu, en tout cas, le 30 juin 1909, si les Puissances prêtes à ratifier peuvent fournir à la Cour neuf juges et neuf juges suppléants, aptes à siéger effectivement. Dans le cas contraire, le dépôt sera ajourné jusqu'au moment où cette condition sera remplie.

Il sera dressé du dépôt des ratifications un procès-verbal dont une copie, certifiée conforme, sera remise par la voie diplomatique à chacune des Puissances désignées à l'alinéa premier.

Article 53

Les Puissances désignées à l'article 15 et dans son annexe sont admises à signer la présente Convention jusqu'au dépôt des ratifications prévu par l'alinéa 2 de l'article précédent.

Après ce dépôt, elles seront toujours admises à y adhérer, purement et simplement. La Puissance qui désire adhérer notifie par écrit son intention au Gouvernement des Pays-Bas en lui transmettant, en même temps, l'acte d'adhésion qui sera déposé dans les archives dudit Gouvernement. Celui-ci enverra, par la voie diplomatique, une copie certifiée conforme de la notification et de l'acte d'adhésion à toutes les Puissances désignées à l'alinéa précédent, en leur faisant savoir la date où il a reçu la notification.

Article 54

La présente Convention entrera en vigueur six mois à partir du dépôt des ratifications prévu par l'article 52, alinéas 1 et 2.

Les adhésions produiront effet soixante jours après que la notification en aura été reçue par le Gouvernement des Pays-Bas et, au plus tôt, à l'expiration du délai prévu par l'alinéa précédent.

Toutefois, la Cour internationale aura qualité pour juger les affaires de prises décidées par la juridiction nationale à partir du dépôt des ratifications ou de la réception de la notification des adhésions. Pour ces décisions, le délai fixé à l'article 28, alinéa 2, ne sera compté que de la date de la mise en vigueur de la Convention pour les Puissances ayant ratifié ou adhéré.

Article 55

La présente Convention aura une durée de douze ans à partir de sa mise en vigueur, telle qu'elle est déterminée par l'article 54, alinéa 1, même pour les Puissances ayant adhéré postérieurement.

Elle sera renouvelée tacitement de six ans en six ans, sauf dénonciation.

La dénonciation devra être, au moins un an avant l'expiration de chacune des périodes prévues par les deux alinéas précédents, notifiée par écrit au Gouvernement des Pays-Bas, qui en donnera connaissance à toutes les autres Parties contractantes.

La dénonciation ne produira ses effets qu'à l'égard de la Puissance qui l'aura notifiée. La Convention subsistera pour les autres Puissances contractantes, pourvu que leur participation à la désignation des juges soit suffisante pour permettre le fonctionnement de la Cour avec neuf juges et neuf juges suppléants.

Article 56

Dans le cas ou la présente Convention n'est pas en vigueur pour toutes les Puissances désignées dans l'article 15 et le tableau qui s'y rattache, le Conseil administratif dresse, conformément aux dispositions de cet article et de ce tableau, la liste des juges et des juges suppléants pour lesquels les Puissances contractantes participent au fonctionnement de la Cour. Les juges appelés à siéger à tour de rôle seront, pour le temps qui leur est attribué par le tableau susmentionné, répartis entre les différentes années de la période de six ans, de manière que, dans la mesure du possible, la Cour fonctionne chaque année en nombre égal. Si le nombre des juges suppléants dépasse celui des juges, le nombre de ces derniers pourra être complété par des juges suppléants désignés par le sort parmi celles des Puissances qui ne nomment pas de juge titulaire.

La liste ainsi dressée par le Conseil administratif sera notifiée aux Puissances contractantes. Elle sera révisée quand le nombre de celles-ci sera modifié par suite d'adhésions ou de dénonciations.

Le changement à opérer par suite d'une adhésion ne se produira qu'à partir du 1er janvier qui suit la date à laquelle l'adhésion a son effet, à moins que la Puissance adhérente ne soit une Puissance belligérante, cas auquel elle peut demander d'être aussitôt représentée dans la Cour, la disposition de l'article 16 étant du reste applicable, s'il y a lieu.

Quand le nombre total des juges est inférieur à onze, sept juges constituent le quorum nécessaire.

Article 57

Deux ans avant l'expiration de chaque période visée par les alinéas 1 et 2 de l'article 55, chaque Puissance contractante pourra demander une modification des dispositions de l'article 15 et du tableau y annexé, relativement à sa participation au fonctionnement de la Cour. La demande sera adressée au Conseil administratif, qui l'examinera et soumettra à toutes les Puissances des propositions sur la suite à y donner. Les Puissances feront, dans le plus bref délai possible, connaître leur résolution au Conseil administratif. Le résultat sera immédiatement, et au moins un an et trente jours avant l'expiration dudit délai de deux ans, communiqué à la Puissance qui a fait la demande.

Le cas échéant, les modifications adoptées par les Puissances entreront en vigueur dès le commencement de la nouvelle période.

En foi de quoi les Plénipotentiaires ont revêtu la présente convention de leurs signatures.

Fait à La Haye, le dix-huit octobre mil neuf cent sept, en un seul exemplaire qui restera déposé dans les archives du Gouvernement des Pays-Bas et dont des copies, certifiées conformes, seront remises par la voie diplomatique aux Puissances désignées à l'article 15 et dans son annexe.

XIII. CONVENTION CONCERNANT LES DROITS ET LES DEVOIRS DES PUISSANCES NEUTRES EN CAS DE GUERRE MARITIME

[Pour les Etats parties, voir convention I, supra, p. 305]

En vue de diminuer les divergences d'opinion qui, en cas de guerre maritime, existent encore au sujet des rapports entre les Puissances neutres et les Puissances belligérantes, et de prévenir les difficultés auxquelles ces divergences pourraient donner lieu;

Considérant que, si l'on ne peut concerter dès maintenant des stipulations s'étendant à toutes les circonstances qui peuvent se présenter dans la pratique, il y a néanmoins une utilité incontestable à établir, dans la mesure du possible, des règles communes pour le cas où malheureusement la guerre viendrait à éclater;

Considérant que, pour les cas non prévus par la présente Convention, il y a lieu de tenir compte des principes généraux du droit des gens;

Considérant qu'il est désirable que les Puissances édictent des prescriptions précises pour régler les conséquences de l'état de neutralité qu'elles auraient adopté;

Considérant que c'est, pour les Puissances neutres, un devoir reconnu d'appliquer impartialement aux divers belligérants les règles adoptées par elles;

Considérant que, dans cet ordre d'idées, ces règles ne devraient pas, en principe, être changées, au cours de la guerre, par une Puissance neutre, sauf dans le cas où l'expérience acquise en démontrerait la nécessité pour la sauvegarde de ses droits;

Sont convenus d'observer les règles communes suivantes qui ne sauraient, d'ailleurs, porter aucune atteinte aux stipulations des traités généraux existants, et ont nommé pour leurs Plénipotentiaires, savoir:

[Dénomination des plénipotentiaires]

Lesquels, après avoir déposé leurs pleins pouvoirs, trouvés en bonne et due forme, sont convenus des dispositions suivantes:

Article premier

Les belligérants sont tenus de respecter les droits souverains des Puissances neutres et de s'abstenir, dans le territoire ou les eaux neutres, de tous actes qui constitueraient de la part des Puissances qui les toléreraient un manquement à leur neutralité.

Article 2

Tous actes d'hostilité, y compris la capture et l'exercice du droit de visite, commis par des vaisseaux de guerre belligérants dans les eaux territoriales d'une Puissance neutre, constituent une violation de la neutralité et sont strictement interdits.

Article 3

Quand un navire a été capturé dans les eaux territoriales d'une Puissance neutre, cette Puissance doit, si la prise est encore dans sa juridiction, user des moyens dont elle dispose pour que la prise soit relâchée avec ses officiers et son équipage, et pour que l'équipage mis à bord par le capteur soit interné.

Si la prise est hors de la juridiction de la Puissance neutre, le Gouvernement capteur, sur la demande de celle-ci, doit relâcher la prise avec ses officiers et son équipage.

Article 4

Aucun tribunal des prises ne peut être constitué par un belligérant sur un territoire neutre ou sur un navire dans des eaux neutres.

Article 5

Il est interdit aux belligérants de faire des ports et des eaux neutres la base d'opérations navales contre leurs adversaires, notamment d'y installer des stations radio-télégraphiques ou tout appareil destiné à servir comme moyen de communication avec des forces belligérantes sur terre ou sur mer.

Article 6

La remise, à quelque titre que ce soit, faite directement ou indirectement par une Puissance neutre à une Puissance belligérante, de vaisseaux de guerre, de munitions, ou d'un matériel de guerre quelconque, est interdite.

Article 7

Une Puissance neutre n'est pas tenue d'empêcher l'exportation ou le transit, pour le compte de l'un ou de l'autre des belligérants, d'armes, de munitions, et, en général, de tout ce qui peut être utile à une armée ou à une flotte.

Article 8

Un Gouvernement neutre est tenu d'user des moyens dont il dispose pour empêcher dans sa juridiction l'équipement ou l'armement de tout navire, qu'il a des motifs raisonnables de croire destiné à croiser ou à concourir à des opérations hostiles contre une Puissance avec laquelle il est en paix. Il est aussi tenu d'user de la même surveillance pour empêcher le départ hors de sa juridiction de tout navire destiné à croiser ou à concourir à des opérations hostiles, et qui aurait été, dans ladite juridiction, adapté en tout ou en partie à des usages de guerre.

Article 9

Une Puissance neutre doit appliquer également aux deux belligérants les conditions, restrictions ou interdictions, édictées par elle pour ce qui concerne l'admission dans ses ports, rades ou eaux territoriales, des navires de guerre belligérants ou de leurs prises.

Toutefois, une Puissance neutre peut interdire l'accès de ses ports et de ses rades au navire belligérant qui aurait négligé de se conformer aux ordres et prescriptions édictés par elle ou qui aurait violé la neutralité.

Article 10

La neutralité d'une Puissance n'est pas compromise par le simple passage dans ses eaux territoriales des navires de guerre et des prises des belligérants.

Article 11

Une Puissance neutre peut laisser les navires de guerre des belligérants se servir de ses pilotes brevetés.

Article 12

A défaut d'autres dispositions spéciales de la législation de la Puissance neutre, il est interdit aux navires de guerre des belligérants de demeurer dans les ports et rades ou dans les eaux territoriales de ladite Puissance, pendant plus de 24 heures, sauf dans les cas prévus par la présente Convention.

Article 13

Si une Puissance avisée de l'ouverture des hostilités apprend qu'un navire de guerre d'un belligérant se trouve dans un de ses ports et rades ou dans ses eaux territoriales, elle doit notifier audit navire qu'il devra partir dans les 24 heures ou dans le délai prescrit par la loi locale.

Article 14

Un navire de guerre belligérant ne peut prolonger son séjour dans un port neutre au-delà de la durée légale que pour cause d'avaries ou à raison de l'état de la mer. Il devra partir dès que la cause du retard aura cessé.

Les règles sur la limitation du séjour dans les ports, rades et eaux neutres, ne s'appliquent pas aux navires de guerre exclusivement affectés à une mission religieuse, scientifique ou philanthropique.

Article 15

A défaut d'autres dispositions spéciales de la législation de la Puissance neutre, le nombre maximum des navires de guerre d'un belligérant qui pourront se trouver en même temps dans un de ses ports ou rades, sera de trois.

Article 16

Lorsque des navires de guerre des deux Parties belligérantes se trouvent simultanément dans un port ou une rade neutres, il doit s'écouler au moins 24 heures entre le départ du navire d'un belligérant et le départ du navire de l'autre.

L'ordre des départs est déterminé par l'ordre des arrivées, à moins que le navire arrivé le premier ne soit dans le cas où la prolongation de la durée légale du séjour est admise.

Un navire de guerre belligérant ne peut quitter un port ou une rade neutres moins de 24 heures après le départ d'un navire de commerce portant le pavillon de son adversaire.

Article 17

Dans les ports et rades neutres, les navires de guerre belligérants ne peuvent réparer leurs avaries que dans la mesure indispensable à la sécurité de leur navigation et non pas accroître, d'une manière quelconque, leur force militaire. L'autorité neutre constatera la nature des réparations à effectuer qui devront être exécutées le plus rapidement possible.

Article 18

Les navires de guerre belligérants ne peuvent pas se servir des ports, rades et eaux territoriales neutres, pour renouveler ou augmenter leurs approvisionnements militaires ou leur armement ainsi que pour compléter leurs équipages.

Article 19

Les navires de guerre belligérants ne peuvent se ravitailler dans les ports et rades neutres que pour compléter leur approvisionnement normal du temps de paix.

Ces navires ne peuvent, de même, prendre du combustible que pour gagner le port le plus proche de leur propre pays. Ils peuvent, d'ailleurs, prendre le combustible nécessaire pour compléter le plein de leurs soutes proprement dites, quand ils se trouvent dans les pays neutres qui ont adopté ce mode de détermination du combustible à fournir.

Si, d'après la loi de la Puissance neutre, les navires ne reçoivent du charbon que 24 heures après leur arrivée, la durée légale de leur séjour est prolongée de 24 heures.

Article 20

Les navires de guerre belligérants, qui ont pris du combustible dans le port d'une Puissance neutre, ne peuvent renouveler leur approvisionnement qu'après trois mois dans un port de la même Puissance.

Article 21

Une prise ne peut être amenée dans un port neutre que pour cause d'innavigabilité, de mauvais état de la mer, de manque de combustible ou de provisions.

Elle doit repartir aussitôt que la cause qui en a justifié l'entrée a cessé. Si elle ne le fait pas, la Puissance neutre doit lui notifier l'ordre de partir immédiatement; au cas où elle ne s'y conformerait pas, la Puissance neutre doit user des moyens dont elle dispose pour la relâcher avec ses officiers et son équipage et interner l'équipage mis à bord par le capteur.

Article 22

La Puissance neutre doit, de même, relâcher la prise qui aurait été amenée en dehors des conditions prévues par l'article 21.

Article 23

Une Puissance neutre peut permettre l'accès de ses ports et rades aux prises escortées ou non, lorsqu'elles y sont amenées pour être laissées sous séquestre en attendant la décision du tribunal des prises. Elle peut faire conduire la prise dans un autre de ses ports.

Si la prise est escortée par un navire de guerre, les officiers et les hommes mis à bord par le capteur sont autorisés à passer sur le navire d'escorte.

Si la prise voyage seule, le personnel placé à son bord par le capteur est laissé en liberté.

Article 24

Si, malgré la notification de l'autorité neutre, un navire de guerre belligérant ne quitte pas un port dans lequel il n'a pas le droit de rester, la Puissance neutre a le droit de prendre les mesures qu'elle pourra juger nécessaires pour rendre le navire incapable de prendre la mer pendant la durée de la guerre et le commandant du navire doit faciliter l'exécution de ces mesures.

Lorsqu'un navire belligérant est retenu par une Puissance neutre, les officiers et l'équipage sont également retenus.

Les officiers et l'équipage ainsi retenus peuvent être laissés dans le navire ou logés, soit sur un autre navire, soit à terre, et ils peuvent être assujettis aux mesures restrictives qu'il paraîtrait nécessaire de leur imposer. Toutefois, on devra toujours laisser sur le navire les hommes nécessaires à son entretien.

Les officiers peuvent être laissés libres en prenant l'engagement sur parole de ne pas quitter le territoire neutre sans autorisation.

Article 25

Une Puissance neutre est tenue d'exercer la surveillance, que comportent les moyens dont elle dispose, pour empêcher dans ses ports ou rades et dans ses eaux toute violation des dispositions qui précèdent.

Article 26

L'exercice par une Puissance neutre des droits définis par la présente Convention ne peut jamais être considéré comme un acte peu amical par l'un ou par l'autre belligérant qui a accepté les articles qui précèdent.

Article 27

Les Puissances contractantes se communiqueront réciproquement, en temps utile, toutes les lois, ordonnances et autres dispositions réglant chez elles le régime des navires de guerre belligérants dans leurs ports et leurs eaux, au moyen d'une notification adressée au Gouvernement des Pays-Bas et transmise immédiatement par celui-ci aux autres Puissances contractantes.

Article 28

Les dispositions de la présente Convention ne sont applicables qu'entre les Puissances contractantes et seulement si les belligérants sont tous parties à la Convention.

Article 29

La présente Convention sera ratifiée aussitôt que possible.

Les ratifications seront déposées à La Haye.

Le premier dépôt de ratifications sera constaté par un procès-verbal signé par les représentants des Puissances qui y prennent part et par le Ministre des Affaires étrangères des Pays-Bas.

Les dépôts ultérieurs de ratifications se feront au moyen d'une notification écrite, adressée au Gouvernement des Pays-Bas et accompagnée de l'instrument de ratification.

Copie certifiée conforme du procès-verbal relatif au premier dépôt de ratifications, des notifications mentionnées à l'alinéa précédent, ainsi que des instruments de ratification, sera immédiatement remise par les soins du Gouvernement des Pays-Bas et par la voie diplomatique aux Puissances conviées à la Deuxième Conférence de la Paix, ainsi qu'aux autres Puissances qui auront adhéré à la Convention. Dans les cas visés par l'alinéa précédent, ledit Gouvernement leur fera connaître en même temps la date à laquelle il a reçu la notification.

Article 30

Les Puissances non signataires sont admises à adhérer à la présente Convention.

La Puissance qui désire adhérer notifie par écrit son intention au Gouvernement des Pays-Bas en lui transmettant l'acte d'adhésion qui sera déposé dans les archives dudit Gouvernement.

Ce Gouvernement transmettra immédiatement à toutes les autres Puissances copie certifiée conforme de la notification ainsi que de l'acte d'adhésion, en indiquant la date à laquelle il a reçu la notification.

Article 31

La présente Convention produira effet, pour les Puissances qui auront participé au premier dépôt des ratifications, soixante jours après la date du procès-verbal de ce dépôt et, pour les Puissances qui ratifieront ultérieurement ou qui adhéreront, soixante jours après que la notification de leur ratification ou de leur adhésion aura été reçue par le Gouvernement des Pays-Bas.

Article 32

S'il arrivait qu'une des Puissances contractantes voulût dénoncer la présente Convention, la dénonciation sera notifiée par écrit au Gouvernement des Pays-Bas qui communiquera immédiatement copie certifiée conforme de la notification à toutes les autres Puissances en leur faisant savoir la date à laquelle il l'a reçue.

La dénonciation ne produira ses effets qu'à l'égard de la Puissance qui l'aura notifiée et un an après que la notification en sera parvenue au Gouvernement des Pays-Bas.

Article 33

Un registre tenu par le Ministère des Affaires étrangères des Pays-Bas indiquera la date du dépôt de ratifications effectué en vertu de l'article 29, alinéas 3 et 4, ainsi que la date à laquelle auront été reçues les notifications d'adhésion (article 30, alinéa 2) ou de dénonciation (article 32, alinéa 1).

Chaque Puissance contractante est admise à prendre connaissance de ce registre et à en demander des extraits certifiés conformes.

En foi de quoi, les Plénipotentiaires ont revêtu la présente Convention de leurs signatures.

Fait à La Haye, le dix-huit octobre mil neuf cent sept, en un seul exemplaire qui restera déposé dans les archives du Gouvernement des Pays-Bas et dont des copies, certifiées conformes, seront remises par la voie diplomatique aux Puissances qui ont été conviées à la Deuxième Conférence de la Paix.

XIV. DÉCLARATION RELATIVE À L'INTERDICTION DE LANCER DES PROJECTILES ET DES EXPLOSIFS DU HAUT DE BALLONS

[Pour les Etats parties, voir convention I, supra, p. 305]

Les soussignés, Plénipotentiaires des Puissances conviées à la Deuxième Conférence internationale de la Paix à La Haye, dûment autorisés à cet effet par leurs Gouvernements,

S'inspirant des sentiments qui ont trouvé leur expression dans la Déclaration de St. Pétersbourg du 29 novembre (11 décembre) 1868, et désirant renouveler la Déclaration de La Haye du 29 juillet 1899, arrivée à expiration,

Déclarent:

Les Puissances contractantes consentent, pour une période allant jusqu'à la fin de la troisième Conférence de la Paix, à l'interdiction de lancer des projectiles et des explosifs du haut de ballons ou par d'autres modes analogues nouveaux.

La présente Déclaration n'est obligatoire que pour les Puissances contractantes, en cas de guerre entre deux ou plusieurs d'entre elles.

Elle cessera d'être obligatoire du moment où, dans une guerre entre des Puissances contractantes, une Puissance non contractante se joindrait à l'un des belligérants.

La présente Déclaration sera ratifiée dans le plus bref délai possible.

Les ratifications seront déposées à La Haye.

Il sera dressé du dépôt des ratifications un procès-verbal, dont une copie, certifiée conforme, sera remise par la voie diplomatique à toutes les Puissances contractantes.

Les Puissances non signataires pourront adhérer à la présente Déclaration. Elles auront, à cet effet, à faire connaître leur adhésion aux Puissances contractantes, au moyen d'une notification écrite, adressée au Gouvernement des Pays-Bas et communiquée par celui-ci à toutes les autres Puissances contractantes.

S'il arrivait qu'une des Hautes Parties contractantes dénonçât la présente Déclaration, cette dénonciation ne produirait ses effets qu'un an après la notification faite par écrit au Gouvernement des Pays-Bas et communiquée immédiatement par celui-ci à toutes les autres Puissances contractantes.

Cette dénonciation ne produira ses effets qu'à l'égard de la Puissance qui l'aura notifiée.

En foi de quoi, les Plénipotentiaires ont revêtu la présente Déclaration de leurs signatures.

Fait à La Haye, le dix-huit octobre mil neuf cent sept, en un seul exemplaire qui restera déposé dans les archives du Gouvernement des Pays-Bas et dont des copies, certifiées conformes, seront remises par la voie diplomatique aux Puissances contractantes.

XV. ACTE FINAL
DE LA DEUXIÈME CONFÉRENCE INTERNATIONALE
DE LA PAIX

La Deuxième Conférence internationale de la Paix, proposée d'abord par Monsieur le Président des Etats-Unis d'Amérique, ayant été, sur l'invitation de Sa Majesté l'Empereur de Toutes les Russies, convoquée par Sa Majesté la Reine des Pays-Bas, s'est réunie le 15 juin 1907 à La Haye, dans la Salle des Chevaliers, avec la mission de donner un développement nouveau aux principes humanitaires qui ont servi de base à l'œuvre de la Première Conférence de 1899.

Les Puissances, dont l'énumération suit, ont pris part à la Conférence, pour laquelle Elles avaient désigné les Délégués nommés ci-après :

[Enumération des puissances et désignation des délégués.
Pour les puissances voir Convention I, supra, p. 305.]

Dans une série de réunions, tenues du 15 juin au 18 octobre 1907, où les Délégués précités ont été constamment animés du désir de réaliser, dans la plus large mesure possible, les vues généreuses de l'Auguste Initiateur de la Conférence et les intentions de leurs Gouvernements, la Conférence a arrêté, pour être soumis à la signature des Plénipotentiaires, le texte des Conventions et de la Déclaration énumérées ci-après et annexées au présent Acte :

    I. Convention pour le règlement pacifique des conflits internationaux.

    II. Convention concernant la limitation de l'emploide la force pour le recouvrement de dettes contractuelles.

    III. Convention relative à l'ouverture des hostilités.

    IV. Convention concernant les lois et coutumes de la guerre sur terre.

    V. Convention concernant les droits et les devoirs des Puissances et des personnes neutres en cas de guerre sur terre.

    VI. Convention relative au régime des navires de commerce ennemis au début des hostilités.

    VII. Convention relative à la transformation des navires de commerce en bâtiments de guerre.

    VIII. Convention relative à la pose de mines sous-marines automatiques de contact.

    IX. Convention concernant le bombardement par des forces navales en temps de guerre.

    X. Convention pour l'adaptation à la guerre maritime des principes de la Convention de Genève.

    XI. Convention relative à certaines restrictions à l'exercice du droit de capture dans la guerre maritime.

    XII. Convention relative à l'établissement d'une Cour internationale des prises.

XIII. Convention concernant les droits et les devoirs des Puissances neutres en cas de guerre maritime.

XIV. Déclaration relative à l'interdiction de lancer des projectiles et des explosifs du haut de ballons.

Ces Conventions et cette Déclaration formeront autant d'actes séparés. Ces actes porteront la date de ce jour et pourront être signés jusqu'au 30 juin 1908 à La Haye par les Plénipotentiaires des Puissances représentées à la Deuxième Conférence de la Paix.

La Conférence, se conformant à l'esprit d'entente et de concessions réciproques qui est l'esprit même de ses délibérations, a arrêté la déclaration suivante qui, tout en réservant à chacune des Puissances représentées le bénéfice de ses votes, leur permet à toutes d'affirmer les principes qu'elles considèrent comme unanimement reconnus:

Elle est unanime,

1) à reconnaître le principe de l'arbitrage obligatoire;

2) à déclarer que certains différends, et notamment ceux relatifs à l'interprétation et à l'application des stipulations conventionnelles internationales, sont susceptibles d'être soumis à l'arbitrage obligatoire sans aucune restriction.

Elle est unanime enfin à proclamer que, s'il n'a pas été donné de conclure dès maintenant une Convention en ce sens, les divergences d'opinion qui se sont manifestées n'ont pas dépassé les limites d'une controverse juridique, et qu'en travaillant ici ensemble pendant quatre mois, toutes les Puissances du monde, non seulement ont appris à se comprendre et à se rapprocher davantage, mais ont su dégager, au cours de cette longue collaboration, un sentiment très élevé du bien commun de l'humanité.

En outre, la Conférence a adopté à l'unanimité la Résolution suivante:

La Deuxième Conférence de la Paix confirme la Résolution adoptée par la Conférence de 1899 à l'égard de la limitation des charges militaires; et, vu que les charges militaires se sont considérablement accrues dans presque tous les pays depuis ladite année, la Conférence déclare qu'il est hautement désirable de voir les Gouvernements reprendre l'étude sérieuse de cette question.

Elle a, de plus, émis les Vœux suivants:

1) La Conférence recommande aux Puissances signataires l'adoption du projet ci-annexé * de Convention pour l'établissement d'une Cour de Justice arbitrale, et sa mise en vigueur dès qu'un accord sera intervenu sur le choix des juges et la constitution de la Cour.

2) La Conférence émet le vœu qu'en cas de guerre, les autorités compétentes, civiles et militaires, se fassent un devoir tout spécial d'assurer et de protéger le maintien des rapports pacifiques et notamment des relations commerciales et industrielles entre les populations des Etats belligérants et les pays neutres.

---

* Non reproduit.

3) La Conférence émet le vœu que les Puissances règlent, par des Conventions particulières, la situation, au point de vue des charges militaires, des étrangers établis sur leurs territoires.

4) La Conférence émet le vœu que l'élaborationd'un règlement relatif aux lois et coutumes de la guerre maritime figure au programme de la prochaine Conférence et que, dans tous les cas, les Puissances appliquent, autant que possible, à la guerre sur mer, les principes de la Convention relative aux lois et coutumes de la guerre sur terre.

Enfin, la Conférence recommande aux Puissances la réunion d'une troisième Conférence de la Paix qui pourrait avoir lieu, dans une période analogue à celle qui s'est écoulée depuis la précédente Conférence, à une date à fixer d'un commun accord entre les Puissances, et elle appelle leur attention sur la nécessité de préparer les travaux de cette troisième Conférence assez longtemps à l'avance pour que ses délibérations se poursuivent avec l'autorité et la rapidité indispensables.

Pour atteindre à ce but, la Conférence estime qu'il serait très désirable que environ deux ans avant l'époque probable de la réunion, un Comité préparatoire fût chargé par les Gouvernements de recueillir les diverses propositions à soumettre à la Conférence, de rechercher les matières susceptibles d'un prochain règlement international et de préparer un programme que les Gouvernements arrêteraient assez tôt pour qu'il pût être sérieusement étudié dans chaque pays. Ce Comité serait, en outre, chargé de proposer un mode d'organisation et de procédure pour la Conférence elle-même.

En foi de quoi, les Plénipotentiaires ont signé le présent acte et y ont apposé leurs cachets.

Fait à La Haye, le dix-huit octobre mil neuf cent sept, en un seul exemplaire qui sera déposé dans les archives du Gouvernement des Pays-Bas et dont les copies, certifiées conformes, seront délivrées à toutes les Puissances représentées à la Conférence.

Annexes

2. ACTS
OF THE SECOND PEACE CONFERENCE

(Signed on 18 October 1907)

[Translation][1]

---

1. The Hague Academy wishes to express appreciation to the Yale Law School and its Avalon Project (http://avalon.law.yale.edu/about/purpose.asp) for its kind permission to publish the English translations of the 1907 Hague Conventions, except Convention XII re-published from *The Laws of Armed Conflicts* by D. Schindler and J. Toman, Martinus Nijhoff, 1988, pp. 825-836.

I. CONVENTION FOR THE PACIFIC SETTLEMENT
OF INTERNATIONAL DISPUTES

His Majesty the German Emperor, King of Prussia ; the President of the United States of America; the President of the Argentine Republic; His Majesty the Emperor of Austria, King of Bohemia, etc., and Apostolic King of Hungary ; His Majesty the King of the Belgians; the President of the Republic of Bolivia; the President of the Republic of the United States of Brazil; His Royal Highness the Prince of Bulgaria; the President of the Republic of Chile; His Majesty the Emperor of China; the President of the Republic of Colombia; the Provisional Governor of the Republic of Cuba; His Majesty the King of Denmark; the President of the Dominican Republic; the President of the Republic of Ecuador; His Majesty the King of Spain; the President of the French Republic; His Majesty the King of the United Kingdom of Great Britain and Ireland and of the British Dominions beyond the Seas, Emperor of India; His Majesty the King of the Hellenes; the President of the Republic of Guatemala; the President of the Republic of Haiti; His Majesty the King of Italy; His Majesty the Emperor of Japan; His Royal Highness the Grand Duke of Luxembourg, Duke of Nassau; the President of the United States of Mexico; His Royal Highness the Prince of Montenegro; the President of the Republic of Nicaragua; His Majesty the King of Norway; the President of the Republic of Panama; the President of the Republic of Paraguay; Her Majesty the Queen of the Netherlands; the President of the Republic of Peru; His Imperial Majesty the Shah of Persia; His Majesty the King of Roumania; His Majesty the Emperor of All the Russias; the President of the Republic of Salvador; His Majesty the King of Servia; His Majesty the King of Siam; His Majesty the King of Sweden; the Swiss Federal Council; His Majesty the Emperor of the Ottomans; the President of the Oriental Republic of Uruguay; the President of the United States of Venezuela;

Animated by the sincere desire to work for the maintenance of general peace ;

Resolved to promote by all the efforts in their power the friendly settlement of international disputes;

Recognizing the solidarity uniting the members of the society of civilized nations;

Desirous of extending the empire of law and of strengthening the appreciation of international justice ;

Convinced that the permanent institution of a Tribunal of Arbitration accessible to all, in the midst of independent Powers, will contribute effectively to this result;

Having regard to the advantages attending the general and regular organization of the procedure of arbitration;

Sharing the opinion of the august initiator of the International Peace Conference that it is expedient to record in an International Agreement the principles of equity and right on which are based the security of States and the welfare of peoples;

Being desirous, with this object, of insuring the better working in practice of Commissions of Inquiry and Tribunals of Arbitration, and of facilitating recourse to arbitration in cases which allow of a summary procedure;

Have deemed it necessary to revise in certain particulars and to complete the work of the First Peace Conference for the pacific settlement of international disputes;

The High Contracting Parties have resolved to conclude a new Convention for this purpose, and have appointed the following as their Plenipotentiaries:

[List of Plenipotentiaries]

Who, after deposited their full powers, found in good and due form, have agreed upon the following:

PART I. THE MAINTENANCE OF GENERAL PEACE

Article 1

With a view to obviating as far as possible recourse to force in the relations between States, the Contracting Powers agree to use their best efforts to ensure the pacific settlement of international differences.

PART II. GOOD OFFICES AND MEDIATION

Article 2

In case of serious disagreement or dispute, before an appeal to arms, the Contracting Powers agree to have recourse, as far as circumstances allow, to the good offices or mediation of one or more friendly Powers.

Article 3

Independently of this recourse, the Contracting Powers deem it expedient and desirable that one or more Powers, strangers to the dispute, should, on their own initiative and as far as circumstances may alow, offer their good offices or mediation to the States at variance.

Powers strangers to the dispute have the right to offer good offices or mediation even during the course of hostilities.

The exercise of this right can never be regarded by either of the parties in dispute as an unfriendly act.

Article 4

The part of the mediator consists in reconciling the opposing claims and appeasing the feelings of resentment which may have arisen between the States at variance.

Article 5

The functions of the mediator are at an end when once it is declared, either by one of the parties to the dispute or by the mediator himself, that the means of reconciliation proposed by him are not accepted.

Article 6

Good offices and mediation undertaken either at the request of the parties in dispute or on the initiative of Powers strangers to the dispute have exclusively the character of advice, and never have binding force.

Article 7

The acceptance of mediation cannot, unless there be an agreement to the contrary, have the effect of interrupting, delaying, or hindering mobilization or other measures of preparation for war.

If it takes place after the commencement of hostilities, the military operations in progress are not interrupted in the absence of an agreement to the contrary.

Article 8

The Contracting Powers are agreed in recommending the application, when circumstances allow, of special mediation in the following form:

In case of a serious difference endangering peace, the States at variance choose respectively a Power, to which they intrust the mission of entering into direct communication with the Power chosen on the other side, with the object of preventing the rupture of pacific relations.

For the period of this mandate, the term of which, unless otherwise stipulated, cannot exceed thirty days, the States in dispute cease from all direct communication on the subject of the dispute, which is regarded as referred exclusively to the mediating Powers, which must use their best efforts to settle it.

In case of a definite rupture of pacific relations, these Powers are charged with the joint task of taking advantage of any opportunity to restore peace.

PART III. INTERNATIONAL COMMISSIONS OF INQUIRY

Article 9

In disputes of an international nature involving neither honour nor vital interests, and arising from a difference of opinion on points of facts, the Contracting Powers deem it expedient and desirable that the parties who have not been able to come to an agreement by means of diplomacy, should, as far as circumstances allow, institute an International Commission of Inquiry, to facilitate a solution of these disputes by elucidating the facts by means of an impartial and conscientious investigation.

Article 10

International Commissions of Inquiry are constituted by special agreement between the parties in dispute.

The Inquiry convention defines the facts to be examined; it determines the mode and time in which the Commission is to be formed and the extent of the powers of the Commissioners.

It also determines, if there is need, where the Commission is to sit, and whether it may remove to another place, the language the Commission shall use and the languages the use of which shall be authorized before it, as well as the date on which each party must deposit its statement of facts, and, generally speaking, all the conditions upon which the parties have agreed.

If the parties consider it necessary to appoint Assessors, the Convention of Inquiry shall determine the mode of their selection and the extent of their powers.

Article 11

If the Inquiry Convention has not determined where the Commission is to sit, it will sit at The Hague.

The place of meeting, once fixed, cannot be altered by the Commission except with the assent of the parties.

If the Inquiry Convention has not determined what languages are to be employed, the question shall be decided by the Commission.

Article 12

Unless an undertaking is made to the contrary, Commissions of Inquiry shall be formed in the manner determined by Articles 45 and 57 of the present Convention.

Article 13

Should one of the Commissioners or one of the Assessors, should there be any, either die, or resign, or be unable for any reason whatever to discharge his functions, the same procedure is followed for filling the vacancy as was followed for appointing him.

Article 14

The parties are entitled to appoint special agents to attend the Commission of Inquiry, whose duty it is to represent them and to act as intermediaries between them and the Commission.

They are further authorized to engage counsel or advocates, appointed by themselves, to state their case and uphold their interests before the Commission.

Article 15

The International Bureau of the Permanent Court of Arbitration acts as registry for the Commissions which sit at The Hague, and shall place its offices and staff at the disposal of the Contracting Powers for the use of the Commission of Inquiry.

Article 16

If the Commission meets elsewhere than at The Hague, it appoints a Secretary-General, whose office serves as registry.

It is the function of the registry, under the control of the President, to make the necessary arrangements for the sittings of the Commission, the preparation of the Minutes, and, while the inquiry lasts, for the charge of the archives, which shall subsequently be transferred to the International Bureau at The Hague.

Article 17

In order to facilitate the constitution and working of Commissions of Inquiry, the Contracting Powers recommend the following rules, which shall be applicable to the inquiry procedure in so far as the parties do not adopt other rules.

Article 18

The Commission shall settle the details of the procedure not covered by the special Inquiry Convention or the present Convention, and shall arrange all the formalities required for dealing with the evidence.

Article 19

On the inquiry both sides must be heard.

At the dates fixed, each party communicates to the Commission and to the other party the statements of facts, if any, and, in all cases, the instruments, papers, and documents which it considers useful for ascertaining the truth, as well as the list of witnesses and experts whose evidence it wishes to be heard.

Article 20

The Commission is entitled, with the assent of the Powers, to move temporarily to any place where it considers it may be useful to have recourse to this means of inquiry or to send one or more of its members. Permission must be obtained from the State on whose territory it is proposed to hold the inquiry.

Article 21

Every investigation, and every examination of a locality, must be made in the presence of the agents and counsel of the parties or after they have been duly summoned.

Article 22

The Commission is entitled to ask from either party for such explanations and information as it considers necessary.

Article 23

The parties undertake to supply the Commission of Inquiry, as fully as they may think possible, with all means and facilities necessary to enable it to become completely acquainted with, and to accurately understand, the facts in question.

They undertake to make use of the means at their disposal, under their municipal law, to insure the appearance of the witnesses or experts who are in their territory and have been summoned before the Commission.

If the witnesses or experts are unable to appear before the Commission, the parties will arrange for their evidence to be taken before the qualified officials of their own country.

Article 24

For all notices to be served by the Commission in the territory of a third Contracting Power, the Commission shall apply direct to the Government of the said Power. The same rule applies in the case of steps being taken on the spot to procure evidence.

The requests for this purpose are to be executed so far as the means at the disposal of the Power applied to under its municipal law allow. They cannot be rejected unless the Power in question considers they are calculated to impair its sovereign rights or its safety.

The Commission will equally be always entitled to act through the Power on whose territory it sits.

Article 25

The witnesses and experts are summoned on the request of the parties or by the Commission of its own motion, and, in every case, through the Government of the State in whose territory they are.

The witnesses are heard in succession and separately in the presence of the agents and counsel, and in the order fixed by the Commission.

Article 26

The examination of witnesses is conducted by the President.

The members of the Commission may however put to each witness questions which they consider likely to throw light on and complete his evidence, or get information on any point concerning the witness within the limits of what is necessary in order to get at the truth.

The agents and counsel of the parties may not interrupt the witness when he is making his statement, nor put any direct question to him, but they may ask the President to put such additional questions to the witness as they think expedient.

Article 27

The witness must give his evidence without being allowed to read any written draft. He may, however, be permitted by the President to consult notes or documents if the nature of the facts referred to necessitates their employment.

Article 28

A Minute of the evidence of the witness is drawn up forthwith and read to the witness. The latter may make such alterations and additions as he thinks necessary, which will be recorded at the end of his statement.

When the whole of his statement has been read to the witness, he is asked to sign it.

Article 29

The agents are authorized, in the course of or at the close of the inquiry, to present in writing to the Commission and to the other party such statements, requisitions, or summaries of the facts as they consider useful for ascertaining the truth.

Article 30

The Commission considers its decisions in private and the proceedings are secret.

All questions are decided by a majority of the members of the Commission.

If a member declines to vote, the fact must be recorded in the Minutes.

Article 31

The sittings of the Commission are not public, nor the Minutes and documents connected with the inquiry published except in virtue of a decision of the Commission taken with the consent of the parties.

Article 32

After the parties have presented all the explanations and evidence, and the witnesses have all been heard, the President declares the inquiry terminated, and the Commission adjourns to deliberate and to draw up its Report.

Article 33

The Report is signed by all the members of the Commission.

If one of the members refuses to sign, the fact is mentioned; but the validity of the Report is not affected.

Article 34

The Report of the Commission is read at a public sitting, the agents and counsel of the parties being present or duly summoned.

A copy of the Report is given to each party.

Article 35

The Report of the Commission is limited to a statement of facts, and has in no way the character of an Award. It leaves to the parties entire freedom as to the effect to be given to the statement.

Article 36

Each party pays its own expenses and an equal share of the expenses incurred by the Commission.

PART IV. INTERNATIONAL ARBITRATION

Chapter I. The System of Arbitration

Article 37

International arbitration has for its object the settlement of disputes between States by Judges of their own choice and on the basis of respect for law.

Recourse to arbitration implies an engagement to submit in good faith to the Award.

Article 38

In questions of a legal nature, and especially in the interpretation or application of International Conventions, arbitration is recognized by the Contracting Powers as the most effective, and, at the same time, the most equitable means of settling disputes which diplomacy has failed to settle.

Consequently, it would be desirable that, in disputes about the above-mentioned questions, the Contracting Powers should, if the case arose, have recourse to arbitration, in so far as circumstances permit.

Article 39

The Arbitration Convention is concluded for questions already existing or for questions which may arise eventually.

It may embrace any dispute or only disputes of a certain category.

Article 40

Independently of general or private Treaties expressly stipulating recourse to arbitration as obligatory on the Contracting Powers, the said Powers reserve to themselves the right of concluding new Agreements, general or particular, with a view to extending compulsory arbitration to all cases which they may consider it possible to submit to it.

Chapter II. The Permanent Court of Arbitration

Article 41

With the object of facilitating an immediate recourse to arbitration for international differences, which it has not been possible to settle by diplomacy, the Contracting Powers undertake to maintain the Permanent Court of Arbitration, as established by the First Peace Conference, accessible at all times, and operating, unless otherwise stipulated by the parties, in accordance with the rules of procedure inserted in the present Convention.

Article 42

The Permanent Court is competent for all arbitration cases, unless the parties agree to institute a special Tribunal.

Article 43

The Permanent Court sits at The Hague.

An International Bureau serves as registry for the Court. It is the channel for communications relative to the meetings of the Court; it has charge of the archives and conducts all the administrative business.

The Contracting Powers undertake to communicate to the Bureau, as soon as possible, a certified copy of any conditions of arbitration arrived at between them and of any Award concerning them delivered by a special Tribunal.

They likewise undertake to communicate to the Bureau the laws, regulations, and documents eventually showing the execution of the Awards given by the Court.

Article 44

Each Contracting Power selects four persons at the most, of known competency in questions of international law, of the highest moral reputation, and disposed to accept the duties of Arbitrator.

The persons thus elected are inscribed, as Members of the Court, in a list which shall be notified to all the Contracting Powers by the Bureau.

Any alteration in the list of Arbitrators is brought by the Bureau to the knowledge of the Contracting Powers.

Two or more Powers may agree on the selection in common of one or more Members.

The same person can be selected by different Powers. The Members of the Court are appointed for a term of six years. These appointments are renewable.

Should a Member of the Court die or resign, the same procedure is followed for filling the vacancy as was followed for appointing him. In this case the appointment is made for a fresh period of six years.

Article 45

When the Contracting Powers wish to have recourse to the Permanent Court for the settlement of a difference which has arisen between them, the Arbitrators called upon to form the Tribunal with jurisdiction to decide this difference must be chosen from the general list of Members of the Court.

Failing the direct agreement of the parties on the composition of the Arbitration Tribunal, the following course shall be pursued:

Each party appoints two Arbitrators, of whom one only can be its national or chosen from among the persons selected by it as Members of the Permanent Court. These Arbitrators together choose an Umpire.

If the votes are equally divided, the choice of the Umpire is intrusted to a third Power, selected by the parties by common accord.

If an agreement is not arrived at on this subject each party selects a different Power, and the choice of the Umpire is made in concert by the Powers thus selected.

If, within two months' time, these two Powers cannot come to an agreement, each of them presents two candidates taken from the list of Members of the Permanent Court, exclusive of the members selected by the parties and not being nationals of either of them. Drawing lots determines which of the candidates thus presented shall be Umpire.

Article 46

The Tribunal being thus composed, the parties notify to the Bureau their determination to have recourse to the Court, the text of their "Compromis", and the names of the Arbitrators.

The Bureau communicates without delay to each Arbitrator the "Compromis", and the names of the other members of the Tribunal.

The Tribunal assembles at the date fixed by the parties. The Bureau makes the necessary arrangements for the meeting.

The members of the Tribunal, in the exercise of their duties and out of their own country, enjoy diplomatic privileges and immunities.

Article 47

The Bureau is authorized to place its offices and staff at the disposal of the Contracting Powers for the use of any special Board of Arbitration.

The jurisdiction of the Permanent Court may, within the conditions laid down in the regulations, be extended to disputes between non-Contracting Powers or between Contracting Powers and non-Contracting Powers, if the parties are agreed on recourse to this Tribunal.

Article 48

The Contracting Powers consider it their duty, if a serious dispute threatens to break out between two or more of them, to remind these latter that the Permanent Court is open to them.

Consequently, they declare that the fact of reminding the parties at variance of the provisions of the present Convention, and the advice given to them, in the highest interests of peace, to have recourse to the Permanent Court, can only be regarded as friendly actions.

In case of dispute between two Powers, one of them can always address to the International Bureau a note containing a declaration that it would be ready to submit the dispute to arbitration.

The Bureau must at once inform the other Power of the declaration.

Article 49

The Permanent Administrative Council, composed of the Diplomatic Representatives of the Contracting Powers accredited to The Hague and of the Netherland Minister for Foreign Affairs, who will act as President, is charged with the direction and control of the International Bureau.

The Council settles its rules of procedure and all other necessary regulations.

It decides all questions of administration which may arise with regard to the operations of the Court.

It has entire control over the appointment, suspension, or dismissal of the officials and employees of the Bureau.

It fixes the payments and salaries, and controls the general expenditure.

At meetings duly summoned the presence of nine members is sufficient to render valid the discussions of the Council. The decisions are taken by a majority of votes.

The Council communicates to the Contracting Powers without delay the regulations adopted by it. It furnishes them with an annual Report on the labours of the Court, the working of the administration, and the expenditure. The Report likewise contains a résumé of what is important in the documents comunicated to the Bureau by the Powers in virtue of Article 43, paragraphs 3 and 4.

Article 50

The expenses of the Bureau shall be borne by the Contracting Powers in the proportion fixed for the International Bureau of the Universal Postal Union.

The expenses to be charged to the adhering Powers shall be reckoned from the date on which their adhesion comes into force.

Chapter III. Arbitration Procedure

Article 51

With a view to encouraging the development of arbritation, the Contracting Powers have agreed on the following rules, which are applicable to arbitration procedure, unless other rules have been agreed on by the parties.

Article 52

The Powers which have recourse to arbitration sign a "Compromis", in which the subject of the dispute is clearly defined, the time allowed for appointing Arbitrators, the form, order, and time in which the communication referred to in Article 63 must be made, and the amount of the sum which each party must deposit in advance to defray the expenses.

The "Compromis" likewise defines, if there is occasion, the manner of appointing Arbitrators, any special powers which may eventually belong to the Tribunal, where it shall meet, the language it shall use, and the languages the employment of which shall be authorized before it, and, generally speaking, all the conditions on which the parties are agreed.

Article 53

The Permanent Court is competent to settle the "Compromis", if the parties are agreed to have recourse to it for the purpose.

It is similarly competent, even if the request is only made by one of the parties, when all attempts to reach an understanding through the diplomatic channel have failed, in the case of:

1. A dispute covered by a general Treaty of Arbitration concluded or renewed after the present Convention has come into force, and providing for a "Compromis" in all disputes and not either explicitly or implicitly excluding the settlement of the "Compromis" from the competence of the Court. Recourse cannot, however, be had to the Court if the other party declares that in its opinion the dispute does not belong to the category of disputes which can be submitted to compulsory arbitration, unless the Treaty of Arbitration confers upon the Arbitration Tribunal the power of deciding this preliminary question.

2. A dispute arising from contract debts claimed from one Power by another Power as due to its nationals, and for the settlement of which the offer of arbitration has been accepted. This arrangement is not applicable if acceptance is subject to the condition that the "Compromis" should be settled in some other way.

Article 54

In the cases contemplated in the preceding Article, the "Compromis" shall be settled by a Commission consisting of five members selected in the manner arranged for in Article 45, paragraphs 3 to 6.

The fifth member is President of the Commission ex officio.

Article 55

The duties of Arbitrator may be conferred on one Arbitrator alone or on several Arbitrators selected by the parties as they please, or chosen by them from the Members of the Permanent Court of Arbitration established by the present Convention.

Failing the constitution of the Tribunal by direct agreement between the parties, the course referred to in Article 45, paragraphs 3 to 6, is followed.

Article 56

When a Sovereign or the Chief of a State is chosen as Arbitrator, the arbitration procedure is settled by him.

Article 57

The Umpire is President of the Tribunal ex officio.

When the Tribunal does not include an Umpire, it appoints its own President.

Article 58

When the "Compromis" is settled by a Commission, as contemplated in Article 54, and in the absence of an agreement to the contrary, the Commission itself shall form the Arbitration Tribunal.

Article 59

Should one of the Arbitrators either die, retire, or be unable for any reason whatever to discharge his functions, the same procedure is followed for filling the vacancy as was followed for appointing him.

Article 60

The Tribunal sits at The Hague, unless some other place is selected by the parties.

The Tribunal can only sit in the territory of a third Power with the latter's consent.

The place of meeting once fixed cannot be altered by the Tribunal, except with the consent of the parties.

Article 61

If the question as to what languages are to be used has not been settled by the "Compromis", it shall be decided by the Tribunal.

Article 62

The parties are entitled to appoint special agents to attend the Tribunal to act as intermediaries between themselves and the Tribunal.

They are further authorized to retain for the defence of their rights and interests before the Tribunal counsel or advocates appointed by themselves for this purpose.

The Members of the Permanent Court may not act as agents, counsel, or advocates except on behalf of the Power which appointed them Members of the Court.

Article 63

As a general rule, arbitration procedure comprises two distinct phases: pleadings and oral discussions.

The pleadings consist in the communication by the respective agents to the members of the Tribunal and the opposite party of cases, counter-cases, and, if necessary, of replies; the parties annex thereto all papers and documents called for in the case. This communication shall be made either directly or through the intermediary of the International Bureau, in the order and within the time fixed by the "Compromis".

The time fixed by the "Compromis" may be extended by mutual agreement by the parties, or by the Tribunal when the latter considers it necessary for the purpose of reaching a just decision.

The discussions consists in the oral development before the Tribunal of the arguments of the parties.

Article 64

A certified copy of every document produced by one party must be communicated to the other party.

Article 65

Unless special circumstances arise, the Tribunal does not meet until the pleadings are closed.

Article 66

The discussions are under the control of the President.

They are only public if it be so decided by the Tribunal, with the assent of the parties.

They are recorded in minutes drawn up by the Secretaries appointed by the President. These minutes are signed by the President and by one of the Secretaries and alone have an authentic character.

Article 67

After the close of the pleadings, the Tribunal is entitled to refuse discussion of all new papers or documents which one of the parties may wish to submit to it without the consent of the other party.

Article 68

The Tribunal is free to take into consideration new papers of documents to which its attention may be drawn by the agents or counsel of the parties.

In this case, the Tribunal has the right to require the production of these papers or documents, but is obliged to make them known to the opposite party.

Article 69

The Tribunal can, besides, require from the agents of the parties the production of all papers, and can demand all necessary explanations. In case of refusal the Tribunal takes note of it.

Article 70

The agents and the counsel of the parties are authorized to present orally to the Tribunal all the arguments they may consider expedient in defence of their case.

Article 71

They are entitled to raise objections and points. The decisions of the Tribunal on these points are final and cannot form the subject of any subsequent discussion.

Article 72

The members of the Tribunal are entitled to put questions to the agents and counsel of the parties, and to ask them for explanations on doubtful points.

Neither the questions put, nor the remarks made by members of the Tribunal in the course of the discussions, can be regarded as an expression of opinion by the Tribunal in general or by its members in particular.

Article 73

The Tribunal is authorized to declare its competence in interpreting the "Compromis", as well as the other Treaties which may be invoked, and in applying the principles of law.

Article 74

The Tribunal is entitled to issue rules of procedure for the conduct of the case, to decide the forms, order, and time in which each party must conclude its arguments, and to arrange all the formalities required for dealing with the evidence.

Article 75

The parties undertake to supply the Tribunal, as fully as they consider possible, with all the information required for deciding the case.

Article 76

For all notices which the Tribunal has to serve in the territory of a third Contracting Power, the Tribunal shall apply direct to the Government of that Power. The same rule applies in the case of steps being taken to procure evidence on the spot.

The requests for this purpose are to be executed as far as the means at the disposal of the Power applied to under its municipal law allow. They cannot be rejected unless the Power in question considers them calculated to impair its own sovereign rights or its safety.

The Court will equally be always entitled to act through the Power on whose territory it sits.

Article 77

When the agents and counsel of the parties have submitted all the explanations and evidence in support of their case the President shall declare the discussion closed.

Article 78

The Tribunal considers its decisions in private and the proceedings remain secret.

All questions are decided by a majority of the members of the Tribunal.

Article 79

The Award must give the reasons on which it is based. It contains the names of the Arbitrators; it is signed by the President and Registrar or by the Secretary acting as Registrar.

Article 80

The Award is read out in public sitting, the agents and counsel of the parties being present or duly summoned to attend.

Article 81

The Award, duly pronounced and notified to the agents of the parties, settles the dispute definitively and without appeal.

Article 82

Any dispute arising between the parties as to the interpretation and execution of the Award shall, in the absence of an Agreement to the contrary, be submitted to the Tribunal which pronounced it.

Article 83

The parties can reserve in the "Compromis" the right to demand the revision of the Award.

In this case and unless there be an Agreement to the contrary, the demand must be addressed to the Tribunal which pronounced the Award. It can only be made on the ground of the discovery of some new fact calculated to exercise a decisive influence upon the Award and which was unknown to the Tribunal and to the party which demanded the revision at the time the discussion was closed.

Proceedings for revision can only be instituted by a decision of the Tribunal expressly recording the existence of the new fact, recognizing in it the character described in the preceding paragraph, and declaring the demand admissible on this ground.

The "Compromis" fixes the period within which the demand for revision must be made.

Article 84

The Award is not binding except on the parties in dispute.

When it concerns the interpretation of a Convention to which Powers other than those in dispute are parties, they shall inform all the Signatory Powers in good time. Each of these Powers is entitled to intervene in the case. If one or more avail themselves of this right, the interpretation contained in the Award is equally binding on them.

Article 85

Each party pays its own expenses and an equal share of the expenses of the Tribunal.

Chapter IV. Arbitration by Summary Procedure

Article 86

With a view to facilitating the working of the system of arbitration in disputes admitting of a summary procedure, the Contracting Powers adopt the following rules, which shall be observed in the absence of other arrangements and subject to the reservation that the provisions of Chapter III apply so far as may be.

Article 87

Each of the parties in dispute appoints an Arbitrator. The two Arbitrators thus selected choose an Umpire. If they do not agree on this point, each of them proposes two candidates taken from the general list of the Members of the Permanent Court exclusive of the members appointed by either of the parties and not being nationals of either of them; which of the candidates thus proposed shall be the Umpire is determined by lot.

The Umpire presides over the Tribunal, which gives its decisions by a majority of votes.

Article 88

In the absence of any previous agreement the Tribunal, as soon as it is formed, settles the time within which the two parties must submit their respective cases to it.

Article 89

Each party is represented before the Tribunal by an agent, who serves as intermediary between the Tribunal and the Government who appointed him.

Article 90

The proceedings are conducted exclusively in writing. Each party, however, is entitled to ask that witnesses and experts should be called. The Tribunal has, for its part, the right to demand oral explanations from the agents of the two parties, as well as from the experts and witnesses whose appearance in Court it may consider useful.

PART V. FINAL PROVISIONS

Article 91

The present Convention, duly ratified, shall replace, as between the Contracting Powers, the Convention for the Pacific Settlement of International Disputes of the 29th July, 1899.

Article 92

The present Convention shall be ratified as soon as possible.

The ratifications shall be deposited at The Hague.

The first deposit of ratifications shall be recorded in a procès-verbal signed by the Representatives of the Powers which take part therein and by the Netherland Minister for Foreign Affairs.

The subsequent deposits of ratifications shall be made by means of a written notification, addressed to the Netherland Government and accompanied by the instrument of ratification.

A duly certified copy of the procès-verbal relative to the first deposit of ratifications, of the notifications mentioned in the preceding paragraph, and of the instruments of ratification, shall be immediately sent by the Netherland Government, through the diplomatic channel, to the Powers invited to the Second Peace Conference, as well as to those Powers which have adhered to the Convention. In the cases contemplated in the preceding paragraph, the said Government shall at the same time inform the Powers of the date on which it received the notification.

Article 93

Non-Signatory Powers which have been invited to the Second Peace Conference may adhere to the present Convention.

The Power which desires to adhere notifies its intention in writing to the Netherland Government, forwarding to it the act of adhesion, which shall be deposited in the archives of the said Government.

This Government shall immediately forward to all the other Powers invited to the Second Peace Conference a duly certified copy of the notification as well as of the act of adhesion, mentioning the date on which it received the notification.

Article 94

The conditions on which the Powers which have not been invited to the Second Peace Conference may adhere to the present Convention shall form the subject of a subsequent Agreement between the Contracting Powers.

Article 95

The present Convention shall take effect, in the case of the Powers which were not a party to the first deposit of ratifications, sixty days after the date of the procès-verbal of this deposit, and, in the case of the Powers which ratify subsequently or which adhere, sixty days after the notification of their ratification or of their adhesion has been received by the Netherland Government.

Article 96

In the event of one of the Contracting Parties wishing to denounce the present Convention, the denunciation shall be notified in writing to the Netherland Government, which shall immediately communicate a duly certified copy of the notification to all the other Powers informing them of the date on which it was received.

The denunciation shall only have effect in regard to the notifying Power, and one year after the notification has reached the Netherland Government.

Article 97

A register kept by the Netherland Minister for Foreign Affairs shall give the date of the deposit of ratifications effected in virtue of Article 92, paragraphs 3 and 4, as well as the date on which the notifications of adhesion (Article 93, paragraph 2) or of denunciation (Article 96, paragraph 1) have been received.

Each Contracting Power is entitled to have access to this register and to be supplied with duly certified extracts from it.

In faith whereof the Plenipotentiaries have appended their signatures to the present Convention.

Done at The Hague, the 18th October 1907, in a single copy, which shall remain deposited in the archives of the Netherland Government, and duly certified copies of which shall be sent, through the diplomatic channel, to the Contracting Powers.

II. CONVENTION RESPECTING THE LIMITATION OF THE EMPLOYMENT OF FORCE FOR THE RECOVERY OF CONTRACT DEBTS

[For the participating States, see Convention I, supra p. 399]

Article 1

The Contracting Powers agree not to have recourse to armed force for the recovery of contract debts claimed from the Government of one country by the Government of another country as being due to its nationals.

This undertaking is, however, not applicable when the debtor State refuses or neglects to reply to an offer of arbitration, or, after accepting the offer, prevents any compromis from being agreed on, or, after the arbitration, fails to submit to the award.

Article 2

It is further agreed that the arbitration mentioned in paragraph 2 of the foregoing Article shall be subject to the procedure laid down in Part IV, Chapter III, of The Hague Convention for the Pacific Settlement of International Disputes. The award shall determine, except where otherwise agreed between the parties, the validity of the claim, the amount of the debt, and the time and mode of payment.

Article 3

The present Convention shall be ratified as soon as possible.

The ratifications shall be deposited at The Hague.

The first deposit of ratifications shall be recorded in a procès-verbal signed by the Representatives of the Powers taking part therein and by the Netherland Minister for Foreign Affairs.

The subsequent deposits of ratifications shall be made by means of a written notification addressed to the Netherland Government and accompanied by the instrument of ratification.

A duly certified copy of the procès-verbal relative to the first deposit of ratifications, of the notifications mentioned in the preceding paragraph, as well as of the instruments of ratification, shall be sent immediately by the Netherland Government, through the diplomatic channel, to the Powers invited to the Second Peace Conference, as well as to the other Powers which have adhered to the Convention. In the cases contemplated in the preceding paragraph, the said Government shall inform them at the same time of the date on which it received the notification.

Article 4

Non-Signatory Powers may adhere to the present Convention.

The Power which desires to adhere notifies its intention in writing to the

Netherland Government, forwarding to it the act of adhesion, which shall be deposited in the archives of the said Government.

The said Government shall forward immediately to all the other Powers invited to the Second Peace Conference a duly certified copy of the notification, as well as of the act of adhesion, mentioning the date on which it received the notification.

Article 5

The present Convention shall come into force, in the case of the Powers which were a party to the first deposit of ratifications, sixty days after the date of the procès-verbal of this deposit, in the case of the Powers which ratify subsequently or which adhere, sixty days after the notification of their ratification or of their adhesion has been received by the Netherland Government.

Article 6

In the event of one of the Contracting Powers wishing to denounce the present Convention, the denunciation shall be notified in writing to the Netherland Government, which shall immediately communicate a duly certified copy of the notification to all the other Powers, informing them at the same time of the date on which it was received.

The denunciation shall only have effect in regard to the notifying Power, and one year after the notification has reached the Netherland Government.

Article 7

A register kept by the Netherland Ministry for Foreign Affairs shall give the date of the deposit of ratifications made in virtue of Article 3, paragraphs 3 and 4, as well as the date on which the notifications of adhesion (Article 4, paragraph 2) or of denunciation (Article 6, paragraph 1) were received.

Each Contracting Power is entitled to have access to this register and to be supplied with duly certified extracts from it.

In faith whereof the Plenipotentiaries have appended their signatures to the present Convention.

Done at The Hague, the 18th October, 1907, in a single copy, which shall remain deposited in the archives of the Netherland Government, and duly certified copies of which shall be sent to the Contracting Powers through the diplomatic channel.

III. CONVENTION RELATIVE TO THE OPENING
OF HOSTILITIES

[For the participating States, see Convention I, supra p. 399]

Considering that it is important, in order to ensure the maintenance of pacific relations, that hostilities should not commence without previous warning;

That it is equally important that the existence of a state of war should be notified without delay to neutral Powers;

Being desirous of concluding a Convention to this effect, have appointed the following as their Plenipotentiaries:

[List of Plenipotentiaries]

Who, after depositing their full powers, found in good and due form, have agreed upon the following provisions:

Article 1

The Contracting Powers recognize that hostilities between themselves must not commence without previous and explicit warning, in the form either of a reasoned declaration of war or of an ultimatum with conditional declaration of war.

Article 2

The existence of a state of war must be notified to the neutral Powers without delay, and shall not take effect in regard to them until after the receipt of a notification, which may, however, be given by telegraph. Neutral Powers, nevertheless, cannot rely on the absence of notification if it is clearly established that they were in fact aware of the existence of a state of war.

Article 3

Article 1 of the present Convention shall take effect in case of war between two or more of the Contracting Powers.

Article 2 is binding as between a belligerent Power which is a party to the Convention and neutral Powers which are also parties to the Convention.

Article 4

The present Convention shall be ratified as soon as possible.

The ratifications shall be deposited at The Hague.

The first deposit of ratification shall be recorded in a procès-verbal signed by the Representatives of the Powers which take part therein and by the Netherland Minister for Foreign Affairs.

The subsequent deposits of ratifications shall be made by means of a written notification addressed to the Netherland Government and accompanied by the instrument of ratification.

A duly certified copy of the procès-verbal relative to the first deposit of ratifications, of the notifications mentioned in the preceding paragraph, as well as of the instruments of ratification, shall be at once sent by the Netherland Government through the diplomatic channel to the Powers invited to the Second Peace Conference, as well as to the other Powers which have adhered to the Convention. In the cases contemplated in the preceding paragraph, the said Government shall at the same time inform them of the date on which it received the notification.

Article 5

Non-Signatory Powers may adhere to the present Convention.

The Power which wishes to adhere notifies in writing its intention to the Netherland Government, forwarding to it the act of adhesion, which shall be deposited in the archives of the said Government.

The said Government shall at once forward to all the other Powers a duly certified copy of the notification as well as of the act of adhesion, stating the date on which it received the notification.

Article 6

The present Convention shall come into force, in the case of the Powers which were a party to the first deposit of ratifications, sixty days after the date of the procès-verbal of that deposit, and, in the case of the Powers which ratify subsequently or which adhere, sixty days after the notification of their ratification or of their adhesion has been received by the Netherland Government.

Article 7

In the event of one of the High Contracting Parties wishing to denounce the present Convention, the denunciation shall be notified in writing to the Netherland Government, which shall at once communicate a duly certified copy of the notification to all the other Powers, informing them of the date on which it was received.

The denunciation shall only have effect in regard to the notifying Power, and one year after the notification has reached the Netherland Government.

Article 8

A register kept by the Netherland Ministry for Foreign Affairs shall give the date of the deposit of ratifications made in virtue of Article 4, paragraphs 3 and 4, as well as the date on which the notifications of adhesion (Article 5, paragraph 2) or of denunciation (Article 7, paragraph 1) have been received.

Each Contracting Power is entitled to have access to this register and to be supplied with duly certified extracts from it.

In faith whereof the Plenipotentiaries have appended their signatures to the present Convention.

Done at The Hague, the 18th October, 1907, in a single copy, which shall remain deposited in the archives of the Netherland Government, and duly certified copies of which shall be sent, through the diplomatic channel, to the Powers which have been invited to the Second Peace Conference.

IV. CONVENTION RESPECTING THE LAWS
AND CUSTOMS OF WAR ON LAND

[For the participating States, see Convention I, supra p. 399]

Seeing that, while seeking means to preserve peace and prevent armed conflicts between nations, it is likewise necessary to bear in mind the case where the appeal to arms has been brought about by events which their care was unable to avert;

Animated by the desire to serve, even in this extreme case, the interests of humanity and the ever progressive needs of civilization;

Thinking it important, with this object, to revise the general laws and customs of war, either with a view to defining them with greater precision or to confining them within such limits as would mitigate their severity as far as possible;

Have deemed it necessary to complete and explain in certain particulars the work of the First Peace Conference, which, following on the Brussels Conference of 1874, and inspired by the ideas dictated by a wise and generous forethought, adopted provisions intended to define and govern the usages of war on land.

According to the views of the High Contracting Parties, these provisions, the wording of which has been inspired by the desire to diminish the evils of war, as far as military requirements permit, are intended to serve as a general rule of conduct for the belligerents in their mutual relations and in their relations with the inhabitants.

It has not, however, been found possible at present to concert regulations covering all the circumstances which arise in practice;

On the other hand, the High Contracting Parties clearly do not intend that unforeseen cases should, in the absence of a written undertaking, be left to the arbitrary judgment of military commanders.

Until a more complete code of the laws of war has been issued, the High Contracting Parties deem it expedient to declare that, in cases not included in the Regulations adopted by them, the inhabitants and the belligerents remain under the protection and the rule of the principles of the law of nations, as they result from the usages established among civilized peoples, from the laws of humanity, and the dictates of the public conscience.

They declare that it is in this sense especially that Articles 1 and 2 of the Regulations adopted must be understood.

The High Contracting Parties, wishing to conclude a fresh Convention to this effect, have appointed the following as their Plenipotentiaries:

[List of Plenipotentiaries]

Who, after having deposited their full powers, found in good and due form, have agreed upon the following:

Article 1

The Contracting Powers shall issue instructions to their armed land forces which shall be in conformity with the Regulations respecting the laws and customs of war on land, annexed to the present Convention.

Article 2

The provisions contained in the Regulations referred to in Article 1, as well as in the present Convention, do not apply except between Contracting Powers, and then only if all the belligerents are parties to the Convention.

Article 3

A belligerent party which violates the provisions of the said Regulations shall, if the case demands, be liable to pay compensation It shall be responsible for all acts committed by persons forming part of its armed forces.

Article 4

The present Convention, duly ratified, shall as between the Contracting Powers, be substituted for the Convention of 29 July 1899, respecting the laws and customs of war on land.

The Convention of 1899 remains in force as between the Powers which signed it, and which do not also ratify the present Convention.

Article 5

The present Convention shall be ratified as soon as possible.

The ratifications shall be deposited at The Hague.

The first deposit of ratifications shall be recorded in a procès-verbal signed by the Representatives of the Powers which take part therein and by the Netherlands Minister for Foreign Affairs.

The subsequent deposits of ratifications shall be made by means of a written notification, addressed to the Netherlands Government and accompanied by the instrument of ratification.

A duly certified copy of the procès-verbal relative to the first deposit of ratifications, of the notifications mentioned in the preceding paragraph, as well as of the instruments of ratification, shall be immediately sent by the Netherlands Government, through the diplomatic channel, to the Powers invited to the Second Peace Conference, as well as to the other Powers which have adhered to the Convention. In the cases contemplated in the preceding paragraph the said Government shall at the same time inform them of the date on which it received the notification.

Article 6

Non-Signatory Powers may adhere to the present Convention.

The Power which desires to adhere notifies in writing its intention to the Netherlands Government, forwarding to it the act of adhesion, which shall be deposited in the archives of the said Government.

This Government shall at once transmit to all the other Powers a duly certified copy of the notification as well as of the act of adhesion, mentioning the date on which it received the notification.

Article 7

The present Convention shall come into force, in the case of the Powers which were a party to the first deposit of ratifications, sixty days after the date of the procès-verbal of this deposit, and, in the case of the Powers which ratify subsequently or which adhere, sixty days after the notification of their ratification or of their adhesion has been received by the Netherlands Government.

Article 8

In the event of one of the Contracting Powers wishing to denounce the present Convention, the denunciation shall be notified in writing to the Netherlands Government, which shall at once communicate a duly certified copy of the notification to all the other Powers, informing them of the date on which it was received.

The denunciation shall only have effect in regard to the notifying Power, and one year after the notification has reached the Netherlands Government.

Article 9

A register kept by the Netherlands Ministry for Foreign Affairs shall give the date of the deposit of ratifications made in virtue of Article 5, paragraphs 3 and 4, as well as the date on which the notifications of adhesion (Article 6, paragraph 2), or of denunciation (Article 8, paragraph 1) were received.

Each Contracting Power is entitled to have access to this register and to be supplied with duly certified extracts.

In faith whereof the Plenipotentiaries have appended their signatures to the present Convention.

Done at The Hague 18 October 1907, in a single copy, which shall remain deposited in the archives of the Netherlands Government, and duly certified copies of which shall be sent, through the diplomatic channel to the Powers which have been invited to the Second Peace Conference.

Annex to the Convention

REGULATIONS RESPECTING THE LAWS AND CUSTOMS OF WAR ON LAND

Section I. On Belligerents

Chapter I. The Qualifications of Belligerents

Article 1

The laws, rights, and duties of war apply not only to armies, but also to militia and volunteer corps fulfilling the following conditions:

To be commanded by a person responsible for his subordinates;
To have a fixed distinctive emblem recognizable at a distance;
To carry arms openly; and
To conduct their operations in accordance with the laws and customs of war.

In countries where militia or volunteer corps constitute the army, or form part of it, they are included under the denomination "army".

Article 2

The inhabitants of a territory which has not been occupied, who, on the approach of the enemy, spontaneously take up arms to resist the invading troops without having had time to organize themselves in accordance with Article 1, shall be regarded as belligerents if they carry arms openly and if they respect the laws and customs of war.

Article 3

The armed forces of the belligerent parties may consist of combatants and non-combatants. In the case of capture by the enemy, both have a right to be treated as prisoners of war.

Chapter II. Prisoners of War

Article 4

Prisoners of war are in the power of the hostile Government, but not of the individuals or corps who capture them.

They must be humanely treated.

All their personal belongings, except arms, horses, and military papers, remain their property.

Article 5

Prisoners of war may be interned in a town, fortress, camp, or other place, and bound not to go beyond certain fixed limits, but they cannot be confined except as in indispensable measure of safety and only while the circumstances which necessitate the measure continue to exist.

Article 6

The State may utilize the labour of prisoners of war according to their rank and aptitude, officers excepted. The tasks shall not be excessive and shall have no connection with the operations of the war.

Prisoners may be authorized to work for the public service, for private persons, or on their own account.

Work done for the State is paid for at the rates in force for work of a similar kind done by soldiers of the national army, or, if there are none in force, at a rate according to the work executed.

When the work is for other branches of the public service or for private persons the conditions are settled in agreement with the military authorities.

The wages of the prisoners shall go towards improving their position, and the balance shall be paid them on their release, after deducting the cost of their maintenance.

Article 7

The Government into whose hands prisoners of war have fallen is charged with their maintenance.

In the absence of a special agreement between the belligerents, prisoners of war shall be treated as regards board, lodging, and clothing on the same footing as the troops of the Government who captured them.

Article 8

Prisoners of war shall be subject to the laws, regulations, and orders in force in the army of the State in whose power they are. Any act of insubordination justifies the adoption towards them of such measures of severity as may be considered necessary.

Escaped prisoners who are retaken before being able to rejoin their own army or before leaving the territory occupied by the army which captured them are liable to disciplinary punishment.

Prisoners who, after succeeding in escaping, are again taken prisoners, are not liable to any punishment on account of the previous flight.

Article 9

Every prisoner of war is bound to give, if he is questioned on the subject, his true name and rank, and if he infringes this rule, he is liable to have the advantages given to prisoners of his class curtailed

Article 10

Prisoners of war may be set at liberty on parole if the laws of their country allow, and, in such cases, they are bound, on their personal honour, scrupulously to fulfil, both towards their own Government and the Government by whom they were made prisoners, the engagements they have contracted.

In such cases their own Government is bound neither to require of nor accept from them any service incompatible with the parole given.

Article 11

A prisoner of war cannot be compelled to accept his liberty on parole; similarly the hostile Government is not obliged to accede to the request of the prisoner to be set at liberty on parole.

Article 12

Prisoners of war liberated on parole and recaptured bearing arms against the Government to whom they had pledged their honour, or against the allies of that Government, forfeit their right to be treated as prisoners of war, and can be brought before the courts.

Article 13

Individuals who follow an army without directly belonging to it, such as newspaper correspondents and reporters, sutlers and contractors, who fall into the enemy's hands and whom the latter thinks expedient to detain, are entitled to be treated as prisoners of war, provided they are in possession of a certificate from the military authorities of the army which they were accompanying.

Article 14

An inquiry office for prisoners of war is instituted on the commencement of hostilities in each of the belligerent States, and, when necessary, in neutral countries which have received belligerents in their territory. It is the function of this office to reply to all inquiries about the prisoners. It receives from the various services concerned full information respecting internments and transfers. releases on parole, exchanges, escapes, admissions into hospital, deaths, as well as other information necessary to enable it to make out and keep up to date an individual return for each prisoner of war. The office must state in this return the regimental number, name and surname, age, place of origin, rank, unit, wounds, date and place of capture, internment, wounding, and death, as well as any observations of a special character. The individual return shall be sent to the Government of the other belligerent after the conclusion of peace.

It is likewise the function of the inquiry office to receive and collect all objects of personal use, valuables, letters, etc., found on the field of battle or left by prisoners who have been released on parole, or exchanged, or who have escaped, or died in hospitals or ambulances, and to forward them to those concerned.

Article 15

Relief societies for prisoners of war, which are properly constituted in accordance with the laws of their country and with the object of serving as the channel for charitable effort shall receive from the belligerents, for themselves and their duly accredited agents every facility for the efficient performance of their humane task within the bounds imposed by military necessities and administrative regulations. Agents of these societies may be admitted to the places of internment for the purpose of distributing relief, as also to the halting places of repatriated prisoners, if furnished with a personal permit by the military authorities, and on giving an undertaking in writing to comply with all measures of order and police which the latter may issue.

Article 16

Inquiry offices enjoy the privilege of free postage. Letters, money orders, and valuables, as well as parcels by post, intended for prisoners of war, or dispatched by them, shall be exempt from all postal duties in the countries of origin and destination, as well as in the countries they pass through.

Presents and relief in kind for prisoners of war shall be admitted free of all import or other duties, as well as of payments for carriage by the State railways.

Article 17

Officers taken prisoners shall receive the same rate of pay as of officers of corresponding rank in the country where they are detained, the amount to be ultimately refunded by their own Government.

Article 18

Prisoners of war shall enjoy complete liberty in the exercise of their religion, including attendance at the services of whatever church they may belong to, on the sole condition that they comply with the measures of order and police issued by the military authorities.

Article 19

The wills of prisoners of war are received or drawn up in the same way as for soldiers of the national army.

The same rules shall be observed regarding death certificates as well as for the burial of prisoners of war, due regard being paid to their grade and rank.

Article 20

After the conclusion of peace, the repatriation of prisoners of war shall be carried out as quickly as possible.

Chapter III. The Sick and Wounded

Article 21

The obligations of belligerents with regard to the sick and wounded are governed by the Geneva Convention.

Section II. Hostilities

*Chapter I. Means of Injuring the Enemy,
Sieges, and Bombardments*

Article 22

The right of belligerents to adopt means of injuring the enemy is not unlimited.

Article 23

In addition to the prohibitions provided by special Conventions, it is especially forbidden:

To employ poison or poisoned weapons;

To kill or wound treacherously individuals belonging to the hostile nation or army;

To kill or wound an enemy who, having laid down his arms, or having no longer means of defence, has surrendered at discretion;

To declare that no quarter will be given;

To employ arms, projectiles, or material calculated to cause unnecessary suffering;

To make improper use of a flag of truce, of the national flag or of the military insignia and uniform of the enemy, as well as the distinctive badges of the Geneva Convention;

To destroy or seize the enemy's property, unless such destruction or seizure be imperatively demanded by the necessities of war;

To declare abolished, suspended, or inadmissible in a court of law the rights and actions of the nationals of the hostile party.

A belligerent is likewise forbidden to compel the nationals of the hostile party to take part in the operations of war directed against their own country, even if they were in the belligerent's service before the commencement of the war.

Article 24

Ruses of war and the employment of measures necessary for obtaining information about the enemy and the country are considered permissible.

Article 25

The attack or bombardment, by whatever means, of towns, villages, dwellings, or buildings which are undefended is prohibited.

Article 26

The officer in command of an attacking force must, before commencing a bombardment, except in cases of assault, do all in his power to warn the authorities.

Article 27

In sieges and bombardments all necessary steps must be taken to spare, as far as possible, buildings dedicated to religion, art, science, or charitable purposes, historic monuments, hospitals, and places where the sick and wounded are collected, provided they are not being used at the time for military purposes.

It is the duty of the besieged to indicate the presence of such buildings or places by distinctive and visible signs, which shall be notified to the enemy beforehand.

Article 28

The pillage of a town or place, even when taken by assault, is prohibited.

Chapter II. Spies

Article 29

A person can only be considered a spy when, acting clandestinely or on false pretences, he obtains or endeavours to obtain information in the zone of operations of a belligerent, with the intention of communicating it to the hostile party.

Thus, soldiers not wearing a disguise who have penetrated into the zone of operations of the hostile army, for the purpose of obtaining information, are not considered spies. Similarly, the following are not considered spies: Soldiers and civilians, carrying out their mission openly, entrusted with the delivery of despatches intended either for their own army or for the enemy's army. To this class belong likewise persons sent in balloons for the purpose of carrying despatches and, generally, of maintaining communications between the different parts of an army or a territory.

Article 30

A spy taken in the act shall not be punished without previous trial.

Article 31

A spy who, after rejoining the army to which he belongs, is subsequently captured by the enemy, is treated as a prisoner of war, and incurs no responsibility for his previous acts of espionage.

Chapter III. Flags of Truce

Article 32

A person is regarded as a parlementaire who has been authorized by one of the belligerents to enter into communication with the other, and who advances bearing a white flag. He has a right to inviolability, as well as the trumpeter, bugler or drummer, the flag-bearer and interpreter who may accompany him.

Article 33

The commander to whom a parlementaire is sent is not in all cases obliged to receive him.

He may take all the necessary steps to prevent the parlementaire taking advantage of his mission to obtain information.

In case of abuse, he has the right to detain the parlementaire temporarily.

Article 34

The parlementaire loses his rights of inviolability if it is proved in a clear and incontestable manner that he has taken advantage of his privileged position to provoke or commit an act of treason.

Chapter IV. Capitulations

Article 35

Capitulations agreed upon between the Contracting Parties must take into account the rules of military honour.

Once settled, they must be scrupulously observed by both parties.

Chapter V. Armistices

Article 36

An armistice suspends military operations by mutual agreement between the belligerent parties. If its duration is not defined, the belligerent parties may resume operations at any time, provided always that the enemy is warned within the time agreed upon, in accordance with the terms of the armistice.

Article 37

An armistice may be general or local. The first suspends the military operations of the belligerent States everywhere; the second only between certain fractions of the belligerent armies and within a fixed radius.

Article 38

An armistice must be notified officially and in good time to the competent authorities and to the troops. Hostilities are suspended immediately after the notification, or on the date fixed.

Article 39

It rests with the Contracting Parties to settle, in the terms of the armistice, what communications may be held in the theatre of war with the inhabitants and between the inhabitants of one belligerent State and those of the other.

Article 40

Any serious violation of the armistice by one of the parties gives the other party the right of denouncing it, and even, in cases of urgency, of recommencing hostilities immediately.

Article 41

A violation of the terms of the armistice by private persons acting on their own initiative only entitles the injured party to demand the punishment of the offenders or, if necessary, compensation for the losses sustained.

SECTION III. MILITARY AUTHORITY OVER THE TERRITORY OF THE HOSTILE STATE

Article 42

Territory is considered occupied when it is actually placed under the authority of the hostile army.

The occupation extends only to the territory where such authority has been established and can be exercised.

Article 43

The authority of the legitimate power having in fact passed into the hands of the occupant, the latter shall take all the measures in his power to restore, and ensure, as far as possible, public order and safety, while respecting, unless absolutely prevented, the laws in force in the country.

Article 44

A belligerent is forbidden to force the inhabitants of territory occupied by it to furnish information about the army of the other belligerent, or about its means of defence.

Article 45

It is forbidden to compel the inhabitants of occupied territory to swear allegiance to the hostile Power.

Article 46

Family honour and rights, the lives of persons, and private property, as well as religious convictions and practice, must be respected.

Private property cannot be confiscated.

Article 47

Pillage is formally forbidden.

Article 48

If, in the territory occupied, the occupant collects the taxes, dues, and tolls imposed for the benefit of the State, he shall do so, as far as is possible, in accordance with the rules of assessment and incidence in force, and shall in consequence be bound to defray the expenses of the administration of the occupied territory to the same extent as the legitimate Government was so bound.

Article 49

If, in addition to the taxes mentioned in the above article, the occupant levies other money contributions in the occupied territory, this shall only be for the needs of the army or of the administration of the territory in question.

Article 50

No general penalty, pecuniary or otherwise, shall be inflicted upon the population on account of the acts of individuals for which they cannot be regarded as jointly and severally responsible.

Article 51

No contribution shall be collected except under a written order, and on the responsibility of a commander-in-chief.

The collection of the said contribution shall only be effected as far as possible in accordance with the rules of assessment and incidence of the taxes in force.

For every contribution a receipt shall be given to the contributors.

Article 52

Requisitions in kind and services shall not be demanded from municipalities or inhabitants except for the needs of the army of occupation. They shall be in proportion to the resources of the country, and of such a nature as not to involve the inhabitants in the obligation of taking part in military operations against their own country.

Such requisitions and services shall only be demanded on the authority of the commander in the locality occupied.

Contributions in kind shall as far as possible be paid for in cash; if not, a receipt shall be given and the payment of the amount due shall be made as soon as possible.

Article 53

An army of occupation can only take possession of cash, funds, and realizable securities which are strictly the property of the State, depots of arms, means of transport, stores and supplies, and, generally, all movable property belonging to the State which may be used for military operations.

All appliances, whether on land, at sea, or in the air, adapted for the transmission of news, or for the transport of persons or things, exclusive of cases governed by naval law, depots of arms, and, generally, all kinds of munitions of war, may be seized, even if they belong to private individuals, but must be restored and compensation fixed when peace is made.

Article 54

Submarine cables connecting an occupied territory with a neutral territory shall not be seized or destroyed except in the case of absolute necessity. They must likewise be restored and compensation fixed when peace is made.

Article 55

The occupying State shall be regarded only as administrator and usufructuary of public buildings, real estate, forests, and agricultural estates belonging to the hostile State, and situated in the occupied country. It must safeguard the capital of these properties, and administer them in accordance with the rules of usufruct.

Article 56

The property of municipalities, that of institutions dedicated to religion, charity and education, the arts and sciences, even when State property, shall be treated as private property.

All seizure of, destruction or wilful damage done to institutions of this character, historic monuments, works of art and science, is forbidden, and should be made the subject of legal proceedings.

V. CONVENTION RESPECTING THE RIGHTS AND DUTIES OF NEUTRAL POWERS AND PERSONS IN CASE OF WAR ON LAND

[For the participating States, see Convention I, supra p. 399]

With a view to laying down more clearly the rights and duties of neutral Powers in case of war on land and regulating the position of the belligerents who have taken refuge in neutral territory;

Being likewise desirous of defining the meaning of the term "neutral", pending the possibility of settling, in its entirety, the position of neutral individuals in their relations with the belligerents;

Have resolved to conclude a Convention to this effect, and have, in consequence, appointed the following as their Plenipotentiaries:

[List of Plenipotentiaries]

Who, after having deposited their full powers, found in good and due form, have agreed upon the following full powers, found in good and due form, have agreed upon the following provisions:

Chapter I. The Rights and Duties of Neutral Powers

Article 1

The territory of neutral Powers is inviolable.

Article 2

Belligerents are forbidden to move troops or convoys of either munitions of war or supplies across the territory of a neutral Power.

Article 3

Belligerents are likewise forbidden to:

(a) Erect on the territory of a neutral Power a wireless telegraphy station or other apparatus for the purpose of communicating with belligerent forces on land or sea;
(b) Use any installation of this kind established by them before the war on the territory of a neutral Power for purely military purposes, and which has not been opened for the service of public messages.

Article 4

Corps of combatants cannot be formed nor recruiting agencies opened on the territory of a neutral Power to assist the belligerents.

Article 5

A neutral Power must not allow any of the acts referred to in Articles 2 to 4 to occur on its territory.

It is not called upon to punish acts in violation of its neutrality unless the said acts have been committed on its own territory.

Article 6

The responsibility of a neutral Power is not engaged by the fact of persons crossing the frontier separately to offer their services to one of the belligerents.

Article 7

A neutral Power is not called upon to prevent the export or transport, on behalf of one or other of the belligerents, of arms, munitions of war, or, in general, of anything which can be of use to an army or a fleet.

Article 8

A neutral Power is not called upon to forbid or restrict the use on behalf of the belligerents of telegraph or telephone cables or of wireless telegraphy apparatus belonging to it or to companies or private individuals.

Article 9

Every measure of restriction or prohibition taken by a neutral Power in regard to the matters referred to in Articles 7 and 8 must be impartially applied by it to both belligerents.

A neutral Power must see to the same obligation being observed by companies or private individuals owning telegraph or telephone cables or wireless telegraphy apparatus.

Article 10

The fact of a neutral Power resisting, even by force, attempts to violate its neutrality cannot be regarded as a hostile act.

Chapter II. Belligerents Interned and Wounded Tended in Neutral Territory

Article 11

A neutral Power which receives on its territory troops belonging to the belligerent armies shall intern them, as far as possible, at a distance from the theatre of war.

It may keep them in camps and even confine them in fortresses or in places set apart for this purpose.

It shall decide whether officers can be left at liberty on giving their parole not to leave the neutral territory without permission.

Article 12

In the absence of a special convention to the contrary, the neutral Power shall supply the interned with the food, clothing, and relief required by humanity.

At the conclusion of peace the expenses caused by the internment shall be made good.

Article 13

A neutral Power which receives escaped prisoners of war shall leave them at liberty. If it allows them to remain in its territory it may assign them a place of residence.

The same rule applies to prisoners of war brought by troops taking refuge in the territory of a neutral Power.

Article 14

A neutral Power may authorize the passage over its territory of the sick and wounded belonging to the belligerent armies, on condition that the trains bringing them shall carry neither personnel nor war material. In such a case, the neutral Power is bound to take whatever measures of safety and control are necessary for the purpose.

The sick or wounded brought under the these conditions into neutral territory by one of the belligerents, and belonging to the hostile party, must be guarded by the neutral Power so as to ensure their not taking part again in the military operations. The same duty shall devolve on the neutral State with regard to wounded or sick of the other army who may be committed to its care.

Article 15

The Geneva Convention applies to sick and wounded interned in neutral territory.

Chapter III. Neutral Persons

Article 16

The nationals of a State which is not taking part in the war are considered as neutrals.

Article 17

A neutral cannot avail himself of his neutrality

(a) If he commits hostile acts against a belligerent;
(b) If he commits acts in favour of a belligerent, particularly if he voluntarily enlists in the ranks of the armed force of one of the parties.

In such a case, the neutral shall not be more severely treated by the belligerent as against whom he has abandoned his neutrality than a national of the other belligerent State could be for the same act.

Article 18

The following acts shall not be considered as committed in favour of one belligerent in the sense of Article 17, letter *(b)*:

(a) Supplies furnished or loans made to one of the belligerents, provided that the person who furnishes the supplies or who makes the loans lives neither in the territory of the other party nor in the territory occupied by him, and that the supplies do not come from these territories;

(b) Services rendered in matters of police or civil administration.

Chapter IV. Railway Material

Article 19

Railway material coming from the territory of neutral Powers, whether it be the property of the said Powers or of companies or private persons, and recognizable as such, shall not be requisitioned or utilized by a belligerent except where and to the extent that it is absolutely necessary. It shall be sent back as soon possible to the country of origin.

A neutral Power may likewise, in case of necessity, retain and utilize to an equal extent material coming from the territory of the belligerent Power.

Compensation shall be paid by one Party or the other in proportion to the material used, and to the period of usage.

Chapter V. Final Provisions

Article 20

The provisions of the present Convention do not apply except between Contracting Powers and then only if all the belligerents are Parties to the Convention.

Article 21

The present Convention shall be ratified as soon as possible.

The ratifications shall be deposited at The Hague.

The first deposit of ratifications shall be recorded in a procès-verbal signed by the representatives of the Powers which take part therein and by the Netherlands Minister for Foreign Affairs.

The subsequent deposits of ratifications shall be made by means of a written notification, addressed to the Netherlands Government and accompanied by the instrument of ratification.

A duly certified copy of the procès-verbal relative to the first deposit of ratifications, of the notifications mentioned in the preceding paragraph, and of the instruments of ratification shall be immediately sent by the Netherlands Government, through the diplomatic channel, to the Powers invited to the Second Peace Conference as well as to the other Powers which have adhered to the Convention. In the cases contemplated in the preceding paragraph, the said Government shall at the same time inform them of the date on which it received the notification.

Article 22

Non-Signatory Powers may adhere to the present Convention.

The Power which desires to adhere notifies its intention in writing to the Netherlands Government, forwarding to it the act of adhesion, which shall be deposited in the archives of the said Government.

This Government shall immediately forward to all the other Powers a duly certified copy of the notification as well as of the act of adhesion, mentioning the date on which it received the notification.

Article 23

The present Convention shall come into force, in the case of the Powers which were a party to the first deposit of ratifications, sixty days after the date of the proces-verbal of this deposit, and, in the case of the Powers which ratify subsequently or which adhere, sixty days after the notification of their ratification or of their adhesion has been received by the Netherlands Government.

Article 24

In the event of one of the Contracting Powers wishing to denounce the present Convention, the denunciation shall be notified in writing to the Netherlands Government, which shall immediately communicate a duly certified copy of the notification to all the other Powers, informing them at the same time of the date on which it was received.

The denunciation shall only have effect in regard to the notifying Power, and one year after the notification has reached the Netherlands Government.

Article 25

A register kept by the Netherlands Ministry of Foreign Affairs shall give the date of the deposit of ratifications made in virtue of Article 21, paragraphs 3 and 4, as well as the date on which the notifications of adhesion (Article 22, paragraph 2) or of denunciation (Article 24, paragraph 1) have been received.

Each Contracting Power is entitled to have access to this register and to be supplied with duly certified extracts from it.

In faith whereof the Plenipotentiaries have appended their signatures to the present Convention.

Done at The Hague, 18 October 1907, in a single copy, which shall remain deposited in the archives of the Netherlands Government and duly certified copies of which shall be sent, through the diplomatic channel, to the Powers which have been invited to the Second Peace Conference.

VI. CONVENTION RELATING TO THE STATUS OF ENEMY MERCHANT SHIPS AT THE OUTBREAK OF HOSTILITIES

[For the participating States, see Convention I, supra p. 399]

Anxious to ensure the security of international commerce against the surprises of war, and wishing, in accordance with modern practice, to protect as far as possible operations undertaken in good faith and in process of being carried out before the outbreak of hostilities,

Have resolved to conclude a Convention to this effect, and have appointed the following persons as their Plenipotentiaries:

[List of Plenipotentiaries]

Who, after having deposited their full powers, found in good and due form, have agreed upon the following provisions:

Article 1

When a merchant ship belonging to one of the belligerent Powers is at the commencement of hostilities in an enemy port, it is desirable that it should be allowed to depart freely, either immediately, or after a reasonable number of days of grace, and to proceed, after being furnished with a pass, direct to its port of destination or any other port indicated.

The same rule should apply in the case of a ship which has left its last port of departure before the commencement of the war and entered a port belonging to the enemy while still ignorant that hostilities had broken out.

Article 2

A merchant ship unable, owing to circumstances of force majeure, to leave the enemy port within the period contemplated in the above article, or which was not allowed to leave, cannot be confiscated.

The belligerent may only detain it, without payment of compensation, but subject to the obligation of restoring it after the war, or requisition it on payment of compensation.

Article 3

Enemy merchant ships which left their last port of departure before the commencement of the war, and are encountered on the high seas while still ignorant of the outbreak of hostilities cannot be confiscated. They are only liable to detention on the understanding that they shall be restored after the war without compensation, or to be requisitioned, or even destroyed, on payment of compensation, but in such cases provision must be made for the safety of the persons on board as well as the security of the ship's papers.

After touching at a port in their own country or at a neutral port, these ships are subject to the laws and customs of maritime war.

Article 4

Enemy cargo on board the vessels referred to in Articles 1 and 2 is likewise liable to be detained and restored after the termination of the war without payment of compensation, or to be requisitioned on payment of compensation, with or without the ship.

The same rule applies in the case of cargo on board the vessels referred to in Article 3.

Article 5

The present Convention does not affect merchant ships whose build shows that they are intended for conversion into war-ships.

Article 6

The provisions of the present Convention do not apply except between Contracting Powers, and then only if all the belligerents are Parties to the Convention.

Article 7

The present Convention shall be ratified as soon as possible. The ratifications shall be deposited at The Hague.

The first deposit of ratifications shall be recorded in a procès-verbal signed by the representatives of the Powers which take part therein and by the Netherlands Minister for Foreign Affairs.

The subsequent deposits of ratifications shall be made by means of a written notification addressed to the Netherlands Government and accompanied by the instrument of ratification.

A duly certified copy of the procès-verbal relative to the first deposit of ratifications, of the notifications mentioned in the preceding paragraph, as well as of the instruments of ratification, shall be at once sent by the Netherlands Government, through the diplomatic channel, to the Powers invited to the Second Peace Conference, as well as to the other Powers which have adhered to the Convention. In the cases contemplated in the preceding paragraph, the said Government shall at the same time inform them of the date on which it received the notification.

Article 8

Non-Signatory Powers may adhere to the present Convention.

The Power which desires to adhere notifies in writing its intention to the Netherlands Government, forwarding to it the act of adhesion, which shall be deposited in the archives of the said Government.

The said Government shall at once transmit to all the other Powers a duly certified copy of the notification as well as of the act of adhesion, stating the date on which it received the notification.

Article 9

The present Convention shall come into force, in the case of the Powers which were a party to the first deposit of ratifications, sixty days after the date of the procès-verbal of that deposit, and, in the case of the Powers which ratify subsequently or which adhere, sixty days after the notification of their ratification or of their adhesion has been received by the Netherlands Government.

Article 10

In the event of one of the Contracting Powers wishing to denounce the present Convention, the denunciation shall be notified in writing to the Netherlands Government, which shall at once communicate a certified copy of the notification to all the other Powers, informing them of the date on which it was received.

The denunciation shall only have effect in regard to the notifying Power, and one year after the notification has reached the Netherlands Government.

Article 11

A register kept by the Ministry of Foreign Affairs shall give the date of the deposit of ratifications made in virtue of Article 7, paragraphs 3 and 4, as well as the date on which the notifications of adhesion (Article 8, paragraph 2) or of denunciation (Article 10, paragraph 1) have been received.

Each Contracting Power is entitled to have access to this register and to be supplied with certified extracts from it.

In faith whereof the Plenipotentiaries have appended to the present Convention their signatures.

Done at The Hague, 18 October 1907, in a single copy, which shall remain deposited in the archives of the Netherlands Government, and duly certified copies of which shall be sent through the diplomatic channel, to the Powers which have been invited to the Second Peace Conference.

VII. CONVENTION RELATING TO THE CONVERSION OF MERCHANT SHIPS INTO WAR-SHIPS

[For the participating States, see Convention I, supra p. 399]

Whereas it is desirable, in view of the incorporation in time of war of merchant ships in the fighting fleet, to define the conditions subject to which this operation may be effected;

Whereas, however, the Contracting Powers have been unable to come to an agreement on the question whether the conversion of a merchant ship into a war-ship may take place upon the high seas, it is understood that the question of the place where such conversion is effected remains outside the scope of this agreement and is in no way affected by the following rules;

Being desirous of concluding a Convention to this effect, have appointed the following as their Plenipotentiaries:

[List of Plenipotentiaries]

Who, after having deposited their full powers, found in good and due form, have agreed upon the following provisions:

Article 1

A merchant ship converted into a war-ship cannot have the rights and duties accruing to such vessels unless it is placed under the direct authority, immediate control, and responsibility of the Power whose flag it flies.

Article 2

Merchant ships converted into war-ships must bear the external marks which distinguish the war-ships of their nationality.

Article 3

The commander must be in the service of the State and duly commissioned by the competent authorities. His name must figure on the list of the officers of the fighting fleet.

Article 4

The crew must be subject to military discipline.

Article 5

Every merchant ship converted into a war-ship must observe in its operations the laws and customs of war.

Article 6

A belligerent who converts a merchant ship into a war-ship must, as soon as possible, announce such conversion in the list of war-ships.

Article 7

The provisions of the present Convention do not apply except between Contracting Powers, and then only if all the belligerents are Parties to the Convention.

Article 8

The present Convention shall be ratified as soon as possible.

The ratifications shall be deposited at The Hague.

The first deposit of ratifications shall be recorded in a procès-verbal signed by the representatives of the Powers who take part therein and by the Netherlands Minister for Foreign Affairs.

The subsequent deposits of ratifications shall be made by means of a written notification, addressed to the Netherlands Government and accompanied by the instrument of ratification.

A duly certified copy of the procès-verbal relative to the first deposit of ratifications, of the notifications mentioned in the to preceding paragraph, as well as of the instruments of ratification, shall be at once sent by the Netherlands Government, through the diplomatic channel, to the Powers invited to the Second Peace Conference, as well as to the other Powers which have adhered to the Convention. In the cases contemplated in the preceding paragraph the said Government shall at the same time inform them of the date on which it received the notification.

Article 9

Non-Signatory Powers may adhere to the present Convention.

The Power which desires to adhere notifies its intention in writing to the Netherlands Government, forwarding to it the act of adhesion, which shall be deposited in the archives of the said Government.

That Government shall at once transmit to all the other Powers a duly certified copy of the notification as well as of the act of adhesion, stating the date on which it received the notification.

Article 10

The present Convention shall come into force, in the case of the Powers which were a party to the first deposit of ratifications, sixty days after the date of the procès-verbal of this deposit, and, in the case of the Powers which ratify subsequently or which adhere, sixty days after the notification of their ratification or of their adhesion has been received by the Netherlands Government.

Article 11

In the event of one of the Contracting Powers wishing to denounce the present Convention, the denunciation shall be notified in writing to the

Netherlands Government, which shall at once communicate a duly certified copy of the notification to all the other Powers, informing them of the date on which it was received.

The denunciation shall only have effect in regard to the notifying Power, and one year after the notification has reached the Netherlands Government.

Article 12

A register kept by the Netherlands Ministry for Foreign Affairs shall give the date of the deposit of ratifications made in virtue of Article 8, paragraphs 3 and 4, as well as the date on which the notifications of adhesion (Article 9, paragraph 2) or of denunciation (Article 11, paragraph 1) have been received.

Each Contracting Power is entitled to have access to this register and to be supplied with duly certified extracts from it.

In faith whereof the Plenipotentiaries have appended their signatures to the present Convention.

Done at The Hague, 18 October 1907, in a single copy, which shall remain deposited in the archives of the Netherlands Government, and duly certified copies of which shall be sent, through the diplomatic channel, to the Powers which have been invited to the Second Peace Conference.

VIII. CONVENTION RELATIVE TO THE LAYING
OF AUTOMATIC SUBMARINE CONTACT MINES

[For the participating States, see Convention I, supra p. 399]

Inspired by the principle of the freedom of sea routes, the common highway of all nations;

Seeing that, although the existing position of affairs makes it impossible to forbid the employment of automatic submarine contact mines, it is nevertheless desirable to restrict and regulate their employment in order to mitigate the severity of war and to ensure, as far as possible, to peaceful navigation the security to which it is entitled, despite the existence of war;

Until such time as it is found possible to formulate rules on the subject which shall ensure to the interests involved all the guarantees desirable;

Have resolved to conclude a Convention for this purpose, and have appointed the following as their Plenipotentiaries:

[List of Plenipotentiaries]

Who, after having deposited their full powers, found in good and due form, have agreed upon the following provisions:

Article 1

It is forbidden — 1. To lay unanchored automatic contact mines, except when they are so constructed as to become harmless one hour at most after the person who laid them ceases to control them; 2. To lay anchored automatic contact mines which do not become harmless as soon as they have broken loose from their moorings; 3. To use torpedoes which do not become harmless when they have missed their mark.

Article 2

It is forbidden to lay automatic contact mines off the coast and ports of the enemy, with the sole object of intercepting commercial shipping.

Article 3

When anchored automatic contact mines are employed, every possible precaution must be taken for the security of peaceful shipping.

The belligerents undertake to do their utmost to render these mines harmless within a limited time, and, should they cease to be under surveillance, to notify the danger zones as soon as military exigencies permit, by a notice addressed to ship owners, which must also be communicated to the Governments through the diplomatic channel.

Article 4

Neutral Powers which lay automatic contact mines off their coasts must observe the same rules and take the same precautions as are imposed on belligerents.

The neutral Power must inform ship owners, by a notice issued in advance, where automatic contact mines have been laid. This notice must be communicated at once to the Governments through the diplomatic channel.

Article 5

At the close of the war, the Contracting Powers undertake to do their utmost to remove the mines which they have laid, each Power removing its own mines.

As regards anchored automatic contact mines laid by one of the belligerents off the coast of the other, their position must be notified to the other party by the Power which laid them, and each Power must proceed with the least possible delay to remove the mines in its own waters.

Article 6

The Contracting Powers which do not at present own perfected mines of the pattern contemplated in the present Convention, and which, consequently, could not at present carry out the rules laid down in Articles 1 and 3, undertake to convert the materiel of their mines as soon as possible, so as to bring it into conformity with the foregoing requirements.

Article 7

The provisions of the present Convention do not apply except between Contracting Powers, and then only if all the belligerents are parties to the Convention.

Article 8

The present Convention shall be ratified as soon as possible.

The ratifications shall be deposited at The Hague.

The first deposit of ratifications shall be recorded in a procès-verbal signed by the representatives of the Powers which take part therein and by the Netherlands Minister for Foreign Affairs.

The subsequent deposits of ratifications shall be made by means of a written notification addressed to the Netherlands Government and accompanied by the instrument of ratification.

A duly certified copy of the procès-verbal relative to the first deposit of ratifications, of the notifications mentioned in the preceding paragraph, as well as of the instruments of ratification, shall be at once sent, by the Netherlands Government, through the diplomatic channel, to the Powers invited to the Second Peace Conference, as well as to the other Powers which have adhered to the Convention. In the cases contemplated in the preceding paragraph, the said Government shall inform them at the same time of the date on which it has received the notification.

Article 9

Non-Signatory Powers may adhere to the present Convention.

The Power which desires to adhere notifies in writing its intention to the Netherlands Government, transmitting to it the act of adhesion, which shall be deposited in the archives of the said Government.

This Government shall at once transmit to all the other Powers a duly certified copy of the notification as well as of the act of adhesion, stating the date on which it received the notification.

Article 10

The present Convention shall come into force, in the case of the Powers which were a party to the first deposit of ratifications, sixty days after the date of the procès-verbal of this deposit, and, in the case of the Powers which ratify subsequently or adhere, sixty days after the notification of their ratification or of their adhesion has been received by the Netherlands Government.

Article 11

The present Convention shall remain in force for seven years, dating from the sixtieth day after the date of the first deposit of ratifications.

Unless denounced, it shall continue in force after the expiration of this period.

The denunciation shall be notified in writing to the Netherlands Government, which shall at once communicate a duly certified copy of the notification to all the Powers, informing them of the date on which it was received.

The denunciation shall only have effect in regard to the notifying Power, and six months after the notification has reached the Netherlands Government.

Article 12

The Contracting Powers undertake to reopen the question of the employment of automatic contact mines six months before the expiration of the period contemplated in the first paragraph of the preceding article, in the event of the question not having been already reopened and settled by the Third Peace Conference.

If the Contracting Powers conclude a fresh Convention relative to the employment of mines, the present Convention shall cease to be applicable from the moment it comes into force.

Article 13

A register kept by the Netherlands Ministry for Foreign Affairs shall give the date of the deposit of ratifications made in virtue of Article 8, paragraphs 3 and 4, as well as the date on which the notifications of adhesion (Article 9, paragraph 2) or of denunciation (Article 11, paragraph 3) have been received.

Each Contracting Power is entitled to have access to this register and to be supplied with duly certified extracts from it.

In faith whereof the Plenipotentiaries have appended their signatures to the present Convention.

Done at The Hague, 18 October 1907, in a single copy, which shall remain deposited in the archives of the Netherlands Government, and duly certified copies of which shall be sent, through the diplomatic channel, to the Powers which have been invited to the Second Peace Conference.

IX. CONVENTION CONCERNING BOMBARDMENT
BY NAVAL FORCES IN TIME OF WAR

[For the participating States, see Convention I, supra p. 399]

Animated by the desire to realize the wish expressed by the First Peace Conference respecting the bombardment by naval forces of undefended ports, towns, and villages;

Whereas it is expedient that bombardments by naval forces should be subject to rules of general application which would safeguard the rights of the inhabitants and assure the preservation of the more important buildings, by applying as far as possible to this operation of war the principles of the Regulation of 1899 respecting the laws and customs of land war;

Actuated, accordingly, by the desire to serve the interests of humanity and to diminish the severity and disasters of war;

Have resolved to conclude a Convention to this effect, and have, for this purpose, appointed the following as their Plenipotentiaries:

[List of Plenipotentiaries]

Who, after depositing their full powers, gound in good and due form, have agreed upon the following provisions:

Chapter I. The Bombardment of Undefended Ports, Towns,
Villages, Dwellings, or Buildings

Article 1

The bombardment by naval forces of undefended ports, towns, villages, dwellings, or buildings is forbidden.

A place cannot be bombarded solely because automatic submarine contact mines are anchored off the harbour.

Article 2

Military works, military or naval establishments, depots of arms or war matériel, workshops or plant which could be utilized for the needs of the hostile fleet or army, and the ships of war in the harbour, are not, however, included in this prohibition. The commander of a naval force may destroy them with artillery, after a summons followed by a reasonable time of waiting, if all other means are impossible, and when the local authorities have not themselves destroyed them within the time fixed.

He incurs no responsibility for any unavoidable damage which may be caused by a bombardment under such circumstances.

If for military reasons immediate action is necessary, and no delay can be allowed the enemy, it is understood that the prohibition to bombard the undefended town holds good, as in the case given in paragraph 1, and that the commander shall take all due measures in order that the town may suffer as little harm as possible.

Article 3

After due notice has been given, the bombardment of undefended ports, towns, villages, dwellings, or buildings may be commenced, if the local authorities, after a formal summons has been made to them, decline to comply with requisitions for provisions or supplies necessary for the immediate use of the naval force before the place in question.

These requisitions shall be in proportion to the resources of the place. They shall only be demanded in the name of the commander of the said naval force, and they shall, as far as possible, be paid for in cash; if not, they shall be evidenced by receipts.

Article 4

Undefended ports, towns, villages, dwellings, or buildings may not be bombarded on account of failure to pay money contributions.

Chapter II. General Provisions

Article 5

In bombardments by naval forces all the necessary measures must be taken by the commander to spare as far as possible sacred edifices, buildings used for artistic, scientific, or charitable purposes, historic monuments, hospitals, and places where the sick or wounded are collected, on the understanding that they are not used at the same time for military purposes.

It is the duty of the inhabitants to indicate such monuments, edifices, or places by visible signs, which shall consist of large, stiff rectangular panels divided diagonally into two coloured triangular portions, the upper portion black, the lower portion white.

Article 6

If the military situation permits, the commander of the attacking naval force, before commencing the bombardment, must do his utmost to warn the authorities.

Article 7

A town or place, even when taken by storm, may not be pillaged.

Chapter III. Final Provisions

Article 8

The provisions of the present Convention do not apply except between Contracting Powers, and then only if all the belligerents are parties to the Convention.

Article 9

The present Convention shall be ratified as soon as possible.

The ratifications shall be deposited at The Hague.

The first deposit of ratifications shall be recorded in a procès-verbal signed by the representatives of the Powers which take part therein and by the Netherlands Minister of Foreign Affairs.

The subsequent deposits of ratifications shall be made by means of a written notification addressed to the Netherlands Government and accompanied by the instrument of ratification.

A duly certified copy of the procès-verbal relative to the first deposit of ratifications, of the notifications mentioned in the preceding paragraph, as well as of the instruments of ratification, shall be at once sent by the Netherlands Government, through the diplomatic channel, to the Powers invited to the Second Peace Conference, as well as to the other Powers which have adhered to the Convention. In the cases contemplated in the preceding paragraph, the said Government shall inform them at the same time of the date on which it received the notification.

Article 10

Non-Signatory Powers may adhere to the present Convention.

The Power which desires to adhere shall notify its intention to the Netherlands Government, forwarding to it the act of adhesion, which shall be deposited in the archives of the said Government.

This Government shall immediately forward to all the other Powers a duly certified copy of the notification, as well as of the act of adhesion, mentioning the date on which it received the notification.

Article 11

The present Convention shall come into force, in the case of the Powers which were a party to the first deposit of ratifications, sixty days after the date of the procès-verbal of that deposit, and, in the case of the Powers which ratify subsequently or which adhere, sixty days after the notification of their ratification or of their adhesion has been received by the Netherlands Government.

Article 12

In the event of one of the Contracting Powers wishing to denounce the present Convention, the denunciation shall be notified in writing to the Netherlands Government, which shall at once communicate a duly certified copy of the notification to all the other Powers informing them of the date on which it was received.

The denunciation shall only have effect in regard to the notifying Power, and one year after the notification has reached the Netherlands Government.

Article 13

A register kept by the Netherlands Minister for Foreign Affairs shall give the date of the deposit of ratifications made in virtue of Article 9, paragraphs 3 and 4, as well as the date on which the notifications of adhesion (Article 10, paragraph 2) or of denunciation (Article 12, paragraph 1) have been received.

Each Contracting Power is entitled to have access to this register and to be supplied with duly certified extracts from it.

In faith whereof the Plenipotentiaries have appended their signatures to the present Convention.

Done at The Hague, 18 October 1907, in a single copy, which shall remain deposited in the archives of the Netherlands Government, and duly certified copies of which shall be sent, through the diplomatic channel, to the Powers which have been invited to the Second Peace Conference.

X. CONVENTION FOR THE ADAPTATION
TO MARITIME WAR OF THE PRINCIPLES
OF THE GENEVA CONVENTION

[For the participating States, see Convention I, supra p. 399]

Animated alike by the desire to diminish, as far as depends on them, the inevitable evils of war; and wishing with this object to adapt to maritime warfare the principles of the Geneva Convention of the 6th July, 1906;

Have resolved to conclude a Convention for the purpose of revising the Convention of the 29th July, 1899, relative to this question, and have appointed the following as their Plenipotentiaries:

[List of Plenipotentiaries]

Who, after having deposited their full powers, found to be in good and due form, have agreed to the following provisions:

Article 1

Military hospital-ships, that is to say, ships constructed or fitted out by States specially and solely with a view to assisting the wounded, sick, and shipwrecked, the names of which shall have been communicated to the belligerent Powers at the commencement or during the course of hostilities, and in any case before they are employed, shall be respected, and cannot be captured while hostilities last.

These ships, moreover, are not on the same footing as ships of war as regards their stay in a neutral port.

Article 2

Hospital-ships, equipped wholly or in part at the expense of private individuals or officially recognized relief societies, shall likewise be respected and exempt from capture, if the belligerent Power to wholly they belong has given them an official commission and has notified their names to the adverse Power at the commencement of or during hostilities, and in any case before they are employed.

These ships must be provided with a certificate from the competent authorities declaring that the ships have been under their control while fitting out and on final departure.

Article 3

Hospital-ships, equipped wholly or in part at the expense of private individuals or officially recognized societies of neutral countries, shall be respected and exempt from capture, on condition that they are placed under the control of one of the belligerents, with the previous consent of their own Government and with the authorization of the belligerent himself, and that the latter has notified their name to his adversary at the commencement of or during hostilities, and in any case, before they are employed.

Article 4

The ships mentioned in Articles 1, 2, and 3 shall afford relief and assistance to the wounded, sick, and shipwrecked of the belligerents without distinction of nationality.

The Governments undertake not to use these ships for any military purpose.

These ships must not in any way hamper the movements of the combatants.

During and after an engagement they will act at their own risk and peril.

The belligerents shall have the right to control and search them; they can refuse their assistance, order them off, make them take a certain course, and put a commissioner on board; they can even detain them, if the gravity of the circumstances requires it.

As far as possible, the belligerents shall enter in the log of the hospital-ships the orders which they give them.

Article 5

Military hospital-ships shall be distinguished by being painted white outside with a horizontal band of green about a metre and a half in breadth.

The ships mentioned in Articles 2 and 3 shall be distinguished by being painted white outside with a horizontal band of red about a metre and a half in breadth.

The boats of the ships above mentioned, as also small craft which may be used for hospital work, shall he distinguished by similar painting.

All hospital-ships shall make themselves known by hoisting, with their national flag, the white flag with a red cross provided by the Geneva Convention, and further, if they belong to a neutral State, by flying at the mainmast the national flag of the belligerent under whose control they are placed.

Hospital-ships which, under the terms of Article 4, are detained by the enemy, must haul down the national flag of the belligerent to whom they belong.

The ships and boats above mentioned which wish to ensure by night the freedom from interference to which they are entitled, must, subject to the assent of the belligerent they are accompanying, take the necessary measures to render their special painting sufficiently plain.

Article 6

The distinguishing signs referred to in Article 5 can be used, whether in time of peace or in time of war, only for protecting or indicating the ships therein mentioned.

Article 7

In the case of a fight on board a vessel of war, the sick-wards shall be respected and spared as far as possible.

The said sick-wards and the matériel belonging to them remain subject to the laws of war, but cannot be used for any purpose other than that for which they were originally intended, so long as they are required for the sick and wounded.

The commander, however, into whose power they have fallen may apply them to other purposes, in case of urgent military necessity, after seeing that the sick and wounded on board are properly provided for.

Article 8

Hospital-ships and sick-wards of vessels arc no longer entitled to protection if they are employed for the purpose of injuring the enemy.

Neither the fact of the personnel of the said ships and sick-wards being armed for maintaining order and for defending the sick and wounded, nor the presence of wireless telegraph apparatus on board, is a sufficient reason for withdrawing protection.

Article 9

Belligerents may appeal to the charity of the commanders of neutral merchant-ships, yachts, or boats to take on board and care for the sick and wounded.

Vessels responding to this appeal, and also vessels which have of their own accord rescued sick, wounded, or shipwrecked men, shall enjoy special protection and certain immunities. In no case can they be captured for having such persons on board, but, apart from special undertakings that may have been made to them, they remain liable to capture for any violations of neutrality they may have committed.

Article 10

The religious, medical, and hospital staff of any captured ship is inviolable, and its members cannot be made prisoners of war. On leaving the ship they take away with them the objects and surgical instruments which are their own private property

This staff shall continue to discharge its duties while necessary, and can afterwards leave, when the commander-in-chief considers it possible.

The belligerents must guarantee to the said staff, when it has fallen into their hands, the same allowances and pay as are given to the staff of corresponding rank in their own navy.

Article 11

Sailors and soldiers on board, when sick or wounded, as well as other persons officially attached to fleets or armies, to whatever nation they belong, shall be respected and cared for by the captors.

Article 12

Any vessel of war belonging to a belligerent may demand the delivery of sick, wounded, or shipwrecked men on board military hospital-ships, hospital-ships belonging to relief societies or to private individuals, merchant-ships, yachts, or boats; whatever the nationality of these vessels.

Article 13

If sick, wounded, or shipwrecked persons are taken on board a neutral vessel of war, every possible precaution must be taken that they can not again take part in the operations of the war.

Article 14

The shipwrecked, wounded, or sick of one of the belligerents who fall into the power of the other are prisoners of war. The captor must decide, according to circumstances, whether to keep them, or to send them to a port of his own country, to a neutral port, or even to an enemy port. In this last case, prisoners thus repatriated cannot serve again while the war lasts.

Article 15

The shipwrecked, sick, or wounded, who are landed at a neutral port with the consent of the local authorities, must, unless an arrangement is made to the contrary between the neutral State and the belligerent States, be guarded by the neutral State so that they can not again take part in the operations of the war.

The expenses of caring for them in hospital and interning them shall be borne by the State to which the shipwrecked, sick, or wounded persons belong.

Article 16

After every engagement, the two belligerents, so far as military interests permit, shall take steps to look for the shipwrecked, sick, and wounded, and to protect them, as well as the dead, against pillage and ill treatment.

They shall see that the burial, whether by land or sea, or cremation of the dead shall be preceded by a careful examination of the corpse.

Article 17

Each belligerent shall send, as early as possible, to the authorities of their country, navy, or army the military marks or documents of identity found on the dead and a list of the names of the sick and wounded gathered up by him.

The belligerents shall keep each other informed as to internments and transfers as well as to the admissions into hospital and deaths which have occurred among the sick and wounded in their hands. They shall collect all the objects of personal use, valuables, letters, &c., which are found in the captured ships, or which have been left by the sick or wounded who died in hospital, in order to have them forwarded to the persons concerned by the authorities of their own country.

Article 18

The provisions of the present Convention do not apply except between Contracting Powers, and only if all the belligerents are parties to the Convention.

Article 19

The commanders in chief of the belligerent fleets must arrange for the details of carrying out the preceding articles, as well as for cases not covered thereby, in accordance with the instructions of their respective Governments and in conformity with the general principles of the present Convention.

Article 20

The Signatory Powers shall take the necessary measures to instruct their naval forces, and especially the protected personnel, in the provisions of the present Convention, and to bring them to the knowledge of the population.

Article 21

The Signatory Powers likewise undertake to enact or to propose to their legislatures, if their criminal laws are inadequate, the measures necessary for checking in time of war individual acts of pillage and ill-treatment of the sick and wounded of the Navy as well as for punishing, as an unjustifiable adoption of naval or military marks, the unauthorized use of the distinctive marks mentioned in Article 5 by vessels not protected by the present Convention.

They will communicate to each other, through the Netherlands Government, the enactments for preventing such acts at the latest within five years of the ratification of the present Convention.

Article 22

In the case of operations of war between the land and the sea forces of belligerents, the provisions of the present Convention do not apply except to the forces actually embarked.

Article 23

The present Convention shall be ratified as soon as possible.

The ratifications shall be deposited at The Hague.

The first deposit of ratifications shall be recorded in a procès-verbal signed by the Representatives of the Powers taking part therein and by the Netherlands Minister for Foreign Affairs.

Subsequent deposits of ratifications shall be made by means of a written notification addressed to the Netherlands Government and accompanied by the instrument of ratification.

A certified copy of the procès-verbal relative to the first deposit of ratifications, of the notifications mentioned in the preceding paragraph, as well as of the instruments of ratification, shall be at once sent by the Netherlands Government through the diplomatic channel to the Powers invited to the Second Peace Conference, as well as to the other Powers which shall have adhered to the Convention. In the cases contemplated in the preceding paragraph the said Government shall inform them at the same time of the date on which it received the notification.

Article 24

Non-signatory Powers which have accepted the Geneva Convention of the 6th July, 1906, may adhere to the present Convention.

A Power which desires to adhere notifies its intention to the Netherlands Government in writing, forwarding to it the act of adherence, which shall be deposited in the archives of the said Government.

The said Government shall at once transmit to all the other Powers a duly certified copy of the notification as well as of the act of adherence mentioning the date on which it received the notification.

Article 25

The present Convention, duly ratified, shall replace as between Contracting Powers, the Convention of the 29th July, 1899, for the adaptation to maritime warfare of the principles of the Geneva Convention.

The Convention of 1899 remains in force as between the Powers which signed it but which do not also ratify the present Convention.

Article 26

The present Convention shall take effect in the case of the Powers which were parties to the first deposit of ratifications, sixty days after the date of the procès-verbal of this deposit, and, in the case of the Powers which ratify subsequently or which adhere, sixty days after the notification of their ratification or of their adherence has been received by the Netherlands Government.

Article 27

In the event of one of the Contracting Powers wishing to denounce the present Convention, the denunciation shall be notified in writing to the Netherlands Government, which shall at once communicate a duly certified copy of the notification to all the other Powers, informing them at the same time of the date on which it was received.

The denunciation shall have effect only in regard to the notifying Power, and one year after the notification has reached the Netherlands Government.

Article 28

A register kept by the Netherlands Ministry for Foreign Affairs shall give the date of the deposit of ratifications made in virtue of Article 23, paragraphs 3 and 4, as well as the date on which the notifications of adherence (Article 24, paragraph 2) or of denunciation (Article 27, paragraph 1) have been received.

Each Contracting Power is entitled to have access to this register and to be supplied with duly certified extracts from it.

In faith whereof the Plenipotentiaries have appended their signatures to the present Convention.

Done at The Hague, the 18th October, 1907, in a single copy, which shall remain deposited in the archives of the Netherlands Government, and duly certified copies of which shall be sent, through the diplomatic channel, to the Powers which have been invited to the Second Peace Conference.

XI. CONVENTION RELATIVE TO CERTAIN RESTRICTIONS WITH REGARD TO THE EXERCISE OF THE RIGHT OF CAPTURE IN NAVAL WAR

[For the participating States, see Convention I, supra p. 399]

Recognizing the necessity of more effectively ensuring than hitherto the equitable application of law to the international relations of maritime Powers in time of war;

Considering that, for this purpose, it is expedient, in giving up or, if necessary, in harmonizing for the common interest certain conflicting practices of long standing, to commence codifying in regulations of general application the guarantees due to peaceful commerce and legitimate business, as well as the conduct of hostilities by sea; that it is expedient to lay down in written mutual engagements the principles which have hitherto remained in the uncertain domain of controversy or have been left to the discretion of Governments;

That, from henceforth, a certain number of rules may be made, without affecting the common law now in force with regard to the matters which that law has left unsettled;

Have appointed the following as their Plenipotentiaries:

[List of Plenipotentiaries]

Who, after having deposited their full powers, found in good and due form, have agreed upon the following provisions:

Chapter I. Postal Correspondence

Article 1

The postal correspondence of neutrals or belligerents, whatever its official or private character may be, found on the high seas on board a neutral or enemy ship, is inviolable. If the ship is detained, the correspondence is forwarded by the captor with the least possible delay.

The provisions of the preceding paragraph do not apply, in case of violation of blockade, to correspondence destined for or proceeding from a blockaded port.

Article 2

The inviolability of postal correspondence does not exempt a neutral mail ship from the laws and customs of maritime war as to neutral merchant ships in general. The ship, however, may not be searched except when absolutely necessary, and then only with as much consideration and expedition as possible.

Chapter II. The Exemption from Capture of Certain Vessels

Article 3

Vessels used exclusively for fishing along the coast or small boats employed in local trade are exempt from capture, as well as their appliances, rigging, tackle, and cargo. They cease to be exempt as soon as they take any part whatever in hostilities.

The Contracting Powers agree not to take advantage of the harmless character of the said vessels in order to use them for military purposes while preserving their peaceful appearance.

Article 4

Vessels charged with religious, scientific, or philanthropic missions are likewise exempt from capture.

Chapter III. Regulations Regarding the Crews of Enemy Merchant Ships Captured by a Belligerent

Article 5

When an enemy merchant ship is captured by a belligerent, such of its crew as are nationals of a neutral State are not made prisoners of war.

The same rule applies in the case of the captain and officers likewise nationals of a neutral State, if they promise formally in writing not to serve on an enemy ship while the war lasts.

Article 6

The captain, officers, and members of the crew, when nationals of the enemy State, are not made prisoners of war, on condition that they make a formal promise in writing, not to undertake, while hostilities last, any service connected with the operations of the war.

Article 7

The names of the persons retaining their liberty under the conditions laid down in Article 5, paragraph 2, and in Article 6, are notified by the belligerent captor to the other belligerent. The latter is forbidden knowingly to employ the said persons.

Article 8

The provisions of the three preceding articles do not apply to ships taking part in the hostilities.

Chapter IV. Final Provisions

Article 9

The provisions of the present Convention do not apply except between Contracting Powers, and then only if all the belligerents are parties to the Convention.

Article 10

The present Convention shall be ratified as soon as possible.

The ratifications shall be deposited at The Hague.

The first deposit of ratifications shall be recorded in a procès-verbal signed by the representatives of the Powers taking part therein and by the Netherlands Minister for Foreign Affairs.

Subsequent deposits of ratifications shall be made by means of a written notification, addressed to the Netherlands Government and accompanied by the instrument of ratification.

A duly certified copy of the procès-verbal relative to the first deposit of ratifications, of the notifications mentioned in the preceding paragraph, as well as of the instruments of ratification, shall be at once sent by the Netherlands Government, through the diplomatic channel, to the Powers invited to the Second Peace Conference, as well as to the other Powers which have adhered to the Convention. In the cases contemplated in the preceding paragraph, the said Government shall inform them at the same time of the date on which it received the notification.

Article 11

Non-Signatory Powers may adhere to the present Convention.

The Power which desires to adhere notifies its intention in writing to the Netherlands Government, forwarding to it the act of adhesion, which shall be deposited in the archives of the said Government.

This Government shall at once transmit to all the other Powers a duly certified copy of the notification as well as of the act of adhesion, mentioning the date on which it received the notification.

Article 12

The present Convention shall come into force in the case of the Powers which were a party to the first deposit of ratifications, sixty days after the procès-verbal of that deposit, and, in the case of the Powers which ratify subsequently or which adhere, sixty days after the notification of their ratification has been received by the Netherlands Government.

Article 13

In the event of one of the Contracting Powers wishing to denounce the present Convention, the denunciation shall be notified in writing to the Netherlands Government, which shall at once communicate a duly certified copy of the notification to all the other Powers informing them of the date on which it was received.

The denunciation shall only have effect in regard to the notifying Power, and one year after the notification has reached the Netherlands Government.

Article 14

A register kept by the Netherlands Ministry for Foreign Affairs shall give the date of the deposit of ratifications made in virtue of Article 10, paragraphs 3 and 4, as well as the date on which the notifications of adhesion (Article 11, paragraph 2) or of denunciation (Article 13, paragraph 1) have been received.

Each Contracting Power is entitled to have access to this register and to be supplied with duly certified extracts from it.

In faith whereof the Plenipotentiaries have appended their signatures to the present Convention.

Done at The Hague, 18 October 1907, in a single copy, which shall remain deposited in the archives of the Netherlands Government, and duly certified copies of which shall be sent, through the diplomatic channel, to the Powers invited to the Second Peace Conference.

XII. CONVENTION RELATIVE TO THE CREATION OF AN INTERNATIONAL PRIZE COURT *

[For the participating States, see Convention I, supra p. 399]

Animated by the desire to settle in an equitable manner the differences which sometimes arise in the course of a naval war in connection with the decisions of national prize courts;

Considering that, if these courts are to continue to exercise their functions in the manner determined by national legislation, it is desirable that in certain cases an appeal should be provided under conditions conciliating, as far as possible, the public and private interests involved in matters of prize;

Whereas, moreover, the institution of an International Court, whose jurisdiction and procedure would be carefully defined, has seemed to be the best method of attaining this object;

Convinced, finally, that in this manner the hardships consequent on naval war would be mitigated; that, in particular, good relations will be more easily maintained between belligerents and neutrals and peace better assured;

Desirous of concluding a Convention to this effect, have appointed the following as their Plenipotentiaries:

[List of Plenipotentiaries]

Who, after depositing their full powers, found in good and due form, have agreed upon the following provisions:

PART I. GENERAL PROVISIONS

Article 1

The validity of the capture of a merchant ship or its cargo is decided before a prize court in accordance with the present Convention when neutral or enemy property is involved.

Article 2

Jurisdiction in matters of prize is exercized in the first instance by the prize courts of the belligerent captor.

The judgments of these courts are pronounced in public or are officially notified to parties concerned who are neutrals or enemies.

---

* Not entered into force.

Article 3

The judgments of national prize courts may be brought before the International Prize Court —

1. When the judgment of the national prize courts affects the property of a neutral Power or individual;
2. When the judgment affects enemy property and relates to—

    (a) Cargo on board a neutral ship;
    (b) An enemy ship captured in the territorial waters of a neutral Power, when that Power has not made the capture the subject of a diplomatic claim;
    (c) A claim based upon the allegation that the seizure has been effected in violation, either of the provisions of a Convention in force between the belligerent Powers, or of an enactment issued by the belligerent captors.

The appeal against the judgment of the national court can be based on the ground that the judgment was wrong either in fact or in law.

Article 4

An appeal may be brought —

1. By a neutral Power, if the judgment of the national tribunals injuriously affects its property or the property of its nationals (Article 3, No. 1), or if the capture of an enemy vessel is alleged to have taken place in the territorial waters of that Power (Article 3, No. 2 *(b)*).
2. By a neutral individual, if the judgment of the national court injuriously affects his property (Article 3, No. 1), subject, however, to the reservation that the Power to which he belongs may forbid him to bring the case before the Court, or may itself undertake the proceedings in his place;
3. By an individual subject or citizen of an enemy Power, if the judgment of the national court injuriously affects his property in the cases referred to in Article 3, No. 2, except that mentioned in paragraph *(b)*.

Article 5

An appeal may also be brought on the same conditions as in the preceding article, by persons belonging either to neutral States or to the enemy, deriving their rights from and entitled to represent an individual qualified to appeal, and who have taken part in the proceedings before the national court. Persons so entitled may appeal separately to the extent of their interest.

The same rule applies in the case of persons belonging either to neutral States or to the enemy who derive their rights from and are entitled to represent a neutral Power whose property was the subject of the decision.

Article 6

When, in accordance with the above Article 3, the International Court has jurisdiction, the national courts cannot deal with a case in more than two instances. The municipal law of the belligerent captor shall decide whether the case may be brought before the International Court after judgment has been given in first instance or only after an appeal.

If the national courts fail to give final judgment within two years from the date of capture, the case may be carried direct to the International Court.

Article 7

If a question of law to be decided is covered by a treaty in force between the belligerent captor and a Power which is itself or whose subject or citizen is a party to the proceedings, the Court is governed by the provisions in the said treaty.

In the absence of such provisions, the Court shall apply the rules of international law. If no generally recognized rule exists, the Court shall give judgment in accordance with the general principles of justice and equity.

The above provisions apply equally to questions relating to the order and mode of proof.

If, in accordance with Article 3, No. 2 *(c)*, the ground of appeal is the violation of an enactment issued by the belligerent captor, the Court will enforce the enactment.

The Court may disregard failure to comply with the procedure laid down in the enactments of the belligerent captor, when it is of opinion that the [consequences] of complying therewith are unjust and inequitable.

Article 8

If the Court pronounces the capture of the vessel or cargo to be valid, they shall be disposed of in accordance with the laws of the belligerent captor.

If it pronounces the capture to be null, the Court shall order restitution of the vessel or cargo, and shall fix, if there is occasion, the amount of the damages. If the vessel or cargo have been sold or destroyed, the Court shall determine the compensation to be given to the owner on this account.

If the national court pronounced the capture to be null, the Court can only be asked to decide as to the damages.

Article 9

The Contracting Powers undertake to submit in good faith to the decisions of the International Prize Court and to carry them out with the least possible delay.

PART II. CONSTITUTION OF THE INTERNATIONAL PRIZE COURT

Article 10

The International Prize Court is composed of judges and deputy judges, who will be appointed by the Contracting Powers, and must all be jurists of known proficiency in questions of international maritime law, and of the highest moral reputation.

The appointment of these judges and deputy judges shall be made within six months after the ratification of the present Convention.

Article 11

The judges and deputy judges are appointed for a period of six years, reckoned from the date on which the notification of their appointment is received by the Administrative Council established by the Convention for the pacific settlement of international disputes of the 29 July 1899. Their appointments can be renewed.

Should one of the judges or deputy judges die or resign, the same procedure is followed for filling the vacancy as was followed for appointing him. In this case, the appointment is made for a fresh period of six years.

Article 12

The judges of the International Prize Court are all equal in rank and have precedence according to the date on which the notification of their appointment was received (Article 11, paragraph 1), and if they sit by rota (Article 15, paragraph 2), according to the date on which they entered upon their duties. When the date is the same the senior in age takes precedence.

The deputy judges when acting are assimilaged to the judges. They rank, however, after them.

Article 13

The judges enjoy diplomatic privileges and immunities in the performance of their duties and when outside their own country.

Before taking their seat, the judges must swear, or make a solemn promise before the Administrative Council, to discharge their duties impartially and conscientiously.

Article 14

The Court is composed of fifteen judges; nine judges constitute a quorum.

A judge who is absent or prevented from sitting is replaced by the deputy judge.

Article 15

The judges appointed by the following Contracting Powers: Germany, the United States of America, Austria-Hungary, France, Great Britain, Italy, Japan, and Russia, are always summoned to sit.

The judges and deputy judges appointed by the other Contracting Powers sit by rota as shown in the table annexed * to the present Conven-

---

* Not reproduced.

tion; their duties may be performed successively by the same person. The same judge may be appointed by several of the said Powers.

Article 16

If a belligerent Power has, according to the rota, no judge sitting in the Court, it may ask that the judge appointed by it should take part in the settlement of all cases arising from the war. Lots shall then be drawn as to which of the judges entitled to sit according to the rota shall withdraw. This arrangement does not affect the judge appointed by the other belligerent.

Article 17

No judge can sit who has been a party, in any way whatever, to the sentence pronounced by the national courts, or has taken part in the case as counsel or advocate for one of the parties.

No judge or deputy judge can, during his tenure of office, appear as agent or advocate before the International Prize Court nor act for one of the parties in any capacity whatever.

Article 18

The belligerent captor is entitled to appoint a naval officer of high rank to sit as assessor, but with no voice in the decision. A neutral Power, which is a party to the proceedings or whose subject or citizen is a party, has the same right of appointment; if as the result of this last provision more than one Power is concerned, they must agree among themselves, if necessary by lot, on the officer to be appointed.

Article 19

The Court elects its president and vice-president by an absolute majority of the votes cast. After two ballots, the election is made by a bare majority, and, in case the votes are equal, by lot.

Article 20

The judges on the International Prize Court are entitled to travelling allowances in accordance with the regulations in force in their own country, and in addition receive, while the Court is sitting or while they are carrying out duties conferred upon them by the Court, a sum of 100 Netherlands florins "per diem".

These payments are included in the general expenses of the Court dealt with in Article 47, and are paid through the International Bureau established by the Convention of the 29 July 1899.

The judges may not receive from their own Government or from that of any other Power any remuneration in their capacity of members of the Court.

Article 21

The seat of the International Prize Court is at The Hague and it cannot, except in the cases of "force majeure", be transferred elsewhere without the consent of the belligerents.

Article 22

The Administrative Council fulfils, with regard to the International Prize Court, the same functions as to the Permanent Court of Arbitration, but only representatives of Contracting Powers will be members of it.

Article 23

The International Bureau acts as registry to the International Prize Court and must place its offices and staff at the disposal of the Court. It has charge of the archives and carries out the administrative work.

The secretary general of the International Bureau acts as registrar.

The necessary secretaries to assist the registrar, translators and short-hand writers are appointed and sworn in by the Court.

Article 24

The Court determines which language it will itself use and what languages may be used before it.

In every case the official language of the national courts which have had cognizance of the case may be used before the Court.

Article 25

Powers which are concerned in a case may appoint special agents to act as intermediaries between themselves and the Court. They may also engage counsel or advocates to defend their rights and interests.

Article 26

A private person concerned in a case will be represented before the Court by an attorney, who must be either an advocate qualified to plead before a court of appeal or a high court of one of the Contracting States, or a lawyer practising before a similar court, or lastly, a professor of law at one of the higher teaching centres of those countries.

Article 27

For all notices to be served, in particular on the parties, witnesses, or experts, the Court may apply direct to the Government of the State on whose territory the service is to be carried out. The same rule applies in the case of steps being taken to procure evidence.

The requests for this purpose are to be executed so far as the means at the disposal of the Power applied to under its municipal law allow.

They cannot be rejected unless the Power in question considers them calculated to impair its sovereign rights or its safety. If the request is complied with, the fees charged must only comprise the expenses actually incurred.

The Court is equally entitled to act through the Power on whose territory it sits.

Notices to be given to parties in the place where the Court sits may be served through the International Bureau.

PART III. PROCEDURE IN THE INTERNATIONAL PRIZE COURT

Article 28

An appeal to the International Prize Court is entered by means of a written declaration made in the national court which has already dealt with the case or addressed to the International Bureau; in the latter case the appeal can be entered by telegram.

The period within which the appeal must be entered is fixed at 120 days, counting from the day the decision is delivered or notified (Article 2, paragraph 2).

Article 29

If the notice of appeal is entered in the national court, this Court, without considering the question whether the appeal was entered in due time, will transmit within seven days the record of the case to the International Bureau.

If the notice of the appeal is sent to the International Bureau, the Bureau will immediately inform the national court, when possible by telegraph. The latter will transmit the record as provided in the preceding paragraph.

When the appeal is brought by a neutral individual the International Bureau at once informs by telegraph the individual's Government, in order to enable it to enforce the rights it enjoys under Article 4, paragraph 2.

Article 30

In the case provided for in Article 6, paragraph 2, the notice of appeal can be addressed to the International Bureau only. It must be entered within thirty days of the expiration of the period of two years.

Article 31

If the appellant does not enter his appeal within the period laid down in Articles 28 or 30, it shall be rejected without discussion.

Provided that he can show that he was prevented from so doing by "force majeure" and that the appeal was entered within sixty days after the circumstances which prevented him entering it before had ceased to operate, the Court can, after hearing the respondent, grant relief from the effect of the above provision.

Article 32

If the appeal is entered in time, a certified copy of the notice of appeal is forthwith officially transmitted by the Court to the respondent.

Article 33

If, in addition to the parties who are before the Court, there are other parties concerned who are entitled to appeal, or if, in the case referred to in Article 29, paragraph 3, the Government who has received notice of an appeal has not announced its decision, the Court will await before dealing with the case the expiration of the period laid down in Articles 28 or 30.

Article 34

The procedure before the International Court includes two distinct parts: the written pleadings and oral discussions.

The written pleadings consist of the deposit and exchange of cases, counter-cases, and, if necessary, of replies, of which the order is fixed by the Court, as also the periods within which they must be delivered. The Parties annex thereto all papers and documents of which they intend to make use.

A certified copy of every document produced by one Party must be communicated to the other Party through the medium of the Court.

Article 35

After the close of the pleadings, a public sitting is held on a day fixed by the Court.

At this sitting the Parties state their view of the case both as to the law and as to the facts.

The Court may, at any stage of the proceedings, suspend speeches of counsel, either at the request of one of the Parties, or on their own initiative, in order that supplementary evidence may be obtained.

Article 36

The International Court may order the supplementary evidence to be taken either in the manner provided by Article 27, or before itself, or one or more of the members of the Court, provided that this can be done without resort to compulsion or the use of threats.

If steps are to be taken for the purpose of obtaining evidence by members of the Court outside the territory where it is sitting, the consent of the foreign Government must be obtained.

Article 37

The Parties are summoned to take part in all stages of the proceedings and receive certified copies of the minutes.

Article 38

The discussions are under the control of the president or vice-president, or, in case they are absent or cannot act, of the senior judge present.

The judge appointed by a belligerent Party cannot preside.

Article 39

The discussions take place in public, subject to the right of a Government who is a Party to the case to demand that they be held in private.

Minutes are taken of these discussions and signed by the president and registrar, and these minutes alone have an authentic character.

Article 40

If a Party does not appear, despite the fact that it has been duly cited, or if a Party fails to comply with some step within the period fixed by the Court, the case proceeds without that Party, and the Court gives judgment in accordance with the material at its disposal.

Article 41

The Court official notifies to the Parties decrees or decisions made in their absence.

Article 42

The Court takes into consideration in arriving at its decision all the facts, evidence, and oral statements.

Article 43

The Court considers its decision in private and the proceedings are secret.

All questions are decided by a majority of the judges present. If the number of judges is even and equally divided, the vote of the junior judge in the order of precedence laid down in Article 12, paragraph 1, is not counted.

Article 44

The judgment of the Court must give the reasons on which it is based. It contains the names of the judges taking part in it, and also of the assessors, if any; it is signed by the president and registrar.

Article 45

The sentence is pronounced in public sitting, the parties concerned being present or duly summoned to attend; the sentence is officially communicated to the Parties.

When this communication has been made, the Court transmits to the national prize court the record of the case, together with copies of the various decisions arrived at and of the minutes of the proceedings.

Article 46

Each Party pays its own costs.

The Party against whom the Court decides bears, in addition, the costs of the trial, and also pays 1 per cent of the value of the subject-matter of the case as a contribution of the general expenses of the International Court. The amount of these payments is fixed in the judgment of the Court.

If the appeal is brought by an individual, he will furnish the International Bureau with security to an amount fixed by the Court, for the purpose of guaranteeing eventual fulfilment of the two obligations mentioned in the preceding paragraph. The Court is entitled to postpone the opening of the proceedings until the security has been furnished.

Article 47

The general expenses of the International Prize Court are borne by the Contracting Powers in proportion to their share in the composition of the Court as laid down in Article 15 and in the annexed table. The appointment of deputy judges does not involve any contribution.

The Administrative Council applies to the Powers for the funds requisite for the working of the Court.

Article 48

When the Court is not sitting, the duties conferred upon it by Article 32, Article 34, paragraphs 2 and 3, Article 35, paragraph 1, and Article 46, paragraph 3, are discharged by a delegation of three judges appointed by the Court. This delegation decides by a majority of votes.

Article 49

The Court itself draws up its own rules of procedure, which must be communicated to the Contracting Powers.

It will meet to elaborate these rules within a year of the ratification of the present Convention.

Article 50

The Court may propose modifications in the provisions of the present Convention concerning procedure. These proposals are communicated, through the medium of the Netherlands Government, to the Contracting Powers, which will consider together as to the measures to be taken.

PART IV. FINAL PROVISIONS

Article 51

The present Convention does not apply as of right except when the belligerent Powers are all parties to the Convention.

It is further fully understood that an appeal to the International Prize Court can only be brought by a Contracting Power or the subject or citizen of a Contracting Power.

In the cases mentioned in Article 5, the appeal is only admitted when both the owner and the person entitled to represent him are equally Contracting Powers or the subjects or citizens of Contracting Powers.

Article 52

The present Convention shall be ratified and the ratifications shall be deposited at The Hague as soon as all the powers mentioned in Article 15 and in the table annexed are in a position to do so.

The deposit of the ratifications shall take place, in any case, on the 30 June 1909, if the Powers which are ready to ratify furnish nine judges and nine deputy judges to the Court, qualified to validly constitute a Court. If not, the deposit shall be postponed until this condition is fulfilled.

A minute of the deposit of ratifications shall be drawn up, of which a certified copy shall be forwarded, through the diplomatic channel, to each of the Powers referred to in the first paragraph.

Article 53

The Powers referred to in Article 15 and in the table annexed are entitled to sign the present Convention up to the deposit of the ratifications contemplated in paragraph 2 of the preceding article.

After this deposit, they can at any time adhere to it, purely and simply. A Power wishing to adhere, notifies its intention in writing to the Netherlands Government transmitting to it, at the same time, the act of adhesion, which shall be deposited in the archives of the said Government. The latter shall send, through the diplomatic channel, a certified copy of the notification and of the act of adhesion to all the Powers referred to in the preceding paragraph, informing them of the date on which it has received the notification.

Article 54

The present Convention shall come into force six months from the deposit of the ratifications contemplated in Article 52, paragraphs 1 and 2.

The adhesions shall take effect sixty days after notification of such adhesion has been received by the Netherlands Government, or as soon as possible on the expiration of the period contemplated in the preceding paragraph.

The International Court shall, however, have jurisdiction to deal with prize cases decided by the national courts at any time after the deposit of the ratifications or of the receipt of the notification of the adhesions. In such cases, the period fixed in Article 28, paragraph 2, shall only be reckoned from the date when the Convention comes into force as regards a Power which has ratified or adhered.

Article 55

The present Convention shall remain in force for twelve years from the time it comes into force, as determined by Article 54, paragraph 1, even in the case of Powers which adhere subsequently.

It shall be renewed tacitly from six years to six years unless denounced.

Denunciation must be notified in writing, at least one year before the expiration of each of the periods mentioned in the two preceding paragraphs, to the Netherlands Government, which will inform all the other Contracting Powers.

Denunciation shall only take effect in regard to the Power which has notified it. The Convention shall remain in force in the case of the other Contracting Powers, provided that their participation in the appointment of judges is sufficient to allow of the composition of the Court with nine judges and nine deputy judges.

Article 56

In case the present Convention is not in operation as regards all the Powers referred to in Article 15 and the annexed table, the Administrative Council shall draw up a list on the lines of that article and table of the judges and deputy judges through whom the Contracting Powers will share in the composition of the Court. The times allotted by the said table to judges who are summoned to sit in rota will be redistributed between the different years of the six-year period in such a way that, as far as possible, the number of the judges of the Court in each year shall be the same. If the number of deputy judges is greater than that of the judges, the number of the latter can be completed by deputy judges chosen by lot among those Powers which do not nominate a judge.

The list drawn up in this way by the Administrative Council shall be notified to the Contracting Powers. It shall be revised when the number of these Powers is modified as the result of adhesions or denunciations.

The change resulting from an adhesion is not made until I January after the date on which the adhesion takes effect, unless the adhering Power is a belligerent Power, in which case it can ask to be at once represented in the Court, the provision of Article 16 being, moreover, applicable if necessary.

When the total number of judges is less than eleven, seven judges form a quorum.

Article 57

Two years before the expiration of each period referred to in paragraphs 1 and 2 of Article 55 any Contracting Power can demand a modification of the provisions of Article 15 and of the annexed table, relative to its participation in the composition of the Court. The demand shall be addressed to the Administrative Council, which will examine it and submit to all the Powers proposals as to the measures to be adopted. The Powers shall inform the Administrative Council of their decision with the least possible delay. The result shall be at once, and at least one year and thirty days before the expiration of the said period of two years, communicated to the Power which made the demand.

When necessary, the modifications adopted by the Powers shall come into force from the commencement of the fresh period.

In faith whereof the Plenipotentiaries have appended their signatures to the present Convention.

Done at The Hague, 18 October 1907, in a single copy, which shall remain deposited in the archives of the Netherlands Government, and duly certified copies of which shall be sent, through the diplomatic channel, to the Powers designated in Article 15 and in the table annexed.

XIII. CONVENTION CONCERNING THE RIGHTS AND DUTIES OF NEUTRAL POWERS IN NAVAL WAR

[For the participating States, see Convention I, supra p. 399]

With a view to harmonizing the divergent views which, in the event of naval war, are still held on the relations between neutral Powers and belligerent Powers, and to anticipating the difficulties to which such divergence of views might give rise;

Seeing that, even if it is not possible at present to concert measures applicable to all circumstances which may in practice occur, it is nevertheless undeniably advantageous to frame, as far as possible, rules of general application to meet the case where war has unfortunately broken out;

Seeing that, in cases not covered by the present Convention, it is expedient to take into consideration the general principles of the law of nations;

Seeing that it is desirable that the Powers should issue detailed enactments to regulate the results of the attitude of neutrality when adopted by them;

Seeing that it is, for neutral Powers, an admitted duty to apply these rules impartially to the several belligerents;

Seeing that, in this category of ideas, these rules should not, in principle, be altered, in the course of the war, by a neutral Power, except in a case where experience has shown the necessity for such change for the protection of the rights of that Power;

Have agreed to observe the following common rules, which cannot however modify provisions laid down in existing general treaties, and have appointed as their Plenipotentiaries, namely:

[List of Plenipotentiaries]

Who, after having deposited their full powers, found in good and due form, have agreed upon the following provisions:

Article 1

Belligerents are bound to respect the sovereign rights of neutral Powers and to abstain, in neutral territory or neutral waters, from any act which would, if knowingly permitted by any Power, constitute a violation of neutrality.

Article 2

Any act of hostility, including capture and the exercise of the right of search, committed by belligerent war-ships in the territorial waters of a neutral Power, constitutes a violation of neutrality and is strictly forbidden.

Article 3

When a ship has been captured in the territorial waters of a neutral Power, this Power must employ, if the prize is still within its jurisdiction, the means at its disposal to release the prize with its officers and crew, and to intern the prize crew.

If the prize is not in the jurisdiction of the neutral Power, the captor Government, on the demand of that Power, must liberate the prize with its officers and crew.

Article 4

A prize court cannot be set up by a belligerent on neutral territory or on a vessel in neutral waters.

Article 5

Belligerents are forbidden to use neutral ports and waters as a base of naval operations against their adversaries, and in particular to erect wireless telegraphy stations or any apparatus for the purpose of communicating with the belligerent forces on land or sea.

Article 6

The supply, in any manner, directly or indirectly, by a neutral Power to a belligerent Power, of war-ships, ammunition, or war material of any kind whatever, is forbidden.

Article 7

A neutral Power is not bound to prevent the export or transit, for the use of either belligerent, of arms, ammunition, or, in general, of anything which could be of use to an army or fleet.

Article 8

A neutral Government is bound to employ the means at its disposal to prevent the fitting out or arming of any vessel within its jurisdiction which it has reason to believe is intended to cruise, or engage in hostile operations, against a Power with which that Government is at peace. It is also bound to display the same vigilance to prevent the departure from its jurisdiction of any vessel intended to cruise, or engage in hostile operations, which had been adapted entirely or partly within the said jurisdiction for use in war.

Article 9

A neutral Power must apply impartially to the two belligerents the conditions, restrictions, or prohibitions made by it in regard to the admission into its ports, roadsteads, or territorial waters, of belligerent war-ships or of their prizes.

Nevertheless, a neutral Power may forbid a belligerent vessel which has failed to conform to the orders and regulations made by it, or which has violated neutrality, to enter its ports or roadsteads.

Article 10

The neutrality of a Power is not affected by the mere passage through its territorial waters of war-ships or prizes belonging to belligerents.

Article 11

A neutral Power may allow belligerent war-ships to employ its licensed pilots.

Article 12

In the absence of special provisions to the contrary in the legislation of a neutral Power, belligerent war-ships are not permitted to remain in the ports, roadsteads, or territorial waters of the said Power for more than twenty-four hours, except in the cases covered by the present Convention.

Article 13

If a Power which has been informed of the outbreak of hostilities learns that a belligerent war-ship is in one of its ports or roadsteads, or in its territorial waters, it must notify the said ship to depart within twenty-four hours or within the time prescribed by local regulations.

Article 14

A belligerent war-ship may not prolong its stay in a neutral port beyond the permissible time except on account of damage or stress of weather. It must depart as soon as the cause of the delay is at an end.

The regulations as to the question of the length of time which these vessels may remain in neutral ports, roadsteads, or waters, do not apply to war-ships devoted exclusively to religious, scientific, or philanthropic purposes.

Article 15

In the absence of special provisions to the contrary in the legislation of a neutral Power, the maximum number of warships belonging to a belligerent which may be in one of the ports or roadsteads of that Power simultaneously shall be three.

Article 16

When war-ships belonging to both belligerents are present simultaneously in a neutral port or roadstead, a period of not less than twenty-four hours must elapse between the departure of the ship belonging to one belligerent and the departure of the ship belonging to the other.

The order of departure is determined by the order of arrival, unless the ship which arrived first is so circumstanced that an extension of its stay is permissible.

A belligerent war-ship may not leave a neutral port or roadstead until twenty-four hours after the departure of a merchant ship flying the flag of its adversary.

Article 17

In neutral ports and roadsteads belligerent war-ships may only carry out such repairs as are absolutely necessary to render them seaworthy, and may not add in any manner whatsoever to their fighting force. The local authorities of the neutral Power shall decide what repairs are necessary, and these must be carried out with the least possible delay.

Article 18

Belligerent war-ships may not make use of neutral ports, roadsteads, or territorial waters for replenishing or increasing their supplies of war material or their armament, or for completing their crews.

Article 19

Belligerent war-ships may only revictual in neutral ports or roadsteads to bring up their supplies to the peace standard.

Similarly these vessels may only ship sufficient fuel to enable them to reach the nearest port in their own country. They may, on the other hand, fill up their bunkers built to carry fuel, when in neutral countries which have adopted this method of determining the amount of fuel to be supplied.

If, in accordance with the law of the neutral Power, the ships are not supplied with coal within twenty-four hours of their arrival, the permissible duration of their stay is extended by twenty-four hours.

Article 20

Belligerent war-ships which have shipped fuel in a port belonging to a neutral Power may not within the succeeding three months replenish their supply in a port of the same Power.

Article 21

A prize may only be brought into a neutral port on account of unseaworthiness, stress of weather, or want of fuel or provisions.

It must leave as soon as the circumstances which justified its entry are at an end. If it does not, the neutral Power must order it to leave at once; should it fail to obey, the neutral Power must employ the means at its disposal to release it with its officers and crew and to intern the prize crew.

Article 22

A neutral Power must, similarly, release a prize brought into one of its ports under circumstances other than those referred to in Article 21.

Article 23

A neutral Power may allow prizes to enter its ports and roadsteads, whether under convoy or not, when they are brought there to be sequestrated pending the decision of a Prize Court. It may have the prize taken to another of its ports.

If the prize is convoyed by a war-ship, the prize crew may go on board the convoying ship.

If the prize is not under convoy, the prize crew are left at liberty.

Article 24

If, notwithstanding the notification of the neutral Power, a belligerent ship of war does not leave a port where it is not entitled to remain, the neutral Power is entitled to take such measures as it considers necessary to render the ship incapable of taking the sea during the war, and the commanding officer of the ship must facilitate the execution of such measures.

When a belligerent ship is detained by a neutral Power, the officers and crew are likewise detained.

The officers and crew thus detained may be left in the ship or kept either on another vessel or on land, and may be subjected to the measures of restriction which it may appear necessary to impose upon them. A sufficient number of men for looking after the vessel must, however, be always left on board.

The officers may be left at liberty on giving their word not to quit the neutral territory without permission.

Article 25

A neutral Power is bound to exercise such surveillance as the means at its disposal allow to prevent any violation of the provisions of the above Articles occurring in its ports or roadsteads or in its waters.

Article 26

The exercise by a neutral Power of the rights laid down in the present Convention can under no circumstances be considered as an unfriendly act by one or other belligerent who has accepted the articles relating thereto.

Article 27

The Contracting Powers shall communicate to each other in due course all laws, proclamations, and other enactments regulating in their respective countries the status of belligerent war-ships in their ports and waters, by means of a communication addressed to the Government of the Netherlands, and forwarded immediately by that Government to the other Contracting Powers.

Article 28

The provisions of the present Convention do not apply except between

Contracting Powers, and then only if all the belligerents are parties to the Convention.

Article 29

The present Convention shall be ratified as soon as possible.

The ratifications shall be deposited at The Hague.

The first deposit of ratifications shall be recorded in a procès-verbal signed by the representatives of the Powers which take part therein and by the Netherlands Minister for Foreign Affairs.

The subsequent deposits of ratifications shall be made by means of a written notification addressed to the Netherlands Government and accompanied by the instrument of ratification.

A duly certified copy of the procès-verbal relative to the first deposit of ratifications, of the ratifications mentioned in the preceding paragraph, as well as of the instruments of ratification, shall be at once sent by the Netherlands Government, through the diplomatic channel, to the Powers invited to the Second Peace Conference, as well as to the other Powers which have adhered to the Convention. In the cases contemplated in the preceding paragraph, the said Government shall inform them at the same time of the date on which it received the notification.

Article 30

Non-Signatory Powers may adhere to the present Convention.

The Power which desires to adhere notifies in writing its intention to the Netherlands Government, forwarding to it the act of adhesion, which shall be deposited in the archives of the said Government.

That Government shall at once transmit to all the other Powers a duly certified copy of the notification as well as of the act of adhesion, mentioning the date on which it received the notification.

Article 31

The present Convention shall come into force in the case of the Powers which were a party to the first deposit of the ratifications, sixty days after the date of the procès-verbal of that deposit, and, in the case of the Powers who ratify subsequently or who adhere, sixty days after the notification of their ratification or of their decision has been received by the Netherlands Government.

Article 32

In the event of one of the Contracting Powers wishing to denounce the present Convention, the denunciation shall be notified in writing to the Netherlands Government, who shall at once communicate a duly certified copy of the notification to all the other Powers, informing them of the date on which it was received.

The denunciation shall only have effect in regard to the notifying Power, and one year after the notification has been made to the Netherlands Government.

Article 33

A register kept by the Netherlands Ministry for Foreign Affairs shall give the date of the deposit of ratifications made by Article 29, paragraphs 3 and 4, as well as the date on which the notifications of adhesion (Article 30, paragraph 2) or of denunciation (Article 32, paragraph 1) have been received.

Each Contracting Power is entitled to have access to this register and to be supplied with duly certified extracts.

In faith whereof the Plenipotentiaries have appended their signatures to the present Convention.

Done at The Hague, 18 October 1907, in a single copy, which shall remain deposited in the archives of the Netherlands Government, and duly certified copies of which shall be sent, through the diplomatic channel, to the Powers which have been invited to the Second Peace Conference.

XIV. DECLARATION PROHIBITING
THE DISCHARGE OF PROJECTILES AND EXPLOSIVES
FROM BALLOONS

[For the participating States, see Convention I, supra p. 399]

The undersigned, Plenipotentiaries of the Powers invited to the Second International Peace Conference at The Hague, duly authorized to that effect by their Governments,

Inspired by the sentiments which found expression in the Declaration of St. Petersburg of 29 November (11 December) 1868, and being desirous of renewing the declaration of The Hague of 29 July 1899, which has now expired,

Declare:

The Contracting Powers agree to prohibit, for a period extending to the close of the Third Peace Conference, the discharge of projectiles and explosives from balloons or by other new methods of a similar nature.

The present Declaration is only binding on the Contracting Powers in case of war between two or more of them.

It shall cease to be binding from the time when, in a war between the Contracting Powers, one of the belligerents is joined by a non-Contracting Power.

The present Declaration shall be ratified as soon as possible.

The ratifications shall be deposited at The Hague.

A "procès-verbal" shall be drawn up recording the receipt of the ratifications, of which a duly certified copy shall be sent, through the diplomatic channel, to all the Contracting Powers.

Non-Signatory Powers may adhere to the present Declaration. To do so, they must make known their adhesion to the Contracting Powers by means of a written notification, addressed to the Netherlands Government, and communicated by it to all the other Contracting Powers.

In the event of one of the High Contracting Parties denouncing the present Declaration, such denunciation shall not take effect until a year after the notification made in writing to the Netherlands Government, and forthwith communicated by it to all the other Contracting Powers.

This denunciation shall only have effect in regard to the notifying Power.

In faith whereof the Plenipotentiaries have appended their signatures to the present Declaration.

Done at The Hague, 18 October 1907, in a single copy, which shall remain deposited in the archives of the Netherlands Government, and duly certified copies of which shall be sent through the diplomatic channel, to the Contracting Powers.

XV. FINAL ACT
OF THE SECOND PEACE CONFERENCE

The Second International Peace Conference, proposed in the first instance by the President of the United States of America, having been convoked, on the invitation of His Majesty the Emperor of All the Russias, by Her Majesty the Queen of the Netherlands, assembled on 15 June 1907, at The Hague, in the Hall of the Knights, for the purpose of giving a fresh development to the humanitarian principles which served as a basis for the work of the First Conference of 1899.

The following Powers took part in the Conference, and appointed the delegates named below:

[List of Powers and names of delegates.
For the Powers, see Convention I, supra p. 399.]

At a series of meetings, held from 15 June to 18 October 1907, in which the above delegates were throughout animated by the desire to realize, in the fullest possible measure, the generous views of the august initiator of the Conference and the intentions of their Governments, the Conference drew up, for submission for signature by the plenipotentiaries, the text of the Conventions and of the Declaration enumerated below and annexed to the present Act:

I. Convention for the pacific settlement of international disputes.
II. Convention respecting the limitation of the employment of force for the recovery of contract debts.
III. Convention relative to the opening of hostilities.
IV. Convention respecting the laws and customs of war on land.
V. Convention respecting the rights and duties of neutral powers and persons in case of war on land.
VI. Convention relative to the status of enemy merchant ships at the outbreak of hostilities.
VII. Convention relative to the conversion of merchant ships into warships.
VIII. Convention relative to the laying of automatic submarine contact mines.
IX. Convention respecting bombardment by naval forces in time of war.
X. Convention for the adaptation to naval war of the principles of the Geneva Convention.
XI. Convention relative to certain restrictions with regard to the exercise of the right of capture in naval war.
XII. Convention relative to the creation of an International Prize Court.

XIII. Convention concerning the rights and duties of neutral Powers in naval war.
XIV. Declaration prohibiting the discharge of projectiles and explosives from balloons.

These Conventions and Declarations shall form so many separate Acts. These Acts shall be dated this day, and may be signed up to 30 June 1908, at The Hague, by the Plenipotentiaries of the Powers represented at the Second Peace Conference.

The Conference, actuated by the spirit of mutual agreement and concession characterizing its deliberations, has agreed upon the following Declaration, which, while reserving to each of the Powers represented full liberty of action as regards voting, enables them to affirm the principles which they regard as unanimously admitted:

It is unanimous:

1. In admitting the principle of compulsory arbitration.
2. In declaring that certain disputes, in particular those relating to the interpretation and application of the provisions of international agreements, may be submitted to compulsory arbitration without any restriction.

Finally, it is unanimous in proclaiming that, although it has not yet been found feasible to conclude a Convention in this sense, nevertheless the divergences of opinion which have come to light have not exceeded the bounds of judicial controversy, and that, by working together here during the past four months, the collected Powers not only have learnt to understand one another and to draw closer together, but have succeeded in the course of this long collaboration in evolving a very lofty conception of the common welfare of humanity.

The Conference has further unanimously adopted the following Resolution:

> "The Second Peace Conference confirms the Resolution adopted by the Conference of 1899 in regard to the limitation of military expenditure; and inasmuch as military expenditure has considerably increased in almost every country since that time, the Conference declares that it is eminently desirable that the Governments should resume the serious examination of this question."

It has besides expressed the following "Voeux":

1. The Conference recommends to the Signatory Powers the adoption of the annexed draft Convention* for the creation of a Judicial Arbitration Court, and the bringing it into force as soon as an agreement has been reached respecting the selection of the judges and the constitution of the Court.

---

* Not reproduced.

2. The Conference expresses the opinion that, in case of war, the responsible authorities, civil as well as military, should make it their special duty to ensure and safeguard the maintenance of pacific relations, more especially of the commercial and industrial relations between the inhabitants of the belligerent States and neutral countries.
3. The Conference expresses the opinion that the Powers should regulate, by special treaties, the position, as regards military charges, of foreigners residing within their territories.
4. The Conference expresses the opinion that the preparation of regulations relative to the laws and customs of naval war should figure in the programme of the next Conference, and that in any case the Powers may apply, as far as possible, to war by sea the principles of the Convention relative to the laws and customs of war on land.

Finally, the Conference recommends to the Powers the assembly of a Third Peace Conference, which might be held within a period corresponding to that which has elapsed since the preceding Conference, at a date to be fixed by common agreement between the Powers, and it calls their attention to the necessity of preparing the programme of this Third Conference a sufficient time in advance to ensure its deliberations being conducted with the necessary authority and expedition.

In order to attain this object the Conference considers that it would be very desirable that, some two years before the probable date of the meeting, a preparatory committee should be charged by the Governments with the task of collecting the various proposals to be submitted to the Conference, of ascertaining what subjects are ripe for embodiment in an international regulation, and of preparing a programme which the Governments should decide upon in sufficient time to enable it to be carefully examined by the countries interested. This committee should further be entrusted with the task of proposing a system of organization and procedure for the Conference itself.

In faith whereof the Plenipotentiaries have signed the present Act and have affixed their seals thereto.

Done at The Hague, 18 October 1907, in a single copy, which shall remain deposited in the archives of the Netherlands Government, and duly certified copies of which shall be sent to all the Powers represented at the Conference.

**PUBLICATIONS DE L'ACADÉMIE
DE DROIT INTERNATIONAL
DE LA HAYE**

**PUBLICATIONS OF THE
HAGUE ACADEMY OF INTERNATIONAL
LAW**

RECUEIL DES COURS

Depuis 1923, les plus grands noms du droit international ont professé à l'Académie de droit international de La Haye. Tous les tomes du *Recueil* qui ont été publiés depuis cette date sont disponibles, chaque tome étant, depuis les tout premiers, régulièrement réimprimé sous sa forme originale. Il en existe un catalogue complet et détaillé.

INDEX

A ce jour, il a paru sept index généraux. Ils couvrent les tomes suivants :

1 à 101	(1923-1960)	379 pages	ISBN 978-90-218-9948-0
102 à 125	(1961-1968)	204 pages	ISBN 978-90-286-0643-2
126 à 151	(1969-1976)	280 pages	ISBN 978-90-286-0630-2
152 à 178	(1976-1982)	416 pages	ISBN 978-0-7923-2955-8
179 à 200	(1983-1986)	260 pages	ISBN 978-90-411-0110-5
201 à 250	(1987-1994)	448 pages	ISBN 978-90-04-13700-4
251 à 300	(1995-2002)	580 pages	ISBN 978-90-04-15387-7

A partir du tome 210 il a été décidé de publier un index complet qui couvrira chaque fois dix tomes du *Recueil des cours*. Le dernier index paru couvre les tomes suivants :

301 à 310	(2003-2004)	380 pages	Tome 310A ISBN 978-90-04-15373-8

COLLOQUES

L'Académie organise également des colloques dont les débats sont publiés. Les derniers volumes parus de ces colloques portent les titres suivants : *L'avenir du droit international de l'environnement* (1984) ; *L'adaptation des structures et méthodes des Nations Unies* (1985) ; *Le règlement pacifique des différends internationaux en Europe : perspectives d'avenir* (1990) ; *Le développement du rôle du Conseil de sécurité* (1992) ; *La Convention sur l'interdiction et l'élimination des armes chimiques : une percée dans l'entreprise multilatérale du désarmement* (1994). (Voir ci-après.)

CENTRE D'ÉTUDE ET DE RECHERCHE

Les travaux scientifiques du Centre d'étude et de recherche de droit international et de relations internationales de l'Académie de droit international de La Haye, dont les sujets sont choisis par le Curatorium de l'Académie, font l'objet, depuis la session de 1985, d'une publication dans laquelle les directeurs d'études dressent le bilan des recherches du Centre qu'ils ont dirigé. Les dernières brochures parues portent les titres suivants : *Le droit international des transports maritimes* (1999) ; *Les sanctions économiques en droit international* (2000) ; *Les ressources en eau et le droit international* (2001) ; *La justice pénale internationale* (2002) ; *La sécurité alimentaire* (2003) ; *Les aspects nouveaux du droit des investissements internationaux* (2004) ; *Le patrimoine culturel de l'humanité* (2005) ; *Terrorisme et droit international* (2006). En outre, lorsque les travaux du Centre se révèlent particulièrement intéressants et originaux, les rapports des directeurs et les articles rédigés par les chercheurs font l'objet d'un ouvrage collectif qui est publié dans la collection Les livres de droit de l'Académie. (Voir ci-après.)

Les demandes de renseignements ou de catalogues et les commandes doivent être adressées à

MARTINUS NIJHOFF PUBLISHERS   B.P. 9000, 2300 PA Leyde
Pays-Bas

COLLECTED COURSES Since 1923 the top names in international law have taught at the Hague Academy of International Law. All the volumes of the *Collected Courses* which have been published since 1923 are available, as, since the very first volume, they are reprinted regularly in their original format. There is a complete and detailed catalogue.

INDEXES Up till now seven General Indexes have been published. They cover the following volumes:

1 to 101	(1923-1960)	379 pages	ISBN 978-90-218-9948-0
102 to 125	(1961-1968)	204 pages	ISBN 978-90-286-0643-2
126 to 151	(1969-1976)	280 pages	ISBN 978-90-286-0630-2
152 to 178	(1976-1982)	416 pages	ISBN 978-0-7923-2955-8
179 to 200	(1983-1986)	260 pages	ISBN 978-90-411-0110-5
201 to 250	(1987-1994)	448 pages	ISBN 978-90-04-13700-4
251 to 300	(1995-2002)	580 pages	ISBN 978-90-04-15387-7

From Volume 210 onwards it has been decided to publish a full index covering, each time, ten volumes of the *Collected Courses*. The latest Index published covers the following volumes:

301 to 310 (2003-2004) 380 pages Volume 310A ISBN 978-90-04-15373-8

WORKSHOPS The Academy publishes the discussions from the Workshops which it organizes. The latest titles of the Workshops already published are as follows: *The Future of the International Law of the Environment* (1984); *The Adaptation of Structures and Methods at the United Nations* (1985); *The Peaceful Settlement of International Disputes in Europe: Future Prospects* (1990); *The Development of the Role of the Security Council* (1992); *The Convention on the Prohibition and Elimination of Chemical Weapons: A Breakthrough in Multilateral Disarmament* (1994). (See below.)

CENTRE FOR STUDIES AND RESEARCH The scientific works of the Centre for Studies and Research in International Law and International Relations of the Hague Academy of International Law, the subjects of which are chosen by the Curatorium of the Academy, have been published, since the Centre's 1985 session, in a publication in which the Directors of Studies report on the state of research of the Centre under their direction. The titles of the latest booklets published are as follows: *The International Law of Maritime Transport* (1999); *Economic Sanctions in International Law* (2000); *Water Resources and International Law* (2001); *International Criminal Justice* (2002); *Food Supply Security* (2003); *New Aspects of International Investment Law* (2004); *The Cultural Heritage of Mankind* (2005); *Terrorism and International Law* (2006). In addition, when the work of the Centre has been of particular interest and originality, the reports of the Directors of Studies together with the articles by the researchers form the subject of a collection published in the series The Law Books of the Academy. (See below.)

Requests for information, catalogues and orders for publications must be addressed to

MARTINUS NIJHOFF PUBLISHERS P.O. Box 9000, 2300 PA Leiden
The Netherlands

TABLE PAR TOME DES COURS PUBLIÉS
CES DERNIÈRES ANNÉES

INDEX BY VOLUME OF THE COURSES PUBLISHED
THESE LAST YEARS

Tome/Volume 285 (2000)

Slaughter, A.-M.: International Law and International Relations, 9-250.
Lucchini, L.: L'Etat insulaire, 251-392.

(ISBN 978-90-411-1606-2)

Tome/Volume 286 (2000)

Boutros-Ghali, B.: Le droit international à la recherche de ses valeurs : paix, développement, démocratisation (conférence inaugurale), 9-38.
Scovazzi, T.: The Evolution of International Law of the Sea: New Issues, New Challenges, 39-244.
Kronke, H.: Capital Markets and Conflict of Laws, 245-386.

(ISBN 978-90-411-1607-9)

Tome/Volume 287 (2000)

González Campos, J. D.: Diversification, spécialisation, flexibilisation et matérialisation des règles de droit international privé. Cours général, 9-426.

(ISBN 978-90-411-1608-6)

Tome/Volume 288 (2001)

Kowalski, W. W.: Restitution of Works of Art pursuant to Private and Public International Law, 9-244.
Caflisch, L.: Cent ans de règlement pacifique des différends interétatiques, 245-468.

(ISBN 978-90-411-1609-3)

Tome/Volume 289 (2001)

Grigera Naón, H. A.: Choice-of-Law Problems in International Commercial Arbitration, 9-396.

(ISBN 978-90-411-1610-9)

Tome/Volume 290 (2001)

Fernández Rozas, J. C.: Le rôle des juridictions étatiques devant l'arbitrage commercial international, 9-224.
Villani, U.: Les rapports entre l'ONU et les organisations régionales dans le domaine du maintien de la paix, 225-436.

(ISBN 978-90-411-1611-6)

Tome/Volume 291 (2001)

Rosenne, Sh.: The Perplexities of Modern International Law. General Course on Public International Law, 9-472.

(ISBN 978-90-411-1746-5)

Tome/Volume 292 (2001)

Momtaz, D.: Le droit international humanitaire applicable aux conflits armés non internationaux, 9-146.
Jacquet, J.-M.: La fonction supranationale de la règle de conflit de loi, 147-248.
Mengozzi, P.: Private International Law and the WTO Law, 249-386.

(ISBN 978-90-411-1854-7)

Tome/Volume 293 (2001)

Fitzmaurice, M. A.: International Protection of the Environment, 9-488.

(ISBN 978-90-411-1855-4)

Tome/Volume 294 (2002)

Camdessus, M.: Organisations internationales et mondialisation (conférence), 9-38.

Zoller, E.: Aspects internationaux du droit constitutionnel. Contribution à la théorie de la fédération d'Etats, 39-166.

McWhinney, E.: Self-determination of Peoples and Plural-ethnic States (Secession and State Succession and the Alternative, Federal Option), 167-264.

Thirlway, H.: Concepts, Principles, Rules and Analogies: International and Municipal Legal Reasoning, 265-406.

(ISBN 978-90-411-1856-1)

Tome/Volume 295 (2002)

Von Mehren, A.: Theory and Practice of Adjudicatory Authority in Private International Law: A Comparative Study of the Doctrine, Policies and Practices of Common- and Civil-Law Systems. General Course on Private International Law (1966), 9-432.

(ISBN 978-90-411-1857-8)

Tome/Volume 296 (2002)

Van der Stoel, M.: The Role of the OSCE High Commissioner on National Minorities in the Field of Conflict Prevention (Address), 9-24.

Hanotiau, B.: L'arbitrabilité, 25-254.

Heiskanen, V.: The United Nations Compensation Commission, 255-398.

(ISBN 978-90-411-1858-5)

Tome/Volume 297 (2002)

Dupuy, P.-M.: L'unité de l'ordre juridique international. Cours général de droit international public (2000), 9-496.

(ISBN 978-90-411-1859-2)

Tome/Volume 298 (2002)

Symeonides, S. C.: The American Choice-of-Law Revolution in the Courts: Today and Tomorrow, 9-448.

(ISBN 978-90-411-1860-8)

Tome/Volume 299 (2002)

Roucounas, E.: Facteurs privés et droit international public, 9-420.

(ISBN 978-90-411-1861-5)

Tome/Volume 300 (2002)

Bennouna, M.: Les sanctions économiques des Nations Unies, 9-78.

Kessedjian, C.: Codification du droit commercial international et droit international privé. De la gouvernance normative pour les relations économiques transnationales, 79-308.

Smits, R.: Law of the Economic and Monetary Union, 309-422.

(ISBN 978-90-411-1862-2)

Tome/Volume 301 (2003)

Meron, T.: International Law in the Age of Human Rights, 9-490.

(ISBN 978-90-04-14020-2)

Tome/Volume 302 (2003)

Black, V.: Foreign Currency Obligations in Private International Law, 9-196.
Leben, Ch.: La théorie du contrat d'Etat et l'évolution du droit international des investissements, 197-386.

(ISBN 978-90-04-14021-9)

Tome/Volume 303 (2003)

Daudet, Y.: Actualités de la codification du droit international, 9-118.
Mezghani, A.: Méthodes de droit international privé et contrat illicite, 119-430.

(ISBN 978-90-04-14022-6)

Tome/Volume 304 (2003)

Mosk, R. M.: The Role of Facts in International Dispute Revolution, 9-180.
Jänterä-Jareborg, M.: Foreign Law in National Courts: A Comparative Perspective, 181-386.

(ISBN 978-90-04-14023-3)

Tome/Volume 305 (2003)

Audit, B.: Le droit international privé en quête d'universalité. Cours général (2001), 9-488.

(ISBN 978-90-04-14307-4)

Tome/Volume 306 (2003)

Casanovas, O.: La protection internationale des réfugiés et des personnes déplacées dans les conflits armés, 9-176.
Reed, L.: Mixed Private and Public Law Solutions to International Crises, 177-410.

(ISBN 978-90-04-14545-0)

Tome/Volume 307 (2004)

Jorda, M. C.: Du Tribunal pénal international pour l'ex-Yougoslavie à la Cour pénale internationale: De quelques observations et enseignements (conférence), 9-24.
Muir Watt, H.: Aspects économiques du droit international privé (Réflexions sur l'impact de la globalisations économique sur les fondements des conflits de lois et de juridictions), 25-384.

(ISBN 978-90-04-456-7)

Tome/Volume 308 (2004)

Rigo Sureda, A.: The Law Applicable to the Activities of International Development Banks, 9-252.
González Lapeyre, E.: Transport maritime et régime portuaire, 253-378.

(ISBN 978-90-04-14547-4)

Tome/Volume 309 (2004)

Karaquillo, J.-P.: Droit international du sport, 9-124.
Maresceau, M.: Bilateral Agreements Concluded by the European Community, 9-452.

(ISBN 978-90-04-14548-1)

Tome/Volume 310 (2004)

Kamto, M.: La volonté de l'Etat en droit international, 9-428.

(ISBN 978-90-04-14552-8)

Tome/Volume 311 (2004)

[A paraître/Forthcoming]

Tome/Volume 312 (2005)

Gaudemet-Tallon, H.: Le pluralisme en droit international privé: richesses et faiblesses (Le funambule et l'arc-en-ciel). Cours général, 9-488.

(ISBN 978-90-04-14554-2)

Tome/Volume 313 (2005)

Mani, V. S.: "Humanitarian" Intervention Today, 9-324.
David, E.: La Cour pénale internationale, 325-454.

(ISBN 978-90-04-14555-9)

Tome/Volume 314 (2005)

Draetta, U.: Internet et commerce électronique en droit international des affaires, 9-232.
Daillier, P.: Les opérations multinationales consécutives à des conflits armés en vue du rétablissement de la paix, 233-432.

(ISBN 978-90-04-14557-3)

Tome/Volume 315 (2005)

Dogauchi, M.: Four-Step Analysis of Private International Law, 9-140.
Mohamed Salah, M. M.: Loi d'autonomie et méthodes de protection de la partie faible en droit international privé, 141-264.
Radicati di Brozolo, L. G.: Arbitrage commercial international et lois de police. Considérations sur les conflits de juridictions dans le commerce international, 265-502.

(ISBN 978-90-04-14558-0)

Tome/Volume 316 (2005)

Cançado Trindade, A. A.: International Law for Humankind: Towards a New *Jus Gentium* (I). General Course on Public International Law, 9-440.

(ISBN 978-90-04-15375-2)

Tome/Volume 317 (2005)

Cançado Trindade, A. A.: International Law for Humankind: Towards a New *Jus Gentium* (II). General Course on Public International Law, 9-312.
Borrás, A.: Le droit international privé communautaire: réalités, problèmes et perspectives d'avenir, 313-536.

(ISBN 978-90-04-15376-9)

Tome/Volume 318 (2005)

Kinsch, P.: Droits de l'homme, droits fondamentaux et droit international privé, 9-332.
Bothe, M.: Environment, Development, Resources, 323-516.

ISBN 978-90-04-15377-6

Tome/Volume 319 (2006)

Hartley, T. C.: The Modern Approach to Private International Law. International Litigation and Transactions from a Common-Law Perspective. General Course on Private International Law, 9-324.
Crawford, J.: Multilateral Rights and Obligations in International Law, 325-482.

(ISBN 978-90-04-15378-3)

Tome/Volume 320 (2006)

Goldstein, G. : La cohabitation hors mariage en droit international privé, 9-390.

(ISBN 978-90-04-15379-0)

Tome/Volume 321 (2006)

Shaker, M. I.: The Evolving International Regime of Nuclear Non-Proliferation, 9-202
Klein, P.: Le droit international à l'épreuve du terrorisme, 203-484.

(ISBN 978-90-04-16100-0)

Tome/Volume 322 (2006)

Loquin, E.: Les règles matérielles internationales, 9-242.
Dinstein, Y.: The Interaction between Customary International Law and Treaties, 243-428.

(ISBN 978-90-04-16101-6)

Tome/Volume 323 (2006)

Fernández Arroyo, D. P.: Compétence exclusive et compétence exorbitante dans les relations privées internationales, 9-260.
Silberman, L. J..: Co-operative Efforts in Private International Law on Behalf of Children: The Hague Children's Conventions, 261-478.

(ISBN 978-90-04-16102-3)

Tome/Volume 324 (2006)

Bedjaoui, M.: L'humanité en quête de paix et de développement (I). Cours général de droit international public, 9-530.

(ISBN 978-90-04-16103-0)

Tome/Volume 325 (2006)

Bedjaoui, M.: L'humanité en quête de paix et de développement (II). Cours général de droit international public, 9-542.

(ISBN 978-90-04-16104-7)

Tome/Volume 326 (2007)

Collins, L.: Revolution and Restitution: Foreign States in National Courts (Opening Lecture, Private International Law Session, 2007), 9-72.
Gotanda, J. Y.: Damages in Private International Law, 73-408.

(ISBN 978-90-04-16616-5)

Tome/Volume 327 (2007)

Mayer, P.: Le phénomène de la coordination des ordres juridiques étatiques en droit privé. Cours général de droit international privé (2003), 9-378.

(ISBN 978-90-04-16617-2)

Tome/Volume 328 (2007)

Garcimartín Alférez, F. J., Cross-border Listed Companies, 9-174.
Vrellis, S., Conflit ou coordination de valeurs en droit international privé. A la recherche de la justice, 175-486.

(ISBN 978-90-04-16618-9)

Tome/Volume 329 (2007)

Pellet, A.: L'adaptation du droit international aux besoins changeants de la société internationale (conférence inaugurale, session de droit international public, 2007), 9-48.
Gaillard, E.: Aspects philosophiques du droit de l'arbitrage international, 49-216.
Schrijver, N.: The Evolution of Sustainable Development in International Law: Inception, Meaning and Status, 217-412.

(ISBN 978-90-04-16619-6)

Tome/Volume 330 (2007)

Pamboukis, Ch. P.: Droit international privé holistique: droit uniforme et droit international privé, 9-474.

(ISBN 978-90-04-16620-2)

Tome/Volume 332 (2007)

Carlier, J.-Y.: Droit d'asile et des réfugiés. De la protection aux droits, 9-354.
Fatouros, A. A.: An International Legal Framework for Energy, 355-446.

(ISBN 978-90-04-17198-5)

CENTRE D'ÉTUDE ET DE RECHERCHE
CENTRE FOR STUDIES AND RESEARCH

1985   La pollution transfrontière et le droit international/Transfrontier Pollution and International Law.

La protection de l'environnement contre la pollution transfrontière et le droit international/International Law and the Protection of the Environment against Transboundary Pollution.

P.-M. Dupuy: Bilan de recherches de la section de langue française.

J. G. Lammers: The Present State of Research Carried out by the English-Speaking Section.   (134 pages — ISBN 978-90-247-3394-1)

1986   L'application du droit humanitaire/The Application of Humanitarian Law.

Y. Sandoz: Bilan de recherches de la section de langue française.

F. Kalshoven: The Present State of Research Carried out by the English-Speaking Section.   (120 pages — ISBN 978-90-247-3508-2)

1987   L'arbitrage transnational et les contrats d'Etat/Transnational Arbitration and State Contracts.

B. Audit: Bilan et perspectives/Findings and Prospects.
   (144 pages — ISBN 978-90-247-3691-1)

1988   Les aspects juridiques du terrorisme international/The Legal Aspects of International Terrorism.

J. A. Carrillo Salcedo: Bilan de recherches de la section de langue française.

J. A. Frowein: The Present State of Research Carried out by the English-Speaking Section.
   (128 pages — ISBN 978-0-7923-0214-8)

1989   Le droit d'asile/The Right of Asylum.

E. Zoller: Bilan de recherches de la section de langue française.

R. Plender: The Present State of Research Carried out by the English-Speaking Section.   (128 pages — ISBN 978-0-7923-0723-5)

1990   Droits et obligations des pays riverains des fleuves internationaux/Rights and Duties of Riparian States of International Rivers.

J. A. Barberis: Bilan de recherches de la section de langue française.

R. D. Hayton: The Present State of Research Carried out by the English-Speaking Section.   (120 pages — ISBN 978-0-7923-1374-8)

1991   Les implications juridiques de 1993 pour les Etats membres et les Etats non membres de la CEE/The Legal Implications of 1993 for Member and Non-Member Countries of the EEC.

D. Vignes: Bilan de recherches de la section de langue française.

A. A. Dashwood: The Present State of Research Carried out by the English-Speaking Section.   (148 pages — ISBN 978-0-7923-1754-8)

1992   La dette extérieure/The External Debt.

D. Carreau: Bilan de recherches de la section de langue française.
F. P. Feliciano: The Present State of Research Carried out by the English-Speaking Section.   (106 pages — ISBN 978-0-7923-2249-8)

1993   Les risques résultant de l'utilisation pacifique de l'énergie nucléaire/The Hazards Arising out of the Peaceful Use of Nuclear Energy.

P. Strohl: Bilan de recherches de la section de langue française.
N. Pelzer: The Present State of Research Carried out by the English-Speaking Section.   (320 pages — ISBN 978-0-7923-3069-1)

1994   La politique de l'environnement: de la réglementation aux instruments économiques/Environmental Policy: From Regulation to Economic Instruments.

M. Bothe: Bilan de recherches de la section de langue française.
P. H. Sand: The Present State of Research Carried out by the English-Speaking Section.   (126 pages — ISBN 978-0-7923-3555-9)

1995   Les aspects internationaux des catastrophes naturelles et industrielles/The International Aspects of Natural and Industrial Catastrophes.

Ch. Leben: Bilan de recherches de la section de langue française.
D. Caron: The Present State of Research Carried out by the English-Speaking Section.   (142 pages — ISBN 978-90-411-0311-6)

1996   La succession d'Etats: la codification à l'épreuve des faits/State Succession: Codification Tested against the Facts.

P. M. Eisemann: Bilan de recherches de la section de langue française.
M. Koskenniemi: The Present State of Research Carried out by the English-Speaking Section.   (192 pages — ISBN 978-90-411-0530-1)

1997   L'Organisation mondiale du commerce/The World Trade Organization.

D. Carreau et P. Juillard: Bilan de recherches de la section de langue française.
P. Mengozzi: The Present State of Research Carried out by the English-Speaking Section.   (128 pages — ISBN 978-90-411-1112-8)

1998   Incidences juridiques des télécommunications globales/Legal Implications of Global Telecommunications.

L. Rapp: Bilan de recherches de la section de langue française.
F. Lyall: The Present State of Research Carried out by the English-Speaking Section.   (116 pages — ISBN 978-90-411-1241-5)

1999   Le droit international des transports maritimes/The International Law of Maritime Transport.

Ph. Delebecque: Bilan de recherches de la section de langue française.
A. von Ziegler: The Present State of Research Carried out by the English-Speaking Section.   (168 pages — ISBN 978-90-411-1674-1)

2000 Les sanctions économiques en droit international/Economic Sanctions in International Law.

L.-A. Sicilianos: Bilan de recherches de la section de langue française.
L. Picchio Forlati: The Present State of Research Carried out by the English-Speaking Section. (272 pages — ISBN 978-90-411-1863-9)

2001 Les ressources en eau et le droit international/Water Resources and International Law.

L. Boisson de Chazournes: Bilan de recherches de la section de langue française.
S. M. A. Salman: The Present State of Research Carried out by the English-Speaking Section. (144 pages — ISBN 978-90-411-1864-6)

2002 La justice pénale internationale/International Criminal Justice.

R. Wedgwood: The Present State of Research Carried out by the English-Speaking Section. (132 pages — ISBN 978-90-04-14031-8)

2003 La sécurité alimentaire/Food Supply Security.

A. Mahiou: Bilan de recherches de la section de langue française.
F. Snyder: The Present State of Research Carried out by the English-Speaking Section. (224 pages — ISBN 978-90-04-14032-5)

2004 Les aspects nouveaux du droit des investissements internationaux/New Aspects of International Investment Law.

Ph. Kahn: Bilan de recherches de la section de langue française.
T. W. Wälde: The Present State of Research Carried out by the English-Speaking Section. (176 pages — ISBN 978-90-04-14544-3)

2005 Le patrimoine culturel de l'humanité/The Cultural Heritage of Mankind.

T. Scovazzi: Bilan de recherches de la section de langue française.
J. A. R. Nafziger: The Present State of Research Carried out by the English-Speaking Section. (304 pages — ISBN 978-90-04-15371-4)

2006 Terrorisme et droit international/Terrorism and International Law.

S. Sur: Bilan de recherches de la section de langue française.
M. J. Glennon: The Present State of Research Carried out by the English-Speaking Section. (176 pages — ISBN 978-90-04-16208-5)

COLLOQUES
WORKSHOPS

Colloque/Workshop 1968

Kojanec, G. (dir. publ./ed.): Les accords de commerce international/International Trade Agreements. (1969, 374 pages.)

(ISBN 978-90-286-1672-1)

Colloque/Workshop 1971

Rideau, R. (dir. publ./ed.): Les aspects juridiques de l'intégration économique/ Legal Aspects of Economic Integration. (1972, 620 pages.)

(ISBN 978-90-286-0053-9)

Colloque/Workshop 1973

Kiss, A.-C. (dir. publ./ed.): La protection de l'environnement et le droit international/ The Protection of the Environment and International Law. (1975, 650 pages.)

(ISBN 978-90-286-0494-0)

Colloque/Workshop 1978

Dupuy, R.-J. (dir. publ./ed.): Le droit à la santé en tant que droit de l'homme/The Right to Health as a Human Right. (1979, 513 pages.)

(ISBN 978-90-286-1028-6)

Colloque/Workshop 1979

Dupuy, R.-J. (dir. publ./ed.): Le droit au développement au plan international/The Right to Development at the International Level. (1980, 458 pages.)

(ISBN 978-90-286-0990-7)

Colloque/Workshop 1980

Dupuy, R.-J. (dir. publ./ed.): Le nouvel ordre économique international. Aspects commerciaux, technologiques et culturels/The New International Economic Order. Commercial, Technological and Cultural Aspects. (1981, 395 pages.)

(ISBN 978-90-247-2602-8)

Colloque/Workshop 1981

Dupuy, R.-J. (dir. publ./ed.): La gestion des ressources pour l'humanité: le droit de la mer/The Management of Humanity's Resources: The Law of the Sea. (1982, 448 pages.)

(ISBN 978-90-247-2762-9)

Colloque/Workshop 1982

Dupuy, R.-J. (dir. publ./ed.): Le règlement des différends sur les nouvelles ressources naturelles/The Settlement of Disputes on the New Natural Resources. (1983, 487 pages.)

(ISBN 978-90-247-2901-2)

Colloque/Workshop 1983

Dupuy, R.-J. (dir. publ./ed.): L'avenir du droit international dans un monde multiculturel/The Future of International Law in a Multicultural World. (1984, 510 pages.)

(ISBN 978-90-247-3070-4)

Colloque/Workshop 1984

Dupuy, R.-J. (dir. publ./ed.): L'avenir du droit international de l'environnement/The Future of the International Law of the Environment. (1985, 536 pages.)
(ISBN 978-90-247-3239-5)

Colloque/Workshop 1985

Bardonnet, D. (dir. publ./ed.): L'adaptation des structures et méthodes des Nations Unies/The Adaptation of Structures and Methods at the United Nations. (1986, 434 pages.)

(ISBN 978-90-247-3441-2)

Colloque/Workshop 1990

Bardonnet, D. (dir. publ./ed.): Le règlement pacifique des différends internationaux en Europe: perspectives d'avenir/The Peaceful Settlement of International Disputes in Europe: Future Prospects. (1991, 704 pages.)
(Relié/Hard-back. ISBN 978-0-7923-1572-8)
(Broché/Soft-cover. ISBN 978-0-7923-1573-5)

Colloque/Workshop 1992

Dupuy, R.-J. (dir. publ./ed.): Le développement du rôle du Conseil de sécurité/The Development of the Role of the Security Council. (1993, 514 pages.)
(ISBN 978-0-7923-2318-1)

Colloque/Workshop 1994

Bardonnet, D. (dir. publ./ed.): La Convention sur l'interdiction et l'élimination des armes chimiques: une percée dans l'entreprise multilatérale du désarmement/The Convention on the Prohibition and Elimination of Chemical Weapons: A Breakthrough in Multilateral Disarmament. (1995, 712 pages.)
(ISBN 978-90-411-0154-9)

LES LIVRES DE DROIT DE L'ACADÉMIE
THE LAW BOOKS OF THE ACADEMY
(Par ordre chronologique de parution) *(By chronological order of publication)*

Dupuy, R.-J. (dir. publ./ed.): Manuel sur les organisations internationales/A Handbook on International Organizations. (1988, 714 pages.)
(ISBN 978-90-247-3658-4)

Dupuy, R.-J., and D. Vignes (eds.): A Handbook on the New Law of the Sea. (2 volumes)
Volume 1: 1991, 900 pages. (ISBN 978-0-7923-0924-3)
Volume 2: 1991, 882 pages. (ISBN 978-0-7923-1063-1)

Bardonnet, D. (dir. publ./ed.): Le règlement pacifique des différends internationaux en Europe: perspectives d'avenir/The Peaceful Settlement of International Disputes in Europe : Future Prospects. (1992, 704 pages.) (Broché/PB.)
(ISBN 978-0-7923-1573-5)

Carreau, D., et/and M. N. Shaw (dir. publ./eds.): La dette extérieure/The External Debt. (1995, 818 pages.)
(ISBN 978-90-411-0083-2)

Dupuy, R.-J. (dir. publ./ed.): Manuel sur les organisations internationales/A Handbook on International Organizations. (2ᵉ éd./2nd ed., 1998, 1008 pages.)
(ISBN 978-90-411-1119-7)

Eisemann, P. M., et/and M. Koskenniemi (dir. publ./eds.): La succession d'Etats : la codification à l'épreuve des faits/State Succession : Codification Tested against the Facts. (2000, 1058 pages.)
(ISBN 978-90-411-1392-4)

Caron, D. D., et/and Ch. Leben (dir. publ./eds.): Les aspects internationaux des catastrophes naturelles et industrielles/The International Aspects of Natural and Industrial Catastrophes. (2001, 912 pages.)
(ISBN 978-90-411-1485-3)

Bothe, M., et/and P. H. Sands (dir. publ./eds.) : La politique de l'environnement. De la réglementation aux instruments économiques/Environmental Policy. From Regulation to Economic Instruments. (2002, 958 pages.)
(ISBN 978-90-411-1604-8)

Forlati Picchio, L., et/and L.-A. Sicilianos (dir. publ./eds.): Les sanctions économiques en droit international/Economic Sanctions in International Law. (2004, 912 pages.)
(ISBN 978-90-04-13701-1)

Boisson de Chazournes, L. et/and S. M. A. Salman (dir. publ./eds.): Les ressources en eau et le droit international/Water Resources and International Law. (2005, 848 pages.)
(ISBN 978-90-04-13702-8)

Mahiou, A., et/and F. Snyder (dir. publ.): La sécurité alimentaire/Food Security and Food Safety. (2006, 992 pages.)

(ISBN 978-90-04-14543-6)

Kahn, Ph., et T. W. Wälde (dir. publ./eds.): Les aspects nouveaux du droit des investissements internationaux/New Aspects of International Investment Law. (2007, 1072 pages.)

(ISBN 978-90-04-15372-1)

Glennon, M. J., et/and S. Sur (dir. publ./eds.): Terrorisme et droit international/ Terrorism and International Law. (2008, 864 pages.)

(ISBN 978-90-04-16107-8)

Nafziger, J. A. R., et/and T. Scovazzi (dir. publ./eds.): Le patrimoine culturel de l'humanité/The Cultural Heritage of Mankind. (2008, 1168 pages.)

(ISBN 978-90-04-16106-1)

LES LIVRES DE POCHE DE L'ACADÉMIE

POCKETBOOKS OF THE ACADEMY

Gaillard, E.: Aspects philosophiques du droit de l'arbitrage international, 2008, 252 pages.

(ISBN 978-90-04-17148-0)

Schrijver, N.: The Evolution of Sustainable Development in International Law: Inception, Meaning and Status, 2008, 276 pages.

(ISBN 978-90-04-17407-8)